The Sunday Telegraph

GOOD WINE GUIDE 2001

ROBERT JOSEPH

A Dorling Kindersley Book

Dorling Kindersley

LONDON, NEW YORK, SYDNEY, DELHI, PARIS,
MUNICH AND JOHANNESBURG

Produced for Dorling Kindersley
by RJ Publishing Services
www.robert-joseph.com

EDITOR Robert Joseph
RESEARCH AND EDITORIAL ASSISTANCE
Terry Copeland, JD Haasbroek, Simon Meads
RETAILER RESEARCH Jane Boyce

PHOTOGRAPHY Steve Gorton
except, E.T. Archive: Correr Museum, Venice p.64
Mary Evans Picture Library pp. 58, 76; Scope: Jacques Guillard p. 63
Telegraph Colour Library: J Sims p. 50

Text film output by Personality, London
Colour reproduced by Colourscan, Singapore
Printed and bound in Spain by
Graficas Estella
First published in Great Britain in 1983 by The Sunday Telegraph

This edition published in 2000 exclusively for WH Smith High Street Stores

ISBN 07513-2978-9

see our complete
catalogue at
www.dk.com

CONTENTS

INTRODUCTION

Welcome to the 16th and biggest ever edition of *The Sunday Telegraph Good Wine Guide* – and the first to boast over 300 pages. As in the past, the Guide is really three books in one. In the first section – *The Basics* – you will find all the grounding you need to get through a dinner party among wine buffs, as well as guidance on styles, flavours, vintages and the most compatible marriages between hundreds of wines and dishes. This year, in recognition of the part the internet is now increasingly playing in the wine world, there is also a feature on *Wine on the Web* introducing a listing of over 120 top web sites.

The following section – *The A–Z of Wine* – is an encyclopedia of some 3,000 wines, terms, regions and producers that will enable you to find your way as easily through the intricacies of an auctioneer's catalogue as around the wine shelves of a supermarket. Unlike any other encyclopedia of its kind, the A–Z goes on to recommend currently available vintages and examples that show off specific wines and winemakers at their best.

The *A–Z* also uniquely tells you how to pronounce the names of all those wines. So, with the book to hand, you will never have to pause before ordering a bottle of Ngatarawa from New Zealand or Beaulieu Napa Valley Cabernet (it's *boh-lyoo* by the way, not *boh-lyuh* as a French-speaker might reasonably expect).

Having chosen your wine, you won't have to search to find a decent merchant from whom to buy it. Simply turn to the third section of the book – the *UK and Eire Merchants* – where you will find details of over 260 British stockists, ranging from quirky one-man-bands and City traditionalists to wine clubs, mail-order specialists, high-street chains and supermarkets.

Taken as a whole, the *guide* should (as a reviewer wrote of a previous edition) be the "only wine book you need" when choosing, buying or drinking wine in 2001.

This year's *Guide* owes a great deal to stalwart researchers/editorial assistants Terry Copeland and Simon Meads, to Jane Boyce who coordinated the merchant section and most particularly to the unflappable JD Haasbroek who almost single-handedly kept the book on track. Lavinia Sanders' organizing skills saved me from the asylum, and Charles Metcalfe and Anthony Downes provided much moral support. I also have to thank Piers Russell-Cobb and, at Dorling Kindersley, Derek Coombes, Sonia Charbonnier and Edward Bunting. Elfreda Pownall at the *Sunday Telegraph* and Richard Davies and Colin Bailey-Wood at *WINE* Magazine and Kim Murphy at the Wine Institute of Asia were all indulgent as ever. All of these people share any credit for this book; the criticism should fall on my shoulders alone.

The
Basics

NEWS

GRAPE EXPECTATIONS

These are – in the words of the Chinese curse – interesting times in the world of wine. No one can say whether we are in the middle of a turbocharged process of evolution or witnessing a full-scale revolution. In either case, the shock to a global wine industry that was accustomed to the more or less predictable transitions of the seasons, has been little short of traumatic.

The Way We Were

In the long-forgotten days of the middle of the 20th century, few people questioned some basic assumptions. Wine grapes could only be grown successfully in a limited number of soils and climates, some of which suited some varieties better than others. The choice of grape naturally influenced the styles of wine that were made, but so did the food the producers and their neighbors were used to eating. Vintages also differed enormously in quality depending on the weather. In Bordeaux and Burgundy, for example, at least one year in three was usually so disastrous that much of the wine was barely drinkable. With a bit of luck, another year in every three, produced decent-to-great wine; the rest was, at best, average.

One of the required characteristics of the good-to-great years was that their wines would improve with age. Winemakers and wine drinkers had, over the centuries, developed a taste for the way the flavor of wine changes as it matures, losing the fruitiness of its youth and taking on interesting characteristics that can best be described as more "winey." Even producers of wines that were supposed to be enjoyed young, such as Beaujolais and Muscadet, would proudly pull out dusty bottles to demonstrate how well their contents had stood the test of time.

The market was driven by the producers and the merchants whom they often allowed to market their wine. In the Old World, that system has, until now, survived remarkably well. "Fine wine" – generally a synonym for Bordeaux and port – was traditionally sold before it went into the bottle and passed through an arcane set of brokers and merchants, and older examples were often hard to find outside the hallowed halls of Christie's and Sotheby's auction rooms.

Any Flavor You Want

So what's changed. Well, first of course, there is the question of where and how wine is now being made. All that stuff about appropriate soils and climates may be respected by the best producers in Napa and Coonawarra, but it has little to do with the carpet of Merlot vines that has recently been laid in California's Central Valley. Often the wrong grape in the wrong place, the Merlot was chosen because it was the "hot" variety. In other words, the wine market is falling into the hands of fickle consumers and the marketeers who seek to read their minds and predict their whims.

Sometimes they get it wrong. Even before some of the new Merlot vines have produced their first grapes, supply is already overtaking demand. Which is why the first white (by which I don't mean pink) Merlots are already beginning to hit the market.

The orgy of planting has not been limited to America. New vines have been going into the ground almost everywhere, from the plains of La Mancha in Spain to pioneering areas of Australia. And since global consumption is actually going *down* (the traditional wine-drinking regions of Europe are pulling fewer corks) we are about to confront the world's first ever glut of drinkable wine.

Satisfaction Guaranteed

And that's the point. Most new wine regions benefit from reliable climates that enable wine of at least decent quality to be produced every year. The Old World has had to fight back to eradicate bad vintages with high-tech machines such as the ones that are legally used by big Bordeaux châteaux to extract the excess water from the juice of rained-on grapes. Other tricks of the trade – include passing young claret through *two* sets of new barrels to maximize the oaky flavor and garner higher marks from all-important wine critics.

Sotheby's auction room – where bidders are paying high prices for young wines.

Castello di Ama in Chianti: an excellent producer, and one of the beneficiaries of the current mania for limited-production wines.

Small is Bountiful

Wines like these are generally made in tiny quantities. And that's another change in the wine world. In the old days, with the exception of Château Pétrus in Bordeaux and the Domaine de la Romanée Conti in Burgundy, the wines most people fought over came from fairly big estates. Château Mouton-Rothschild, for example, might produce a quarter of a million bottles per year. The players in the New Economy, such as the 64 dollar millionaires spawned every day by silicon valley, prefer a little more exclusivity. The wines that attract them come in annual harvests of just 2,000 bottles or so – from Bordeaux, Burgundy, California, the Rhône or Tuscany

Out With the Old

Some of these Bonsai wines from new Bordeaux estates such as le Pin and Valandraud, or from new California wineries such as Screaming Eagle and Harlan Estate, have no track record of course. No one knows how their wines will taste in 30 years – because they haven't been going long enough to find out. Historically, this would have excluded them from the hallowed circle of wines that were recognised as great by the critics. But we live in a youth culture. Actors like Leonardo di Caprio make two or three movies and almost instantly command far higher wage packets than any number of tried-and-tested Oscar-winners. Besides, as the head of Sotheby's, Serena Sutcliffe pointed out recently, many of the people buying wine today simply aren't used to the flavour of old wine, and don't really like it when it is offered to them. Which is why, in early 2000, there was often very little difference in the price of mature 1986 Bordeaux and young 1996s from the same châteaux.

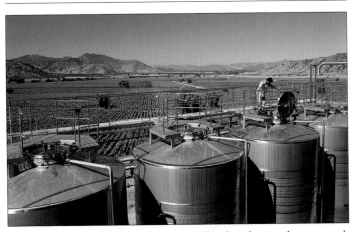

The huge vineyards of the Central Valley in Chile, where the wine glut is expected over the next few years.

What's Bad for GM...

One of the unexpected side-effects of the anti-GM (genetically modified) farming protests in Europe was a sudden international rise in interest in more environmentally-friendly forms of agriculture. Steady rather than swift-selling organic wines such as Fetzer's Californian Bonterra range suddenly began to attract attention. The Australian giant Penfolds, which was reportedly considering halting the production of its Clare Valley organic wines, started to receive calls eagerly asking when the next vintage would be released.

Watch out over the next year or so for a growing number of branded organic wines from the New and Old Worlds – and watch out for "green"ness being used as a marketing tool by big wineries.

Brand Aid

The way a wine is made and even the way it tastes, however, today sometimes seem to be of less importance than the means of promoting a brand and getting it from the producer to the consumer. The makers of California's bonsai wines are ingeniously cutting out the middleman completely by selling their wares by subscription (you'll almost never see a bottle of Screaming Eagle in a shop). Other producers are looking to the internet. Château Haut-Brion has a great website, and observers are beginning to wonder why this and other châteaux don't simply offer their new wine over the net via an online auction site like winebid.com.

One of Bordeaux' biggest merchants has just been partly bought by a consortium including the owner of Fiat cars, the maker of France's Mirage jet fighters, and a Saudi Arabian businessman. These are, as I said, interesting times.

A PERSONAL SELECTION

An unashamedly quirky list of wines that, out of the thousands I have tasted this year, have caught my attention. I have generally attempted to limit myself to one example per style or region and have given full rein to alternatives to the ubiquitous Chardonnay and Merlot. Wines are listed alphabetically. Prices are rounded to the nearest dollar.

RED WINES FOR DAILY DRINKING

1999 Pedras do Monte, Terras do Sad $10 Great, new-wave red from Portugal, bursting with brambley flavor.

1999 Primitivo di Puglia, A Mano $10 Zinfandel's Italian cousin. Really serious herby wine from Puglia in the warm south.

1996 Sotelo, Telmo Rodriguez $10 Lovely blackcurranty, maturing Navarra Cabernet Sauvignon from the maker of Remelluri in the neighboring region of Rioja.

1997 Canyon Road California Cabernet Sauvignon $12 Terrific value – by California terms – from the Geyser Peak winery. Pure, juicy blackcurrant fruit to spare.

1999 Rosemount Estate Shiraz $12 Australian red wine at its fruit-packed, oaky best.

1999 MontGras Reserva Single Vineyard Carmenere $15 This Chilean wine would once have been sold as Merlot, but this peppery, berryish wine is typical Carmenère.

1999 Terrazas Alto Malbec $17 Moët & Chandon's Argentinian offshoot is now making delicious, peppery, plummy reds like this well-oaked Malbec.

1998 Vacqueyras Perrin $15 The owners of the great Châteauneuf du Pape estate Château Beaucastel prove that they can make great peppery, gamey red down the road in Vacqueyras.

1997 Bonterra Zinfandel $16 Organic wines will be the thing of the near future. Fetzer got there before the rest of the gang and deserves credit for this lovely spicy wine.

1998 Errazuriz Sangiovese $18 If California can use this Italian grape, so can Chile – as this delicious herb-packed wine proves.

1997 Marqués de Riscal Reserva $20 One of the historic names in Rioja is now really back on form with efforts like this impeccably made strawberry-mulberryish wine.

RED WINES FOR SPECIAL OCCASIONS

1996 Château de Pibarnon, Bandol $32 One of France's greatest reds – unmatched anywhere else, for the simple reason that nowhere else has mastered the tricky Mourvèdre grape. Lovely, spicy, minerally wine to drink now or in five years' time.

1997 Nocetto Shenandoah Valley Sangiovese $32 California Sangiovese is often disappointing, but this chocolatey, tobaccoey effort really hits the top Chianti-style target.

1988 Côte Rôtie, Dom Boucharey $35 Textbook traditional Côte-Rôtie, with the smell and flavor of smoke, pheasant, and wild berries, and little evidence of new oak barrels. Gorgeously exotic wine.

1998 Felton Road Central Otago Pinot Noir $38 The great, raspberryish wine that proves how well this grape can perform on the South Island of New Zealand.

1995 Amarone della Valpolicella Classico Brigaldara $40 Classic, raisiny, curranty wine with wonderful lingering intensity.

1997 Clos de l'Obac, Priorat $40 One of Spain's new stars, from the up-and-coming region of Priorat(o). Lovely spicy, gamey wine with more than a hint of licorice.

1995 Cain Five $42 The five classic Bordeaux grape varieties are used here to produce a really stylish, blackcurranty-cedary wine.

1995 Yalumba The Signature $45 A classic Australian blend of Cabernet and Shiraz with plenty of sweet oaky spice. Great now, but well worth waiting for.

1998 Archery Summit Pinot Noir $47 Silky-rich Oregon Pinot from the same stable as Pine Ridge. Dangerously easy to drink.

1997 Casa Lapostolle Clos Apalta $48 Vying with Rothschild's Almaviva, Mondavi's Seña, Montes Alpha M, Bordeaux superstar Michel Rolland's intensely plummy Chilean effort still gets the top prize from me.

1997 Clos du Val Stag's Leap Cabernet Sauvignon $50 Everything California Cabernet in general – and Stag's Leap in particular – is supposed to be: wonderfully packed with cassis and minty flavors and just enough oak.

1997 Duckhorn Merlot $50 This used to be tough stuff that took eons to soften. But look at it now: rich, silky, and voluptuously plummy and chocolatey – and it will still improve with keeping.

1994 Barolo Vigneto Bric Sant'Ambrogio, Eredi Lodai $53 Sweetly ripe, seductively spicy wine, with the irresistible appeal of old walnut furniture with deep, velvet cushions.

1986 Château Palmer $60 Bordeaux at its mature best – for those who enjoy the way the berry fruit of youth evolves into flavors of tar and cigar boxes.

WHITE WINES FOR DAILY DRINKING

1998 Gaia Thalassitis £7 Oddbins. Made from the local Assyrtiko grape, this new wave Greek wine has refreshing, lemony-honeyed flavours that scream for a plate of Mezze.

1998 Montagny Château de Cray £8 Majestic. Fresh, nutty white Burgundy produced in a village sandwiched between the famous Côte d'Or and Pouilly Fuissé.

1999 Laithwaite Sauvignon Blanc £6 Bordeaux Direct. This merchant's boss's "own" wine from Bordeaux. Great, modern stuff, with gooseberries, apples and just a touch of mineral.

1999 Sainsbury's Classic Selection Chablis £8 Sainsbury. Made by Dom Brocard, one of the most reliable producers in Chablis, this is the kind of subtle, steely Chardonnay to run back to when you've had enough juicy-fruity New World wines.

1998 Jindalee Chardonnay £5 Safeway. Juicy Aussie Chardonnay, with lots of toasty oak and tropical fruit. Really good value barbecue fare.

1998 Dona Beatriz Sauvignon Blanc £5 Asda. Produced in Rueda, one of Spain's few successful regions for white wine, this is a mouthwateringly fresh modern wine with bags of grassy, limey flavour.

1999 Villiera Gewürztraminer £6 Thresher. The world needs more funkily individual wines like Gewürztraminer, so this fresh, floral dry example from South Africa is very, very welcome.

1995 Marques de Murrieta, Bianco Reserva Especial £9 Majestic. A really traditional – not to say old-fashioned – Spanish white that's lovely, nutty and woody. Like old Chardonnay.

1999 Cono Sur Viognier £5 Somerfield. Viognier doesn't *have* to be ferociously expensive – or ferociously oaky. This fairly priced Chilean example is packed with apricot and violets.

1994 Mount Pleasant Elizabeth Semillon £8 Tesco. A classic, maturing lemony-nutty Aussie white from the Hunter Valley, made without even a glimpse at an oak barrel. Great with food.

1999 Trulli Chardonnay £5 Tesco. Fresh, creamy, great value Italian Chardonnay to serve by the bucket at parties – or to enjoy with chicken cooked with tarragon.

1999 Nepenthe Unoaked Chardonnay £9 Oddbins. Yes, this is "unoaked" – so just like traditional Burgundy, this cool-climate Aussie tastes of the pineapppley fruit rather than the wooden barrel.

1999 Zenato Cortechiara Soave Classico £5 Safeway. Serious, creamy, almondy Soave that has nothing to do with the watery stuff usually sold under this name.

WHITE WINES FOR SPECIAL OCCASIONS

1997 Seresin Marlborough Estate Chardonnay £13 John Armit. From a new star in Marlborough, this wine proves that New Zealand's most famous region for Sauvignon can also produce Chardonnay that combines tropical fruit with elegance.

1996 Amigne du Valais, Jean Bonvin £12 Tanners. Swiss wine? Well, why not, when the Swiss have exciting spicy grapes like this Amigne. A refreshingly different experience.

1998 Riesling Furstentum Vielles Vignes Grand Cru Schoffit £20 Lay & Wheeler. A stylish but deceptively intense example of the Riesling grape, combining baked apple, spice and a hint of minerals.

1997 Clos la Chance Napa Valley Chardonnay £15 Berry Bros & Rudd. Full marks to this Napa producer for offering a Chardonnay with subtlety and style. Peachy, with just enough melon and oak.

1998 Jermann Pinot Bianco £15 Valvona & Crolla. From one of Italy's – and the world's – top white wine producers, this is wonderful rich wine that somehow manages to combine brazil nuts with flowers.

1997 Eileen Hardy Chardonnay 1997 £13 Morrisons. A superstar that regularly offers the gorgeous and unique Aussie combination of rich peachy, pineappley fruit and spicy oak.

1997 Condrieu, Lys de Volan, Alain Paret £26 Berry Bros & Rudd. From the man who makes Condrieu every year with the highly enthusiastic Gérard Départdieu, an impeccable apricot and lime blossom-flavoured wine with a great "oily" texture.

1998 Jasper Hill, Georgia's Paddock Riesling £12. Yapp Bros. An intense, organic wine made by one of Australia's most committed producers. Rich, limey and very long.

1998 Domaine de Chevalier, Pessac-Léognan £35 Wine Society. Great white Bordeaux is an under-appreciated style. Lovely subtle wine with grapefruit, white peach and greengage flavours.

1998 Pinot Gris Heimbourg, Domaine Zind Humbrecht £17 Anthony Byrne. The quintessence of Pinot Gris: rich, creamy stuff, with flavours of ripe pear and subtle spice.

1996 Gewurztraminer Grand Cru Furstentum Cuveé Laurence £30 Justerini & Brooks. A textbook example of the way this potentially showy variety can produce, fine, elegant wine with the seductive appeal of liquid flowers.

1997 Chevalier-Montrachet, Château de Puligny-Montrachet £58 Oddbins Fine Wine. Top class intensely biscuity white Burgundy with layers of subtly lingering appley, pineappley and nutty flavours.

SPARKLING WINES AND ROSÉ

1996 Seaview Chardonnay Blanc de Blancs $12 Tremendous value pure Chardonnay from Australia. Creamy and with just enough tropical fruit.

Raventos I Blanc Cava Brut Reserva $18 One of the best examples of Cava, Spain's Champagne-method sparkling wine. Rich, and attractively yeasty.

Charles Melton Sparkling Red $35 Funky fizzy, slightly off-dry, plummy-chocolatey red Shiraz from Australia.

1998 Cave de Pfaffenheim Crémant d'Alsace Blanc de Blancs $25 Sparkling Alsace that's creamy enough to live up to its "Crémant" name. Subtly floral and peary.

Charles Heidsieck Brut Réserve Mis en Cave 1995 $45 The best nonvintage Champagne around? This blend of several years that was put together in 1995 has real vintage character.

1993 Moët & Chandon Brut Impérial Vintage Rosé $60 People who've shelled out twice this price to get a Dom Perignon Rosé will hate me for saying so, but this seductive raspberryish wine is not only a better buy at the moment – it's a better wine altogether.

R. de Ruinart Champagne $60 Often overlooked, this smaller producer under the same ownership as Moët & Chandon, Veuve Clicquot, Krug, etc. produces lovely toast wine.

1992 J. Schram Napa Valley $70 Schramsberg was the first winery to master sparkling wine in California. This nutty, ripe appley vintage example shows that this is still the place to come to discover recent examples of that mastery.

1990 Taittinger Comtes de Champagne Blanc de Blancs Brut $120 There aren't many bottles of the 1990 left, but grab one when you see it. Great, rich, lingering, buttery yeasty stuff.

1990 Pol Roger Sir Winston Churchill Cuvée $130 Named after one of this wine's greatest fans, this is supremely stylish stuff with the richness of a decade's maturity.

ROSÉ

1999 Bonny Doon Vin Gris de Cigare $10 While others produce sugary commercial, "white" pink wines, Randall Grahm thankfully goes on with his deliciously peppery dry efforts.

1999 Château le Raz Bergerac Rosé $10 Lovely dry, berryish wine made from Merlot and Cabernet Sauvignon grapes.

1999 Enate Rosado $10 Refreshing, lightly spicy pink wine from a go-ahead winery in the go-ahead Spanish region of Somontano.

SWEET AND FORTIFIED WINES

1996 Clos d'Yvigne Saussignac $25 Sauternes is often very disappointing. Wines like this luscious apricotty effort produced nearby can be a far, better buy.

1993 Royal Tokaji Wine Co. Tokaji Aszú 4 Putts $35 Not the sweetest example of this orangey wine, but a wonderful, clean, exciting drink to sip by itself, or with cheese.

1989 Ch. Filhot $52 Great sweet Bordeaux is a bargain, and maturing examples like this are an absolute steal. Relish the subtle exotic layers of spicy and ripe fruit flavors.

1997 Brauneberger Juffer Sonnenuhr Riesling Auslese, Fritz Haag $55 Fine, intense yet supremely delicate wine from a master craftsman. The kind of wine that can only be achieved in Germany, and with the Riesling, and in the Mosel.

1991 Blauer Zweigelt Beerenauslese, Martin Haider $65 Weird and wonderful, bronze-hued, blackberryish, late-picked wine made from black grapes.

1994 Gewurztraminer Grand Cru Rangen de Thann Sélection des Grains Nobles, Schoffit $85 Imagine violets, lychees and roses. Add some honey and just a little extract of apricot, and you'll have an idea of how this tastes.

1997 Kühling Gillot Bodenheim Heitersbrunnchen Scheurebe Eiswein $110 Made from the Scheurebe, a grape little known outside Germany and Austria, using grapes picked while frozen by the winter chill, this is extraordinarily intense wine.

FORTIFIED

Barbadillo Obispo Gascon Palo Cortado $30 The least well-known style of sherry, this is brilliant, nutty but fresh, light dry wine that would go wonderfully with smoked salmon.

Terre Arse Marsala Vergine, Florio $35 Most Marsala should go straight into the saucepan, but this is a voluptuous, concentrated, fruity, nutty exception to the rule.

Henriques & Henriques 15 YO Verdelho $37 Madeira deserves to make a comeback, and here's an example to start with. Great dry, marmaladey wine. Rich but with a bite!

1986 Guimaraens $50 Save your money! Grab a few bottles of this instead of the bigger names and more famous vintages. Under the same ownership as Taylor's, this is a silky, plummy delight.

González Byass Noë $45 Another sherry – but very different. This is intense raisiny stuff made from the Pedro Ximenez grape.

Seppelt DP63 Rutherglen Show Muscat $50 Australia's unique wine style. Liquid plum pudding, with a sprinkling of spice.

WINE ON THE WEB

A QUIET REVOLUTION

First things first. I have a fierce, inbuilt, resistance to hype. While others were noisily declaring *Titanic* to be one of the greatest movies ever made, I thought it an overblown load of tosh with some good special effects and an annoyingly memorable theme song. So, when the Internet came along, I was naturally suspicious of the lofty claims that it would revolutionise our lives. But it didn't take long for me to realise that the hype has, if anything, understated the impact of the new technology. And few areas of our lives will be affected more than the way we choose, buy and learn about wine.

Opinion Formers

In the old, pre-Net, days, wine was stuff you could discuss with a few like-minded friends and the person who sold it to you. For wine-loving individuals who picked bottles from the shelves of the local supermarket, this sometimes made for a pretty uncommunicative existence. Since the very earliest days of the Internet, however, long before anyone began to tap its commercial potential, large numbers of people divided by geography got together to chew the metaphorical fat over the respective merits of their favourite wines.

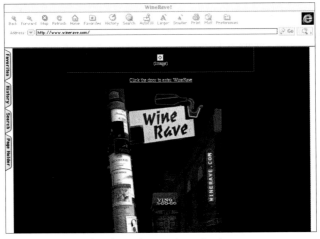

Want to chat about Chianti? This is the place to come.

Checking the winners on the International Wine Challenge site.

The basic chat-rooms where these discussions took place are still to be found – on *aol.com*, *excite.com* etc. – but there are now far more sophisticated places to swap vinous opinions. *winerave.com,* for example, offers a lively environment for all kinds of vinous chat, while other sites, such as the the *Wine Spectator* magazine's *winespectator. com* or the International Wine Challenge's *intlwinechallenge.com* and *winepros.com*, invite you to add your tasting notes to those written by professionals and other browsers. Other sites like my own *coonawarra.com* and *zinfans.com* and *anythingbutchardonnay.com* are conceived to serve as meeting points for lovers of – or people who are bored with – particular styles of wine.

Information Overload

Then there are the information-based sites. Go to *winepros.com* and you'll find an online version of Jancis Robinson's *Oxford Companion* – as well as James Halliday's *Australian Wine Encyclopedia* and regularly contributed tasting notes and features from writers like Halliday, Len Evans, Clive Coates and myself. The *New York Times'* *winetoday.com* appropriately enough offers news of who's about to take over whom and *wine-and-health.com* provides updates on the pros and cons of pouring yourself another glass of red. Other sites, like the smart ones run by wineries ranging from Chateau Haut-Brion (*haut-brion.com*) to Robert Mondavi (*robertmondavi.com*) give you the producers' view, while unashamedly retail-based operations like *chateauonline.com*, *planetwine.com*, *wine.com*, *everywine.com*, *orgasmicwine.com* and Berry Bros & Rudd's *bbr.co.uk* all do their best to sell you wine. It is the notion of buying wine over the net that will do the most to revolutionise our lives – just as *amazon.com* has revolutionised our reading. And for the same reasons. Where a shop can offer a few hundred different wines and a mail order catalogue

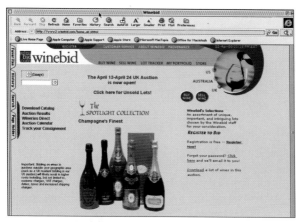

Top left: the Australian, expert-based winepros site; Middle left: Berry Bros & Rudd, a top-class online wine merchant. Bottom left: Haut-Brion, a Bordeaux Grand Cru on the web. Above: the innovative auctioneer, winebid.com

run to perhaps a couple of thousand, a website is almost unlimited in the range it can present. We'll all get mightily confused of course – and most likely still buy the bottles we've read about or drunk elsewhere, but the bigger playing field must improve the chances for smaller producers who were often overlooked in the past. Eventually, it'll also break down legal barriers that stop people in many US states buying wine from stockists elsewhere in their own country – and prevent people in the UK from ordering their Burgundy directly from the grower across the Channel.

To Bid or Not to Bid?

Just as online share dealing has helped to bring the stock market to ordinary mortals, the launch of *winebid.com* enables wine drinkers to sidestep the auction rooms. Now, it's as easy to buy and sell a case of Château Margaux as Microsoft shares. But at this point, I think a warning is in order. When bidding online, never lose sight of the dangers implicit in buying any wine. That seductive double-magnum of 1945 Pétrus on offer on *eBay* is almost certainly a fake (there were few if any produced) and the case of 1990 Latour may well have spent the last few years cooking in an uninsulated attic. So be as careful about where you do your buying as you are about the wine you buy.

Apart from the sites already mentioned, I have to declare an interest in winepros.com (for which I write), the International Wine Challenge (of which I am chairman), wine-and-health.com and wine-school.com

A full list of recommended websites begins on page 319

TASTING & BUYING

SPOILED FOR CHOICE

Buying wine today has become wonderfully – and horribly – like buying a gallon of paint. Just as the manufacturer's helpful chart can become daunting with its endless shades of subtly different white, the number of bottles and the information available on the supermarket shelves can make you want to give up and reach for the one that is most familiar, or most favourably priced.

If you're not a wine buff, why should you know the differences in flavour to be found in wines made from the same grape in Meursault in France, Mendocino in California and Maipo in Chile? Often, the merchant has helpfully provided descriptive terms to help you to imagine the flavour of the stuff in the bottle. But, these too can just add to the confusion. Do you want the one that tastes of strawberries or raspberries, the "refreshingly dry", or the "crisp, lemony white"?

I can't promise to clear a six-lane highway through this jungle but, with luck, I shall give you a path to follow when you are choosing a wine, and one from which you can confidently stray.

Arm yourself with a good corkscrew (see page 66) and let's get tasting.

THE LABEL

Wine labels should reveal the country or region where the wine was produced (see page 26), and possibly the grape variety (see page 50) from which it was made. Both region and grape, however, offer only partial guidance as to what you are likely to find when you pull the cork.

Bear in mind the following:

1) Official terms such as Appellation Contrôlée, Grand or Premier Cru, Qualitätswein and Reserva are often as trustworthy as official pronouncements by politicians.

2) Unofficial terms such as Réserve Personnelle and Vintner Selection are, likewise, as trustworthy as unofficial pronouncements by the producer of any other commodity.

3) Knowing where a wine comes from is often like knowing where a person was born; it provides no guarantee of how good the wine will be. Nor, how it will have been made (though there are often local rules). There will be nothing to tell you, for instance, whether a Chablis is oaky nor, quite possibly, whether an Alsace or Vouvray is sweet.

4) "Big name" regions don't always make better wine than supposedly lesser ones. Cheap Bordeaux is far worse than similarly priced wine from Bulgaria.

5) Don't expect all wines from the same grape variety to taste the same: a South African Chardonnay may taste far drier than one from California and less fruity than one from Australia. The flavour and style will depend on the climate, soil and producer.

6) Just because a producer makes a good wine in one place, don't trust him to make others either there or elsewhere. The team at Lafite Rothschild produce less classy Los Vascos wines in Chile; Robert Mondavi's inexpensive Woodbridge wines bear no relation to the quality of his Reserve wines from Napa.

7) The fact that there is a château on a wine label has no bearing on the quality of the contents.

8) Nor does the boast that the wine is bottled at said château.

9) Nineteenth-century medals look pretty on a label; they say nothing about the quality of the 20th-century stuff in the bottle.

10) Price provides some guidance to a wine's quality: a very expensive bottle may be appalling, but it's unlikely that a very cheap one will be better than basic.

A WAY WITH WORDS

Before going any further, I'm afraid that there's no alternative to returning to the thorny question of the language you are going to use to describe your impressions.

When Washington Irving visited Bordeaux 170 years ago, he noted that Château Margaux was "a wine of fine flavour – but not of equal body". Lafite on the other hand had "less flavour than the former but more body – an equality of flavour and body". Latour, well, that had "more body than flavour". He may have been a great writer, but he was evidently not the ideal person to describe the individual flavours of the great Bordeaux – and how they actually tasted.

Michelangelo was more poetic, writing that the white wine of San Gimignano "kisses, licks, bites, thrusts, and stings...". Modern pundits refer to wines as having "gobs of fruit" and tasting of "kumquats and suede." Each country and each generation comes up with its own vocabulary. Some descriptions, such as the likening to gooseberry and asparagus of wines made from the Sauvignon Blanc, can be justified by scientific analysis, which confirms that the same aromatic chemical compound is found in the fruit, vegetable, and wine.

Then there are straightforward descriptions. Wines can be fresh or stale, clean or dirty. If they are acidic, or overfull of tannin, they will be "hard"; a "soft" wine, by contrast might be easier to drink, but boring.

There are other less evocative terms. While a downright watery wine is "dilute" or "thin," subtle ones are called "elegant." A red or white whose flavor is hard to discern is described as "dumb." Whatever the style of a wine, it should have "balance." A sweet white, for example, needs enough acidity to keep it from cloying. No one will ever enjoy for long a wine that is too fruity, too dry, too oaky, or too anything.

The flavor that lingers in your mouth long after you have swallowed or spat it out is known as the "finish." Wines whose flavor – pleasant or unpleasant – hangs around, are described as "long"; those whose flavor disappears quickly are "short."

Finally, there is "complex," the word that is used to justify why one wine costs ten times more than another. A complex wine is like a well-scored symphony, while a simpler one could be compared to a melody picked out on a single instrument.

TASTING

Wine tasting is surrounded by mystery and mystique. And it shouldn't be – because all it really consists of is paying attention to the stuff in the glass, whether you're in the formal environment of a wine tasting, or drinking the house white in your local bar. The key questions are: do you like the wine? And is it a good example of what it claims to be. Champagne costs a lot more than basic Spanish Cava, so it should taste recognizably different. Some do, some don't.

See

The look of a wine can tell you a lot. Assuming that it isn't cloudy (in which case send it straight back), it will reveal its age and may give some hint of the grape and origin. Some grapes, like Burgundy's Pinot Noir, make naturally paler wines than, say, Bordeaux's Cabernet Sauvignon; wines from warmer regions tend to have deeper colors. Tilt the glass away from you over a piece of white paper and look at the rim of the liquid. The more watery and brown it is, the older the wine (Beaujolais Nouveau will be violet through and through).

Swirl

Vigorously swirl the wine around the glass for a moment or so to release any reluctant smells.

Sniff

You sniff a wine before tasting it for the same reason that you sniff a carton of milk before pouring its contents into coffee. The smell can tell you more about a wine than anything else. If you don't believe me, try tasting anything while holding your nose, or while you've got a cold. When sniffing, concentrate on whether the wine seems fresh and clean, and on any smells that indicate how it is likely to taste.

What are your first impressions? Is the wine fruity, and, if so, which fruit does it remind you of? Does it have the vanilla smell of a wine that has been fermented and/or matured in new oak barrels? Is it spicy? Or herbaceous? Sweet or dry? Rich or lean?

A brief look then swirl the wine round in the glass to release the aromas.

Sip

Take a small mouthful and – this takes practice – suck air between your teeth and through the liquid. Look in a mirror while you're doing this: if your mouth looks like a cat's bottom and sounds like a child trying to suck the last few drops of soda through a straw, then you're doing it right. Hold the wine in your mouth for a little longer to release as much of its flavor as possible.

Focus on the flavor. Ask yourself the same questions about whether it tastes sweet, dry, fruity, spicy, herbaceous. Is there just one flavor, or do several contribute to a "complex" overall effect?

Now concentrate on the texture of the wine. Some like – Chardonnay – are mouth-coatingly buttery, while others – e.g., Gewürztraminer – are almost oily. Muscadet is a good example of a wine with a texture that is closer to that of water.

Reds, too, vary in texture, some seeming tough and tannic enough

Does the wine smell fresh and inviting? Simple or complex? Let it wash around your palate, and focus on the range of flavours it has to offer.

to make the inside of one cheek want to kiss the inside of the other. Traditionalists rightly claim tannin is necessary to a wine's longevity, but modern winemakers distinguish between the harsh tannin and the "fine" (non-aggressive) tannin to be found in wine carefully made from ripe grapes. A modern Bordeaux often has as much tannin as old-fashioned examples – but is far easier to taste and drink.

Spit

The only reason for spitting a wine out – unless it is actively repellent – is quite simply remain upright at the end of a lengthy tasting. I have notes I took during a banquet in Burgundy at which there were dozens of great wines and not even the remotest chance to do anything but swallow. The descriptions of the first few are perfectly legible; the thirtieth apparently tasted "very xgblorefjy". If all you are interested in is the taste, not spitting is an indulgence; you should have got 90% of the flavour while the wine was in your mouth.

Pause for a moment or two after spitting the wine out. Is the flavour still there? How does what you are experiencing now compare with the taste you had in your mouth? Some wines have an unpleasant aftertaste; others have flavours that linger deliciously in the mouth.

SHOULD I SEND IT BACK?

Wines are subject to all sorts of faults, though far less than they were even as recently as a decade ago.

Acid

All wines, like all fruit and vegetables, contain a certain amount of acidity. Without it they would go very stale very quickly. Wines made from unripe grapes will, however, taste unpalatably "green" and like unripe apples or plums – or like chewing stalky leaves or grass.

Bitter

Bitterness is quite different. On occasion, especially in Italy, a touch of bitterness may not only be forgivable, it may even be an integral part of a wine's character, as in the case of Amarone. Of course, the Italians like Campari too. Even so, a little bitterness goes a very long way.

Cloudy

Wine should be transparent. The only excuse for cloudiness is in a wine like an old Burgundy whose deposit has been shaken up.

Corked

Ignore any cork crumbs you may find floating on the surface of a wine. Genuinely corked wines have a musty smell and flavour that comes from mouldy corks. Some corks are mouldier, and wines mustier, than others, but all corked wines become nastier with exposure to air. Around 6% of wines – irrespective of their price – are corked.

Crystals

Not a fault, but people often think there is something wrong with a white wine if there is a layer of fine white crystals in the bottom of the bottle. These are just tartrates that fall naturally.

Maderised/Oxidised

Madeira is fortified wine, that has been intentionally exposed to the air and heated in a special oven. Maderised wine is stale, unfortified stuff which has been accidentally subjected to warmth and air.

Oxidised is a broader term, referring to wine that has been exposed to the air – or made from grapes that have cooked in the sun. The taste is reminiscent of poor sherry or vinegar – or both.

Sulphur (SO_2/H_2S)

Sulphur dioxide is used as a protection against bacteria that would oxidise (qv) a wine. In excess, sulphur dioxide, may make you cough or sneeze. Even worse, though, is hydrogen sulphide and mercaptans, its associated sulphur compounds, which are created when sulphur dioxide combines with wine. Wines with hydrogen sulphide smell of rotten eggs, while mercaptans reek of nastiness, ranging from rancid garlic to burning rubber. Decanting the wine or popping a copper coin in your glass may help to clear up these characteristics.

Vinegary/Volatile

Volatile acidity is present in all wines, but only in small proportions. In excess – usually the result of careless winemaking – what can be a pleasant component (like a touch of balsamic vinegar in a sauce) tastes downright vinegary.

READING THE LABEL

INTRODUCTION

Labels – in all their different forms – are so much part of the business of wine that it may come as a surprise that, even a century ago, they barely existed. Wine was sold by the barrel and served by the jug or decanter. Indeed, the original "labels" were silver tags that hung on a chain around the neck of a decanter and were engraved with the word "claret," "hock," "port," or whatever.

Today, however, printed wine labels include legally required information such as the amount of liquid in the bottle, its strength, the place where it was made and the name of the producer, brand-owner or importer. Confusingly, though, the rules governing what may be said on a label can vary between countries and between regions. Labels may also reveal a wine's style – the grape variety, oakiness or sweetness, for example. And lastly, they are part of the packaging that helps to persuade you to buy one wine rather than another. The following examples should help you through the maze.

CHAMPAGNE

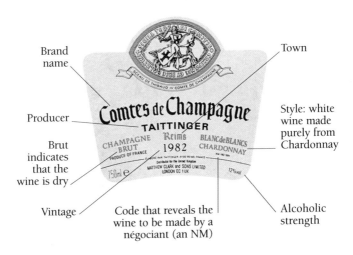

Brand name

Town

Producer

Style: white wine made purely from Chardonnay

Brut indicates that the wine is dry

Comtes de Champagne
TAITTINGER
CHAMPAGNE BRUT — Reims 1982 — BLANC de BLANCS CHARDONNAY
PRODUCE OF FRANCE
750ml e — 12%vol

Vintage

Code that reveals the wine to be made by a négociant (an NM)

Alcoholic strength

WHITES

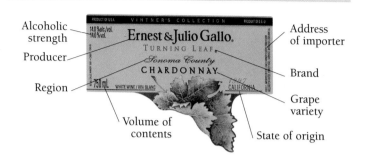

Alcoholic strength

Producer

Region

Volume of contents

Address of importer

Brand

Grape variety

State of origin

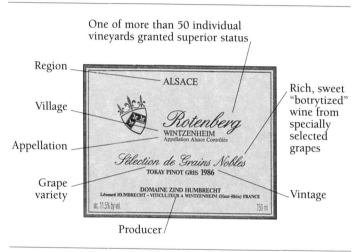

One of more than 50 individual vineyards granted superior status

Region

Village

Appellation

Grape variety

Rich, sweet "botrytized" wine from specially selected grapes

Vintage

Producer

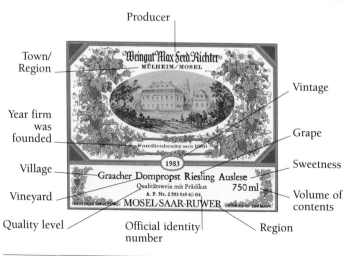

Producer

Town/ Region

Year firm was founded

Village

Vineyard

Quality level

Vintage

Grape

Sweetness

Volume of contents

Region

Official identity number

REDS

Grape variety

Region

Brand

IGT, the recently introduced designation for wines that fall outside DOC legislation

Vintage

Country of origin

Alcoholic strength

Volume of contents

Winemaker and address

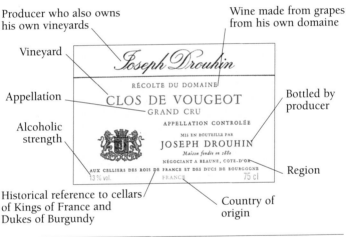

Producer who also owns his own vineyards

Wine made from grapes from his own domaine

Vineyard

Appellation

Bottled by producer

Alcoholic strength

Region

Historical reference to cellars of Kings of France and Dukes of Burgundy

Country of origin

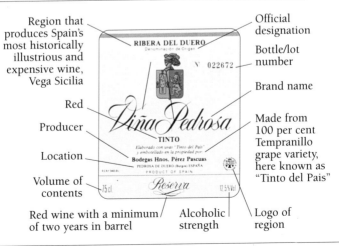

Region that produces Spain's most historically illustrious and expensive wine, Vega Sicilia

Official designation

Bottle/lot number

Red

Brand name

Producer

Made from 100 per cent Tempranillo grape variety, here known as "Tinto del Pais"

Location

Volume of contents

Red wine with a minimum of two years in barrel

Alcoholic strength

Logo of region

DESSERTS/FORTIFIEDS

A *puttonyo* is the "hod" of Aszú sweet grape paste used to sweeten tokaji – the number of puttonyos indicates the sweetness of the wine

Wine name

Producer

Paste made from "nobly-rotten" grapes

Producer's crest

Volume of contents – smaller than standard wine bottle size

Alcoholic strength

Country of origin

Producer's crest

Producer

Style of sherry, Old Amontillado

Brand name

Produced and bottled in principal sherry town, Jerez

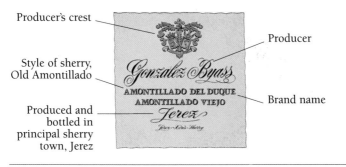

Producer

"Traditional" means "unfiltered", like real vintage port. Other late bottled vintage is filtered so as to remove the need for decanting

History and credentials of producer

Vintage

LBV ports bottled 4 to 6 years after the vintage (rather than 2 for vintage port)

Unlike "tawny" which is matured in bottle

Bottling date – obligatory for LBV labels

Alcoholic strength

Company's name and address

Volume of contents

COUNTRIES

WHERE IN THE WORLD?

Despite the plethora of bottles whose labels bear the name of the same grape variety, the country and region in which a wine is made – with its climate, traditions and local taste – still largely dictate the style of the stuff that ends up in your glass. In the next few pages, we'll take a whirlwind tour of the wine world, which should give you a clearer idea of what to expect from all of the most significant winemaking nations. (For more information on grapes, terms and regions, see the A–Z, which starts on page 97.)

AUSTRALIA

Reading the label: Late harvest/noble harvest – *sweet*. Show Reserve – *top-of-the-range wine, usually with more oak.* Tokay – *Australian name for the Muscadelle grape, used for rich liqueur wines.* Verdelho – *Madeira grape used for limey dry wines.* Mataro – *Mourvèdre.* Shiraz – *Syrah.* Tarrango – *local success story, fresh, fruity, and Beaujolais-like.*

Twenty or so years ago, Australian wines were the butt of a Monty Python sketch. Today, these rich and often intensely fruity wines are the reliable vinous equivalent of Japanese hi-fi and cameras. It is hard to explain quite how this switch happened, but I would attribute much of the credit to the taste the Australians themselves have developed for wine. Having a populace that treats wine the way many Americans treat milk or beer has provided the impetus for two of the best wine schools in the world – and for a circuit of fiercely fought competitions in which even the humblest wines battle to win medals.

Another strength has been the spirit of exploration which led to the establishment of areas like the Barossa and Hunter Valleys, and which is now fueling the enthusiastic planting of vines in new regions such as Orange, Robe, Mount Benson, Young, and Pemberton.

Remember these names; they are already appearing on a new generation of subtler Australian reds and whites that will make some of today's stars look like amateurs. And look out too for unconventional blends of grape varieties, as well as delicious new flavors none of us has ever tasted. Australia is the only region or country to have

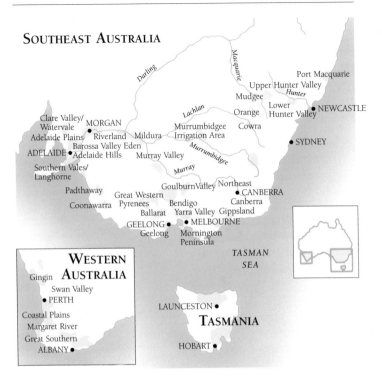

SOUTHEAST AUSTRALIA

Darling · Macquarie · Lachlan · Murrumbidgee · Murray

Port Macquarie
Upper Hunter Valley
Mudgee
Orange · Lower Hunter Valley · NEWCASTLE
Cowra
Clare Valley/ Watervale · MORGAN
Adelaide Plains · Riverland · Mildura
Barossa Valley Eden
ADELAIDE · Adelaide Hills · Murray Valley
Southern Vales/ Langhorne
Murrumbidgee Irrigation Area
SYDNEY
Padthaway · Great Western · Goulburn Valley · Northeast
Coonawarra · Pyrenees · Bendigo · Canberra · CANBERRA
Ballarat · Yarra Valley · Gippsland
GEELONG · MELBOURNE
Geelong · Mornington Peninsula

TASMAN SEA

WESTERN AUSTRALIA
Gingin
Swan Valley
PERTH
Coastal Plains
Margaret River
Great Southern
ALBANY

LAUNCESTON
TASMANIA
HOBART

drawn up a master plan to dominate the world's premium wines within 25 years. Judging by what's been achieved so far, I think the Austalians may well be on track to achieving their ambitions.

AUSTRIA

Reading the label: Ausbruch – *late-harvested, between Beerenauslese and Trockenbeerenauslese.* Erzeugerabfüllung – *estate bottled.* Morillon – *Chardonnay.* Schilfwein – *made from grapes dried on mats.*

Austrian winemakers are riding high, with brilliant, late harvest wines, dry whites and increasingly impressive reds. Names to look out for include Alois Lang, Kracher, and Willi Opitz.

CANADA

Reading the label: VQA (Vintners Quality Alliance) – *local designation seeking to guarantee quality and local provenance.*

The icewines, made from grapes picked when frozen on the vine, are the stars here, though the Chardonnays and other light reds are fast improving.

EASTERN EUROPE

Some parts of Eastern Europe are coming to terms with life under capitalism a lot more successfully than others, but throughout the region, winemaking is improving fitfully.

BULGARIA

The pioneer of good Iron Curtain reds, Bulgaria remains a reliable source of inexpensive, ripe Cabernet Sauvignon and Merlot, as well as creditable examples of the earthy local Mavrud. Whites are getting better too, thanks largely to the efforts of visiting Australian winemakers.

HUNGARY

Still probably best known for its red Bull's Blood, Hungary's strongest card today lies in the rich Tokajis, the best of which are being made by foreign investors.

Reds are improving, as are affordable Australian-style Sauvignons and Chardonnays.

ROMANIA, MOLDOVA AND FORMER YUGOSLAVIA

It is too early to see whether the new Yugoslav republics can export as many bottles of wine as used to go out under the Laski Rizling label, but Romania produces decent if atypical Pinot Noir, while Moldova's strength lies in whites.

ENGLAND AND WALES

Despite an unhelpful climate and government, the vineyards of England and Wales are steadily developing a potential for using recently developed German grape varieties to make Loire-style whites, high-quality, late harvest wines and good sparkling wines. There are reds too, but these are only really of curiosity value and are likely to remain so until global warming takes effect.

FRANCE

Reading the label: Appellation Contrôlée (or AOC) – *designation covering France's (supposedly) better wines.* Blanc de Blancs/Noirs – *white wine made from white/black grapes.* Cave – *cellar.* Cave des Vignerons de – *usually a co-operative.* Cépage – *grape variety.* Château – *wine estate.* Chêne – *oak barrels, as in Fûts de Chêne.* Clos – *(historically) walled vineyard.* Côte(s)/Coteaux – *hillside.* Crémant – *sparkling.* Cuvée – *a specific blend.* Demi-sec – *medium sweet.* Domaine – *wine estate.* Doux – *sweet.* Grand Cru – *higher quality, or specific vineyard.* Gris – *pale rosé, as in Vin Gris.* Jeunes Vignes – *young vines (often ineligible for Appellation Contrôlée).*

Méthode Classique – *used to indicate the Champagne method of making sparkling wine.* Millésime – *year or vintage.* Mis en Bouteille au Château/Domaine – *bottled at the estate.* Moelleux – *sweet.* Monopole – *a vineyard owned by a single producer.* Mousseux – *sparkling.* Négociant (Eleveur) – *a merchant who buys, matures, bottles and sells wine.* Pétillant – *lightly sparkling.* Premier Cru – *"first growth", a quality designation that varies from area to area.* Propriétaire (Récoltant) – *vineyard owner/manager.* Réserve (Personelle) – *legally meaningless phrase.* Sur Lie – *aged on the lees (dead yeast).* VDQS (Vin Délimité de Qualité Supérieur) – *"soon-to-be-abolished" official designation for wines which are better than Vin de Pays but not good enough for Appellation Contrôlée.* Vieilles Vignes – *old vines (any age from 20–80 years), should indicate higher quality.* Villages – *supposedly best part of a larger region, as in Beaujolais-Villages.* Vin de Pays – *wine with regional character.* Vin de Table – *basic table wine.*

Still the benchmark, or set of benchmarks, against which winemakers in other countries test themselves. This is the place to find the Chardonnay in its finest oaked (white Burgundy) and unoaked (traditional Chablis) styles; the Sauvignon (from Sancerre and Pouilly

FRANCE

Fumé in the Loire, and in blends with the Sémillon, Bordeaux); the
Cabernet Sauvignon and Merlot (red Bordeaux); the Pinot Noir (red
Burgundy and Champagne); the Riesling, Gewurztraminer, and Pinots
Blanc and Gris (Alsace). The Chenin Blanc still fares better in the Loire
than anywhere else and, despite their successes in Australia, the Syrah
(aka Shiraz) and Grenache are still at their finest in the Rhône.

France is handicapped by the unpredictability of the climate in
most of its best regions and by the unreliability of many of its winemakers, who are often happy to coast along on the reputation of their
region. Unfortunately, a set of (Appellation Contrôlée) laws on the
one hand prevent producers from combatting climatic problems (by
irrigating, for example) and, on the other, legally allow them to get
away with selling their poor wine.

ALSACE

Reading the label: Sélection de Grains Nobles – *Sweet wine from
noble rot-affected grapes*. Vendange Tardive – *late harvested*.
Edelzwicker – *blend of white grapes, usually Pinot Blanc and Sylvaner*.

Often underrated, and confused with German wines from the other
side of the Rhine, Alsace deserves to be more popular. Its odd assort-
ment of grapes make wonderfully rich, spicy wine, both in their customary dry and more unusual, late harvest styles. This is my bet to
follow the success of its spicy red counterparts in the Rhône.

BORDEAUX

Reading the label: Chai – *cellar.* Cru Bourgeois – *level beneath Cru
Classé but possibly of similar quality.* Cru Classé – *"Classed Growth",
a wine featured in the 1855 classification of the Médoc and Graves, provides no guarantee of current quality.* Grand Cru/Grand Cru Classé –
*confusing terms, especially in St. Emilion, where the former is allo-
cated annually on the basis of a sometimes less-than-arduous tasting,
while the latter is reassessed every decade.*

For all but the keenest wine buff, Bordeaux is one big region (producing almost as much wine as Australia) with a few dozen châteaux
that have become internationally famous for their wine.

Visit the region, or take a look at the map, however, and you will
find that this is essentially a collection of quite diverse sub-regions,
many of which are separated by farmland, forest or water.

Heading north from the city of Bordeaux, the Médoc is the region
which includes the great communes of St. Estèphe, Pauillac, St. Julien,
and Margaux where some of the finest reds are made. Largely gravel
soil suiting the Cabernet Sauvignon, though lesser Médoc wines, of
which there are more than enough, tend to have a higher proportion

BORDEAUX

SOULAC-SUR-MER

Gironde

Médoc

St. Estèphe

PAUILLAC ● Côtes de Blaye

St. Julien ● BLAYE
Margaux
Listrac Côtes de Bourg
Moulis ● BOURG

Haut-Médoc Fronsac Pomerol
● LIBOURNE Libournais
St. Emilion
Côtes de Francs
Côtes de Castillon

BORDEAUX ●
Premières Côtes
de Bordeaux

Pessac-Léognan

Graves Entre-Deux-Mers

Cérons Loupiac
Ste. Croix-du-Mont
Barsac
LANGON ●
Sauternes

Garonne

Dordogne

– – – – AOC Bordeaux

of the Merlot. For the best examples of wines made principally from this variety, though, you have to head eastwards to St. Emilion and Pomerol and the regions of Bourg and Blaye where the Merlot is usually blended with the Cabernet Franc.

To the south of Bordeaux lie Pessac-Léognan and the Graves which produce some of Bordeaux's lighter, more delicate reds. This is also dry white country, where the Sémillon and Sauvignon Blanc hold sway. A little farther to the southeast, the often misty climate provides the conditions required to produce the noble rot required for the great sweet whites of Sauternes and Barsac.

Each of these regions produces its own individual style of wine. In some years, the climate suits one region and/or grape variety more than others. So, beware of vintage charts that seek to define the quality of an entire vintage across the whole of Bordeaux.

BURGUNDY

> **Reading the label:** Hospices de Beaune – *wines made and sold at auction by the charitable Hospices de Beaune.* Passetoutgrains – *a blend of Gamay and Pinot Noir.* Tasteviné – *a special label for wines that have* passed a tasting by the Confrérie des Chevaliers de Tastevin.

The heartland of the Pinot Noir and the Chardonnay and wines such as Chablis, Nuits-St-Georges, Gevrey-Chambertin, Beaune, Meursault, Puligny-Montrachet, Mâcon Villages, Pouilly-Fuissé and Beaujolais. According to the official quality pyramid, the best wines come from the Grands Crus vineyards; next are the Premiers Crus, followed by plain village wines and, last of all, basic Bourgogne Rouge or Blanc.

The region's individual producers make their wines with varying luck and expertise, generally selling in bulk to merchants who are just as variable in their skills and honesty. So, one producer's supposedly humble wine can be finer than another's pricier Premier or Grand Cru.

CHAMPAGNE

> **Reading the label:** Blanc de Blancs – *white wine from white grapes, i.e.*
> *pure Chardonnay.* Blancs de Noirs – *white wine made from black*
> *grapes.* Brut Sauvage/Zéro – *bone dry.* Extra-Dry – *(surprisingly)*
> *sweeter than Brut.* Grand Cru – *from a top-quality vineyard.*
> Négociant-manipulant (NM) – *buyer and blender of wines.* Non-
> Vintage – *a blend of wines usually based on wine of a single vintage.*
> Récoltant manipulant (RM) – *individual estate.*

Top-class Champagne has a unique blend of toasty richness and subtle fruit. Beware cheap examples, however, and poor wine from big-
name Champagne houses who should know better.

LOIRE

> **Reading the label:** Moelleux – *sweet.* Sur Lie – *on its lees (dead yeast),*
> *usually only applied to Muscadet.* Côt – *local name for the Malbec.*

This is the heartland of fresh, dry Sauvignons as well as honeyed sweet
wines from Vouvray, Quarts de Chaume and Bonnezeaux, fresh
sparkling wine in Saumur and Vouvray, and juicy, blackcurranty reds
in Chinon and Bourgeuil. Buy with care. Shoddy winemaking and
sulphur dioxide abuse can give wines – particularly late harvest, sweet
ones – an unpleasantly "woolly" character.

RHÔNE

> **Reading the label:** Vin Doux Naturel – *fortified wine, such as Muscat*
> *de Beaumes de Venise.* Côtes du Rhône Villages – *wine from one of a*
> *number of better sited villages in the overall Côtes du Rhône appella-*
> *tion, and thus, supposedly finer wine than plain Côtes du Rhône.*

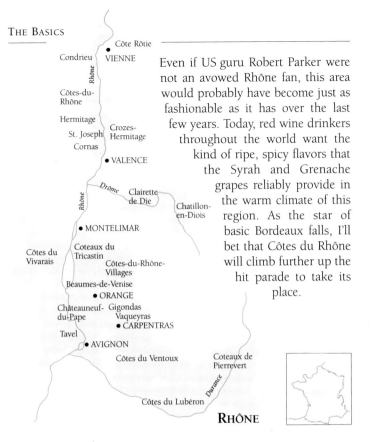

Even if US guru Robert Parker were not an avowed Rhône fan, this area would probably have become just as fashionable as it has over the last few years. Today, red wine drinkers throughout the world want the kind of ripe, spicy flavors that the Syrah and Grenache grapes reliably provide in the warm climate of this region. As the star of basic Bordeaux falls, I'll bet that Côtes du Rhône will climb further up the hit parade to take its place.

RHÔNE

THE SOUTHWEST

Reading the label: Perlé or Perlant – *gently sparkling, used in one of the styles of Gaillac.*

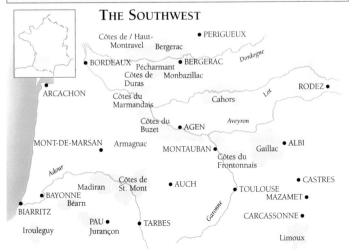

This conservative corner of France, heading inland from Bordeaux, is the home of sweet and dry Jurançon, Gaillac, Cahors, and Madiran. Once upon a time these wines, though famous among French wine buffs, were often quite old-fashioned in the worst sense of the term.

Today, a new wave of winemakers is learning how to extract unsuspected fruit flavors from grapes like the Gros and Petit Manseng, the Tannat, the Mauzac, and the Malbec. These wines are worth the detour for anyone bored with the ubiquitous Cabernet Sauvignon and Chardonnay and dissatisfied with poor quality claret.

THE SOUTH

Reading the label: Vin de Pays d'Oc – *country wine from the Languedoc region. Often some of the best stuff in the region.* Rancio – *woody, slightly volatile character in Banyuls and other fortified wines that have been aged in the barrel.*

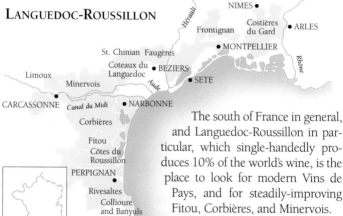

LANGUEDOC-ROUSSILLON

NIMES •

Frontignan Costières du Gard • ARLES

St. Chinian Faugères

Coteaux du Languedoc • BEZIERS • MONTPELLIER

Limoux

Minervois Aude • SETE

CARCASSONNE Canal du Midi • NARBONNE

Corbières

Fitou

Côtes du Roussillon

PERPIGNAN •

Rivesaltes

Collioure and Banyuls

The south of France in general, and Languedoc-Roussillon in particular, which single-handedly produces 10% of the world's wine, is the place to look for modern Vins de Pays, and for steadily-improving Fitou, Corbières, and Minervois.

The poor wines to be found here can be blamed on the conservatism of the producers. Even so, the combination of an ideal climate and increasingly dynamic winemaking is raising the quality here, as well as in Provence to the east, where classics such as Cassis and Bandol now attract as much attention as the ubiquitous rosé.

EASTERN FRANCE

Reading the label: Vin de Paille – *sweet, golden wine from grapes dried on straw mats.* Vin Jaune – *sherrylike, slightly oxidized wine.*

Savoie's zingy wines are often only thought of as skiing fare but, like Arbois' nutty, sherry-style whites, they are characterfully different, and made from grape varieties that are grown nowhere else.

GERMANY

Reading the label: Amtliche Prüfungsnummer (AP number) – *official identification number*. Auslese – *sweet wine from selected grapes above a certain ripeness level*. Beerenauslese – *luscious, sweet wines from selected, ripe grapes (Beeren), hopefully affected by botrytis*. Erzeugerabfüllung – *bottled by the grower/estate*. Halbtrocken – *off-dry*. Hock – *English name for Rhine wines*. Kabinett – *first step in German quality ladder, for wines which fulfil a certain natural sweetness*. Kellerei/Kellerabfüllung – *cellar/producer/estate-bottled*. Landwein – *a relatively recent quality designation – the equivalent of a French Vin de Pays*. QbA (Qualitätswein bestimmter Anbaugebiete) – *basic quality German wine, meeting certain standards*. QmP (Qualitätswein mit Prädikat) – *QbA wine with "special qualities" subject to (not very) rigorous testing. The QmP blanket designation is broken into five sweetness rungs, from Kabinett to Trockenbeerenauslese plus Eiswein*. Schloss – *literally "castle", the equivalent of Château, designating a vineyard or estate*. Sekt – *very basic, sparkling wine*. Spätlese – *second step in the QmP scale, late harvested grapes, a notch drier than Auslese*. Staatsweingut – *state-owned wine estate*. Tafelwein – *table wine, only the prefix "Deutscher" guarantees German origin*. Trocken – *dry*. Trockenbeerenauslese – *wine from selected dried grapes which are usually botrytis-affected*. Weingut – *estate*. Weinkellerei – *cellar or winery*. VDP – *the emblem of a group of quality-conscious producers*.

Ignore the oceans of sugar-water cynically exported by Germany under such labels as Liebfraumilch, Piesporter Michelsberg and Niersteiner Domtal. Ignore too, some of the big-name estates that still seem to get away with producing substandard fare. For real quality, look for Mosel Rieslings from producers like Dr Loosen and Richter, and new wave Rhine wines now being made by winemakers such as Künstler, Müller Catoir and Kurt Darting, not to mention the occasional successful red from Karl Lingenfelder. But, however convincing an explanation anyone might offer you for them, avoid dry "Trocken" Kabinett wines from northern Germany unless you want the tartar and enamel removed from your teeth.

ITALY

Reading the label:
Abboccato – *semi-dry*.
Amabile – *semi-sweet*.
Amaro – *bitter*. Asciutto
– *dry*. Azienda – *estate*.
Classico – *best vineyards at the heart of a DOC*. Colle/ colli – *hills*.
DOC(G) Denominazione di Origine Controllata (e Garantita) – *designation, based on grape variety and/or origin*.

Dolce – *sweet*. Frizzante – *semi-sparkling*. IGT, Indicazione Geografica Tipica – *new designation for quality Vino da Tavola*. Imbottigliato nel'origine – *estate-bottled*. Liquoroso – *rich, sweet*. Passito – *raisiny wine made from sun-dried grapes*. Recioto – *strong, sweet (unless designated Amarone)*. Vino da Tavola – *table wine outside the DOC system. Includes basic stuff as well as some of Italy's top wines. Now replaced by IGT*.

Three facts about Italy. **1)** It is more a set of regions than a single country. **2)** There is a tradition of interpreting laws fairly liberally. **3)** Style is often valued as highly as content. So when it comes to wine, this can be a confusing place. Producers do their own frequently delicious thing, using indigenous and imported grape varieties and designer bottles and labels in ways that leave legislators – and humble wine drinkers – exhilarated and exasperated in equal measure.

NEW ZEALAND

This New World country has one of the most unpredictable climates, but produces some of the most intensely flavored wines. There are gooseberryish Sauvignon Blancs, Chardonnays and innovative Rieslings and Gewürztraminers, as well as some impressive Pinot Noirs.

Hawke's Bay seems to be the most consistent region for reds, while Gisborne, Marlborough, Auckland, and Martinborough share the honors for white wine (though the last produces very classy Pinot Noir).

NORTH AFRICA

Islamic fundamentalism has done little to encourage winemaking of any description in North Africa. Even so, Algeria, Morocco, and Tunisia can all offer full-flavored, old-fashioned reds that will probably delight people who liked Burgundy when it routinely included a slug of Algerian blackstrap.

PORTUGAL

Reading the label: Adega – *winery*. Branco – *white*. Colheita – *vintage*. Engarrafado na origem – *estate-bottled*. Garrafeira – *a vintage-dated wine with a little more alcohol and minimum aging requirements*. Quinta – *vineyard or estate*. Reserva – *wine from a top-quality vintage, made from riper grapes than the standard requirement*. Velho – *old*. Vinho de Mesa – *table wine*.

Like Italy, Portugal has grapes grown nowhere else in the world. Unlike Italy, however, until recently the Portuguese had done little to persuade foreigners of the quality of these varieties.

But now, thanks to a new generation of innovative producers like Luis Pato in Bairrada and Jose Neiva, with a bit of help from Australians like David Baverstock and Peter Bright we can see what the native grapes can do.

Try any of Pato's Bairradas, Bright's new-wave Douro reds, and Baverstock's tasty Quinta do Crasto red wines from the Douro.

PORTUGAL

SOUTH AFRICA

Reading the label: Cap Classique – *South African term for Champagne method sparklers*. Cultivar – *grape variety*. Edel laat-oes – *noble late harvest*. Edelkeur – *"noble rot", a fungus affecting grapes and producing sweet wine*. Gekweek, gemaak en gebottel op – *estate-bottled*. Landgoedwyn – *estate wine*. Laat-oes – *late harvest*. Oesjaar – *vintage*. Steen – *local name for Chenin Blanc*.

Until recently, as visitors from Bordeaux, Britain and Australia have noticed, too many wines have had the "green" flavour of over-cropped and underripe grapes. Wineries like Thelema, Saxenburg, Plaisir de Merle, Vergelegen and Fairview show what can be done, while Grangehurst, Kanonkop and Vriesenhof support the cause for South Africa's own spicy red grape, the Pinotage.

Chardonnays and Sauvignons are often very European in style – as are late harvest and sparkling wines.

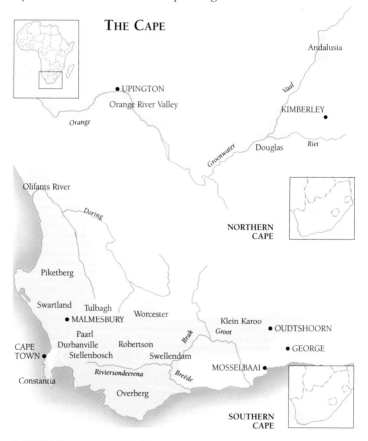

THE CAPE

SOUTH AMERICA

BOLIVIA

• BRASILIA

• LA PAZ

BRAZIL

Parana

PACIFIC
OCEAN

PARAGUAY

RIO DE JANEIRO

Salta *Teuco*

SAO PAULO •

Catamarca   Tucamán

Salado

ASUNCION

La Rioja

ATLANTIC
OCEAN

Aconcagua   San Juan   • CORDOBA   URUGUAY

Casablanca   Mendoza   • ROSARIO

• SANTIAGO

Rapel   Maipo   BUENOS

Curicó   AIRES   MONTEVIDEO

Maule   ARGENTINA   La Pampa

Itata   *Colorado*

Bio Bio

Rio

CHILE   Negro

Negro

Chico

SOUTH
AMERICA

ARGENTINA

> **Reading the label:** Malbec – *spicy red grape*. Torrontes – *unusual grapey white*.

As it chases Chile, this is a country to watch. The wines to look for now are the spicy reds made from the Malbec, a variety once widely grown in Bordeaux and still used in the Loire. Cabernets can be good too, as can the grapey but dry white Torrontes.

CHILE

> **Reading the label:** Envasado en Origen – *estate-bottled*. Carmenère/Grand Vidure – *grape variety once used in Bordeaux*.

One of the most exciting wine-producing countries in the world, thanks to ideal conditions, skilled local winemaking and plentiful investment. The most successful grape at present is the Merlot, but the Cabernet, Chardonnay, Pinot Noir and Sauvignon can all display ripe fruit and subtlety often absent in the New World.

SOUTHEASTERN EUROPE

GREECE

Finally casting off its image as purveyor of Europe's worst wines, Greece is beginning to show what can be done with "international" grapes and highly characterful indigenous varieties. Prices are high (so is demand in smart Athens restaurants), but as the new-wave wines trickle out into the outside world, producers like Château Lazaridi, Gentilini, and Hatzimichali are set for international success.

CYPRUS

Still associated with cheap sherry-substitute and dull wine, but things are changing. Look out for the traditional rich Commandaria.

TURKEY

Lurching out of the vinous dark ages, Turkey has yet to offer the world red or white wines that non-Turks are likely to relish.

LEBANON

Château Musar has survived all the tribulations of the last few years, keeping Lebanon on the map as a wine-producing country.

ISRAEL

Israel's best Cabernet and Muscat now comes from the Yarden winery in the Golan Heights – a region which may soon lose its Israeli nationality as part of a new peace agreement.

SPAIN

> **Reading the label**: Abocado – *semi-dry*. Año – *year*. Bodega – *winery or wine cellar*. Cava – *Champagne method sparkling wine*. Criado y Embotellado (por) – *grown and bottled (by)*. Crianza – *aged in wood*. DO(Ca) (Denominacion de Origen (Calificada)) – *Spain's quality designation, based on regional style. Calificada (DOC) indicates superior quality*. Elaborado y Anejado Por – *made and aged for*. Gran Reserva – *wine aged for a designated number of years in wood; longer than for Reserva*. Joven – *young wine, specially made for early consumption*. Reserva – *official designation for wine that has been aged for a specific period*. Sin Crianza – *not aged in wood*. Vendemia – *harvest or vintage*. Vino de Mesa – *table wine*. Vino de la Tierra – *designation similar to the French "Vin de Pays."*

Spain used to be relied on for a certain style of highly predictable wine: soft, oaky reds with flavors of strawberry and vanilla, and whites that were either light, dry and unmemorable (Marqués de Cáceres Rioja Blanco), oaky and old-fashioned (traditional Marqués de Murrieta Rioja), or sweet and grapey (Moscatel de

SPAIN

Valencia). Suddenly, however, like a car whose driver has just found an extra gear, Spanish wines have begun to leap ahead – into often largely uncharted territory. The first region to hail the revolution was Penedés, where winemaker Miguel Torres made a specialty of using both traditional and imported grape varieties.

Others have overtaken Torres, in regions like Somontano, Rueda, and Navarra. In Rioja itself experiments are quietly going on to see whether the Cabernet Sauvignon can improve the flavor of this traditional wine. There are traditionalists who would prefer all this pioneering business to stop, but the wine genie is out of the Spanish bottle and there seems little chance of anyone forcing it back inside again.

SWITZERLAND

> **Reading the label:** Gutedel, Perlan, Fendant – *local names for the Chasselas*. Grand Cru – *top designation which varies from one canton to the next*. Süssdruck – *off-dry, red wine*.

Notable for being the only place in the world where the Chasselas produces anything even remotely memorable – and the country that has sensibly switched from corks to screwcaps for many of its wines. Other grapes worth looking out for are the white (Petite) Arvigne and Amigne (de Vétroz) and the red Cornalin, as well as the Gamay, Syrah, Pinot Noir, and Merlot, a variety that is used to make white wines here.

USA

Reading the label: Blush – *rosé*. Champagne – *any sparkling wine.* Fumé – *oak-aged white wine, especially Sauvignon (Blanc Fumé).* Meritage – *popular, if pretentious, name for a Bordeaux blend (white or red).* Vinted – *made by (a vintner, or winemaker).* White Grenache/Zinfandel, etc) – *refers to the unfashionable rosé, slightly pink wines, sometimes also referred to as "blush".*

CALIFORNIA

These are busy days for the best-known winemaking state of the Union. After 20 years of almost single-minded devotion to the Chardonnay and Cabernet Sauvignon and to the Napa Valley, the focus has broadened to take in a wider range of grapes (particularly Italian and Rhône varieties) and regions (Sonoma, Santa Barbara, especially for the Pinot Noir, plus San Luis Obispo, Santa Cruz, Mendocino and Monterey).

CALIFORNIA

Within the Napa Valley too, where vineyards are being replanted in the wake of the damage caused by the phylloxera louse, there is growing acknowledgement that some sub-regions produce better wines than others. Carneros is already famous for its Pinot Noir, Oakville for its Chardonnay, while Rutherford and Stag's Leap are known for their Cabernet. But do try other worthwhile areas, such as Mount Veeder and Howell Mountain.

THE PACIFIC NORTH-WEST

Outside California, head north to Oregon for some of the best Pinot Noirs in the US (at a hefty price) and improving, but rarely earth-shattering Chardonnays, Rieslings and Pinot Gris. Washington State has some Pinot too, on the cooler, rainy west side of the Cascade mountains. On the east, the irrigated vineyards produce great Sauvignon and Riesling, as well as top-flight Chardonnay, Cabernet Sauvignon and – especially impressive Syrah and Merlot.

NEW YORK AND OTHER STATES

Once the source of dire "Chablis" and "Champagne", New York State is now producing worthwhile wines, particularly in the microclimate of Long Island, where the Merlot thrives. The Finger Lakes are patchier but worth visiting, especially for the Rieslings and cool-climate Chardonnays. Elsewhere Virginia, Missouri, Texas, Maryland and even Arizona are all producing wines to compete with California and indeed some of the best that Europe can offer.

THE GRAPES

BLENDS OR SINGLE VARIETIES?

Some wines are made from single grape varieties – e.g., red or white Burgundy, Sancerre, German Riesling, and Barolo – while others, such as red or white Bordeaux, California "Meritage" wines, port, and Châteauneuf-du-Pape, are blends of two or more types of grape. Champagne can fall into either camp, as can New World "varietal" wines which, though labeled as "Chardonnay," "Cabernet Sauvignon," etc., can contain up to 25 percent of other grape varieties. Blends are not, per se, superior to single varietals – or vice versa.

Freshly picked black grapes ready for crushing.

WHITE WINE GRAPES

CHARDONNAY

Ubiquitous but hard to define because of the influences of climate, the soil and the particular clone type. Burgundy and the best California examples, (Kistler, Peter Michael, Sonoma Cutrer) taste of butter and hazelnuts; lesser New World efforts are often sweet and simple and often very melony (a flavor which comes from the clone). Australians range from subtle buttery pineapple to oaky tropical fruit juice. Petaluma, Coldstream Hills, and Leeuwin show how it can be done. New Zealand's efforts are tropical too, but lighter and fresher (Te Mata, Cloudy Bay). Elsewhere, Chile is beginning to hit the mark, as is South Africa (Jordan). In Europe, look around southern France, Italy, Spain, and Eastern Europe, but beware of watery cheaper versions.

CHENIN BLANC

Loire variety producing fresh sparkling wine, dry, and luscious honeyed wines; also raw stuff like unripe apples and, when over-sulfured, old socks. Most California Chenins are semisweet and ordinary. South Africans call it the Steen and use it for sweet wines. There are few good Australians (but try Moondah Brook) or New Zealanders (Millton).

GEWÜRZTRAMINER

Outrageous stuff that smells of parma violets and tastes of lychee nuts. At its best in Alsace, dry and sweet, as a Vendange Tardive or Sélection de Grains Nobles (Zind Humbrecht, Schlumberger, Faller). Try examples from Germany, New Zealand, and Italy too.

Chenin Blanc   *Gewürztraminer*

MARSANNE

A classic, flowery, lemony variety used in the Rhône in wines like Hermitage (from producers like Guigal), and in Australia – especially in Goulburn in Victoria (Chateau Tahbilk and Mitchelton); in southern France (from Mas de Daumas Gassac); Switzerland (late harvest efforts from Provins) and in innovative wines from California. At its best young or after five or six years.

MUSCAT

The only variety whose wines actually taste as though they are made of grapes, rather than some other kind of fruit or vegetable. In Alsace, southern France, and northeast Italy it is used to make dry wines. Generally, though, it performs best as sparkling wine (Moscatos, and Asti Spumantes from Italy and Clairette de Die Tradition from France) and as sweet fortified wine. Look out for Beaumes de Venise and Rivesaltes in southern France, Moscatel de Setúbal in Portugal, Moscatel de Valencia in Spain, and Christmas-puddingy Liqueur Muscat in Australia (Morris, Chambers, Yalumba).

PINOT BLANC/PINOT BIANCO

As rich as Chardonnay, but with less fruit. At its worst – when overcropped in Alsace and Italy, it makes neutral wine. At its best, however (also in Alsace), it can develop a lovely cashew nut flavour. When well handled it can also do well in Italy, where it is known as Pinot Bianco (Jermann), and in Germany, where it is called Weissburgunder. Most California Pinot Blancs are really made from the duller Melon de Bourgogne of Muscadet fame.

PINOT GRIS

An up-and-coming Alsace variety also known as Tokay but unrelated to any of the world's other Tokays. Its wines can be spicy, and appear in both sweet and dry versions. In Italy, where it is often used to make dilute wine, it is called Pinot Grigio, and in Germany it is known as Grauerburgunder. Look for New World examples from Oregon (Eyrie), California and New Zealand.

RIESLING

For purists this, not the Chardonnay, is the king of white varieties. Misunderstood – and often mispronounced as Rice-ling rather than Rees-ling – it carries the can for torrents of cheap German wine made from quite different grapes. At its best, it makes dry and sweet grapey, appley, limey wines that develop a spicy "petrolly" character with age. Quality and character depend on soil – ideally slate – more than climate and while the best examples come from Germany, in the Mosel (Maximin Grünhaus), the Rhine (Schloss Johannisberg) and Alsace (Zind-Humbrecht, Faller), this variety can perform equally well in such different environments as Washington State (Arbor Crest), Australia (Grossett, Tim Adams) and New Zealand (Matua Valley). Don't confuse the Riesling with such unrelated varieties as Lazki, Lutomer, Welsch, Emerald or White Riesling.

Riesling   *Sauvignon Blanc*

SAUVIGNON BLANC

The grape of Loire wines, such as Sancerre and Pouilly Fumé, and white Bordeaux, where it is often blended with the Sémillon. This gooseberryish variety now performs brilliantly in Marlborough in New Zealand (where the flavours can include asparagus and pea-pods), in South Africa (Thelema) and Australia (Shaw & Smith, Cullens). Chile has some good examples (from Casablanca) – and poor ones, made from a different variety called the Sauvignonasse. Washington State can get it right, but in California it is often horribly sweet or overburdened by the flavour of oak. (Oaked versions here and elsewhere are usually labelled Fumé Blanc.) Only the best ones improve after the first couple of years.

SÉMILLON

A distinctive peachy variety with only two successful homes. In Bordeaux, usually in blends with the Sauvignon Blanc, it produces sublime dry Graves and sweet Sauternes – and over-sulphured stuff that tastes like old dishcloths. In Australia there are brilliant, long-lived dry wines which are made purely from the Sémillon in the Hunter Valley (often unoaked) and Barossa Valley (usually oaked). Good "noble" late-harvest examples have also been produced (by de Bortoli) in Riverina. Elsewhere in Australia the grape is sometimes blended with the Chardonnay, a cocktail which has proved popular in California (in Geyser Peak's Semchard). Progress is being made in Washington State but most examples from California, New Zealand and Chile are disappointing.

SYLVANER

A characterful grape rarely found outside Alsace and Franken in Germany, the Sylvaner has a recognisably "earthy" character at odds with most modern wines. Crossing the Sylvaner with the Riesling, incidentally, produced both the Scheurebe and the Müller-Thurgau.

Sémillon   *Viognier*

VIOGNIER

A cult grape, the Viognier was once only found in Condrieu and Château Grillet in the Rhône, where small numbers of good examples showed off its extraordinary perfumed, peach-blossomy character, albeit at a high price. Today, however, it has been widely introduced to the Ardèche and Languedoc-Roussillon, California (where it is sometimes confused with the Roussanne) and made with loving care (and generous exposure to oak barrels) – Eastern Europe, Argentina, and Australia (Yalumba). While affordable examples are welcome, many are disappointing. Buy with care.

RED WINE GRAPES

BARBERA

A wild-berryish Italian variety at its best in Piedmont. Increasingly successful in blends with the Nebbiolo and Cabernet. Good in Argentina; making inroads into California and Australia (Brown Bros.)

CABERNET SAUVIGNON

A remarkable success story, historically associated with the great red wines of the Médoc and Graves (where it is blended with the Merlot) and, more recently, with some of the best reds from the New World, especially California, Chile, and Australia. Eastern Europe has good value examples (Bulgaria), as does southern France (Vin de Pays). Spain is rapidly climbing aboard (in the Penedès, Navarra, and – though this is kept quiet – Rioja). The hallmark to look for is blackcurrant, though unripe versions taste like a blend of weeds and bell peppers. There are some great Cabernets in Italy, though the "Italian wine" flavor somehow always dominates the grape. Good New World Cabernets can smell and taste of fresh mint, but with time, like the best Bordeaux, they develop a rich, leathery "cigar box" character.

Cabernet Sauvignon   *Grenache/Garnacha*

GRENACHE/GARNACHA

Pepper – freshly ground black pepper – is the distinguishing flavor here, sometimes with the fruity tang of penny candy. At home in Côtes du Rhône and Châteauneuf-du-Pape, it is also used in Spain (as the Garnacha) in blends with the Tempranillo. Seek out "Old Vine" or "Bush" examples from Australia.

Merlot

Nebbiolo/Spanna

MERLOT

The most widely planted variety in Bordeaux and the subject of eager planting in California. In Bordeaux it is at its best in Pomerol, where wines can taste of ripe plums and spice, and in St. Emilion, where the least successful wines show the Merlot's less lovable dull and earthy character. Wherever it is made, the Merlot should produce softer wines than the Cabernet Sauvignon, though some California examples have been tough. Elsewhere, Washington State and Chile are places to look, along with Italy and Eastern Europe.

NEBBIOLO/SPANNA

The red wine grape of Barolo and Barbaresco in Piedmont now, thanks to modern winemaking, increasingly reveals a lovely cherry and rose-petal character, often with the sweet vanilla of new oak casks.

PINOT NOIR

The wild raspberryish, plummy, and licoricey grape of red Burgundy, is also a major component of white and pink Champagne. It makes red and pink Sancerre, as well as light reds in Alsace and Germany (where it is called Spätburgunder). Italy makes a few good examples, but for the best, modern efforts, look to California – especially Carneros (Saintsbury) and Santa Barbara (Au Bon Climat) – Oregon (Domaine Drouhin), Australia (Coldstream Hills), New Zealand (Martinborough), Chile (Cono Sur, Valdivieso), and South Africa.

PINOTAGE

Almost restricted to South Africa, this cross between the Pinot Noir and the Cinsaut can make berryish young wines that may develop rich gamey-spicy flavours. Try Kanonkop and Vriesenhof.

SANGIOVESE

The grape of Chianti, Brunello di Montalcino and of a host of popular Vino da Tavola wines in Italy, not to mention 'new wave' Italian-style wines in California. The recognisable flavour is of sweet tobacco, wild herbs and berries.

SYRAH/SHIRAZ

The spicy, brambly grape of the Northern Rhône (Hermitage, Cornas, etc) and the best reds of Australia (Henschke Hill of Grace and Penfolds Grange), where it is also blended with the Cabernet Sauvignon (just as it once was in Bordeaux). Marqués de Griñon has a great Spanish example, and Isole e Olena has made an unofficial one in Tuscany. Increasingly successful in California and Washington State.

Syrah/Shiraz   *Zinfandel*

TEMPRANILLO

Known under all sorts of names around Spain, including Cencibel (in Navarra) and Tinto Fino (in Ribeira del Duero), the grape gives Spanish reds their recognisable strawberry character. Often blended with the Garnacha, it works well with the Cabernet Sauvignon.

ZINFANDEL

California's "own", related to the Italian Primitivo. In California, it makes rich spicy blueberryish reds (see Ridge Vineyards) and "ports" and, when blended with sweet Muscat, sweet pink "White Zinfandel". Outside California, Cape Mentelle makes a good example in Western Australia and Delheim a floral one in South Africa.

OTHER GRAPES

WHITE

Albariño/Alvarinho Floral. Grown in Spain and Portugal.
Aligoté Lean Burgundy grape.
Arneis Perfumed variety in Piedmont.
Colombard Appley, basic; grown in S.W. France, US and Australia.
Furmint Limey variety, traditionally used for Tokaji.
Grüner Veltliner Limey. Restricted to Austria and Eastern Europe.
Kerner Dull German grape. Can taste leafy.
Müller-Thurgau/Rivaner Dull variety, grown in Germany and England. Can have a similar "cat's pee" character to Sauvignon.
Roussanne Fascinating Rhône variety that deserves more attention.
Scheurebe Exciting grapefruity grape grown in Germany.
Torrontes Grapey, Muscat-like variety of Argentina.
Ugni Blanc/Trebbiano Basic grape of S.W. France and Italy.
Verdejo Interesting Spanish variety of Rueda.
Verdelho Limey grape found in Madeira and Australian table wine.
Viura Widely planted, so-so Spanish variety.
Welschriesling Basic. Best in late harvest Austrians.

RED

Cabernet Franc Kid-brother of Cabernet Sauvignon, grown alongside it in Bordeaux and by itself in the Loire and Italy.
Carmenère/Grand Vidure Exciting spicy smoky variety.
Charbono Fun spicy-berryish grape only grown in California.
Cinsaut Spicy Rhône variety; best in blends.
Carignan Toffeeish non-aromatic variety widely used in S. France.
Concord US grape better used for grape juice or jelly.
Dolcetto Cherryish Piedmont grape.
Dornfelder Successful juicy variety grown in Germany.
Gamay The Beaujolais grape; less successful in the Loire and Gaillac.
Gamay Beaujolais/Valdiguié Mulberryish cousin of the Pinot Noir, grown in California. Confusingly unrelated to the Gamay.
Lemberger/Limberger/Blaufränkisch Berryish; successful in Washington State.
Malbec/Côt Once in Bordeaux blends; now Cahors, Loire, Argentina.
Mourvèdre (Mataro) Spicy Rhône grape; good in California and Australia, but can be hard and "metallic".
Petit Verdot Spicy ingredient of Bordeaux. Now being used neat.
Petite-Sirah Spicy; thrives in California and Mexico. Durif in Australia.
Ruby Cabernet Basic Carignan-Cabernet Sauvignon cross.
Tannat Tough variety of Madiran and Uruguay.

Styles

1880 A formal dinner party, by Georges du Maurier.

Style Counsel

In simple terms, wine can be separated into a few easily recognizable styles: red, white and pink; still and sparkling; sweet and dry; light and fortified. To say that the contents of a bottle are red and dry does little, however, to convey the way a wine tastes. It could be a fruity Beaujolais, a mature Rioja, a blueberryish California Zinfandel, or a tough young Bordeaux.

Knowing the grape and origin of a wine can give a clearer idea of what it is like, but it won't tell you everything. The human touch is as important in wine as it is in the kitchen. Some chefs like to assemble eclectic flavors while others prefer more conservative ingredients. The wine world is similarly divided between producers who focus on obvious fruit flavors, and winemakers, in France for example, who go for the *goût de terroir* – the taste of the earth or soil.

In a world that is increasingly given to instant sensations, it is perhaps unsurprising that it is the fruit-lovers rather than the friends of the earthy flavor who are currently in the ascendant.

New World/Old World

Until recently, these two philosophies broadly belonged to the New and Old World. Places like California and Australia made wine that was approachably delicious when compared with the more serious wine being produced in Europe, which demanded time and food.

Life is never quite that cut-and-dried, however. Today, there are Bordeaux châteaux that are taking a decidedly New World approach and South Africans who take a pride in making wine as resolutely tough and old-fashioned as a Bordeaux of a hundred years ago.

Flying Winemakers

One phenomenon that has contributed to these changes has been the "flying winemakers" – mostly Antipodeans, who are contracted to produce wine all over the world. Today, you can choose between a white Loire made by a Frenchman – or one bearing the fruity fingerprint of Australian-rules winemaking.

Fruit of Knowledge

European old timers like to claim that the Australians use alchemy to obtain those fruity flavors. In fact, their secret lies in the winemaking process. Picking the grapes when they are ripe (rather than too early); preventing them from cooking beneath the midday sun (as often happens in Europe while work stops for lunch); pumping the juice through pipes that have been cleaned daily rather than at each end of the harvest; fermenting at a cool temperature (overheated vats can cost a wine its freshness); and storing and bottling it carefully, will all help a wine made from even the dullest grape variety to taste fruitier.

COME HITHER

If the New Worlders want their wines to taste of fruit, they are – apart from some reactionary South Africans and Californians – just as eager to make wine that can be drunk young. They take care not to squeeze the red grapes too hard, so as not to extract bitter, hard tannins, and they try to avoid their white wines being too acidic.

Traditionalists claim these wines do not age well. It is too early to say whether this is true, but there is no question that the newer wave red Bordeaux of, say 1985, have given more people more pleasure since they were released, than the supposedly greater 1970 vintage, whose wines remained dauntingly hard throughout their lifetime. A wine does not have to be undrinkable in its youth to be good later on; indeed, wines that start out tasting unbalanced go on tasting that way.

SPOTTING THE WOOD FROM THE TREES

Another thing that sets many new wave wines apart has nothing to do with grapes. Wines have been matured in oak barrels since Roman times, and traditionally new barrels were only bought to replace old ones that had begun to fall apart. Old casks have little flavor but, for the first two years or so of their lives, the way the staves are bent over flames gives new ones a recognizable vanilla and caramel character. Winemakers once used to rinse out their new casks with dilute ammonia to remove this flavour. Today, however, they often take the choice of forest, cooper and charring (light, medium or heavy "toast") as seriously as the quality of their grapes.

Oak-mania began when Bordeaux châteaux began to spend the income from the great vintages of the 1940s on replacements for their old barrels – and when New World pioneers like Mondavi noticed the contribution the oak was making to these wines. Ever since, top producers and would-be top producers internationally have introduced new barrels, while even the makers of cheaper wine have found that dunking giant "teabags" filled with small oak chips into wine vats could add some of that vanilla flavour too.

If you like oak, you'll find it in top-flight Bordeaux and Burgundy (red and white), Spanish Crianza, Reserva, or Gran Reserva and Italians whose labels use the French term "Barrique". The words "Elevé en fût de Chêne" on a French wine could confusingly refer to new or old casks. Australian "Show Reserve" will be oaky, as will Fumé Blanc and New World Reserve and "Barrel Select" wines.

RED WINES – FRUITS, SPICE AND . . . COLD TEA

If you enjoy your red wines soft and juicily fruity, the styles to look for are Burgundy and other wines made from the Pinot Noir, Rioja, and reds from Spain, inexpensive Australians, Pomerol, good St. Emilion from Bordeaux, and Merlots from almost anywhere. Look too for Nouveau, Novello, and Joven (young wines).

The Kitchen Cupboard
Italy's Sangiovese is not so much fruity as herby, while the Syrah/Shiraz of the Rhône and Australia, the peppery Grenache and – sometimes – the Zinfandel and Pinotage can be surprisingly spicy.

Some Like it Tough
Most basic Bordeaux and all but a few wines from St. Estèphe and Listrac in Bordeaux are more tannic, as are most older-style wines from Piedmont, California, and most South Africans. The Cabernet Sauvignon will make tougher wines than the Merlot or Pinot Noir.

WHITE WINES – HONEY AND LEMON

If dry wines with unashamedly fruity flavours are what you want, try the Muscat, the Torrontes in Argentina, basic Riesling and Chardonnay, and New World and Southern French Sauvignon Blanc.

Non-Fruit
For more neutral styles, go for Italian Soave or Frascati, Grenache Blanc, Muscadet, and most traditional wines from Spain and Southern France.

Riches Galore

The combination of richness and fruit is to be found in white Burgundy, better dry white Bordeaux and in Chardonnays, Semillons, and oaked Sauvignon (Fumé) wines from the New World.

Aromatherapy

Some perfumed, spicy grapes, like the Gewürztraminer, are frankly aromatic. The Tokay-Pinot Gris, the Gewürztraminer's neighbour in Alsace, fits the bill, as do the Viognier in France, the Arneis in Italy, the Albariño in Spain and the Grüner Veltliner in Austria.

Middle of the Road

Today, people want wine that is – or says it is – either dry or positively sweet. The Loire can get honeyed semisweet wine right. Otherwise, head for Germany and Kabinett and Spätlese wines.

Pure Hedonism

Sweet wine is making a comeback as people rebel against the health fascism that sought to outlaw such pleasures. The first places to look are Bordeaux, the Loire (Moelleux), Alsace (Vendange Tardive or Sélection des Grains Nobles); Germany (Auslese, Beerenauslese Trockenbeerenauslese); Austria (Ausbruch); the New World (late harvest and noble late harvest); and Hungary (Tokaji 6 Puttonyos).

All of these wines should not only taste sweet, but have enough fresh acidity to prevent them from being in the least cloying. Also, they should have the additional, characteristic dried-apricot flavour that comes from grapes that have been allowed to be affected by a benevolent fungus known as "botrytis" or "noble rot".

Other sweet wines such as Muscat de Beaumes de Venise are fortified with brandy to raise their strength to 15% or so. These wines can be luscious too, but they never have the flavour of "noble rot".

PINK

Tread carefully. Provence and the Rhône should offer peppery-dry rosé just as the Loire and Bordeaux should have wines that taste deliciously of blackcurrant. Sadly, many taste dull and stale. Still, they are a better bet than California's dire sweet "white" or "blush" rosé. Look for the most recent vintage and the most vibrant colour.

SPARKLING

If you find Champagne too dry, but don't want a frankly sweet grapey fizz like Asti Spumante, try a fruity New World sparkler like the Cuvée Napa from California or Seaview from Australia. If you don't like that fruitiness, try traditional Cava from Spain, Prosecco from Italy, and Blanquette de Limoux from France.

STORING

Keep track of your bottles.

STARTING A CELLAR

THE RESTING PLACE

Not so long ago, when winemaking was less sophisticated and there were fewer ways to counter tricky vintages, there were two kinds of wines: the basic stuff to drink immediately, and the cream of the crop that was left in the barrel and/or bottle to age. So, a good wine was an old wine. And vice versa. Young wine and old wine had as much in common as hamburgers and *haute cuisine*.

Today there are brilliant wines that never improve beyond the first few years after the harvest, and are none the worse for that. On the other hand, some wines – German Riesling, fine claret, and top Australian Shiraz, for example – by their very nature, still repay a few years' patience in the cellar.

While many of us live in homes that are ill-suited for storing wine, one can often find an unused grate or a space beneath the stairs that offers wine what it wants: a constant temperature of around 44–60°F (never lower than 40°F nor more than 68°F), reasonable humidity (install a cheap humidifier or leave a sponge in a bowl of water), sufficient ventilation to avoid a musty atmosphere and, ideally, an absence of vibration (wines stored beneath train tracks – or beds – age faster). Alternatively, invest in a fridgelike Eurocave that guarantees perfect conditions – or even adapt an old freezer.

RACKS AND CELLAR BOOKS

Purpose-built racks can be bought "by the hole" and cut to fit. Square chimney pots can be used too. If you have plenty of space, simply allocate particular racks to specific styles of wine. Unfortunately, even the best-laid cellar plans tend to fall apart when two cases of Australian Shiraz has to be squeezed into a space big enough just for one.

If the size of the cellar warrants it, give each hole in the rack a cross-referenced identity, from A1 at the top left to, say, Z100 at the bottom right. As bottles arrive, they can then be put in any available hole, and their address noted in a cellar book in which you can record when and where you obtained it, what it cost and how each bottle tasted (is it improving or drying out?). Some people, like me, prefer to use a computer program (Filemaker Pro or Microsoft Excel).

TO DRINK OR KEEP?

A guide to which corks to pop soon and which bottles to treasure for a few years in the rack:

Drink as Soon as Possible
Most wine at under $8, particularly Muscadet, Vins de Pays, white Bordeaux; Nouveau/Novello/Joven reds; Bardolino, Valpolicella; light Italian whites; most Sauvignon Blanc; almost all rosé.

Less than 5 Years
Most Petit-Château Bordeaux and Cru Bourgeois, and lesser Cru Classés clarets from poorer vintages; basic Alsace, Burgundy and better Beaujolais; Chianti, Barbera, basic Spanish reds; good mid-quality Germans; English wines; cheaper New World Chardonnays; all but the finest New and Old World Sauvignons; basic South African, Chilean, and Australian reds.

5-10 Years
Most Cru Bourgeois Bordeaux from good years; better châteaux from lesser vintages; all but the best red and white Burgundy and Pinot and Chardonnay from elsewhere; middle-quality Rhônes; southern-French higher flyers; good German, Alsace, dry Loire and white Bordeaux; Portuguese reds; California and Washington State; South African, Chilean, and New Zealand Merlots.

Over 10 Years
Top-class Bordeaux, Rhône, Burgundy, and sweet Loire from ripe years; top-flight German late harvest, Italian Vino da Tavola and Barolo; best Australian Shiraz, Cabernet, Rieslings and Semillon, and California Cabernet.

SERVING

From the Correr Museum in Venice. Graeco-Venetian School,
16th Century: "The Marriage Feast at Cana".

THE RULES OF THE GAME

"The art in using wine is to produce the greatest possible
quantity of present gladness, without any future depression."
The Gentleman's Table Guide, 1873

The Romans used to add salt to their wine to preserve it, while the
Greeks favoured pine resin (which helps to explain the popularity of
pine-flavoured Retsina today). Burgundians often refer to Napoleon's
taste for Chambertin, but rarely mention that he used to dilute his red
wine with water. A century ago, the English used to add ice to claret
and – in winter, in Europe today, skiers – drink hot "mulled" wine,
adding sugar, fruit, and spices. Today, Chinese wine drinkers
apparently prefer their Mouton Cadet with a dash of Sprite. And why
not? Millions of British wine drinkers got their first taste of wine in the
form of sangria – a blend of wine, lemonade and fresh fruit. I'm sure
the addition of lemonade would do many a skinny Bordeaux a world
of good – it's just rather a pity when it's added to a classier glass of
Médoc or St. Emilion. It's well worth questioning accepted rules –
especially when they vary between cultures. Have no fear, the advice
that follows is based on common sense and experience – and offered
only to help you to decide how you enjoy serving and drinking wine.

SOME LIKE IT HOT

Particular styles of wine taste better at particular temperatures. At many restaurants, though, white and sparkling wine are more often served too cold than too hot. Paradoxically, it is the reds that suffer most from being drunk too warm. Few of the people who serve wines at "room temperature" recall that, when that term was coined, there wasn't a lot of central heating. Be ready to chill a fruity red in a bucket of ice and water for five to ten minutes before serving.

Don't cook your reds – or freeze your whites...

Red Wine

When serving red, focus on the wine's flavour. Tough wines are best slightly warmer. The temperatures given are a rule-of-thumb guide:
1) Beaujolais and other fruity reds: 10–13°C (an hour in the fridge).
2) Younger red Burgundy and Rhônes and older Bordeaux, Chianti, younger Rioja, New World Grenache, and Pinotage: 14–16°C.
3) Older Burgundy, tannic young Bordeaux, and Rhônes, Zinfandel, bigger Cabernet Sauvignon, Merlot, and Shiraz, Barolo, and other bigger Italian and Spanish reds: 16–18°C.

Rosé

Rosé should be chilled at 12–13°C, or for five to ten minutes in a bucket of ice and water.

White Wine

The cooler the wine, the less it will smell or taste. Subtler, richer wines deserve to be drunk a little warmer.
1) Lighter sweeter wines and everyday sparklers: 4–8°C (two or three hours in the fridge or 10–15 minutes in ice and water).
2) Fuller-bodied, aromatic, drier, semidry, lusciously sweet whites; Champagne, simpler Sauvignons, and Chardonnays: 8–11°C.
3) Richer dry wines: Burgundy, California Chardonnay: 12–13°C.

THE PERFECT OUTCOME

The patented Screwpull is still the most reliable way to get a cork out of bottle. The "waiter's friend" is the next best thing; otherwise choose a corkscrew that comes in the form of a wire spiral rather than that looks like a large screw.

Good corkscrews all have spirals rather than screws.

WHICH GLASSES?

On occasions when no other glass was available I have enjoyed great wine from a toothbrushing mug. I suspect I'd have gotten more out of the experience if something a bit more stylish had come to hand. Glasses should be narrower across the rim than the bowl. Red ones should be bigger than white because whites are best kept chilled in the bottle rather than warming in the glass. If you like bubbles in your sparkling wine, serve it in a flute rather than a saucer from which they will swiftly escape. Dartington Crystal, Schott, and Riedel are among a number of companies that now produce attractive glasses that are specially designed to bring out the best in particular styles of wine.

Wines definitely benefit from purpose-designed glasses like these.

To Breathe or Not to Breathe?

Some reds have an unwelcome mudlike deposit; some reds and whites may benefit from the aeration of being poured into a decanter or another bottle. But don't decant every red wine you encounter. A tannic young Cabernet or Italian may soften to reveal unexpected flavors, but old Burgundy or Rioja will have very little deposit and may be too light-bodied to gain from decanting.

Stand the bottle for up to a day before decanting it. Pour it very slowly, in front of a flashlight or candle, watching for the first signs of the deposit. Coffee filters suit those with less steady hands.

Airing a wine by simply opening it a few hours in advance of serving achieves little (the contact with oxygen offered by the neck of the bottle is far too limited). So, to be aired properly a wine normally needs to be poured out of the bottle. A small device exists however, that bubbles air into wine to mimic the effect of decanting.

Although this is not often appreciated, white wine can also sometimes benefit from the aeration that comes from being poured into a decanter. Try it for any wine that seems to smell of throat-tickling sulfur dioxide or one that seems to smell and taste more restrained than you might have anticipated.

Decant red – or white – wine to bring out the flavor.

Order of Service

The rules say that white wines and youth respectively precede red wines and age; dry goes before sweet (most of us prefer our main course before the dessert); the lighter the wine, the earlier. These rules are often impossible to follow. What are you to do, for example, if the red Loire is lighter-bodied than the white Burgundy? Can the claret follow the Sauternes that you are offering with the foie gras? Ignore the absolutes but bear in mind the common sense that lies behind them. Work gently up the scale of fullness, "flavorsomeness," and quality, rather than swinging wildly between styles.

Investing

Liquid Assets

Bottles of wine and high-tech stocks have one thing in common: the prices they command may have little to do with their true current worth or future potential. The 1997 Bordeaux, for example, though undeniably inferior to the 1996s, sold for higher prices *en primeur* – in the barrel – as producers took advantage of the wine boom in Asia. Trendy wine buyers today pay four times as much for a hyped, limited-production bottle of California Cabernet from a recently launched winery than for one from an established Bordeaux château – simply because of its rarity. Young 1996 Bordeaux now sells for more than mature 1986 which may well taste better now and live longer. There is often little logic in the no-man's land where wine and money meet.

Supply and Demand

The New Economy has created obscene amounts of New Money – and New Tastes. Buyers are going for limited-production, young wine whose immediately attractive oaky-fruity flavours they understand better than the more complex ones of older, more mature stuff. So, apart from the "blue chips" (Latour, Pétrus etc) with a guaranteed following, the Bordeaux that are attracting interest are wines from small estates in Pomerol (such as l'Eglise Clinet) and recently launched "micro-wines" produced in tiny quantities such as le Pin and Valandraud. This enthusiasm for rarity is also evident in the unprecedented growth of interest in limited-production wines from Burgundy, the Rhône as well as the US (Harlan Estate, Screaming Eagle) and Australia (Clarendon Hills). It remains to be seen whether the micro-wines will sustain their ludicrously high prices any more successfully than overpriced stocks on the NASDAQ.

My guess is that, quite often, they won't. The few surviving older bottles may well prove that some of the new stars are fundamentally not as fine as some of the older ones. We'll see. In the meantime bear the following rules in mind.

The Rules

1) The popularity and value of any wine can vary from one country to another. 2) Wines are not like works of art; they don't last forever, so be ready to see their value fall. 3) Tread carefully among wines like le Pin

from Bordeaux and Screaming Eagle from California which have yet to prove their long-term potential. **4)** When buying *en primeur*, deal with financially solid merchants. **5)** At auction, favour wines that are known to have been carefully cellared. **6)** Store your wines carefully and securely – and insure them. **7)** Follow their progress; read critics' comments, and watch auction prices. **8)** Never forget that – even in an age of internet auctions – a case of wine is tougher to sell instantly than stocks or a piece of jewellery. **9)** Beware of falling reputations: the 1975 Bordeaux came after a series of poor vintages and sold at high prices; within a decade they had been eclipsed by the 1970 and 1982 vintages. The 1974 Californian Cabernets, once heavily hyped, are now similarly questioned. The following wines are worth investing in:

FRANCE

Bordeaux

Châteaux l'Angélus, Ausone, Cheval Blanc, Cos d'Estournel, Ducru-Beaucaillou, Eglise-Clinet, Figeac, Grand-Puy-Lacoste, Gruaud-Larose, Haut-Brion, Lafite, Lafleur, Latour, Léoville Barton, Léoville Las Cases, Lynch Bages, Margaux, la Mission-Haut-Brion, la Mondotte, Montrose, Mouton-Rothschild, Palmer, Pétrus, Pichon Lalande, Pichon Longueville, le Pin, Rauzan Ségla (recent vintages) Rol Valentin, Valandraud. Vintages: 1982, 1983 (for Margaux), 1985, 1986, 1988, 1989, 1990, 1995, 1996. Top properties only in 1998 and 1999.

Burgundy

Drouhin Marquis de Laguiche, Gros Frères, Hospices de Beaune (from négociants such as Drouhin, or Jadot), Méo-Camuzet, Romanée-Conti (la Tâche, Romanée-Conti), Lafon, Leflaive, Leroy, de Vogüé.

Rhône

Chapoutier, Chave, Guigal (top wines), Jaboulet Aîné "La Chapelle".

PORTUGAL (PORT)

Cockburn's, Dow's, Fonseca, Graham's, Noval, Taylor's, Warre's.

CALIFORNIA

Beaulieu Private Reserve, Diamond Creek, Dominus, Duckhorn, Dunn Harlan Estate, Howell Mountain, Grace Family, Heitz Martha's Vineyard, (varied in the late 1980s and early 1990s), Matanzas Creek, Robert Mondavi Reserve, Opus One, Ridge, Spottswoode, Stag's Leap.

AUSTRALIA

Jim Barry "The Armagh", Henschke Hill of Grace and Mount Edelstone, Leeuwin Chardonnay, Penfolds Grange and Bin 707, Petaluma Cabernet, Wynns "John Riddoch", Virgin Hills, Yarra Yering.

VINTAGES

TIME WILL TELL

Twenty-five years ago, a vintage chart was as necessary for the enjoyment of wine as a corkscrew and a glass. But that was in the days when wine of quality was produced only in a limited number of places, and in years when the climate was just right. Man had yet to develop ways – physical, chemical, and organic – of combatting pests and diseases that used to spoil wine with dreadful regularity.

Really disastrous vintages are a rarity now. Though frost can cut production, every year the most skilled and the luckiest producers in almost every region manage to make drinkable wines. Some places, however, are naturally more prone to tricky vintages than others. Northern Europe, for example, suffers more from unreliable sun and untimely rain than more southerly regions, let alone the warm, irrigated vineyards of Australia and the Americas.

A dependable climate does not necessarily make for better wine, however. Just as plants often bloom best in tough conditions, grapes develop more interesting flavors in what is known as a "marginal" climate – which is why New World producers are busily seeking out cooler, higher-altitude sites in which to plant their vines.

IT'S AN ILL WIND

Some producers can buck the trend of a climatically poor year – by luckily picking before the rainstorms, carefully discarding rotten grapes, or even using equipment to concentrate the flavor of a rain-diluted crop. In years like these, well-situated areas within larger regions can, in any case, make better wines than their neighbors. So, Grand and Premier Cru vineyards in France, for example, owe their prestige partly to the way their grapes ripen. The difference in quality between regions can, however, also be attributed to the types of grapes that are grown. Bordeaux had a fair-to-good vintage for red wine in 1997, but a great one for Sauternes. Similarly, there are vintages where, for example, the St. Emilion and Pomerol châteaux have already picked their Merlot grapes in perfect conditions before rainstorms arrive to ruin the prospects of their counterparts' later-ripening Cabernet Sauvignon in the Médoc, only a few miles away. The following pages suggest regions and wines for the most significant vintages of this century.

THE LAST FIVE YEARS

2000 (SOUTHERN HEMISPHERE)

A mixed vintage, with intense heat (including bush fires) in South Africa at harvest time making for high-alcohol wines. New Zealand's best wines were Hawke's Bay reds and Marborough Sauvignons and Australia did well in Western Australia and in the Hunter Valley. Victoria and South Australia had varied results. Argentina and Chile both produced large quantities of good wine.

1999

A generally patchy year. There were great Sauternes, but red Bordeaux, like red Burgundy was very variable, with good and disappointing wines having been produced throughout both regions. There were some worthwile Rhônes, Loires, and Alsaces but white Burgundy was more generally fine. Top Italians – especially from Chianti are worth looking out for, as are German wines from the Mosel-Saar-Ruwer. The vintage in Spain was good rather than great. In Australia, the finest wines were from Coonawarra and Victoria. New Zealand made far better whites than in 1998 and both Chile and Argentina had one of their best years.

1998

Untimely rain made for a very mixed vintage almost everywhere in the northern hemisphere. There were some great red Bordeaux (St. Emilion, Pomerol, and top châteaux in the Médoc and Graves), lovely Sauternes and Alsace, and a few fine Burgundies (especially Chablis) and ports. California reds varied enormously.

1997

Bordeaux produced light, attractive reds and some brilliant sweet whites, and there were good white Burgundies and variable reds. Elsewhere in Europe, though, the vintage was variable. Alsace, Italy, Germany, and Austria, however, made terrific wines, as did the port houses of the Douro and producers in California, Washington, Australia, and New Zealand. South African reds will be slow to mature.

1996

A classic vintage for the Médoc, Graves, and Sauternes (though less so in Pomerol and St. Emilion) and for white Burgundy and the Loire. There were vintage-quality Champagnes, but Alsace and the Rhône were patchy. Germany made good but austere Kabinett and Spätlese wines, while Italy, Spain, and Portugal had a fair vintage. California, New Zealand, and Australia produced top-class red and white wines.

1995

Attractive, approachable, classy red Bordeaux and white Burgundy. Italian and Loire reds, Rhône, Alsace, German, Rioja, and Ribera del Duero are all worth buying, as are wines from Australia, New Zealand, South Africa, North and South America.

1994

Red Bordeaux tended to be unripe-tasting. There were fine northern Rhône reds, red Burgundy for early drinking and great Vintage port. Italy's reds were average-to-good. Germany did better. California had a great vintage, while the wines in Australia were good to very good.

1993

Red Bordeaux is tiring now. There are excellent Tokaji, Alsace, and Loires (red and white), good red Burgundy and top-class whites. Wines were better in South Africa and New Zealand than in Australia.

1992

Bordeaux was poor but white Burgundy was good. Red Burgundy is for early drinking. Taylor's and Fonseca produced great vintage port. Californian Cabernets are fine – finer than efforts from Australia.

1991

Bordeaux are ready to drink, but reds from the Northern Rhône are as good. Fine vintage port. Spain, South Africa, California, New Zealand, and Australia all had a good vintage.

1990

Great red and white Bordeaux, Champagne, German Rieslings, and Alsace, Loire whites, red Rhônes, Burgundies, Australians, and Californians, Barolo and Spanish reds, especially from the Duero.

1985-1989

1989 Top-class, juicy ripe red and good white Bordeaux and Champagne. Stunning German wines (from Kabinett to TBA) and excellent Alsace. Outstanding Loires (especially red), good red and superb white Rhône, good red Burgundy. **1988** Slow-evolving claret, fine Sauternes and Champagne, long-lasting Italian reds, Tokaji, German, Alsace, Loire reds and sweet whites, good red and white Rhône, and red Burgundy. **1987** Fading claret and Burgundy. **1986** Fine red and white Bordeaux, Australian reds, white Burgundy. **1985** California reds, claret, vintage port, Champagne, Spanish and Italian reds, Alsace, sweet Loire, red Rhône, Burgundy.

1980-1985

1984 South African reds, Australian reds, and Rieslings. **1983** claret, red Rhône, Portuguese reds, Sauternes, Madeira, vintage port, Tokaji, Alsace. **1982** Claret, Champagne, Australian, Portuguese and Spanish reds, Italian reds, red and white Burgundy, and Rhône. **1981** Champagne, Alsace. **1980** California and Australian Cabernet, Madeira, port.

1970-1979

1979 Champagne, Sassicaia, sweet Austrians. **1978** Red and white Rhône, Portuguese reds, Bordeaux, Burgundy, Barolo, Tuscan and Loire reds. **1977** Port, sweet Austrians. **1976** Champagne, Loire reds and sweet whites, sweet Germans, Alsace, Sauternes. **1975** Top claret and port, Sauternes, Penfolds Grange. **1974** California and Portuguese reds. **1973** Napa Cabernet, sweet Austrians. **1972** Tokaji. **1971** Bordeaux, Burgundy, Champagne, Barolo and Tuscan reds, sweet Germans, red Rhône, Penfolds Grange. **1970** Port, Napa Cabernet, claret, Champagne, Rioja, Ch. Musar.

1960-1969

1969 Sweet Austrians, red Rhône, Burgundy. **1968** Madeira, Rioja, Tokaji. **1967** Sauternes, Tuscan reds, Châteauneuf-du-Pape, German TBA. **1966** Port, Burgundy, Champagne, claret, Australian Shiraz, **1965** Barca Velha. **1964** Claret, Tokaji, Champagne, Vega Sicilia, Rioja, sweet Loire, red Rhône. **1963** Vintage port, Tokaji. **1962** Champagne, top Bordeaux and Burgundy, Rioja, Australian Cabernet and Shiraz. **1961** Claret, Sauternes, Champagne, Brunello, Barolo, Alsace, red Rhône. **1960** Port, top claret.

1950-1959

1959 Claret, Sauternes, Champagne, Tokaji, sweet Germans, Loire, Alsace, Rhône, Burgundy. **1958** Barolo. **1957** Madeira, Vega Sicilia, Chianti, Tokaji. **1956** Château Yquem. **1955** Claret, Sauternes, port, Champagne, Brunello. **1954** Madeira. **1953** Claret, Tokaji, Champagne, sweet Germans, Côte Rôtie, Burgundy. **1952** Claret, Madeira, Champagne, Barolo, Tokaji, red Rhône, red and white Burgundy. **1951** Terrible. **1950** Madeira.

1940-1949

1949 Red and white Bordeaux, Champagne, Tokaji, sweet Germans; red Rhône, Burgundy. **1948** Port, Vega Sicilia. **1947** Bordeaux and Burgundy, port, Champagne, Tokaji, sweet Loire. **1946** Armagnac. **1945** Brunello, port, Bordeaux, Champagne, Chianti, sweet Germans, Alsace, red Rhônes and Burgundy. **1944** Madeira, port. **1943** Champagne, red Burgundy. **1942** Port, Rioja, Vega Sicilia. **1941** Madeira, Sauternes. **1940** Madeira.

Anniversary Wines

1931 Madeira. **1921** Port, Bordeaux. **1911** Madeira. **1901** Madeira, Claret.

WINE & HEALTH

WINE AND HEALTH

"Wine is fit for man in a wonderful way, provided that it is taken
with good sense by the sick as well as the healthy."

Hippocrates

RED OR DEAD ?

Sometime around 2200 BC a Sumerian produced the oldest known
medical handbook, a pharmacopeia written on a clay tablet which
recommends wines for various ailments.

It has taken us a remarkably long time to rediscover the healthy
qualities of moderate wine consumption, but since the CBS
Television *60 Minutes* "French Paradox" program revealed how much
healthier Gallic wine drinkers were than Anglo-Saxon teetotallers,
researchers throughout the world have been busily analyzing the
link between wine and well-being.

WINE AND HEART DISEASE

Research at the Université de Bourgogne suggest that wine combats
heart disease in two ways. People who daily drink up to half a liter
of red wine have higher levels of HDL (high density lipoproteins) –
"good" cholesterol which escorts "bad" cholesterol away from the
artery walls and to the liver where it is destroyed. Also Resveratrol,
an antifungal compound found in high concentration in grape skins,
especially in the Pinot Noir grape, has been shown to improve the
lipid profile of volunteers, drinking three glasses of red wine a day
for two weeks. Resveratrol appears to be 20 times more powerful in
its antioxidant affect than Vitamin E.

WINE AND DIGESTION

Wine of both colors counters both constipation and diarrhea, while
white wine in particular stimulates the urinary functions. Wine also
kills cholera bacteria and combats typhoid and trichinella, the
poisonous compound in "bad" pork. Surprisingly, one researcher, Dr.
Heinrich Kliewe, actually recommends that moderate amounts of
wine can counteract some of the side effects of antibiotics.

WINE AND AGING

Antioxidants in red wine inhibit the effects of degenerative oxidation, such as graying and the clogging of arteries leading to strokes. Wine may also offer protection against Alzheimer's Disease.

WINE AND VIRUSES

According to Dr. Jack Konowalchuk and Joan Speirs of Canada's Bureau of Microbial Hazards, the polyphenols in tannic red wine, derived mainly from the skins, are effective against such viruses as cold sores, and possibly – though this remains hypothetical – even against the supposedly incurable genital Herpes 2.

WINE AND PREGNANCY

Despite the fears it arouses, Fetal Alcohol Syndrome is rare outside the poorer inner cities of the US. In 1997, the UK Royal College of Obstetricians and Gynecologists reported that up to 15 units of alcohol per week should do no harm to a fetus.

WINE AND CALORIES

There is no difference in calories between a Muscadet and a claret (around 110 per glass). Sweeter, but less alcoholic Liebfraumilch has about 79. A Stanford University survey suggests the action of the wine on the metabolism somehow makes its calories less fattening.

HANGOVERS

All alcohol – especially vintage port – is hangover fare. The only way to avoid this fate is to drink plenty of water before going to bed.

WINE AND CANCER

Alcohol has been linked to rare occurrences of mouth and throat cancer – but only among smokers. Red wine is rich in gallic acid, an acknowledged anticarcinogenic, and wine's role in reducing stress has been associated with a lower incidence of certain forms of cancer.

WINE AND MIGRAINE

Red wine, like chocolate, can inhibit an enzyme called phenosulfotransferase-P, or PST-P, which naturally detoxifies all sorts of bacteria in the gut. An absence of PST-P is linked to migraine. In some people, red wine is also associated with episodic skin allergies.

WINE AND ASTHMA

Wines that are heavily dosed with sulfur dioxide (used to combat bacteria in most dried, bottled, and canned foods) can trigger asthma attacks. New World and organic wines have lower sulfur levels.

FOOD & WINE

Suspicions of a previously uncorked bottle, Paris, 1890's.

MATCHMAKING FOR BEGINNERS

One of the most daunting aspects of wine has always been the traditional obsession with serving precisely the right wine with any particular dish – of only ever drinking red with meat and white with fish or shellfish.

It may be reassuring to learn that some of these time-honoured rules are just plain wrong. In Portugal, for example, fishermen love to wash down their sardines and salt cod with a glass or two of harsh red wine. In Burgundy they even poach fish in their local red.

On the other hand, the idea that a platter of cheese is somehow incomplete without a bottle of red wine can be exploded in an instant. Just take a mouthful of claret immediately after eating a little goat's cheese or Brie. The wine will taste metallic and unpleasant because the creaminess of the cheese reacts badly with the tannin – the toughness – in the wine. A fresh, dry white would be far more successful (its acidity would cut through the fat), while the claret would be shown to its best advantage alongside a harder, stronger cheese. If you don't want to offer a range of wines, try sticking to one or two cheeses that really will complement the stuff in the glass.

Don't take anything for granted. Rare beef and Bordeaux surprisingly fails the test of an objective tasting. The protein of the meat somehow makes all but the fruitiest wines taste tougher. If you're looking for a perfect partner for beef, uncork a Burgundy. If it's the claret that takes precedence, you'd be far better off with lamb.

The difference between an ideal and a passable food-and-wine combination can be very subtle. Most of us have after all happily quaffed claret with our steak, but just as a keen cook will tinker with a recipe until it is just right, there's a lot to be said for making the occasional effort to find a pairing of dish and wine that really works. Like people who are happier in a couple than separately, some foods and wines simply seem to bring out the best in each other.

A SENSE OF BALANCE

There is no real mystery about the business of matching food and wine. Some flavours and textures are compatible, and some are not. Strawberry mousse is not really delicious with chicken casserole, but apple sauce can do wonders for roast pork.

The key to spotting which relationships are marriages made in heaven, and which have the fickleness of Hollywood romances, lies in identifying the dominant characteristics of the contents of the plate and the glass. And learning which are likely to complement each other, either through their similarities or through their differences.

LIKELY COMBINATIONS

It is not difficult to define particular types of food and wine, and to guess how they are likely to get along. A buttery sauce is happier with something tangily acidic, like a crisp Sauvignon Blanc, rather than a rich, buttery Chardonnay. A subtly poached fish won't appreciate a fruit-packed New World white, and you won't do pheasant pie any favours by pulling the cork on a delicate red.

WHAT TO AVOID

Some foods and their characteristics, though, make life difficult for almost any drink. Sweetness, for example, in a fruity sauce served with a savoury dish seems to strip some of the fruitier flavours out of a wine. This may not matter if the stuff in your glass is a blackcurranty New World Cabernet Sauvignon, but it's bad news if it is a bone-dry white or a tough red with little fruit to spare.

Cream is tricky too. Try fresh strawberries with Champagne – delicious; now add a little whipped cream to the equation and you'll spoil the flavour. Creamy sauces can have the same effect on a wine.

Spices are problematical – due to the physical sensation of eating them rather than any particular flavour. A wine won't seem nasty after a mouthful of chilli sauce; it will simply lose its fruity flavour and taste of nothing at all. The way a tannic red dries out the mouth will also accentuate the heat of the spice. The ideal wine for most Westerners to drink with any spicy dish would be a light, possibly slightly sweet, white. Chinese palates often react differently to these combinations. They like the burning effect of the chili and see no point in trying to put out the fire with white wine.

ALWAYS WORTH A TRY

Some condiments actually bring out the best in wines. A little freshly ground pepper on your meat or pasta can accentuate the flavor of a wine, just as it can with a sauce. Squeezing fresh lemon onto your fish will reduce the apparent acidity of a white wine – a useful tip if you have inadvertently bought a case of tooth-strippingly dry Muscadet. And, just as lemon can help to liven up a dull sauce, it will do the same for a dull white wine, such as a basic Burgundy or a Soave by neutralizing the acidity and allowing other flavors to make themselves apparent. Mustard performs a similar miracle when it is eaten with beef, somehow nullifying the effect of the meat protein on the wine.

MARRIAGE GUIDANCE

In the following pages, I have suggested wines to go with a wide range of dishes and ingredients, taking the dominant flavor as the keypoint. Don't treat any of this advice as gospel – use it instead as a launchpad for your own food and wine experiments.

And, if no wine seems to taste just right, don't be too surprised. Heretical as it may seem, some dishes are actually more enjoyable with other drinks. The vinegar which is a fundamental part of a good pickle, for example, will do no wine a favor. Even keen wine lovers might well find beer a far more pleasurable accompaniment.

COOKING WITH WINE

Finally, a word or two about how to make best use of wine in the kitchen (apart from its role as refreshment following a vigorous session of egg-beating, and as a tranquilizer for the moments when sauces curdle and soufflées refuse to rise). The first – and most often forgotten – rule to remember is that wine that's not good enough to drink is probably not good enough to pour into the frying pan or casserole. At least, not unless you take a perverse pleasure in using and eating substandard ingredients. On the other hand, despite the advice of classic French recipes, your "coq au vin" won't be spoiled by your unwillingness to make it with a pricy bottle of Grand Cru Burgundy. A decent, humbler red will do perfectly well, though it is worth trying to use a similar style to the one suggested.

Second – and just as important – remember that, with the exception of a few dishes such as sherry trifle or zabaglione, in which wine is enjoyed in its natural state, wine, used as an ingredient needs to be cooked in order to remove the alcohol. So, add it early enough for the necessary evaporation to take place.

A

Almond Liqueur Muscats or Beaumes de Venise.
   Trout with Almonds Bianco di Custoza, Pinot Blanc.
Anchovies
   Salted Anchovies Rioja red or white, Manzanilla or Fino sherry.
   Fresh Anchovy (Boquerones) Albariño, Vinho Verde, Aligoté.
   Salade Niçoise Muscadet, Vinho Verde, or Beaujolais.
   Tapenade Dry sherry or Madeira.
Aniseed Dry white.
Apple
   Apple Pie or Strudel Austrian off-dry white.
   Blackberry and Apple Pie Late harvest Riesling, Vouvray demi-sec.
   Roast Pork with Apple Sauce Off-dry Vouvray or Riesling.
   Waldorf Salad Dry Madeira.
Apricot Late harvest Sémillon or Riesling, Jurançon Moelleux.
Artichoke White Rhône.
   Artichoke Soup Dry Loire whites, Pinot Gris.
Arroz con Pollo Côtes du Rhône, young Zinfandel, Navarra or Rioja "Joven."
Arugula Pinot Grigio, young Viognier.
Asparagus
   Asparagus Soup Fresh dry whites, Sauvignon Blanc.
   Asparagus Crêpes au Gratin Muscadet, Vinho Verde, Cider.
Avocado
   Avocado Mayonnaise Unoaked Chardonnay, Chablis.
   Avocado Stuffed with Crab Champagne, Riesling Kabinett,
      Sauvignon Blanc, Pinot Gris, Australian Chardonnay.
   Guacamole Fumé Blanc or unoaked Sauvignon Blanc.

B

Bacon Rich Pinot Gris or Alsace Riesling.
   Bacon with Marinated Scallops Fino sherry or mature Riesling,
      Shiraz-based Australians, Zinfandel from the States, or a heavy Cape red.
   Warm Bacon Salad New World Sauvignon Blanc, California Fumé Blanc
      or a good Pouilly Fumé.

Warm Bacon Salad

Banana
    Flambéed Banana with Rum Jurançon, Tokaji, Pedro Ximénez sherry, rum.
    Banoffee Pie Sweet Tokaji.
Barbecue Sauce Inexpensive off-dry white or a simple fruity Cabernet.
    Spare Ribs with Barbecue Sauce Fruity Australian Shiraz, Grenache or
        Zinfandel, spicy Côtes du Rhône from a ripe vintage or an off-dry white.
Basil Slightly sweet Chardonnay (ie California, commercial Australian).
Beans
    Baked Beans Light Zinfandel, Beaujolais, dry rosé or beer.
    Bean Salad Spanish reds such as Rioja Reserva and Rueda or New Zealand
        Sauvignon Blanc.
    Bean Stew Chunky Portuguese or Spanish reds.
    Cassoulet Serious white Rhône, Marsanne or Roussanne, or reds including
        Grenache and Syrah from the Rhône, crunchy Italian reds or Zinfandel.
Beef
    Beef with Green Peppers in Black Bean Sauce Off-dry German Riesling
        or characterful dry white like white Rhône or Marsanne.
    Beef Stew Pomerol or St. Emilion, good Northern Rhône like Crozes-
        Hermitage, Shiraz or Pinot Noir from the New World.
    Beef Stroganoff Tough beefy reds like Amarone, Brunello di Montalcino,
        Barolo, Côte Rôtie or really ripe Zinfandel.

Beef Stroganoff

    Beef Wellington Top Burgundy, Châteauneuf-du-Pape.
    Beefburger Tasty country reds, from Italy or Southern France eg Corbières.
    Boeuf Bourguignon Australian Bordeaux-style, Barolo or other robust reds
        with sweet fruit.
    Boiled Beef and Carrots Bordeaux Rouge, Valpolicella Classico, Australian
        Shiraz.
    Bresaola (Air Dried Beef) Beaujolais, Barbera and tasty reds from the
        Languedoc.
    Carpaccio of Beef Chardonnay, Champagne, Cabernet Franc and other
        Loire reds, Pomerol.
    Chilli Con Carne Robust fruity reds, Beaujolais Crus, Barbera or
        Valpolicella, spicy reds like Zinfandel or Pinotage.
    Corned Beef Hash Characterful spicy reds from the Rhône or Southern
        France.
    Daube of Beef Cheap Southern Rhône reds or Côtes du Rhône.
    Goulash East European reds, Bulgarian Cabernet or Mavrud and Hungarian
        Kadarka or Australian Shiraz.
    Meatballs Spicy rich reds from the Rhône, Zinfandel, Pinotage and
        Portuguese reds.
    Panang Neuk (Beef in Peanut Curry) New World Chardonnay, New

Zealand Sauvignon Blanc, or a spicy aromatic white Rhône.

Pastrami Zinfandel, good Bardolino, light Côtes du Rhône.

Rare Chargrilled Beef Something sweetly ripe and flavoursome, but not too tannic. Try Chilean Merlot.

Roast Beef Côte Rôtie, good Burgundy.

Salt Beef Loire reds from Gamay or Cabernet Franc.

Steak Pinot Noir and Merlot from the New World, Australian Shiraz, Châteauneuf-du-Pape, good ripe Burgundy.

Steak with Dijon Mustard Bordeaux, Cabernet Sauvignon from the New World or Australian Shiraz.

Steak and Kidney Pie/Pudding Bordeaux, Australian Cabernet Sauvignon, Southern Rhône reds or Rioja.

Steak au Poivre Cabernet Sauvignon, Chianti, Rhône reds, Shiraz or Rioja.

Steak Tartare Bourgogne Blanc, fruity reds, light on tannin; Beaujolais, Bardolino, etc, or traditionally vodka.

Thai Beef Salad New Zealand or South African Sauvignon Blanc, Gewürztraminer, Pinot Blanc.

Beer
Carbonnade à la Flamande Cheap Southern Rhône or Valpolicella.

Beetroot
Borscht Rich, dry Alsace Pinot Gris, Pinot Blanc or Italian Pinot Grigio.

Blackberry
Blackberry and Apple Pie Late harvest Riesling, Vouvray demi-sec.

Black Cherry
Black Forest Gâteau Fortified Muscat, Schnapps or Kirsch.

Blackcurrant
Blackcurrant Cheesecake Sweet grapey dessert wines.

Blackcurrant Mousse Sweet sparkling wines.

Black Pudding
Chablis, New Zealand Chardonnay, Zinfandel or Barolo.

Brandy
Christmas Pudding Australian Liqueur Muscat, tawny port, rich (sweet) Champagne, Tokaji.

Crêpe Suzette Asti Spumante, Orange Muscat, Champagne cocktails.

Bream (freshwater)
Chablis or other unoaked Chardonnay.

Bream (sea)
White Rhône, Sancerre.

Brie
Sancerre or New Zealand Sauvignon.

Brill
Dry white, Soave, Albariño, Vinho Verde.

Broccoli
Broccoli and Cheese Soup Slightly sweet sherry – Amontillado or Oloroso.

Butter
Béarnaise Sauce Good dry Riesling.

Beurre Blanc Champagne Blanc de Blancs, dry Vinho Verde.

Butternut Squash
Butternut Soup Aromatic Alsace Gewürztraminer.

C

Cabbage
Stuffed Cabbage East European Cabernet.

Cajun Spices
Beaujolais Crus.

Gumbo Zinfandel or maybe beer.

Camembert
Dry Sauvignon Blanc or unoaked Chablis.

Capers
Sauvignon Blanc.

Skate with Black Butter Crisply acidic whites like Muscadet or Chablis.

Tartare Sauce Crisply fresh whites, particularly Sauvignon.

Caramel
Caramelized Oranges Asti Spumante, Sauternes.
Crème Caramel Muscat or Gewürztraminer Vendange Tardive.

Crème Caramel

Carp Franken Sylvaner, dry Jurançon, Hungarian Furmint.
Carrot
Carrot and Orange Soup Madeira or perhaps an Amontillado sherry.
Carrot and Coriander Soup Aromatic, dry Muscat, Argentinian Torrontes.
Cashew Nuts Pinot Blanc.
Chicken with Cashew Nuts Rich aromatic white, Pinot Gris, or Muscat.
Cauliflower
Cauliflower Cheese Fresh crisp Côtes de Gascogne white, Pinot Grigio,
softly plummy Chilean Merlot or young, unoaked Rioja.
Caviar Champagne or chilled vodka.
Celery
Celery Soup Off-dry Riesling
Cheddar (mature) Good Bordeaux, South African Cabernet, port.
Cheese (general – see individual entries)
Cheeseburger Sweetly fruity oaky reds – Australian Shiraz, Rioja.
Cheese Fondue Swiss white or Vin de Savoie.
Cheese Platter Match wines to cheeses; don't put too tannic a red with too
creamy a cheese, and offer white wines – which go well with all but the hardest
cheese. Strong creamy cheeses demand fine Burgundy, blue cheese is made for
late harvest wines, goat cheese is ideal with Sancerre, Pouilly Fumé, or other
dry, unoaked Sauvignons. Munster is best paired with Alsace Gewurztraminer.
Cheese Sauce (Mornay) Oaky Chardonnay.
Cream Cheese, Crème Fraîche, Mozzarella, Mascarpone Fresh light dry
whites – Frascati, Pinot Grigio.
Raclette Swiss white or Vin de Savoie.
Cheesecake Australian botrytized Semillon.
Cherry Valpolicella, Recioto della Valpolicella, Dolcetto.
Roast Duck with Cherry Sauce Barbera, Dolcetto or Barolo.
Chestnut
Roast Turkey with Chestnut Stuffing Côtes du Rhône, Merlot, or soft and
mature Burgundy.
Chicken
Barbecued Chicken Rich and tasty white, Chardonnay.
Chicken Casserole Mid-weight Rhône such as Crozes-Hermitage or Lirac.
Chicken Chasseur Off-dry Riesling.
Chicken Kiev Chablis, Aligoté, or Italian dry white.
Chicken Pie White Bordeaux, simple Chardonnay, or else a light Italian
white.
Chicken Soup Soave, Orvieto, or Pinot Blanc.

Chicken Vol-au-Vents White Bordeaux.

Coq au Vin Shiraz-based New World reds, red Burgundy.

Curry Chicken Gewürztraminer, dry white Loire, fresh Chinon.

Devilled Chicken Australian Shiraz.

Fricassée Unoaked Chardonnay.

Lemon Chicken Muscadet, Chablis, or basic Bourgogne Blanc.

Roast/Grilled Chicken Reds or whites, though nothing too heavy –
  Burgundy is good, as is Barbera, though Soave will do just as well.

Roast/Grilled Chicken with Sage and Onion Stuffing Italian reds,
  especially Chianti, soft, plummy Merlots, and sweetly fruity Rioja.

Roast/Grilled Chicken with Tarragon Dry Chenin (Vouvray or perhaps a
  good South African).

Saltimbocca (Cutlet with Mozzarella and Ham) Flavorsome, dry
  Italian whites, Lugana, Bianco di Custoza, Orvieto.

Smoked Chicken Oaky Chardonnay, Australian Marsanne, or Fumé Blanc.

Southern Fried Chicken White Bordeaux, Muscadet, Barbera, light
  Zinfandel.

Tandoori Chicken White Bordeaux, New Zealand Sauvignon Blanc.

Chicken Liver (Sauté) Softly fruity, fairly light reds including Beaujolais,
  Italian Cabernet or Merlot, or perhaps an Oregon Pinot Noir.

Chicken Liver Pâté Most of the above reds plus Vouvray Moelleux,
  Monbazillac, or Amontillado sherry.

Chili Cheap wine or cold lager beer.

Chili Chipped Beef Robust fruity reds, Beaujolais Crus, Barbera or
  Valpolicella, spicy reds like Zinfandel or Pinotage.

Hot and Sour Soup Crisply aromatic English white, Baden Dry.

Szechuan-Style Dry, aromatic whites, Alsace Pinot Gris, Riesling,
  Grenache rosé, beer.

Thai Beef Salad New Zealand or South African Sauvignon Blanc,
  Gewürztraminer, Pinot Blanc.

Chinese (general) Aromatic white (Gewürztraminer, Pinot Gris, English).

Chives Sauvignon Blanc.

Chili Chipped Beef

Chocolate Orange Muscat, Moscatel de Valencia.

Black Forest (Chocolate and Cherry) Gâteau Fortified Muscat or Kirsch.

Chocolate Cake Beaumes de Venise, Bual or Malmsey Madeira, Orange
  Muscat, sweet German, or fine Champagne.

Chocolate Profiteroles with Cream Muscat de Rivesaltes.

Dark Chocolate Mousse Sweet Black Muscat or other Muscat-based wines.

Milk Chocolate Mousse Moscato d'Asti.

Chorizo (Sausage) Red or white Rioja, Navarra, Manzanilla sherry, Beaujolais,
  or Zinfandel.

Cinnamon Riesling Spätlese, Muscat.

Chorizo (Pork) Red or white Rioja, Navarra, Manzanilla sherry, Beaujolais or Zinfandel.
Cinnamon Riesling Spätlese, Muscat.
Clams Chablis or Sauvignon Blanc.
   Clam Chowder Côtes de Gascogne blanc, Amontillado sherry or Madeira.
   Spaghetti Vongole Pinot Bianco or Lugana.
Cockles Muscadet, Gros Plant, Aligoté, dry Vinho Verde.
Coconut (milk) California Chardonnay.
   Green Curry Big-flavoured New World whites or Pinot Blanc from Alsace.
Cod Unoaked Chardonnay, good white Burgundy, dry Loire Chenin.
   Cod and Chips Any light crisp dry white, such as a Sauvignon from Bordeaux or Touraine. Alternatively, try dry rosé or Champagne. Remember, though, that heavy-handedness with the vinegar will do no favours for the wine. For vinegary chips, stick to tea.
   Cod in Crumb Bake Lugana, Pinot Bianco, Pinot Blanc.
   Salt Cod (Bacalhão de Gomes) Classically Portuguese red or white – Vinho Verde or Bairrada reds.
   Smoked Cod Vinho Verde.
Cod's Roe (smoked) Well-oaked New World Chardonnay.
Coffee
   Coffee Gâteau Asti Spumante.
   Coffee Mousse Asti Spumante, Liqueur Muscat.
   Tiramisu Sweet fortified Muscat, Vin Santo, Torcolato.
Coriander
   Coriander Leaf Dry or off-dry English white.
   Coriander Seed Dry herby Northern Italian whites.
Courgette
   Courgette Gratin Good dry Chenin from Vouvray or South Africa.
Couscous Spicy Shiraz, North African reds or earthy Southern French Minervois.
Crab Chablis, Sauvignon Blanc, New World Chardonnay.
   Crab Bisque Chablis, Pinot Gris or dry sherry.
   Crab Pâté Crisp dry whites – Baden Dry or Soave.
   Crab and Sweetcorn Soup Sancerre, other Sauvignon Blanc.
   Dressed Crab Chablis or Mâcon Chardonnay
Cranberry
   Roast Turkey with Cranberry and Orange Stuffing Richly fruity reds like Shiraz from Australia, Zinfandel or modern Rioja.
Crayfish
   Freshwater Crayfish South African Sauvignon, Meursault.
   Salad of Crayfish Tails with Dill Rich South African Chenin blends or crisp Sauvignon, white Rhône.
Cream When dominant, not good with wine, particularly bad with tannic reds.
Cucumber Soup Dry Madeira.
Cumin Soave, Lugana.
Curry
   Coronation Chicken Gewürztraminer, dry aromatic English wine or a fresh Chinon.
   Curried Beef Beefy, spicy reds; Barolo, Châteauneuf-du-Pape and Shiraz/Cabernet or off-dry aromatic whites – Gewürztraminer, Pinot Gris. Or try some Indian sparkling wine or cold Cobra lager.
   Curried Turkey New World Chardonnay.
   Tandoori Chicken Young white Bordeaux or fruity New Zealand Sauvignon Blanc.
   Thai Green Chicken Curry Big New World whites or young Alsace Pinot Blanc or Italian Pinot Bianco.

D

Dill Sauvignon Blanc.
   Gravadlax Ice cold vodka, Pinot Gris or Akvavit.
Dover Sole Sancerre, good Chablis, unoaked Chardonnay.
Dried Fruit Sweet sherry, tawny port.
   Bread and Butter Pudding Barsac or Sauternes, Monbazillac, Jurançon, Muscat de Beaumes de Venise or Australian Orange Muscat.
Duck Pinot Noir from Burgundy, California or Oregon, or perhaps an off-dry German Riesling.
   Cassoulet Serious white Rhônes, Marsanne or Roussanne, or try reds including Grenache and Syrah from the Rhône, berryish Italian reds or Zinfandel.
   Confit de Canard Alsace Pinot Gris or a crisp red like Barbera.
   Duck Pâté Chianti or other juicy herby red, Amontillado sherry.
   Duck Pâté with Orange Riesling or Rioja.
   Peking Duck Rice wine, Alsace Riesling, Pinot Gris.
   Roast Duck with Orange Sauce Loire red or, surprisingly, a sweet white like Vouvray demi-sec.
   Smoked Duck California Chardonnay or Fumé Blanc.
Duck Liver
   Foie Gras de Canard Champagne, late harvest Gewürztraminer or Riesling, Sauternes.

E

Eel
   Jellied Eels A pint of stout.
   Smoked Eel Pale, dry sherry, simple, fresh white Burgundy.
Egg
   Baked Eggs Bordeaux Blanc, Côtes de Gascogne or young, fruity red.
   Crème Brûlée Jurançon Moelleux, Tokaji.
   Eggs Benedict Unoaked Chardonnay, Blanc de Blancs, Bucks Fizz, Bloody Mary.
   Eggs Florentine Unoaked Chardonnay, Pinot Blanc, Aligoté, Sémillon.
   Omelettes Cheap Beaujolais, Bardolino.
   Tortilla Young, juicy Spanish reds and fresher whites from La Mancha or Rueda.

F

Fennel Sauvignon Blanc.
Fig Liqueur Muscat.
Frankfurter Côtes du Rhône or Budweiser beer.
Fish (general – see individual entries)
   Bouillabaisse Red or white Côtes du Rhône, dry rosé or peppery dry white from Provence, California Fumé Blanc, Viognier, Marsanne or Verdicchio.
   Cumberland Fish Pie California Chardonnay, Alsace Pinot Gris, Sauvignon Blanc.
   Fish Cakes White Bordeaux, Chilean Chardonnay, or dry rosé from Provence.

Fish and Chips Most fairly simple, crisply acidic dry whites (white Bordeaux, Sauvignon Blanc) or maybe a rosé or Champagne (See Cod). In any case, go easy with the vinegar.

Fish Soup Manzanilla, Chablis, Muscadet.

Kedgeree Aligoté, crisp Sauvignon.

Mediterranean Fish Soup Provençal reds and rosés, Tavel, Côtes du Rhône, Vin de Pays d'Oc.

Seafood Salad Soave, Pinot Grigio, Muscadet, or a lightly oaked Chardonnay.

Sushi Saké.

Fruit (general – see individual entries)

Fresh Fruit Salad Moscato d'Asti, Riesling Beerenauslese, or Vouvray Moelleux.

Fruit Flan Vouvray Moelleux, Alsace Riesling Vendange Tardive.

Summer Pudding Late harvest Riesling, German or Alsace.

G

Game (general – see individual entries)

Cold Game Fruity Northern Italian reds – Barbera or Dolcetto – good Beaujolais or light Burgundy.

Roast Game Big reds, Brunello di Montalcino, old Barolo, good Burgundy.

Well-hung Game Old Barolo or Barbaresco, mature Hermitage, Côte Rôtie or Châteauneuf-du-Pape, fine Burgundy.

Game Pie Beefy reds, Southern French, Rhône, Australian Shiraz.

Garlic

Aïoli A wide range of wines go well including white Rioja, Provence rosé, California Pinot Noir.

Garlic Sausage Red Rioja, Bandol, Côtes du Rhône.

Gazpacho Fino sherry, white Rioja.

Roast/Grilled Chicken with Garlic Oaky Chardonnay or red Rioja.

Roast Lamb with Garlic and Rosemary Earthy soft reds like California Petite Sirah, Rioja, or Zinfandel.

Snails with Garlic Butter Aligoté and light white Burgundy or perhaps a red Gamay de Touraine.

Ginger Gewürztraminer or Riesling.

Beef with Onions and Ginger Off-dry German Riesling, one of the more serious Beaujolais Crus.

Chicken with Ginger White Rhône, Gewürztraminer.

Ginger Ice Cream Asti Spumante or late harvest Sémillon.

Goat Cheese Sancerre, New World Sauvignon, Pinot Blanc.

Grilled Goat Cheese Loire reds.

Goose A good Rhône red like Hermitage, Côte Rôtie, or a crisp Barbera, Pinot Noir from Burgundy, California or Oregon, or even off-dry German Riesling.

Confit d'Oie Best Sauternes, Monbazillac.

Goose Liver

Foie Gras Best Sauternes, Monbazillac.

Gooseberry

Gooseberry Fool Quarts de Chaume.

Gooseberry Pie Sweet Madeira, Austrian Trockenbeerenauslese.

Grapefruit Sweet Madeira or sherry.

Grouse

Roast Grouse Hermitage, Côte Rôtie, robust Burgundy, or good mature red Bordeaux.

Guinea Fowl Old Burgundy, Cornas, Gamay de Touraine, St. Emilion.

H

Haddock White Bordeaux, Chardonnay, Pinot Blanc.
  Mousse of Smoked Haddock Top white Burgundy.
  Smoked Haddock Fino sherry or oaky Chardonnay.
Hake Soave, Sauvignon Blanc.
Halibut White Bordeaux, Muscadet.
  Smoked Halibut Oaky Spanish white/Australian Chardonnay, white Bordeaux.
Ham
  Boiled/Roasted/Grilled/Fried Ham Beaujolais-Villages, Gamay de
    Touraine, slightly sweet German white, Tuscan red, lightish Cabernet
    (e.g., Chilean), Alsace Pinot Gris, or Muscat.
  Braised Ham with Lentils Light, fruity Beaujolais, Côtes du Rhône.
  Honey-Roast Ham Riesling.
  Oak-Smoked Ham Oaky Spanish reds.
  Parma Ham (Prosciutto) Try a dry Lambrusco, Tempranillo Joven, or Gamay
    de Touraine.
  Pea and Ham Soup Beaujolais.
Hare
  Hare Casserole Good Beaujolais Crus or, for a stronger flavor, try an
    Australian red.
  Jugged Hare Argentinian reds, tough Italians like Amarone, Barolo and
    Barbaresco, inky reds from Bandol or the Rhône.
Hazelnut Vin Santo, Liqueur Muscat.
  Warm Bacon, Hazelnut, and Sorrel Salad New World Sauvignon Blanc,
    California Fumé Blanc, or a good Pouilly Fumé.
Herbs (see individual entries)
Herring
  Fresh Herrings Sauvignon Blanc, Muscadet, Frascati, or cider.
  Roll-Mop Herring Savoie, Vinho Verde, Akvavit, cold lager.
  Salt Herring White Portuguese.
  Sprats Muscadet, Vinho Verde.
Honey Tokaji.
  Baklava Moscatel de Setúbal.
Horseradish
  Roast Beef with Horseradish California Pinot Noir or mature Burgundy.
Houmous French dry whites, Retsina, Vinho Verde.

I

Ice Cream Try Marsala or Pedro Ximénez sherry.
Indian (general) Gewürztraminer (spicy dishes); New World Chardonnay
  (creamy/yogurt dishes); New Zealand Sauvignon Blanc (Tandoori).

J

Japanese Barbecue Sauce
  Teriyaki Spicy reds like Zinfandel or Portuguese reds.
John Dory Good, white Burgundy or Australian Chardonnay.

K

Kedgeree New World Sauvignon Blanc or Sauvignon.

Kidney
    Lambs' Kidneys Rich spicy reds; Barolo, Cabernet Sauvignon, Rioja reserva.
    Steak and Kidney Pie/Pudding Bordeaux, Australian Cabernet Sauvignon, Southern Rhône reds or Rioja.

Kipper New World Chardonnay or a good fino sherry. Or, if you are having it for breakfast, Champagne, a nice cup of tea or Dutch gin.

L

Lamb
    Casserole Rich and warm Cabernet-based reds from France or California Zinfandel.
    Cassoulet Serious white Rhône, Marsanne or Roussanne, or reds including Grenache and Syrah from the Rhône, berryish Italian reds or Zinfandel.
    Cutlets or Chops Cru Bourgeois Bordeaux, Chilean Cabernet.
    Haggis Beaujolais, Côtes du Rhône, Côtes du Roussillon, Spanish reds, malt whisky.
    Irish Stew A good simple South American or Eastern European Cabernet works best.
    Kebabs Modern (fruity) Greek reds or sweetly ripe Australian Cabernet/Shiraz.
    Kleftiko (Lamb Shanks Baked with Thyme) Greek red from Nemea, Beaujolais, light Cabernet Sauvignon.
    Lancashire Hotpot Robust country red – Cahors, Fitou.
    Moussaka Brambly Northern Italian reds (Barbera, Dolcetto, etc), Beaujolais, Pinotage, Zinfandel, or try some good Greek wine from a modern producer.
    Roast Lamb Bordeaux (especially Médoc and Graves) New Zealand Cabernet Sauvignon or Merlot, South African Cabernet, Cahors, Rioja crianza or reserva, Merlot or Cabernet from Chile and Malbec from Argentina. Alternatively try a new wave Greek red (especially made from the St George).
    Roast Lamb with Thyme Try a New Zealand or South African Merlot or Cabernet Sauvignon, Bourgeuil or Chinon.
    Shepherd's Pie Barbera, Cabernet Sauvignon, Minervois, Zinfandel, Beaujolais, Southern French red.

Langoustine Muscadet, Soave, South African Sauvignon.

Leek
    Leek and Potato Soup Dry whites, Côtes de Gascogne.
    Leek in Cheese Sauce Dry white Bordeaux, Sancerre or fruity Australian Semillon.
    Vichyssoise Dry whites, Chablis, Bordeaux Blanc.

Lemon
    Lemon Cheesecake Moscato d'Asti.
    Lemon Meringue Pie Malmsey Madeira.
    Lemon Sorbet Late harvest Sémillon or sweet Tokaji.
    Lemon Tart Sweet Austrian and German wines.

Lemon Grass New Zealand Sauvignon, Sancerre, Viognier.

Lemon Sole Chardonnay.

Lentils Earthy country wines, Côtes du Rhône.
  Chicken Dhansak Sémillon or New Zealand Sauvignon.
  Dhal Soup Try Soave or Pinot Bianco.
Lime Australian Verdelho, Grüner Veltliner, Furmint.
  Kaffir Lime Leaves (in Thai Green Curry, etc.) Big-flavoured New World whites or Pinot Blanc from Alsace.
Liver
  Calves' Liver Good Italian Cabernet, St Emilion, New World Merlot or mature Chianti.
  Fegato alla Veneziana Nebbiolo, Zinfandel or Petite Sirah.
  Lambs' Liver Chianti, Aussie Shiraz or Merlot.
  Liver and Bacon Côtes du Rhône, Zinfandel, Pinotage.
Lobster Good white Burgundy.
  Lobster Bisque Grenache rosé, fresh German white, Chassagne-Montrachet, dry Amontillado sherry.
  Lobster in a Rich Sauce Champagne, Chablis, fine white Burgundy, good white Bordeaux.
  Lobster Salad Champagne, Chablis, German or Alsace Riesling.
  Lobster Thermidor Rich beefy Côtes du Rhône, oaky Chardonnay or a good deep-coloured rosé from Southern France.

M

Mackerel Best with Vinho Verde, Albariño, Sancerre and New Zealand Sauvignon.
  Smoked Mackerel Bourgogne Aligoté, Alsace Pinot Gris.
  Smoked Mackerel Pâté Sparkling Vouvray.

Mackerel

Mallard Côte Rôtie, Ribera del Duero or Zinfandel.
Mango Best eaten in the bath with a friend and a bottle of Champagne. Otherwise, go for Asti Spumante or Moscato.
Marjoram Provençal reds.
Marsala
  Chops in Marsala Sauce Australian Marsanne or Verdelho.
Mascarpone
  Tiramisu Sweet fortified Muscat, Vin Santo, Torcolato.
Meat (general – see individual entries)
  Cold Meats Juicy, fruity reds, low in tannin ie Beaujolais, Côtes du Rhône, etc.
  Consommé Medium/Amontillado sherry.

Meat Pâté Beaujolais, Fumé Blanc, lesser white Burgundy.

Mixed Grill Versatile uncomplicated red – Australian Shiraz, Rioja, Bulgarian Cabernet.

Melon Despite its apparently innocent, juicy sweetness, melon can be very unfriendly to most wines. Try tawny port, sweet Madeira or sherry, Quarts de Chaume, late harvest Riesling.

Mincemeat

Mince Pie Rich, sweet, late-harvest wine or botrytis-affected Sémillon.

Mint Beaujolais, young Pinot Noir, or try a New Zealand or Australian Riesling.

Thai Beef Salad New Zealand or South African Sauvignon Blanc, Gewürztraminer, Pinot Blanc.

Monkfish A light, fruity red such as Bardolino, Valpolicella, La Mancha Joven, or most Chardonnays.

Mushroom Merlot-based reds, good Northern Rhône, top Piedmontese reds.

Mushroom Soup Bordeaux Blanc, Côtes de Gasgogne.

Mushrooms à la Greque Sauvignon Blanc or fresh, modern Greek white.

Mushroom Soup

Risotto with Fungi Porcini Top-notch Piedmontese reds – mature Barbera, Barbaresco, or earthy Southern French reds.

Stuffed Mushrooms Chenin Blanc, Sylvaner.

Wild Mushrooms Nebbiolo, red Bordeaux.

Mussels Sauvignon Blanc, light Chardonnay, Muscadet Sur Lie.

Moules Marinières Bordeaux Blanc or Muscadet Sur Lie.

New Zealand Green-Lipped Mussels New Zealand Sauvignon Blanc.

Mustard Surprisingly, can help red Bordeaux and other tannic reds to go with beef which might otherwise accentuate their tough, tannic character.

Dijon Mustard Beaujolais.

English Wholegrain Mustard Beaujolais, Valpolicella.

French Mustard White Bordeaux.

Steak with Dijon Mustard Cabernet Sauvignon from the New World or Australian Shiraz.

Nectarine Sweet German Riesling.

Nutmeg Rioja, Australian Shiraz or, for sweet dishes, Australian late harvest Semillon.

Nuts Amontillado sherry, Vin Santo, and Tokaji.

O

Octopus Rueda white or a fresh, modern Greek white.
Olives Dry sherry, Muscadet, Retsina.
   Salade Niçoise Muscadet, Vinho Verde or Beaujolais.
   Tapenade Dry sherry or Madeira.
Onion
   Caramelized Onions Shiraz-based Australians, Zinfandel from the States, or a good Pinotage.
   French Onion Soup Sancerre or dry, unoaked Sauvignon Blanc, Aligoté, white Bordeaux.
   Onion/Leek Tart Alsace Gewurztraminer, New World Riesling or a good unoaked Chablis.
Orange
   Caramelized Oranges Asti Spumante, Sauternes or Muscat de Beaumes de Venise.
   Crêpe Suzette Sweet Champagne, Moscato d'Asti.
   Orange Sorbet Moscato or sweet Tokaji.
   Orange Zest Dry Muscat, Amontillado sherry.
Oregano Provençal reds, red Lambrusco, serious Chianti, or lightish Zinfandel.
Oxtail Australian Cabernet, good Bordeaux.
Oyster Sauce
   Beef and Snow Peas in Oyster Sauce Crisp, dry whites like Muscadet or a Northern Italian Lugana or Pinot Bianco, white Rhône, Gewürztraminer.
   Oysters Champagne, Chablis, or other crisp, dry white.

P

Paprika
   Goulash Eastern European red like Bulgarian Cabernet or Mavrud, Hungarian Kadarka, or Australian Shiraz.
Parmesan Salice Salentino, Valpolicella.
   Baked Chicken Parmesan with Basil Chenin Blanc, Riesling.
Parsley Dry, Italian whites – Bianco di Custoza, Nebbiolo, or Barbera.
   Parsley Sauce Pinot Grigio, Hungarian Furmint, lightly oaked Chardonnay.
Partridge
   Roast Partridge Australian Shiraz, Gevrey-Chambertin, Pomerol, or St. Emilion.
Pasta
   Lasagne Valpolicella, Barbera, Teroldego, Australian Verdelho or Sauvignon.
   Pasta with Meat Sauce Chianti, Bordeaux Rouge.
   Pasta with Pesto Sauce New Zealand Sauvignon Blanc, Valpolicella.
   Pasta with Seafood Sauce Soave, Sancerre.
   Ravioli with Spinach and Ricotta Pinot Bianco/Grigio, Cabernet d'Anjou.
   Spaghetti with Tomato Sauce California Cabernet, Zinfandel, Chianti.
   Spaghetti Vongole Pinot Bianco, Lugano.
   Tagliatelle Carbonara Pinot Grigio or a fresh, red Bardolino or Beaujolais.
Peach Sweet German Riesling.
   Peaches in Wine Riesling Auslese, Riesling Gewürztraminer Vendange Tardive, sweet Vouvray.
Peanuts
   Beef in Peanut Curry New World Chardonnay, an aromatic, white Rhône.

Satay Gewürztraminer.

Pepper (corns)

Steak au Poivre Cabernet Sauvignon, Chianti, Rhône reds, Shiraz or Rioja.

Peppers (fresh green, red) New Zealand Cabernet, Loire reds, crisp Sauvignon Blanc, Beaujolais, Tuscan red.

Peppers (yellow) Fruity Italian reds, Valpolicella, etc.

Stuffed Peppers Hungarian red – Bull's Blood, Chianti or spicy Rhône reds.

Pheasant Top-class red Burgundy, good American Pinot Noir, mature Hermitage.

Pheasant Casserole Top class red Burgundy, mature Hermitage.

Pheasant Pâté Côtes du Rhône, Alsace Pinot Blanc.

Pigeon Good red Burgundy, rich Southern Rhône. Chianti also goes well.

Warm Pigeon Breasts on Salad Merlot-based Bordeaux or Cabernet Rosé.

Pike Eastern European white.

Pine Nuts

Pesto Sauce New Zealand Sauvignon Blanc, Valpolicella.

Pizza

Fiorentina Pinot Bianco, Pinot Grigio, Vinho Verde, Verdicchio, Sauvignon Blanc.

Napoletana Verdicchio, Vernaccia di San Gimignano, white Rhône.

Quattro Formaggi Pinot Grigio, Frascati, Bianco di Custoza, Lugana, serious single-vineyard Soave.

Quattro Stagioni Valpolicella, Bardolino, light Chianti, good single-vineyard Soave.

Plaice White Burgundy, South American Chardonnay, Sauvignon Blanc.

Plum

Plum Pie Trockenbeerenauslese, Côteaux du Layon.

Pork

Cassoulet Serious white Rhône, Marsanne or Roussanne, or reds including Grenache and Syrah from the Rhône, berryish Italian reds or Zinfandel.

Pork Casserole Mid-weight, earthy reds like Minervois, Navarra or Montepulciano d'Abruzzo.

Pork Pie Spicy reds, Shiraz, Grenache.

Pork with Prunes Cahors, mature Chinon or other Loire red or rich southern French wine such as Corbières, Minervois or Faugères.

Pork Rillettes Pinot Blanc d'Alsace, Menetou-Salon Rouge.

Pork Sausages Spicy Rhône reds, Barbera.

Pork and Sage Sausages Barbera, Côtes du Rhône.

Pork Spare Ribs Zinfandel, Aussie Shiraz.

Roast Pork Rioja reserva, New World Merlot or Pinot Noir, Chenin Blanc, dry Vouvray.

Roast Pork with Apple Sauce Off-dry Vouvray or Riesling, or good South African Chenin Blanc.

Saucisson Sec Barbera, Cabernet Franc, Alsace Pinot Blanc or Beaujolais (Villages or Crus).

Szechuan-Style Pork Dry aromatic whites, Alsace Pinot Gris, Riesling, Grenache rosé, beer.

Prawns White Bordeaux, dry Australian Riesling, Gavi.

Prawn Cocktail Light fruity whites – German Riesling.

Prawns in Garlic Vinho Verde, Pinot Bianco.

Prawn Vol-au-Vents White Bordeaux, Muscadet.

Thai Prawns Gewürztraminer, dry aromatic Riesling or New Zealand Sauvignon Blanc.

Prunes Australian late harvest Semillon.

Pork with Prunes and Cream Sweet Chenin-based wines.

Prune Ice Cream Muscat de Beaumes de Venise.

Q

Quail Light red Burgundy, full-flavoured white Spanish wines.
Quince Lugana.
  Braised Venison with Quince Jelly Rich and fruity Australian or Chilean
    reds, good ripe Spanish Rioja or a Southern French red.

R

Rabbit
  Rabbit Casserole New World Pinot Noir or mature Châteauneuf-du-Pape.
  Rabbit in Cider Muscadet, demi-sec Vouvray, cider or Calvados.
  Rabbit with Mustard Franken wine or Czech Pilsner beer.
  Rabbit in Red Wine with Prunes Good mature Chinon or other Loire red.
Raspberries New World late harvest Riesling or Champagne, Beaujolais,
    demi-sec Champagne.
  Raspberry Fool Vouvray Moelleux.
Raspberry Vinegar Full-bodied Pinot Noir.
  Warm Bacon and Sorrel Salad New World Sauvignon Blanc,
    California Fumé Blanc or a good Pouilly Fumé.
Ratatouille Bulgarian red, Chianti, simple Rhône or Provence
    red, Portuguese reds, New Zealand Sauvignon Blanc.

Ratatouille

Redcurrant
  Cumberland Sauce Rioja, Australian Shiraz.
Red Mullet Dry rosé, New World Chardonnay, Sauvignon Blanc.
Rhubarb
  Rhubarb Pie Moscato d'Asti or late harvest Riesling.
Rice
  Rice Pudding Monbazillac, sweet Muscat, Asti Spumante or California
    Orange Muscat.
Rocket Lugana, Pinot Blanc.
Roquefort The classic match is Sauternes or Barsac, but almost any full-
    flavoured, botrytised sweet wine will be a good partner.
Rosemary Light red Burgundy or Pinot Noir.
Rum
  Flambéed Banana with Rum Jurançon, Tokaji, Pedro Ximénez sherry, rum.

S

Saffron Dry whites especially Chardonnay.
  Bass in Saffron Sauce Riesling (German, Australian, or Austrian), Viognier.
  Paella with Seafood White Penedés, unoaked Rioja, Navarra, Provence rosé.
Sage Chianti, or country reds from the Languedoc. Otherwise Sauvignon
    Blancs are great, especially Chilean.
  Roast Chicken, Goose, or Turkey with Sage and Onion Stuffing Italian
    reds, especially Chianti, soft, plummy Merlots, sweetly fruity Rioja, and
    brambly Zinfandel.
Salami Good, beefy Mediterranean rosé, Sardinian red, Rhône red, Zinfandel,
    dry aromatic Hungarian white.
Salmon
  Carpaccio of Salmon Cabernet Franc, Chardonnay, Australian reds, red
    Loire, Portuguese reds, Puligny-Montrachet.
  Grilled Salmon White Rhône (especially Viognier).
  Poached Salmon Chablis, good, white Burgundy, other Chardonnay, Alsace
    Muscat, white Bordeaux.
  Poached Salmon with Hollandaise Muscat, Riesling, good Chardonnay.
  Salmon Pâté Best white Burgundy.
Salmon Trout Light Pinot Noir from the Loire, New Zealand, good, dry,
    unoaked Chardonnay, Chablis, etc.
Sardines Muscadet, Vinho Verde, light and fruity reds such as Loire, Gamay.
Scallops Chablis and other unoaked Chardonnay.
  Coquilles St. Jacques White Burgundy.
  Marinated Scallops with Bacon Fino sherry or mature Riesling.
  Scallops Mornay White Burgundy, Riesling Spätlese.
Sea Bass Good white Burgundy.
  Bass in Saffron Sauce Riesling (German, Austrian or Australian), Viognier.
Seafood (general – see individual entries)
  Platter of Seafood Sancerre, Muscadet.
  Seafood Salad Soave, Pinot Grigio, Muscadet, lightly oaked Chardonnay.
Sesame Seeds Oaked Chardonnay.
Shrimps Albariño, Sancerre, New World Sauvignon, Arneis.
  Potted Shrimps New World Chardonnay, Marsanne.
Skate Bordeaux white, Côtes de Gascogne, Pinot Bianco.
Smoked Salmon Chablis, Alsace Pinot Gris, white Bordeaux.

Sole

Avocado and Smoked Salmon Lightly oaked Chardonnay, Fumé Blanc or Australian Semillon.

Smoked Salmon Paté English oaked Fumé Blanc, New Zealand Chardonnay.

Smoked Trout

Smoked Trout Paté Good, white Burgundy.

Snapper Australian or South African, dry white.

Sole Chablis, Muscadet.

Sorbet Like ice cream, these can be too cold/sweet for most wines. Try Australian fortified Muscats or see under individual entries (orange, lemon)

Sorrel Dry Loire Chenin or Sauvignon Blanc.

Soy Sauce Zinfandel or Australian Verdelho.

Spinach Pinot Grigio, Lugana.

Eggs Florentine Chablis or unoaked Chardonnay, Pinot Blanc, Sémillion.

Spinach/Pasta Bakes Soft, Italian reds (Bardolino, Valpolicella) rich whites.

Spring Rolls Pinot Gris, Gewürztraminer, or other aromatic whites.

Squab Good, red Burgundy, rich Southern Rhône. Chianti also goes well.

Warm Squab Breasts on Salad Merlot-based Bordeaux or Cabernet Rosé.

Squid Gamay de Touraine, Greek or Spanish white.

Squid in Batter Crisp and neutral dry white – Muscadet.

Squid in Ink Nebbiolo or Barbera.

Stilton Tawny port.

Strawberries – No Cream Surprisingly, red Rioja, Burgundy (or other young Pinot Noir). More conventionally, sweet Muscats or fizzy Moscato.

Strawberries and Cream Vouvray Moelleux, Monbazillac

Strawberry Meringue Late harvest Riesling.

Strawberry Mousse Sweet or fortified Muscat.

Sweet and Sour Dishes (general) Gewürztraminer, Sauvignon Blanc (unoaked) or beer.

Sweetbreads Lightly oaked Chablis, Pouilly-Fuissé, or light, red Bordeaux.

Sweetbreads in Mushroom, Butter and Cream sauce Southern French whites, Vin de Pays Chardonnay.

T

Taramasalata Oaked Chardonnay or Fumé Blanc.

Tarragon White Menetou-Salon or South African Sauvignon Blanc.

Roast/Grilled Chicken with Tarragon Dry Chenin Blanc, Vouvray, South African whites.

Thyme Ripe and fruity Provençal reds, Rioja, Northern Italian whites.

Roast Lamb with Thyme New Zealand Cabernet Sauvignon, Bourgeuil.

Toffee Moscatel de Setúbal, Eiswein.

Banoffee Pie Sweet Tokaji.

Tomato

Gazpacho Fino sherry, white Rioja.

Pasta in a Tomato Sauce California Cabernet, Zinfandel, Chianti.

Tomato Soup Sauvignon Blanc.

Tripe Earthy, French country red, Minervois, Cahors, Fitou.

Trout Pinot Blanc, Chablis.

Smoked Trout Bourgogne Aligoté, Gewürztraminer, Pinot Gris.

Trout with Almonds Bianco di Custoza, Pinot Blanc.

Truffles Red Burgundy, old Rioja, Barolo or Hermitage.

Tuna

Carpaccio of Tuna Australian Chardonnay, red Loire, Beaujolais.

Fresh Tuna Alsace Pinot Gris, Australian Chardonnay, Beaujolais.

Turbot Best white Burgundy, top California or Australian Chardonnay.

Turkey
    Roast Turkey Beaujolais, light Burgundy and quite rich or off-dry whites.
    Roast Turkey with Chestnut Stuffing Rhône, Merlot or mature Burgundy.

Vanilla Liqueur Muscat.
    Custard Monbazillac, sweet Vouvray.
Veal
    Blanquette de Veau Aromatic, spicy whites from Alsace or from the
        Northern Rhône.
    Roast Veal Light Italian whites or fairly light reds – Spanish, Loire or
        St Emilion.
    Wienerschnitzel Austrian Grüner Veltliner or Alsace or Hungarian Pinot
        Blanc.
Vegetables
    Roasted and Grilled Light juicy reds, Beaujolais, Sancerre and Sauvignon
        Blanc. Unoaked and lightly oaked Chardonnay.
    Vegetable Soup Pinot Blanc or rustic reds such as Corbières, or Southern
        Italian reds
    Vegetable Terrine Good New World Chardonnay.
Venison Pinotage, rich red Rhône, mature red Burgundy, earthy Italian reds.
    Venison Casserole Australian Shiraz, Zinfandel, South African red.
Vinegar
    Choucroute Garnie White dry Alsace (especially Riesling), Italian Pinot
        Grigio or Beaujolais.
    Sauerkraut Pilsner beer.

Walnut Tawny port, sweet Madeira.
Watercress
    Watercress Soup Aromatic dry Riesling (Alsace or Australia).
Whitebait Fino sherry, Spanish red/white (Garnacha) single-vineyard Soave.

Yams Depends on the sauce. When subtly prepared, try Alsace Pinot Blanc.
Yoghurt Needs full-flavoured wines, such as Australian Semillon or New World
    Chardonnay.

Zabaglione Marsala is an obvious choice, but also try Australian Liqueur
    Muscat or a fortified French Muscat such as Muscat de Beaumes de Venise
    or Muscat de Rivesaltes.

A-Z
of
WINE

HOW TO READ THE ENTRIES

Names of wines are accompanied by a glass symbol (🍷); grape varieties by a bunch of grapes (🍇). Wine regions appear in an orange band.

Words that have their own entry elsewhere in the A–Z appear in italics. Recommended wines may also be cross-referenced.

Poor vintages are not listed. Particularly good years that are ready to drink now are featured in bold; vintages that will improve with keeping are in orange

🍷 **Ch. l'Angélus** [lon jay-loos] (*St. Emilion Grand Cru Classé, Bordeaux,* France) Flying high since the late 1980s, this is a lovely, plummy *St. Emilion* to watch. The *second label* Carillon d'Angélus is also well worth seeking out. **79 82 83 85 86** 87 88 89 90 **92 93** 94 95 96 97 98 ☆☆☆☆☆ **1990 ££££;** ☆☆☆ **1991 £££**

Throughout this section, examples are given of recommended vintages, producers or wines which represent good examples of the region, style or maker.

Recommended wines are accompanied by stars.
☆☆☆☆☆ = outstanding in their style.
☆☆☆☆ = excellent in their style.
☆☆☆ = good in their style.

Prices are indicated, using the following symbols:

£	Under £5
££	£5–10
£££	£10–20
££££	Over £20

PRONUNCIATION GUIDE

All but the most common words are followed by square [ ] brackets, which enclose pronunciation guides. These use the "sounding-out" phonetic method, with the accented syllable (if there is one) indicated by capital letters. For example, **Spätlese** is pronounced as *SHPAYT-Lay-Zuh.* The basic sounds employed in this book's pronunciations are as follows:

a as in **can**	ah as in **father**	ay as in **day**	ur as in **turn**
ch as in **church**	kh as in **loch**	y as in **yes**	zh as in **vision**
ee as in **see**	eh as in **get**	g as in **game**	i as in **pie**
ih as in **if**	j as in **gin**	k as in **cat**	o as in **hot**
oh as in **soap**	oo as in **food**	ow as in **cow**	uh as in **up.**

Foreign sounds: eu is like a cross between oo and a; an italicised n or m is silent and the preceding vowel sounds nasal; an ñ is like an n, followed by a y (as in Bourgogne); an italicised r sounds like a cross between r and w; rr sounds like a rolled r.

A

🍷 **Abadia Retuerta** [ah-bah-dee-yah Reh-twehr-tah] (Spain) Close to *Ribera del Duero,* this large new venture benefits from the expertise of Pascal Delbeck of *Ch. Belair* in *St. Emilion.* Several equally recommendable cuvées, include Palomar, Pago Negralato, Valdebon and Campanario.

🍷 **Abazzia Sant'Anastasia** [ah-baht-zee-yah San-tan-nah-stah-zee-yah] (*Sicily* Italy) The hottest new star in Sicily, this estate makes a Cabernet – Litra – that can beat the *Super-Tuscans,* some pretty fine *Chardonnay* – Baccante – as well as reds from the local Nero d'Avola. ☆☆☆☆ **1996 Litra £££**

Abboccato [ah-boh-kah-toh] (Italy) Semi-dry.

🍷 **Abel-Lepitre** [ah-bel luh-pee-tre] (*Champagne,* France) The wine to look for here is the Réserve Blanc de Blanc Cuvée 'C' 1990.

Abfüller/Abfüllung [ab-few-ler/ ab-few-lerng] (Germany) Bottler/bottled by.
Abocado [ah-boh-kah-doh] (Spain) Semi-dry.
☠ **Abreu Vineyards** [Eh-Broo] (*Napa*, California) Cult St Helena winery with
vineyards whose grapes go to such top *Napa* names as *Harlan Estate*. Don't
bother to go looking in the shops, though, to lay your hands on a bottle.
you'll have to be on the mailing list.

Abruzzi/zzo [ah-broot-zee/zoh] (Italy) Region on the east coast, with
often dull *Trebbiano* whites and fast-improving *Montepulciano* reds. **Barone
Cornacchia; Farnese, Castello di Salle; Cantina Tollo; Edoardo Valentini.**

AC (France) See *Appellation Contrôlée.*
☠ **Acacia** [a-kay-shah] (*Carneros*, California) Fine producer of *Chardonnay*
and *Pinot Noir.* Under the same ownership as the similarly excellent
Chalone, Edna Valley and *Carmenet.* ☆☆☆☆☆ **1995 Pinot Noir ££££;**
☆☆☆☆☆ **1995 Chardonnay £££**
☠ **Accordini** [a-kor-DEE-nee] (*Veneto*, Italy) New *Valpolicella* star with fine
vineyards. ☆☆☆ **1994 Amarone Acinatico £££**
Acetic acid [ah-see-tihk] This volatile acid (CH3COOH) features in small
proportions in all wines. Careless winemaking can result in wine being
turned into acetic acid, a substance most people know as vinegar.
Acidity Naturally occurring (*tartaric* and malic) acids in the grapes are vital
to contributing freshness, and also help to preserve the wine while it ages.
In reds and many cool region whites, the malic is often converted to lactic
by a natural process known as *malolactic fermentation,* which gives the
wines a buttery texture and flavour. In hotter countries (and sometimes
cooler ones) the acid level may (not always legally) be adjusted by adding
tartaric and citric acid.
☠ **Ackerman-Laurance** [ah-kehr-man Loh-ronss] (*Loire*, France) One of
Loire's most reliable sparkling wine producers. Privilège is the top wine.

Aconcagua Valley [ah-kon-kar-gwah] (*Central Valley*, Chile) Region
noted for blackcurrant *Cabernet Sauvignon.* The sub-region is
Casablanca. Grapes from both are used by many Chilean producers.
Concha y Toro, Errazuriz.

☠ **Tim Adams** (*Clare Valley*, Australia) Highly successful producer of
Riesling, rich peachy *Semillon* and deep-flavoured Aberfeldy *Shiraz* and
intense peppery Fergus *Grenache.* ☆☆☆☆☆ **1998 The Aberfeldy £££;**
☆☆☆☆ **1999 Riesling ££**
☠ **Adanti** [ah-dan-ti] (*Umbria*, Italy) Star producer of spicy reds and herby
Grechetto whites. ☆☆☆☆ **1994 Rosso di Montefalco £££**
Adega [ah-day-gah] (Portugal) Winery – equivalent to Spanish *bodega.*

Adelaide Hills [ah-dur-layd] (*South Australia*) High-altitude region, long
known for classy, lean *Riesling* and *Semillon*; now famous for *Sauvignon
Blanc* and *Chardonnay* from *Ashton Hills, Petaluma* and *Nepenthe* and *Shaw
& Smith, Croser sparkling wine* and the occasional *Pinot Noir.* See also the
new sub-region of *Lenswood. Ashton Hills;* **Chain of Ponds; Grosett;
Heggies; Henschke; Mountadam; Penfolds.**

☠ **Weingut Graf Adelmann** [graf-ah-del-man] (*Württemberg*, Germany)
One of the region's best estates, making good reds from grapes such as the
Trollinger, Lemberger and Urban. Look for Brüssele'r Spitze wines.
☠ **Adelsheim** [a-del-sime] (*Oregon*, USA) Classy, long-lived but non-showy,
quite old-fashioned, Pinot Noir from a producer with the look of an Old
Testament prophet. ☆☆☆☆☆ **1996 Oregon Pinot Noir £££**
☠ **Age** [ah-khay] (*Rioja*, Spain) Big, modern, highly commercial winery.

🌿 **Aglianico** [ah-lee-AH-nee-koh] (Italy) Thick-skinned grape grown by the Ancient Greeks. Now used to make hefty *Taurasi* and *Aglianico del Vulture*.

🍷 **Aglianico del Vulture** [ah-lee-AH-nee-koh del vool-TOO-reh] (*Basilicata*, Italy) Tannic liquoricey-chocolatey blockbusters made in Southern Italy on the hills of an extinct volcano. Older examples are labelled as Vecchio (3 years+) and Riserva (5 years+). **D'Angelo; Basilium; Casele; Paternoster; Sasso.**

Agricola vitivinicola (Italy) Wine estate.

Ahr [ahr] (Germany) Northernmost *Anbaugebiet*, making light-bodied reds.

Ajaccio [ah-JAK-see-yoh] (*Corsica*, France) Very mixed fare, but *Comte Peraldi* makes intense reds and whites. See also: *Gie Les Rameaux.*

🌿 **Airén** [i-REHN] (Spain) The world's most planted variety. Dull and fortunately more or less restricted to the region of *La Mancha*.

🍷 **Albana di Romagna** [ahl-BAH-nah dee roh-MAN-yah] (*Emilia-Romagna*, Italy) Inexplicably, Italy's first white *DOCG*. Traditionally dull but improving white. Passita, sweeter whites are best. **Celli; Umberto Cesari; Fattoria Paradiso; Zerbina.**

🌿 **Albariño** [ahl-BAH-ree-nyoh] (*Galicia*, Spain) The Spanish name for the Portuguese *Alvarinho* and the peachy-spicy wine made from it in *Rias Baixas*. **Lagar de Cervera; Martin Codex; *Pazo de Barrantes*; Salnesu; Valdamor.**

🍷 **Castello d'Albola** [KAS-teh-loh DAL-boh-la] (*Tuscany*, Italy) Top Tuscan Estate belonging to the increasingly dynamic firm of *Zonin*.
Alcohol This simple compound, technically known as ethanol, is formed by the action of yeast on sugar during fermentation.

🌿 **Aleatico** [ah-lay-AH-tee-koh] (Italy) Red grape producing sweet, *Muscat*-style, often fortified wines. Produces *DOCs* A. di Puglia and A. di Gradoli.

Alella [ah-LEH-yah] (*Catalonia*, Spain) *DO* district producing better whites (from grapes including the *Xarel-lo*) than reds. **Marfil; Marqués de Alella; Parxet.** ☆☆☆☆ **1998 Marqués de Alella Clasico £££**

Alenquer [ah-lehn-kehr] (*Oeste*, Portugal) Coolish region producing good *Periquita* reds and *Muscat*-style *Fernão Pires* whites. Also making successful efforts from French varietals. ☆☆☆ **1998 Quinta de Parrotes ££**

Alentejo [ah-lehn-TAY-joh] (Portugal) Province north of the Algarve whose elevation from its status as a source of bulk wine has recently been recognised by its division into five DOCs: Borba, Portalegre, Redondo, Reguengos, Vidigueira. This is the region where *JM da Fonseca* makes Morgado de Reguengo, *JP Vinhos* produces Tinta da Anfora and *Ch. Lafite* has its Quinta do Carmo. Cooperatives, such as the one at *Borba*, are improving too and this will increasingly be recognised as a place to find both quality and value. *Borba*; Cartuxa; *Esporão*; Herdade de Mouchao; *Quinta do Carmo*; Redondo, Jose de Sousa.

Alexander Valley (*Sonoma*, California) *Appellation* in which *Simi, Jordan, Murphy Good*, and *Geyser Peak* are based. *Turley* makes big Zinfandels here too. Red: 86 89 **90** 91 92 **94** 95 96 97 98 White: **92** 95 **96** 97 98 *Arrowood, Ch. St Jean; Clos du Bois; Geyser Peak; Jordan; Marcassin; Simi; Stonestreet.*

Ⓧ Caves Aliança [ah-lee-an-sah] (Portugal) Modern *Bairrada, Douro* and better-than-average *Dão*. ☆☆☆ 1997 Dão Reserva ££

Alicante (*Valencia*, Spain) Hot region producing generally dull stuff apart from the sweetly honeyed *Moscatels* that appreciate the heat.

❦ Alicante-Bouschet [al-ee-KONT- boo-SHAY] Unusual dark-skinned and fleshed grapes traditionally used (usually illegally) for dyeing pallid reds made from nobler fare. *Rockford* in Australia uses it to make a good rosé.

❦ Aligoté [Al-lee-GOH-tay] (*Burgundy*, France) Lesser white grape, making dry wine that is traditionally mixed with *cassis* for *Kir*. With care and a touch of oak it can imitate basic *Bourgogne* Blanc, especially in the village of *Bouzeron*. La Digoine; *Domaine Dujac;* G & J-H Goisot; Aubert de Vilaine.

Ⓧ Alion [ah-lee-yon] (*Ribera del Duero*, Spain) New venture by the owners of *Vega Sicilia*, with fruitier, more modern wines. ☆☆☆☆☆ 1994 Reserva £££

Ⓧ All Saints (*Rutherglen*, Australia) Good producer of *Liqueur Muscat, Tokay* and *late harvest* wines.

Ⓧ Allegrini [ah-leh-GREE-nee] (*Veneto*, Italy) Top-class producer of single-vineyard *Valpolicella* and *Soave*. ☆☆☆☆ 1997 la Grola £££

Ⓧ Thierry Allemand [al-mon] (*Rhône*, France) Producer of classic, concentrated, single-vineyard *Cornas* from a small 2.5-hectare (6-acre) estate. ☆☆☆☆☆ 1997 Cornas Chaillot £££

Allier [a-lee-yay] (France) Spicy oak favoured by makers of white wine.

Ⓧ Almaviva [al-mah-vee-vah] (*Maipo*, Chile) New, pricy red co-production between *Mouton Rothschild* and *Concha y Toro*. ☆☆☆☆ 1996 £££

Almacenista [al-mah-theh-nee-stah] (*Jerez,* Spain) Fine unblended sherry from a single *solera* – the *sherry* equivalent of a single malt whisky. Lustau.

Ⓧ Aloxe-Corton [a-loss kawr-ton] (*Burgundy*, France) *Côte de Beaune commune* with tough, slow-maturing, sometimes uninspiring reds (including the *Grand Cru Corton*) and potentially sublime whites (including *Corton-Charlemagne*). Louis Latour's pricy whites can be fine. White: **85 86 88** 89 90 92 95 96 97 Red: **78 85** 86 87 **88 89 90** 95 96 97 98 Arnoux; *Bonneau du Martray;* Denis Bousse; Capitan-Gagnerot; *Drouhin;* Michel Gay; Antonin Guyon; *Jadot; Patrick Javillier;* Daniel Largeot; *Leflaive;* Prince de Mérode; André Nudant; Comte Senard; *Tollot-Beaut; Michel Voarick.*

Alsace [al-sas] (France) Northerly region whose warm micro-climate enables producers to make riper-tasting wines than their counterparts across the Rhine. Wines are named after the grapes – *Pinot Noir, Gewurztraminer, Riesling, Tokay/Pinot Gris, Pinot Blanc* (known as Pinot d'Alsace), *Sylvaner* and (rarely) *Muscat*. In the right hands, the 50 or so *Grand Cru* vineyards yield better wines. *Late harvest* sweet wines are labelled *Vendange Tardive* and *Sélection des Grains Nobles*. White: 85 86 88 89 90 93 94 95 96 97 *Léon Beyer; Paul Blanck;* Bott-Geyl; Albert Boxler; *Ernest J & F Burn;* Joseph Cattin; Marcel Deiss; Jean-Pierre Dirler; *Dopff au Moulin;* Faller; *Hugel; Josmeyer; André Kientzler; Kreydenweiss; Albert Mann; Meyer-Fonné, Mittnacht-Klack; René Muré; Ostertag; Rolly Gassmann; Schlumberger;* Schoffit; *Bruno Sorg; Marc Tempé; Trimbach; Weinbach; Zind Humbrecht.*

Ⅰ **Elio Altare** [Ehl-lee-yoh al-TAh-ray] (*Piedmont*, Italy) The genial, Svengali-like leader of the *Barolo* revolution and inspirer of *Clerico* and *Roberto Voerzio*. ☆☆☆☆☆ **1996 Langhe Arborina; £££** ☆☆☆☆☆ **1994 Barolo £££**

Ⅰ **Altesino** [al-TEH-see-noh] (*Tuscany*, Italy) First-class producers of *Brunello di Montalcino*, *Cabernet* ("Palazzo") and *Sangiovese* ("Altesi"). ☆☆☆☆☆ **1995 Palazzo d'Altesi £££**

> **Alto-Adige** [ahl-toh ah-dee-jay] (Italy) Aka Italian Tyrol and Südtirol. *DOC* for a huge range of whites often from Germanic grape varieties; also light and fruity reds from the *Lagrein* and Vernatsch. Cooperatives are particularly successful here. **Appiano; Cant. Prod. di Cortaccia; Cant. Prod. di Termeno; Cant. Vit. di Caldaro; Gaierhof; Hofstätter;** *Alois Lageder;* **Maddalena;** *Pojer & Sandri;* **Tiefenbrunner;** Viticoltori Alto Adige.

🌱 **Alvarinho** [ahl-vah-reen-yoh] (Portugal) White grape aka *Albariño*; at its lemony best in *Vinho Verde* and in the *DO* Alvarinho de Monção. **Amabile** [am-MAH-bee-lay] (Italy) Semi-sweet.

Ⅰ **Castello di Ama** [ah-mah] (*Tuscany*, Italy) Brilliant small *Chianti* estate. Great single vineyard Vigna l'Apparita wines and very fine *Chardonnay*. ☆☆☆☆☆ **1995 Vigna l'Apparita £££**

> **Amador County** [am-uh-dor] (*California*) Intensely-flavoured, old-fashioned *Zinfandel*. Look for Amador Foothills Winery's old-vine *Zinfandels* and top-of-the-range stuff from *Sutter Home* and *Monteviña*. **Red: 86 87 88 89 90 91 92** 94 95 96 97 **White: 94** 95 96 97 *Quady.*

Ⅰ **Amarone** [ah-mah-ROH-neh] (*Veneto*, Italy) Literally "bitter"; used particularly to describe *Recioto*. Best known as *Amarone della Valpolicella*. *Allegrini; Boscaini; Masi;* **Angelo Nicolis;** *Quintarelli;* **Romano dal Forno;** *Speri; Tedeschi; Vignalta; Zenato.*

Ⅰ **Bodegas Amézola de la Mora** [ah-meh-THOH-lah deh lah MAW-rah] (*Rioja*, Spain) Eight-year-old estate producing unusually classy red *Rioja*.

Ⅰ **Amity** [am-mi-tee] (*Oregon*, US) Maker of very high quality berryish *Pinot Noir*, good dry *Gewürztraminer* and *late-harvest* whites. **Amontillado** [am-mon-tee-yah-doh] (*Jerez*, Spain) Literally "like Montilla". Often pretty basic medium-sweet *sherry*, but ideally fascinating dry, nutty wine. *Gonzalez Byass; Lustau; Sanchez Romate.*

Ⅰ **Ampelones Vassilou** [am-peh-loh-nehs vas-see-loo] (*Attica*, Greece) Producer of good new-wave Greek wines **Amtliche Prüfungsnummer** [am-tlish-eh proof-oong-znoomer] (Germany) Identification number on all *QbA/QmP* labels. **Anbaugebiet** [ahn-bow-geh-beet] (Germany) Term for 11 large regions (e.g. *Rheingau*). *QbA* and *QmP* wines must include the name of their *Anbaugebiet* on their labels.

Anderson Valley (*Mendocino*, California) Small, cool area, good for white and sparkling wines including the excellent *Roederer.* Do not confuse with the less impressive Anderson Valley, New Mexico. Red: **88 89 90 91 94** 95 96 97 White: 91 92 **94** 95 **96** 97 **Edmeades; Roederer; Steele; Williams Selyem.**

�>**Anderson Vineyard** (*Napa*, California) Stag's Leap producer of intense blackcurranty Cabernet and rich, full-flavoured *Chardonnay.*

�>**Andrew Will** (*Washington State*, US) Superstar producer of some of *Washington State's* – not to say North America's – best *Cabernet Sauvignon* and *Merlot.* ☆☆☆☆☆ **1997 Merlot £££**

�>**Ch. l'Angélus** [lon jay-loos] (*St. Emilion Grand Cru Classé, Bordeaux,* France) Flying high since the late 1980s, this is a lovely plummy, oaky *St. Emilion.* The *second label* Carillon d'Angélus is also well worth seeking out. 79 81 **82 83 85 86 87 88** 89 90 **93 94** 95 96 97 98 99 ☆☆☆☆☆ **1998 ££££**

�>**Marquis d'Angerville** [don-jehr-veel] (*Burgundy*, France) Long-established *Volnay* estate with rich, long-lived traditional wines from here and from *Pommard.* ☆☆☆☆ **1997 Volnay £££**

�>**Ch d'Angludet** [don gloo-day] (*Cru Bourgeois, Margaux, Bordeaux,* France) Made by the late *Peter Sichel,* classy cassis-flavoured, if slightly earthy, wine that can generally be drunk young but is worth waiting for. 78 **82 83** 85 **86** 88 89 90 **91** 93 94 95 96 97 98

�>**Angoves** [an-gohvs] (*Padthaway*, Australia) *Murray River* producer with improving, inexpensive *Chardonnay* and *Cabernet* and great brandy.

�>**Weingut Paul Anheuser** [an-hoy-zur] (*Nahe*, Germany) One of the most credible supporters of the *Trocken* movement, and a strong proponent of the *Riesling*, this excellent estate is also unusually successful with its *Ruländer* and *Pinot Noir.*

�>**Finca la Anita** [feen-kah lah an-nee-tah] (*Mendoza*, Argentina) An organic, small-scale winery to watch. Innovative wines include a tasty *Syrah-Malbec* blend.

�>**Anjou** [on-joo] (*Loire*, France) Dry and *Demi-Sec* whites, mostly from *Chenin Blanc*, with up to 20 per cent *Chardonnay* or *Sauvignon Blanc.* The rosé is almost always awful but there are good, light reds. Look for *Anjou-Villages*, in which *Gamay* is not permitted. Within Anjou, there are smaller, more specific ACs, most importantly *Savennières* and *Coteaux du Layon.* Red: **88** 89 90 95 96 97 White: 88 89 **90 94** 95 96 97 98 Sweet White: **76 83 85 88 89 90 94** 95 96 97 **Arnault et Fils, Bouvet-Ladubay; Ch. du Breuil; Dom. du Closel; Ch. de Fesles; Gaudard; Genaiserie Lebreton; Richou; Ch. la Varière.**

�>**Anjou-Coteaux de la Loire** [Koh-toh duh lah Lwarh] (*Loire*, France) Small, lesser-known appellation for varied styles of Chenin Blanc, including quite luscious late-harvest examples. Do not confuse with *Coteaux du Loir.* **Ch. de Putille.**

�>**Anjou-Villages** [on-joo vee-larj] (*Loire*, France) Increasingly famous red wine appellation, thanks partly to Gérard Dépardieu's presence here as a (seriously committed) winemaker at Ch. de Tigné, and partly to the impressive quality of the juicy, potentially long-lived Cabernet-based red wines. **Bablut; Ch. de Coulaine; Ch. de Fesles; Ogereau; Richou; Rochelles; Pierre Bise; Ogereau; Montigilet; Dom. de Sablonettes; Pierre Soulez; Ch. de Tigné.**

Annata [ahn-nah-tah] (Italy) *Vintage.*

ℤ **Roberto Anselmi** [an-sehl-mee] (*Veneto*, Italy) Source of classy dry
Soave Classico wines as well as some extremely serious sweet examples.
☆☆☆☆ **1996 I Capitelli Recioto di Soave £££**

ℤ **Antinori** [an-tee-NOR-ree] (*Tuscany*, Italy) Pioneer merchant-producer
who has improved the quality of *Chianti*, with his Villa Antinori and
Pèppoli, while spearheading the *Super-Tuscan* revolution with *Tignanello*,
Sassicaia and *Solaia* and producing around 15,000,000 bottles of wine per
year. There are also joint ventures in California (*Atlas Peak*), Washington
State and Hungary ☆☆☆☆ **1995 Chianti Classico Tenute del Marchese
Riserva £££; ☆☆☆☆☆ 1995 Solaia ££££; ☆☆☆☆ 1993 Tignanello ££££**

AOC (France) See *Appellation Contrôlée*.

AP (Germany) See *Amtliche Prüfungsnummer.*

Appellation Contrôlée (AC/AOC) [AH-pehl-lah-see-on kon troh-lay]
(France) Official designation guaranteeing origin, grape varieties and
method of production and – in theory – quality, though tradition and
vested interest combine to allow pretty appalling wines to receive the
rubber stamp. Increasingly questioned by quality-conscious producers.

Aprémont [ah-pray-mon] (Eastern France) Floral, slightly *petillant* white
from skiing region. **Ch. de la Violette.**

Apulia [ah-pool-ee-yah] (Italy) See *Puglia.*

Aquileia [ah-kwee-lay-ah] (*Friuli-Venezia Giulia,* Italy) *DOC* for easy-
going, single-variety wines. The *Refosco* can be plummily refreshing.
Ca'Bolani and Corvignano Cooperatives; Franco-Clementin; *Zonin.*

ℤ **Agricola Aquitania**. [ah-gree-koh-lah ah-kee-tah-nee-ya] (*Maipo*, Chile)
Estate founded by Paul Pontallier (of *Ch. Margaux*) and Bruno Prats
(formerly of *Ch. Cos d'Estournel*) and overlooking the city of Santiago and
close to premium housing land. Early vintages of the *Cabernet* were rather
forbidding (and suffered from being unoaked). More recent efforts are
richer, thanks partly to older vines and partly to a sojourn in cask. The top
wine is Paul Bruno and the second wine, Uno Fuera.

Arbois [ahr-bwah] (Eastern France) *AC* region with light *Trousseau* and
Pinot Noir reds and nutty dry Savignan (not to be confused with the
Sauvignon) and *Chardonnay* whites. Also *sherry*-like *Vin Jaune,* sweet *Vin
de Paille,* and sparkling wine. **Aviet; Dugois; Fruitière Viticole; Lornet;
Puffeney; Rolet; Tissot.**

ℤ **Ch. d' Arche** [dahrsh] (*Sauternes 2ème Cru Classé, Bordeaux,* France)
Greatly improved, but still slightly patchy. 83 **86 88 89** 90 93 94 95 97 98

ℤ **Archery Summit** (*Oregon*, USA) A recent venture in Yamhill County in
Oregon by Gary Andrus of *Pine Ridge* in *Napa*. Both *Pinot Noir* and
Pinot Gris are impressive – if pricy. ☆☆☆☆☆ **1998 Arcus Estate Pinot
Noir Premier Cuvée ££££**

ℤ **Viña Ardanza** [veen-yah ahr-dan-thah] (*Rioja*, Spain) Highly reliable,
fairly full-bodied, long-lived, classic red *Roija* made with a high
proportion (40 per cent) of *Grenache*; good, *oaky* white, too. ☆☆☆☆
1990 Tinto Reserva ££

ℤ **d'Arenberg** [dar-ren-burg] (*McLaren Vale*, Australia) Excellent up-and-
coming producer with memorably named, impressive sweet and dry table
wines and unusually dazzling fortifieds. ☆☆☆☆☆ **1997 The Dead Arm £££;**
☆☆☆☆☆ **1997 The Ironstone Pressings £££; ☆☆☆☆ 1998 The Broken
Fishplate £££**

Argentina Fast up-and-coming nation with fine *Malbec*. *Cabernet* and *Merlot* have a touch more backbone than many efforts from Chile and there are interesting wines made from Italian red varieties. *Chardonnays* and grapey whites from the *Muscat*-like *Torrontes* are worthwhile too. **la Agricola; *Finca la Anita; Leoncio Arizu; Balbi; Luigi Bosca;* Canale; *Catena;* M Chandon (Paul Galard; Terrazas); Esmeralda; *Etchart; Lurton; Morande;* Navarro Correas; *Norton; la Rural;* San Telmo; Santa Ana; Torino; Trapiche; Weinert.**

🍷 **Tenuta di Argiano** [teh-noo-tah dee ahr-zhee-ahn-noh] (*Tuscany*, Italy) Instant success story, with top-class vineyards, and lovely juicy reds. ☆☆☆☆ **1996 Rosso di Montalcino £££;** ☆☆☆☆☆ **1993 Solengo ££££**

🍷 **Argyle** (*Oregon*, US) Classy sparkling wine and still wines from Brian Croser (of *Petaluma*). ☆☆☆☆ **1995 Blanc de Blancs £££;** ☆☆☆☆ **1995 Willamette Valley Reserve Chardonnay £££**

🍷 **Ch. d'Arlay** [dahr-lay] (*Jura*, France) Reliable producer of nutty *Vin Jaune* and light, earthy-raspberry *Pinot Noir*. ☆☆☆☆ **1995 Côtes du Jura £££**

🍷 **Leoncio Arizu** [Ah-ree-zoo] (*Mendoza*, Argentina) Variable, old-established producer. Also owns *Luigi Bosca*

🍷 **Dom. de l'Arlot** [dur-lahr-loh] (*Burgundy*, France) Brilliant, award-winning *Nuits-St.-Georges* estate under the same – insurance company – ownership as *Ch. Pichon-Longueville*. Delicate modern reds (including an increasingly impressive *Vosne-Romanée*) and a rare example of white *Nuits-St.-Georges*. ☆☆☆☆ **1997 Nuits-St.-Georges Clos de l'Arlot £££**

🍷 **Ch. d'Armailhac** [darh-mi-yak] (*Pauillac 5ème Cru Classé, Bordeaux*, France). In the same stable as *Mouton-Rothschild*, and showing similar rich flavours, though never the same elegance. 82 83 85 **86 88 89** 90 92 93 **94** 95 96 **97** 98 99 ☆☆☆☆ **1995 ££££**

🍷 **Dom. du Comte Armand** [komt-arh-mon] (*Burgundy*, France) The top wine from the Canadian-born winemaker here is the exceptional *Pommard* Clos des Epeneaux, but the *Auxey Duresses* and *Volnay* les Fremiets are fine too. ☆☆☆☆ **1998 £££**

🥂 **Arneis** [ahr-nay-ees] (*Piedmont*, Italy) Spicy white; makes good, young, unoaked wine. *Bava; Ceretto; Bruno Giacosa;* Malvira; Serafino; *Voerzio.*

🍷 **Ch. l' Arrosée**, [lah-roh-say] (*St. Emilion Grand Cru Classé, Bordeaux*, France) Small, well-sited property with fruity intense wines. 79 81 **82** 83 **85 86 88** 89 90 **93 94** 95 96 **97** 98 99 ☆☆☆☆ **1990 ££££**

🍷 **Arrowood** (*Sonoma Valley*, California) Fine *Chardonnay, Merlot, Pinot Blanc, Viognier* and *Cabernet* from former *Ch. St. Jean* winemaker. ☆☆☆☆ **1995 Sonoma Special Reserve Cabernet Sauvignon ££££**

🍷 **Ismael Arroyo** [uh-Roy-oh] (*Ribera del Duero*, Spain) A name to watch for flavoursome reds. ☆☆☆☆ **1995 Val Sotillo Reserva £££**

♈ **Artadi** [ahr-tah-dee] (*Rioja*, Spain) Up-and-coming producer with particularly good *Crianza* and *Reserva* wines – and fast-rising prices ☆☆☆☆ 1995 Rioja Pagos Viejos Reserva ££££

♈ **Arvine** [ah-veen] (Switzerland) Delicious, spicy white indigenous grape which has reminded some visiting Italians of their *Arneis*. Bonvin; Provins; Rochaix

♈ **Bodegas Arzuaga** [Ahr-thwah-gag] (*Ribera del Duero*, Spain) One of the growing number of new wave estates in Ribera del Duero, with large acreage of vines and emphatically modern winemaking that is catching the attention of US critics. ☆☆☆☆☆ 1994 Ribera del Duero Reserva £££

♈ **Giacomo Ascheri** [ash-sheh-ree] (*Piedmont*, Italy) Pioneering producer. Impressive single-vineyard, tobacco 'n berry wines, also *Nebbiolo*, *Syrah* and *Viognier* and Freisa del Langhe. ☆☆☆☆☆ 1996 Montelupa Rosso £££
Asciutto [ah-shoo-toh] (Italy) Dry.

Asenovgrad [ass-seh-nov-grad] (Bulgaria) Demarcated northern wine region with rich plummy *Cabernet Sauvignon*, *Merlot* and *Mavrud*.

♈ **Ashton Hills** (*Adelaide Hills*, Australia) Small up-and-coming winery producing good Pinot Noir as well as subtle, increasingly creditable *Chardonnay* and *Riesling*. ☆☆☆☆ 1998 Pinot Noir £££
Assemblage [ah-sehm-blahj] (France) The art of blending wine from different grape varieties. Associated with *Bordeaux* and *Champagne*.

Assmanhausen [ass-mahn-how-zehn] (*Rheingau*, Germany) If you like sweet *Pinot Noir*, this is the place to come looking for it.

🍷 **Asti** (*Piedmont*, Italy) Town famous for sparkling *Spumante*, lighter *Moscato d'Asti* and red *Barbera d'Asti*. Red: 82 **85 88** 89 90 **93 94** 95 96 97 White: 98 Bera; Bersano; Contratto; *Fontanafredda; Gancia; Martini.*

Astringent Mouth-puckering. Associated with young red wine. See *tannin*.
Aszu [ah-soo] (Hungary) The sweet syrup made from dried and "nobly rotten" grapes (see *botrytis*) used to sweeten *Tokaji*.

♈ **Ata Rangi** [ah-tah ran-gee] (*Martinborough*, New Zealand) Small estate with high-quality *Pinot Noir* and *Shiraz*. ☆☆☆☆ 1998 Pinot Noir £££

♈ **Atlas Peak** (*Napa*, California) Antinori's US venture is proving more successful with Cabernet than with Sangiovese.

♈ **Au Bon Climat** (oh bon klee-Mat] (*Santa Barbara*, California) Top-quality producer of characterful and flavoursome *Pinot Noir* and particularly classy *Chardonnay*. ☆☆☆☆ 1997 Talley Reserve Pinot Noir £££

♈ **Dom. des Aubuisières** [day Soh-bwee-see-yehr] (*Loire*, France) Bernard Fouquet produces impeccable wines ranging from richly dry to lusciously sweet. ☆☆☆☆ 1997 Vouvray Sec le Marigny £££

Auckland (New Zealand) An all-embracing designation which once comprised over a quarter of the country's vineyards. Often derided, despite the fact that some vintages favour this region over starrier areas such as *Marlborough*. *Collards; Goldwater Estate; Kumeu River; Matua Valley;* Sacred Hill.

Aude [ohd] (South-West France) Prolific *département* traditional source of ordinary wine. Now *Corbières* and *Fitou* are improving as are the *Vins de Pays*, thanks to new grapes (such as the *Viognier*) and the efforts of firms like *Skalli Fortant de France, Val d'Orbieu* and *Domaine Virginie*.

Ausbruch [ows-brook] (Austria) Term for rich *botrytis* wine which is sweeter than *Beerenauslese* but less sweet than *Trockenbeerenauslese*.

Auslese [ows-lay-zuh] (Germany) Mostly sweet wine from selected ripe grapes, usually affected by *botrytis*. Third rung on the *QmP* ladder.

Ⴎ Ch. Ausone [oh-zohn] (*St. Emilion Premier Grand Cru Classé, Bordeaux,* France) Pretender to the crown of top *St. Emilion*. The estate owes its name to the Roman occupation and can produce fine complex *claret*. Until the wine-making was taken over by *Michel Rolland* in 1995, the wine lacked the intensity demanded by critics. The 1998 is delicious, if less delicately perfumed than in the past, but the 1999 is one of the wines of the vintage. 79 81 **82 83 85 86** 88 89 90 92 93 94 95 96 **97** 98 99 ☆☆☆☆☆ **1990 ££££**

Austria Home of all sorts of whites, ranging from dry *Sauvignon Blancs,* greengagey *Grüner Veltliners* and ripe *Rieslings* to especially luscious *late harvest* wines. Reds are increasingly successful too – particularly the *Pinot-Noir*-like *St Laurents.* Brundlmayer; *Feiler-Artinger; Freie Weingärtner;* Holler; Juris; Knoll; *Alois Kracher;* Alois Lang; Münzenrieder; Nicolaihof; *Willi Opitz; Pichler;* Johan Tschida; *Prager; Ernst Triebaumer; Umathum.*

⚑Auxerrois [oh-sehr-wah] (France) Named after the town in northern *Burgundy*, this is the Alsatians' term for a fairly dull local variety that may be related to the *Sylvaner, Melon de Bourgogne* or *Chardonnay*. South Africa's winemakers learned about it when cuttings were smuggled into the *Cape* and planted there under the misapprehension that they were *Chardonnay*. In Luxembourg it is called the *Luxembourg Pinot Gris.*

Ⴎ Auxey-Duresses [oh-say doo-ress] (*Burgundy*, France) *Côtes de Beaune* village best known for buttery whites, but producing rather more rustic, raspberryish, reds. A slow developer. **Robert Ampeau; Dom. d'Auvenay; Dom. Chassorney;** *Coche-Dury; Comte Armand;* Jean-Pierre Diconne; Louis Jadot; Olivier Leflaive; Michel Prunier; Vincent Prunier; Guy Roulot.

AVA (US) Acronym for American Viticultural Areas, a recent attempt to develop an American *appellation* system. It makes sense in smaller, climatically coherent *appellations* like *Mount Veeder* and *Carneros;* much less so in larger, more heterogenous ones like *Napa.*

Ⴎ Quinta da Aveleda (*Vinho Verde,* Portugal) Famous estate producing disappointing dry *Vinho Verde.*

Avelsbach [ahr-vel-sarkh] (*Mosel,* Germany) *Ruwer* village producing delicate, light-bodied wines. Qba/Kab/Spät: 85 87 **88** 89 90 **91** 92 **93 94** 95 96 97 Aus/Beeren/Tba: **83** 85 **88 89 90** 91 92 **93 94** 95 97 98

Ⴎ Avignonesi [ahr-veen-yon-nay-see] (*Tuscany,* Italy) Ultra-classy producer of *Vino Nobile di Montepulciano, Super-Tuscans* such as *Grifi,* a pure *Merlot* described by an American critic as Italy's *Pétrus*. There are also serious *Chardonnay* and *Sauvignon* whites – plus an unusually good *Vin Santo.* ☆☆☆☆☆ **1996 Grifi £££**

Ⴎ Ayala [ay-yah-lah] (*Champagne,* France) Underrated producer which takes its name from the village of Ay. ☆☆☆ **Non Vintage £££**

Ayl [ihl] (*Mosel,* Germany) Distinguished *Saar* village producing steely wines. Qba/Kab/Spät: 86 88 **89** 90 **91** 92 **93 94** 95 96 97 Aus/Beeren/Tba: **83** 85 88 89 90 91 92 **93 94** 95 97 98

Azienda [ad-see-en-dah] (Italy) Estate.

B

Babich [ba-bitch] (*Henderson*, New Zealand) Family winery with wines from Auckland, Marlborough and Hawkes Bay, source of the rich "Irongate" and Patriarch *Chardonnays*. The *Sauvignon Blanc* is good too. The reds improve with every vintage.
☆☆☆☆☆ 1998 Irongate Chardonnay £££

Quinta da Bacalhôa [dah ba-keh-yow] (*Setúbal*, Portugal) The innovative *Cabernet-Merlot* made by *Peter Bright* at *JP Vinhos*.

Bacchus [ba-kuhs] White grape. A *Müller-Thurgau-Riesling* cross, making light, flowery wine. *Denbies; Tenterden.*

Dom. Denis Bachelet [dur-nee bash-lay] (*Burgundy*, France) Classy, small *Gevrey-Chambertin* estate with cherryish wines that are great young – and with five or six years of age. ☆☆☆☆☆ 1996 Vieilles Vignes Gevrey-Chambertin £££

Backsberg Estate [bax-burg] (*Paarl*, South Africa) *Chardonnay* pioneer, with good, quite *Burgundian* versions. ☆☆☆ 1998 Merlot ££

Bad Dürkheim [baht duhr-kime] (*Pfalz*, Germany) Chief *Pfalz* town, producing some of the region's finest whites, plus some reds.
Qba/Kab/Spät: **85 86 88 89** 90 91 92 **93 94 95** 96 97 98 Aus/Beeren/Tba: **83 85 88 89** 90 91 92 **93 94 95** 96 97 *Kurt Darting;* Fitz-Ritter; Karl Schäfer.

Bad Kreuznach [baht kroyts-nahkh] (*Nahe*, Germany) The chief and finest wine town of the region, giving its name to the entire lower *Nahe*.
75 76 **83 85** 86 88 **89 90** 91 92 **93** 94 95 96 97 *Paul Anheuser;* von Plettenberg.

Baden [bah-duhn] (Germany) Warm southern region of Germany, with ripe grapes to make dry (*Trocken*) wines. Some of these, such as "Baden Dry", are good, as are some of the *Pinot Noirs*. The huge *Winzerkeller* cooperative makes good wines, as do: *Dr Heger; Karl Heinz Johner;* R Zimmerlin.

Baden Winzerkeller (ZBW) [bah-den vin-zehr-keh-luhr] (*Baden*, Germany) Huge co-op whose reliability has set *Baden* apart from the rest of Germany.

Badia a Coltibuono [bah-dee-yah ah kohl-tee-bwoh-noh] (*Tuscany*, Italy) One of Italy's most reliable producers of *Chianti*, fairly priced pure *Sangiovese* and *Chardonnay*. Great mature releases. ☆☆☆☆ 1995 Chianti Classico Riserva ££; ☆☆☆☆☆ 1996 Sangioveto £££

Badia di Morrona [bah-dee-yah dee Moh-ROH-nah] (*Tuscany*, Italy) Up-and-coming estate with a notable Super-Tuscan in the shape of the N'Antia Cabernet-Sangiovese blend.

Baga [bah-gah] (*Bairrada*, Portugal) The spicily fruity red variety of *Bairrada*.

Ch. Bahans-Haut-Brion [bah-on oh-bree-on] (*Graves, Bordeaux,* France) The second label of *Ch. Haut Brion*. Red: 82 83 85 **86** 87 88 **89** 90 92 93 94 95 96 97 98 99 ☆☆☆☆ 1995 ££££

Bailey's (*Victoria*, Australia) Traditional, good *Liqueur Muscat* and hefty, old-fashioned *Shiraz*. Current wines are a little more subtle but still pack a punch. ☆☆☆☆ 1996, 1920's Block Shiraz £££

Ŧ Bairrada [bi-rah-dah] (Portugal) *DO* region south of Oporto, traditionally making dull whites and tough reds. Revolutionary producers like *Sogrape, Luis Pato* and *Alianca* are proving what can be done. Look for spicy blackberryish reds and creamy whites. Red: 85 86 87 88 90 91 92 94 95 96 97

Baja California [bah-hah] (*Mexico*) The part of *Mexico* abutting the Californian border, best known for exporting illegal aliens and importing adventurous Californians and hippies. Also a successful, though little known, wine region; home to the Santo Tomas, Casa de Piedra and *LA Cetto* wineries.

Balance Harmony of fruitiness, *acidity, alcohol and tannin.* Balance can develop with age but should be evident (if sometimes hard to discern) in youth.

Balaton [bah-la-ton] (*Hungary*) Wine region frequented by *flying winemakers,* and producing fair-quality reds and whites.

Ŧ Anton Balbach [an-ton bahl-barkh] (*Rheinhessen,* Germany) Potentially one of the best producers in the *Erden* region – especially for *late harvest* wines. ☆☆☆☆☆ 1996 Niersteiner Delberg Eiswein ££££

Ŧ Bodegas Balbás [bal-bash] (*Ribera del Duero,* Spain) Small producer of juicy *Tempranillo* reds, *Bordeaux*-style *Cabernet* blends and a lovely rosé.

Ŧ Balbi [bal-bee] (*Mendoza,* Argentina) Producer of good, inexpensive modern wines, including particularly appealing *Malbecs* and dry rosés.

Ŧ Ch. Balestard-la-Tonnelle [bah-les-star lah ton-nell] (*St. Emilion Grand Cru Classé, Bordeaux,* France) Good, quite traditional *St. Emilion* built to last. 81 83 85 86 87 88 89 90 92 93 94 95 96 97 98

Ŧ Balgownie Estate [bal-Gow-nee] (*Bendigo,* Australia) One of Victoria's most reliable producers of lovely, intense, blackcurranty *Cabernet* in *Bendigo. Chardonnays* are big and old-fashioned and *Pinot Noirs* are improving. ☆☆☆☆☆ 1996 Cabernet Sauvignon, Bendigo £££

Ŧ Bandol [bon-dohl] (*Provence,* France) *Mourvèdre*-influenced plummy, herby reds, and rich whites. **Ch. de Pibarnon; Dom. Tempier; Dom Tour de Bon; Ch la Rouvière; Ch. Vannières.**

Ŧ Villa Banfi [veel-lah ban-fee] (*Tuscany,* Italy) US-owned producer with improving *Brunello* and *Vini da Tavola.* ☆☆☆☆☆ 1995 Merlot Toscana Mandrielle £££

Ŧ Bannockburn (*Geelong,* Australia) Gary Farr uses his experience of making wines at *Dom. Dujac* in *Burgundy* to produce concentrated, *Pinot Noir* and *Shiraz* at home. The *Chardonnay* is also pretty good, if slightly big for its boots, and the *Bordeaux* blends are impressive too. ☆☆☆☆ 1997 Shiraz ££

Ŧ Banyuls [bon-yools] (*Provence,* France) France's answer to *tawny port.* Fortified, *Grenache*-based, *Vin Doux Naturel,* ranging from off-dry to lusciously sweet. The *Rancio* style is rather more like *Madeira.* **L'Etoile; Dom. Mas Amiel; Dom. du Mas Blanc; Clos de Paulilles; Dom. de la Rectorie; Dom. la Tour Vieille; Vial Magnères.**

Ŧ Barancourt [bah-ron-koor] (*Champagne,* France) Improving *Champagne* brand, since its purchase by Vranken. Cuvée des Fondateurs is the top wine.

♀ Antonio Barbadillo [bahr-bah-deel-yoh] (*Jerez*, Spain) Great producer of *Fino* and *Manzanilla*. ☆☆☆☆☆ Obispo Gascon Palo Cortado ££

♀ Barbaresco [bahr-bah-ress-koh] (*Piedmont*, Italy) *DOCG Nebbiolo* red, with spicy fruit, depth and complexity. Approachable earlier (three to five years) than neighbouring *Barolo* but, in the right hands – and in the best vineyards – of almost as high a quality. 82 **85 88** 89 90 **93 94** 95 96 97. *Ceretto; Gaja; di Gresy; Castello di Neive; Paitin; Pelissero; Alfredo Prunotto;* Albino Rocca.

♀ Cascina la Barbatella [kah-shh-nah lah bahr-bah-teh-lah] (*Piedmont*, Italy) Rising star, focusing its attention firmly on the *Barbera* (as Barbera d'Asti and single-vineyard Vigna di Sonvico and Vigna dell'Angelo) as well as a good Cortese-Sauvignon blend called Noè after one of its makers.

🌱 Barbera [Bar-Beh-Rah] (*Piedmont*, Italy) Grape making fruity, spicy, characterful wine (e.g. *B. d'Alba* and *B. d'Asti*), with a flavour reminiscent of cheesecake with raisins. Now in *California*, *Mexico* and (at *Brown Bros and Crittenden*) Australia.

♀ René Barbier [ren-Nay Bah-Bee-yay] (*Penedès*, Spain) Dynamic producer of commercial wines and fine *Priorato*. ☆☆☆☆☆ 1997 Priorato Clos Mogador ££

♀ Barca Velha [bahr-kah vayl-yah] (*Douro*, Portugal) Portugal's most famous red, made from port varieties by *Ferreira*. It's tough stuff, but plummy enough to be worth keeping – and paying for. Also look out for Reserva Especial released in more difficult years.

♀ Bardolino [bar-doh-lee-noh] (*Veneto*, Italy) Cherryish red. Can be dull – or fruity alternatives to *Beaujolais*. Also comes as Chiaretto Rosé. Best young unless from an exceptional producer. *Boscaini;* Fabiano Masi; Portalupi.

♀ Gilles Barge [bahzh] (*Rhône*, France) Son of Pierre who won an international reputation for his fine, classic *Côte Rôtie*. Gilles, who now runs the estate, has also shown his skill with *St. Joseph*.

♀ Guy de Barjac [gee dur bar-jak] (*Rhône*, France) A master of the *Syrah* grape, producing some of the best – and most stylish – *Cornas* around.

♀ Barolo [bah-Roh-loh] (*Piedmont*, Italy) Noble *Nebbiolo* reds with extraordinary berryish, floral and spicy flavours. Old-fashioned versions are dry and tannic when young but, from a good producer and year, can develop extraordinary complexity. Modern versions are oakier and more accessible. 82 **85 88** 89 90 **93** 95 96 97 *Elio Altare; Batasiolo; Borgogno; Chiarlo; Clerico; Aldo Conterno; Giacomo Conterno; Conterno Fantino; Fontanafredda; Gaja; Bartolo Mascarello; Giuseppe Mascarello;* Pio Cesare; Pira; *Prunotto;* Ratti; *Sandrone; Scavino;* Vietti; Roberto Voerzio.

♀ Baron de Ley [bah-rohn duh Lay] (*Rioja*, Spain) Small *Rioja* estate whose wines, partly aged in French oak, can be worth waiting for. ☆☆☆☆ 1996 Rioja Reserva ££

Barossa Valley [bah-ros suh] (Australia) Big, warm region north-east of Adelaide which is famous for traditional, old vine *Shiraz* and *Grenache*, "*ports*" and *Rieslings* which age to oily richness. *Chardonnay* and *Cabernet* make subtler, classier wines along with *Riesling* in the higher altitude vineyards of the *Eden Valley* and *Adelaide Hills*. *Barossa Valley Estate; Basedow; Bethany;* Charles Cimicky; *E&E; Elderton; Wolf Blass; Grant Burge; Hardy's; Henschke; Krondorf; Peter Lehmann; Melton; Orlando; Penfolds; Rockford; St. Hallett; Turkey Flat; Yalumba.*

♀ Barossa Valley Estate (*Barossa Valley*, Australia) Top end of *BRL Hardy* with good old-vine *Barossa* reds. ☆☆☆☆☆ 1996 E&E Black Pepper Shiraz £££

♊ **Daniel Barraud** [Bah-roh] (*Burgundy*, France) Dynamic producer of single-*cuvée Pouilly-Fuissé*. ☆☆☆☆☆ 1997 Pouilly Fuissé la Verchère £££

Barrique [ba-reek] (France) French barrel, particularly in *Bordeaux*, holding 225 litres. Term used in Italy to denote (new) barrel ageing.

♊ **Jim Barry** (*Clare Valley*, Australia) Producer of the dazzling, spicy, mulberryish *Armagh Shiraz* and great, floral Watervale Riesling. ☆☆☆☆☆ 1998 Watervale Riesling £££; ☆☆☆☆ 1996 Armagh £££

♊ **Barsac** [bahr-sak] (*Bordeaux*, France) *AC* neighbour of *Sauternes* with similar, though not quite so rich, *Sauvignon/Sémillon* dessert wines. 71 75 76 78 79 80 81 82 83 85 86 88 89 90 95 97 98 99 *Ch. Broustet; Ch. Climens; Ch. Coutet; Ch. Doisy-Dubroca; Ch. Doisy-Daëne; Ch. Nairac.*

♊ **Ghislaine Barthod-Noëllat** [jee-lenn Bar-Toh Noh-Way-Lah] (*Burgundy*, France) Top class Chambolle-Musigny estate. ☆☆☆☆☆ 1997 Chambolle-Musigny Beaux Bruns £££ ☆☆☆☆☆ 1997 Chambolle-Musigny les Charmes £££

♊ **De Bartoli** [day bahr-toh-lee] (*Sicily*, Italy) *Marsala* for drinking rather than cooking from a revolutionary producer who has voluntarily removed his Vecchio Samperi from the DSOC system. ☆☆☆☆ Vecchio Samperi ££

♊ **Barton & Guestier** [bahr-ton ay geht-tee-yay] (*Bordeaux*, France) Highly commercial *Bordeaux* shipper. ☆☆☆ 1998 Fondation 1725 ££

♊ **Barwang** [bahr-wang] (*New South Wales*, Australia) *McWilliams* label for cool-climate wines produced in newly-planted vineyards near Young in eastern *New South Wales*. ☆☆☆☆ 1997 Cabernet Sauvignon ££

♊ **Basedow** [baz-zeh-dohs] (South Australia) Producer of big, concentrated *Shiraz* and *Cabernet* and ultra-rich *Semillon* and *Chardonnays*.

Basilicata [bah-see-lee-kah-tah] (Italy) Southern wine region chiefly known for *Aglianico del Vulture* and improving *IGT wines*. **Basilium.**

Basket Press Traditional wine press, favoured for quality reds by Australian producers such as *Chateau Reynella*.

♊ **Bass Philip** (*Victoria*, Australia) Fanatical South *Gippsland* pioneer Philip Jones's fine *Burgundy*-like *Pinot*. ☆☆☆☆☆ 1997 Premium Pinot Noir ££££

♊ **Von Bassermann-Jordan** [fon bas-suhr-man johr-dun] (*Pfalz*, Germany) A traditional producer often using the fruit of its brilliant vineyards to produce *Trocken Rieslings* with more ripeness than is often to be found in this style. ☆☆☆☆ 1998 Riesling Kabinett Pfalz Forster Jesuitengarten ££

🍇 **Bastardo** [bas-tahr-doh] (Portugal) Red grape traditionally used widely in *port* and previously in *Madeira*.

♊ **Ch. Bastor-Lamontagne** [bas-tohr-lam-mon-tañ] (*Sauternes, Bordeaux,* France) Remarkably reliable classy *Sauternes*; inexpensive alternative to the big-name properties. 85 86 88 89 90 94 95 96 97 98 99

Ch. Batailley [bat-ti-yay] (*Pauillac 5ème Cru Classé, Bordeaux,* France) Approachable, quite modern tobacco-cassis-cedar *claret* from the same stable as *Ch. Ducru-Beaucaillou*. Shows more class than its price might lead one to expect. 70 78 79 **82 83 85 86** 87 **88** 89 90 94 **95** 96 **97** 98 99

Bâtard-Montrachet [bat-tahr mon-rah-shay] (*Burgundy,* France) Wonderful, biscuity-rich white *Grand Cru* which straddles the border between the appellations of *Chassagne-* and *Puligny-Montrachet*. Often very fine; invariably expensive. *Cailot; Colin-Deleger; Joseph Drouhin; Jean-Noel Gagnard; Gagnard-Delagrange; Dom. Leflaive; Ch. de la Maltroye; Pierre Morey; Michel Niellon; Ramonet; Sauzet.*

Batasiolo [bat-tah-see-oh-loh] (*Piedmont,* Italy) Producer of top-class *Barolo,* impressive cherryish *Dolcetto,* fresh *Moscato,* intense berryish *Brachetto* and a subtle *Chardonnay.* ☆☆☆☆ 1993 Barolo Bofani £££, ☆☆☆☆ 1995 Langhe Chardonnay Morino £££

Dom. des Baumard [day boh-marh] (*Loire,* France) Superlative producer of great *Coteaux du Layon, Quarts de Chaume* and *Savennières.* ☆☆☆☆☆ 1995 Savennières Clos du Papillon ££££; ☆☆☆☆☆ 1997 Coteaux du Layon ££££

Bava [bah-vah] (*Piedmont,* Italy) Innovative producer making good *Moscato Barbera,* reviving indigenous grapes such as the rarely grown raspberryish *Ruche* as well as a rather wonderful traditional curious herb-infused *Barolo Chinato Cocchi.* Try it with one of Roberto Bava's other enthusiasms: black chocolate. ☆☆☆☆ 1995 Stradivario Barbera d'Asti Superiore ££

Béarn [bay-ar'n] (*South West,* France) Highly traditional and often dull region. Lapeyre is the name to look out for.

Ch. Beau-Séjour (-Bécot) [boh-say-zhoor bay-koh] (*St. Emilion Grand Cru Classé, Bordeaux,* France) Reinstated in 1996 after a decade of demotion. Now making fairly priced, greatly improved wine. **82** 83 85 **86** 88 89 90 92 93 94 95 96 97 98

Ch. Beau-Site [boh-seet] (*St. Estèphe Cru Bourgeois, Bordeaux,* France) Benchmark *St. Estèphe* in the same stable as *Ch. Batailley.* 78 **82** 83 85 **86** 88 89 90 92 93 94 95 96 97 98

Ch. de Beaucastel [boh-kas-tel] (*Rhône,* France) The top *Châteauneuf-du-Pape* estate, using organic methods to produce richly gamey (for some, too gamey) long-lived, spicy reds which reflect the presence in the blend of an unusually high proportion of Mourvèdre. There are also rare but fine creamy-spicy whites. ☆☆☆☆☆ 1998 Château de Beaucastel Blanc, Vieilles Vignes ££££

Y Beaujolais [boh-zhuh-lay] (*Burgundy*, France) Light fruity *Gamay* red. Good chilled and for early drinking. *Beaujolais-Villages* is better, and the 10 *Crus* better still. With age, these can taste like (fairly ordinary) *Burgundy* from the *Côte d'Or*. *Beaujolais Blanc* made from *Chardonnay* is now mostly sold as *St. Véran*. See *Crus: Morgon; Chénas; Brouilly; Côte de Brouilly; Juliénas; Fleurie; Regnié; St. Amour; Chiroubles; Moulin-à-Vent.*

Y Beaujolais-Villages (*Burgundy*, France) From the north of the region, fuller-flavoured and more alcoholic than plain *Beaujolais*, though not necessarily from one of the named *Cru* villages. *Duboeuf;* Dubost; Ch. es Jacques; Janin; Pivot; Large.

Y Beaulieu Vineyard [bohl-yoo] (*Napa Valley*, California) Historic winery getting back on its feet after years of neglect/abuse by its multinational owners. The wines to look for are the Georges de Latour Private Reserve *Cabernets* which have been consistently good (as a recent tasting of old vintages proved) and the new Signet ranger. Recent vintages of the Beau Tour *Cabernet Sauvignon* have been good too. Other wines are unexciting.
☆☆☆☆☆ **1994 Georges de Latour Private Reserve ££££**

Y *Beaumes de Venise* [bohm duh vuh-neez] (*Rhône*, France) *Côtes du Rhône* village producing spicy dry reds and sweet, grapey, fortified *Vin Doux Naturel* from the *Muscat.* Dom. des Bernardins; *Chapoutier*; Dom de Coyeux; Durban; de Fenouillet; *Paul Jaboulet Aîné*; la Soumade; Vidal-Fleury.

Y Ch. Beaumont [boh-mon] (*Haut-Médoc Cru Bourgeois, Bordeaux*, France) Impressive estate back on form since 1998. **82 85 86 88 89 90 93 95 96** 98 99

Y Beaune [bohn] (*Burgundy*, France) Large commune that gives its name to the *Côte de Beaune* and produces soft, raspberry-and-rose-petal *Pinot Noir*. As in *Nuits-St.-Georges*, there are plenty of *Premier Crus*, but no *Grands Crus*. The walled city is the site of the famous *Hospices* charity auction. Reds are best from *Michel Prunier, Louis Jadot, Bouchard Père et Fils* (since 1996), Ch. de Chorey; Albert Morot and *Joseph Drouhin* who also make a very successful example of the ultra-rare white. Other good producers: Robert Ampeau; Arnoux Père et Fils; *Pascal Bouley*; Dubois; Génot-Boulanger; Germain (Ch. de Chorey); *Michel Lafarge*; Daniel Largeot; Laurent; *Jacques Prieur*; Rapet Père et Fils; Thomas-Moillard; *Tollot-Beaut*.

Y Ch. Beauregard [boh-ruh-gahr] (*Pomerol, Bordeaux*, France) Estate producing juicy oaky *Pomerol*. **82 85 86** 88 89 90 **93** 95 96 97 98 99

Y Ch. Beauséjour-Duffau-Lagarosse [boh-say-zhoor doo-foh lag-gahr-ros] (*St. Emilion Premier Grand Cru Classé, Bordeaux*, France) Traditional tough, *tannic St. Emilion*. 82 93 85 86 88 89 90 93 94 95 96 98

Y Beaux Frères [boh frair] (*Oregon,* US) *Pinot Noir* winery launched by wine guru Robert Parker and his brother-in-law (hence the name).

Y Graham Beck (Robertson, South Africa) Associated with *Bellingham*, and producer of some of South Africa's best fizz. A Coastal Range of still wines are looking good too. ☆☆☆☆ **1993 Blanc de Blancs ££**
Beerenauslese [behr-ren-ows-lay-zuh] (Austria/Germany) Sweet wines from selected, ripe grapes (Beeren), hopefully affected by *botrytis*.

Y Ch. de Bel-Air [Bel-ehr] (*Lalande-de-Pomerol, Bordeaux*, France) Impressive property making wines to make some *Pomerols* blush. **82 85** 86 88 **89** 90 93 **94** 95 96 97 98 99

� **Ch. Bel-Orme-Tronquoy-de-Lalande** [bel-orm-tron-kwah-duh-la-lond] (*Haut-Médoc Cru Bourgeois, Bordeaux,* France) Highly old-fashioned estate and wines. Under the same ownership (and philosophy) as *Rauzan Gassies*. Could do (much) better.

�) **Ch. Belair** [bel-lehr] (*St. Emilion Premier Grand Cru Classé, Bordeaux,* France) Classy, delicate, long-lived, *St. Emilion* with a very impressive 1998 and 1999. Compare and contrast with more "modern" neighbour *Ausone* which used to be produced by Pascal Delbeck who still produces Belair. Don't confuse with the *Lalande-de-Pomerol Ch. de Bel-Air* – or any of the countless lesser Belairs scattered around *Bordeaux*). 78 **79 82 83 85 86** 88 89 90 93 95 96 97 98 99.

�) **Bellavista** (*Lombardy,* Italy) Commercial Franciacorta producers of classy sparkling and still wines. The Riserva Vittorio Moretti, which is only produced in top years, is the star of the show. ☆☆☆☆ **1995 Gran Cuvée Brut £££**

�)** Albert Belle** [bel] (*Rhône,* France) An estate that has recently begun to bottle its own excellent red and – oaky – white Hermitage.

�) **Bellet** [bel-lay] (*Provence,* France) Tiny *AC* behind Nice producing fairly good red, white and rosé from local grapes including the Rolle, the *Braquet* and the *Folle Noir*. Pricey and rarely seen outside France. **Ch. de Bellet.**

�) **Bellingham** (South Africa) Highly commercial winery that has just been bought out by its management and is focusing increasingly on quality. Cabernet Franc is a particular success. Look for the Premium Range labels. ☆☆☆☆ **1997 Premium Cabernet Sauvignon ££**

Bendigo [ben-dig-goh] (*Victoria,* Australia) Warm region producing big-boned, long-lasting reds with intense berry fruit. *Balgownie;* **Heathcote;** *Jasper Hill; Mount Ida; Passing Clouds;* **Water Wheel.**

�) **Benziger** [ben-zig-ger] (*Sonoma,* California) Classy wines at the top end of the *Glen Ellen* range. ☆☆☆☆ **1996 Chardonnay Carneros Yamakawa Vineyards Reserve ££**

�) **Berberana** [behr-behr-rah nah] (*Rioja,* Spain) Increasingly dynamic producer of a range of fruitier young-drinking styles, as well as the improving Carta de Plata and Carta de Oro and Lagunilla *Riojas,* plus sparkling Marquès de Monistrol and the excellent Marquès de Griñon range. ☆☆☆☆ **1996 Viña Alarde Reserva £££;** ☆☆☆☆ **1995 Rioja Reserva ££**

�) **Bercher** [behr-kehr] (*Baden,* Germany) Dynamic estate, producing impressive modern *Burgundy*-style reds and whites.
Bereich [beh-ri-kh] (Germany) Vineyard area, subdivision of an *Anbaugebiet*. On its own indicates *QbA* wine, e.g. *Niersteiner*. Finer wines are followed by the name of a (smaller) *Grosslage*, better ones by that of an individual vineyard.

�) **Bergerac** [behr-jur-rak] (France) Traditionally *Bordeaux's* "lesser" neighbour but possibly soon to be assimilated into that regional *appellation*. The wines, though often pretty mediocre, can still be better value than basic red or white *Bordeaux*, while the *Monbazillac* can outclass basic *Sauternes*. **Ch. Belingard; Court-les-Muts; des Eyssards; Grinou; la Jaubertie; de Raz; Tour des Gendres.**

�) **Bergkelder** [berg-kel-dur] (*Cape,* South Africa) Huge firm best known for its *Stellenryck* wines. Its cheaper *Fleur du Cap* range is likeable enough and the best of the *JC Le Roux* sparkling wines are first class. ☆☆☆ **1995 Stellenryck Cabernet Sauvignon ££**

Beringer Vineyards [ber-rin-jer] (*Napa Valley*, California) Big Swiss-owned producer, increasingly notable for its single-vineyard *Cabernet Sauvignons* (Knights Valley, *Howell Mountain, Spring Mountain* and Private Reserve), *Cabernet Francs* and *Merlots, Burgundy*-like *Chardonnays* and *late harvest* wines. ☆☆☆☆☆ 1994 Cabernet Sauvignon Napa Valley St. Helena Home Vineyard £££

Bernkastel [berhrn-kah-stel] (*Mosel*, Germany) Town and area on the *Mittelmosel* and source of some of the finest *Riesling* (like the famous Bernkasteler Doktor), and a lake of poor-quality stuff. QbA/Kab/Spät: 85 86 88 89 90 91 92 93 94 95 96 97 98 Aus/Beeren/Tba: 83 85 88 89 90 91 92 93 94 95 96 97 Dr Loosen; JJ Prum; Von Kesselstadt; *Wegeler Deinhard.*

Bernardus (*Monterey*, California) Producer of rich, unsubtle, fairly-priced, unashamedly New World-style *Sauvignon Blanc, Chardonnay* and *Pinot Noir.* ☆☆☆☆ 1996 Chardonnay Monterey County ££

Berri Renmano [ber-ree ren-mah-noh] (*Riverland*, Australia) The controlling force behind the giant *BRL Hardy*, with quality brands like *Thomas Hardy, Barossa Valley Estates, Château Reynella* and *Houghton.* Under its own name, it is better known for inexpensive reds and whites.

Dom Bertagna [behr-tan-ya] (*Vougeot*, France) Recently improved estate notable for offering the rare, (relatively) affordable *Premier Cru Vougeot* alongside its own version of the easier-to-find *Clos de Vougeot Grand Cru.* ☆☆☆☆ 1997 Vougeot Clos de la Perrière £££

Bertani [behr-tah-nee] (*Veneto*, Italy) Producer of good *Valpolicella* and innovative wines such as the Le Lave Garganega-Chardonnay blend. ☆☆☆☆ 1996 Cabernet Sauvignon Villa Novare £££

Best's Great Western (*Victoria*, Australia) Under-appreciated winery in *Great Western* making delicious concentrated *Shiraz* from old vines, attractive *Cabernet, Dolcetto, Pinot Noir, Colombard* and rich *Chardonnay* and *Riesling.* ☆☆☆☆☆ 1997 Great Western Pinot Meunier £££

Bethany [beth-than-nee] (*Barossa Valley*, Australia) Impressive small producer of knockout *Shiraz.* ☆☆☆☆☆ 1997 Shiraz £££

Bethel Heights (*Oregon*, California) Long-established but now a rising star, with good Pinot Noir and particularly impressive Pinot Blanc and Chardonnay.

Dom. Henri Beurdin [bur-dan] (*Loire*, France) White and rosé from *Reuilly.*

Ch. Beychevelle [bay-shur-vel] (*St. Julien 4ème Cru Classé, Bordeaux*, France) A fourth growth that achieves the typical cigar-box character of *St. Julien* but fails to excite. The *second label Amiral de Beychevelle* can be a worthwhile buy. 82 83 85 86 88 89 90 94 95 96 97 98 ☆☆☆☆ 1990 ££££

Léon Beyer [bay-ur] (*Alsace*, France) Serious producer of lean long-lived wines. ☆☆☆☆ 1997 Riesling Comtes d'Eguisheim ££

Beyerskloof [bay-yurs-kloof] (*Stellenbosch*, South Africa) Newish venture, with Beyers Truter (of Kanonkop) on its way to producing South Africa's top *Cabernet* and *Stellenbosch Pinotage.* ☆☆☆☆ 1997 Cabernet ££

Bianco di Custoza [bee-yan-koh dee koos-toh-zah] (*Veneto*, Italy) Widely exported *DOC*. A reliable, crisp, light white from a blend of grapes. A better-value alternative to most basic *Soave.* **Gorgo; Portalupi;** *Tedeschi;* le Vigne di San Pietro; *Zenato.*

Maison Albert Bichot [bee-shoh] (*Burgundy*, France) Big *négociant* with excellent *Chablis* and *Vosne-Romanée*, plus adequate wines sold under a plethora of other labels. ☆☆☆☆ 1997 Chablis Grand Cru Vaudésir £££

♈ **Biddenden** [bid-den-den] (*Kent*, England) Producer showing impressive mastery of the peachy *Ortega*. ☆☆☆ **1998 Ortega £**

♈ **Bienvenue-Batard-Montrachet** [bee-yen-veh-noo bat-tahr mon ra-rhay] (*Burgundy*, France) Fine white *Burgundy* vineyard with potentially gorgeous biscuity wines. **Carillon;** *Henri Clerc*; **Dom Leflaive;** *Sauzet*.

♈ **Weingut Josef Biffar** [bif-fah] (*Pfalz*, Germany). *Deidesheim* estate that is on a roll at the moment with its richly spicy wines. ☆☆☆☆ **1997 Riesling Spätlese Pfalz Wachenheimer Altenburg ££**

♈ **Billecart-Salmon** [beel-kahr sal-mon] (*Champagne*, France) Producer of the stylish winners (the 1959 and 1961 vintages) of the Champagne of the Millennium competition held in Stockholm in 1999 at which I was a taster. Possibly the best all-rounder for quality and value, and certainly the *Champagne* house whose subtle but decidedly ageable *non-vintage, vintage* and rosé I buy without hesitation. Superlative. ☆☆☆☆☆ **1990 Cuvée Nicolas François Billecart ££££**

♈ **Billiot** [bil-lee-yoh] (*Champagne*, France) Impressive small producer with classy rich fizz. ☆☆☆☆ **Cuvée de Reserve NV £££**

Bingen [bing-urn] (*Rheinhessen*, Germany) Village giving its name to a *Rheinhessen Bereich* that includes a number of well-known *Grosslage*. QbA/Kab/Spät: **85** 86 **88 89 90** 91 **92 93** 94 95 96 97 98
Aus/Beeren/Tba: **83 85** 88 89 90 91 **92 93 94** 95 96 97

Binissalem [bin-nee-sah-lem] (*Mallorca*, Spain) The holiday island is proud of its demarcated region, though why, it's hard to say. José Ferrer's and Jaime Mesquida's wines are the best of the bunch.

♈ **Biondi-Santi** [bee-yon-dee san-tee] (*Tuscany*, Italy) Big-name estate making absurdly expensive and sometimes disappointing *Brunello di Montalcino* that can be bought – after a period of vertical storage at room temperature – at the local trattoria. ☆☆☆☆ **1993 Brunello Di Montalcino ££££**

Biscuity Flavour of savoury crackers often associated with the *Chardonnay* grape, particularly in *Champagne* and top-class mature *Burgundy*, or with the yeast that fermented the wine.

♈ **Bitouzet-Prieur** [bee-too-zay pree-yur] (*Burgundy*, France) If you like classic *Meursault*, built to last rather than seduce instantly with ripe fruit and oak, try this estate's 1997 *Meursault Perrières*. The *Volnays* are good too.

♈ **Dom. Simon Bize** [beez] (*Burgundy*, France) Intense, long-lived and good-value wines produced in *Savigny-lès-Beaune*. ☆☆☆☆ **1997 Savigny-lès-Beaune les Vergelesses £££**

♈ **Blaauwklippen** [blow-klip-pen] (*Stellenbosch*, South Africa) Recently sold, large estate, veering between commercial and top quality. The *Cabernet* and *Zinfandel* are the strong cards. ☆☆☆ **1996 Cabernet Sauvignon ££**

♈ **Blagny** [blan-yee] (*Burgundy*, France) Tiny source of unsubtle red (sold as Blagny) and potentially top-class white (sold as *Meursault, Puligny-Montrachet*, Blagny, Hameau de Blagny or la Pièce sous le Bois). Red: 83 **85** 86 **88 89 90** 92 95 96 97 **Ampeau;** Chavy-Chouet; *Jobard; Thierry Matrot.*

♈ **Blain-Gagnard** [blan gan-yahr] (*Burgundy*, France) Excellent creamy modern *Chassagne-Montrachet*. ☆☆☆☆ **1997 Chassagne-Montrachet ££££**

Blanc de Blancs [blon dur blon] A white wine, made from white grapes – hardly worth mentioning except in the case of *Champagne*, where *Pinot Noir*, a black grape, usually makes up 30–70 per cent of the blend. In this case, *Blanc de Blancs* is pure *Chardonnay*.

Blanc de Noirs [blon dur nwahrr] A white (or frequently very slightly pink-tinged wine) made from red grapes by taking off the free-run juice, before pressing to minimise the uptake of red pigments from the skin. Paul Bara; Duval-Leroy (Fleur de Champagne); Egly-Ouiriet.

℉ **Paul Blanck** [blank] (*Alsace*, France) Top-class *Alsace* domaine, specialising in single *Cru* wines. ☆☆☆☆ 1997 Pinot Gris Furstentum £££

℉ **Blandy's** [blan-deez] (*Madeira*, Portugal) Brand owned by the Madeira Wine Company and named after the sailor who began the production of fortified wine here. Brilliant old wines. ☆☆☆☆ 5 Year Old Malmsey ££

℉ **Blanquette de Limoux** [blon ket dur lee-moo] (*Midi*, France) *Méthode Champenoise* sparkling wine, which, when good, is appley and clean. Best when made with a generous dose of *Chardonnay*, as the local *Mauzac* tends to give it an earthy flavour with age. ☆☆☆☆ Domaine de l'Aigle ££

℉ **Wolf Blass** (*Barossa Valley*, Australia) Part of the huge Mildara-Blass operation (and thus, owned by Fosters), this brand was founded by a German immigrant who prides himself on producing "sexy" (his term) reds and whites, by blending wines from different regions of *South Australia* and allowing them plentiful contact with new oak. ☆☆☆☆ 1996 President's Selection Cabernet Sauvignon £££

❦ **Blauburgunder** [blow-boor-goon-durh] (Austria) The name the Austrians give their light, often sharp, *Pinot Noir*.

❦ **Blauer Portugieser** [blow-urh por-too-gay-suhr] (Germany) Red grape used in Germany and Austria to make light, pale wine.

❦ **Blaufrankisch** [blow-fran-kish] (Austria) Grape used to make refreshingly berryish wines that can – in the right hands – compete with the reds of the *Loire*.

℉ **Quinta da Boavista** [keen-tah dah boh-wah-vees-tah] (*Alenquer*, Portugal) Starry estate producing a range of red and white wines, including Palha Canas, Quinta das Sete and Espiga.

℉ **Boccagigabbia** [Bbok-kah-ji-gah-bee-yah] (*Marche*, Italy) Top class estate, producing delicious *Pinot Noir* (Girone), *Cabernet* (Akronte) and *Chardonnay* (Aldonis).

Bocksbeutel [box-boy-tuhl] (*Franken,* Germany) The famous flask-shaped bottle of *Franken*, adopted by the makers of *Mateus* Rosé.

Bodega [bod-day-gah] (Spain) Winery or wine cellar; producer.

℉ **Bodegas y Bebidas** [bod-day-gas ee beh-bee-das] (Spain) One of Spain's most dynamic wine companies, and maker of *Campo Viejo*.

Body Usually used as "full-bodied", meaning a wine with mouth-filling flavours and probably a fairly high alcohol content.

℉ **Jean-Marc Boillot** [bwah-yoh] (*Burgundy*, France) Small *Pommard* domaine run by the son of the winemaker at *Olivier Leflaive*, and offering really good examples from neighbouring villages. ☆☆☆☆☆ 1997 Volnay £££

℉ **Jean-Claude Boisset** [bwah-say] (*Burgundy*, France) Dynamic *négociant* which now owns a long list of *Burgundy négociants*, including the excellent *Jaffelin* and the improved though still far from dazzling *Bouchard Aîné*. Boisset also makes passable wines in *Languedoc-Roussillon*.

℉ **Boisson-Vadot** [bwah-son va-doh] (*Burgundy*, France) Classy, small *Meursault domaine*. ☆☆☆☆☆ 1997 Meursault ££££

℉ **Bolgheri** [bol-geh-ree] (*Tuscany*, Italy) Increasingly exciting region made famous by red superstars such as *Antinori's Sassicaia* and *Ornellaia*. Other impressive producers now include: *Belvedere, Grattamacco; Guado al Tasso;* Le Macchiole and Satta, and there are some top class whites made from the *Vermentino*.

Bolla [bol-lah] (*Veneto*, Italy) Producer of plentiful, adequate *Valpolicella* and *Soave*, and of smaller quantities of impressive single vineyard wines like Jago and Creso.

Bollinger [bol-an-jay] (*Champagne*, France) Great family-owned firm at Ay, whose wines need age. The luscious and rare *Vieilles Vignes* is made from pre-*phylloxera* vines, while the nutty *RD* was the first late-disgorged *Champagne* to hit the market. ☆☆☆☆ **1990 Grande Année ££££**

Bommes [bom] (*Bordeaux*, France) *Sauternes commune* and village containing several *Premiers Crus* such as *la Tour Blanche, Lafaurie-Peyrauguey, Rabaud-Promis* and *Rayne Vigneau*. 70 **71 75** 76 83 85 86 88 89 90 95 96 97 98

Ch. le Bon-Pasteur [bon-pas-stuhr] (*Pomerol, Bordeaux*, France) The impressive private estate of *Michel Rolland*, who acts as consultant – and helps to make fruit-driven wines – for half his neighbours, as well as producers in almost every other wine-growing region in the universe. 76 **82 83 85 86** 87 **88** 89 90 92 93 94 95 96 97 98

Domaine de la Bongran [bon-grah] See *Jean Thevenet*.

Henri Bonneau [bon-noh] (*Rhône*, France) *Châteauneuf-du-Pape* producer with two special *cuvées* – "Marie Beurrier" and "des Celestins" – and a cult following. ☆☆☆☆☆ **1995 Cuvée Marc Beurrier ££££**

Dom. Bonneau du Martray [bon-noh doo mahr-tray] (*Burgundy*, France) Largest grower of *Corton-Charlemagne* and impressive producer thereof. Also makes a classy red *Grand Cru Corton*. ☆☆☆☆☆ **1997 Corton ££££**

Bonnes Mares [bon-mahr] (*Burgundy*, France) Rich *Morey St. Denis Grand Cru*. Dom. d'Auvenay; Bouchard Père; Clair Daü; Drouhin; Dujac; Fougeray de Beauclair; Groffier; Jadot; Laurent; Roumier; de Vogüé.

Ch. Bonnet [bon-nay] (*Bordeaux*, France) Top-quality *Entre-Deux-Mers château* whose wines are made by *Jacques Lurton*.

F. Bonnet [bon-nay] (*Champagne*, France) Reliable producer under whose own and customers' names Winemaker, Daniel Thibault also makes *Charles Heidsieck*. ☆☆☆☆ **Bonnet Rosé £££**

Bonnezeaux [bonn-zoh] (*Loire*, France) Within the *Coteaux du Layon*, this is one of the world's greatest sweet wine producing areas, though the wines have often tended to be spoiled by heavy-handedness with sulphur dioxide. 76 83 85 86 **88 89** 90 93 94 95 96 97 *Ch. de Fesles*; Dom. Godineau; René Renou; Ch. la Varière.

Bonny Doon Vineyard (*Santa Cruz,* California) Randall Grahm, sorcerer's apprentice, and original "Rhône Ranger" also has an evident affection for unfashionable French and Italian varieties, which he uses for characterful red, dry and *late harvest* whites. The sheep-like Californian wine industry needs more mavericks like Grahm. ☆☆☆☆☆ **1997 Ca del Solo Malvasia ££**

☥ **Bonvin Jean** [bon-van] (*Valais*, Switzerland) Top producer of traditional local varieties ☆☆☆☆ **1996 Amigne du Valais**

☥ **Bonterra** Recommendable organic brand launched by *Fetzer*.

☥ **Tenuta Bonzara** [bont-zah-rah] (*Emilia Romagna*, Italy) *Cabernet Sauvignon* and *Merlot* specialists producing wines that compete with the starriest of *Super-Tuscans*.

Borba [Bohr-bah] (*Alentejo*, Portugal) See *Alentejo*.

☥ **Bordeaux** [bor-doh] (France) Largest (supposedly) quality wine region in France, producing reds, rosés and deep pink *Clairets* from *Cabernet Sauvignon, Cabernet Franc, Petit Verdot* and *Merlot*, and dry and sweet whites from (principally) blends of *Sémillon* and *Sauvignon*, with a little *Muscadelle*. *Bordeaux Supérieur* denotes (relatively) riper grapes. The rare dry whites from regions like the *Médoc* and *Sauternes* are (curiously) sold as *Bordeaux Blanc*, so even the efforts by Châteaux d'Yquem and Margaux are sold under the same label as basic supermarket white. See *Graves, Médoc, Pomerol, St. Emilion etc.*

☥ **Borgo del Tiglio** [bor-goh dehl tee-lee-yoh] (*Friuli*, Italy) One of the classiest wineries in this region, hitting the target with a range of varieties that includes *Merlot, Sauvignon Blanc, Chardonnay* and Tocai Friulano.

☥ **Giacomo Borgogno** [baw-gon-yoh] (*Piedmont*, Italy) Hitherto old-fashioned *Barolo* producer which is now embracing modern winemaking and producing fruitier, more immediately likeable wines. ☆☆☆☆ **1984 Barolo Sarmassa ££££**

☥ **De Bortoli** [baw-tol-lee] (*Yarra* and *Riverina*, Australia) Fast-developing firm which startled the world by making a *botrytised*, peachy, honeyed "Noble One" *Semillon* in the unfashionable *Riverina*, before shifting its focus to the very different climate of the *Yarra Valley*. Top wines here include trophy-winning *Pinot Noirs* and impressive *Shirazes*. ☆☆☆☆ **1998 Yarra Valley Chardonnay ££**

☥ **Bodega Luigi Bosca** [bos-kah] (*Mendoza*, Argentina) Good producer with particularly good *Sauvignons* and *Cabernets*. ☆☆☆☆ **1996 Cabernet Sauvignon ££**

☥ **Boscaini** [bos-kah-yee-nee] (*Veneto*, Italy) Innovative producer linked to *Masi* and making better-than-average *Valpolicella* and *Soave*. Look out for individual-vineyard wines such as the starry Ca' de Loi Valpolicella. ☆☆☆☆ **1995 Amarone Della Valpolicella Classico £££**

☥ **Boscarelli** [bos-kah-reh-lee] (*Tuscany*, Italy) The star producer of *Vino Nobile de Montepulciano* is also the place to find its own delicious Boscarelli *Super-Tuscan* and the exciting new De Ferrari blend of *Sangiovese* with the local Prugnolo Gentile. ☆☆☆☆☆ **1995 Boscarelli £££**

☥ **Boschendal Estate** [bosh-shen-dahl] (*Cape*, South Africa) Recent investment by its Anglo-American owners are helping to raise the game here. This is the place to find some of the *Cape's* best sparkling wine and one of its most European-style *Shirazes* ☆☆☆☆ **1997 Shiraz ££**

☥ **Ch. le Boscq** [bosk] (*St. Estèphe Cru Bourgeois, Bordeaux*, France) Improving property that excels in good vintages, but still tends to make tough wines in lesser ones. 82 83 85 86 87 88 **89** 90 92 **93** 95 96 98

☥ **Le Bosquet des Papes** [bos-kay day pap] (*Rhône*, France) Serious *Châteauneuf-du-Pape* producer, making a range of styles that all last. The pure *Grenache* example is particularly impressive.

Botrytis [boh-tri-tiss] Botrytis cinerea, a fungal infection that attacks and shrivels grapes, evaporating their water and concentrating their sweetness. Vital to *Sauternes*, the finer German and Austrian sweet wines and *Tokaji*. See *Sauternes, Trockenbeerenauslese, Tokaji*.

Bott-Geyl [bott-gihl] (*Alsace*, France) Young producer, whose impressive *Grand Cru* wines suit those who like their *Alsace* big and rich. The oaked *Pinot Gris* is particularly unusual. ☆☆☆☆ **1997 Riesling Mandelberg £££**

Bottle-fermented Commonly found on the labels of US sparkling wines to indicate the *Méthode Champenoise*, and gaining wider currency. Beware, though – it can indicate inferior *"transfer method"* wines.

Pascal Bouchard [boo-shahrr d] (*Burgundy*, France) One of the best small producers in *Chablis*. ☆☆☆☆ **1996 Chablis Blanchot ££**

Bouchard Aîné [boo-shahrr day-nay] (*Burgundy*, France) Once unimpressive merchant, now taken over by *Boisset* and improving under the winemaking control of the excellent Bernard Repolt.

Bouchard-Finlayson [boo-shard] (*Walker Bay*, South Africa) *Burgundy*-style joint-venture between Peter Finlayson and Paul Bouchard, formerly of *Bouchard Aîné* in France. ☆☆☆☆ **1997 Galpin Peak Pinot Noir ££**

Bouchard Père & Fils [boo-shahrr pehrr ay fees] (*Burgundy*, France) Traditional merchant with great vineyards. Bought in 1996 by the *Champagne* house of *Henriot*. The best wines are the *Beaunes*, especially the Beaune de l'Enfant Jésus, as well as the La Romanée from *Vosne-Romanée*. ☆☆☆☆ **1997 Meursault Genevrières £££**

Vin de Pays des Bouches du Rhône (*Midi*, France) dynamic region around *Aix* en *Provence*, focusing on *Rhône* and *Bordeaux* varieties. Top wines here include the great *Dom. de Trévallon*. **Dom. des Gavelles.**

Pascal Bouley [boo-lay] (*Burgundy*, France) Producer of good, if not always refined *Volnay*. ☆☆☆☆ **1997 Volnay Champans £££**

Bouquet Overall smell, often made up of several separate aromas. Used by Anglo-Saxon enthusiasts more often than by professionals.

Henri Bourgeois [on-ree boor-jwah] (*Loire*, France) High quality *Sancerre* and *Pouilly-Fumé* grower-négociant wih a sense of humour (a top wine is called "la Bourgeoisie"). Also owns Laporte.

Ch. Bourgneuf-Vayron [boor-nurf vay-roh] (*Pomerol, Bordeaux*, France) Fast-rising star with deliciously rich plummy *Merlot* fruit.

Bourgogne [boorr-goyñ] (*Burgundy*, France) French for *Burgundy*.

Bourgueil [boorr-goyy] (*Loire*, France) Red *AC* in the *Touraine*, producing crisp, grassy-blackcurranty, 100 per cent *Cabernet Franc* wines that can age well in good years like 1995. **Amirault; Boucard; Caslot-Galbrun; Cognard; Delaunay; Druet.**

Ch. Bouscassé [boo-ska-say] (*Madiran*, France) See *Ch. Montus*.

Ch. Bouscaut [boos-koh] (*Pessac-Léognan, Bordeaux*, France) Good, rather than great *Graves* property; better white than red.

J. Boutari [boo-tah-ree] (*Greece*) One of the most reliable names in Greece, producing good, traditional red wines in *Nemea* and *Naoussa*.

� **Bouvet-Ladubay** [boo-vay lad-doo-bay] (*Loire*, France) Producer of good *Loire* sparkling wine and better *Saumur-Champigny* reds. A welcome new move has been the introduction of top-quality mini-cuvées, labelled as "les Non Pareils". ☆☆☆☆☆ 1997 Saumur-Champigny les Non Pareils £££

🍇 **Bouvier** [boo-vee-yay] (Austria) Characterless variety used to produce tasty but mostly simple *late harvest* wines.

Bouzeron [booz-rron] (*Burgundy*, France) *Côte Chalonnaise* village known for *Aligoté*. ☆☆☆☆☆ 1997 Aligoté Aubert de Villaine ££

� **Bouzy Rouge** [boo-zee roozh] (*Champagne*, France) Sideline of a black grape village: an often thin-bodied, rare and overpriced red wine which, can occasionally age well. Paul Bara, *Barancourt*, Brice, Ledru.

� **Bowen Estate** [boh-wen] (*Coonawarra*, Australia) An early *Coonawarra* pioneer proving that the region can be as good for *Shiraz* as for *Cabernet*.

� **Domaines Boyar** [boy-yahr] (*Bulgaria*) Privatised producers, especially in the *Suhindol* region, selling increasingly worthwhile "Reserve" reds under the Lovico label. Other wines are less reliably recommendable. ☆☆☆☆ 1999 Lambol Merlot ££

� **Ch. Boyd-Cantenac** [boyd-kon-teh-nak] (*Margaux 3ème Cru Classé*, *Bordeaux*, France) A third growth generally performing at the level of a fifth – or less. 78 **82 83 85 86** 88 89 90 93 **94** 95 96 97 98

🍇 **Brachetto d'Acqui** [brah-KET-toh dak-wee] (*Piedmont*, Italy) Eccentric *Muscatty* red grape. Often *frizzante*. Banfi; *Batasiolo;* Marenco.

� **Braida** [brih-dah] (*Piedmont*, Italy) A big producer whose range includes Barberas galore and some highly recommendable *Dolcetto* and *Chardonnay*.

�wine **Dom Brana** [brah-nah] (*South West*, France) One of the best producers of Irouleguy.

� **Ch. Branaire(-Ducru)** [brah-nehr doo-kroo] (*St.-Julien 4ème Cru Classé, Bordeaux*, France) New owners are doing wonders for this estate. Red: **82** 83 85 86 87 88 89 90 91 92 93 **95 96 97 98** ☆☆☆☆ 1998 £££

� **Brand's Laira** [lay-rah] (*Coonawarra*, Australia) Traditional producer, much improved since its purchase by *McWilliams*. Delving into the world of *Pinot Noir* and sparkling *Grenache* rosé.

� **Ch. Brane-Cantenac** [brahn kon teh-nak] (*Margaux 2ème Cru Classé, Bordeaux*, France) Often under-achieving *Margaux*, which made a better wine than usual in 1999. The unprepossessingly named second-label Ch. Notton can be a good buy. 78 79 82 83 85 **86** 87 88 89 90 95 96 98 ☆☆☆☆ 1999 £££

🍇 **Braquet** [brah-ket] (*Midi*, France) Grape variety used in *Bellet*.

Brauneberg [brow-nuh-behrg] (*Mosel*, Germany) Village best known for the *Juffer* vineyard. ☆☆☆☆☆ 1997 Riesling Auslese Gold Cap Brauneberger Juffer-Sonnenuhr Fritz Haag ££££

Brazil Large quantities of light-bodied wine (including *Zinfandel* that is sold in the US under the Marcus James label) are produced in a rainy region close to Puerto Allegre. The Palomas vineyard on the *Uruguayan* border has a state-of-the-art winery and a good climate but has yet to make exciting wine.

�wine **Breaky Bottom** (Sussex, England) One of Britain's best, whose *Seyval Blanc* rivals dry wines made in the *Loire* from supposedly finer grapes.

� **Marc Bredif** [bray-deef] (*Loire*, France) Big, and quite variable *Loire* producer, with still and sparkling wine, including some good *Vouvray*.

Ⓣ **Breganze** (*Veneto*, Italy) Little-known *DOC* for characterful reds and whites. Maculan is the star here.

Ⓣ **Ch. du Breuil** [doo breuh-yee] (*Loire*, France) Source of good *Coteaux de Layon*, and relatively ordinary examples of other *appellations*. ☆☆☆☆ 1997 Coteaux de Layon, Vieilles Vignes ££

Ⓣ **Palacio de Brejoeira** [breh-sho-reh-yah] (*Vinho Verde*, Portugal) Top class pure *Alvarinho Vinho Verde*.

Ⓣ **Weingut Georg Breuer** [broy-yer] (*Rheingau*, Germany) Innovative producer with classy *Rieslings* and high-quality *Rülander*.

Ⓣ **Bricco Manzoni** [bree-koh man-tzoh-nee] (*Piedmont*, Italy) Non-*DOC* oaky red blend made by Rocche dei Manzoni from *Nebbiolo* and *Barbera* grapes grown in *Monforte* vineyards which could produce *Barolo*. ☆☆☆☆☆ 1995 £££

Ⓣ **Brick House** (*Oregon*, US) A small organic slice of *Burgundy* in Yamhill County founded by a former television reporter. The *Gamay* can be as good as the *Pinot* and the *Chardonnay*.

Ⓣ **Bricout** [bree-koo] (*Champagne*, France) A cleverly marketed range of good-to-very good wines including the Cuvée Spéciale Arthur Bricout.

Ⓣ **Bridgehampton** (*Long Island*, US) Producer of first class *Merlot* and *Chardonnay* to worry a Californian.

Ⓣ **Bridgewater Mill** (*Adelaide Hills*, Australia) More modest sister winery and brand to *Petaluma*. Recently bought by a US winery, so likely to be keenly distributed there. Its fair prices should make it popular.

Ⓣ **Peter Bright** Australian-born Peter Bright of the *JP Vinhos* winery produces top-class Portuguese wines, including Tinta da Anfora and Quinta da Bacalhoa, plus a growing range in countries such as Spain, Italy and Chile, under the Bright Brothers label. ☆☆☆☆ 1998 Bright Brothers Barrel Aged Nero d'Avola ££

Ⓣ **Bristol Cream** (*Jerez*, Spain) See *Harvey's*.

Ⓣ **Jean-Marc Brocard** [broh-kahrr] (*Burgundy*, France) Very classy *Chablis* producer with well-defined individual vineyard wines, also producing unusually good *Aligoté*. ☆☆☆☆☆ 1998 Chablis Dom. Ste-Claire Malantes £££, ☆☆☆☆ 1998 Bourgogne Kimmeridgian £££

Ⓣ **Brokenwood** (*Hunter Valley*, Australia) Long-established, source of great *Semillon*, *Shiraz* and even (unusually for the *Hunter Valley*) *Cabernet*. Look for the "Cricket Pitch" bottlings. ☆☆☆☆ 1997 Rayner's Vineyard Shiraz ££

Ⓣ **Brouilly** [broo-yee] (*Burgundy*, France) Largest of the ten *Beaujolais Crus* producing pure, fruity *Gamay*. 94 95 96 97 98 *Duboeuf;* Cotton; *Sylvain Fessy;* Laurent Martray; Michaud; Piron; Roland; Ch. des Tours.

Ⓣ **Ch. Broustet** [broo-stay] (*Barsac 2ème Cru Classé, Bordeaux*, France) Rich, quite old-fashioned, well-oaked *Barsac* second growth. 70 **71 75** 76 **83** 85 **86 88 89 90** 95 96 97 98 99

Ⓣ **Brown Brothers** (*Victoria*, Australia) Proudly family-owned and *Victoria*-focused winery with a penchant for new wine regions and grapes. The wines are reliably good, though for excitement you should look to the *Shiraz* and the *Liqueur Muscat*. The *Orange Muscat* and *Flora* remains a delicious mouthful of liquid marmalade, the *Tarrango* is a good alternative to *Beaujolais* and the sparkling wine is a new success. ☆☆☆☆☆ 1997 Shiraz £££

Ⓣ **David Bruce** (*Santa Cruz*, California) Long established *Zinfandel* specialist whose fairly-priced *Petite Sirah* and *Pinot Noir* are also worth seeking out. ☆☆☆☆☆ 1997 Central Coast Pinot Noir £££

Ⓣ **Bruisyard Vineyard** [broos-syard] (*Suffolk*, England) High-quality vineyard. ☆☆☆ 1998 Müller-Thurgau ££

☿ **Le Brun de Neuville** [bruhn duh nuh-veel] (*Champagne,* France) Good little-known producer with classy *vintage* and excellent rosé, non-vintage and *Blanc de Blancs.* ☆☆☆☆ Cuvée Selection Brut ££

☿ **Willi Bründlmayer** [broodl-mi-yurh] (Austria) Oaked *Chardonnay* and *Pinots* of every kind, *Grüner Veltliner* and even a fair shot at *Cabernet.* ☆☆☆☆ 1997 Grüner Veltliner Kamptal Alte Reben Qualitätswein Trocken £££

☿ **Lucien & André Brunel** [broo-nel] (*Rhône,* France) The Brunels' "Les Caillous" produces good, traditional, built-to-last *Châteauneuf-du-Pape.*

☿ **Brunello di Montalcino** [broo-nell-oh dee mon-tahl-chee-noh] (*Tuscany,* Italy) *DOCG* red from a *Sangiovese* clone. 78 79 81 82 85 88 90 93 94 95 96 97 *Altesino; Argiano; Villa Banfi;* Barbi; *Tenuta Caparzo; Costanti;* Lambardi; Col d'Orcia; *Poggio Antico;* Talenti; Val di Suga.

Brut [broot] Dry, particularly of *Champagne* and sparkling wines. Brut nature/sauvage/zéro are even drier, while *"Extra-Sec"* is perversely applied to (slightly) sweeter sparkling wine.

🍇 **Bual** [bwahl] (*Madeira*) Grape producing soft, nutty wine – wonderful with cheese. *Blandy's; Cossart Gordon; Henriques & Henriques.*

☿ **Buçaco Palace Hotel** [boo-sah-koh] (Portugal) Red and white wines made from grapes grown in *Bairrada* and *Dão*, which last forever but cannot be bought outside the Disneyesque hotel itself.

Bucelas [boo-sel-las] (Portugal) *DO* area near Lisbon, best known for its intensely coloured, aromatic, bone-dry white wines. *Caves Velhas.*

☿ **Buena Vista** [bway-nah vihs-tah] (*Carneros,* California) One of the biggest estates in *Carneros,* this is an improving producer of California *Chardonnay, Pinot Noir* and *Cabernet.* Look out for Grand Reserve wines.

Bugey [boo-jay] (*Savoie,* France) *Savoie* district producing a variety of wines, including spicy white *Roussette de Bugey,* from the grape of that name.

☿ **Reichsrat von Buhl** [rihk-srat fon bool] (*Pfalz,* Germany) One of the area's best estates, due partly to vineyards like the *Forster Jesuitengarten.* ☆☆☆☆ 1997 Forster Kirchenstuck Riesling Spätlese £££

☿ **Buitenverwachting** [biht-turn-fur-vak-turng] (*Constantia,* South Africa) Enjoying a revival since the early 1980s, a show-piece organic *Constantia* winery making tasty organic whites.

Bulgaria Developing slowly since the advent of privatisation and *flying wine-makers.* Bulgaria's reputation still relies on its country wines and affordable *Cabernet Sauvignons* and *Merlots.* Mavrud is the traditional red variety and *Lovico, Rousse, Iambol, Suhindol* and *Haskovo* the names to look out for.

☿ **Bull's Blood** (*Eger,* Hungary) The gutsy red wine, aka Egri Bikaver, which gave defenders the strength to fight off Turkish invaders, is mostly anaemic stuff now, but privatisation has brought some improvement. ☆☆☆ 1998 Hilltop Neszmely Bulls Blood ££

☿ **Bernard Burgaud** [boor-goh] (*Rhône,* France) Serious producer of *Côte Rôtie.* ☆☆☆☆ 1995 Côte Rôtie £££

☿ **Grant Burge** (*Barossa Valley,* Australia) Dynamic producer and – since 1993 – owner of *Basedows.* ☆☆☆☆☆ 1991 Meshach £££

Burgenland [boor-gen-lund] (Austria) Wine region bordering *Hungary,* climatically ideal for fine sweet *Auslese* and *Beerenauslese. Feiler-Artinger;* Kollwentz-Römerhof; Helmut Lang; *Kracher; Opitz;* Wachter

♀ **Weinkellerei Burgenland** [vin-kel-ler-rih boor-gen-lund]
(*Neusiedlersee,* Austria) Cooperative with highly commercial *late harvest* wines.

♀ **Alain Burguet** [al-lan boor-gay] (*Burgundy,* France) One-man *domaine* proving how good plain *Gevrey-Chambertin* can be without heavy doses of new oak. ☆☆☆☆ 1995 Gevrey-Chambertin £££

♀ **Burgundy** (France) Home to *Pinot Noir* and *Chardonnay*; wines range from banal to sublime, but are never cheap. See *Chablis, Côte de Nuits, Côte de Beaune, Mâconnais, Beaujolais* and individual villages.

♀ **Leo Buring** [byoo-ring] (*South Australia*) One of the many labels used by the Southcorp (*Penfolds* etc.) group, specialising in ageable *Rieslings* and mature *Shiraz's.* ☆☆☆☆☆ 1994 Watervale Riesling £££

♀ **Weingut Dr Bürklin**-Wolf [boor-klin-volf] (*Pfalz,* Germany) Impressive estate with great organic *Riesling* vineyards and fine, dry wines.

♀ **Ernest J&F Burn** [boorn] (*Alsace,* France) Classy estate with vines in the Goldert *Grand Cru.* Great traditional *Gewurztraminer, Riesling* and *Muscat.* ☆☆☆☆ 1996 Gewurztraminer Goldert £££

Buttery Rich, fat smell often found in good *Chardonnay* (often as a result of *malolactic fermentation*) or in wine that has been left on its *lees.*

♀ **Buzet** [boo-zay] (*South-West,* France) Eastern neighbour of *Bordeaux,* using the same grape varieties to make generally basic wines. *Buzet;* co-operative; Ch. de Gueyze; Tissot.

♀ **Byron Vineyard** [bi-ron] (*Santa Barbara,* California) Impressive *Santa Barbara* winery with investment from *Mondavi,* and a fine line in *Pinots* and *Chardonnays.* ☆☆☆☆ 1997 Santa Maria Chardonnay £££

C

♀ **Ca' del Bosco** [kah-del-bos-koh] (*Lombardy,* Italy) Classic, if pricey, *barrique*-aged *Cabernet/Merlot* blends and fine *Chardonnay Pinot Noir* and *Pinot Bianco/Pinot Noir/Chardonnay Méthode Champenoise Franciacorta.* ☆☆☆☆☆ 1995 Maurizio Zanella ££££

♀ **Luis Caballero** [loo-is cab-ih-yer-roh] (*Jerez,* Spain) Quality *sherry* producer responsible for the *Burdon* range; also owns *Lustau.*

♀ **Château La Cabanne** [la ca-ban] (*Pomerol, Bordeaux,* France) Up-and-coming *Pomerol* property. 82 83 **85 86** 88 89 90 92 93 94 95 96 97 98

♀ **Cabardès** [cab-bahr-des] (*South-West* France) Region north of Carcassonne using Southern and *Bordeaux* varieties to produce good, if rustic, reds.

♀ **Cabernet d'Anjou/de Saumur** [cab-behr-nay don-joo / dur soh-moor] (*Loire,* France) Light, fresh, grassy, blackcurranty rosés, typical of their grape, the *Cabernet Franc.* **96 97** 98

❦ **Cabernet Franc** [ka-behr-nay fron] Kid brother of *Cabernet Sauvignon*; blackcurrant but more leafy. Best in the *Loire,* Italy, and increasingly in Australia, California and Washington, of course, as a partner of the *Cabernet Sauvignon* and particularly *Merlot* in Bordeaux. See *Chinon* and *Trentino.*

🍇 **Cabernet Sauvignon** [ka-ber-nay soh-vin-yon] The great blackcurranty, cedary, green peppery grape of *Bordeaux*, where it is blended with *Merlot*. Despite increasing competition from the *Merlot*, this is still by far the most successful red varietal, grown in every reasonably warm winemaking country on the planet. See *Bordeaux, Coonawarra, Chile, Napa*, etc.

🍷 **Marqués de Cáceres** [mahr-kehs day cath-thay-res] (*Rioja*, Spain) Modern French-influenced *bodega* making fresh-tasting wines. A good, if anonymous, new-style white has been joined by a promising oak-fermented version and a recommendable rosé (*rosado*), plus a grapey *Muscat*-style white. ☆☆☆☆ 1994 Rioja Tinto ££

🍷 **Ch. Cadet-Piola** [ka-day pee-yoh-lah] (*St. Emilion Grand Cru Classé, Bordeaux*, France) Wines that are made to last, with fruit and *tannin* to spare. 79 **82 83 85** 86 88 89 **90** 92 **93** 94 95 96 97 98

Cadillac [kad-dee-yak] (*Bordeaux*, France) Sweet but rarely luscious (non-botrytis) *Sémillon* and *Sauvignon* whites. Ch. Fayau is the star wine. Its *d'Yquem*-style label is pretty smart too. **88 89 90** 94 95 96 97 98

🍷 **Cahors** [kah-orr] (*South-West*, France) Often rustic wines produced from the local *Tannat* and the *Cot* (*Malbec*). Some are *Beaujolais*-like, while others are *tannic* and full-bodied, though far lighter than in the days when people spoke of "the black wines of Cahors". **Ch. de Caix; la Caminade; du Cèdre; Clos la Coutale; Clos de Gamot; Gautoul; de Hauterivem; Haute-Serre; Lagrezette; Lamartine; Latuc; Prieuré de Cenac; Rochet-Lamother; Clos Triguedina.**

🍷 **Cain Cellars** (*Napa*, California) Spectacular *Napa* hillside vineyards devoted to producing a classic *Bordeaux* blend of five varieties – hence the name of the wine. ☆☆☆☆☆ 1995 Cain Five £££

🍷 **Cairanne** [keh-ran] (*Rhône*, France) Named *Côtes du Rhône* village known for good peppery reds. **85 88** 89 **90** 92 93 **95 96** 97 98 **Dom d'Ameilhaud; Aubert; Brusset; Oratoire St-Martin; Richaud; Tardieu-Laurent.**

🍷 **Cakebread** (*Napa*, California) Long-established producer of rich reds, *Sauvignon Blanc, Chardonnay* and improving *Pinot Noir*. ☆☆☆☆ 1997 Chardonnay ££££

Calabria [kah-lah-bree-ah] (Italy) The "toe" of the Italian boot, making Cirò from the local Gaglioppo reds and *Greco* whites. *Cabernet* and *Chardonnay* are promising, too, especially those made by *Librandi*.

�X **Calem** [kah-lin] (*Douro*, Portugal) Quality-conscious, small *port* producer. The speciality *Colheita tawnies* are among the best of their kind. ☆☆☆☆ **1977 Vintage Port ££££**

�X **Calera Wine Co.** [ka-lehr-uh] (*Santa Benito*, California) Maker of some of *California's* best, longest-lived *Pinot Noir* from individual vineyards such as Jensen, Mills, Reed and Selleck. The *Chardonnay* and *Viognier* are pretty special too. ☆☆☆☆☆ **1997 Mount Harlan Viognier £££**

California (US) Major wine-producing area of the US. See *Napa, Sonoma, Santa Barbara, Amador, Mendocino*, etc, plus individual wineries. Red: 84 **85** 86 87 **90 91** 92 93 95 96 97 98 White: **85 90 91** 92 **95** 96 **97 98**

�X **Viña Caliterra** [kal-lee-tay-rah] (*Curico*, Chile) Sister company of *Errazuriz*. Now a 50-50 partner with *Mondavi* and co-producer of *Seña*. ☆☆☆☆☆ **1996 Tribute Chardonnay £££**

�X **Callaway** (*Temecula* California) An unfashionable part of California, and a deliciously unfashionable style of – unoaked – *Chardonnay*. What a pity others aren't as ready to buck the wood-crazy trend.

�X **Ch. Calon-Ségur** [kal-lon say-goor] (*St. Estèphe 3ème Cru Classé, Bordeaux*, France) Traditional *St. Estèphe* that has recently begun to surpass its third growth status. 78 **82** 83 **85 86 88** 89 **90** 91 93 94 95 96 97 98 ☆☆☆☆☆ **1995 ££££**

�X **Cambria** (*Santa Barbara*, California) Huge operation in the *Santa Maria Valley* belonging to the dynamic *Kendall Jackson* and producing fairly priced and good, if rarely complex, *Chardonnay, Pinot Noir, Syrah, Viognier* and *Sangiovese*. ☆☆☆☆☆ **1997 Late Harvest Viognier £££**

�X **Ch. Camensac** [kam-mon-sak] (*Haut-Médoc 5ème Cru Classé, Bordeaux*, France) Improving property following investment in 1994. **82** 85 **86** 88 89 90 91 92 93 **94 95** 96 97 98 ☆☆☆☆ **1995 £££**

�X **Cameron** (*Oregon*, US) John Paul makes terrific *Pinot Noir* in this Yamhill estate - plus some impressive *Pinot Blanc*.

Campania [kahm-pan-nyah] (Italy) Region surrounding Naples, known for *Taurasi, Lacryma Christi* and *Greco di Tufo* and wines from *Mastroberadino*.

�X **Campbells** (*Rutherglen*, Australia) Classic producer of fortified *Muscat* and rich, concentrated reds under the Bobbie Burns label. ☆☆☆☆☆ **Merchant Prince Rare Rutherglen Muscat £££**

�X **Campillo** [kam-pee-yoh] (*Rioja*, Spain) A small estate producing *Rioja* made purely from *Tempranillo*, showing what this grape can do. The white is less impressive. ☆☆☆☆ **1995 Rioja Riserva ££**

�X **Bodegas Campo Viejo** [kam-poh vyay-hoh] (*Rioja*, Spain) A go-ahead, if underrated *bodega* whose *Reserva* and *Gran Reserva* are full of rich fruit. Albor, the unoaked red (pure *Tempranillo*) and white (*Viura*) are first-class examples of modern Spanish winemaking. ☆☆☆☆ **1997 Reserva ££**

Canada Surprising friends and foes alike, British Columbia and, more specifically, *Ontario* are producing good *Chardonnay, Riesling,* improving *Pinot Noirs* and intense *Icewines,* usually from the *Vidal* grape. **Cave Springs;** *Chateau des Charmes; Henry of Pelham;* Hillebrand; *Inniskillin;* Jackson-Triggs; Konzelmann; Magnotta; *Mission Hill;* Pelee Island; Peller Estates; Pilliteri; *Reif Estate;* Stoney Ridge; Sumac Ridge; Vineland Estates.

Ⓣ **Canard Duchêne** [kan-nah doo-shayn] (*Champagne,* France) Improving subsidiary of *Veuve Clicquot.* ☆☆☆☆ **Grande Cuvée Charles VII £££**

Ⓣ **Canberra District** (*New South Wales,* Australia) Confounding the critics, a small group of producers led by *Doonkuna, Helm's* and *Lark Hill* are making good *Rhône*-style reds and *Rieslings* in high-altitude vineyards here.

Ⓣ **Candido** [kan-dee doh] (*Apulia,* Italy) Top producer of deliciously chocolatey Salice Salentino and sweet Aleatico di Puglia.

Ⓣ **Canépa** [can-nay-pah] (Chile) Good rather than great winery, making progress with *Chardonnays* and *Rieslings* as well as reds that suffer from over-generous exposure to oak. ☆☆☆☆ **1998 Chardonnay ££**

🍇 **Cannonau** [kan-non-now] (*Sardinia,* Italy) A red *clone* of the *Grenache,* producing a variety of wine styles from sweet to dry, mostly in *Sardinia.*

Ⓣ **Cannonau di Sardegna** [kan-non-now dee sahr-den-yah] (*Sardinia,* Italy) Heady, robust, dry-to-sweet, *DOC* red made from the *Cannonau.*

Ⓣ **Ch. Canon** [kan-non] (*St. Emilion Premier Grand Cru Classé, Bordeaux,* France) Back on form after a tricky patch in the 1990s. The keynote here is elegance rather than power. **82 83 85 86** 87 88 89 90 93 95 96 97 98

Ⓣ **Ch. Canon de Brem** [kan-non dur brem] (*Canon-Fronsac, Bordeaux,* France) A very good *Moueix*-run *Fronsac* property. 81 **82** 83 85 86 88 89 90 92 93 **95** 96 97 ☆☆☆☆ **1998 ££**

Ⓣ **Canon-Fronsac** [kah-non fron-sak] (*Bordeaux,* France) Small *appellation* bordering on *Pomerol,* with attractive plummy, *Merlot*-based reds from increasingly good value, if rustic, petits *châteaux.* **82** 83 85 86 **88 89** 90 94 95 96 96 97 98 *Ch. Canon-Moueix;* Ch. Moulin Pey-Labrie.

Ⓣ **Ch. Canon-la-Gaffelière** [kan-non lah gaf-fel-yehr] (*St. Emilion Grand Cru Classé, Bordeaux,* France) High-flying estate run by an innovative, quality-conscious Austrian who, in 1996, created the instant superstar *la Mondotte.* Rich, ultra-concentrated wine. 82 83 **85 86** 88 89 90 92 **93** 94 95 96 97 98

Ⓣ **Ch. Canon-Moueix** [kan-non mwex] (*Canon-Fronsac, Bordeaux,* France) A characteristically stylish addition to the *Moueix* empire in *Canon-Fronsac.* A wine to beat many a pricier *St. Emilion.*

Ⓣ **Ch. Cantemerle** [kont-mehrl] (*Haut-Médoc 5ème Cru Classé, Bordeaux,* France) A *Cru Classé* situated outside the main villages of the *Médoc.* Classy, perfumed wine with bags of blackcurrant fruit. **61** 78 81 82 **83** 85 88 89 90 92 93 95 **96** ☆☆☆☆ **1992 ££**

Ⓣ **Ch. Cantenac-Brown** [kont-nak brown] (*Margaux 3ème Cru Classé, Bordeaux,* France) Now under the same ownership as Ch. Pichon Baron but never quite showing the same class. 85 **86** 87 88 89 90 93 94 95 97 98

Canterbury (New Zealand) Following *St. Helena's* early success with *Pinot Noir,* Waipara in this region of the South Island has produced highly aromatic *Riesling, Pinot Blanc* and *Chablis*-like *Chardonnay. Giesen;* Pegasus Bay; Melness; Mark Rattray; St. Helena; Sherwood Estate; *Waipara Springs.*

Cantina (Sociale) [kan-tee-nuh soh-chee-yah-lay] (Italy) Winery (cooperative).

☥ **Capannelle** Good producer of rich *Super Tuscan* wine near Gaiole.

Cap Corse [kap-korss] (*Corsica*, France) 17 villages in the north of the island produce great, floral Muscat as well as some attractive herby dry Vermentino. **Antoine Arena; Dom de Catarelli; Clos Nicrosi.**

Cap Classique [kap-klas-seek] (South Africa) Now that the term *"Méthode Champenoise"* has unreasonably been outlawed, this is the phrase developed by the South Africans to describe their Champagne-method sparkling wine.

☥ **Ch. Cap-de-Mourlin** [kap-dur-mer-lan] (*St. Emilion Grand Cru Classé, Bordeaux,* France) Until 1983 when they were amalgamated, there were, confusingly, two different *châteaux* with this name. Good mid-range stuff. 79 81 **82 83** 85 86 88 89 90 93 94 95 96 98 ☆☆☆☆ **1990 ££**

☥ **Caparzo** [ka-pahrt-zoh] (*Tuscany,* Italy) Classy, *Brunello di Montalcino* estate producing wines that age brilliantly. ☆☆☆☆☆ **1993 La Casa £££**

Cape (South Africa) All of the vineyard areas of South Africa are located in the Western Cape, most of them close to Cape Town. See under *Stellenbosch, Paarl, Franschhoek, Walker Bay, Robertson, Tulbagh, Worcester* etc. Red: 89 **91 92** 93 94 95 96 97 White: 94 95 96 97 98 99

☥ **Cape Mentelle** [men-tel] (*Margaret River,* Western Australia) Brilliant French-owned winery, founded, like *Cloudy Bay,* by David Hoehnen. Impressive *Semillon-Sauvignon, Shiraz, Cabernet* and, remarkably, a wild berryish *Zinfandel,* to shame many a Californian. ☆☆☆☆ **1998 Cabernet Sauvignon £££**

☥ **Capel Vale** [kay-puhl vayl] (*South West Coat,* Western Australia) Just to the north of the borders of *Margaret River. Good Riesling, Gewürztraminer* and an improving Baudin blended red. ☆☆☆☆ **1998 CV Shiraz ££**

☥ **Capezzana** [kap-pay-tzah-nah] (*Tuscany,* Italy) Conte Ugo Contini Bonacossi not only got *Carmignano* its *DOCG,* he also helped to promote the notion of *Cabernet* and *Sangiovese* as compatible bedfellows, helping to open the door for all those priceless – and pricy – *Super-Tuscans.* ☆☆☆☆☆ **1997 Barco Reale £££**

Capsule The sheath covering the cork. Once lead, now plastic, or tin. In the case of "flanged" bottles, though, it is noticeable by its transparency or absence.

☥ **Caramany** [kah-ram-man-nee] (*Midi,* France) New *AC* for an old section of the *Côtes du Roussillon*-Villages, near the *Pyréneés.* **Vignerons Catalans.**

Carbonic Maceration See *Macération Carbonique.*

☥ **Ch. Carbonnieux** [kar-bon-nyeuh] (*Graves Cru Classé, Bordeaux,* France) Since 1991, the whites have greatly improved and the raspberryish reds are among the most reliable in the region. Red: 82 85 **86** 88 89 90 91 92 94 95 96 97 98 99 White: 93 **94** 95 96 97 98 99 ☆☆☆☆ **1998 Red £££**

☥ **Carcavelos** [kar-kah-veh-losh] (Portugal) *DO* region in the Lisbon suburbs producing usually disappointing fortified wines.

☥ **Cardinale** (California) *Kendall-Jackson's* top line, produced by a former star Mondavi winemaker from grapes grown on mostly hillside vines. The Royale white is impressively *Bordeaux*-like.

☥ **Ch. la Cardonne** [kar-don] (*Bordeaux,* France) *Cru Bourgeois* whose quality is improving since its sale by the Rothschilds of *Ch. Lafite.*

℗ **Carema** [kah-ray-mah] (*Piedmont,* Italy) Wonderful perfumed *Nebbiolo* produced in limited quantities largely by Cantina dei Produttori Nebbiolo.

🍇 **Carignan** [kah-ree-nyon] Prolific red grape making usually dull, coarse wine for blending, but classier fare in *Corbières, Minervois* and *Fitou.* The key to good Carignan, as its Californian fan Randall Grahm of *Bonny Doon* says, lies in getting low yields from old vines. In Spain it is known as *Cariñena* and Mazuelo, while Italians call it Carignano.

℗ **Carignano del Sulcis** [ka-reen-yah-noh dehl sool-chees] (*Sardinia,* Italy) Dynamic *DOC* spearheaded by the Santadi cooperative.

℗ **Louis Carillon & Fils** [ka-ree-yon] (*Burgundy,* France) Great modern *Puligny* estate. ☆☆☆☆☆ **1997 Puligny-Montrachet Les Perrières ££££**

℗ **Cariñena** [kah-ree-nyeh-nah] (Spain) Important *DO* of Aragon for rustic reds, high in alcohol and, confusingly, made not from the *Cariñena* (or *Carignan*) grape, but mostly from the *Garnacha Tinta.* Also some whites.

🍇 **Cariñena** [kah-ree-nyeh-nah] (Spain) The Spanish name for *Carignan.*
℗ **Carmel** (Israel) Huge producer offering a wide range of pleasant but generally unremarkable wines.
℗ **Viña Carmen** [veen-yah kahr-men] (*Maipo,* Chile) Quietly developing a reputation as one of the best red wine producers in Chile. Increasingly organic. ☆☆☆☆ **1998 Nativa Chardonnay ££**

🍇 **Carmenère** [kahr-meh-nehr] (Chile) Smoky-spicily distinctive grape that although almost extinct in Bordeaux is still a permitted variety for claret. Widely planted in Chile where it has traditionally been sold as Merlot. Look for examples like the Santa Inès Carmenère, *Carmen* Grand Vidure or *Veramonte Merlot.* ☆☆☆☆ **1998 Carmen Grand Vidure ££**
℗ **Carmenet Vineyard** [kahr-men-nay] (*Sonoma Valley,* California) Excellent and unusual winery tucked away in the hills and producing long-lived, very *Bordeaux*-like but approachable reds, fairly-priced *Chardonnay,* and also (even more unusually for California) good *Semillon-Sauvignon* and *Cabernet Franc.* ☆☆☆☆☆ **1996 Moon Mountain Reserve ££**
℗ **Les Carmes-Haut-Brion** [lay kahrm oh bree-yon] (*Bordeaux,* France) Small property neighbouring *Ch. Haut-Brion* in *Pessac-Léognan.* Good in 1999.

℗ **Carmignano** [kahr-mee-nyah-noh] (*Tuscany,* Italy) Nearby alternative to *Chianti,* with the addition of more *Cabernet* grapes. See *Capezzana.*

℗ **Quinta do Carmo** [Keen-tah doh Kar-moh] (*Alentejo,* Portugal) The Ch. Lafite Rothschilds' best foreign venture. Rich, tastily modern reds.

Carneros [kahr-neh-ros] (California) Small, fog-cooled, high-quality region shared between the *Napa* and *Sonoma Valleys* and used by just about everybody as a source for cool-climate grapes. Producing top-class *Chardonnay, Pinot Noir* and now, *Merlot*. Some of the best examples are from from Hudson and Hyde vineyards. Red: **85 86 87 90 91 92 93** 95 96 97. White: **95 96** 97 98. *Acacia; Carneros Creek; Cuvaison; Domaine Carneros; Domaine Chandon; Kistler;* Macrostie; *Marcassin; Mondavi; Mumm Cuvée Napa; Patz & Hall; Pine Ridge;* Ramey; *Saintsbury; Shafer; Swanson;* Truchard.

℞ **Domaine Carneros** (*Napa Valley,* California) *Taittinger's* US fizz – produced in a perfect and thus ludicrously incongruous replica of their French HQ. The wine, however, is one of the best New World efforts by the Champenois. ☆☆☆☆ **1993 le Reve £££**

℞ **Carneros Creek** (*Carneros,* California) Producer of ambitious *Pinot Noir* under this name and the rather better (and cheaper) berryish Fleur de Carneros.

℞ **Caronne-Ste-Gemme** [kah-ronn-sant jem] (*Bordeaux,* France) Reliable Cru Bourgeois that delivers value – even in poorer vintages.

℞ **Carpineto** [Kah-pi-neh-toh] (*Tuscany,* Italy) High-quality producer of *Chianti,* and *Chardonnay* and *Cabernet* that are sold under the Farnito label. ☆☆☆☆☆ **1995 Farnito £££**

℞ **Carr Taylor** (*Sussex,* England) One of England's more business-like estates. Sparkling wines are the best buys.

℞ **Ch. Carras** [kar-ras] (*Macedonia,* Greece) Greece's best-known estate, left behind by more modern producers. Now in new hands: we'll see.

℞ **Les Carruades de Lafite** [kah-roo-ahd-dur la-feet] (*Pauillac, Bordeaux,* France) The second label of *Ch. Lafite.* Rarely (quite) as good as *les Forts de Latour,* nor *Ch. Margaux's Pavillon Rouge.* ☆☆☆☆ **1998 £££**

℞ **Ch. Carsin** [kahr-san] (*Bordeaux,* France) Finnish-owned, Aussie-style *Premières Côtes de Bordeaux* estate, proving that this *appellation* is capable of producing wines of class and complexity. Australian-born Mandy Jones makes particularly tasty whites using the Sauvignon Gris. 95 96 97 98 ☆☆☆ **1999 Cuvée Prestige Blanc ££**

Casa [kah-sah] (Italy, Spain, Portugal) Firm or company.

Casablanca [kas-sab-lan-ka] (*Aconcagua,* Chile) New region in *Aconcagua;* a magnet for quality-conscious winemakers and producing especially impressive *Sauvignons, Chardonnays* and *Gewürztraminers.* *Caliterra; Viña Casablanca; Concha y Toro; Errazuriz; Santa Carolina; Santa Emiliana; Santa Rita; Veramonte; Villard.*

℞ **Viña Casablanca** [veen-yah kas-sab-lan-ka] (*Casablanca,* Chile) Go-ahead winery in the region of the same name. A showcase for the talents of winemaker *Ignacio Recabarren.* ☆☆☆☆ **1998 Santa Isabel Barrel-fermented Chardonnay ££**

℞ **Casanova di Neri** [kah-sah-NOH-vah dee NAY-ree] (*Tuscany,* Italy) Fine producer of *Brunello* and *Rosso di Montalcino.* ☆☆☆☆ **1996 Rosso ££**

℞ **Casse Basse** [kah-seh-bas-say] (*Tuscany,* Italy) Soldera's hard-to-find *Brunello di Montalcino* is developing a cult following in the US – and fetching crazily high prices.

℞ **Caslot-Galbrun** [kah-loh gal-bruhn] (*Loire,* France) Top-class producer of serious, long-lived red *Loires.*

℞ **Cassegrain** [kas-grayn] (*New South Wales,* Australia) Tucked away in the Hastings Valley on the East Coast, but also drawing grapes from elsewhere. The wines can be variable, but are often impressive. ☆☆☆☆ **1994 Semillon Hastings Valley ££**

Cassis [ka-sees] (*Provence,* France) Small coastal *appellation* producing (variable) red, (often dull) white and (good) rosé. **Clos Ste. Magdeleine; la Ferme Blanche.**

Ⅰ **Castel del Monte** [Ka-stel del mon-tay] (*Puglia,* Italy) Interesting southern region where Rivera makes excellent Il Falcone reds and Bianca di Svevia whites. Grapes grown include the local *Aglianico*, Pampanuto, Bombino Bianco and Nero, and Nero di Troia.

Ⅰ **Castelgiocondo** [kas-tel-jee-yah-kon-doh] (*Tuscany,* Italy) High-quality *Brunello* estate owned by *Frescobaldi.*

Ⅰ **Castellare** [kas-teh-LAH-ray] (*Tuscany*, Italy) Innovative small *Chianti Classico* estate whose *Sangiovese-Malvasia* blend, Nera I Sodi di San Niccoló, *Vino da Tavola*, is worth seeking out.

Ⅰ **Castellblanch** [kas-tel-blantch] (*Catalonia,* Spain) Producer of better-than-most *Cava* – but catch it young. ☆☆☆ **Cava Brut Zero ££**

Ⅰ **Casteller** [kas-teh-ler] (*Trentino-Alto-Adige,* Italy) Pale red, creamy-fruity wines for early drinking, made from *Schiava*. See *Ca'Vit.*

Ⅰ **Castello di Ama** [kas-tel-loh-dee-ah-mah] (*Tuscany,* Italy) Producer of great single-vineyard *Chianti Classico* (esp. the Bellavista Riserva) plus the stunning Vigna l'Apparita Merlot and delicious Chardonnay.

Ⅰ **Castell'sches, Fürstlich Domänenamt** [kas-tel-shs foorst-likh Doh-mehn-en-ahmt] (*Franken,* Germany) Good Auslese Scheurebe and Rieslaner and dry Sylvaner. Dornfelder reds are interesting too.

Ⅰ **Castillo de Monjardin** [kas-tee-yoh deh mon-har-deen] (*Navarra,* Spain). Navarra rising star with good *Chardonnay, Pinot Noir* and *Merlot.. Cat's pee* Describes the tangy smell frequently found in typical *Müller-Thurgau* and unripe *Sauvignon Blanc.*

Catalonia [kat-tal-loh-nee-yah] (Spain) Semi-autonomous region that includes *Penedés, Priorato, Conca de Barberá, Terra Alta* and *Costers del Segre.*

Ⅰ **Catena Estate** [kat-tay-nah] (Argentina) Quality-focused part of the giant Catena-Esmeralda concern, helped by the expertise of ex-*Simi* Californian winemaker Paul Hobbs. ☆☆☆☆ **1999 Argento Malbec ££*f***

Ⅰ **Cattier** [Kat-ee-yay] (*Champagne,* France) Up-and-coming producer with good non-vintage wines.

Ⅰ **Dom. Cauhapé** [koh-ap-pay] (*South-West* France) Extraordinary *Jurançon* producer of excellent *Vendange Tardive* and dry wines from the *Manseng* grape. ☆☆☆☆ **1997 Jurançon Noblesse du Temps ££**

Ⅰ **Cava** [kah-vah] (*Catalonia,* Spain) Fizz produced in *Penedés* by the *Methode Champenoise*, but handicapped by innately dull local grapes and ageing, which deprives it of freshness. Avoid *vintage* versions and look instead for Anna de *Codorníu* and *Raimat* Cava – both made from *Chardonnay* – or such well-made exceptions to the earthy rule as *Juvé y Camps, Conde de Caralt, Cava Chandon* and *Segura Viudas.*
Cava (Greece) Legal term for wood- and bottle-aged wine.

Ⅰ **Cavalleri** [kah-vah-yah-ree] (*Lombardy,* Italy) One of the top sparkling wines in Italy. ☆☆☆☆ **Franciacorta Brut ££**
Cave [kahv] (France) Cellar.

Ⅰ **Cave Spring** (*Ontario,* Canada) One of Canada's most reliable producers, with especially good Chardonnay.

Ⅰ **Caymus Vineyards** [kay-muhs] (*Napa Valley*, California) Traditional producer of concentrated Italianate reds (including a forceful *Zinfandel*) and a characterful *Cabernet Franc*. Liberty School is the *second label.* ☆☆☆☆☆ **1996 Cabernet Sauvignon £££**

T Dom. Cazes [kahrs] (*Midi*, France) Maker of great *Muscat de Rivesaltes*, rich marmaladey stuff which makes most *Beaumes de Venise* seem dull.

T Cellier le Brun [sel-yay luh-bruhn] (*Marlborough*, New Zealand) Specialist producer of *Méthode Champenoise* sparkling wine originally founded by Daniel Le Brun, an expatriate Frenchman. ☆☆☆ **Brut NV £££**

🍇 Cencibel [sen-thee-bel] (*Valdepeñas*, Spain) Alternative name for *Tempranillo*.

Central Coast (California) Increasingly interesting, varied set of regions south of San Francisco, including *Santa Barbara, Monterey, Santa Cruz* and *San Luis Obispo*.

T Central Otago [oh-tah-goh] (*South Island*, New Zealand) Exciting "new" region where *Pinot Noir* and *Riesling* flourish. Increasingly attracting a similar cult following to *Marlborough*. **Black Ridge; Chard Farm;** *Felton Road*; **Gibbston Valley; Rippon Vineyards.**

Central Valley (California) Huge irrigated region controlled by giants who make three-quarters of the state's wines without, so far, matching the efforts of similar regions Down Under. New vineyards and a concentration on cooler parts of the region are paying off for the *Sauvignon Blanc* but I doubt the potential of the increasingly widely planted *Merlot*. Smaller-scale winemaking is beginning to help (this is wine-factory country), but good wines are still the exception to the rule. *Quady's* fortified and sweet wines are still by far the best wines here.

Central Valley (Chile) The region in which most of *Chile's* wines are made. It includes *Maipo, Rapel, Maule* and *Curico*, but not the new cool-climate region of *Casablanca*, which is in *Aconcagua*, further north.

Cépage [say-pahzh] (France) Grape variety.

T Cepparello [chep-par-rel-loh] (*Tuscany*, Italy) Brilliant pure *Sangiovese Vino da Tavola* made by Paolo de Marchi of *Isole e Olena*. ☆☆☆☆ **1997 £££**

T Ceretto [cher-ret-toh] (*Piedmont*, Italy) Producer of good modern *Barolos* and increasingly impressive single-vineyard examples, plus excellent La Bernardina varietals (Syrah, Pinot Noir etc) ☆☆☆☆ **1995 Barolo Brunate ££££**

T Ch. de Cérons [say-ron] (*Bordeaux*, France) One of the best properties in *Cérons*. White: 83 86 **88** 89 **90** ☆☆☆☆ **1990 Château de Cerons £££**

T Ch. Certan de May [sehr-ton dur may] (*Pomerol, Bordeaux*, France) Top-class *Pomerol* estate with subtly plummy wine. 70 75 78 **79 81 82 83 85 86** 87 88 89 90 94 95 96 98 ☆☆☆☆☆ **1990 ££££**

T Ch. Certan-Giraud [sehr-ton zhee-roh] (*Pomerol, Bordeaux*, France) *Pomerol* estate recently bought by JP Moueix and – in part – providing the grapes for his new Hosanna superstar wine. Wines sold after 1998 under the Certan-Giraud will presumably be less exciting.

🍇 César [say-zahr] (*Burgundy*, France) The forgotten plummy-raspberryish red grape of *Burgundy*, still vinified near *Chablis* by Simonnet-Fèvre.

T LA Cetto [chet-toh] (*Baja California*, Mexico) With wines like LA Cetto's tasty *Cabernet* and spicy-soft *Petite Sirah*, it's hardly surprising that *Baja California* is now beginning to compete with a more northerly region across the US frontier. ☆☆☆☆ **1997 Petite Sirah ££**

Chablais [shab-lay] (*Vaud*, Switzerland) A good place to find *Pinot Noir* rosé and young *Chasselas* (sold as *Dorin*).

🍷 **Chablis** [shab-lee] (*Burgundy*, France) When not overpriced, *Chablis* offers a steely European finesse that New World *Chardonnays* rarely capture. *Petits* and, more particularly *Grands Crus* should (but do not always) show extra complexity. A new Union des Grands Crus de Chablis, founded in 2000 is intended to promote quality. We'll see. 85 **86** 88 89 **90** 92 94 **95** 96 97 98 *Bichot; J-M Brocard; La Chablisienne;* René Dauvissat; *Joseph Drouhin; Durup; William Fèvre; Laroche; Louis Michel; Raveneau; Servin; Verget; Vocoret.*

🍷 **La Chablisienne** [shab-lees-yen] (*Burgundy*, France) Cooperative making wines from *Petit Chablis* to *Grands Crus* under a host of labels. Rivals the best estates in the *appellation*. ☆☆☆☆ **1998 Chablis – Les Vignerons de Chablis £££**

Chai [shay] (France) Cellar/winery.

🍷 **Chalk Hill** (*Sonoma*, California) Producer of rich *Chardonnay*, stylish *Sauvignon Blanc*, lovely berryish *Cabernet* and great *Sauternes*-style whites. Chalk is ideal soil for Chardonnay. Here in California though, the only chalk you would find is in the winery name. ☆☆☆☆ **1997 Estate-bottled Chardonnay £££**

🍷 **Chalone** [shal-lohn] (*Monterey*, California) Under the same ownership as *Acacia, Edna Valley* and *Carmenet*, this 25-year old winery is one of the big names for *Pinot Noir* and *Chardonnay*. Unusually *Burgundian*, long-lived. ☆☆☆☆ **1996 Chardonnay £££**

Chalonnais/Côte Chalonnaise [shal-lohn-nay] (*Burgundy*, France) Source of lesser-known, less complex *Burgundies – Givry, Montagny, Rully* and *Mercurey*. Potentially (rather than always actually) good value, but the Bourgougne Rouge is often a good buy.

🍷 **Chambers** (*Rutherglen*, Australia) Competes with *Morris* for the crown of best *Liqueur Muscat* maker. The Rosewood is great.

🍷 **Ch. Chambert-Marbuzet** [shom-behr mahr-boo-zay] (*St. Estèphe Cru Bourgeois, Bordeaux*, France) Characterful *Cabernet*-based *St. Estèphe*.

🍷 **Chambertin** [shom-behr-tan] (*Burgundy*, France) Ultra-cherryish, damsony *Grand Cru* whose name was adopted by the village of Gevrey. Famous in the 14th century, and Napoleon's favourite. Chambertin Clos-de-Bèze, Charmes-Chambertin, Griottes-Chambertin, Latricières-Chambertin, Mazis-Chambertin and Ruchottes-Chambertin are neighbouring *Grands Crus*. 76 **78** 79 83 **85** 87 **88 89 90 92** 93 **94** 95 96 97 Pierre Amiot; *Bachelet; Alain Burguet; Bruno Clair;* Pierre Damoy; *Drouhin; Dugat-Py; Dujac; Engel; Faiveley; Groffier;* Raymond Launay; *Leroy; Denis Mortet;* Bernard Meaume; Jean Raphet; *Roty;* Henri Rebourseau; *Armand Rousseau;* Jean Trapet.

♈ **Chambolle-Musigny** [shom-bol moo-see-nyee] (*Burgundy*, France) *Côte de Nuits* village whose wines can be like perfumed examples from the *Côte de Beaune*. *Georges Roumier* is the local star, and *Drouhin*, *Dujac* and *Ponsot* are all reliable, as are *Bertagna*, *Drouhin*; *Anne Gros*, *Ghislaine Barthod*, *Dominique Laurent Mugnier, de Vogüe* and *Leroy*. Red: 78 83 **85 88 89 90 92** 93 **94** 95 96 97 98

♈ **Champagne** [sham-payn] (France) Source of potentially the greatest sparkling wines, from *Pinot Noir*, *Pinot Meunier* and *Chardonnay* grapes. See individual listings. **81 82 83 85** 86 **88** 89 90 91 92 93

♈ **Didier Champalou** [dee-dee-yay shom-pah-loo] (*Loire*, France) Estate with serious sweet, dry and sparkling *Vouvray*. ☆☆☆☆ **Brut Méthode Traditionelle £££**

♈ **Champy** [shom-pee] (*Burgundy*, France) Long-established, recently much-improved *Beaune négociant*. ☆☆☆☆ **1997 Savigny-lès-Beaune £££**

♈ **Dom. Chandon** [doh-mayn shahn-dahn] (*Napa Valley*, California) *Moët & Chandon*'s Californian winery, until recently under-performing, has finally been allowed to compete with its counterpart at *Dom. Chandon* in Australia. Wines are sold in the UK as Shadow Creek. ☆☆☆☆ **Etoile Napa Valley Non-Vintage £££**

♈ **Dom. Chandon** [doh-mihn shon-don] (*Yarra Valley*, Australia) Sold as *Green Point* in the UK and proving that Australian grapes, grown in a variety of cool climates can compete with *Champagne*. Now joined by a creditable, *Chablis*-like, still Colonades *Chardonnay*. ☆☆☆☆ **1996 £££**

♈ **Dom. Chandon de Briailles** [shon-don dur bree-iy] (*Burgundy*, France) Good *Savigny-lès-Beaune* estate whose owner is related to the *Chandon* of *Champagne*. ☆☆☆☆ **1997 Savigny-lès-Beaune Lavières ££££**

♈ **Clos la Chance** (*Napa*, California) Up-and-coming producer of good value Chardonnay.

♈ **Chanson** [shon-son] (*Burgundy*, France) Improving *Beaune* merchant. Go for the *domaine* wines. ☆☆☆ **1998 Côte de Beaune Villages ££**

♈ **Ch. de Chantegrive** [shont-greev] (*Graves*, *Bordeaux*, France) Large modern *Graves* estate with excellent modern reds and whites. Red: 82 83 85 87 88 93 94 95 96 97 98 White: 89 90 92 93 **94 95** 96 97 98 99

♈ **Chapel Down** (*Kent*, England) David Cowdroy's impressive winery-only operation uses grapes sourced from vineyards throughout southern England. ☆☆☆ **1995 Vintage Brut Sparkling Wine £££**

♈ **Chapel Hill Winery** (*McLaren Vale*, Australia) Pam Dunsford's impressively rich – some say too rich – reds and whites have recently been joined by a leaner, unoaked *Chardonnay*. ☆☆☆☆☆ **1996 The Vicar Cabernet Shiraz £££**

♈ **Chappellet** (*Napa*, California) Innovative winery with beautiful vineyards and the courage to make wines such as an oaked *Chenin Blanc*, Tocai Friulano, "Moelleux" late harvest wines rather than stick to mainstream *Chardonnay* and *Merlot*.

♈ **Chapoutier** [shah-poo-tyay] (*Rhône*, France) Family-owned merchant rescued from its faded laurels by a new generation who are using more or less organic methods. Not all wines live up to their early promise but credit is deserved for the initiative of printing labels in braille. Now making wine in Australia. ☆☆☆☆ **1998 Crozes-Hermitage La Petite Ruche £££**

Chaptalisation [shap-tal-lih-zay-shuhn] The legal (in some regions) addition of sugar during fermentation to boost a wine's *alcohol* content.

🍇 **Charbono** [shar-boh-noh] (California) Obscure grape variety grown in California but thought to come from France. Makes interesting, very spicy, full-bodied reds at *Inglenook*, *Duxoup* and *Bonny Doon*.

🍇 **Chardonnay** [shar-don-nay] The great white grape of *Burgundy*, *Champagne* and now just about everywhere else. Capable of fresh simple charm in *Bulgaria* and buttery hazelnutty richness in *Meursault* in the *Côte d'Or*. Given the right chalky soil, in regions like *Chablis*, it can also make wines with an instantly recognisable "mineral" character. In the New World, it tends to produce tropical flavours, partly thanks to warmer climates and partly thanks to the use of clones and cultured yeasts. Almost everywhere, its innate flavour is often married to that of new oak. See regions and producers.

🍷 **Vin de Pays du Charentais** [shar-ron-tay] (*South-West*, France) Competing with its brandy-producing neighbour Gasgogne, this region now makes pleasant light reds and whites. **Blanchard.**

Charmat [shar-mat] The inventor of the *Cuve Close* method of producing cheap fizz. See *Cuve Close*.

🍷 **Ch. des Charmes** [day sharm] (*Ontario,* Canada) Good maker of *Chardonnay*, *Pinot* and *Icewine*. ☆☆☆☆ **1997 Paul Bosc Estate Riesling Icewine £££**

Charta [kahr-tah] (*Rheingau*, Germany) Syndicate formed in the *Rheingau* using an arch as a symbol to indicate (often searingly) dry (*Trocken*) styles designed to be suitable for ageing and drinking with food. Recently reborn with (thankfully) less rigorously dry aspirations, as part of the *VDP.*

🍷 **Chartron & Trébuchet** [shar-tron ay tray-boo-shay] (*Burgundy,* France) Good small merchant specialising in white *Burgundies*.

🍷 **Chassagne-Montrachet** [shah-san mon-rash-shay] (*Burgundy,* France) *Côte de Beaune* commune making grassy, *biscuity*, fresh yet rich whites and mid-weight often rustic-tasting wild fruit reds. Pricey but sometimes less so than neighbouring *Puligny* and as recommendable. White: **85 86 87 88 89 90 92 93 94** 95 96 97 98 .Red: 78 83 **85** 86 87 **88 89 90** 92 93 94 95 96 97 98 98 *Carillon; Marc Colin;* Colin-Déleger; *Jean-Noël Gagnard; Henri Germain, Ch de Maltroye; M Morey; Michel Niellon; J. Pillot;* Roux; *Ramonet.*

🍷 **Ch. Chasse-Spleen** [shas spleen] (*Moulis Cru Bourgeois, Bordeaux,* France) *Cru Bourgeois château* whose wines can, in good years, rival those of many a *Cru Classé*. Went into a slightly dull patch in the 1990s but is now back on form. **70 78 79 81** 82 **83 85 86** 87 88 89 90 **94 95 96 97 98** 99 ☆☆☆☆ **1990 £££**

🍇 **Chasselas** [shas-slah] Widely grown, prolific white grape making light often dull wine principally in Switzerland, eastern France and Germany. Good examples are rare. *Pierre Sparr.*

🍷 **Ch. du Chasseloir** [shas-slwah] (*Loire,* France) Makers of good *domaine Muscadets*. ☆☆☆☆ **1999 Muscadet de Sèvre et Maine Sur Lie ££**

Château [sha-toh] (*Bordeaux,* France) Literally means "castle". Some châteaux are extremely grand, many are merely farmhouses. A building is not required; the term applies to a vineyard or wine estate. Château names cannot be invented, but there are plenty of defunct titles that are used unashamedly by large cooperative wineries to market their members' wines.

🍷 **Château-Chalon** [sha-toh sha-lo'n] (*Jura,* France) Like *Château Grillet,* this is, confusingly, the name of an appellation. Unlike *Château Grillet,* however, here there isn't even a vinous château. The name applies to top flight *Vin Jaune,* the nutty, sherry-like wine which is aged for six years before hitting the market.

� **Châteauneuf-du-Pape** [shah-toh-nurf-doo-pap] (*Rhône*, France) Traditionally the best reds (rich and spicy) and whites (rich and floral) of the southern *Rhône*. Thirteen varieties can be used for the red, though purists favour *Grenache*. 78 81 **83 85 88** 89 90 93 94 95 96 Pierre André; *Ch. de Beaucastel; Beaurenard; Henri Bonneau; Bosquet des Papes; Lucien & André Brunel;* Cabrières; *Chapoutier; la Charbonnière; Clos des Mont-Olivet; Clos des Papes; Delas; Font de Michelle;* Fortia la Gardine; *Guigal; Jaboulet Aîné;* la Mordorée; *La Nerthe;* du Pegaü; *Rayas;* Reserve des Célestins; Tardieu-Laurent; Vieux Télégraphe.

☟ **Jean-Claude Chatelain** [shat-lan] (*Loire*, France) Producer of classy individual *Pouilly-Fumés* and *Sancerre* ✫✫✫✫ 1996 Pouilly-Fume Pilou £££

☟ **Jean-Louis Chave** [sharv] (*Rhône*, France) Gérard Chave and his son Jean-Louis run the best estate in *Hermitage*. These are great wines but they demand patience and are easily overlooked by those looking for richer, more instantly accessible fare. There is a first-class *St. Joseph* too which can be drunk earlier. ✫✫✫✫✫ 1996 Hermitage ££££

☟ **Dom Gérard Chavy** [shah-vee] (*Burgundy*, France) High-quality estate. ✫✫✫✫✫ 1997 Puligny-Montrachet les Charmes ££££

☟ **Chehalem** [sheh-hay-lem] (*Oregon*, US) Top class Yamhill producer of *Pinot Noir, Chardonnay* and *Pinot Gris*, and benefitting from collaborating with the go-ahead Patrice *Rion* from Burgundy.

☟ **Chenas** [shay-nass] (*Burgundy*, France) Good but least well-known of the *Beaujolais Crus*. Daniel Robin, Hubert Lapierre, Bernard Santé and *Duboeuf* make worthy examples.

☟ **Dom. du Chêne** [doo-shehn] (*Rhône*, France) Small estate producing rich ripe *Condrieu* and top-class *St. Joseph*. The best *cuvée* is "Anais". **Chêne** [shehn] (France) Oak, as in *Fûts de Chêne* (oak barrels).

🌿 **Chenin Blanc** [shur-nah-blo'n for France, shen nin blonk elsewhere] Honeyed white grape of the *Loire*. Wines vary from bone-dry to sweet and long-lived. High acidity makes it ideal for sparkling wine, while sweet versions benefit from *noble rot*. French examples are often marred by green unripe flavours and heavy handedness with *sulphur dioxide*. Grown in South Africa (where it is known as *Steen*), in New Zealand (where it is lovingly – and successfully – grown by *Millton*) and Australia (where it is skilfully oaked by *Moondah Brook Steen*). It is generally disappointing in California (but see *Chappellet*). See *Vouvray, Quarts de Chaumes, Bonnezeaux, Saumur.*
Chêne [shayn] (*Loire*, France) Tourist attraction chateau that also produces high quality still and sparkling *Chenin Blanc*.

☟ **Ch. Cheval Blanc** [shuh-vahl blon] (*St. Emilion Premier Grand Cru Classé, Bordeaux*, France) Supreme *St. Emilion* property, unusual in using more *Cabernet Franc* than *Merlot*. 75 76 78 79 80 **81 82 83 85 86** 87 88 89 90 92 93 94 95 96 98 99 ✫✫✫✫ 1995 ££££

♆ Dom. de Chevalier [shuh-val-yay] (*Graves Cru Classé, Bordeaux,* France) Great *Pessac-Léognan* estate which proves itself in difficult years for both red and white. Very fine 1999s Red: **70 78** 79 **81 83** 85 86 87 88 89 90 92 93 94 95 96 98 99 White: **83 85 87** 88 89 90 92 93 94 95 96 98 99 ☆☆☆☆☆ **1996 Blanc, Pessac-Léognan ££££**
   Chevaliers de Tastevin [shuh-val-yay duh tast-van] (*Burgundy,* France) A brotherhood – *confrérie* – based in *Clos de Vougeot,* famed for grand dinners and fancy robes. Wines approved at an annual tasting may carry a special "tasteviné" label.

♆ Cheverny [shuh-vehr-nee] (*Loire,* France) Light floral whites from *Sauvignon* and *Chenin Blanc* and now, under the new "Cour Cheverny" *appellation,* wines made from the limey local *Romarantin* grape. 97 **Caves Bellier; François Cazin; Ch de la Gaudronnière.**

♆ Robert Chevillon [roh-behr shuh-vee-yon] (*Burgundy,* France) Produces long-lived wines. ☆☆☆☆☆ **1996 Nuits-St.-Georges Les Chaignots £££**

♆ Chianti [kee-an-tee] (*Tuscany,* Italy) (*Classico/Putto/Rufina*) *Sangiovese*-dominant, now often *Cabernet*-influenced, *DOCG.* Generally better than pre-1984, when it was customary to add wine from further south, and to put dull white grapes into the vat with the black ones. Wines labelled with the insignia of the *Classico, Putto* or the *Rufina* areas are supposed to be better too, as are wines from *Colli Fiorentini* and *Colli Senesi.* Trusting good producers, however, is a far safer bet. 79 **82, 85, 88, 90, 94,** 95 96 97 98 *Castello di Ama; Antinori; Frescobaldi; Castellare; Castell'in Villa; Isole e Olena; Ruffino; Rocca di Castagnoli; Selvapiana; Castello dei Rampolla; Castello di Volpaia.*

♆ Chiaretto di Bardolino [kee-ahr-reh-toh dee bahr-doh-lee-noh] (*Lombardy,* Italy) Berryish, light reds and rosés from around Lake Garda. **Corte Gardoni; Guerrieri Rizzardi; Nicolis e Figli; Santi; Valleselle-Tinazzi.**

♆ Michele Chiarlo [Mee-Kay-leh kee-Ahr-loh] (*Piedmont,* Italy) Increasingly impressive modern producer of *Barolo, Barbaresco* and *Barbera.* ☆☆☆☆☆ **1996 Barbaresco Rabaja £££**

Chile Rising source of juicy blackcurrant *Cabernet* and (potentially even better) *Merlot, Carmenère, Semillon, Chardonnay. Almaviva; Santa Rita; Casablanca; Carmen; Concha y Toro; Errazuriz; Caliterra; Casa Lapostolle; Montes; Veramonte.*

♆ Chimney Rock (*Stag's Leap District,* California) Producer of serious, fairly priced, *Cabernet.* ☆☆☆☆ **1995 Cabernet Sauvignon £££**

♆ Chinon [shee-non] (*Loire,* France) An *AC* within *Touraine* for (mostly) red wines from the *Cabernet Franc* grape. Excellent and deliciously long-lived from good producers in ripe years; otherwise potentially thin and green. *Olga Raffault* makes one of the best, Otherwise: **Philippe Alliet; Bernard Baudry; Couly-Dutheil; Delauney; Ch. de la Grille;** *Charles Joguet;* **Logis de la Bouchardière.**

♆ Chiroubles [shee-roo-bl] (*Burgundy,* France) Fragrant and early-maturing *Beaujolais Cru,* best expressed by the likes of Bernard Méziat. 85 87 **88 89** 90 **91** 93 94 95 97 98 **Emile Cheyson; Georges Duboeuf; Hubert Lapierre; Alain Passot; Ch de Raousset.**

Chivite [shee-vee-tay] (*Navarra*, Spain) Innovative producer which can outclass many a big name *Rioja bodega*. ☆☆☆ 1998 Gran Feudo Reserva ££

Chorey-lès-Beaune [shaw-ray lay bohn] (*Burgundy*, France) Modest raspberry and damson reds once sold as *Côte de Beaune Villages*, and now appreciated in their own right. 85 87 **88 89 90** 92 93 94 95 96 97 Allexant; Arnoux; Ch. de Chorey; *Drouhin;* Gay; Maillard; *Tollot-Beaut.*

JJ Christoffel [kris-tof-fell] (*Mosel*, Germany) Fine producer of Riesling in Erden and Urzig. ☆☆☆☆☆ 1998 Erdener Treppchen Auslese ££

Churchill (*Douro*, Portugal) Small, dynamic young firm founded by Johnny Graham, whose family once owned a rather bigger *port* house. Unusually good White Port. Red: 82 **85** 91 92 85 96 97 ☆☆☆☆☆ 1996 Aua Alta Vintage Port £££

Chusclan [shoos-klon] (*Rhône*, France) Named village of *Côtes du Rhône* with maybe the best rosé of the area. ☆☆☆☆ 1998 Caves de Chusclan ££

Cinque Terre [chin-kweh-TEH-reh] (*Liguria*, Italy) Traditionally dull, dry and sweet holiday whites. The regional cooperative is making good examples now, however.

Cinsaut/Cinsault [san-soh] Fruity-spicy red grape with high acidity, often blended with *Grenache*. One of 13 permitted varieties of *Châteauneuf-du-Pape*, and also in the blend of *Ch. Musar* in the *Lebanon*. Widely grown in South Africa and Australia.

Cirò [chih-Roh] (*Calabria*, Italy) Thanks to the efforts of pioneering producer Librandi, these southern reds (made from Gaglioppo) and whites (made from Greco) can be well worth buying. ☆☆☆ 1998 Rosso Classico Riserva Duca Sam Felice, Librandi ££

Ch. Cissac [see-sak] (*Haut-Médoc Cru Bourgeois, Bordeaux*, France) Traditional *Cru Bourgeois*, close to *St. Estèphe*, making tough wines that last. Those who dislike *tannin* should stick to ripe vintages. 70 75 78 81 82 83 85 86 88 89 90 93 95 96 97 98 99 ☆☆☆☆ 1990 £££

Ch. Citran [see-tron] (*Haut-Médoc Cru Bourgeois, Bordeaux*, France) Improving – though still not dazzling – *Cru Bourgeois*, thanks to major investment by the Japanese. 82 85 86 87 88 **89 90** 91 92 93 **94 95 96**

Bruno Clair [klehr] (*Burgundy*, France) *Marsannay* estate with good *Fixin, Gevrey-Chambertin, Morey-St.-Denis* (inc. a rare white) and *Savigny*. ☆☆☆☆ 1997 Marsannay Les Vaudenelles £££

Clairet [klehr-ray] (*Bordeaux*, France) The word from which we derived *claret* – originally a very pale-coloured red from *Bordeaux*. Seldom used.

Clairette [klehr-ret] (*Midi*, France) Dull white grape of southern France.

Clairette de Die [klehr-rheht duh dee] (*Rhône*, France) The dry Crémant de Die is unexciting sparkling wine, but the "Méthode Dioise Traditionelle" (previously known as "Tradition") made with *Muscat* is invariably far better; grapey and fresh – like a top-class French *Asti Spumante*. Cave Diose.

Auguste Clape [klap] (*Rhône*, France) Almost certainly the supreme master of *Cornas*. Great, intense, long-lived traditional wines. ☆☆☆☆☆ 1995 Cornas ££££

La Clape [la klap] (*Languedoc-Roussillon,* France) Little-known *cru* within the *Coteaux de Languedoc* with tasty *Carignan* reds and soft, creamy whites.

Clare Valley [klehr] (South Australia) Old slatey soil region enjoying a renaissance with high-quality *Rieslings* that age well, and deep-flavoured *Shiraz, Cabernet* and *Malbec. Tim Adams; Jim Barry; Leo Buring; Grosset; Knappstein; Leasingham; Penfolds; Petaluma; Mitchell; Mount Horrocks; Pike;* Sevenhill; *Wendouree.*

Clarendon Hills (*Blewitt Springs,* South Australia) Self-confident estate which scores highly with US critics who like the ripe intensity and overlook what sometimes strikes me as unwelcome *volatility.* Like some Australians, I'm impressed but (still) not that impressed – and not really ready to pay the price these wines command ☆☆☆☆ **1996 Australis ££££**

Claret [klar-ret] English term for red *Bordeaux.*

Clarete [klah-reh-Tay] (Spain) Term for light red – frowned on by the EU.

Classed Growth (France) Literal translation of *Cru Classé,* commonly used when referring to the status of *Bordeaux châteaux.*

Classico [kla-sih-koh] (Italy) A defined area within a *DOC* identifying what are supposed to be the best vineyards, e.g. *Chianti* Classico, *Valpolicella* Classico.

Henri Clerc et fils [klehr] (*Burgundy,* France) Top-class white *Burgundy* estate. ☆☆☆☆ **1997 Puigny-Montrachet Folatières £££**

Ch. Clerc-Milon [klehr mee-lon] (*Pauillac 5ème Cru Classé, Bordeaux,* France) Juicy member of the *Mouton-Rothschild* stable. 78 81 **82** 83 85 **86** 87 88 89 90 92 93 94 95 96 98 99 ☆☆☆☆ **1993 £££**

Domenico Clerico [doh-meh-nee-koh Klay-ree-koh] (*Piedmont,* Italy) Makes great *Barolo* and *Dolcetto* and Arte, a *Nebbiolo, Barbera* blend. ☆☆☆☆☆ **1995 Barolo Pajana £££**

Climat [klee-mah] (*Burgundy,* France) An individual named vineyard – not always a *Premier Cru.*

Ch. Climens [klee-mons] (*Barsac Premier Cru Classé, Bordeaux,* France) Gorgeous, but delicate *Barsac* which easily outlasts many heftier *Sauternes.* 75 78 79 **80** 81 82 **83** 85 86 88 89 90 95 96 97 98 99 ☆☆☆☆☆ **1998 ££££**

Ch. Clinet [klee-nay] (*Pomerol, Bordeaux,* France) Starry property with lovely, complex, intense wines. 82 83 85 **86** 87 88 89 90 91 92 93 95 96 97 98 99

Clone [klohn] Specific strain of a given grape variety. For example, more than 300 clones of *Pinot Noir* have been identified.

Clos [kloh] (France) Literally, a walled vineyard.

Clos de Gamot [kloh duh gah-moh] (*South West,* France) One of the most reliable producers in *Cahors.*

Ⴈ Clos de la Roche [kloh duh lah rosh] (*Burgundy*, France) One of the most richly reliable *Côte d'Or Grands Crus*. **85 86** 88 89 90 95 97 *Drouhin; Dujac; Faivelay*; Lecheneault; *Leroy*; Perrot-Minot; *Ponsot*; Jean Raphet; Louis Rémy; *Rousseau.*

Ⴈ Clos de Mesnil [kloh duh may-neel] (*Champagne*, France) *Krug's* single vineyard *Champagne* made entirely from *Chardonnay* grown in the Clos de Mesnil vineyard. ☆☆☆☆☆ **1989 ££££**

Ⴈ Clos de Tart [kloh duh tahr] (*Burgundy*, France) *Grand Cru* vineyard in *Morey-St.-Denis*, exclusive to Mommessin. ☆☆☆☆ **1997 ££££**

Ⴈ Clos de Vougeot [kloh duh voo-joh] (*Burgundy*, France) *Grand Cru* vineyard, once a single monastic estate but now divided among more than 70 owners, some of whom are decidedly uncommitted to quality. **Amiot-Servelle; Robert Arnoux; *Bertagna; Bouchard Père et Fils; Champy; Jean-Jacques Confuron; Joseph Drouhin; Engel; Jean Grivot; Anne Gros; Jean Gros; Faiveley; Leroy*; Méo Camuzet; *Mugneret-Gibourg; Jacques Prieur; Prieuré Roch; Jean Raphet; Henri Rebourseau; Dom. Rion*; Ch. de la Tour.**

Ⴈ Ch. Clos des Jacobins [kloh day zha-koh-Ban] (*St. Emilion Grand Cru Classé, Bordeaux*, France) Rich and ripe, if not always very complex .

Ⴈ Clos des Mont-Olivet [kloh day mon-to-lee-vay] (*Rhône*, France) *Châteauneuf-du-Pape* estate with a rare mastery of white wine.

Ⴈ Clos des Papes [kloh day pap] (*Rhône*, France) Producer of serious *Châteauneuf-du-Pape* which – in top vintages – rewards cellaring.

Ⴈ Clos du Bois [kloh doo bwah] (*Sonoma Valley*, California) Top-flight producer whose "Calcaire" *Chardonnay* and Marlstone *Cabernet Merlot* are particularly fine. ☆☆☆☆ **1996 Briarcrest Cabernet Sauvignon £££**

Ⴈ Clos du Ciel [kloh doo see-yel] (*Stellenbosch*, South Africa) Inspiring *Chardonnay* from South African wine critic John Platter.

Ⴈ Clos du Clocher [kloh doo klosh-shay] (*Pomerol, Bordeaux*, France) Reliably rich, plummy wine. 93 **94** 95 **96** 97 98 99 ☆☆☆☆ **1998 £££**

Ⴈ Clos du Marquis [kloh doo mahr-kee] (*St. Julien, Bordeaux*, France) The *second label* of *Léoville-Las-Cases*. 93 94 95 96 97 98

Ⴈ Clos du Roi [kloh doo rwah] (*Burgundy*, France) *Beaune Premier Cru* that is also part of *Corton Grand Cru*. ☆☆☆☆ **1997 Château de Santenay £££**

Ⴈ Clos du Val [kloh doo vahl] (*Napa Valley*, California) Bernard Portet, brother of Dominique who used to run *Taltarni* in Australia, makes stylish *Stag's Leap* reds – including *Cabernet* and *Merlot*. They develop with time. ☆☆☆☆☆ **1997 Stag's Leap Cabernet Sauvignon £££**

Ⴈ Clos l'Eglise [klos lay-gleez] (*Pomerol, Bordeaux*, France) Spicy wines from a consistent small *Pomerol* estate. 83 85 86 88 89 **90 93** 95 96 97 98

Ⴈ Clos Floridène [kloh floh-ree-dehn] (*Graves, Bordeaux*, France) Classy, oaked, white *Graves* made by superstar *Denis Dubourdieu*.

Ⴈ Clos Fourtet [kloh-for-tay] (*Bordeaux*, France) Shifting from one branch of the Lurton family to another, this long-time under-performer is now part of André Lurton's portfolio. Watch this space. **81 82 83 85 86 88 89 90** 93 95 96 97 98 99

Ⴈ Clos Mogador [klohs-fmoh-gah-dor] (*Priorato*, Spain) *René Barbier's* rich, modern, juicy red from Priorato.

Ⴈ Clos Pegase (*Napa*, California) The architectural masterpiece-cum-winery is worth a visit. The wines are less exciting.

Ⴈ Clos René [kloh ruh-nay] (*Pomerol, Bordeaux*, France) Estate making increasingly concentrated though approachable wines.

Ⴈ Clos St.-Landelin [kloh San lon-duhr-lan] (*Alsace*, France) Long-lived wines; the sister label to *Muré*.

  Cloudy Bay (*Marlborough,* New Zealand) Under the same French ownership as *Cape Mentelle*, this cult winery has a waiting list for every vintage of its *Sauvignon* (though the 1999 was less than dazzling). The *Chardonnay* is reliably impressive, as are the rare *late harvest* wines. The *Pelorus* sparkling wine, made by an American winemaker, is less of a buttery mouthful than it used to be.

  Clusel-Roch [kloo-se rosh] (*Rhône,* France) Good, traditional *Côte Rôtie* and *Condrieu* producer. ☆☆☆☆ **1996 Côte Rôtie £££**

  la Clusière [kloo-see-yehr]] (*Bordeaux,* France) Recent, tiny-production (250-300 case) *St Emilion* micro-wine from the new owners of *Ch. Pavie*

  JF Coche-Dury [kosh doo-ree] (*Burgundy,* France) A superstar *Meursault* producer whose basic reds and whites outclass his neighbours' supposedly finer fare. ☆☆☆☆☆ **1997 Meursault £££**

  Cockburn-Smithes [koh burn] (*Douro,* Portugal) Unexceptional Special Reserve but producer of great *vintage* and superlative *tawny port*. 55 60 **63** 67 **70** 75 83 **85** 91 94 97 ☆☆☆☆ **10 Year Old Tawny £££**

  Codorníu [kod-dor-nyoo] (*Catalonia,* Spain) Huge sparkling wine maker whose Anna de Codorníu is good *Chardonnay*-based *Cava*. The Raventos wines are recomendable too, as are the efforts of the *Raimat* subsidiary. The Californian offshoot Codorníu Napa's sparkling wine is *Cava*-ish and dull despite using *Champagne* varieties. The *Pinot Noirs* are more impressive.

  BR Cohn (*Sonoma,* California) A reliable source of Sonoma Valley Cabernet Sauvignon. ☆☆☆☆ **1997 Olive Hill Estate Vineyards Cabernet Sauvignon £££**

  Colchagua Valley [kohl-shah-gwah] (*Central Valley,* Chile) Up-and-coming sub-region. **Bisquertt; *Casa Lapostolle; Undurraga; Los Vascos;***

  Coldstream Hills (*Yarra Valley,* Australia) Founded by lawyer-turned winemaker and wine writer *James Halliday*, now still run by him but in the same stable as *Penfolds*. Stunning *Pinot Noir, Chardonnay,* fine *Cabernets* and *Merlots*. Proof that critics can make as well as break a wine! ☆☆☆☆ **1998 Reserve Pinot Noir £££**

  Colheita [kol-yay-tah] (Portugal) Harvest or vintage – particularly used to describe **tawny port** of a specific year.

  Marc Colin [mahrk koh-lan] (*Burgundy,* France) Family estate with affordable wines from St Aubin and a small chunk of (rather pricier) *Le Montrachet*. ☆☆☆☆ **1997 St.-Aubin En Remilly £££**

  Michel Colin-Deleger [koh-lah day-lay-jay] (*Burgundy,* France) Up-and-coming *Chassagne-Montrachet* estate. ☆☆☆☆☆ **1996 Chassagne-Montrachet Morgeot ££££**

  Collards [kol-lards] (*Auckland,* New Zealand) Small producer of lovely pineappley *Chardonnay* and appley *Chenin Blanc*.

  Collegiata [koh-lay-jee jah-tah] (*Toro,* Spain) Rich, red wine from the *Tempranillo* produced in a little-known region.

  Colle/colli [kol-lay/kol-lee] (Italy) Hill/hills.

Colli Berici [kol-lee bay-ree-chee] (*Veneto*, Italy) Red and white *DOC*.

Colli Orientali del Friuli [kol-lee oh-ree yehn-tah-lee del free-yoo-lee] (*Friuli-Venezia Giulia*, Italy) Lively, single-variety whites and reds from near the *Slovenian* border. Subtle, honeyed and very pricy *Picolit* too.

Colli Piacentini [kol-lee pee-yah-chayn-tee-nee] (*Emiglia-Romagna*, Italy) A very varied *DOC*, covering characterful, off-dry Malvasia sparkling wine and the Bonarda-*Barbera*-based Guttiunio. **Fugazza; la Tosa.**

Vin de Pays des Collines Rhodaniennes [kol-leen roh-dah nee-enn] (*Rhône*, France) The *Vin de Pays* region of the northern *Rhône*, using *Rhône* varieties, *Gamay* and *Merlot*. **St Désirat Cooperative.**

Collio [kol-lee-yoh] (*Friuli-Venezia Giulia*, Italy) High-altitude region with a basketful of white varieties, plus those of *Bordeaux* and red *Burgundy*. Refreshing and often restrained.

Collioure [kol-yoor] (*Midi*, France) Intense *Rhône*-style *Languedoc-Roussillon* red, often marked by the presence of *Mourvèdre* in the blend. **Clos de Paulilles.**

Colombard [kol-om-bahrd] White grape grown in *South-West* France for making into Armagnac and good, light, modern whites by *Yves Grassa* and *Plaimont*. Also planted in Australia (*Primo Estate* and *Best's*) and the US, where it is known as French Colombard.

Jean-Luc Colombo [kol-lom-boh] (*Rhône*, France) Oenologist guru to an impressive number of *Rhône* estates – and producer of his own modern, oaky *Côtes du Rhône* and *Cornas*. ☆☆☆☆ 1996 Cornas Les Ruchets £££

Columbia Crest (*Washington State*, US) *Second label* of *Ch. Ste. Michelle*. ☆☆☆☆ 1996 Reserve Syrah £££

Columbia Winery (*Washington State*, US) Producer of good, fairly priced *Chablis* style *Chardonnay* and *Graves* like *Semillon*, subtle single-vineyard *Cabernet*, especially good *Merlot*, *Syrah* and *Burgundian Pinot Noir*. ☆☆☆☆ 1997 Otis Vineyard Chardonnay ££

Commandaria [com-man-dah-ree-yah] (Cyprus) Traditional dessert wine with rich, raisiny fruit. Now hard to find.

Commune [kom-moon] (France) Small demarcated plot of land named after its principal town or village. Equivalent to an English parish.

Vin de Pays des Comtés Tolosan [kom-tay toh-loh-so'n] (*South West* France) Fast-improving blends of *Bordeaux* and indigenous grapes.

Conca de Barberá [kon-kah deh bahr-beh-rah] (*Catalonia*, Spain) Cool region where *Torres's* impressive Milmanda *Chardonnay* is made.

Viña Concha y Toro [veen-yah kon-chah ee tohr-roh] (*Maipo*, Chile) Steadily improving, thanks to winemaker *Ignacio Recabarren* and investment in *Casablanca*. Best wines are Don Melchior, Marques de Casa Concha, Trio, Casillero del Diablo and *Almaviva*, its joint-venture with *Mouton Rothschild*.

♀ **Condado de Haza** [kon-dah-doh deh hah-thah] (*Ribera del Duero*, Spain) Impressive new venture from the owner of *Pesquera*.

♀ **Conde de Caralt** [kon-day day kah-ralt] (*Catalonia*, Spain) One of the best names in *Cava*. Catch it young.

♀ **Condrieu** [kon-dree-yuhh] (*Rhône*, France) One of the places where actor Gérard Depardieu owns vines. Fabulous, pricy, pure *Viognier*: a cross between dry, white wine and perfume. Far better than the hyped and high-priced *Ch. Grillet* next door. 82 85 **88 89 90** 91 94 95 96 94 98 **Ch. d'Ampuis; Patrick & Christophe Bonneford; Louis Chèze; Gilbert Chirat; Yves Cuilleron;** Pierre Dumazet; **Philippe Faury; Pierre Gaillard; Michel Gerin; Etienne Guigal;** de Monteillet; **Antoine Montez; Robert Niero;** Alain Parent (& Gérard Depardieu); **André Perret;** Phillipe & Christophe Pichon; **Hervé Richard; Georges Vernay;** Francois Villand; Gérard Villano.**

Confréries [kon-fray-ree] (France) Promotional brotherhoods linked to a particular wine or area. Many, however, are nowadays more about pomp and pageantry, kudos and backslapping, than active promotion.

♀ **Jean-Jacques Confuron** [con-foor-ron] (*Burgundy*, France) Go-ahead producer with good *Nuits-St.-Georges, Vosne-Romanée* and *Clos Vougeot*. ☆☆☆☆☆ 1996 Nuits-St.-Georges £££

♀ **Cono Sur** [kon-noh soor] (Chile) *Concha y Toro* subsidiary with a range of varietals including a classy *Pinot Noir* from *Casablanca*. Returning to form after the arrival of a new winemaker (in 1998). The Isla Negra wines are good too. ☆☆☆☆☆ 1998 Zo Barrel Cabernet Sauvignon Reserve ££

♀ **Ch. la Conseillante** [lah kon-say-yont] (*Pomerol, Bordeaux*, France) Brilliant property with lovely, complex, perfumed wines. **70 75** 76 79 **81 82** 83 84 **85** 88 89 90 91 93 94 95 96 97 98

Consejo Regulador [kon-say-hoh ray-goo-lah-dohr] (Spain) Administrative body responsible for *DO* laws.

Consorzio [kon-sohr-zee-yoh] (Italy) Producers' syndicate.

Constantia [kon-stan-tee-yah] (South Africa) The first New World wine region. Until recently, the big name was *Groot Constantia*. Now *Constantia Uitsig, Klein Constantia, Buitenverwachting* and *Steenberg* explain the enduring reputation. ☆☆☆☆☆ 1999 Klein Constantia Sauvignon Blanc ££

♀ **Aldo Conterno** [al-doh kon-tehr-noh] (*Piedmont*, Italy) Truly top-class *Barolo* estate with similarly top-class *Barbera*. Nobody does it better. ☆☆☆☆☆ 1995 Barolo Cicala ££££

♀ **Conterno Fantino** [kon-tehr-noh fan-tee-noh] (*Piedmont*, Italy) Another worthwhile Conterno. ☆☆☆☆ 1995 Barolo Sori Ginestra £££

♀ **Viñedos del Contino** [veen-yay-dos del con-tee-no] (*Rioja*, Spain) CVNE-owned *Rioja* Alavesa estate whose wines can have more fruit and structure than most. ☆☆☆☆ 1989 Rioja Reserva ££

Controliran (Bulgaria) Bulgarian version of *Appellation Contrôlée*

Coonawarra [koon-nah-wah-rah] (*South* Australia) Internationally acknowledged top-class mini-region, stuck in the middle of nowhere, with a cool(ish) climate, terra rossa (red) soil, and a long-brewed controversy over where precisely its boundaries ought to be drawn. (There are nearby "islands" of red soil whose wines have been excluded from the Coonawarra designation). The best Coonawarra reds are great, blackcurranty-minty *Cabernet* Sauvignons and underrated *Shirazes. Whites are less impressive;* big *Chardonnays* and full-bodied *Rieslings. Bowen Estate; Hardy's; Katnook; Lindemans; Mildara; Orlando; Petaluma; Parker Estate; Penfolds; Penley Estate; Ravenswood (Hollick); Rosemount; Rouge Homme; Yalumba; Wynns.*

℞ **Coopers Creek** (*Auckland,* New Zealand) Individualistic whites including a *Chenin-Semillon* blend, *Chardonnay, Sauvignon* and *Riesling*.

℞ **Copertino** [kop-per-tee-noh] (*Apulia,* Italy) Fascinating berryish wine made from the "bitter-black" *Negroamaro*. ☆☆☆☆ 1997 Riserva Cantina Sociale ££

℞ **Corbans** (*Henderson,* New Zealand) Big producer (encompassing *Cooks*) making wines in several regions. Good, rich *Merlot* reds (even, occasionally, from *Marlborough*). ☆☆☆☆ 1997 Cottage Block Marlborough Chardonnay ££

℞ **Corbières** [kawr-byayr] (*Languedoc-Roussillon,* France) Region where a growing number of small estates are now making tasty red wines. Ch. d'Aguilhar; Aiguilloux; Caraguilhes; des Chandelles; Etang des Colombes; Grand Caumont; Hélène de Lastours; *Mont Tauch;* Pech-Latt; Vignerons de la Méditerranée; Meunier St Louis; d'Ornaisons; les Palais du Révérend; St Auriol; St Estève; Celliers St Martin; Salvagnac; Villemajou; *la Voulte Gasparets.*

℞ **Cordon Negro** [kawr-don nay-groh] (*Catalonia,* Spain) Brand name for *Freixenet's* successful *Cava*. The recognisable matte-black bottle and generous marketing must account for sales. Not a sparkling wine I voluntarily drink.

℞ **Corino** [koh-ree-noh] (*Piedmont,* Italy) Up-and-coming winery, winning particular applause for the quality of its Barbera d'Alba.

℞ **Coriole** [koh-ree-ohl] (*McLaren Vale,* Australia) *Shiraz* specialist that has diversified into *Sangiovese*. The *Semillons* and *Rieslings* are pretty good too. ☆☆☆☆ 1997 McLaren Vale Shiraz ££

℞ **Corison** [kaw-ree-son] (*Napa,* California) Winery specialising in juicy *Cabernet*. ☆☆☆☆☆ 1996 Cabernet Sauvignon Napa Valley £££

Corked Unpleasant, musty smell and flavor, caused by (usually invisible) mould in the cork. Affects at least 6% of bottles.

℞ **Cornas** [kaw-re-nas] (*Rhône,* France) Smoky, spicy *Syrah; tannic* when young, but worth keeping. 76 78 82 83 85 88 89 90 91 95 96 97 98 *Thierry Allemand; de Barjac; Chapoutier; Auguste Clape; Jean-Luc Colombo; Courbis; Eric & Joël Durand;* Durvieu; Jaboulet Aîné; *Juge;Jacques Lemercier; Jean Lionnet; Robert Michel; Michel Rochepertuis; de St Pierre; Serette;* Tain Cooperative; *Tardieu-Laurent; Noël Verset; Alain Voge.*

℞ **Fattoria Coroncino** [kawr-ron-chee-noh] (*Marche,* Italy) One of the best producers of *Verdicchio Castello dei Jesi Classico Superiore.*

Corsica (France) Mediterranean island making robust reds, whites and rosés under a raft of *appellations* (doled out generously to assuage rebellious islanders). *Vins de Pays (de l'Ile de Beauté)* are often more interesting.

℞ **Dom. Corsin** [kawr-san] (*Burgundy,* France) Reliable *Pouilly-Fuissé* and *St. Véran* estate. ☆☆☆☆ 1997 Pouilly Fuissé ££

🍇 **Cortese** [kawr-tay-seh] (*Piedmont,* Italy) Herby grape used in *Piedmont* and to make *Gavi.* Drink young.

🍷 **Corton** [kawr-ton] (*Burgundy,* France) *Grand Cru* hill potentially making great, intense, long-lived reds and – as *Corton-Charlemagne* – whites. The supposedly uniformly great vineyards run a suspiciously long way round the hill. Reds can be very difficult to taste young; many never develop. White: **78 85 87 88** 89 **90 92** 95 96 97 98 Red: **78 83 85** 86 87 **88 89 90 92** 95 96 97 98 Bertrand Ambroise; *Bonneau du Martray; Chandon de Briailles; Dubreuil-Fontaine; Faiveley;* Laleur-Piot; *Louis Latour (white); Leroy;* Maillard; Nudant; *Jacques Prieur; Tollot-Beaut; Thomas-Moillard.*

🍷 **Corzano & Paterno** [kawrt-zah-noh eh pah-tehr-noh] (*Tuscany,* Italy) Fine Chianti Colli Fiorentini and Vin Santo.

🍷 **Corvo** [kawr-voh] (*Sicily,* Italy) Brand used by Duca di Salaparuta for its recently re-packaged pleasant reds and whites.

🍷 **Ch. Cos d'Estournel** [koss-des-tawr-nel] (*St. Estèphe 2ème Cru Classé Bordeaux,* France) Recently sold *estate* making top-class wines with *Pauillac* richness and fruit. Spice is the hallmark. **61** 70 **75 76 78** 79 **82 83 85** 86 88 **89** 90 91 92 93 94 95 96 97 98 99

🍷 **Ch. Cos Labory** [koss la-baw-ree] (*St. Estèphe 5ème Cru Classé, Bordeaux,* France) Good, traditional, if tough, wines. 89 90 92 93 95 96 97 98
Cosecha [coh-seh-chah] (Spain) Harvest or *vintage.*

🍷 **Cosentino** (*Napa,* California) Producer of serious, long-lived reds. ☆☆☆☆ 1997 Chardonnay ££££

🍷 **Cossart Gordon** (*Madeira,* Portugal) High-quality brand used by the *Madeira* Wine Co. ☆☆☆☆☆ 5 year old Sercial £££

🍷 **Costanti** (*Tuscany,* Italy) Serious *Brunello di Montalcino* producer with classy, long-lived wines.

Costers del Segre [kos-tehrs del say-greh] (*Catalonia,* Spain) *DO* created for the excellent *Raimat,* whose irrigated vineyards helped to persuade Spain's wine authorities to allow other producers to give thirsty vines a drink. ☆☆☆☆☆ 1994 Raimat Cabernet Sauvignon Réserva £££

Costers de Siurana [kos-tehrs deh see-yoo-rah-nah] (*Priorato,* Spain) One of the stars of *Priorato.* Grape varieties for the Clos de l'Obac include *Syrah, Cabernet* and *Merlot,* plus the local *Garnacha, Cariñena* and *Tempranillo.*

🍷 **Costières de Nîmes** [kos-tee-yehr duh neem] (*Midi,* France) An up-and-coming region whose *Syrah*-based reds can match the best of the Northern Rhône. Ch. de l'Amarine; de Campuget; Dom. des Cantarelles; Mas de Bressades; Ch Mourges du Grès; de Nages; Tuilerie de Pazac; Valcombe.

🍷 **Costières du Gard** [kos-tee-yehr doo gahr] (*South-West,* France) Fruity reds, rarer whites and rosés.

🍇 **Cot** [koh] (France) The grape of *Cahors* and the *Loire* (aka *Malbec*).
🍷 **Cotat Frères** [koh-tah] (*Loire,* France) One of the few *Loire Sauvignon* producers to achieve superstar status in the US. The Cotats' *Sancerres* repay ageing and deserve their success. ☆☆☆☆☆ 1997 La Grande Côte £££

Côte d'Or [koht dor] (*Burgundy,* France) Geographical designation for the finest slopes, encompassing the *Côte de Nuits* and *Côte de Beaune.*

☨ **Côte de Beaune (Villages)** [koht duh bohn] (*Burgundy*, France) The southern half of the *Côte d'Or*. With the suffix *"Villages"*, indicates red wines from one or more of the specified *communes*. Confusingly, wine labelled simply *"Côte de Beaune"* comes from a small area around *Beaune* itself and often tastes like wines of that *appellation*. White: **86 87 88** 89 **90 92 95 96 97 98 99** Red: **78 85 88 89 90 91 92** 95 96 97 98

☨ **Côte de Brouilly** [koht duh broo-yee] (*Burgundy*, France) *Beaujolais Cru*: distinct from *Brouilly* – often finer. Floral and ripely fruity; will keep for a few years. **88 89** 90 **91** 94 95 **96** 97 98 *Duboeuf;* Pivot; **Ch. Thivin.**

☨ **Côte de Nuits (Villages)** [koht duh nwee] (*Burgundy*, France) Northern, and principally "red" end of the *Côte d'Or*. The suffix *"Villages"* indicates wine from one or more specified *communes*.

☨ **Côte Rôtie** [koh troh tee] (*Rhône*, France) Smoky yet refined *Syrah* (possibly with some white *Viognier*) from the northern *Rhône appellation* divided into the "Brune" and "Blonde" hillsides. Most need at least six years. **76 78 80 82 83 85 86 88** 89 90 **91** 95 96 **Ch. d'Ampuis.** *Barge;* Bonnefond; *Burgaud;* Champet; *Cuilleron; Clusel-Roch;* Gallet; *Gasse;* Gentaz-Dervieux; *Gerin; Guigal; Jamet; Jasmin;* Ogier; *Rostaing;* Saugère; L. de Vallouit; *Vernay; Vidal Fleury.*

Côte(s), *Coteaux* [koht] (France) Hillsides.

☨ **Coteaux d'Aix-en-Provence** [koh-toh dayks on prov vons] (*Provence*, France) A recent *AC* region producing light floral whites, fruity reds and dry rosés using *Bordeaux* and *Rhône* varieties. **Château Calissanne; Ch. Revelette; Mas Ste-Berthe; Ch. Vignelaure.**

☨ **Coteaux d'Amazone** [koh-toh dah-mah-zohn] Most of the network of vineyards here have yet to bear fruit; but investment is excitedly piling into the highly costly Dottes-Commes region between the Bay of Biscay and the Alta Vista hills. Freya Hood is planning a hot mail-order wine business here.

☨ **Coteaux d'Ancenis** [koh-toh don-suh-nee] (*Loire*, France) So far, only *VDQS* status for this region near Nantes, producing light reds and deep pinks from the *Cabernet Franc* and *Gamay* and also *Muscadet*-style whites.

☨ **Coteaux d'Ardèche** [koh-toh dahr-desh] (*Rhône*, France) Light country wines, mainly from the *Syrah* and *Chardonnay*. A popular place with *Burgundians* to produce affordable alternatives to their own white wine.

☨ **Coteaux Champenois** [koh-toh shom-puh-nwah] (*Champagne*, France) Over-priced, mostly thin, acidic, still wine. *Laurent Perrier's* is better than most.

☨ **Coteaux du Languedoc** [koh-toh doo long-dok] (*Midi*, France) A big *appellation*, and a source of fast-improving rich reds such as *Pic St Loup*.

☷ **Coteaux du Layon** [koh-toh doo lay-yon] (*Loire*, France) *Chenin Blancs* that are slow to develop and long lived. Lots of lean, dry wine and great, sweet *Bonnezeaux* and *Quarts de Chaume*. Sweet White: **76 83 85 86 88 89** 90 **94** 95 96 97 **98** Perre Aguilas; Patrick Baudoin; Dom. des Baumard; Ch. Pierre Bise; Ch. du Breuil; Cady; Delesvaux; des Forges; Godineau; Guimoniere; Ch la Plaisance; Ch des Rochettes; de la Roulerie; des Sablonettes; Ch Soucherie; la Varière.

PRODUCE OF FRANCE

La vinée **1987** a compo...é 8300 bouteilles cette bouteille porte le No 002932

CLOS DE SAINTE CATHERINE

APPELLATION COTEAUX DU LAYON CONTRÔLÉE

75 cl ... 13% Vol.

Jean Baumard, Propriétaire-Viticulteur, Rochefort-sur-Loire Maine-&-Loire

MISE EN BOUTEILLES A LA PROPRIÉTÉ

☷ **Coteaux du Loir** [koh-toh doo lwahr] (*Loire*, France) Clean, vigorous whites from a *Loire* tributary. 96 97 98

☷ **Coteaux du Lyonnais** [koh-toh doo lee-ohn-nay] (*Rhône*, France) Just to the south of *Beaujolais*, making some very acceptable good-value wines from the same grapes. Descottes; *Duboeuf;* Fayolle; Sain Bel Co-operative.

☷ **Coteaux du Tricastin** [koh-toh doo tris-kass-tan] (*Rhône*, France) Southern *Rhône appellation*, emerging as a source of good-value, peppery-blackcurranty reds. Dom de Grangeneuve; de Rozets; du Vieux Micoulier.

☷ **Coteaux Varois** [koh-toh vahr-rwah] (*Provence*, France) Inexpensive, fruity reds, whites and rosés. Deffends.

☷ **Côtes de/Premières Côtes de Blaye** [koht duh/pruh-myerh koht duh blih] (*Bordeaux*, France) A ferry-ride across the river from *St. Julien*. Poor winemaking prevents many *estates* from living up to their potential. Premières are usually red; Côtes, white. **88 89** 90 **94** 95 96 97 **98** Ch. Bertinerie; Gigault; Haut-Sociondo; les Jonqueyres; Segonzac; des Tourtes.

☷ **Côtes de Bourg** [koht duh boor] (*Bordeaux*, France) Clay-soil region just across the water from the *Médoc* and an increasingly reliable source of good-value, *Merlot*-dominated, plummy reds. Red: 85 86 **88 89** 90 **94** 95 96 97 **98** Brulesécaille; Falfas; Fougas; Guerry; les Jonquières; Maldoror; Repimplet; Robin; Roc-de-Cambes; Rousset; Tayac.

☷ **Côtes de Castillon** [koht duh kass-tee-yon] (*Bordeaux*, France) Region where the *Merlot* is often a lot more lovingly handled than in nearby *St. Emilion*. Ch. d'Aiguilhe; de Belcier; Cap de Faugères; Champ de Mars; Côte Montpezat; Grande Maye; Lapeyronie; de Parenchère; Pitray; Poupille; Robin.

Ⴅ Côtes de Duras [koht duh doo-rahs] (*Bordeaux*, France) Inexpensive *Sauvignons*, often better value than basic *Bordeaux* Blanc. **Amblard; Duras Cooperative; Moulin des Groyes.**

Ⴅ Côtes de Francs [koht duh fron] (*Bordeaux*, France) Up-and-coming region close to *St. Emilion* producing increasingly good reds. **Charmes-Godard; de Francs; la Claverie; la Prade;** *Puygeraud.*

Ⴅ Vin de Pays des Côtes de Gascogne [koht duh gas-koyn] (*South West* France) Armagnac-producing region where dynamic producers *Yves Grassa* and the *Plaimont* cooperative used modern winemaking techniques on grapes that would in the past have been used for brandy. *Ugni Blanc* and *Colombard* are giving way to *Sauvignon Blanc.* **Grassa;** *Plaimont.*

Ⴅ Côtes de Provence [koht dur prov-vonss] (*Provence*, France) Improving, good-value, fruity whites and ripe, spicy reds. The famous rosés, however, are often carelessly made and stored, but holidaymakers rarely notice that the so-called pink wine is a deep shade of bronze and decidedly unrefreshing. A region with as much appeal to organic winemakers as to fans of Mr Mayle's rural tales. **Dom la Bernarde; la Courtade; d'Esclans; Gavoty; de Mireille; Ott; Rabiega; Richeaume.**

Ⴅ Côtes de St. Mont [koht duh san-mon] (*South-West*, France) Large *VDQS* area encompassing the whole of the Armagnac region. *Plaimont* is the largest and best-known producer.

Ⴅ Vin de Pays des Côtes de Tarn [koht duh tarn] (*South-West*, France) Fresh, fruity, simple reds and whites, mostly for drinking *in-situ* rather than outside France. **Labastide-de-Levis Cooperative.**

Ⴅ Vin de Pays des Côtes de Thau [koht duh toh] (*Languedoc-Roussillon*, France) Fresh whites to drink with seafood in the canalside restaurants of *Sète.* **Les Vignerons des Garrigues.**

Ⴅ Vin de Pays des Côtes de Thongue [koht duh tong] (*Languedoc-Roussillon*, France) Up-and-coming region between Béziers and Toulouse where the Domaines d'Arjolle, Condamine, l'Eveque, Teisserenc and Deshenrys are making tasty modern wines.

Ⴅ Côtes du Frontonnais [koht doo fron-ton-nay] (*South-West*, France) Up-and-coming, inexpensive red (and some rosé); fruitily characterful wines. **Ch. Baudare; Bellevue la Forêt; Cave de Fronton; le Roc; Viguerie de Beulaygue**

Ⴅ Côtes du Jura [koht duh joo-rah] (France) *Vin Jaune* and *Vin de Paille* are the styles to look for in this area close to Arbois, as well as sparkling wine and light Poulsard and Trousseau reds and *Ch d'Arlay;* **Jean Bourdy; Couret; Delay.**

Côtes du Marmandais [koht doo mahr-mon-day] (*South-West* France)
Uses the *Bordeaux* red grapes plus *Gamay*, *Syrah* and others to make
pleasant, fruity, inexpensive wines. **Ch. de Beaulieu; Les Vignerons de
Beaupuy; Cave de Cocument**

Côtes du Rhône (Villages) [koht doo rohn] (*Rhône*, France) Spicy reds
mostly from the southern part of the *Rhône* Valley. The best supposedly come
from a set of better *Villages* (and are sold as *CdR Villages*), though some
single *domaine* "simple" *Côtes du Rhônes* outclass many *Villages* wines.
Grenache is the key grape, though recent years have seen a growing use of the
Syrah. Whites, which can include new-wave *Viogniers*, are improving. Red:
89 **90 93 94** 95 96 **97** 98 99 **Dom. de Beaurenard; Cabasse; les Goubert;
Grand Moulas; Guigal;** Richaud; la Soumade; Ste. Anne.

Côtes du Roussillon (Villages) [koht doo roo-see-yon] (*Midi*, France)
Appellation for red, white and rosé of pretty variable quality. *Côtes du
Roussillon Villages* is generally better. **Brial; Força Réal;** *Gauby;* **de Jau;
Vignerons Catalans.**

Côtes du Ventoux [koht doo von-too] (*Rhône*, France) Improving
everyday country reds that are similar to *Côtes du Rhône*. 85 88 89 **90** 94
95 96 97 98 **Jaboulet Aîné;** Pascal; Perrin; *la Vieille Ferme.*

Côtes du Vivarais [koht doo vee-vah-ray] (*Provence*, France) Light
southern *Rhône*-like reds, fruity rosé and fragrant light whites.

Cotesti [kot tesh-tee] (Romania) Easterly vineyards growing varieties such
as *Pinots Noir, Blanc, Gris* and *Merlot*.

Cotnari [kot nah-ree] (Romania) Traditional and now very rare white
dessert wine. Has potential.

Bodegas el Coto [el kot-toh] (*Rioja*, Spain) Small *estate* producing good,
medium-bodied El Coto and Coto de Imaz reds. ☆☆☆ **1994 El Coto
Crianza ££**

Cottin Frères [cot-tah] (*Burgundy*, France) A new name that has been
adopted by the Cottin Brothers who run the dynamic *Nuits-St.-Georges
négociant* firm of *Labouré Roi*. ☆☆☆☆ **1996 Chassagne-Montrachet £££**

Quinta do Côtto [keen-tah doh kot-toh] (*Douro*, Portugal) Ports and
intense, tannic, berryish red wines – labelled as Grande Escolha – produced
in a more southerly part of the Douro river than most other vintage *ports*.

☥ **Coulée de Serrant** [koo-lay duh seh-ron] (*Loire*, France) Great dry *Chenin* from a top property in *Savennières* run by *Nicolas Joly*, a leading champion of "biodynamique" winemaking. The Becherelle vineyard is fine too. ☆☆☆☆ **1998 ££££**

☥ **Paul Coulon et Fils** [Koo-lon] (*Rhône*, France) Serious *Rhône* producer. ☆☆☆☆ **1996 Dom. de Beaurenard, Châteauneuf-du-Pape ££££**

Coulure [koo-loor] Climate-related wine disorder which causes reduced yields (and possibly higher quality) as grapes shrivel and fall off the vine.

☥ **Couly-Dutheil** [koo-lee doo-tay] (*Loire*, France) High-quality *Chinon* from single-vineyards just behind the *château* in which Henry II of England imprisoned his wife, Eleanor of Aquitaine. ☆☆☆☆ **1997 Clos de L'Echo £££**

☥ **Viña Cousiño Macul** [koo-sin-yoh mah-kool] (*Maipo*, Chile) The most traditional producer in Chile. Reds are more successful than whites. ☆☆☆ **1995 Finis Terrae ££**

☥ **Ch. Coutet** [koo-tay] (*Barsac Premier Cru Classé, Bordeaux*, France) Delicate neighbour to *Ch. Climens*, often making comparable wines: Cuvée Madame is top flight. **71 75 76 81 82 83 85 86 87 88 89** 90 95 96 97 98 99

☥ **Ch. Couvent-des-Jacobins** [koo-von day zhah-koh-ban] (*St. Emilion Grand Cru Classé, Bordeaux*, France) Producer of juicy plummy-spicy wines. **82** 83 85 86 88 89 90 **92 93** 94 95 96 98 99 ☆☆☆ **1995 £££**

Cowra [kow-rah] (*New South Wales*, Australia) Up-and-coming region, making a name for itself with *Chardonnay*, for which it will one day eclipse its better known but less viticulturally ideal neighbour, the *Hunter Valley*.

☥ **Dom. de Coyeux** [duh cwah-yuh] (*Rhône*, France) One of the best producers of *Côtes du Rhône* and *Muscat de Beaumes de Venise*.

☥ **Cranswick Estate** (*Riverina, NSW*, Australia) Successful producer making reliable, fairly-priced wines under its own and the Barramundi label and some great *late harvest* whites. ☆☆☆☆ **1996 Botrytis Semillon ££**

☥ **Quinta do Crasto** [kin-tah doh cras-toh] (*Douro*, Portugal) An up-and-coming small port producer with good red table wines too. ☆☆☆☆ **1998 Douro Reserva ££**

☥ **Cream Sherry** (*Jerez*, Spain) Popular style (though not in Spain) produced by sweetening an *oloroso*. A visitor to *Harvey's* apparently preferred one of the company's *sherries* to the then popular "Bristol Milk". "If that's the milk," she joked, "this must be the Cream."

Crémant [kray-mon] (France) Term used in *Champagne*, denoting a slightly sparkling style due to a lower pressure of gas in the bottle. Elsewhere, a term to indicate sparkling wine, e.g. Crémant de *Bourgogne*, de *Loire* and d'*Alsace*.

Crème de Cassis [kraym duh kas-seess] (*Burgundy*, France) Fortified fruit essence perfected in *Burgundy* using blackcurrants from around Dijon. Commonly drunk mixed with sharp local *Aligoté* as *Kir*, or sparkling wine, as *Kir Royale*. Crème de Mûre (blackberries), Framboise (raspberries), Fraise (strawberries) and Pêche (peaches) are also delicious. **Vedrenne**

☥ **Crépy** [kray-pee] (*Savoie*, France) Crisp floral white from *Savoie*.

Criado y Embotellado (por) [kree-yah-doh ee em-bot-tay-yah-doh] (Spain) Grown and bottled (by).

Crianza [kree-yan-thah] (Spain) Literally keeping "con Crianza" means aged in wood – often preferable to the *Reservas* and *Gran Reservas*, which are highly prized by Spaniards but can taste dull and dried-out.

☥ **Crichton Hall** [krih-ton] (*Rutherford*, California) Small winery specialising in top-class *Chardonnay*. ☆☆☆☆ **1997 Merlot £££**

Crisp Fresh, with good *acidity*.

♆ **Ch. le Crock** [lur krok] (*St. Estèphe Cru Bourgeois, Bordeaux,* France) Traditional property which, like *Léoville-Poyferré,* its stablemate, has shown great recent improvement. 82 83 85 86 88 **89** 90 92 93 95 96 98

♆ **Croft** (Spain/Portugal) *Port* and *sherry* producer making highly commercial but rarely memorable wines. The *vintage port* is back on form. 55 60 **63** 66 67 **70** 75 77 82 85 94 97 ☆☆☆☆ **1997 Quinta de Roeda £££**

♆ **Ch. La Croix** [la crwah] (*Pomerol, Bordeaux,* France) Producer of long-lasting traditional wines.

♆ **Ch. la Croix-de-Gay** [la crwah duh gay] (*Pomerol, Bordeaux,* France) Classy *estate* whose complex wines have good, blackcurranty-plummy fruit. 81 **82 83** 85 86 **88** 89 90 91 **92** 93 94 95 96 99

♆ **Ch. Croizet-Bages** [krwah-zay bahzh] (*Pauillac 5ème Cru Classé, Bordeaux,* France) Underperformer showing some signs of improvement. 82 83 85 86 87 88 **90** 92 93 94 95 96 98

♆ **Croser** [kroh-sur] (*Adelaide Hills,* Australia) Made by *Brian Croser* of *Petaluma* in the Piccadilly Valley, this is one of the New World's most *Champagne*-like sparkling wines. ☆☆☆☆ **1996 Brut £££**

🍇 **Crouchen** [kroo-shen] (France) Obscure white grape known as Clare Riesling in Australia and Paarl Riesling in South Africa.

♆ **Crozes-Hermitage** [krohz ehr-mce-tahzh] (*Rhône,* France) Up-and-coming *appellation* in the hills behind supposedly greater *Hermitage.* Smoky, blackberryish reds are pure *Syrah.* Whites (made from *Marsanne* and *Roussanne*) are creamy but less impressive. And they rarely keep. Red: **83 85 88 89 90** 91 95 96 97 98 White: **89 90** 91 94 **95** 96 97 98 *Dom Belle; Chapoutier;* Colombier; *Combier; Delas; Alain Graillot; Paul Jaboulet Aîné;* Dom. du Pavilion-Mercure; Pochon; *Sorrel; Tain l'Hermitage Cooperative.*

Cru Bourgeois [kroo boor-zhwah] (*Bordeaux,* France) Wines beneath the *Crus Classés,* supposedly satisfying certain requirements, which can be good value for money and, in certain cases, better than more prestigious *classed growths.* Since around half the wine in the *Médoc* comes from Crus Bourgeois (and a quarter from *Crus Classés*), don't expect the words to mean too much. *d'Angludet; Beaumont; Chasse-Spleen; Citran; Haut-Marbuzet; Gloria; la Gurgue; Labégorce; Labégorce-Zédé; Marbuzet; Meyney; Monbrison; de Pez; Phélan-Ségur; Pibran; Potensac; Poujeaux; Siran; Sociando-Mallet; la Tour Haut-Caussin.*

Cru Classé [kroo klas-say] (*Bordeaux,* France) The best wines of the *Médoc* are crus classés, split into five categories from first (top) to fifth growth (or *Cru*) for the Great Exhibition in 1855. The *Graves, St. Emilion* and *Sauternes* have their own classifications. Some châteaux make better or worse wines than others of the same classification.

♆ **Weingut Hans Crusius** [hans skroos-yuhs] (*Nahe,* Germany) Family-run *estate* prized for the quality of its highly traditional wines. Some of the best, ripest *Trocken* wines around.

Crusted Port (*Douro,* Portugal) An affordable alternative to *vintage* port – a blend of different years, bottled young and allowed to throw a deposit. *Churchill's;* Graham's; Dow's.

♆ **Yves Cuilleron** [Kwee-yehr-ron] (*Rhône,* France) Rising star producing great (red and white) *St. Joseph* and (sweet and dry) *Condrieu.* ☆☆☆☆ **1997 St. Joseph Blanc £££**

♆ **Cullen** (*Margaret River,* Australia) Brilliant pioneering *estate* showing off the sensitive winemaking skills of Vanya Cullen. Source of stunning *Sauvignon-Semillon* blends, *claret*-like reds, a highly individual *Pinot Noir* and a *Burgundian*-style *Chardonnay.* ☆☆☆☆☆ **1998 Chardonnay £££**

Cultivar [kul-tee-vahr] (South Africa) South African for grape variety.

☫ **Ch. Curé-Bon-la-Madelaine** [koo-ray bon lah mad-layn] (*St. Emilion Grand Cru Classé, Bordeaux,* France) Very small *St. Emilion estate* next to *Ausone.* 78 81 **82** 83 **85** 86 88 **89 90 94** 95 96 97 98

Curico [koo-ree-koh] (Chile) Region in which *Torres, San Pedro* and *Caliterra* have vineyards. Now being eclipsed by *Casablanca* as a source for cool-climate whites, but still one of Chile's best wine areas for red and white. *Caliterra;* Echeverria; la Fortuna; *Montes; Miguel Torres; Valdivieso.*

☫ **Cuvaison Winery** [koo-vay-san] (*Napa Valley,* California) Reliable Swiss-owned winery with high-quality *Carneros Chardonnay,* increasingly approachable *Merlot* and now good *Pinot Noir.* Calistoga Vineyards is a *second label.* ☆☆☆☆ 1997 Pinot Noir Napa Valley Carneros ££

Cuve close [koov klohs] The third-best way of making sparkling wine, in which the wine undergoes secondary fermentation in a tank and is then bottled. Also called the *Charmat* or *Tank method.*

Cuvée (de Prestige) [koo-vay] Most frequently a blend put together in a process called *assemblage.* Prestige *Cuvées* are (particularly in *Champagne*) supposed to be the best a producer has to offer.

☫ **Cuvée Napa** (*Napa,* California) The well-established Californian venture launched by by *Mumm Champagne,* and still offering significantly better quality and value for money than the mother-ship back in France.

☫ **CVNE** [koo-nay] (*Rioja,* Spain) The Compania Vinicola del Norte de Espana (usually referred to as "koo-nay") is a large high-quality operation, run by the owners of *Contino* and producing the excellent Viña Real in *Crianza, Reserva, Imperial* or *Gran Reserva* forms in the best years, as well as a light *CVNE Tinto.* Some recent releases have been slightly less dazzling. ☆☆☆☆ 1995 Rioja Reserva ££

Cyprus Shifting its focus away from making ersatz 'sherry'. Even so, the best wine is still the fortified *Commandaria.*

D

☫ **Didier Dagueneau** [dee-dee-yay dag-guhn-noh] (*Loire,* France) The iconoclastic producer of some of the best steely and oak-aged *Pouilly-Fumé,* and even the occasional *late harvest* effort that upsets the authorities. Look out for the "Pur Sang" (made from rare, ungrafted vines) and "Silex" bottlings. ☆☆☆☆ 1998 Silex £££

☫ **Romano Dal Forno** [roh-mah-noh dal for-noh] (*Veneto,* Italy) Up-and-coming estate for top class Valpolicella (with some particularly good Amarones)

☫ **Ch. Dalem** [dah-lem] (*Fronsac, Bordeaux,* France) Maker of rich full-bodied *Fronsac* that easily matches many a St Emilion. 82 83 **85** 86 88 **89 90** 91 93 95 96 97 98 99

☫ **Dalla Valle** (*Napa,* California) One of the leading lights in the new trend towards Italian flavours, this small winery makes a delicious Super Tuscan lookalike in the shape of the Sangiovese-based Pietre Rosso.

☫ **Dalwhinnie** [dal-win-nee] (*Pyrenees, Victoria,* Australia) Quietly classy producer close to *Taltarni* whose reds and whites are made to last. ☆☆☆☆ 1998 Estate Shiraz £££

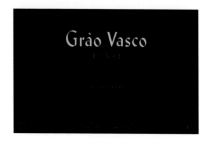

Dão [downg] (Portugal) Once Portugal's best-known region – despite the traditional dullness of its wines. Thanks to pioneering producers like *Sogrape* and *Aliança*, and the introduction of better grape varieties such as the *Touriga Nacional*, both reds and whites are improving. Sogrape's Quinta dos Carvalhais is particularly recommendable. Red: **80 85 88 90 91 93** 94 95 96 97 **98 Boas Quintas; Duque de Viseu; Porta dos Cavaleiros; Quinta dos Roques; Casa de Santar.**

Kurt Darting [koort dahr-ting] (*Pfalz,* Germany) New-wave producer who cares more about ripe flavour than making the tooth-scouringly dry wine favoured by some of his neighbours. Rieslings are terrific, but so are examples of other varieties. Great *late harvest* wines. ☆☆☆☆ **1998 Pfalz Dürkheimer Michelsberg Riesling Spätlese ££**

Ch. Dassault [das-soh] (*St. Emilion Grand Cru Classé, Bordeaux,* France) Named after the producer of France's fighter planes, this is good, juicy *St. Emilion.* 82 83 **85** 86 88 89 **90** 92 93 94 95 96 97 98

Ch. de la Dauphine [duh lah doh-feen] (*Fronsac, Bordeaux,* France) Proof that *Fronsac* really did deserve its reputation in the days when it was better-regarded than *St. Emilion.* **85** 86 87 88 **89 90** 92 93 94 95 96 97 98 99

Domaine d'Auvenay [Dohv-nay] (*Burgundy,* France) *Estate* belonging to Lalou Bize Leroy, former co-owner of the *Dom. de la Romanée-Conti,* and now at *Dom. Leroy.* Great, if pricy, long-lived, examples of *Auxey-Duresses, Meursault, Puligny-Montrachet* and *Grands Crus of the Côtes de Nuits.*

René and Vincent Dauvissat [doh-vee-sah] (*Burgundy,* France) One of the best *estates* in *Chablis.* Watch for other Dauvissats though, the name is also used by the *La Chablisienne* cooperative. ☆☆☆☆ 1997 **Chablis les Preuses ££**

Ch. Dauzac [doh-zak] (*Margaux 5ème Cru Classé, Bordeaux,* France) Rejuvenated, following its purchase in 1993 by André Lurton of *Ch. la Louvière.* **82 83 85** 86 **88 89 90** 93 94 95 96 97 98.

Dealul Mare [day-al-ool mah-ray] (Romania) Carpathian region once known for whites, now producing surprisingly good *Pinot Noir.*

Etienne & Daniel Defaix [duh-fay] (*Burgundy,* France) Classy traditional *Chablis* producer, making long-lived wines with a steely bite. ☆☆☆ **1997 Chablis Vieilles Vignes ££**
Dégorgée (dégorgement) [day-gor-jay] The removal of the deposit of inert yeasts from *Champagne* after maturation.

Dehlinger (*Sonoma,* California) *Russian River Pinot Noir* and *Chardonnay* specialist (with some great single-vineyard examples) that is proving highly successful with *Syrah* and *Cabernet Sauvignon.* ☆☆☆☆ **1996 Russian River Valley Chardonnay ££**

Deidesheim [di-dess-hime] (*Pfalz,* Germany) Distinguished wine town noted for flavoursome *Rieslings.* QbA/Kab/Spät: **85 86 88 89 90** 91 92 93 94 95 96 97 98 Aus/Beeren/Tba: **83 85** 88 89 90 91 92 93 94 95 96 97 98 *Bassermann-Jordan; Josef Biffar; Reichsrat von Buhl; JL Wolf.*

Ⓣ **Deinhard** [dine-hard] (*Mosel,* Germany) See *Wegeler Deinhard.*

Ⓣ **Marcel Deiss** [dise] (*Alsace,* France) Tiny property producing some of the best wine in the region, including some unusually good *Pinot Noir.* ☆☆☆☆☆ 1997 Riesling Altenberg de Bergheim ££££

Ⓣ **Delaforce** [del-lah-forss] (*Douro,* Portugal) Small *port* house with lightish but good *vintage* and *tawny.* 58 60 **63 66** 70 74 75 77 85 94 97 ☆☆☆ 1995 Quinta da Corte Vintage Port £££

Ⓣ **Delas Frères** [del-las] (*Rhône,* France) *Négociant* with great *Hermitage* vineyards and now promising much since its purchase by *Louis Roederer.* ☆☆☆ 1997 Côte Rôtie Seigneur de Maugiron £££

Ⓣ **Delatite** [del-la-tite] (*Victoria,* Australia) Producer of lean-structured, long-lived wines. ☆☆☆☆ 1998 Dead Man's Hill Gewürztraminer ££

Ⓣ **Delbeck** [del-bek] (*Champagne,* France) Underrated little producer, whose wines are strongly *Pinot*-influenced.

Ⓣ **Delegats** [del-leg-gats] (*Auckland,* New Zealand) Family firm which has hit its stride recently with impressively (for New Zealand) ripe reds, especially plummy *Merlots.* The *second label* is "*Oyster Bay*". ☆☆☆☆ 1998 Hawke's Bay Reserve Chardonnay £££

Ⓣ **Philippe Delesvaux** [Dels-voh] (*Loire,* France) Quality-conscious *Coteaux de Layon* estate with some good red too.

Ⓣ **Delheim Wines** [del-hihm] (*Stellenbosch,* South Africa) A commercial *estate* with lean, quite traditional reds and white. ☆☆☆☆ 1999 Pinotage ££

Ⓣ **DeLille Cellars** (*Washington State,* US) A small producer of very classy Bordeaux-style reds and whites under this and the Chaleur Estate labels.

Ⓣ **André Delorme** [del-lorm] (*Burgundy,* France) Little-known négociant based in the Côte Chalonnaise and specialising in sparkling wines. *Demi-sec* [duh-mee sek] (France) Medium-dry.

Ⓣ **Demoiselle** [duh-mwah-zel] (*Champagne,* France). A new *Champagne* name to watch with attractive, light, creamy wines.

Ⓣ **Denbies Wine Estate** [den-bees] (*Surrey,* England) Part tourist attraction, part winery, the largest wine *estate* England has so far produced. Sweet wines are the best of the batch so far. ☆☆☆☆ Special Late Harvest £££ *Deutscher Tafelwein* [doyt-shur tah-fuhl-vihn] (Germany) Table wine, guaranteed German as opposed to Germanic-style EC *Tafelwein.* Can be good value – and often no worse than *Qualitätswein,* the supposedly "quality" wine designation that includes every bottle of *Liebfraumilch.* *Deutsches Weinsiegel* [doyt-shus vihn-see-gel] (Germany) Seals of various colours – usually neck labels – awarded for merit to German wines. Treat with circumspection.

Ⓣ **Deutz** [duhtz] (*Champagne,* France, and also Spain, New Zealand, California) Reliable small but dynamic producer at home and abroad, now owned by *Roederer.* The *Montana Marlborough* Cuvée from New Zealand was created with the assistance of *Deutz,* as was the *Yalumba "D"* in Australia. Maison Deutz is a 150-acre cool-climate vineyard joint venture in California with Nestlé and *Deutz* where unusually, a bit of *Pinot Blanc* goes into the – generally – excellent blend. The *Cuvée William Deutz* is the star wine.

Ⓣ **Devaux** [duh-voh] (*Champagne,* France) Small producer with a knack of producing fairly-priced wine and unusually good rosé and *Blanc de Noirs.*

Dézaley [days-lay] (*Vaud,* Switzerland) One of the few places in the world where the Chasselas (here called the *Dorin*) makes decent wine.

Diabetiker Wein [dee-ah-beh-ti-ker vihn] (Germany) Very dry wine with most of the sugar fermented out (as in a Diat lager); suitable for diabetics, but daunting for others.

⚺ Diamond Creek (*Napa Valley,* California) Big Name producer with a set of very good vineyards (Gravelly Meadow, Red Rock Terrace and Volcanic Hill) that produce toughly intense red wines which demand, but don't always repay, patience. ☆☆☆☆ **1995 Cabernet Sauvignon Volcanic Hill ££££**

Schlossgut Diel [shloss-goot deel] (*Nahe,* Germany) Wine writer Armin Diel makes sublime dry and sweet Rieslings as well as some pioneering oaked Rülander and Weissburgunder.

⚺ Dieu Donné Vineyards [dyur don-nay] (*Franschhoek,* South Africa) Variable producer of quality varietals in the Franschhoek valley. The 1992 *Chardonnay* was legendary. ☆☆☆☆ **1998 Merlot £££**

⚺ Dom. Disznókó [diss-noh-koh] (*Tokaji,* Hungary) Newly-constituted *estate* belonging to *AXA* and run by Jean-Michel Cazes of *Ch. Lynch-Bages.* Top-class modern sweet *Tokaji* and dry lemony *Furmint.* ☆☆☆☆☆ **1993 Tokaji Aszu 6 Puttonyos £££**

DLG (Deutsche Landwirtschaft Gesellschaft) (Germany) Body awarding medals for excellence to German wines – far too generously.

DO Denominac/ion/ão de Origen (Spain, Portugal) Demarcated quality area, guaranteeing origin, grape varieties and production standards (everything, in other words except the quality of the stuff in the bottle).

⚺ DOC Denominación de Origem Controlada (Portugal) Replacing the old RD (Região Demarcada) as Portugal's equivalent of Italy's *DOCG.*

DOC Denominacion de Origen Califacada (Spain) Ludicrously, and confusingly, Spain's recently launched higher quality equivalent to Italy's *DOCG* shares the same initials as Italy's lower quality *DOC* wines. So far, restricted to *Rioja* – good, bad and indifferent. In other words, this official designation should be treated – like Italy's *DOCs* and *DOCGs* and France's *Appellation Contrôlée* – with something less than total respect.

DOC(G) Denominazione di Origine Controllata (e Garantita) (Italy) Quality control designation based on grape variety and/or origin. "Garantita" is supposed to imply a higher quality level, but all too often it does no such thing and has more to do with regional politics than with tasty wines. It is worth noting, that, while the generally dull wines of *Albana di Romagna* received the first white *DOCG* (ahead of all sorts of more worthy candidates), the new efforts to bring *Vini da Tavola* into the system left such internationally applauded wines as *Tignanello* out in the cold among the most basic *DOCs.*

⚺ Ch. Doisy-Daëne [dwah-zee di-yen] (*Barsac 2ème Cru Classé, Bordeaux,* France) Fine *Barsac* property whose wines are typically more restrained than many a *Sauternes.* The top wine is L'Extravagance. **76** 78 79 81 82 83 85 86 **88 89 90** 91 94 95 96 97 98

⚺ Ch. Doisy-Dubroca [dwah-zee doo-brohkah] (*Barsac 2ème Cru Classé, Bordeaux,* France) Underrated *estate* producing ultra-rich wines at often attractively low prices. **75** 76 78 79 **81 83** 85 86 87 88 89 90 95 96 97 98

⚺ Ch. Doisy-Védrines [dwah-zee vay-dreen] (*Barsac 2ème Cru Classé, Bordeaux,* France) Reliable *Barsac* property which made a stunningly concentrated 1989 (and a less impressive 1990). 70 **75 76** 78 79 81 **82 83** 85 86 **88** 89 90 92 93 95 96 97 98 99

🍇 **Dolcetto** (d'Alba, di Ovada) [dohl-cheh-toh] (*Piedmont,* Italy) Grape producing anything from soft everyday red to very robust and long-lasting examples. Generally worth catching quite young though. *Bests* use it to good effect in Australia *Bava; Aldo Conterno;* **Cortese;** *Vajra.*

Dôle [Dohl] (Switzerland) *Appellation* of *Valais* producing attractive reds from *Pinot Noir* and/or *Gamay* grapes. **Germanier.**

Ⅰ **Dom Pérignon** [dom peh-reen-yon] (*Champagne,* France) *Moët et Chandon's Prestige Cuvée,* named after the cellarmaster who is erroneously said to have invented the *Champagne* method. Impeccable white and (rare) rosé. (*Moët* will disgorge older *vintages* to order.) ☆☆☆☆ 1992 ££££
Domaine (Dom.) [doh-mayn] (France) Wine estate.

Ⅰ **Domecq** [doh-mek] (*Jerez/Rioja,* Spain) Producer of (disappointing) *La Ina Fino* and the rare, wonderful *511A Amontillado* and Sibarita *Palo Cortado.*

Ⅰ **Ch. la Dominique** [lah doh-mee-neek] (*St. Emilion Grand Cru Classé, Bordeaux,* France) High-flying property; one of the finest in *St. Emilion.* 70 **71** 78 79 81 **82** 83 **86** 88 89 90 93 94 95 96 97 98 99

Ⅰ **Dominus** [dahm-ih-nuhs] (*Napa Valley,* California) *Christian Moueix* of *Ch. Petrus's* modestly named competitor to *Opus One* has now developed an accessibility that was lacking in early years. Even so, it is concentrated stuff that is built to last. ☆☆☆☆☆ 1996 ££££

Ⅰ **Hermann Dönnhoff** (*Nahe,* Germany) Brilliant winemaker who crafts great *late harvest* wine and *Eiswein* from his Hermannshöhle vineyard.

Ⅰ **Doonkuna** [doon-koo-nah] (*New South Wales,* Australia) Small winery making decent red wine close to the capital. ☆☆☆☆ 1992 Shiraz ££

Ⅰ **Dopff "Au Moulin"** [dop-foh-moo-lan] (*Alsace,* France) *Négociant* with concentrated *Grand Crus.* ☆☆☆☆ 1996 Riesling Riquewihr £££

Ⅰ **Dopff & Irion** [dop-fay-ee-ree-yon] (*Alsace,* France) Greatly improved; not to be confused with Dopff "Au Moulin", its namesake. ☆☆☆ 1997 Riesling Schoenenbourg £££

Ⅰ **Vin de Pays de la Dordogne** [dor-doyn] (*South West,* France) To the East of *Bordeaux,* this improving region offers light *Bordeaux*-style wines.

Ⅰ **Girolamo Dorigo** [Jee-roh-lah-moh doh-ree-goh] (*Friuli-Venezia Giulia,* Italy) Classy Collio Orientali del Friuli producer with good reds (made from grapes such as the local Pignolo and *Refosco*) and even more impressive whites including a *Chardonnay, Verduzzo* and Picolit

🍇 **Dorin** [doh-ran] (*Vaud,* Switzerland) The Swiss name for *Chasselas* in the *Vaud* region.

🍇 **Dornfelder** [dorn-fel-duh] (Germany) Sadly underrated early-ripening, juicy, berryish grape which is beginning to attract some interest among pioneering winemakers in the southern part of Germany.
Dosage [doh-sazh] The addition of sweetening syrup to naturally dry *Champagne* after *dégorgement* to replace the wine lost with the yeast, and to set the sugar to the desired level (even *Brut Champagne* requires up to four grammes per litre of sugar to make it palatable).

Douro [doo-roh] (Portugal) The *port* region and river, with increasingly good table wines thanks to the efforts of the long-established *Barca Velha, Quinta do Cotto (Grande Escolha), Sogrape,* and Australians *David Baverstock* and *Peter Bright.* Port house *Ramos Pinto's* Duas Quintas wines are good too. ☆☆☆☆ 1996 Ferreirinha, Quinta da Leda £££

Dourthe [doort] (*Bordeaux,* France) Dynamic négociant whose Dourthe No.1 offers unusually reliable red and – particularly white Bordeaux.
Doux [doo] (France) Sweet.

Dow [dow] (*Douro*, Portugal) One of the big two (with *Taylor's*) and under the same family ownership as *Warre, Smith Woodhouse* and *Graham*. Great *vintage port* and similarly impressive *tawny*. The *single-quinta* Quinta do Bomfim wines offer a chance to taste the Dow's style affordably. 63 66 70 72 75 77 85 91 94 97 ☆☆☆☆ 1995 Quinta do Bomfim Vintage Port £££

Drappier [drap-pee-yay] (*Champagne*, France) Small, reliably recommendable producer. ☆☆☆☆☆ 1995 Champagne Cuvée du Millenaire £££

Jean-Paul Droin [drwan] (*Burgundy*, France) Good, small *Chablis* producer with approachable "modern" wines. ☆☆☆ 1996 Chablis Grand Cru Les Clos £££

Dromana Estate [droh-mah-nah] (*Mornington Peninsula*, Australia) Viticulturalist Gary Crittenden makes good, if light, *Chardonnay* and raspberryish *Pinot Noir*, as well as an impressive range of Italian varietals sold under the "I" label.

Domaine Drouhin [droo-an] (*Oregon*, US) Top *Burgundy* producer's highly expensive investment in the US that's increasingly producing world-beating reds – thanks to Veronique Drouhin's skill and commitment and some of *Oregon's* best vineyards. ☆☆☆☆ 1997 Pinot Noir ££££

Joseph Drouhin [droo-an] (*Burgundy*, France) Probably *Burgundy's* best *négociant*, with first-class red and white wines that are unusually representative of their particular *appellations*. Also look out for the rare white *Beaune* from its own Clos des Mouches, top-class *Clos de Vougeot* and unusually (for a *négociant*) high-quality *Chablis*. The Marquis de Laguiche *Montrachet* is sublime. ☆☆☆☆☆ 1997 Beaune Clos des Mouches £££

Pierre-Jacques Druet [droo-ay] (*Loire*, France) Wonderfully reliable *Bourgueil* producer making characterful individual cuvées. ☆☆☆☆ 1996 Grand Mont £££

Dry Creek (*Sonoma*, California) A rare example of a Californian *AVA* region whose wines have an identifiable quality and style. Look out for *Sauvignon Blanc* and *Zinfandel*. Red: 84 85 86 87 90 91 92 93 95 96 97 98 White: 85 90 91 92 95 96 97 98. *Beaulieu Vineyard; Collier Falls; Dry Creek; Duxoup; Gallo Sonoma; Nalle; Quivira; Rabbit Ridge; Rafanell; Turley.*

Dry Creek Vineyard (*Sonoma*, California) Eponymous vineyard within the *Dry Creek AVA* making well-known *Fumé Blanc*, great *Chenin Blanc* and impressive reds. ☆☆☆☆☆ 1997 Heritage Clone Zinfandel £££

Dry River (*Martinborough*, New Zealand) Small *estate* with particularly impressive *Pinot Noir* and *Pinot Gris* and a delicious line in *late harvest* wines. ☆☆☆☆☆ 1998 Gewürztraminer £££

Duboeuf [doo-burf] (*Burgundy,* France) The "King of *Beaujolais*", who introduced the world to the penny candy flavour of young *Gamay.* Offers a range of good examples from individual growers, vineyards and villages. Reliable *nouveau,* good straightforward *Mâconnais* white, single *domaine Rhônes* and now the world's biggest plantation of *Viognier.* (Though this last style needs more work before it's really recommendable).

Dubreuil-Fontaine [doo-broy fon-tayn] (*Burgundy,* France) Quite traditional *estate,* producing full-flavoured red and white individual cuvées from the *Corton* hillsides. ☆☆☆☆☆ **1997 Pernand Vergelesses Blanc £££**

Duckhorn (*Napa Valley,* California) Once the producer of dauntingly tough Merlot, Duckhorn is now making deliciously approachable examples of this and other varieties. ☆☆☆☆ **1997 Napa Valley Merlot £££**

Ch. Ducru-Beaucaillou [doo-kroo boh-ki-yoo] (*St. Julien 2ème Cru Classé, Bordeaux,* France) *"Super Second"* with a decidedly less obvious style than peers such as *Léoville-Las-Cases* and *Pichon-Lalande.* Especially back on form in 1996, 1997 and (brilliantly in) 1998 and 1999 after a disappointing patch in the late 1980s and early 1990s. Second wine is Croix-Beaucaillou. **70 75 76 78 79 80 81 82 83 85** 86 87 88 89 90 91 **93** 95 96 97 98 99

Dom. Bernard Dugat-Py [doo-gah pee] (*Burgundy,* France) Superstar *Gevrey-Chambertin estate* with great vineyards, from which M. Dugat makes delicious and unusually fairly priced wines *Grand Cru* ☆☆☆☆☆ **1997 Gevrey-Chambertin Lavaux St-Jacques £££**

Ch. Duhart-Milon-Rothschild [doo-ahr mee-lon rot-sheeld] (*Pauillac 4ème Cru Classé, Bordeaux,* France) Under the same management as *Lafite* and benefiting from heavy investment. 78 79 80 81 **82** 83 **85** 86 87 88 89 90 91 92 93 95 96 97 98 99

Dom. Dujac [doo-zhak] (*Burgundy,* France) Cult *Burgundy* producer Jacques Seysses makes fine, long-lived and quite modern wines from *Morey-St.-Denis,* (including a particularly good *Clos de la Roche*) that are packed with intense *Pinot Noir* flavour. Now helped by Gary Farr of the excellent *Bannockburn* in Australia and busily investing time and effort into vineyards in southern France. ☆☆☆☆☆ **1997 Clos de la Roche ££££**

Dulong [doo-long] (*Bordeaux,* France) Reliable negociant which has broken ranks – and shocked some of its neighbours – by producing *International Wine Challenge* medal-winning multi-regional Vin de Table blends under the "Rebelle" label.

Dumb As in dumb nose, meaning without smell.

Dunn Vineyards (*Napa Valley,* California) Randy Dunn makes tough, forbidding *Cabernets* from *Howell Mountain* for patient collectors. Give them time, though; eventually, they yield extraordinary spicy, berryish flavours. ☆☆☆☆☆ **1995 Cabernet Sauvignon Howell Mountain ££££**

Durbach [door-bahk] (*Baden,* Germany) Top vineyard area of this *Anbaugebiet.* **Wolf-Metternich.**

Ch. Durfort-Vivens [door-for vee-va'ns] (*Margaux 2ème Cru Classé, Bordeaux,* France) Never really starry, but sometimes very classic, elegant wine from the owners of Ch. *Brane-Cantenac.* Recent vintages show decided improvement. 78 79 81 **82** 83 **85** 86 87 88 89 90 91 93 95 96 97 98 99

Durif [dyoor-if] See *Petite Sirah.*

Jean Durup [doo-roop] (*Burgundy,* France) Modern *estate* whose owner controversially believes in extending vineyards of *Chablis* into what some claim to be less distinguished soil, and not using new oak. Wines are good rather than great. The best are sold as Ch. de Maligny. ☆☆☆ **1996 Chablis Vieilles Vignes ££**

�‌ **Duval-Leroy** [doo-val luh-rwah] (*Champagne,* France) Finally beginning to develop a reputation for itself outside France, Duval-Leroy was previously highly popular among retailers and restaurateurs to whom it supplied excellent own-label wines. Fleur de Champagne and Cuvée des Rois are worth looking out for.

�‌ **Duxoup Wine Works** [duk-soop] (*Sonoma Valley,* California) Inspired winery-in-a-shed, producing very good characterful *Charbono* and fine *Syrah* from bought-in grapes.

E

�‌ **E&E** (*Barossa,* South Australia) Top wine produced by *Barossa Valley Estate.*

�‌ **Maurice Ecard** [Ay-car] (*Burgundy,* France) Very recommendable *Savigny-lès-Beaune* estate with good *Premier Cru* vineyards. ✩✩✩✩ **1997 Savigny-les-Beaune les Peuillets £££**

�‌ **Echeverria** [eh-che-veh-ree-yah] (*Maule,* Chile) Impressive Curico producer with good *Cabernets, Chardonnays* and *Sauvignon Blancs.*

�‌ **Echézeaux** [ay-shuh-zoh] (*Burgundy,* France) *Grand Cru* between *Clos de Vougeot* and *Vosne-Romanée* and more or less an extension of the latter *commune. Flagey-Echézeaux,* a village on the relatively vineless side of the Route Nationale, takes its name from the "flagellation" used by the peasants to gather corn in the 6th century. *Grands-Echézeaux* should be finer. **Dom. de la Romanée-Conti; Henri Jayer; Dom. Dujac; Dom. Thierry Vigst.**

L'Ecole Nº 41
1997
Walla Walla Valley
CABERNET SAUVIGNON

�‌ **L' Ecole No. 41** [ay-kohl] (*Washington State,* US) Superlative producer of classy *Chardonnay* and *Merlot.* as well as some lovely rich *Semillon.* ✩✩✩✩ **1996 Cabernet Sauvignon ££££**

Edelfäule [ay-del-fow-luh] (Germany) *Botrytis cinerea,* or *"noble rot".*

Edelzwicker [ay-del-zwik-kur] (*Alsace,* France) Generic name for a blend of grapes. The idea of blends is coming back – but not the name (see *Hugel*).

�‌ **Edmunds St. John** (*Alameda,* California) Producer with his heart in the *Rhône* – and a taste for rich, spicy *Syrah* and *Zinfandel* reds. ✩✩✩✩✩ **1995 Durell Vineyard Syrah ££££**

�‌ **Edna Valley Vineyard** (California) Long-standing maker of rich, buttery *Chardonnay* in the *AVA* of the same name. In the same stable as *Chalone, Carmenet* and *Acacia* and now in an ambitious joint Californian venture with *Penfolds.*

Eger [eg-gur] (Hungary) Region of Hungary where *Bull's Blood* is made.

Dom. de l'Eglise [duh lay glees] (*Pomerol, Bordeaux,* France) Fairly priced, mid-range, wines.**79 82** 83 85 86 88 89 90 95 96 97 98

Ch. l'Eglise-Clinet [Lay gleez klee-nay] (*Pomerol, Bordeaux,* France) Terrific tiny estate that has gained – and earned – recent superstar status. 70 71 75 76 78 **79** 81 82 83 85 86 **88** 89 **90** 91 92 93 **94** 95 96 97 98 99 ☆☆☆☆☆ 1995 ££££

Egri Bikaver [eh-grih bih-kah vehr] (*Eger,* Hungary) See *Bull's Blood.*

Cave Vinicole d'Eguisheim [Eh-gees-hime] (*Alsace,* France) One of the most dynamic cooperatives in Alsace, with a range of grand cru vineyards (including Hengst and Speigel) and alternative brands: *Wolfberger* and Willm. Look for the Sigillé wines.

Eiswein / Eiswein [ihs-vihn] (Germany/Austria/Canada) Ultra-concentrated *late harvest* wine, made from grapes naturally frozen on the vine and often picked a long time after the rest of the crop. (Some German vintages are harvested in the January of the following year!). Hard to make (and consequently very pricey) in Germany but much easier and more affordable in *Canada.* Unlike other top quality sweet wines, Eiswein does not rely on *noble rot.* In fact, this characteristic is normally absent because winemakers need frozen grapes in a perfect state.

Eitelsbach [ih-tel-sbahk] (*Mosel,* Germany) One of the top two *Ruwer* wine towns, and the site of the famed Karthäuserhofberg vineyard.

Elaborado y Anejado Por [ay-lah-boh-rah-doh ee anay-hahdo pohr] (Spain) "Made and aged for".

Elderton (*Barossa Valley,* Australia) Highly commercial maker of big, rich, competition-winning wines, especially *Shiraz* and *Cabernet.*

Elever/éleveur [ay-leh-vay/ay-leh-vuhr] To mature or "nurture" wine, especially in the cellars of the *Burgundy négociant*s, who act as éléveurs after traditionally buying in wine made by small estates.

Elgin [el-gin] (South Africa) Coolish – *Burgundy*-like – apple-growing country which is increasingly attracting the interest of big wine producers. Watch out for the Paul Cluver reds and whites from *Neil Ellis.* May eventually overshadow all but the best parts of *Stellenbosch* and *Paarl.*

Neil Ellis (*Stellenbosch,* South Africa) New-wave Cape winemaker – and a pioneer of the new region of *Elgin.* ☆☆☆ 1999 Sauvignon Blanc ££

Eltville [elt-vil] (*Rheingau,* Germany) Town housing the *Rheingau* state cellars and the German Wine Academy, producing good *Riesling* with backbone. QbA/Kab/Spät: **85** 86 **88 89 90** 91 **92 93 94** 95 96 97 98 Aus/Beeren/Tba: **83 85 88 89 90** 91 92 93 94 95 96 97 98

Elyse Wine Cellars (*Napa,* California) *Zinfandel* specialist with *Howell Mountain vineyards.* Look out for the fine Cabernet and a Nero Misto spicy *Zinfandel-Petite Sirah* blend. ☆☆☆☆☆ 1997 Morisoli Zinfandel £££

Emilia-Romagna [eh-mee-lee-yah roh-ma-nya] (Italy) Region around Bologna best known for *Lambrusco*; also the source of *Albana, Sangiovese* di Romagna and *Pagadebit.*

Enate [eh-nah-tay] (*Somontano,* Spain) Dynamic modern winery specialising in varietals, including particularly successful Chardonnays. ☆☆☆ 1999 Rosado ££

En primeur [on pree-muh] New wine, usually *Bordeaux*. Producers and specialist merchants buy and offer wine *en primeur* before it has been released. In the US and Australia, where producers like *Mondavi* and *Petaluma* are selling their wine in this way, the process is known as buying "futures".

☙ **Ch. l'Enclos** [lon kloh] (*Pomerol, Bordeaux*, France) Gorgeously rich, fairly priced wines. 79 **82** 83 85 86 88 **89** 90 91 92 93 94 95 96 97 98.

☙ **René Engel** [On-jel] (*Burgundy*, France) Producer of rich, long-lived wines in *Vosne-Romanée* and *Clos Vougeot*. ☆☆☆☆☆ 1996 Echézeaux ££££

English wine Quality has improved in recent years, as winemakers have moved from making semi-sweet, mock-Germanic to dry mock-*Loire* and, increasingly, sparkling, aromatic-but-dry and *late harvest*. **Breaky Bottom; Thames Valley Vineyards; Nyetimber, Bruisyard; Three Choirs; Carr Taylor; Chiltern Valley.**

Enoteca [ee-noh-teh-kah] (Italy) Literally wine library or, now, wine shop.

☙ **Entre-Deux-Mers** [on-truh duh mehr] (*Bordeaux*, France) Once a region of appalling sweet wine from vineyards between the cities of *Bordeaux* and Libourne. Now a source of basic *Bordeaux* Blanc and principally dry *Sauvignon*. Reds are sold as *Bordeaux* Rouge. Both reds and whites suffer from the difficulty grapes have in ripening in cool years. *Ch. Bonnet* is the star.

☙ **Erath Vineyards** [ee-rath] (*Oregon*, US) One of *Oregon's* pioneering *Pinot Noir* producers, now better than ever. ☆☆☆☆☆ 1996 Pinot Noir £££

Erbach [ayr-bahkh] (*Rheingau*, Germany) Town noted for fine full *Riesling*, particularly from the Marcobrunn vineyard. QbA/Kab/Spät: **85** 86 **88 89 90** 91 92 93 94 95 96 97 98 Aus/Beeren/Tba: **83 85** 88 89 90 91 92 93 94 95 96 97 98 **Schloss Reinhartshausen; Schloss Schönborn.**

🍇 **Erbaluce** [ehr-bah-loo-chay] (*Piedmont*, Italy) White grape responsible for the light dry wines of the *Caluso*, and the sweet sun-dried *Caluso Passito*.

☙ **Erbaluce di Caluso** [ehr-bah-loo-chay dee kah-loo-soh] (*Piedmont*, Italy) Dry, quite herby white made from the *Erbaluce* grape (*Bava* makes a good one, blending in a little *Chardonnay*). Also used to make sparkling wine. ☆☆☆☆ 1997 Cieck, Vigna Misobolo £££

Erden [ehr-durn] (*Mosel-Saar-Ruwer*, Germany) In the *Bernkastel bereich*, this northerly village produces some of the finest full, crisp, *Riesling* in the *Mosel*, and includes the famous Treppchen vineyard. QbA/Kab/Spät: **85** 86 **88 89 90** 92 93 94 95 96 97 98 Aus/Beeren/Tba: **83 85** 88 89 90 91 92 93 94 95 97 98 **JJ Christoffel; Dr Loosen; Mönchhof; Peter Nicolay.**

☙ **Errazuriz** [ehr-raz-zoo-riz] (*Aconcagua Valley*, Chile) One of Chile's big name producers and owner of *Caliterra*. Wines have been improved by input from *Mondavi*. Look out for the "Wild Ferment" *Chardonnay* and recently launched *Syrah*. The top wine, Don Maximiano is one of Chile's very best reds. ☆☆☆☆ 1998 Sangiovese ££

Erzeugerabfüllung [ayr-tsoy-guhr-ab-foo-loong] (Germany) Bottled by the grower/estate.

☙ **Esk Valley** (*Hawke's Bay*, New Zealand) Under the same ownership as *Vidal* and *Villa Maria*. Successful with *Bordeaux*-style reds and juicy rosé. ☆☆☆☆☆ 1997 Réserve Merlot/Malbec/Cabernet Sauvignon ££

Esporão [esp-per-row] (*Alentejo*, Portugal) Revolutionary wines made by Australian-born, Portuguese-based David Baverstock. ☆☆☆☆ 1998 Cabernet Sauvignon ££

Espum/oso/ante [es-poom-mo-soh/san-tay] (Spain/Portugal) Sparkling.

Est! Est!! Est!!! [ehst-ehst-ehst] (*Lazio*, Italy) Red named after the repeated exclamation of a bishop's servant when he found a good wine. Apart from the ones made by *Falesco*, today's examples rarely offer much to exclaim about.

Esters Chemical components in wine responsible for all those extraordinary odours of fruits, vegetables, hamster cages and trainers.

Estremadura [ehst-reh-mah-doo-rah] (Portugal) Huge area producing mostly dull wine. Quintas da Pancas and Boavista are showing what can be done.

Estufa [esh-too-fah] (*Madeira*, Portugal) The vats in which *Madeira* is heated, speeding maturity and imparting its familiar "cooked" flavour.

Eszencia [es-sen-tsee-yah] (*Tokaji*, Hungary) Incredibly concentrated syrup made by piling around 100kg of *late harvested*, *botrytised* grapes into *puttonyos* and letting as little as three litres of incredibly sticky treacle dribble out of the bottom. This will only ferment up to about 4 per cent alcohol, over several weeks, before stopping completely. It is then stored and used to sweeten normal *Aszú* wines. The Tzars of Russia discovered the joys of Eszencia, and it has been prized for its effects on the male libido. It is incredibly hard to find, even by those who can see the point in doing anything with the expensive syrup other than pouring it on ice-cream. The easier-to-find *Aszú Essencia* (one step sweeter than *Aszú 6 puttonyos*) is far better value.

Arnaldo Etchart [et-shaht] (*Cafayate*, Argentina) Dynamic producer, benefiting from advice by *Michel Rolland* of *Pomerol* fame, and also investment by its French owners Pernod Ricard. The key wine here, though, is the grapey white *Torrontes*. ☆☆☆ 1999 Rio de Plata Torrontes £

l'Etoile [eh-twahl} (*Jura*, France) Theoretically the best *appellation* in the *Jura*. *Chardonnay* and *Savagnin* whites and sparkling wines can be good, and the *sherry*-like *Vin Jaune* is of interest. Ch de l'Etoile; Michel Geneletti; Montbo

Etude [ay-tewd] (*Napa*, California) Thoughtful superstar consultant Tony Soter experiments by marrying specific sites and clones of *Pinot Noir*. Apart from these wines, there are good rich *Napa Cabernets* and *Carneros Chardonnays*. ☆☆☆☆ 1996 Pinot Noir Napa Valley £££

Ch. l' Evangile [lay-van-zheel] (*Pomerol, Bordeaux*, France⸵ A classy and increasingly sought-after property that can, in great *vintages* like 1988, 1989 and 1990, sometimes rival its neighbour *Pétrus*, but in a more *tannic* style. 75 78 79 **82 83 85 86** 87 88 89 90 92 93 95 96 97 98 ☆☆☆☆ 1990 ££££

Evans Family/Evans Wine Co (*Hunter Valley*, Australia) Len Evans' (founder, and ex-chairman of *Rothbury Vineyards*) own estate and company. Rich *Chardonnay* and *Semillon* as characterful and generous as their maker.

Evans & Tate (*Margaret River*, Australia) Much improved producer with good *Chardonnay* and *Shiraz*. ☆☆☆☆ 1998 Redbrook Shiraz £££

Eventail de Vignerons Producteurs [ay-van-tih] (*Burgundy*, France) Reliable source of *Beaujolais*.

♈ **Eyrie Vineyards** [i-ree] (*Oregon*, US) Pioneering *Pinot Noir* producer in the *Willamette Valley*, whose success in a blind tasting of *Burgundies* helped to attract *Joseph Drouhin* to invest his francs in a vineyard here. ☆☆☆☆ **1996 Pinot Gris ££**

F

♈ **Fabre Montmayou** [fab-re mon-mey-yoo] (*Mendoza*, Argentina) Luján de Cuyo winery to watch for rich *Michel Rolland*-influenced reds.
♈ **Fairview Estate** (*Paarl*, South Africa) Go-ahead estate where Charles Back – both under his own name and under that of Fairview makes wines such as the wittily named and labelled "Goats do Roam". Also a good cheese producer.
♈ **Joseph Faiveley** [fay-vlay] (*Burgundy*, France) Impressive modern *négoçiant* with particular strength in vineyards in the *Côte de Nuits* and *Nuits-St.-Georges*. ☆☆☆☆ **1997 Corton Clos des Corton ££££**
♈ **Falchino** [fal kee-noh] (*Tuscany*, Italy) One of the key producers of *Vernacchia di San Gimignano*.
♈ **Falesco** [fah leh-skoh] (*Lazio*, Italy) Producer of fine – Montiano – *Merlot*, *Grechetto* and *Est Est Est*.
♈ **Bodegas Fariña** [fah ree-nah] (*Toro*, Spain) Top producer in *Toro*, making cask-aged (Gran Colegiata) and fruitier, non-cask-aged Colegiata.
♈ **Far Niente** [fah nee-yen-tay] (*Napa Valley*, California) Well regarded producer of sometimes over-showy *Chardonnay* and *Cabernet*.
♈ **Ch. de Fargues** [duh-fahrg] (*Sauternes*, *Bordeaux*, France) Elegant wincs made by the winemaker at *Ch. d'Yquem* – and a good alternative. **70 71 75 76** 78 79 80 83 **85** 86 88 89 90 95 96 97 98 ☆☆☆☆ **1997 ££££**
♈ **Gary Farrell** (*Sonoma*, California) A Russian River *Pinot Noir* maker to watch. ☆☆☆☆ **1997 Pinot Noir ££££**
Fat Has a silky texture which fills the mouth. More fleshy than meaty.
Fattoria [fah-tor-ree-ah] (Italy) *Estate*, particularly in *Tuscany*.

♈ **Faugères** [foh-zhehr] (*Midi*, France) With neighbouring *St. Chinian*, this gently hilly region is a major cut above the surrounding *Coteaux du Languedoc*, and potentially the source of really exciting red. For the moment, however, most still taste pretty rustic. **Ch. des Adouzes; Gilbert Alquier; Ch. Chenaie; des Estanilles; Grézan; Cave Cooperative de Laurens; la Liquière; de Météore; Moulin Couderc; des Peyregran; du Rouge Gorge; St. Antonin.**

Ⅰ Bernard Faurie [fow-ree] (*Rhône*, France) Tournon-based producer who makes intense perfumed wines with great longevity.

Ⅰ Bodegas Faustino Martinez [fows-tee-noh mahr-tee-nehth] (*Rioja*, Spain) Dependable *Rioja* producer with excellent (*Gran*) *Reservas*, fair whites and a decent *cava*. ☆☆☆ 1995 Reserva £££

Favorita [fahvoh-ree-tah] (*Piedmont*, Italy) Traditional variety from *Piedmont* transformed by modern winemaking into delicate floral whites. Conterno; Villa Lanata; *Bava*.

Ⅰ Weingut Feiler-Artinger [fi-luh arh-ting-guh] (*Rust*, Austria) Superlative innovative producer of dry and, especially, *late harvest* wines. ☆☆☆☆ 1999 Ruster Ausbruch Traminer £££

Ⅰ Fattoria di Felsina Berardenga [fah-toh-ree-ah dee fehl-see-nah beh-rah-den-gah] (*Tuscany*, Italy) Very high-quality *Chianti* estate. ☆☆☆☆ 1997 Chianti Classico Vigneto Rancia £££

Ⅰ Felton Road (*Central Otago*, New Zealand) This is an instant superstar, producing what may be New Zealand's top *Pinot Noir* as well as some very smart *Riesling*. ☆☆☆☆☆ 1998 Pinot Noir £££

Fendant [fon-don] (Switzerland) See *Chasselas*.

Fer [fehr] (*South-West*, France) Grape used to make *Marcillac*.

Fermentazione naturale [fehr-men-tat-zee-oh-nay] (Italy) "Naturally sparkling" but, in fact, indicates the *cuve close* method.

Fernão Pires [fehr-now pee-rehsh] (Portugal) *Muscat*ty grape, used to great effect by *Peter Bright* of the João Pires winery.

Ⅰ Ch. Ferrand [feh-ron] (*St. Emilion, Bordeaux*, France) Not to be confused with *Ferrand Lartigue*, this is a big estate, producing rather tough wines.

Ⅰ Ch. Ferrand Lartique [feh-ron lah-teek] (*St. Emilion Grand Cru, Bordeaux*, France) Small 5-acre estate producing full-bodied rich wines.

Ⅰ Luigi Ferrando (*Piedmont* Italy) Producer in the Carema *DOC* of good *Nebbiolo*-based wines that are surprisingly and attractively light and elegant in style.

Ⅰ Ferrari [feh-rah-ree] (*Trentino*, Italy) A sexy name for some really rather sexy *Champagne*-method fizz. The Riserva del Fondatore is the star of the show.

Ⅰ Ferrari-Carano (*Sonoma*, California) Improving winery best known for its oaky, crowd-pleasing *Chardonnay, Cabernet Sauvignon, Zinfandel* and rich *Merlot*. All these are good in their unsubtle way, but Siena, the Italianate *Sangiovese*-Cabernet blend and the Syrah are both more interesting.

Ⅰ AA Ferreira [feh-ray-rah] (*Douro*, Portugal) Associated with *Sogrape*, this traditional Portuguese *port* producer is as famous for its excellent *tawnies* as for its *Barca Velha*, Portugal's best traditional unfortified red. ☆☆☆☆ Duque de Braganca 20 Year Old Tawny ££; ☆☆☆☆ 1998 Vallado Douro Tinto £££

Ⅰ Gloria Ferrer (*Sonoma*, California) New World offshoot of *Freixenet* (the people behind *Cordon Negro*) making generally unmemorable sparkling wine and rather more interesting *Chardonnay* and *Pinot Noir* from its *Carneros* vineyards.

Ⅰ Ch. Ferrière [feh-ree-yehr] (*Margaux 3ème Cru Classé, Bordeaux*, France) Once small, now rather bigger, thanks to the convenience of belonging to the same owners as the *Margaux Cru Bourgeois, Ch. la Gurgue* – and the legal right to swap land between estates in the same appellation. 89 90 91 92 93 94 95 96 97 98 ☆☆☆☆ 1995 £££

Ⅰ Ch. de Fesles [dur fel] (*Loire*, France) Classic *Bonnezeaux* has now been joined by *Anjou* and *Savennières*. ☆☆☆☆ 1997 Bonnezeaux ££££

Ⅰ Sylvain Fessy [seel-van fes-see] (*Burgundy*, France) Reliable small *Beaujolais* producer with wide range of *crus*.

Ⅰ Henry Fessy [on-ree fes-see] (*Burgundy*, France) Consistent *négociant*, vineyard owner and producer of *Beaujolais*.

Fetzer [fet-zuh] (*Mendocino*, California) Confusingly, this big producer offers quite different ranges of wines in the UK and US – which helps to explain why the name is more respected overseas. Fortunately, the whole world can buy the excellent "Bonterra" range which are among the best examples of commercial organic wine in the world. ☆☆☆☆ **1996 Bonterra Chardonnay ££;** ☆☆☆☆ **1997 Bonterra Zinfandel ££**

Nicolas Feuillatte [fuh-yet] (*Champagne*, France) Quietly rising star with good-value wine. ☆☆☆☆ **1992 Palmes d'Or £££**

William Fèvre [weel-yum feh-vr] (*Burgundy*, France) Quality *Chablis* producer who has been a revolutionary in his use of new oak. His efforts in Chile have been improving with each *vintage*. ☆☆☆☆ **1996 Chablis Montée de Tonnerre ££££**

Ch. Feytit-Clinet [fay-tee klee-nay] (*Pomerol, Bordeaux*, France) A *Moueix* property with good, delicate wines. 79 81 **82** 83 **85** 86 87 88 89 90 94 95 96 97 98

Fiano [fee-yah-noh] (Italy) Herby white grape variety used to make Fiano di Avellino in the south.

Les Fiefs-de-Lagrange [fee-ef duh lag-ronzh] (*St. Julien, Bordeaux*, France) Recommendable *second label* of *Ch. Lagrange*.

Fiefs Vendéens [fee-ef von-day-yi'n] (*Loire*, France) One of the few surviving VDQS regions, this area close to Muscadet offers a wide range of grape varieties – and fresh, light wines that are worth buying in ripe vintages.

Ch. de Fieuzal [duh fyuh-zahl] (*Pessac-Léognan Grand Cru* Classé, *Bordeaux*, France) *Pessac-Léognan* property which can produce great whites and lovely raspberryish reds. Abeille de Fieuzal is the (excellent) *second label*. Red: 75 79 81 **82** 83 **85** 86 88 89 90 91 92 93 94 **95** 96 97 98   White: **85** 88 89 90 91 **92 93** 96 97 98

Ch. Figeac [fee-zhak] (*St. Emilion Premier Grand Cru, Bordeaux*, France) Forever in the shadow of its neighbour, *Cheval Blanc*, and often quite unpredictable in its evolution, but still one of the most characterful *St. Emilions*. **64 70** 78 **82** 83 84 **85** 86 88 89 90 92 93 **94** 95 96 97 98 ☆☆☆☆ **1994 ££££**

Granxa Fillaboa [gran-shah fee-yah-boh-wah] (*Galicia*, Spain) one of the best *Albariño* producers in *Rias Baixas*.

Filliatreau (*Loire*, France) Exemplary producer of Saumur Champigny which shows how tasty the *Cabernet* Franc can be – and how it can age.

Ch. Filhot [fee-yoh] (*Sauternes*, France) Rarely among the most complex examples of Sauternes, this is nonetheless one of the most reliable sources of well-made, good value wine. ☆☆☆☆ **1989 £££**

Finger Lakes (*New York State,* US) Cold region whose producers struggle (sometimes effectively) to produce good *vinifera,* including *late harvest Riesling.* Hybrids such as *Seyval Blanc* are more reliable. *Fox Run.*

Fining The clarifying of young wine before bottling to remove impurities, using a number of agents including *isinglass* and *bentonite.*

Finish What you can still taste after swallowing.

☨ **Fino** [fee-noh] (*Jerez,* Spain) Dry, delicate *sherry* which gains its distinctive flavour from the *flor* or yeast which grows on the surface of the wine during maturation. Drink chilled, with tapas, preferably within two weeks of opening. *Lustau; Barbadillo; Hidalgo; Gonzalez Byass.*

☨ **Firestone** (*Santa Ynez,* California) Good producer – particularly of good value *Chardonnay, Merlot* and *Sauvignon* and *late harvest Riesling* – in southern California. ☆☆☆ **1997 Merlot £££**

☨ **Fisher** (*Sonoma,* California) Top-class producer of limited-production, single-vineyard *Cabernets* and *Chardonnays* from hillside vineyards. ☆☆☆☆ **1996 Lamb Vineyard Cabernet Sauvignon ££££**

☨ **Fitou** [fee-too] (*Midi,* France) Long considered to be an up-market *Corbières* but actually rather a basic southern *AC,* making reds largely from the *Carignan* grape. The wines here may have become more refined, with a woody warmth, but they never quite shake off their rustic air. *Ch. d'Espigne; Lepaumier; Lerys; de Nouvelles; Mont Tauch; de Rolland; Val d'Orbieu.*

☨ **Fixin** [fee-san] (*Burgundy,* France) Northerly village of the *Côte de Nuits,* producing lean, tough, uncommercial reds which can mature well. 78 79 **80** 82 83 **85** 86 87 **88 89 90** 92 95 96 97 98 Vincent Berthaut; *Bruno Clair;* Michel Defrance; Derey Frères; Fougeray de Beauclair; Pierre Gelin; André Geoffroy; J-P Guyard; *Louis Jadot;* Philippe Joliet; Denis Philibert.

Flabby Lacking balancing acidity.

Flagey-Echézeaux [flah-jay ay-shuh-zoh] (*Burgundy,* France) Village on the wrong (non-vine) side of the Route National 74 that lends its name to the *appellations* of *Echézeaux* and *Grands Echézeaux.*

☨ **Ch. La Fleur** [flur] (*St. Emilion, Bordeaux,* France) Small *St. Emilion* property producing softly fruity wines. **82** 83 85 86 88 **89** 90 92 94 95 96 97 98

☨ **Ch. la Fleur de Gay** [flur duh gay] (*Pomerol, Bordeaux,* France) *Ch. Croix de Gay's* best wine and thus heavily sought after. Showed improvement in 1998. **82 86** 88 89 90 94 95 96 97 98

☨ **Ch. la Fleur-Pétrus** [flur pay-trooss] (*Pomerol, Bordeaux,* France) For those who find *Pétrus* a touch unaffordable, this next-door neighbour offers gorgeously accessible *Pomerol* flavour for (in *Pétrus* terms) a bargain price. 70 **75** 78 79 **81 82 83 85 86** 87 **88 89 90** 92 **93** 95 96 97 98

☨ **Fleurie** [fluh-ree] (*Burgundy,* France) One of the 10 *Beaujolais Crus,* ideally fresh and fragrant, as its name suggests. Best vineyards include La Madonne and Pointe du Jour. Dom. Bachelard and Guy Depardon are names to watch. 90 95 96 **97 98** Berrod; Chignard; Després; *Duboeuf;* Ch. Labourons; Métrat; Andre Vaisse.

Flor [flawr] Yeast which grows naturally on the surface of some maturing *sherries*, making them potential *finos*.

🍇 **Flora** [flor-rah] A cross between *Semillon* and *Gewürztraminer*, best known in *Brown Brothers Orange Muscat* and Flora.

🍷 **Flora Springs** (*Napa Valley,* California) One Good, unusual *Sauvignon Blanc* (Soliloquy) and classy *Merlot, Cabernet Sauvignon* & *Cabernet Franc* blend (Trilogy). ☆☆☆☆ **1996 trilogy £££**

🍷 **Emile Florentin** [floh-ron-tan] (*Rhône,* France) Maker of ultra-traditional, ultra-*tannic*, chewy *St. Joseph.*

Flying winemakers Young (usually) Australians and New Zealanders who have, since the 1980s, been despatched like vinous mercenaries to wineries worldwide to make better and more reliable wine than the home teams can manage. Often, as they have proved, all it has taken to improve the standards of a European cooperative has been a more scrupulous attitude towards picking ripe grapes (rather than impatiently harvesting unripe ones) and keeping tanks and pipes clean.

🍷 **Ch. Fombrauge** [fom-brohzh] (*St. Emilion, Bordeaux,* France) Middling *St. Emilion.* **82 83 85 86 88 89 90** 92 93 **94 95** 96 97 98 ☆☆☆ **1996 £££**

🍷 **Ch. Fonplégade** [fon-pleh-gahd] (*St. Emilion Grand Cru Classé, Bordeaux,* France) If you like your *St. Emilion* tough, this is for you. 78 **82** 83 85 86 87 88 89 90 94 95 96 97 98 ☆☆☆ 1995 **££££**

🍷 **Ch. Fonroque** [fon-rok] (*St. Emilion Grand Cru Classé, Bordeaux,* France) Property with concentrated wines, but not always one of *Moueix*'s very finest. 70 **75** 78 **79 82 83 85** 86 88 89 90 92 93 94 95 96 97 98

🍷 **Fonseca Guimaraens** [fon-say-ka gih-mah-rans] (*Douro,* Portugal) Now a subsidiary of *Taylor*'s but still independently making great *port.* In blind tastings the 1976 and 1978 and 1984 regularly beat supposedly classier houses' supposedly finer vintages. See also *Guimaraens.* Fonseca: 60 **63 66** 70 75 77 80 83 **84** 85 95 Fonseca Guimaraens: **76 78** 82 84 88 92 94 98 ☆☆☆☆☆ **1984 Fonseca Guimaraens Vintage Port £££**

🍷 **JM da Fonseca Internacional** [fon-say-ka in-tuhr-nah-soh-nahl] (*Setúbal Peninsula,* Portugal) Highly commercial firm whose wines include Lancers, the *Mateus*-taste-alike sold in mock-crocks.

🍷 **JM da Fonseca Successores** [fon-say-ka suk-ses-saw-rays] (*Estremadura,* Portugal) Unrelated to the *port* house of the same name and no longer connected to *JM da Fonseca Internacional.* Family-run firm, which with *Aliança* and *Sogrape* is one of Portugal's big three dynamic wine companies. Top reds include Pasmados, *Periquita* (from the grape of the same name), *Quinta da Camarate,* Terras Altas Dão and the *Cabernet*-influenced "TE" *Garrafeiras.* Dry whites are less impressive, but the sweet old *Moscatel de Setúbals* are luscious classics. ☆☆☆☆ **1991 Moscatel de Setúbal, Terras do Sado ££££**

🍷 **Dom. Font de Michelle** [fon-duh-mee shel] (*Rhône,* France) Reliable producer of medium-bodied red *Châteauneuf-du-Pape* and small quantities of brilliant, almost unobtainable, white. ☆☆☆☆ **1998 Châteauneuf-du-Pape £££**

🍷 **Fontana Candida** [fon-tah-nah kan-dee-dah] (*Lazio,* Italy) Good producer, especially for *Frascati.* The top wine is Colle Gaio which is good enough to prove the disappointing nature of most other wines from this area. ☆☆☆ **1999 Frascati Superiore ££**

🍷 **Fontanafredda** [fon-tah-nah-freh-dah] (*Piedmont,* Italy) Big producer with impressive *Asti Spumante* and very approachable (especially single-vineyard) *Barolo.* ☆☆☆☆ **1996 Barolo d'Serralunga d'Alba ££££**

🍷 **Domaine de Font Sane** [fon-sen] (*Rhône,* France) Producer of fine *Gigondas* in a very underrated *AC.* Very traditional and full-bodied.

🍷 **Castello di Fonterutoli** (*Tuscany,* Italy) *Chianti* Classico producer of real class, which also produces great non-*DOC* blends: Concerto and Siepi. ☆☆☆☆☆ **1997 Chianti Classico Riserva £££**

☒ **Fontodi** [Fon-toh-dee] (*Tuscany,* Italy) Classy *Tuscan* producer with Flaccianello, a good *Vino da Tavola.* ☆☆☆☆☆ **1998 Chianti Classico ££££**

☒ **Foradori** [Foh-rah-doh-ree] (*Trentino,* Italy) Specialist producer of *Teroldego* (Granato is the reserve wine) plus an inventive *Pinot Bianco-Pinot Grigio-Chardonnay* white blend.

☒ **Forman** (*Napa Valley,* California) Rick Forman makes good *Cabernet* and *Merlot* and refreshingly crisp *Chardonnay.* ☆☆☆☆ **1997 Cabernet ££££**

Forst [Fawrst] (*Pfalz,* Germany) Wine town producing great concentrated *Riesling.* Famous for the *Jesuitengarten* vineyard. QbA/Kab/Spät: **85** 86 **88** 91 92 93 94 95 96 97 98 Aus/Beeren/Tba: **83 85** 88 89 90 91 92 93 94 95 96 97 98 ☆☆☆☆ **1996 Forster Jesuitengarten, Dr V Basserman-Jordan £££**

☒ **Fortant de France** [faw-tan duh frons] (*Languedoc-Roussillon,* France) Good-quality revolutionary brand owned by *Skalli* and specialising in varietal *Vin de Pays d'Oc.* ☆☆☆☆ **1999 Merlot ££**

☒ **Les Forts de Latour** [lay faw duh lah-toor] (*Pauillac, Bordeaux,* France) *Second label* of *Ch. Latour.* Not, as is often suggested, made exclusively from the fruit of young vines and wine which might otherwise have ended up in *Ch. Latour* – there are several vineyards whose grapes are grown specially for Les Forts – but, like the *second labels* of other top châteaux, this is still often better than lesser *classed growth châteaux*' top wines. Indeed in 1999, it was one of the best wines of the vintage. **82 83 85 86** 88 **90** 91 92 **93 94** 95 96 97 98

☒ **Ch. Fourcas-Dupré** [faw-kass doo-pray] (*Listrac Cru Bourgeois, Bordeaux,* France) Tough, very traditional *Listrac.* **70** 75 **78** 81 **82 83** 85 **86** 87 88 89 90 91 92 95 96 97 98

☒ **Ch. Fourcas-Hosten** [faw-kass hos-ten] (*Listrac Cru Bourgeois, Bordeaux,* France) Firm, old-fashioned wine with plenty of 'grip' for *tannin* fans. 75 78 81 **82 83 85 86** 87 88 89 90 91 92 95 96 97 98

☒ **Fox Run Vineyards** (*New York,* US) One of the most successful producers in the Finger Lakes, offering good fizz, *Riesling* and *Chardonnay.*

☒ **Foxen** (*Santa Ynez,* California) Highly successful producer of single-vineyard *Pinot* and *Chardonnay,* now moving successfully into *Syrah.* ☆☆☆☆☆ **1997 Syrah £££**

☒ **Ch. Franc-Mayne** [fron-mayn] (*St. Emilion Grand Cru Classé, Bordeaux,* France) Dry, austere, traditional wines for those who like them that way. 85 86 87 88 **89 90** 94 95 96 ☆☆☆ **1990 £££**

☒ **Franciacorta** [fran-chee yah-kor-tah] (*Lombardy,* Italy) *DOC* for good, light, French-influenced reds but better noted for varied sparklers made to sell at the same price as – if not more than – *Champagne. Bellavista; Ca' Del Bosco; Cavalleri; Monte Rossa; Uberti.*

Franciscan Vineyards [fran-sis-kan] (*Napa Valley,* California) Now part of the huge Canandaigua company, reliable *Napa* winery whose Chilean boss Augustin Huneeus, has pioneered natural yeast wines with his *Burgundy*-like "Cuvée Sauvage" *Chardonnay* and has punctured the pretentious balloons of some of his neighbours. Now also making wine in Chile – at *Veramonte*. ☆☆☆☆ 1996 Chardonnay Cuvée Sauvage £££

Ch. de Francs [day fron] (*Côtes de Francs, Bordeaux,* France) Well-run estate which makes great-value crunchy, blackcurranty wine and, with *Ch. Puygeraud*, helps to prove the worth of this little-known region.

Franken [fran-ken] (Germany) *Anbaugebiet* making characterful, sometimes earthy, dry whites, traditionally presented in the squat flagon-shaped "*Bocksbeutel*" on which the *Mateus* bottle was modelled. One of the key varieties is the *Sylvaner* which explains the earthiness of many of the wines. The weather here does make it easier to make dry wine than in many other regions.

Franschhoek [fran-shook] (South Africa) Valley leading into the mountains away from Paarl (and thus cooler). The soil is a little suspect, however, and the best producers are mostly clustered at the top of the valley, around the picturesque eponymous town. Red: 84 86 **87** 89 **91 92** 93 94 95 96 White: **87 91** 92 93 94 95 96 97

Frascati [fras-kah-tee] (*Latium,* Italy) Clichéd dry or semi-dry white from *Latium*. At its best it is soft and clean with a fascinating 'sour cream' flavour. Drink within 12 months of *vintage*. **Fontana Candida; Colli di Catone.**

Ca' dei Frati [kah day-yee frah-tee] (*Lombardy,* Italy) Fine producers, both of *Lugana* and *Chardonnay*-based sparkling wine.

Freemark Abbey (*Napa Valley,* California) Well-regarded (in the US) producer of good *Cabernet*. The Bosche examples are the ones to look for. ☆☆☆☆ 1993 Cabernet Sauvignon Bosche ££££

Freie Weingärtner Wachau [fri-eh-vine-gehrt-nur vah-kow] (*Wachau,* Austria) Unusually fine cooperative with great vineyards, dry and sweet versions of the indigenous *Grüner Veltliner* and gloriously concentrated *Rieslings* that outclass the efforts of many a big-name estate in Germany. ☆☆☆☆ 1998 Beerenauslese £££

Freisa [fray-ee-sah] (Italy) Characterful perfumed red wine grape with lovely cherryish, raspberryish flavours, popular with Hemingway and grown in *Piedmont* by producers like Gilli and *Vajra*. Drink young.

Freixenet [fresh-net] (*Catalonia,* Spain) Giant in the *cava* field and proponent of traditional *Catalonia*n grapes in sparkling wine. Its dull, off-dry big-selling *Cordon Negro* made from traditional grapes is a perfect justification for adding *Chardonnay* to the blend.

Marchesi de' Frescobaldi [mah-kay-see day fres-koh-bal-dee] (*Tuscany,* Italy) Family estate with classy wines including *Castelgiocondo*, Mormoreto, a *Cabernet Sauvignon* based wine, the rich white Pomino Il Benefizio *Chardonnay*, *Pomino Rosso* using *Merlot* and *Cabernet Sauvignon*, and Nippozano in *Chianti*. Now in joint venture to make *Luce* with *Mondavi*. ☆☆☆☆ 1997 Montesodi Chianti Rufina £££ ☆☆☆☆ 1996 La Maione £££

Freycinet [fres-sih-net] (*Tasmania,* Australia) Small East Coast winery with some of Australia's best *Pinot Noir* and great *Chardonnay*. Sadly, the giant Spanish sparkling wine firm *Freixenet* has striven to prevent this label appearing outside Australia, despite the facts that *Freycinet* is an historic name in *Tasmania* and that this winery makes no sparkling wine. ☆☆☆☆ 1996 Pinot Noir £££

♟ **Friuli-Venezia Giulia** [free-yoo-lee veh-neht-zee-yah zhe-yoo-lee-yah]
(Italy) Northerly region containing a number of *DOCs* such as *Colli Orientali*,
Collio, Friuli Grave and Aquileia and *Isonzo* which focus on single-variety
wines like *Merlot*, *Cabernet Franc*, *Pinot Bianco*, *Pinot Grigio* and *Tocai*.
Quality varies enormously, ranging from dilute, over-cropped efforts to the
complex masterpieces of producers like *Jermann; Bidoli; Puiatti; Zonin.*

Frizzante [freet-zan-tay] (Italy) Semi-sparkling especially *Lambrusco*.

♟ **Frog's Leap** (*Napa Valley*, California) Winery whose owners combine
organic winemaking skill with a fine sense of humour (their slogan is "Time's
fun when you're having flies"). Tasty *Zinfandel*, "wild yeast" *Chardonnay* and
unusually good *Sauvignon Blanc.* ☆☆☆☆ 1997 Sauvignon Blanc £££

♟ **Fronsac/Canon Fronsac** [fron-sak] (*Bordeaux*, France) *Pomerol*
neighbours, who regularly produce rich, intense, affordable wines. They
are rarely subtle; however, with some good winemaking from men like
Christian Moueix of *Ch. Pétrus* (he is a great believer in these regions),
they can often represent some of the best buys in *Bordeaux*. Canon Fronsac
is thought by some to be the better of the pair. 83 85 86 **88 89** 90 94 95
96 97 98 *Ch. Canon;* Cassagne; *Dalem;* Fontenil; Moulin Haut Laroque;
Moulin Pey-Labrie; Vieille Cure.

♟ **Ch. de Fuissé** [duh fwee-say] (*Burgundy*, France) Jean-Jacques Vincent is
probably the best producer in this *commune*, making wines comparable to
some of the best of the *Côte d'Or*. The *Vieilles Vignes* can last as long as a
good *Chassagne-Montrachet*; the other *cuvées* run it a close race.
☆☆☆☆ 1996 Pouilly Fuissé £££

Fumé Blanc [fyoo-may blahnk] Name originally adapted from *Pouilly Blanc
Fumé* by *Robert Mondavi* to describe his California oaked *Sauvignon*. Now
widely used – though not exclusively – in the New World for this style.

🍇 **Furmint** [foor-mint] (*Tokaji*, Hungary) Lemony white grape, used in
Hungary for *Tokaji* and, given modern winemaking, good dry wines. See
Royal Tokaji Wine Co and *Disznókö.* ☆☆☆☆ 1996 Disznókö Fürmint ££

♟ **Rudolf Fürst** [foorst] (*Fraken*, Germany) One of Germany's best producers
of ripe red Pinot Noir Spätburgunder, and some lovely floral *Riesling*.

♟ **Fürstlich Castell'sches Domänenamt** [foorst-likh kas-tel-shes doh-
meh-nehn-amt] (*Franken*, Germany) Prestigious producer of typically full-
bodied dry whites from the German *Anbaugebiet* of *Franken*.

Fûts de Chêne (élévé en) [foo duh shayne] (France) Oak barrels (aged in).

Futures See *En Primeur*

G

♟ **Ch. la Gaffelière** [gaf-fuh-lyehr] (*St. Emilion Premier Grand Cru*,
Bordeaux, France) Lightish-bodied but well-made wines. Not to be
confused with *Ch. Canon la Gaffelière*. 82 83 85 86 88 89 90 92 93 94
95 96 97 98

♟ **Dom. Jean-Noël Gagnard** [jon noh-wel gan-yahr] (*Burgundy*, France) A
reliable *domaine* with vineyards which spread across *Chassagne-
Montrachet*. There is also some *Santenay.* ☆☆☆☆ 1996 Chassagne-
Montrachet ££££

♟ **Jacques Gagnard-Delagrange** [gan-yahr duh lag-ronzh] (*Burgundy*,
France) A top-class producer to follow for those traditionalists who like their
white *Burgundies* delicately oaked. ☆☆☆☆☆ 1995 Montrachet ££££

Gaia [gay-ee-yahr] (*Nemea*, Greece) Up-and-coming modern estate.

Gaillac [gi-yak] (*South-West* France) Light, fresh, good-value reds and (sweet, dry and slightly sparkling) whites, produced using *Gamay* and *Sauvignon* grapes, as well as the indigenous *Mauzac*. The reds can rival *Beaujolais*. **Ch. Clement Ternes; Labastide de Levis; Robert Plageoles.**

Pierre Gaillard [gi-yahr] (*Rhône*, France) A good producer of *Côte Rôtie*, *St. Joseph* and *Condrieu*. ☆☆☆☆ **1997 Condrieu ££££**

Gainey Vineyard [gay-nee] (*Santa Barbara*, California) Classy reds and whites, especially *Pinot* and *Chardonnay*. ☆☆☆☆ **1996 Merlot £££**

Gaja [gi-yah] (*Piedmont*, Italy) In 1999, Angelo Gaja, the man who proved that wines from the previously modest region of *Barbaresco* could sell for higher prices than top-class *clarets*, let alone the supposedly classier neighbours *Barolo*, surprised the wine world by announcing that his highly prized – and priced – individual vineyard reds from these regions would henceforth be sold under the simpler *Langhe* denomination. This would, he argued, focus attention on his excellent blended Barolo and Barbaresco. Whatever their legal handle, asking whether the Gaja wines are worth their prices is like questioning the cost of a Ferrari.

Galestro [gah-less-troh] (*Tuscany*, Italy) The light white of the *Chianti* region. **Antinori; Frescobaldi.**

E & J Gallo [gal-loh] (*Central Valley*, California) The world's biggest wine producer; with around 60 per cent of the total Californian harvest. The top end *Cabernet* and (particularly impressive) *Chardonnay* from individual "ranch" vineyards and Gallo's own "Northern *Sonoma* Estate", a piece of land which was physically re-contoured by their bulldozers. The new Turning Leaf wines are good too, at their level. The rest of the basic range, though much improved and very widely stocked, is still pretty ordinary. ☆☆☆☆☆ **1996 Stefani Ranch Chardonnay £££**

Gamay [ga-may] (*Beaujolais*, France) Light-skinned grape traditional to *Beaujolais* where it is used to make fresh and fruity reds for early drinking, usually by the *carbonic maceration* method, and more serious *cru* wines that resemble light *Burgundy*. Also successful in California (*J Lohr*), Australia (*Sorrenberg*) and South Africa (*Fairview*).

Gamay [ga-may] (California) Confusingly unrelated to the *Gamay*.

Gamey Smell or taste oddly, reminiscent of hung game – associated with *Pinot Noir* and *Syrah*. Sometimes at least partly attributable to the combination of those grapes' natural characteristics with careless use of *sulphur dioxide*. Modern examples are less gamey than in the past. Another explanation can be the presence of a vineyard infection called Brettanomyces which is feared in California but often goes unnoticed in France where gamey wines are (sometimes approvingly) said to "renarder" – to smell of fox.

Gancia [gan-chee-yah] (*Piedmont,* Italy) Reliable producer of *Asti Spumante* and good dry *Pinot* di *Pinot,* as well as *Pinot Blanc* sparkling wine.

Vin de Pays du Gard [doo gahr'] (*Languedoc-Roussillon,* France) Fresh, undemanding red and rosé wines from the southern part of the *Rhône.* Drink young, and quite possibly chilled.

Garganega [gahr-gah-nay-gah] (Italy) White grape at its best – and worst – in *Soave* in the *Veneto.* In the right site and when not overcropped, it produces interesting almondy flavours. Otherwise the wines it makes are simply light and dull. Now being blended with *Chardonnay.*

Garnacha [gahr-na-cha] (Spain and France) See *Grenache.*

Garrafeira [gah-rah-fay-rah] (Portugal) Indicates a producer's *"reserve"* wine, which has been selected and given extra time in cask (minimum 2 years) and bottle (minimum 1 year).

Vincent Gasse [gass] (*Rhône,* France) Next to the La Landonne vineyard and producing superb, concentrated, inky black wines.

Gattinara [Gat-tee-nah-rah] (*Piedmont,* Italy) Red *DOC* from the *Nebbiolo* – varying in quality but generally full-flavoured and dry. 78 79 82 **85 88 89 90 93 94** 95 96 97 98 Travaglini.

Domaine Gauby [Goh-Bee] (*Côtes de Roussillon,* France) Serious *Roussillon* reds and (*Muscat*) whites. The Muntada *Syrah* is the top *cuvée.* ☆☆☆☆☆ **1998 Villages Vieilles Vignes ££;** ☆☆☆☆ **1998 Côtes du Roussillon-Villages Muntada ££**

Gavi [gah-vee] (*Piedmont,* Italy) Often unexceptional white wine from the *Cortese* grape. Compared by Italians to white *Burgundy,* with which it and the creamily pleasant Gavi di Gavi share a propensity for high prices. ☆☆☆☆ **1997 Minaia, Bergaglio ££££**

Ch. le Gay [luh gay] (*Pomerol, Bordeaux,* France) Good *Moueix* property with intense complex wine. 70 **75 76** 78 79 **82 83 85** 86 88 89 90 94 95 96 97 98 ☆☆☆☆ **1995 £££**

Ch. Gazin [Ga-zan] (*Pomerol, Bordeaux,* France) Increasingly polished since the mid 1980s. 85 86 **87** 88 89 90 92 93 94 95 96 97 98 ☆☆☆☆ **1995 ££££**

Geelong [zhee-long] (*Victoria,* Australia) Cool region pioneered by Idyll Vineyards (makers of old-fashioned reds) and rapidly attracting notice with Clyde Park and with *Bannockburn's* and *Scotchman Hill's Pinot Noirs.*

Geisenheim [gi-zen-hime] (*Rheingau,* Germany) Home of the German Wine Institute wine school, once one of the best in the world, but now overtaken by more go-ahead seats of learning in France, California and Australia. Qba/Kab/Spät: **85** 86 **88 89 90** 91 92 93 94 95 96 97 Aus/Beeren/Tba: **83 85** 88 89 90 91 92 93 94 95 96 97

Ch. de la Genaiserie [Jeh-nay-seh-ree] (*Loire,* France) Classy, lusciously honeyed, single-vineyard wines from *Coteaux du Layon.* ☆☆☆☆☆ **1995 Coteaux du Layon Chaume ££££**

Generoso [zheh-neh-roh-soh] (Spain) Fortified or dessert wine.

Genève [jer-nev] (Switzerland) Region best known for high quality, if often lightweight, *Gamay* and slightly sparkling "Perlan" *Chasselas.*

ℤ **Gentilini** [zhen-tee-lee-nee] (*Cephalonia*, Greece) Nick Cosmetatos's impressive modern white wines, made using both classic Greek grapes and French varieties, should be an example to those of his countrymen who are still happily making and drinking stuff which tastes as fresh as an old election manifesto. ☆☆☆ **1997 Gentilini Fumé ££££**

ℤ **JM Gerin** [ger-an] (*Rhône*, France) A producer of good modern *Côte Rôtie* and *Condrieu*; uses new oak to make powerful, long-lived wines. ☆☆☆☆☆ **1997 Côte Rôtie La Landonne ££££**

ℤ **Gerovassilou** [jeh-roh-vah-see-loo] (*Cephalonia*, Greece) Producer of successful new wave whites, including impressive *Viognier.*

ℤ **Gevrey-Chambertin** [zheh-vray shom-behr-tan] (*Burgundy*, France) Best-known big red *Côte de Nuits commune*; very variable, but still capable of superb, plummy, cherryish wine. The top *Grand Cru* is *Le Chambertin* but, in the right hands, *Premiers Crus* like Les Cazetiers can beat this and the other *Grands Crus*. 78 83 **85 88 89 90** 92 95 96 97 98 *Denis Bachelet; Alain Burguet;* Bourrée (Vallet); *Champy,* Charlopin; *Bruno Clair;* P. Damoy; *Joseph Drouhin; Dugat-Py; Dujac; Leroy; Denis Mortet;* Henri Rebourseau; *Roty; Rossignol-Trapet; Armand Rousseau.*

🍸 **Gewürztraminer** [geh-voort-strah-mee-nehr] White (well, slightly pink) grape, making dry-to-sweet, full, oily-textured, spicy wine. Best in *Alsace* (where it is spelled Gewurztraminer, without the umlaut accent) but also grown in Australasia, Italy, the US and Eastern Europe. Instantly recognisable by its parma-violets-and-lychees character. *Alsace; Casablanca.*

ℤ **Geyser Peak** [Gih-Suhr] (*Alexander Valley*, California) Australian winemaker Darryl Groom revolutionised Californian thinking in this once Australian-owned winery with his *Semillon-Chardonnay* blend ("You mean *Chardonnay*'s not the only white grape?"), and with reds which show an Australian attitude towards ripe *tannin*. A name to watch. Canyon Road is the good-value *second label*. ☆☆☆☆ **1997 Geyser Peak Zinfandel £££;** ☆☆☆☆ **1997 Canyon Road California Cabernet Sauvignon £££**

ℤ **Ghemme** [gem-may] (*Piedmont*, Italy) Spicy *Nebbiolo* usually unfavourably compared to its neighbour Gatinara. Cantalupo is the star producer.

ℤ **Ghiaie della Furba** see *Capezzana.*

ℤ **Giaconda** [zhee-ya-kon-dah] (*Victoria*, Australia) Small winery hidden away high in the hills. Sells out of its impressive *Pinot Noir* and *Chardonnay en primeur.* ☆☆☆☆☆ **1997 Pinot Noir £££**

ℤ **Bruno Giacosa** [zhee-yah-koh-sah] (*Piedmont*, Italy) Stunning winemaker with a large range, including *Barolos* (Vigna Rionda in best years) and *Barbarescos* (Santo Stefano, again, in best years). Recent success with whites, including a *Spumante.* ☆☆☆☆ **1995 Barbaresco £££**

ℤ **Gie les Rameaux** [lay ram-moh] (*Corsica*, France) One of this island's top producers.

ℤ **Giesen** [gee-sen] (*Canterbury*, New Zealand) Small estate, with particularly appley *Riesling* from *Canterbury*, and *Sauvignon* from *Marlborough.* ☆☆☆☆ **1999 Sauvignon Blanc ££**

ℤ **Gigondas** [zhee gon-dass] (*Rhône*, France) *Côtes du Rhône commune*, with good-value, spicy/peppery, blackcurranty reds which show the *Grenache* at its best. A good competitor for nearby Châteauneuf. 78 79 **83 85 88** 89 90 **93 94** 95 96 Dom des Bosquets; Brusset; de Cabasse; du Cayron; *Delas;* Font-Sane; Entrefaux; des Espiers; les Goubert; *Guigal;* Pochon; *Sorrel;* de Thalabert; *Vidal-Fleury.*

♈ **Ch. Gilette** [djil-lette] (*Sauternes, Bordeaux,* France) Eccentric, unclassified but of classed-growth quality *Sauternes* kept in tank (rather than cask) for 20 or 30 years. Rare, expensive, worth it. 49 53 59 **61 62 67 70 75 76 78**

♈ **Sandro & Claudio Gini** [djee-nee] (*Veneto,* Italy) Producers of great "basic" and individual single-vineyard *Soaves.*

Gippsland [gip-sland] (*Victoria,* Australia) Up-and-coming coastal region where *Bass Philip* and *Nicholson River* are producing fascinating and quite European-style wines. Watch out for some of Australia's finest *Pinot Noirs.*

♈ **Vincent Girardin** [van-son zhee-rahr-dan] (*Burgundy,* France) Reliable, dynamic *Santenay* producer and (since 1996) *negociant,* with vines in several other *communes.* ☆☆☆☆ **1997 Santenay Gravièrs £££**

Giropalette [zhee-roh-pal-let] Large machine which automatically and highly efficiently replaces the human beings who used to perform the task of *remuage.* Used by most *Champagne* houses which, needless to say, prefer to conceal them from visiting tourists.

♈ **Camille Giroud** [kah-mee zhee-roo] (*Burgundy,* France) Laudably old-fashioned family-owned *négociant* with no love of new oak and small stocks of great mature wine that go a long way to prove that good *Burgundy* really doesn't need it to taste good. ☆☆☆☆ **1996 Volnay ler Cru £££**

Gisborne [giz-bawn] (New Zealand) North Island vine-growing area since the 1920s. Cool, wettish climate, mainly used for New Zealand's best *Chardonnay.* An ideal partner for *Marlborough* in blends. White: **89 91 94 95 96 97** 98 *Coopers Creek; Corbans;* Matawhero; *Matua Valley; Millton; Montana.*

♈ **Ch. Giscours** [zhees-koor] (*Margaux 3ème Cru Classé, Bordeaux,* France) Recently-bought *Margaux* property which is only (since 1999) beginning to offer the quality associated with the vintages of the late 1970s. **71 75 76 78 79 81** 82 85 86 88 89 90 91 92 96 97 98 ☆☆☆ **1982 ££££**

♈ **Louis Gisselbrecht** [gees-sel-brekt] (*Alsace,* France) Recommendable grower and *negociant* which, like cousin Willy, has good vines in the Frankstein *Grand Cru.*

♈ **Givry** [zheev-ree] (*Burgundy,* France) *Côte Chalonnaise commune,* making typical and affordable, if rather jammily rustic, reds and creamy whites. French wine snobs recall that this was one of King Henri IV's favourite wines, forgetting the fact that a) he had many such favourites dotted all over France and b) his mistress − of whom he also probably had several − happened to live here. Red: **78 85** 88 89 90 92 93 94 95 96 97 98 **Bourgeon; Derain;** *Joblot;* Lumpp; Mouton; Ragot; Clos Salomon; Steinmaier; Thénard.

♈ **Glen Carlou** [kah-loo] (*Paarl,* South Africa) Small-scale winery with rich, oily, oaky *Chardonnay* and less convincing reds. ☆☆☆ **1996 Chardonnay ££**

♈ **Glen Ellen** (*Sonoma Valley,* California) Dynamic firm producing large amounts of commercial tropical fruit juice-like *Chardonnay* under its "Proprietor's Reserve" label. Reds are better value. The *Benziger* range is more worthwhile.

Glenrowan [glen-roh-wan] (*Victoria,* Australia) Area near *Rutherglen* with a similar range of excellent *liqueur Muscats* and *Tokays.*

♈ **Ch. Gloria** [glaw-ree-yah] (*St. Julien Cru Bourgeois, Bordeaux,* France) One of the first of the super *Crus Bourgeois.* Now back on form.

♈ **Golan Heights Winery** [goh-lan] (Israel) Californian expertise is used to produce good *Kosher Cabernet* and *Muscat.*

♈ **Goldwater Estate** (*Auckland*, New Zealand) *Bordeaux*-like red wine specialist on *Waiheke Island* whose wines are expensive but every bit as good as many similarly-priced Californian offerings. ☆☆☆☆ **1998 Esslin Merlot ££££**

♈ **Gonzalez Byass** [gon-zah-lez bih-yas] (*Jerez*, Spain) If *sherry* is beginning to enjoy a long awaited comeback, this is the company that should take much of the credit. Producer of the world's best-selling *fino*, *Tío Pepe* – and a supporting cast of the finest, most complex, traditional *sherries* available to mankind. ☆☆☆☆☆ **Matusálem Oloroso Dulce Muy Viejo ££££**

♈ **Gosset** [gos-say] (*Champagne*, France) The oldest house in *Champagne* producing some marvellous and very long-lived *cuvées*, particularly the Celebris. ☆☆☆☆ **1993 Grand Millésime ££££**

♈ **Henri Gouges** [Gooj] (*Burgundy*, France) Long-established estate, producing some truly classic long-lived wines. ☆☆☆☆☆ **1997 Nuits-St.-Georges les St.-Georges ££££**

♈ **Marquis de Goulaine** [goo-layn] (*Loire*, France) One of the best producers of *Muscadet* – and a butterfly museum, to boot.

Goulburn Valley [gohl-boorn] (*Victoria*, Australia) Small, long-established region reigned over by the respectively ancient and modern *Ch. Tahbilk* and *Mitchelton*, both of whom make great *Marsanne*, though in very different styles.

♈ **Gould Campbell** [goold] (*Douro*, Portugal) Underrated member of the same stable as *Dow's*, *Graham's* and *Warre's*. 60 63 66 70 75 77 80 83 85 91 94 97 ☆☆☆ **1994 Late Bottled Vintage Port ££**

♈ **Goundrey** [gown-dree] (*Western* Australia) Winery in the up-and-coming region of *Mount Barker*, bought by an American millionaire who has continued the founder's policy of making fruity but not overstated *Chardonnay* and *Cabernet*. ☆☆☆☆ **1997 Mount Barker Chardonnay ££**

Graach [grahkh] (*Mosel-Saar-Ruwer*, Germany) *Mittelmosel* village producing fine wines. Best known for its *Himmelreich* vineyard. QbA/Kab/Spät: **85 86 88 89 90 92 93 94** 95 96 97 98 Aus/Beeren/Tba: **83 85 88 89 90** 92 93 94 95 96 97 98 *Deinhard; JJ Prüm; Max Ferd Richter; Von Kesselstadt.*

♈ **Grace Family Vineyards** (*Napa*, California) Tiny quantities – occasionally fewer than 100 – of Cabernet whose rarity makes for prices of $300-400 per bottle. (Remember, if potatoes were harder to grow, they'd cost more too).

♈ **Graham** [gray-yam] (*Douro*, Portugal) Sweetly delicate wines, sometimes outclassing the same stable's supposedly finer but heftier *Dow's*. Malvedos is erroneously thought of as the Single *Quinta*. **55** 60 **63 66 70** 75 77 85 91 94 97 ☆☆☆☆ **1994 Late Bottled Vintage Port £££;** ☆☆☆☆ **1997 Vintage Port £££**

☆ **Alain Graillot** [al-lan gri-yoh] (*Rhône,* France) Producer who should be applauded for shaking up the sleepy, largely undistinguished *appellation* of *Crozes-Hermitage,* using grapes from rented vineyards. All the reds are excellent, and La Guiraude is the wine from the top vineyard. ☆☆☆☆ **1996 Crozes Hermitage la Guiraude £££**

Grampians (*Victoria,* Australia) New name for *Great Western.*

Gran Reserva [gran rays-sehr-vah] (Spain) Quality wine aged for a designated number of years in wood and, in theory, only produced in the best *vintages.* Can be dried out and less worthwhile than *Crianza* or *Reserva.*

Grand Cru [gron kroo] (France) Prepare to be confused. Term referring to the finest vineyards and the – supposedly – equally fine wine made in them. It is an official designation in *Bordeaux, Burgundy, Champagne* and *Alsace,* but its use varies. In *Alsace* where there are 50 or so *Grand Cru* Vineyards, some are more convincingly grand than others. In *Burgundy Grand Cru* vineyards with their own *ACs,* e.g. *Montrachet,* do not need to carry the name of the village (e.g. *Chassagne-Montrachet*) on their label. Where these regions apply the designation to pieces of soil, in *Bordeaux* it applies to châteaux whose vineyards can be bought and sold. More confusingly, still *St. Emilion* can be described as either *Grand Cru, Grand Cru Classé* – or both – or *Premier Grand Cru Classé.*

☆ **Ch. Grand Mayne** [gron-mayn] (*St. Emilion Grand Cru, Bordeaux,* France) Producer of rich, deeply flavoursome, modern *St. Emilion.* Not for traditionalists perhaps, but still due for promotion to *Premier Grand Cru* status. 82 83 85 86 87 88 89 90 92 93 94 95 96 97 98

☆ **Ch. du Grand Moulas** [gron moo-lahs] (*Rhône,* France) Very classy *Côtes du Rhône* property with unusually complex red wines. ☆☆☆☆ **1995 ££**

Grand Vin [gron van] (*Bordeaux,* France) The first (quality) wine of an estate – as opposed to its *second label.*

☆ **Ch. Grand-Pontet** [gron pon-tay] (*St. Emilion Grand Cru Classé, Bordeaux,* France) Rising star with showy wines. 86 88 89 90 92 93 94 95 96 97 98.

☆ **Ch. Grand-Puy-Ducasse** [gron pwee doo-kass] (*Pauillac 5ème Cru Classé, Bordeaux,* France) Reliably excellent wines from an over-performing fifth growth *Pauillac* property. 79 81 **82** 83 **85 86** 88 89 90 91 92 93 94 95 96 **97** 98

☆ **Ch. Grand-Puy-Lacoste** [gron pwee lah-kost] (*Pauillac 5ème Cru Classé, Bordeaux,* France) Top-class fifth growth owned by the Borie family of *Ducru-Beaucaillou* and now right up there among the *Super Seconds.* 79 81 **82 83 85** 86 88 89 90 91 92 **93** 94 95 96 97 98 ☆☆☆☆☆ **1996 £££**

☆ **Grande Rue** [grond-roo] (*Burgundy,* France) Recently promoted *Grand Cru* in Vosne-Romanée, across the way from Romanée-Conti (hence the promotion). Sadly, the Dom. Lamarche to which this *monopole* belongs is an improving but long-term under-performer.

Grandes Marques [grond mahrk] (*Champagne,* France) Once-official designation for "big name" *Champagne* houses, irrespective of the quality of their wines. Now, although the "Syndicat" of which they were members has been disbanded, the expression is still quite widely used.

☆ **Grands-Echézeaux** [grons AY-sheh-zoh] (*Burgundy,* France) One of the best *Grand Crus* in *Burgundy*; and supposedly better than the neighbouring *Echézeaux.* The *Domaine de la Romanée-Conti* is a famous producer here.

Grange [graynzh] (*South* Australia) *Penfolds'* and Australia's greatest wine – "The Southern Hemisphere's only first growth" – pioneered by Max Schubert in the early 1950s following a visit to Europe. From the outset, although Schubert was aiming to match top *Bordeaux,* he used *Shiraz* and American (rather than French) oak barrels and a blend of grapes from 70-year-old vines sited in several South Australian regions. Recently discovered in the US and thus a collector's item that sells out as soon as each *vintage* hits the streets. **55 63 66 71 76 78 81 83 86 88** 90 91 93 ☆☆☆☆☆ **1993 ££££**

Grangehurst [graynzh-huhrst] (*Stellenbosch,* South Africa) Concentrated modern reds from a small winery converted from the family squash court! Expanding. Good *Cabernet* and *Pinotage.* ☆☆☆☆ **1997 Pinotage ££**

Weingut Grans-Fassian [grans-fass-yan] (*Mosel,* Germany) Improving estate with some really fine, classic wine – especially at a supposedly basic level. ☆☆☆☆ **1997 Riesling ££**

Yves Grassa [gras-sah] (*South-West,* France). Pioneering producer of *Vin de Pays des Côtes de Gascogne* – now moving from *Colombard* and *Ugni Blanc* into *Sauvignon Blanc.* ☆☆☆ **1999 Dom. de Tariquet £**

Elio Grasso [eh-lee-yoh grah-so] (*Piedmont,* Italy) Producer of high quality, single-vineyard *Barolo* (Casa Maté and Chiniera), *Barbera, Dolcetto* and *Chardonnay.*

Alfred Gratien [gras-see-yen] (*Champagne,* France) Good *Champagne* house, using traditional methods. Also owner of *Loire* sparkling wine-maker Gratien et Meyer, based in *Saumur.* ☆☆☆ **1990 Vintage Champagne £££**

🍇 **Grauerburgunder** [grow-urh-buhr-goon-duhr] (Germany) Another name for *Pinot Gris. Müller-Catoir.*

Dom. la Grave [lah grahv] (*Graves, Bordeaux,* France) Small property in the *Graves* with a growing reputation for 100 per cent *Sémillon* whites.

La Grave à Pomerol [lah grahv ah pom-rohl] (*Pomerol, Bordeaux,* France) One of the excellent Christian *Mouiex's* characteristically stylish estates that shows off *Pomerol's* plummy-cherry fruit at its best.

Grave del Friuli [grah-veh del free-yoo-lee] (*Friuli-Venezia Giulia,* Italy) *DOC* for young-drinking reds and whites. *Cabernet, Merlot* and *Chardonnay* are increasingly successful.

Graves [grahv] (*Bordeaux,* France) Large region producing vast quantities of red and white, ranging from good to indifferent. The best whites come from *Pessac-Léognan* in the northern part of the region and are sold under that *appellation.* Reds can have a lovely raspberryish character. Red: **70** 78 79 81 82 83 85 86 88 89 90 94 95 97 98 96 White: 78 79 82 **83 85 86** 88 89 90 93 94 95 96 97 98 *Ch. d'Archambeau; de Chantegrive; Clos Floridène;* Rahoul; du Seuil; Villa Bel Air.

☲ **Gravner** [grahv-nehr] (*Friuli-Venezia Giulia*, Italy) Innovative producer with brilliant oaked *Chardonnay* and *Sauvignon Blanc* produced in *Collio* but not under the rules of that denomination. The blended white Breg is good too.

Great Western (*Victoria*, Australia) Old name for region noted for *Seppelt's* sparkling wines including the astonishing "Sparkling *Burgundy*" *Shirazes*, for *Best's* and for the wines of *Mount Langi Ghiran*. Now renamed *Grampians*, though I suspect it will take time for enthusiasts to get used to the new name.

🍇 **Grechetto** [grek-keh-toh] (Italy) Subtly spicy white grape used to fine effect in *Umbria* by *Adanti*, *Falesco*, Goretti and Palazzone.

☲ **Greco di Tufo** [greh-koh dee too-foh] (*Campania*, Italy) From *Campania*, best-known white from the ancient Greco grape; dry, characterfully herby southern wine. **Botomagno;** *Librandi;* **Mastroberardino; Vignadora.**

Greece Finally, if belatedly, beginning to modernise its wine industry – and to exploit the potential of a set of grapes grown nowhere else. Unfortunately, as Greece begins to rid itself of its taste for the stewed, oxidised styles of the past, the modern wines are so popular in the smart restaurants in Athens that they tend to be both expensive and hard to find overseas. Oddbins and the Greek Wine Center in the UK have a good range. **Amethystos;** *Antonopoulos; Boutari; Ch. Carras; Gaia; Gentilini; Gerovassilou; Hatzimichalis;* Ktima; *Lazarides;* Papantonis; *Skouras;* Strofilia.

☲ **Green Point** (*Yarra Valley*, Australia) See *Dom. Chandon*.

☲ **Green & Red** (*Napa Valley*, California) Fast-rising star with impressive *Zinfandel*. ✰✰✰✰ **1997 Chiles Valley Zinfandel £££**

🍇 **Grenache** [greh-nash] Red grape of the *Rhône* (aka *Garnacha* in Spain) making spicy, peppery, full-bodied wine, provided yields are kept low. Also used to make rosés across Southern France, Australia and California.

☲ **Marchesi de Gresy** [mah-kay-see day greh-see] (*Piedmont*, Italy) Good producer of single-vineyard *Barbaresco*. ✰✰✰✰ **1995 Martinenga ££££**

☲ **Grgich Hills** [guhr-gich] (*Napa Valley*, California) Pioneering producer of *Cabernet Sauvignon*, *Chardonnay* and *Fumé Blanc*. The name is a concatenation of the two founders – Mike Grgich and Austin Hills, rather than a topographical feature. ✰✰✰✰ **1997 Napa Valley Chardonnay £££**

☲ **Miljenko Grgich** [mell-yen-koh guhr-gich] (Croatia) The coast of Dalmatia gets the *Grgich Hills* treatment – and a Californian rediscovers his Eastern European roots.

🍇 **Grignolino** [green-yoh-lee-noh] (*Piedmont*, Italy) Red grape and modest but refreshing cherryish wine, e.g. the *DOC* Grignolino d'Asti. Drink young.

☲ **Ch. Grillet** [gree-yay] (*Rhône*, France) *Appellation* consisting of a single estate and producer of improving *Viognier* white. Neighbouring *Condrieu* is still better value. ✰✰✰ **1996 Ch. Grillet ££££**

☲ **Marqués de Griñon** [green-yon] (*La Mancha*, *Rioja*, *Ribera del Duero*, Spain/Argentina) Dynamic exception to the dull *La Mancha* rule, making wines, with the help of *Michel Rolland*, which can outclass *Rioja*. The juicy *Cabernet Merlot* and fresh white *Rueda* have been joined by Durius, a blend from *Ribera del Duero*, an exceptional new *Syrah* and an extraordinary *Petit Verdot*. Look out too for new wines from Argentina. ✰✰✰✰✰ **1996 Dominio de Valdespusa Syrah ££;** ✰✰✰✰ **1998 Dominio de Veldespusa Petit Verdot ££**

�275 **Bernard Gripa** [gree-pah] (*Rhône*, France) Maker of top-notch *St. Joseph* – ripe, thick, *tarry* wine that could age forever. ☆☆☆☆ 1997 St. Joseph £££

�275 **Jean-Louis Grippat** [gree-pah] (*Rhône*, France) An unusually great white *Rhône* producer in *Hermitage* and *St. Joseph*. His reds in both *appellations* are less stunning, but still worth buying in their subtler-than-most way. Look out too for his ultra-rare Cuvée des Hospices, *St. Joseph* Rouge. ☆☆☆☆ 1997 Hermitage ££££

�275 **Dom. Jean Grivot** [gree-voh] (*Burgundy*, France) Top-class *Vosne-Romanée* estate whose winemaker Etienne has one of the most sensitive touches in Burgundy. ☆☆☆☆ 1997 Vosne-Romanée Les Beaux Monts ££££

�275 **Robert Groffier** [grof-fee-yay] (*Burgundy*, France) Up-and-coming estate with top-class wines from *Chambolle-Musigny*. ☆☆☆☆☆ 1996 Bonnes Mares ££££

�275 **Groot Constantia** [khroot-kon-stan-tee-yah] (*Constantia*, South Africa) Government-run, 300-year-old wine estate and national monument that is finally making worthwhile wines. ☆☆☆ 1995 Cabernet Sauvignon £££

�275 **Dom. Anne Gros** [groh] (*Burgundy*, France) Unfortunately for one's wallet, the best wines from this *Vosne-Romanée domaine* are as expensive as they are delicious – but they are worth every cent. ☆☆☆☆ 1997 Clos de Vougeot ££££

�275 **Jean Gros** [groh] (*Burgundy*, France) Slightly less impressive *Vosne-Romanée* producer, but the *Clos Vougeots* are good. ☆☆☆☆ 1995 Clos du Vougeot ££££

�275 **Michel Gros** [groh] (*Burgundy*, France) Least recommendable of the Gros clan – unless you love toasty new oak as much as some US critics.

🍇 **Gros Lot/Grolleau** [groh-loh] (*Loire*, France) The workhorse black grape of the *Loire*, particularly in *Anjou*, used to make white, rosé and sparkling *Saumur*.

🍇 **Gros Plant (du Pays Nantais)** [groh-plon doo pay-yee non-tay] (*Loire*, France) Light, sharp white *VDQS* wine from the western *Loire*. In all but the best hands, serves to make even a poor *Muscadet* look good.

�275 **Grosset** [gros-set] (*Clare Valley*, South Australia) Terrific white (*Chardonnay*, *Semillon* and especially *Riesling*) specialist now making great reds too (the Gaia red *Bordeaux*-blend and lovely *Pinot Noir*). Give all wines time to develop. (Mrs Grosset, incidentally, is responsible for the similarly brilliant *Mount Horrocks* wines). ☆☆☆☆ 1998 Polish Hill Riesling £££

Grosslage [gross-lah-guh] (Germany) Wine district, the third subdivision after *Anbaugebiet* (e.g. *Rheingau*) and *Bereich* (e.g. *Nierstein*). For example, *Michelsberg* is a *Grosslage* of the *Bereich Piesport*.

�275 **Groth** [grahth] (*Napa Valley*, California) Serious producer of quality *Cabernet* and *Chardonnay*. ☆☆☆☆ 1995 Napa Valley Cabernet Reserve £££

�275 **Grove Mill** (New Zealand) Young *Marlborough* winery with good *Sauvignon Blanc*, *Chardonnay* and *Riesling*. ☆☆☆☆ 1999 Sauvignon Blanc ££

�275 **Ch. Gruaud-Larose** [groo-oh lah-rohz] (*St. Julien 2ème Cru Classé*, *Bordeaux*, France) One of the stars of the *Cordier* stable. Rich but potentially slightly unsubtle. The second wine is "Le Sarget".

🍇 **Grüner Veltliner** [groo-nuhr felt-lee-nuhr] Spicy white grape of Austria and Eastern Europe, producing light, fresh, aromatic wine – and for *Willi Opitz* an extraordinary *late harvest* version. *Knoll; Kracher;* Lang; Metternich-Sándor; *Opitz; Pichler; Prager;* Schuster; Steininger.

�275 **Bodegas Guelbenzu** [guhl-bent-zoo] (*Navarra*, Spain) Starry new-wave producer of rich red wines using local grapes and *Cabernet*. ☆☆☆☆ 1998 Garnacha ££; ☆☆☆☆ 1996 Guelbenzu Evo ££

�275 **Guerrieri-Rizzardi** [gwer-reh-ree rit-zar-dee] (*Veneto*, Italy) Solid organic producer, with good rather than great *Amarone* and single-vineyard *Soave Classico*. ☆☆☆☆ 1995 Rosso £££

🍷 **Guffens-Heynen** [goof-fens ay-na(n)] (*Burgundy*, France) Rising star in *Pouilly-Fuissé.* ☆☆☆☆ 1998 Mâcon Pierreclos £££

🍷 **E Guigal** [gee-gahl] (*Rhône*, France) Still the yardstick for *Rhône* reds, despite increased competition from *Chapoutier.* His extraordinarily pricy single-vineyard La Mouline, La Landonne and La Turque wines from *Côte Rôtie* and Château d'Ampuis wines are still ahead of the young turks and the "Brune et Blonde" blend of grapes from two hillsides remains a benchmark for this **appellation**. The basic red and white *Côtes du Rhône* are also well worth looking out for. ☆☆☆☆☆ 1995 Côte Rôtie la Landonne ££££; ☆☆☆☆ 1995 Côte Rôtie Brune et Blonde ££

🍷 **Guimaraens** [gee-mah-rens] (*Douro*, Portugal) Associated with *Fonseca*; under-rated *port*-house making good wines. ☆☆☆☆☆ 1984 Fonseca Guimaraens Vintage Port ££££

🍷 **Ch. Guiraud** [gee-roh] (*Sauternes Premier Cru Classé, Bordeaux*, France) *Sauternes* classed growth, recently restored to original quality. Good wines but rarely among the most complex sweet *Bordeaux.* 67 79 81 82 **83** 85 86 87 88 89 90 92 93 94 95 96 97 98 99 ☆☆☆☆ 1997 ££££

🍷 **Weingut Gunderloch** [goon-duhr-lokh] (*Rheinhessen*, Germany) One of the few estates to make *Rheinhessen* wines of truly reliable quality. ☆☆☆☆ 1997 Nackenheimer Rothenbergl Riesling Gold Cap Auslese £££

🍷 **Gundlach-Bundschu** [guhnd-lakh buhnd-shoo] (*Sonoma Valley*, California) Good, well-made, juicy *Merlot* and spicy *Zinfandel.*

🍷 **Louis Guntrum** [goon-troom] (*Rheinhessen*, Germany) Family-run estate with a penchant for *Sylvaner.* ☆☆☆☆ 1997 Oppenheimer Herrenberg Silvaner Eiswein ££££

🍷 **Ch. la Gurgue** [lah guhrg] (*Margaux Cru Bourgeois, Bordeaux*, France) *Cru Bourgeois* across the track from *Ch. Margaux.* Less impressive since the same owner's neighbouring *Ch. Ferrière* has both improved and increased its production, but the 1999 is a winner. **83 85** 86 88 89 90 95 96

🍇 **Gutedel** [goot-edel] (Germany) German name for the *Chasselas* grape.

🍷 **Friedrich-Wilhelm Gymnasium** [free-drikh vil-helm-gim-nahz-yuhm] (*Mosel*, Germany) Big-name estate that ought to be making better wine. ☆☆☆☆ 1996 Graacher Himmelreich Riesling Spätlese £££

H

🍷 **Weingut Fritz Haag** [hahg] (*Mosel-Saar-Ruwer*, Germany) Superlative small estate with classic *Rieslings.* ☆☆☆☆☆ 1997 Brauneberger Juffer Sonnenuhr Riesling Auslese Gold Cap ££££

🍷 **Weingut Reinhold Haart** [rihn-hohld hahrt] (*Mosel*, Germany) Fast rising *Piesport* star. ☆☆☆☆ 1997 Piesporter Goldtröpfchen Riesling Auslese £££ **Halbtrocken** [hahlb-trok-en] (Germany) Off-dry. Usually a safer buy than *Trocken* in regions like the *Mosel*, *Rheingau* and *Rheinhessen*, but still often aggressively *acidic.* Look for *QbA* or *Auslese* versions.

Hallgarten [hal-gahr-ten] (*Rheingau*, Germany) Important town near *Hattenheim* producing robust wines including the (in Germany) well-regarded produce from *Schloss Vollrads.* QbA/Kab/Spät: **85 88 89 90** 91 92 93 95 96 97 98   Aus/Beeren/Tba: **83 85 88 89 90** 92 93 94 95 96 97 98

🍷 **Hamilton Russell Vineyards** (*Walker Bay*, South Africa) Pioneer of impressive *Pinot Noir* and *Chardonnay* at a winery in Hermanus at the southernmost tip of the *Cape.* Now expanded to include a *second label* – Southern Right – to produce a varietal *Pinotage*, and a *Chenin*-based white.

☨ **Handley Cellars** (*Mendocino,* California) Fine sparkling wine producer with a particularly good pure *Chardonnay Blanc de Blancs.* The still *Chardonnay* is pretty impressive too.

☨ **Hanging Rock** (*Victoria,* Australia) As in the movie, "Picnic at....", this winery makes Australia's biggest, butteriest sparkling wine and some pretty good reds and whites. ☆☆☆☆ 1997 Heathcote Shiraz £££

☨ **Hanzell** (*Sonoma,* California) One of the great old names of Californian wine, and a pioneer producer of *Chardonnay* and *Pinot Noir.* The former grape is still a major success story – in its broad-shouldered, traditional Californian style.

☨ **BRL Hardy** (*South* Australia) The second biggest wine producer in Australia, encompassing *Houghton* and *Moondah Brook* in *Western Australia, Leasingham* in the *Clare Valley, Redman* in *Coonawarra, E& E* in *Barossa,* Hardy's itself and *Ch. Reynella. Hardy's* reliable range includes the commercial Nottage Hill, new Bankside and Banrock Station, and multi-regional blends, but the wines to look for are the top-of-the-range Eileen and Thomas Hardy. The *Ch. Reynella* wines from *McLaren Vale* fruit (and, in the case of the reds, using *basket presses*) are good, quite lean examples of the region. Hardy's ventures in Italy (d'Istinto) and France (la Baume) are less impressive. ☆☆☆☆ 1999 Nottage Hill ££; ☆☆☆☆☆ 1997 Eileen Hardy Shiraz £££

☨ **Hargrave Vineyard** (*Long Island,* New York, US) Alex Hargrave's recently-sold, nearly 30 year-old winery put the North Fork of Long Island – not to say the island as a whole – on the wine map with its Chardonnay and Merlot. And it so impressed the owner of *Ch. Pichon-Lalande* when she visited that she apparently briefly considered making wine here.

☨ **Harlan Estate** (*Napa Valley,* California) Fiercely pricy, small quantities of *Bordeaux*-style reds, made with input from *Michel Rolland,* and using grapes from hillside vineyards.

🍇 **Hárslevelü** [harsh-leh-veh-loo] (Hungary) White grape used in *Tokaji* and for light table wines.

☨ **Harveys** (*Jerez,* Spain) Maker of the ubiquitous *Bristol Cream.* Other styles are unimpressive apart from the 1796 range and Club Classic.

☨ **Haskovo** [hash-koh-voh] (Bulgaria) Along with the more frequently seen Stambolovo and Sakar, this is a name to look out for. All three are newly privatised cooperatives that can make good, rich, red wine.

☨ **Hattenheim** [hat-ten-hime] (*Rheingau,* Germany) One of the finest villages in the *Rheingau,* with wines from producers such as *Balthasar Ress,* Von Simmern, *Schloss Rheinhartshausen* and *Schloss Schönborn.*

☨ **Hatzimichalis** [hat-zee-mikh-ahlis] (*Atalanti,* Greece) The face of future Greek winemaking? Hopefully. This self-taught producer's small estate makes variable but often top-notch *Cabernet Sauvignon, Merlot, Chardonnay* and fresh dry Atalanti white. ☆☆☆☆ 1997 Merlot ££.

☨ **Ch. Haut-Bages-Averous** [oh-bahj-aveh-roo] (*Pauillac Cru Bourgeois, Bordeaux,* France) *Second label* of *Ch. Lynch-Bages.* Good-value black-curranty *Pauillac.* 82 83 85 86 88 89 90 93 94 95 96 97 98

☨ **Ch. Haut-Bages-Libéral** [oh-bahj-lib-ay-ral] (*Pauillac 5ème Cru Classé, Bordeaux,* France) Classy small property in the same stable as *Chasse-Spleen.* 75 78 82 83 85 86 87 88 89 90 91 93 94 95 96 97 98

☨ **Ch. Haut-Bailly** [oh bih-yee] (*Pessac-Léognan Cru Classé, Bordeaux,* France) Recently sold: brilliant *Pessac-Léognan* property consistently making reliable, excellent-quality, long-lived red wines. A stunning 1998. 61 64 70 78 79 81 83 85 86 87 88 89 90 92 93 94 95 96 97 98

☨ **Ch. Haut-Batailley** [oh-ba-tih-yee] (*Pauillac 5ème Cru Classé, Bordeaux,* France) Subtly-styled wine from the same stable as *Ducru-Beaucaillou* and *Grand-Puy-Lacoste.* 85 86 88 89 90 91 92 93 95 96 97 98

Ch. Haut-Brion [oh bree-yon] (*Pessac-Léognan Premier Cru Classé, Bordeaux*, France) Pepys' favourite and still the only non-*Médoc* first growth. Situated in the *Graves* on the outskirts of *Bordeaux* in the shadow of the gasworks. Wines can be tough and hard to judge when young, but at their best they develop a rich, fruity, perfumed character which sets them apart from their peers. 1996, 1998 and 1999 were especially good, as – comparatively – were 1993, 1994 and 1995.The white is rare and often sublime. Red: **61 70 71 75 78 79 82** 85 86 88 89 90 91 92 93 94 95 96 97 98 99 White: 85 87 88 89 90 91 92 93 94 95 96 97 98 99

Ch. Haut-Marbuzet [oh-mahr-boo-zay] (*St. Estèphe Cru Bourgeois, Bordeaux*, France) *Cru bourgeois* which thinks it's a *cru classé*. Immediately imposing wine with bags of oak. Decidedly new-wave *St. Estèphe*.

Haut-Médoc [oh-may-dok] (*Bordeaux*, France) Large *appellation* which includes nearly all of the well-known *crus classés*. Basic *Haut-Médoc* should be better than plain *Médoc*. **82** 83 **85 86** 88 89 90 94 95 96 97 98

Haut-Montravel [oh-mo'n rah-vel] (*South West*, France) A potentially good alternative to *Monbazillac* and even *Sauternes*.

Haut-Poitou [oh-pwa-too] (*Loire*, France) A source of basic inexpensive *Sauvignon*.

Hautes Côtes de Beaune [oht-coht-duh-bohn] (*Burgundy*, France) Rustic wines from the hills above the big-name *communes*. Worth buying in good *vintages*; in poorer ones the grapes have problems ripening. The Cave des Hautes Côtes cooperative makes good examples.

Hautes Côtes de Nuits [oht-coht-duh-nwee] (*Burgundy*, France) Mostly red wines that are slightly tougher than *Hautes Côtes de Beaune*.

Hawke's Bay (New Zealand) Major North Island vineyard area which is finally beginning to live up to the promise of producing top-class reds. Whites can be fine too, though rarely achieving the bite of *Marlborough*. *Babich;* Brookfields; Church Road; *Cleview; Delegats; Esk Valley; Matua Valley,* Mills Reef; *Mission; Montana; Morton Estate; Ngatarawa;* CJ Pask; Sacred Hill; *Te Mata; Vidal; Villa Maria.*

Hedges (*Washington State*, US) Producer of good, rich, berryish reds from a number of the best vineyards in Washington State. ☆☆☆☆ **1997 Three Vineyards Red Mountain Reserve £££**

Ⱦ Heemskerk [heems-kuhrk] (*Tasmania*, Australia) Generally underperforming winery until its purchase by its neighbour *Pipers Brook*. The *Jansz* sparkling wine label (originally launched as a joint venture with *Roederer*) now belongs to *Yalumba*, while Heemskerk's own (excellent) sparkling wine has been renamed *Pirie*, after the owner of *Pipers Brook*.

Ⱦ Dr Heger [hay-gehr] (*Baden*, Germany) A brilliant exponent of the *Grauerburgunder* which ripens well in this warm region of Germany.
☆☆☆☆ **1997 Ihringer Winkleberg Grauer Burgunder Spätlese Trocken £££**

Ⱦ Heggies [heg-gees] (*South* Australia) Impressive *Adelaide Hills* label in the same camp as *Yalumba*. Lovely *Riesling*, *Viognier*, *Merlot*, *Pinot Noir* and stickies. ☆☆☆☆ 1997 **Botrytis-Affected Riesling ££**

🍇 Heida [hi-da] (Switzerland) Spicy Swiss grape variety, thought to be related to the *Gewürztraminer*. When carefully handled, produces wonderfully refreshing wines .

Ⱦ Charles Heidsieck [hihd-seek] (*Champagne*, France) Go-ahead producer whose winemaker Daniel Thibaut (*Bonnet, Piper Heidsieck*) has recently introduced the clever notion of labelling non-*vintage* wine with a "mis en cave" bottling date. Wines are all recommendable. ☆☆☆☆☆ **Brut Réserve Mis en Cave 1995 £££**

Ⱦ Heidsieck Dry Monopole [hihd-seek] (*Champagne*, France) A subsidiary of *Mumm* and thus until 1999 controlled by Seagrams. Wines with the same quality aspirations as that brand. Even so, recent *vintages* have shown some improvement. ☆☆☆ **Diamant Bleu ££££**

Ⱦ Heitz Cellars [hihtz] (*Napa Valley*, California) One of the great names of California and the source of stunning reds in the 1970s. More recent (pre 1992) releases of the flagship Martha's Vineyard *Cabernet* have tasted unacceptably musty, however, as have the traditionally almost-as-good Bella Oaks. At the winery and among some critics, such criticisms are apparently treated as lèse-majesté. Recent (post 1996) *vintages* of Martha's Vineyard wines are made from newly replanted (post-Californian *phylloxera*) vines.

Ⱦ Joseph Henriot [on-ree-yoh] (*Champagne*, France) Modern *Champagne* house producing soft, rich wines. Now also shaking things up and improving wines at its recently purchased *Bouchard Père et Fils négociant* in *Burgundy*. ☆☆☆☆ **Champagne Blanc de Blancs ££££**

Ⱦ Henriques & Henriques [hen-reeks] (*Madeira*, Portugal) One of the few independent producers still active in *Madeira*. Top quality. ☆☆☆☆☆ **15 Year Old Verdelho £££**

Ⱦ Henry of Pelham (*Ontario*, Canada) One of Canada's better producers of Chardonnay – plus a rare recommendable example of the Baco Noir grape.

Ⱦ Henschke [hench-kee] (*Adelaide Hills*, Australia) One of the world's best. From the long-established Hill of Grace with its 130-year-old vines and (slightly less intense) Mount Edelstone *Shirazes* to the new Abbott's Prayer *Merlot-Cabernet* from *Lenswood*, the *Riesling* and Tilly's Vineyard white blend, there's not a poor wine here; the reds last forever. ☆☆☆☆☆ **1996 Mount Edelstone £££**

Ⱦ Vin de Pays de l'Hérault [Eh-roh] (*Languedoc-Roussillon*, France) Large region made famous by the Aimé Guibert's *Mas de Daumas Gassac*. Other producers such as Domaine Limbardie are following in his footsteps.

Ⱦ Hermitage [ayr-mee-tazh] (*Rhône*, France) Supreme Northern *Rhône appellation* for long-lived pure *Syrah*. Whites are less reliable. Red: **76 78 82 83 85 88** 89 90 91 95 96 97 98 White: **82 85** 87 **88 89 90** 91 94 **95** 96 97 98 *Belle Père & Fils;* Michel Bernard; *Chapoutier; Chave; Dom. Colombier; Grippat; Guigal; Delas; Bernard Faurie; Jaboulet Aîné; Sorrel; Cave de Tain l'Hermitage;* Tardieu-Laurent.

♟ James Herrick [heh-rick] (*Languedoc-Roussillon*, France) Dynamic Briton who brought an Australian philosophy to southern France, planting extensive *Chardonnay* vineyards and producing good-value varietal wine. Now part of Southcorp (*Penfolds* etc).

♟ The Hess Collection (*Napa Valley*, California) High-class *Cabernet* producer high in the *Mount Veeder* hills named after the owner's art collection (see *Vinopolis*). The lower-priced Hess Select *Monterey* wines are worth buying too. ☆☆☆☆☆ 1997 Mount Veeder Cabernet Sauvignon £££

Hessische Bergstrasse [hess-ishuh behrg-strah-suh] (Germany) Smallest *Anbaugebiet* capable of fine *Eisweins* and dry *Sylvaners* which can surpass those of nearby *Franken*. QbA/Kab/Spät: **85 88 89 90** 91 92 93 94 95 96 97 98 Aus/Beeren/Tba: **83 85** 88 89 90 91 92 93 94 95 96 97 98

♟ Heuriger [hoy-rig-gur] (Austria) Austria's equivalent of *Beaujolais* Nouveau – except that this new-born wine is white and sold by the jug in cafés. Of interest if only as a taste of the way most wine used to be drunk.

♟ Heyl zu Herrnsheim [highl zoo hehrn-sime] (*Rheinhessen*, Germany) Organic estate in *Nierstein* with good *Riesling* from the Plettenthal vineyard.

♟ Heymann-Löwenstein [hay-mun low-ven-stine] (*Mosel-Saar-Ruwer*, Germany) A rising star with bone dry to lusciously sweet Rieslings.

♟ Vinicola Hidalgo y Cia [hid-algoh ee-thia] (*Jerez*, Spain) Specialist producer of impeccable dry "La Gitana" *sherry* and a great many own-label offerings. ☆☆☆☆ Manzanilla Pasada Pastrada Single Vineyard Sherry ££

♟ Cavas Hill [kah-vas heel] (*Penedés*, Spain) Best-known for its sparkling wine, but also producing rich, fruity *Tempranillo* reds.

♟ Hill-Smith (South Australia) Dynamic but still very classy firm, under the same family ownership as *Pewsey Vale*, *Yalumba* and *Heggies* Vineyard, and now active in Tasmania (Jansz sparkling wine), New Zealand (*Nautilus*) and California (where its *Voss* wines are made). ☆☆☆ 1997 Estate Chardonnay.

♟ Hillstowe [hil-stoh] (*South Australia*) Up-and-coming producer in the *McLaren Vale*, using grapes from various parts of the region to produce unusually stylish *Chardonnay*, *Sauvignon Blanc* and *Cabernet-Merlot*. ☆☆☆☆ 1998 Mary's Hundred Shiraz £££

Himmelreich [him-mel-rihkh] (*Mosel*, Germany) One of the finest vineyards in *Graach*. See JJ Prum. QbA/Kab/Spät: **85 86 88 89** 90 **91 92 93** 94 95 96 97 98 Aus/Beeren/Tba: **83 85 88 89 90 91** 92 93 94 95 96 97 98

Franz Hitzberger [fruntz hits-ber-gur] (*Wachau*, Austria) A name to remember for reliable dry *Grüner Veltliner* and *Riesling*.

♟ Paul Hobbs (*Sonoma*, California) Former winemaker at *Simi*, and now a consultant at *Catena* and *Valdivieso*, Paul Hobbs makes fine *Pinot Noir*, lean *Cabernet* and rich *Chardonnay* from the memorably-named "Dinner Vineyard".

Hochfeinste [hokh-fihn-stuh] (Germany) "Very finest".

Hochgewächs QbA [hokh-geh-fex] (Germany) Recent official designation for *Rieslings* which are as ripe as a *QmP* but can still only call themselves *QbA*. This from a nation supposedly dedicated to simplifying what are acknowledged to be the most complicated labels in the world.

Hochheim [hokh-hihm] (*Rheingau,* Germany) Village whose fine *Rieslings* gave the English the word *"Hock"*. QbA/Kab/Spät: **85 86 88 89 90** 91 92 93 94 95 96 97 98 Aus/Beeren/Tba: **83 85** 88 89 90 91 92 93 94 95 96 97 98 **Geh'rat Aschrott; Konigen Victoria Berg.**

☫ **Reichsgraf zu Hoensbroech** [rike-sgrahf tzoo hoh-ern sbroh-urch] (*Baden,* Germany) A large estate specialising in *Pinot Blanc* (Weissburgunder) and *Gris* Grauburgunder

☫ **Höffstatter** [Hurf-shtah-ter] (*Alto Adige,* Italy) Star, new wave producer with unusually good *Pinot Noir.*

☫ **Hogue Cellars** [hohg] (*Washington State,* US) Highly dynamic, family-owned *Yakima Valley* producer of good *Chardonnay, Riesling, Merlot* and *Cabernet.* ☆☆☆☆ **1996 Barrel Select Merlot £££**

☫ **Hollick** (*Coonawarra,* Australia) A good, traditional producer; the *Ravenswood* is particularly worth seeking out. ☆☆☆☆ **1994 Coonawarra Cabernet-Merlot £££**

☫ **Dom. de l'Hortus** [Or-Toos] (*Languedoc-Roussillon,* France) Exciting spicy reds from *Pic St. Loup* in the *Coteaux de Languedoc* that easily outclass many an effort from big-name producers in the *Rhône.* ☆☆☆☆ **1997 £££**

☫ **Hosanna** [Oh-zah-nah] (*Pomerol, Bordeaux,* France) Christian Moueix's sleek new stablemate for *Petrus* – produced from the best part of the *Certan-Guiraud* vineyard,

☫ **Hospices de Beaune** [os-peess duh bohn] (*Burgundy,* France) Hospital whose wines (often *cuvées* or blends of different vineyards) are sold at an annual charity auction, the prices of which are erroneously thought to set the tone for the *Côte d'Or* year. In the early 1990s, wines were generally sub-standard, improving instantly in 1994 with the welcome return of winemaker André Porcheret who, before leaving once again, proved controversial by (in 1997) making wines that struck some critics (not this one) as too big and rich. In any case, be aware that although price lists often merely indicate "Hospices de Beaune" as a producer, all of the wines bought at the auction are matured and bottled by local merchants, some of whom are a great deal more scrupulous than others.

☫ **Houghton** [haw-ton] (*Swan Valley,* Australia) Long-established subsidiary of *Hardy's.* Best known in Australia for its *Chenin*-based rich white blend traditionally sold down under as "White *Burgundy*" and in Europe as "HWB". The Wildflower Ridge commercial wines are good, as are the ones from *Moondah Brook.* Look out too for the more recently launched *Cabernet-Shiraz-Malbec* "Jack Mann", named after one of *Western Australia's* pioneering winemakers. ☆☆☆☆ **1995 Jack Mann £££.**

☫ **Weingut von Hovel** [fon huh-vel] (*Mosel-Saar-Ruwer,* Germany) A 200-year-old estate with fine *Rieslings* from great vineyards. These repay the patience that they demand. ☆☆☆☆ **1997 Oberemmeler Hütte Riesling Auslese Gold Cap £££**

☫ **Howard Park** (*Western Australia*) John Wade is one of the best winemakers in *Western Australia* and one of the finest *Riesling* producers in Australia. Madfish Bay is the *second label.* ☆☆☆☆ **1998 Riesling £££**

Howell Mountain [how-wel] (*Napa Valley*, California) Increasingly well-respected hillside region in the north of the *Napa Valley*, capable of fine whites and reds that justify its *AVA*. Red: **85** 86 87 **90 91** 92 93 95 96 97 98. White: **85 90 91** 92 95 96 97 98 *Beringer; Duckhorn; Dunn; la Jota; Turley.*

�T **Huadong Winery** (*Shandong Province*, China) Dynamic joint venture producing the basic commercial Tsing Tao brand of wines. Recent *vintages* have shown a marked improvement.

�T **Alain Hudelot-Noëllat** [ood-uh-loh noh-el-lah] (*Burgundy*, France) A great winemaker whose generosity with oak is matched, especially in his *Grand Cru Richebourg* and *Romanée St.Vivant*, by intense fruit flavours. ☆☆☆☆☆ 1995 Vosne-Romanée les Suchots ££££

Huelva [wel-vah] (*Extremadura,* Spain) *DO* of the *Extremadura* region, producing rather heavy whites and fortified wines.

☆T **Gaston Huët** [oo-wet] (*Loire*, France) Winemaker Noël Pinguet produces top-quality individual vineyard examples of *Sec, Demi-Sec* and *Moëlleux* wines. The non-*vintage* sparkling wine, though only made occasionally, is top class too. ☆☆☆☆ 1997 le Haut-Lieu Sec ££££

☆T **Hugel et Fils** [oo-gel] (*Alsace*, France) Reliable *négociant*. Best are the *late harvest* and Jubilee wines. The wine "Gentil" revives the tradition of blending different grape varieties. ☆☆☆☆ 1997 Pinot Gris "Jubilée" £££

Hungary Country too long known for its infamous *Bull's Blood* and *Olasz Rizling*, rather than *Tokaji. Disznókö;* Egervin; *Megyer; Kym Milne;* Nagyrede; *Neszmély;* Pajsos; *Royal Tokay; Hugh Ryman.*

Hunter Valley (*New South Wales*, Australia) The best-known wine region in Australia is ironically one of the least suitable places to make wine. When the vines are not dying of heat and thirst they are drowning beneath the torrential rains which like to fall at harvest time. Even so, the *Shirazes* and *Semillons* – traditionally sold as *"Hermitage", "Claret", "Burgundy"*, *"Chablis"* and *"Hunter Valley Riesling"* – develop remarkably. Allandale; Allanmere; *Brokenwood;* Evans Family; Lake's Folly; Lindemans; McWilliams; Petersons; Reynolds; *Rosemount; Rothbury Estate; Tyrrells;* Wilderness Estate.

☆T **Hunter's** (*Marlborough*, New Zealand) One of *Marlborough's* most consistent producers of ripe fruity *Sauvignon Blancs* and now a quality sparkling wine. ☆☆☆☆☆ 1997 Miru Miru Brut £££; ☆☆☆☆☆ 1999 Sauvignon Blanc £££

☆T **Ch. de Hureau** [oo-roh] (*Loire*, France) One of the few producers to excel in all styles of *Saumur*, from rich red to sparkling white.

❦ **Huxelrebe** [huk-sel-ray-buh] Minor white grape, often grown in England but proving what it can do when harvested late in Germany. Anselmann (Germany); Barkham Manor; Nutbourne Manor (England).

Hybrid [hih-brid] Cross-bred grape *Vitis vinifera* (European) x *Vitis labrusca* (North American) – an example is *Seyval Blanc.*

Hydrogen sulphide Naturally occurring rotten egg-like gas produced by yeasts as a by-product of fermentation, or by *reductive* conditions. Before bottling, may be cured by *racking*. If left untreated, hydrogen sulphide will react with other components in the wine to form *mercaptans*. Stinky bottled wines may often be "cleaned up" by decanting or by the addition of a copper coin. Unfortunately, too many (especially in *Ribera del Duero* for some reason) go unnoticed.

I

Iambol [yam-bohl] (*Southern Region,* Hungary) Large, former cooperative which now makes commercial *Merlot* and *Cabernet Sauvignon* reds, particularly for sale overseas under the Domaines Boyar label.

Icewine Increasingly popular Anglicisation of the German term *Eiswein,* used particularly by Canadian producers making luscious, spicily exotic wines from the frozen grapes of varieties like *Vidal.*

IGT – Indicazione Geografiche Tipici (Italy) New designation designed to create a home for quality non-*DOC/DOCG* wines that were previously sold as *Vino da Tavola.*

Vin de Pays de l'Île de Beauté [eel-duh-bow-tayl] (*Corsica,* France) Designation that includes varietal wines (including *Pinot Noir, Cabernet, Syrah,* and *Merlot* as well as local grapes). Often better than the island's *ACs.*

Imbottigliato nel'origine [im-bot-til-yah-toh neh-loh-ree-zhee-nay] (Italy) Estate-bottled.

Imperial(e) [am-pay-ray-ahl] (*Bordeaux,* France) Bottle containing almost six and a half litres of wine (eight and a half bottles). Cherished by collectors partly through rarity, partly through the longevity that large bottles give their contents.

India Source of generally execrable table wine and surprisingly reliable sparkling wine, labelled as Marquis de Pompadour or *Omar Khayam.*

Inferno [een-fehr-noh] (*Lombardy,* Italy) *Lombardy DOC. Nebbiolo* red that needs ageing for at least five years. ☆☆☆ **1994 Nino Negri ££**

Inglenook Vineyards [ing-gel-nook] (*Napa Valley,* California) Once-great winery which, like *Beaulieu,* fell into the hands of the giant Grand Metropolitan. The Gothic building and vineyards now belong appropriately to Francis Ford-Coppola. The now far from dazzling brand has been sold to the giant Canandaigua which has also recently bought *Franciscan* and *Simi.*

Inniskillin (*Ontario,* Canada) Long-established, pioneering winery with good *Icewines* (from the Vidal grape), highly successful *Chardonnay,* improving *Pinot Noir* and a rare example of a good *Maréchal Foch*

Institut National des Appellations d'Origine (INAO) (France) French official body which designates and (half-heartedly) polices quality, and outlaws sensible techniques like irrigation and the blending of *vintages,* which are permitted elsewhere. Which is why *Appellation Contrôlée* wines are often inferior to – and sell at lower prices than – the newer *Vins de Pays.*

International Wine Challenge (England) Wine competition, held in London by WINE Magazine and in, Tokyo, China, Hong Kong, and Singapore. (The author is founder chairman.)

International Wine & Spirit Competition (England) Wine competition, held in London.

Iphofen (*Franken*, Germany) One of the finest places to sample wines made from the *Sylvaner*. Modern wine drinkers may, however, prefer the *Rieslings* which are fruitier and less earthy in style.

IPR - Indicação de Proveniência Regulamentada (Portugal) Designation for wines that fall beneath the top – *DOC* – grade and above the basic Vinho Regional.

Irancy [ee-ron-see] (*Burgundy*, France) Little-known light reds and rosés made near *Chablis* from a blend of grapes including the *Pinot Noir* and the little-known *César*. Curiously, Irancy has *AC* status whereas nearby *Sauvignon de St. Bris* is merely a VDQS region. **Brocard;** Simonnet-Febvre.

Iron Horse Vineyards (*Sonoma* Valley, California) One of the best sparkling wine producers in the New World, thanks to cool-climate vineyards. Reds and still whites are increasingly impressive too.
☆☆☆ 1993 Chardonnay Estate Cuvée Joy £££

Irouléguy [ee-roo-lay-gee] (*South-West*, France) Earthy, spicy reds and rosés, and improving whites from Basque country where names seem to include an abundance of the letter "x". **Dom. Brana;** Etxegaraya; Irouléguy **Cooperative.**

Isinglass [Ih-sing-glahs] *Fining* agent derived from sturgeon bladders.

Isole e Olena [ee-soh-lay ay oh-lay-nah] (*Tuscany*, Italy) Brilliant pioneering small *Chianti* estate with a pure *Sangiovese Super-Tuscan, Cepparello* and Italy's first (technically illegal) *Syrah*. ☆☆☆☆ 1995 Cepparello £££

Isonzo [Ih-son-zoh] (*Friuli-Venezia Giulia*, Italy) One of the best *DOCs* in this region, offering a wide range of varietal wines from some very go-ahead producers. **Lis Neris-Pecorari; Ronco del Gelso;** *Vie di Romans;* Villanova.

Israel Once the source of appalling stuff, but the new-style varietal wines are increasingly impressive. **Golan Heights; Carmel.**

Ch. d'Issan [dee-son] (*Margaux 3ème Cru Classé, Bordeaux*, France) Recently revived *Margaux* third growth with lovely, recognisable blackcurrant *Cabernet Sauvignon* intensity.

꜀ **Italian Riesling/Riesling Italico** [ee-tah-lee-koh] Not the great *Rhine Riesling*, but another name for an unrelated variety, which also goes by the names *Welschriesling, Lutomer* and *Laski Rizling*, and is widely grown in Northern and Eastern Europe. At its best in Austria.

Italy Tantalising, seductive, infuriating. In many ways the most exciting wine nation in the world, though, as ever, in a state of change as it reorganises its wine laws. See individual regions.

J

꜀ **J** (Sonoma, California) One of California's most reliable sparkling wines – originally produced by *Jordan* in the winery where the dire Piper Sonoma used to be made.

꜀ **JP Vinhos** (Portugal) See *Peter Bright*.

꜀ **Paul Jaboulet Aîné** [zha-boo-lay ay-nay] (*Rhône,* France) The wine world was saddened to learn of the death last year from a heart attack of Gérard Jaboulet, the highly popular international face of this family *négociant* which owns the illustrious *Hermitage* La Chapelle vineyard. Despite being overshadowed nowadays by *Guigal*, this remains a reliable producer of a wide range of wines apart from the La Chapelle, including white *Hermitage*, chunky *St. Joseph*, good *Côtes du Rhône* and *Châteauneuf-du-Pape*. ☆☆☆☆☆ 1996 Hermitage la Chapelle £££

꜀ **Jackson Estate** (*Marlborough,* New Zealand) Neighbour of *Cloudy Bay* and producer of *Sauvignon*, which gives that superstar estate a run for its money. The fizz is good too. ☆☆☆☆ 1999 Chardonnay ££

꜀ **Jacob's Creek** (*South Australia*) Brilliantly commercial *South Australian* wines made by *Orlando*. Try the recently launched sparkling wine.

꜀ **Jacquart** [zha-kahr] (*Champagne,* France) Large cooperative with some top-class wines. ☆☆☆☆ 1988 Cuvée Nominée ££££

꜀ **Jacquère** [zha-kehr] The slightly citrusy grape of *Savoie.*

꜀ **Jacquesson et Fils** [jak-son] (*Champagne,* France) A small *Champagne* house that deserves to be better known, particularly for its delicately stylish *Blanc de Blancs*. ☆☆☆☆ 1990 Blanc de Blancs ££££

꜀ **Louis Jadot** [zha-doh] (*Burgundy,* France) Good, sometimes great, *Beaune négociant* with a growing number of its own top-class vineyards in *Beaune*, *Chassagne-* and Puligny-Montrachet. Jadot has also been a pioneering producer of *Rully* in the *Côte Chalonnaise*. Whites are most impressive. ☆☆☆☆ 1996 Beaune Premier Cru £££

꜀ **Jaffelin** [zhaf-lan] (*Burgundy,* France) Small *négociant*, particularly good at supposedly "lesser" *appellations* – *Rully Blanc* and *Monthélie* are particularly good – but winemaker Bernard Repolt (who is now also responsible for the improving wines at *Bouchard Aîné*) is now showing his skills across the board. ☆☆☆☆ 1998 St. Romain £££

꜀ **Joseph Jamet** [zha-may] (*Rhône,* France) Top-class *Côte Rôtie* estate, making unusually stylish wines for this *appellation*. ☆☆☆☆ 1997 Côte Rôtie ££££

꜀ **Jamieson's Run** (*Coonawarra,* Australia) *Mildara's* prize-winning, good-value red and white wines. Just what commercial wine should be. ☆☆☆☆ 1998 Jamieson's Run Merlot ££

꜀ **Dom. de la Janasse** [ja-nass] (*Rhône,* France) High-quality *Châteauneuf-du-Pape* estate, producing three individual wines under this *appellation*, plus a good *Côtes du Rhône* les Garrigues. ☆☆☆☆ 1998 Côtes du Rhône les Tradition £££

꜀ **Jansz** [yantz] (*Tasmania,* Australia) See *Yalumba* and *Pirie*.

♟ **Vin de Pays du Jardin de la France** [jar-da'n duh lah fronss] (*Loire*, France) Large *Loire* region that can produce alternatives to the region's *appellations*, but tends to offer light, unripe whites. ☆☆☆☆☆ **1999 Pierre Fuery Chardonnay £££**

♟ **Robert Jasmin** [zhas-man] (*Rhône*, France) Traditionalist *Côte Rotie* estate, producing great wine despite (or thanks to) his dislike of new oak. ☆☆☆☆☆ **1994 Côte Rôtie ££££**

Jasnières [zhan-yehr] (*Loire*, France) On rare occasions bone-dry and – even rarer – *Moelleux*, sweet *Chenin Blanc* wines from *Touraine*. Buy carefully. Poorly made, over-sulphured efforts offer a pricy chance to taste the *Chenin* at its worst. White: 86 88 89 90 94 95 96 97 98 Sweet White: 76 83 85 86 **88 89 90 94** 95 96 97 98

♟ **Jasper Hill** (*Bendigo,* Australia) Winery in Heathcote with a cult following for both reds and whites – especially those from the Georgia's Paddock vineyard. ☆☆☆☆ **1997 Georgia's Paddock Riesling, Heathcote ££**

♟ **Jaume Serra** [how-may seh-rah] (*Penedès*, Spain) Privately owned company which recently relocated from *Alella* to *Penedès*, and is doing good things with *Xarel-lo*.

♟ **Patrick Javillier** [zha-vil-yay] (*Burgundy*, France) Reliable, small merchant making meticulous village *Meursault* and good reds. ☆☆☆☆ **1997 Meursault Les Tillets ££££**

♟ **Henri Jayer** [zha-yay] (*Burgundy*, France) Now retired cult winemaker who is still represented on labels referring to Georges et Henri. Also an influence on the wines of *Méo-Camuzet*.

♟ **Robert Jayer-Gilles** [zhah-yay-zheel] (*Burgundy*, France) *Henri Jayer's* cousin, whose top wines – including an *Echézeaux* – bear comparison with those of his more famous relative. (His whites – particularly the *Aligoté* – are good too.)) ☆☆☆☆☆ **1997 Echézeaux ££££**

Jerez (de la Frontera) [hay-reth] (Spain) Center of the *sherry* trade, giving its name to entire *DO* area. **Gonzalez Byass; Lustau; Hidalgo; Barbadillo.**

♟ **Jermann** [zhehr-man] (*Friuli-Venezia Giulia,* Italy) Brilliant winemaker who gets outrageous flavours – and prices – out of every white grape variety he touches. Look out for the *Vintage* Tunina blend of *Tocai*, *Picolit* and *Malvasia*, and the "Dreams" white blend plus the single-vineyard Capo Martino. Also good at *Chardonnay*, *Pinot Gris* and *Pinot Blanc*. ☆☆☆☆ **1998 Pinot Bianco £££**

Jeroboam [zhe-roh-bohm] Large bottle; in *Champagne* holding three litres (four bottles); in *Bordeaux*, four and a half (six bottles). Best to make sure before writing your cheque.

Jesuitengarten [zhes-yoo-wi-ten-gahr-ten] (*Rheingau*, Germany) One of Germany's top vineyards – well handled by *Bassermann-Jordan*. QbA/Kab/Spät: 85 86 **88 89 90** 91 92 93 94 95 96 97 Aus/Beeren/Tba: 83 85 88 89 90 91 92 93 94 95 96 97

Jeunes Vignes [zhuhn veen] Denotes vines too young for their crop to be sold as an *Appellation Contrôlée* wine.

♟ **Dom. François Jobard** [fron-swah joh-bahr] (*Burgundy*, France) Great white wine estate in *Meursault*. ☆☆☆☆ **1995 Meursault Genevrières £££**

♟ **Dom. Joblot** [zhob-loh] (*Burgundy*, France) One of the top *domaines* in *Givry*. ☆☆☆ **1996 Cellier Aux Moines £££**

☨ **Charles Joguet** [zho-gay] (*Loire*, France) One of the finest producers of red *Loire*, making *Chinon* wines that last. He is also notable in having some of the only quality vines in France that have not been grafted onto *phylloxera*-resistant American rootstock.
☆☆☆☆ 1998 Chinon, Clos de la Cure ££

Johannisberg [zho-han-is-buhrg.] (*Rheingau*, Germany) Village making superb *Riesling*, which has lent its name to a *Bereich* covering all the *Rheingau*. QbA/Kab/Spät: **85 86 88 89 90** 91 **92** 93 94 95 96 97 98
Aus/Beeren/Tba: **83 85 88 89** 90 91 92 93 94 95 96 97 98

🍾 **Johannisberg Riesling** [rees-ling] Californian name for *Rhine Riesling*.
☨ **Johannishof** [zhoh-hah-niss-hoff] (*Rheingau*, Germany) Family-owned estate with fine examples of wines from *Johannisberg* and *Rüdesheim*.
☨ **Weingut Karl-Heinz Johner** [karl-hihntz yoh-nuh] (*Baden*, Germany) Former winemaker at *Lamberhurst*, now making exceptional oaky *Pinot Noir* in southern Germany.
☨ **Pascal Jolivet** [zhol-lee-vay] (*Loire*, France) Superstar producer of modern *Sancerre* and *Pouilly-Fumé*. ☆☆☆☆ 1998 Sancerre Grand Cuvée £££
☨ **Nicolas Joly** [Zhoh-lee] (*Loire*, France) The biodynamic owner-winemaker behind the *Coulée de Serrant* in *Savennières*.
☨ **Jordan** (*Stellenbosch*, South Africa) Young winery whose Californian-trained winemakers are hitting the mark with their *Sauvignon* and *Chardonnay*. ☆☆☆☆ 1999 Jordan Estate Chardonnay £££
☨ **Jordan** (*Sonoma Valley*, California) *Sonoma* winery surrounded by the kind of hype more usually associated with *Napa*. Table wines – from the *Alexander Valley* – are mostly good rather than great, though *J* the sparkling wine is of *Champagne* quality. ☆☆☆☆☆ 1991 "J", Sonoma County ££££
☨ **Joseph** (*South Australia*) *Primo Estate's* label for its top wines and olive oils.
☨ **Josmeyer** [jos-mi-yur] (*Alsace*, France) Estate producing wines that are more delicate and restrained than those of some of its neighbours.
☆☆☆☆ 1998 Gewürztraminer Les Folastries £££
☨ **Weingut Toni Jost** [toh-nee yohst] (*Mittelrhein*, Germany) A new-wave producer with (well-sited) vines in Bacharach, good reds and a penchant for experimenting (often successfully) with new oak barrels. ☆☆☆☆☆ 1998 Riesling Spätlese Mittelrhein Bacharacher Hahn £££
☨ **La Jota** [lah hoh-tah] (*Napa Valley*, California) Small *Howell Mountain* producer with stylish reds, including an unusually good *Cabernet Franc*.
☆☆☆☆ 1997 Howell Mountain Cabernet Sauvignon £££
☨ **Judd's Hill** (*Napa Valley*, California) Young winery with dazzling *Cabernets*. ☆☆☆☆ 1995 Cabernet Sauvignon Napa Valley £££.

Juffer [yoof-fuh] (*Mosel*, Germany) Famous vineyard in the village of *Braunberg*. QbA/Kab/Spät: **85 86 88 89 90** 91 **92** 93 94 95 96 97 98
Aus/Beeren/Tba: **83 85 88 89 90** 91 92 93 94 95 96 97 98

Jug wine (California) American term for quaffable *Vin Ordinaire*.
☨ **Marcel Juge** [zhoozh] (*Rhône*, France) Producer of one of the subtlest, classiest examples of *Cornas*. ☆☆☆☆ 1995 Cornas £££

☨ **Juliénas** [joo-lee-yay-nas] (*Burgundy*, France) One of the ten *Beaujolais Crus*, producing classic, vigorous wine which often benefits from a few years in bottle. **85 87 88 89** 90 **91** 93 94 95 96 97 98 E. Aujas; Jean Benon; Bernard Broyer; François Condemine; Georges Descombes; *Georges Duboeuf;* Eventail des Producteurs; Pierre Ferraud; Paul Granger; Ch. de Juliénas; Henri Lespinasse; Dom. Michel Tête; Raymond Trichard.

☥ **Weingut Juliusspital** [yoo-lee-yoos-shpit-ahl] (*Franken,* Germany) Top-class estate whose profits benefit the poor and sick. A good source of *Riesling* and *Sylvaner*.

Jumilla [hoo-mee-yah] (Spain) *DO* region, traditionally known for heavy high-alcohol wines but increasingly making lighter *Beaujolais*-style ones.

☥ **Jurançon** [zhoo-ron-son] (*South-West,* France) Rich, dry apricoty white and excellent sweet wines made from the *Gros* and *Petit Manseng* 83 85 86 **89 90 92 93** 95 **96 98 99 Bellegarde; Dom. J-P Bousquet;** *Brana;* **Bru-Baché; Castera;** *Cauhapé;* **Clos Guirouilh; Clos Lapeyre; Cru Lamouiroux; Clos Uroulat.**

☥ **Justin** (*San Luis Obispo,* California) A winery to watch, with stunning reds, including a great *Cabernet Franc* and Isosceles, a *Bordeaux* blend. ☆☆☆☆ **1994 Isosceles San Luis Obispo County Reserve.**

☥ **Juvé y Camps** [hoo-vay ee kamps] (*Catalonia,* Spain) The exception which proves the rule – by making and maturing decent cava from traditional grapes and excellent *vintage Brut*.

K

Kabinett (Germany) First step in German quality ladder, for wines which achieve a certain natural sweetness.

Kaiserstuhl-Tuniberg [ki-sehr shtool too-nee-behrg] (*Baden,* Germany) Supposedly the finest *Baden* Bereich (actually it covers a third of *Baden's* vineyards) with top villages producing rich, spicy *Riesling* and *Sylvaner* from volcanic slopes. QbA/Kab/Spät: **85 88 89 90** 91 **92** 93 94 95 96 97 98 Aus/Beeren/Tba: **83 85 88 89** 90 91 92 93 94 95 96 97 98

Kallstadt [kahl-shtaht] (*Pfalz,* Germany) Village containing the best-known and finest vineyard of Annaberg, making luscious full *Riesling*. QbA/Kab/Spät: **85 86 88 89 90** 91 92 93 94 95 96 97 98 Aus/Beeren/Tba: **83 85** 88 89 90 91 92 93 94 95 96 97 98

☥ **Kamptal** [kamp-tal] (*Niederösterreich,* Austria) Up-and-coming region for rich dry white *Grüner Veltliners* and *Rieslings,* thanks largely to the efforts of star producer Brundlmayer.

☥ **Kanonkop Estate** [ka-non-kop] (*Stellenbosch,* South Africa) An estate with largely traditional equipment, but a modern approach to its unusually classy *Pinotage*. The light red blend, "Kadette", is good too, and *Bordeaux*-style "Paul Sauer" is one of the *Cape's* best. ☆☆☆☆ **1995 Pinotage ££**

☥ **Kanzem** [kahnt-zem] (*Mosel-Saar-Ruwer,* Germany) Less well-known commune near Wiltingen.

☥ **Karlsmühle** [kahl-smoo-lur] (*Mosel-Saar-Ruwer,* Germany) Very high class estate producing good Riesling in the heart of the *Ruwer*.

Y Karthäuserhof [kart-oy-ser-hof] (*Mosel-Saar-Ruwer,* Germany)
This *Ruwer* estate is not only the producer of great dry Rieslings in
Eitelsbach, its bottles are also a very welcome exception to the generally
uniform presentation of German labels. They are naked – apart from a
stylish neck label. ☆☆☆☆ 1997 Riesling Kabinett Eitelsbacher
Karthäuserhofberg Karthäuserhof £££

Y Katnook Estate (*Coonawarra,* Australia) Small estate making the highly
commercial Deakin Estate wines as well as plenty of such innovative stuff
as a *late harvest Coonawarra Chardonnay* and top-class *Coonawarra
Merlot* and *Cabernet.* ☆☆☆ 1998 Cabernet Sauvignon £££

Y Katsaros [kaht-sah-rohs] (Greece) One of the classiest new wave Cabernet
Sauvignon producers in Greece.

Y Ch. Kefraya [keh-frah-ya] (Lebanon) *Ch. Musar* is not the only Lebanese
winery; this is the other one worth taking seriously. ☆☆☆ 1996 Ch. Kefraya ££
Kellerei/Kellerabfüllung [kel-luh-rih/kel-luh-rab-foo-loong] (Germany)
Cellar/producer/estate-bottled.

Y Kendall-Jackson (*Clear Lake,* California) Extraordinarily dynamic, fast-
growing producer with popular, consistent but decidedly off-dry "Vintner's
Reserve" *Chardonnay* and *Sauvignon,* of which millions of cases are
produced. Reds and "Grand Reserve" wines are better. Other associated
brands include Cambria and (the more generally impressive) *Stonestreet.*
☆☆☆☆ 1998 Vintners Reserve Viognier ££

Y Kenwood Vineyards (*Sonoma Valley,* California) Classy Sonoma
winery with good single-vineyard *Chardonnay*s and impressive, if
sometimes rather tough, *Cabernets* (including one made from the author
Jack London's vineyard). The other star is the brilliant *Zinfandel.*
☆☆☆☆ 1997 Sauvignon Blanc Reserve ££; ☆☆☆☆☆ 1997 Valley of the
Moon £££

❦ Kerner [kehr-nuh] A white grape variety. A *Riesling*-cross that is grown in
Germany and also widely in England. **Anselmann.**

Y Weingut Reichsgraf von Kesselstatt [rikh-sgraf fon kes-sel-shtat]
(*Mosel-Saar-Ruwer,* Germany) Large, impressive collection of four *Riesling*
estates spread between the *Mosel, Saar,* and *Ruwer.* ☆☆☆ Ockfener
Bockstein Riesling ££

Kiedrich [kee-drich] (*Rheingau,* Germany) Top village high in the hills
whose vineyards can produce great intense *Rieslings.* QbA/Kab/Spät: **85** 86
88 89 90 91 **92 93** 94 95 96 97 98 Aus/Beeren/Tba: **83 85 88 89** 90 91
92 93 94 95 **96** 97 98

Kientzheim [keents-him] (*Alsace,* France) Village noted for its *Riesling.*

Y André Kientzler [keent-zluh] (*Alsace,* France) Classy producer with
better-than-average *Pinot Blanc.* ☆☆☆ 1996 Pinot Blanc d'Alsace ££

℣ **JF Kimich** [kih-mikh] (*Pfalz*, Germany) Fast-rising star making rich spicy wines typical of the *Pfalz*. *Gewürztraminers* are as good as *Rieslings*.

℣ **King Estate** (*Oregon*, US) Glitzy new investment in part of the state that has yet to produce top-class wine. ☆☆☆ 1997 Chardonnay £££

℣ **Kingston Estate** (*Murray Valley*, South Australia) Controversial commercial producer in the Riverland.

℣ **Kiona** [kih-yoh-nah] (*Washington State*, US) Small producer in the middle of nowhere with a penchant for berryish reds and intensely flavoured *late harvest* wines. ☆☆☆☆ 1997 Late Harvest Riesling ££££

Kir (*Burgundy*, France) A mixture of sweet fortified *Crème de Cassis* (regional speciality of *Burgundy*) with simple and often rather *acidic* local white wine (*Aligoté*, or basic *Bourgogne Blanc*) to produce a delicious summertime drink.

℣ **Ch. Kirwan** [keer-wahn] (*Margaux 3ème Cru Classé, Bordeaux*, France) Belatedly coming out of prolonged doldrums. Still doesn't warrant its third growth status. **82 83** 85 86 88 89 90 **93** 95 96 97 98

℣ **Kistler** [kist-luh] (*Sonoma Valley*, California) Probably California's top *Chardonnay* producer, with a really dazzling range of uncompromising complex single-vineyard wines and fast-improving *Pinot Noirs*. *Burgundy* quality at *Burgundy* prices. ☆☆☆☆☆ 1996 Chardonnay Carneros Hyde Vineyard ££££

℣ **Klein Constantia** [klihn kon-stan-tee-yah] (*Constantia*, South Africa) Small go-ahead estate on the site of the great 17th-century *Constantia* vineyard. After a slightly disappointing patch, wines seem to be right back on form and proving a credit to the *Constantia* region. The star wine is the sweet "Vin de Constance" which is sadly hard to find outside South Africa. ☆☆☆☆☆ 1999 Sauvignon Blanc ££; ☆☆☆☆☆ 1998 Shiraz £££

Klüsserath [kloo-seh-raht] (*Mosel-Saar-Ruwer*, Germany) Small village best known for *Sonnenuhr* and Königsberg vineyards.

℣ **Knappstein** [nap-steen] (*Clare Valley*, South Australia). Now part of the *Mildara-Blass* stable and no longer associated with founder Tim (see *Knappstein Lenswood*) but still producing good *Clare Valley* wines.

℣ **Knappstein Lenswood** [nap-steen] (*Lenswood*, South Australia) Tim Knappstein's brilliant *Sauvignon, Semillon, Chardonnay, Pinot Noir* and *Cabernets* from *Lenswood* label. ☆☆☆☆ 1998 Semillon £££

℣ **Emerich Knoll** [knowl] (*Wachau*, Austria). Maker of stunning new wave *Riesling* and *Grüner Veltliner* wines.

Koehler-Ruprecht [kurler-roop-recht] (*Pfalz*, Germany) Classy estate in Kallstadt, producing good *Riesling* and unusually fine *Spätburgunder*.

℣ **Konocti Cellars** [ko-nok-tih] (*Lake County*, California) Dynamic producer with good straightforward wines.

Kosher (Israel) Wine made under complex rules. Every seventh vintage is left unharvested and non-Jews are barred from the winemaking process.

℣ **Korbel** [Kor-BEL] (*Sonoma*, California) Big producer of basic California sparkling wine. Better wines like Le Premier Reserve show what can be done.

℣ **Kourtakis** [koor-tah-kis] (Greece) One of Greece's growing number of dynamic wine companies with unusually recommendable whites and the characterful native *Mavrodaphnes*. ☆☆☆☆ 1996 Kouros Nemea £££

℣ **Weinlaubenhof Weingut Alois Kracher** [Ah-loys krah-kuh] (*Neusiedlersee*, Austria) Source of world-class, (very) *late harvest* wines including a very unusual effort which blends the *Chardonnay* with the *Welschriesling*. ☆☆☆☆☆ 1996 Chardonnay Welschriesling Nouvelle Vague Trockenbeerenauslese No.4 ££££

Krems [krems] (*Wachau*, Austria) Town and *Wachau* vineyard area producing Austria's most stylish *Rieslings* from terraced vineyards.

Kreuznach [kroyt-znahkh] (*Nahe,* Germany) Northern *Bereich,* boasting fine vineyards situated around the town of *Bad Kreuznach.* QbA/Kab/Spät: **85 86 88 89 90** 91 92 93 94 95 96 97 98 Aus/Beeren/Tba: **83 85 88 89** 90 91 92 93 94 95 96 97 98

☡ **Dom. Kreydenweiss** [krih-den-vihs] (*Alsace,* France) Top-class organic producer with particularly good *Muscat, Pinot Gris,* and *Riesling.*

☡ **Krondorf** [kron-dorf] (*Barossa Valley,* Australia) Innovative viticulturists and winery specialising in traditional, big *Barossa* style wines. ☆☆☆☆ **1996 Semillon £££**

☡ **Krug** [kroog] (*Champagne,* France) The *Ch. Latour* of *Champagne.* Great vintage wine, extraordinary rosé, and pure *Chardonnay* from the *Clos de Mesnil* vineyard. Theoretically the best non-vintage, thanks to the greater proportions of aged Reserve wine. ☆☆☆☆☆ **1989 Vintage ££££**

☡ **Kruger-Rumpf** [kroo-gur roompf] (*Nahe,* Germany) *Nahe* estate, demonstrating the potential of varieties like the *Scheurebe.* ☆☆☆☆☆ **1997 Riesling Eiswein Nahe Münsterer Pittersberg Kruger-Rumpf ££££**

☡ **Kuentz-Bas** [koontz bah] (*Alsace,* France) Reliable producer for *Pinot Gris* and *Gewurztraminer.* ☆☆☆☆ **1998 Gewurztraminer Cuvée Tradition £££**

☡ **Kuhling-Gillot** [koo-ling gil-lot] (*Rheinhessen,* Germany) Hitherto little-known producer, now fast developing a reputation for rich concentrated wines. ☆☆☆☆ **1997 Bodenheim Heitersbrunnchen Scheurebe Eiswein ££££**

☡ **Kumeu River** [koo-myoo] (*Auckland,* New Zealand) Michael Brajkovich is successful with a wide range of wines, including a very unusual dry *botrytis Sauvignon* which easily outclasses many a dry wine from *Sauternes.* ☆☆☆☆☆ **1998 Mate's Vineyard Chardonnay £££**

☡ **Kunde** [koon-day] (*Sonoma,* California) Producer of good *Chardonnay* and *Zinfandel.* ☆☆☆☆ **1995 Zinfandel Sonoma Valley Robusto £££**

☡ **Weingut Franz Künstler** [koonst-luh] (*Rheingau,* Germany) A new superstar producer with superlative *Riesling.* ☆☆☆☆ **1996 Rheingau Hochheimer Kirchenstück Riesling Spätlese ££**

☡ **KWV** (*Cape,* South Africa) Huge cooperative formed by the South African government at a time when surplus wine seemed set to flood the industry and, for a long time, maintained by the National Party when it needed to keep the members of the big wine cooperatives, well, cooperative. Winemaking has improved recently – especially the wines sold under the Cathedral Cellars label. ☆☆☆☆☆ **1997 Cathedral Cellars Shiraz £££**

L

☡ **Ch. Labégorce** [la-bay-gors] (*Bordeaux,* France) Good traditional *Margaux.* 75 79 81 **82 83 85** 86 88 **89** 90 94 95 96 97 98

☡ **Ch. Labégorce-Zédé** [la-bay-gors zay-day] (*Margaux Cru Bourgeois, Bordeaux,* France). An estate that belongs to the same Thienpont family as *Vieux Château Certan* and *le Pin.* A name to remember for wine beyond its Bourgeois class. 81 82 **83 85 86** 88 89 90 92 94 95 96 97 98

☡ **Labouré-Roi** [la-boo-ray rwah] (*Burgundy,* France) A highly successful and very commercial *négociant,* responsible for some quite impressive wines. See *Cottin Frères.* ☆☆☆☆ **1995 Meursault Clos de la Baronne £££**

🍇 **Labrusca** [la-broo-skah] *Vitis labrusca,* the North American species of vine, making wine which is often referred to as "foxy". All *vinifera* vine stocks are grafted on to *phylloxera*-resistant *labrusca* roots, though the vine itself is banned in Europe and its wines, thankfully, are almost unfindable.

☀ **Ch. Lacoste-Borie** [la-cost-bo-ree] (*Pauillac, Bordeaux*, France) The reliable *second label* of *Grand-Puy-Lacoste*.
☆☆☆ 1995 Ch. Lacoste-Borie £££

Lacryma Christi [la-kree-mah kris-tee] (*Campania*, Italy) Literally, "tears of Christ", the melancholy name for some amiable, light, rather rustic reds and whites. Those from Vesuvio are *DOC*. Caputo; Mastroberardino.

☀ **Ladoix-Serrigny** [la-dwah-seh-reen-yee] (*Burgundy*, France) Village including parts of *Corton* and *Corton-Charlemagne*. The village wines are not well known and some bargains are still to be found. White: 79 **85 86 88** 89 **90 92** 95 96 97 98 Red: 78 83 **85** 87 **88 89 90** 92 94 95 96 97 98 Capitain-Gagnerot; Chevalier Père et Fils; *Dubreuil-Fontaine;* Gay; Launay; Maréchale; André Nudant.

☀ **Patrick de Ladoucette** [duh la-doo-set] (*Loire*, France) Fine intense *Pouilly-Fumé*, sold as "Baron de L." Other wines are greatly improved in recent years. ☆☆☆☆ 1997 Comte Lafond Blanc £££

☀ **Michel Lafarge** [la-farzh] (*Burgundy*, France) One of the very best producers in *Volnay* – and indeed *Burgundy*. Fine, long-lived, modern wine. ☆☆☆☆ 1995 Volnay Clos des Chênes £££

☀ **Ch. Lafaurie-Peyraguey** [la-foh-ree pay-rah-gee] (*Sauternes Premier Cru Classé, Bordeaux*, France) Much-improved *Sauternes* estate that has produced creamy, long-lived wines in the 1980s and in the 1990s. 78 80 81 82 83 85 86 88 89 90 96 95 97 98 ☆☆☆☆ 1990 ££££

☀ **Ch. Lafite-Rothschild** [la-feet roh-chihld] (*Pauillac Premier Cru Classé, Bordeaux*, France) Often almost impossible to taste young, this *Pauillac* first growth is still one of the monuments of the wine world – especially since the early 1980s. A brilliant 1998 and a fine 1999. The *Carruades*, *second-wine* is worth looking out for too. **61 75 76** 78 79 **81 82** 83 84 85 **86 87** 88 89 90 91 92 **93 94** 95 96 97 98 ☆☆☆☆ 1994 ££££

☀ **Ch. Lafleur** [la-flur] (*Pomerol, Bordeaux*, France) *Christian Moueix's* pet *Pomerol*, often on a par with the wine *Moueix* makes at *Pétrus* – though in a more understated way. **61 62 66 70 75** 78 79 **82 83 85 86** 88 89 90 **92 93** 94 95 96 97 98

☀ **Ch. Lafleur-Gazin** [la-flur-ga-zan] (*Pomerol, Bordeaux*, France) Another good *Moueix* wine. **82 83 85 86** 88 89 90 92 93 94 95 96 97 98

☀ **Dom. des Comtes Lafon** [day comt la-fon] (*Burgundy*, France) The best domaine in *Meursault* (and one of the very best in the whole of Burgundy) with great vineyards in *Volnay* and a small slice of *Montrachet*. Wines last forever. ☆☆☆☆ 1995 Meursault Clos de la Barre £££

☀ **Ch. Lafon-Rochet** [la-fon-ro-shay] (*St. Estèphe 4ème Cru Classé, Bordeaux*, France) Very classy modern *St. Estèphe*. Impressive in 1998. **70** 79 81 82 83 85 86 88 89 90 91 92 93 94 95 96 97 98

☀ **Alois Lageder** [la-gay-duh] (*Trentino-Alto-Adige*, Italy) New-wave producer of the kind of wine the *Alto-Adige* ought to make.

Lago di Caldaro [la-goh dih kahl-deh-roh] (*Trentino-Alto Adige,* Italy) Also known as the *Kalterersee*, using the local *Schiava* grape to make cool light reds with slightly unripe, though pleasant, fruit.

☀ **Ch. Lagrange** [la-gronzh] (*St. Julien 3ème Cru Classé, Bordeaux*, France) A once underperforming third growth rejuvenated by Japanese cash and local know-how (for a while from Michel Delon of *Léoville-Las-Cases*). Look out for *Les Fiefs de Lagrange*, the impressive *second wine*.

🍷 **Ch. Lagrange** [la-gronzh] (*Pomerol, Bordeaux,* France) Yet another *Moueix* property – and yet another good wine. **70 75** 78 81 **82** 83 **85** 86 87 88 89 90 92 93 94 95 96 97 98 ☆☆☆ **1993 £££**

🌿 **Lagrein** [la-grayn] (Italy) Cherryish red grape of north-east Italy.

🍷 **Ch. la Lagune** [la-goon] (*Haut-Médoc 3ème Cru Classé, Bordeaux,* France) Lovely accessible wines which last well and are worth buying even in poorer years. **70 75 78** 79 **82** 85 86 88 89 90 92 93 94 95 96 97 98

Lake County (California) Vineyard district salvaged by improved irrigation techniques and now capable of some fine wines as well as *Kendall Jackson's* highly commercial efforts.

🍷 **Lake's Folly** (*Hunter Valley,* Australia) Meet Max Lake, surgeon-turned-winemaker/writer/researcher who has great theories about the sexual effects of sniffing various kinds of wine. He is also a leading Australian pioneer of *Chardonnay*, with an unusually successful *Hunter Valley Cabernet Sauvignon.* Wines now made by Max's son, Stephen. ☆☆☆☆ **1995 Hunter Valley Cabernet Sauvignon £££**

LAKE'S FOLLY
HUNTER VALLEY
Cabernet
1987
WINE OF AUSTRALIA
BOTTLE NO. 26936   Alcohol by volume 11.6%   750 ml

🍷 **Lalande de Pomerol** [la-lond duh po-meh-rol] (*Bordeaux,* France) Bordering on *Pomerol* with similar, but less fine wines. Still generally better than similarly priced *St. Emilions.* Some good-value *Petits-Châteaux.* **70 82 83 85** 86 **88 89** 90 92 93 94 95 96 97 98

Ch. Lalande-Borie [la-lond bo-ree] (*St. Julien, Bordeaux,* France) In the same stable as *Ch. Ducru-Beaucaillou.* Reliable wines. 82 85 86 88 89 90 91 92 93 94 95 **96** 97 98 ☆☆☆☆ **1989 £££**

🍷 **Ch. Lamarque** [la-mahrk] (*Haut-Médoc Cru Bourgeois, Bordeaux,* France) Spectacular *château* with good, quite modern, wines. 82 **83** 85 **86** 88 89 90 91 92 93 94 95 96 97 98 ☆☆☆ **1992 £££;** ☆☆☆ **1993 ££**

🍷 **Lamberhurst** (*Kent,* England) One of the first English vineyards and once one of the more reliable.

🍷 **Lamborn Family** (*Napa Valley,* California) Small *Howell Mountain* producer, focusing on rich, concentrated, long-lived *Zinfandel.*

🍷 **Dom. des Lambrays** [lom-bray] (*Burgundy,* California) Under new ownership and promising further improvements in quality. Already very worthwhile, though. ☆☆☆☆ **1995 Clos des Lambrays £££**

🍷 **Lambrusco** [lam-broos-koh] (*Emilia-Romagna,* Italy) Famous/infamous low-strength (7.5 per cent) sweet, sparkling UK and North American version of the sparkling, dry, red wine favoured in Italy. The real thing, less commercial, but far more fascinating with its dry, unripe, cherry flavour – comes with a cork rather than a screw-cap. ☆☆☆ **1997 Don Bosco Escuela Vitivinicola £**

✠ **Lamouroux Landing** [lam-moh-roh] (*New York State*, USA) Impressive young *Chardonnay* specialist in the *Finger Lakes*.

✠ **Landmark** (*Sonoma*, California) Small *Chardonnay* specialist with rich, fruity, buttery wines from individual "Damaris" and "Overlook" vineyards, and blends of Chardonnay from Sonoma, Santa Barbara and Monterey.

Landwein [land-vihn] (Germany) The equivalent of a French *Vin De Pays* from one of 11 named regions (*Anbaugebiete*). Often dry.

✠ **Ch. Lanessan** [la-neh-son] (*Haut-Médoc Cru Bourgeois*, *Bordeaux*, France). Recommendable *Cru Bourgeois* now more influenced by new oak than it used to be, but still quite traditional fare.

Langelois [lung-ger-loyss] (*Kamptal*, Austria).One of the best wine communes in Austria – the place to find producers like Hiedler and Brundelmayer.

Langhe [lang-gay] (*Piedmont*, Italy) A range of hills; when preceded by "*Nebbiolo* delle", indicates declassified *Barolo* and *Barbaresco*. Also, the denomination now used by Angelo *Gaja* for his single-vineyard wines.

✠ **Ch. Langoa-Barton** [lon-goh-wah-bahr-ton] (*St. Julien 3ème Cru Classé*, *Bordeaux*, France) *Léoville-Barton's* (slightly) less complex kid brother. Often one of the best bargain classed growths in *Bordeaux*. Well made in poor years. **70 75** 76 **78** 79 **82** 83 85 **86** 88 89 90 91 92 93 **94** 95 96 97 98 99 ☆☆☆☆ **1993 ££££**

Languedoc-Roussillon [long-dok roo-see-yon] (*Midi*, France) One of the world's largest wine regions and, until recently, a major source of the wine lake. But a combination of government-sponsored uprooting and keen activity by *flying winemakers* and (a few) dynamic producers is beginning to turn this into a worrying competitor for the New World. The region includes appellations like *Fitou*, *Corbières* and *Minervois*, *Faugères*, *St. Chinian*, *Coteaux de Languedoc*, *Côtes de Roussillon*, and a torrent of *Vin de Pays d'Oc*. Sadly, many of the best, more ambitious, wines are hard to find outside France where they are developing a cult following among consumers who relish the value they often offer.

✠ **Lanson** [lon-son] (*Champagne*, France) Much-improved *Champagne* house with decent non-vintage "Black Label", good *Demi-Sec*, and fine *vintage champagne*. ☆☆☆☆ **1988 Noble Cuvée Vintage ££££**

✠ **Casa Lapostolle** [la-pos-tol] (*Colchagua Valley*, Chile) Instant superstar. Belongs to the owners of Grand Marnier and benefits from the expertise of *Michel Rolland*. Cuvée Alexandre *Merlot* reds have been a classy instant success, though the whites need more work. The 1997 Clos Apalta *Merlot*-Carmenère blend is one of the (relatively) cheapest of Chile's new-wave flagship reds. It easily justifies its (£20 / $35) price tag. ☆☆☆☆☆ **1997 Clos Apalta ££££**

✠ **Ch. Larcis-Ducasse** [lahr-see doo-kass] (*St. Emilion Grand Cru Classé*, *Bordeaux*, France) Property whose lightish wines rarely live up to the potential of its hillside site. 66 78 79 81 **82** 83 85 86 88 89 90 94 95 96 97 98 ☆☆☆ **1996 £££**

✠ **Ch. Larmande** [lahr-mond] (*St. Emilion Grand Cru Classé*, *Bordeaux*, France) A property to watch for well-made ripe-tasting wines. 85 86 **88 89** 90 **92 93** 94 95 96 97 98

✠ **Dom. Laroche** [la-rosh] (*Burgundy*, France) Highly reliable *Chablis* négociant with some enviable vineyards of its own, including some top-class *Premiers* and *Grands Crus*. At more affordable prices, there are also reliable southern French *Chardonnay Vin de Pays d'Oc* and innovative wines from *Corsica*. ☆☆☆☆ **1998 Chablis £££**

⚱ **Ch. Lascombes** [las-komb] (*Margaux 2ème Cru Classé, Bordeaux,* France) Subtle second growth *Margaux* which can exemplify the perfumed character of this *appellation*, but could still do better. **70 75** 82 83 85 **86 88** 89 90 91 92 93 94 95 96 97 98 ☆☆☆☆ **1995 ££££**

🌿 **Laski Riesling/Rizling** [lash-kee riz-ling] (Former Yugoslavia) Yugoslav name for white grape, unrelated to the *Rhine Riesling*, aka *Welsch, Olasz* and *Italico.*

⚱ **Ch. de Lastours** [duh las-toor] (*Languedoc-Roussillon,* France) Combined winery and home for people with mental disabilities which frequently provides ample proof that *Corbières* can rival *Bordeaux.* Look out for the *cuvée* Simone Descamps. ☆☆☆ **1995 Simone Descamps ££**

Late harvest Made from (riper) grapes picked after the main vintage. Should have at least some *botrytis.*

Late-Bottled Vintage (Port) (LBV) (*Douro,* Portugal) Officially, bottled four or six years after a specific (usually non-declared) *vintage.* Until the late 1970s, this made for a *vintage port*-style wine that matured earlier, was a little lighter and easier to drink, but still needed to be decanted. Until recently, the only houses to persevere with this style were *Warres* and *Smith Woodhouse,* who labelled their efforts *"Traditional" LBV.* Almost every other LBV around, however, was of the filtered, "modern" style pioneered by *Taylors.* These taste pretty much like up-market *ruby* and *vintage character ports,* need no decanting, and bear very little resemblance to real *vintage* or even *crusted port.* Belatedly, a growing number of producers are now confusingly offering "Traditional" as well as modern LBV. For the moment, buyers can tell one style from the other by reading the small print on the label, but there are proposals from the port shippers to ban the use of the word "Traditional". If they do so, precisely the same name will be used for these two very different styles of wine. As one very prominent retired *port* maker smilingly admitted, he and his competitors have always done well out of confusing their clients.

Latium/Lazio [lah-tee-yoom] (Italy) The vineyard area surrounding Rome, including *Frascati* and Marino. *Fontana Candida;* Colli di Catone.

⚱ **Louis Latour** [loo-wee lah-toor] (*Burgundy,* France) Underperforming *négociant* who still pasteurises his – to my mind, consequently muddy-tasting – reds, treating them in a way no quality-conscious New World producer would contemplate. Some whites, however, including *Corton-Charlemagne,* can be sublime, and Latour deserves credit for pioneering regions such as *Mâcon Lugny* and the *Ardèche.* ☆☆☆☆ **1993 Montrachet ££££;** ☆☆☆☆ **1996 Corton Charlemage ££££**

⚱ **Ch. Latour** [lah-toor] (*Pauillac Premier Cru Classé, Bordeaux,* France) Recently bought – from its British owners, Allied Domecq – by the same self-made French millionaire who recently bought Christie's. First growth *Pauillac* which can be very tricky to judge when young, but which develops majestically. *Les Forts de Latour* is the – often worthwhile – *second label.* The 1992 is a good example of a generally disappointing vintage and the 1999 is possibly the wine of the vintage. **61** 62 64 **66** 67 **70** 73 **75** 76 **78** 79 80 81 **82** 83 **85 86** 88 89 90 **91 92 93** 94 95 96 97 98 99

⚱ **Ch. Latour-à-Pomerol** [lah-toor ah po-meh-rol] (*Pomerol, Bordeaux,* France) A great-value, small (3,500-case) *Pomerol* estate under the same ownership as *Ch. Pétrus* and the same *Moueix* winemaking team. It is a little less concentrated than its big brother, but then it is around a quarter of the price, too. **82** 83 **85** 86 88 89 90 92 93 94 95 96 98 ☆☆☆☆ **1990 ££££**

⚱ **Ch. Latour-Martillac** [la-toor mah-tee-yak] (*Graves Cru Classé, Bordeaux,* France) Good, sometimes overlooked reds and whites. Red: **85** 86 88 89 90 91 92 93 94 95 96 White: **89** 90 93 94 96 97 98 99

Laudun [loh-duhn] (*Rhône,* France) Named village of *Côtes du Rhône,* with peppery reds and attractive rosés.

℥ **Laurel Glen** (*Sonoma Mountain,* California) Small hillside estate with *claret*-style reds that are respected by true Californian wine lovers. Terra Rosa is the accessible *second label.* ☆☆☆☆ 1997 Sonoma Mountain Cabernet ££

℥ **Dominique Laurent** [Loh-ron] (*Burgundy,* France) A young *négociant* founded a few years ago by a former pastry chef who has rapidly shown his skills at buying and maturing top-class wines from several *appellations.*

℥ **Laurent-Perrier** [law-ron pay-ree-yay] (*Champagne,* France) Historically one of the more reliable larger houses, though some recent bottlings have seemed variable. Grand Siècle is the most interesting wine.

℥ **Lavaux** [la-voh] (Switzerland) A major wine region to the north of Lake Geneva, broken down into several communal appellations such as Dezaleym Epesses and St-Saphorin. This is a good place to taste varied examples of *Chasselas* (known here as "*Fendant*") and Pinot Noir.

℥ **Ch. Laville Haut-Brion** [la-veel oh-bree-yon] (*Graves Cru Classé, Bordeaux,* France) Exquisite white *Graves* that lasts for 20 years or more. 62 **66 75** 82 **83 85** 86 88 89 90 92 93 94 95 96 97 98 99

℥ **Lawson's Dry Hills** (*Marlborough,* New Zealand) Producer of New Zealand's best 1999 *Sauvignon Blanc* and an unusually good Gewürztraminer.

℥ **Ch. Lazaridi** (Greece) One of Greece's best producerrs of red wines, making no use of the national appellation system.

℥ **Kostas Lazarides** (Greece) An up-and-coming producer of various styles of wine, including an unusually good rosé.

Lazio [lat-zee-yoh] (Italy) See *Latium.*

LBV (*Douro,* Portugal) See *Late-Bottled Vintage.*
Lean Lacking body.

℥ **Leasingham** (*South Australia*) BRL Hardy subsidiary in the *Clare Valley* that makes top-flight reds and whites, including great *Shiraz, Cabernet* and *Chardonnay.* ☆☆☆☆ 1997 Classic Clare Cabernet Sauvignon £££

Lebanon Best known for the remarkable *Ch. Musar* from the *Bekaa Valley.*

℥ **Leconfield** [leh-kon-feeld] (*South Australia*) Reliable producer of intense *Coonawarra* reds. (Ralph Fowler, the man behind the award-winning recent vintages, has his own wine now and works for *Chapoutier,* Australia).
Lees or lie(s) The sediment of dead yeasts that fall in the barrel or vat as a wine develops. *Muscadet* – like some other white wines – is aged *Sur Lie.* Producers of modern *Chardonnay* also leave their wine in its lees, stirring it occasionally to maximise richness - the rich flavour provided by the yeasts.

℥ **Leeuwin Estate** [loo-win] (*Margaret River,* Western Australia) Showcase winery (and concert venue) whose vineyards were originally picked out by *Robert Mondavi.* The genuinely world-class ("art label") *Chardonnay* is one of Australia's priciest and longest-lived. Other wines are less dazzling. ☆☆☆☆☆ 1995 Art Series Chardonnay £££

℥ **Dom. Leflaive** [luh-flev] (*Burgundy,* France) A new generation of Leflaives is using organic methods – and making better wines than ever. ☆☆☆☆☆ 1996 Puligny-Montrachet Les Combettes ££££

℥ **Olivier Leflaive** [luh-flev] (*Burgundy,* France) The *négociant* business launched by Vincent Leflaive's nephew. High-class white wines, ☆☆☆☆ Rully Premier Cru les Clous £££

☲ **Peter Lehmann** [lee-man] (*Barossa Valley*, Australia) The grand old man of the *Barossa*, Peter Lehmann and his son Doug make intense *Shiraz*, *Cabernet*, *Semillon*, and *Chardonnay* which make up in character (and value) what they lack in subtlety. Stonewell is the best red.
Length How long the taste lingers in the mouth.

Lenswood (*South Australia*) New high-altitude region near *Adelaide*, proving its potential with *Sauvignon*, *Chardonnay*, *Pinot Noir*, and even (in the case of *Henschke's* Abbott's Prayer) *Merlot* and *Cabernet Sauvignon*. Pioneers include *Stafford Ridge, Shaw & Smith, Knappstein Lenswood* and *Nepenthe*.

☲ **Lenz Vineyards** [lentz] (*New York State*, US) One of the best wineries on Long Island, with particularly recommendable *Merlot* and *Chardonnay*.

León [lay-on] (Spain) Northwestern region producing acceptable dry, fruity reds and whites.

☲ **Jean León** [zhon lay-ON] (*Catalonia*, Spain) American pioneer of Spanish *Chardonnay* and *Cabernet*, whose wines have greatly improved since its purchase by *Torres*.
✩✩✩✩ 1993 Cabernet Sauvignon £££

☲ **Leone de Castris** [lay-oh-nay day kah-striss] (*Puglia*, Italy) A leading exponent of Salice Santino, Copertino, Salento Chardonnay and pink Salento rosato. A name to watch as this region gathers prestige over the next few years.

☲ **Leonetti Cellars** [lee-oh-net-tee] (*Washington State*, US) One of the best red wine producers in the US. Now showing its skills with *Sangiovese* and an innovative "American" (Washington State / Dry Creek) *Merlot*.

☲ **Ch. Léoville-Barton** [lay-oh-veel bahr-ton] (*St. Julien 2ème Cru Classé*, *Bordeaux*, France) The charming Anthony Barton produces one of the most reliably classy wines in *Bordeaux*, without – unlike a great many of his neighbours – recourse to the machines that concentrate the juice to provide "bigger" flavours.. Then, again, unlike them, he has the temerity to ask a reasonable rather than extortionate price for it. *Langoa Barton* is the sister property. 61 70 78 **82** 83 85 86 88 89 90 91 93 94 95 96 97 98 99 ✩✩✩✩✩ 1996 ££££

☲ **Ch. Léoville-Las-Cases** [lay-oh-veel las-kahz] (*St. Julien 2ème Cru Classé*, *Bordeaux*, France) Impeccably made *St. Julien Super Second* whose quality now often matches its neighbour *Ch. Latour* – a fact that its owner Michel Delon tries to reflect in his prices. The *Clos du Marquis second label* is also good. 76 **78 82 83 85** 86 88 89 90 93 94 95 96 97 98 99

♀ Ch. Léoville-Poyferré [lay-pwah-feh-ray] (*St. Julien 2ème Cru Classé, Bordeaux,* France) 1995, 1996 and 1997 showed the touch of *Michel Rolland* here. A rising star. The *second label* is Moulin Riche. 82 83 84 85 86 87 88 89 90 91 93 94 95 96 97 98 ☆☆☆☆ 1995 ££££

♀ Dom. Leroy [luh-rwah] (*Burgundy,* France) Organic domaine in *Vosne-Romanée* founded by the former co-owner of the *Dom. de la Romanée-Conti* and making wines as good as those of that estate. Prices are stratospheric, but the humblest wines are better than other producers' *Grands Crus.* ☆☆☆☆☆ 1996 Volnay Santenots ££££

♀ Maison Leroy [luh-rwah] (*Burgundy*) If you want to buy a really great old bottle of *Burgundy,* no matter the cost, this is the place to come.

❦ Lexia [lex-ee-yah] See *Muscat d'Alexandrie*.

♀ Librandi [lee-bran-dee] (*Calabria,* Italy) Another flagship winery from the fast-improving regions of Southern Italy. There are terrific examples of the Cirò grape, as well as Gravello, a great blend of the local Gaglioppo and the *Cabernet Sauvignon*.

Lie(s) See *Lees/Sur Lie.*

Liebfraumilch [leeb-frow-mihlch] (Germany) Seditious exploitation of the *QbA* system. Good examples are pleasant; most are alcoholic sugar-water bought on price alone.

♀ Lievland [leev-land] (*Stellenbosch,* South Africa) Estate which has a reputation in South Africa as a high-quality speciality producer of *Shiraz* and *late harvest* wines. ☆☆☆ 1997 Shiraz ££

♀ Hubert Lignier [Lee-nee-yay] (*Burgundy,* France) Producer of classic long-lived *Morey-St.-Denis*. ☆☆☆☆☆ 1997 Gevrey-Chambertin £££

♀ Limestone Ridge (*South Australia*) *Lindemans'* often excellent *Coonawarra* red blend. ☆☆☆☆ 1996 Shiraz Cabernet £££

Limousin [lee-moo-zan] (France) Oak forest that provides barrels that are high in wood *tannin*. Better, therefore, for red wine than for white.

Limoux [lee-moo] (*Midi,* France) (Relatively) cool-climate, chalky soil *appellation* that was recently created for increasingly *Chardonnay* which was previously sold as *Vin de Pays d'Oc*. Stories of tankers of wine being driven north by night to *Burgundy* are hotly denied (in the latter region). See *Blanquette*.

♀ Lindauer [lin-dowr] (*Marlborough,* New Zealand) Good-value Montana sparkling wine. ☆☆☆☆ Special Reserve ££

♀ Lindemans (*South Australia*) Once *Penfolds'* greatest rival, now (like so many other once-independent Australian producers) its subsidiary. Noted for long-lived *Hunter Valley Semillon* and *Shiraz, Coonawarra* reds, and good-value multi-region blends, such as the internationally successful *Bin 65 Chardonnay, Bin 45 Cabernet* and Cawarra wines.

♀ Weingut Karl Lingenfelder [lin-gen-fel-duh] (*Pfalz,* Germany) Great new-wave *Rheinpfalz* producer of a special *Riesling, Dornfelder, Scheurebe* and an unusually successful *Pinot Noir*. ☆☆☆☆ 1997 Freisenheimer Riesling Spätlese ££

♀ Jean Lionnet [lee-oh-nay] (*Rhône,* France) Classy *Cornas* producer whose Rochepertius is a worthwhile buy. The *St. Péray* is an unusually good example of its *appellation* too. ☆☆☆☆ 1997 Cornas £££

♀ Ch. Liot [lee-yoh] (*Barsac, Bordeaux,* France) Good light and elegant *Barsac.* 75 76 82 83 86 88 89 90 92 94 96 97 98 ☆☆☆☆ 1996 £££

Liqueur Muscat (*Rutherglen,* Australia) A wine style unique to Australia. Other countries make fortified *Muscats,* but none achieve the caramelised marmalade and Christmas pudding flavours that *Rutherglen* can achieve. Mick Morris; Campbell's.

Liqueur d'Expédition [lee-kuhr dex-pay-dees-see-yon] (*Champagne,* France) Sweetening syrup for *dosage*.

Liqueur de Tirage [lee-kuhr duh tee-rahzh] (*Champagne*, France) The yeast and sugar added to base wine to induce secondary fermentation (and hence the bubbles) in bottle.

Liquoreux [lee-koh-ruh] (France) Rich and sweet.

Liquoroso [lee-koh-roh-soh] (Italy) Rich and sweet.

Ⴑ Lirac [lee-rak] (*Rhône*, France) Peppery, *Tavel*-like rosés, and increasingly impressive, deep berry-fruit reds. Red: 90 95 96 97 98 Ch. D'Aqueria; Bouchassy; Delorme; Ch. Mayne Lalande; André Méjan; Perrin.

Ⴑ Listel [lees-tel] (*Languedoc-Roussillon*, France) Recently taken over, improving pioneer with vineyards on beaches close to Sète. Best wines: rosé ("Grain de Gris") and sparkling *Muscat* (Pétillant de Raisin).

Listrac-Médoc [lees-trak] (*Bordeaux*, France) Small *Haut-Médoc commune* near *Moulis*, though quite different in style. Clay makes this *Merlot* country, though this isn't always reflected in the vineyards. Wines tend to be toughly unripe and fun-free even in warm vintages. 82 83 85 86 88 89 90 94 95 96 97 98 99 Ch. Clarke; Fonréaud; *Fourcas-Dupré; Fourcas-Hosten.*

Livermore (Valley) [liv-uhr-mohr] (California) Warm-climate vineyard area with fertile soil producing full rounded whites, including increasingly fine *Chardonnay*. Red: 84 85 86 87 90 91 92 93 95 96 97 98 99 White: 92 95 96 97 98 *Bonny Doon;* Concannon; Livermore Cellars; *Wente.*

Ⴑ Los Llanos [los yah-nos] (*Valdepeñas*, Spain) Commendable modern exception to the tradition of dull *Valdepeñas*, with quality mature reds.

Ⴑ De Loach [duh lohch] (*Sonoma*, California) Look for the letters OFS – Our Finest Selection – on the *Chardonnay* and *Cabernet*. But even these rarely surpass the stunning individual vineyard *Zinfandels*.

Ⴑ J Lohr [lohr] (*Santa Clara*, California) Winery noted for its well-made affordable wines, particularly the Wildflower and now more classic noble styles. ☆☆☆☆ 1998 Cyprus Chardonnay ££

Loire [lwahr] (France) An extraordinary variety of wines come from this area – dry whites such as *Muscadet* and the classier *Savennières, Sancerre* and *Pouilly-Fumé*; grassy summery reds (*Chinon* and *Bourgueil*); buckets of rosé – some good, most dreadful; glorious sweet whites (*Vouvray* etc.) ; and very acceptable sparkling wines (also *Vouvray* plus *Crémant de Loire*). Stick to growers and *domaines*. White: 86 88 89 90 94 95 97 98 Sweet White: 85 88 89 90 94 95 96 97 Red: 85 86 88 89 90 95 96 97 98

Lombardy [lom-bahr-dee] (Italy) Region (and vineyards) around Milan, known mostly for sparkling wine but also for increasingly interesting reds, such as Valcalepio and Oltrepò Pavese and the whites of *Lugana*. Red: 78 79 82 85 88 90 94 95 96 97 98 ☆☆☆☆ 1998 Lugana Ca' Dei Frati ££££

Long Island (*New York State*, US) A unique microclimate where fields once full of potatoes are now yielding classy *Merlot* and *Chardonnay*. *Bridgehampton; Hargrave; Lenz;* Palmer Vineyards.

Ⴑ Long Vineyards (*Napa*, California) High quality producer of long-lived *Cabernet Sauvignon, Chardonnay* and late-harvest *Riesling*.

Ⴑ Longridge (*Stellenbosch*, South Africa) Designer winery tailoring three ranges (Longridge, Bay View, and Capelands) to export markets.

Lontue [lon-too-way] (Chile) Region where some of Chile's best *Merlots* are being made. *Lurton; San Pedro; Santa Carolina; Valdevieso.*

⚑ **Weingut Dr. Loosen** [loh-sen] (*Mosel-Saar-Ruwer*, Germany) New-wave *Riesling* producer. Probably the best and most reliable in the *Mosel*, and certainly one of the most successful promoters of good modern German wine. (I only wish he'd use a little less *sulphur dioxide*).

⚑ **Lopez de Heredia** [loh-peth day hay-ray-dee-yah] (*Rioja*, Spain) Ultra-traditional winery producing old-fashioned Viña Tondonia white and *Gran Reserva* reds. ☆☆☆ **1993 Vina Tondonia Tinto Crianza £££**

⚑ **Louisvale** [loo-wis-vayl] (*Stellenbosch*, South Africa) Once avowed *Chardonnay* specialists, Louisvale's range has expanded to include some *Cabernet*-based reds. ☆☆☆ **1997 Cabernet Merlot ££**

⚑ **Loupiac** [loo-peeyak] (*Bordeaux*, France) *Sauternes* neighbour with similar but less fine wines. **83 85 86 88** 89 90 95 96 97 98 *Clos-Jean; Ch du Cros; Loupiac-Gaudiet; Mazarin;* du Noble; de Ricaud.

⚑ **Ch. Loupiac-Gaudiet** [loo-pee-yak goh-dee-yay] (*Loupiac, Bordeaux,* France) A reliable producer of *Loupiac*. 83 85 86 88 89 90 95 96 97 98
Loureiro [loh-ray-roh] (Portugal) Good Vinho Verde grape.

⚑ **Ch. la Louvière** [lah loo-vee-yehr] (*Graves, Bordeaux,* France) André Lurton's best known *Graves* property. Reliable, rich, modern whites and reds. The second wine is called "L" de Louvière. Red: 81 **82** 83 **85 86** 88 89 90 **91 92** 93 94 95 96 97 98 99 White: 86 88 **89 90** 91 92 93 94 95 96 97 98 99 ☆☆☆☆ **1996 Red £££**

⚑ **Fürst Lowenstein** [foorst ler-ven-shtine] (*Franken*, Germany) One of the very top producers of *Sylvaner*.

⚑ **Van Loveren** [van loh-veh-ren] (*Robertson*, South Africa) Family-owned estate producing good value for money wine. Concentrating primarily on classic fresh whites and soft reds. ☆☆☆ **1998 Binnode Noir Muscadelle ££**

Côtes du Lubéron [koht doo LOO-bay-ron] (*Rhône*, France) Reds like light *Côtes du Rhône*, pink and sparkling wines and *Chardonnay*-influenced whites. A new *appellation* and still good value.

⚑ **Luce** [loo-chay] (Tuscany, Italy) Co-production between *Mondavi* and *Frescobaldi* who have combined forces to produce a good, if pricy, red.

⚑ **Lugana** [loo-gah-nah] (*Lombardy*, Italy) Potentially appley, almondy whites made from the *Trebbiano*, grown on the shores of Lake Garda. ☆☆☆☆ **1999 Villa Flora, Zenato ££**

Lugny [loo-nee] (*Burgundy*, France) See *Mâcon*.

Ⴑ **Pierre Luneau** [loo-noh] (*Loire*, France) A rare beast: a top-class *Muscadet* producer. M. Luneau likes to try out wacky ideas with his wines, like keeping juice under nitrogen for a few years to see what happens.

Ⴑ **Cantine Lungarotti** [kan-tee-nah loon-gah-roh-tee] (*Umbria*, Italy) Highly innovative producer, and the man who single-handedly created the *Torgiano* denomination. ☆☆☆☆ **1986 Il Vessillo Rosso Dell'Umbria ££££**

Ⴑ **Jacques & François Lurton** [loor-ton] Having made a success at his father's *Ch. la Louvière* and *Ch. Bonnet in Entre-Deux-Mers* (especially with the whites), Jacques now makes wine all over the world. Look out for Hermanos Lurton labels from Spain and Bodega Lurton wines from Argentina. ☆☆☆☆ **1997 Gran Araucano Cabernet Sauvignon Reserva ££**

Ⴑ **Ch. de Lussac** [loo-sak] (*Lussac St. Emilion, Bordeaux*, France) A name to watch out for in *Lussac St. Emilion*. 86 **89** 90 **94** 95 96 97 98

Ⴑ **Lussac St. Emilion** [loo-sak sant-ay-mee-yon] (*Bordeaux*, France) Potentially worthwhile satellite of *St. Emilion*. 82 83 **85** 86 88 **89** 90 **94** 95 96

Ⴑ **Emilio Lustau** [loos-tow] (*Jerez*, Spain) Top-class *sherry* producer with great *almacanista* wines. ☆☆☆☆ **Palo Cortado Almacenista Vides ££**

Lutomer [loo-toh-muh] (Slovenia) Area still known mostly for its (very basic) Lutomer *Laski Riesling*. Now doing better things with *Chardonnay*.

Luxembourg [luk-sehm-burg] Source of some pleasant, fresh, white wines from *Alsace*-like grape varieties, and generally dire sparkling wine.

Ⴑ **Ch. Lynch-Bages** [lansh bazh] (*Pauillac 5ème Cru Classé, Bordeaux*, France) Reliably over-performing fifth growth *Pauillac* belonging to Jean-Michel Cazes of *Ch. Pichon-Longueville*. The (very rare) white is worth seeking out too. 70 75 78 **82 83 85 86** 88 89 90 91 92 93 94 95 96 97 98

Ⴑ **Ch. Lynch-Moussas** [lansh moo-sahs] (*Pauillac 5ème Cru Classé, Bordeaux*, France) Slowly improving. 85 86 88 89 **90** 91 **94 95 96**

M

Ⴑ *Macération carbonique* [ma-say-ra-see-yon kahr-bon-eek] Technique of *fermenting* uncrushed grapes under pressure of a blanket of carbon dioxide gas to produce fresh fruity wine. Used in *Beaujolais*, southern France and, increasingly, the New World.

Ⴑ **Machard de Gramont** [ma-shahr duh gra-mon] (*Burgundy*, France) Producer of fine *Nuits-St.-Georges*, *Vosne-Romanée* and *Savigny-lès Beaune*.

Mâcon/Mâconnais [ma-kon/nay] (*Burgundy*, France) Avoid unidentified "rouge" or "blanc" on wine lists. Mâcons with the suffix *Villages, Superieur,* or Prissé, *Viré, Lugny* or *Clessé* should be better. The region contains the *appellations St.-Véran* and *Pouilly-Fuissé*. For straight Mâcon try *Jadot* or *Duboeuf*, but the *Dom. Thevenet Dom. de la Bongran* from Clessé is of *Côte d'Or* quality. Red: **95 96 97 98** White: **90 92 95 96 97** 98
Roger Lasserat; Caves de Lugny; Cave de Prissé.

Ⴘ Maculan [mah-koo-lahn] (*Veneto,* Italy) A superstar producer of blackcurranty *Cabernet* Breganze, an oaked *Pinot Bianco-Pinot Grigio-Chardonnay* blend called Prato di Canzio and the lusciously sweet *Torcolato.* ☆☆☆☆ **1996 Breganze Cabernet Sauvignon Ferrata ££**

Ⴘ Madeira [ma-dee-ruh] (Portugal) Atlantic island producing fortified wines, usually identified by style: *Bual, Sercial, Verdelho,* or *Malmsey.* Most is ordinary stuff for use by mainland European cooks and, more rarely, finer fare for those who appreciate the unique marmalady character of good Madeira. **Blandy; Cossart-Gordon; Barros e Souza; Henriques & Henriques.**

Maderisation [mad-uhr-ih-zay-shon] Deliberate procedure in *Madeira,* produced by the warming of wine in *estufas.* Otherwise undesired effect, commonly produced by high temperatures during transport and storage, resulting in a dull flat flavour, tinged with a *sherry* taste and colour. A frequent problem in Asia – and, unfortunately in the US where wines are occasionally handled quite carelessly during the hot summer.

Ⴘ Madiran [ma-dee-ron] (*South-West,* France) Robust country reds made from the *Tannat* grape; *tannic* when young, but worth ageing. **Aydie; Barréjat; Berthoumieu;** *Bouscassé;* **Dom. du Crampilh;** *Ch. Montus; Producteurs de Plaimont.*

Ⴘ Ch. Magdelaine [Mag-duh-layn] (*St. Emilion Premier Grand Cru, Bordeaux,* France) *St. Emilion* estate owned by *JP Moueix* and neighbour to *Ch. Ausone,* producing impeccable, perfumed wines that are now, however, closer in style to those of the other nearby estate, Ch. *Belair.* **61 70 71** 75 78 79 81 **82 83** 85 86 88 **89** 90 92 93 94 95 96 97 98 ☆☆☆☆ **1989 £££**

Ⴘ Maglieri [mag-lee-yeh-ree] (*McLaren Vale,* South Australia) Dynamic *Shiraz* specialist recently taken over by *Mildara-Blass.*

Magnum Large bottle containing the equivalent of two bottles of wine (one and a half litres in capacity). Wines age slower in big bottles, and fewer are produced. For both reasons, Magnums tend to cost more – especially at auction.

Maipo [mih-poh] (Chile) Historic region in which are found many good producers. Reds are most successful, especially *Cabernet* and *Merlot,* and softer *Chardonnays* are also made. New varieties and enterprising organic vineyards are moving in, but vineyards close to Santiago, the capital, increasingly have to compete with the needs of housing developers. **Aquitania (Paul Bruno); Canepa;** *Carmen;* **Concha y Toro;** Cousino Macul; Peteroa; *Santa Carolina;* Santa Inés; *Santa Rita;* **Undurraga;** Viña Carmen.

Maître de Chai [may-tr duh chay] (France) Cellar master.

Malaga [ma-la-gah] (Spain) A semi-moribund Andalusian *DO* producing raisiny dessert wines of varying degrees of sweetness, immensely popular in the 19th century. Sadly very hard to find nowadays. **Lopez Hermanos.**

Ⴘ Ch. Malartic-Lagravière [mah-lahr-teek lah-gra-vee-yehr] (*Pessac-Léognan Cru Classé, Bordeaux,* France) Previously slumbering estate, bought in 1994 by *Laurent Perrier,* improving new-wave whites; reds need time. Red: 81 **82** 83 85 **86** 88 89 90 91 92 93 94 95 96 97 98 White: 85 **87** 88 89 90 91 92 94 95 96 97 98

🍇 **Malbec** [mal-bek] Red grape, now rare in *Bordeaux* but widely planted in Argentina, the *Loire* (where it is known as the *Côt*), *Cahors* and also in Australia. Producing rich, plummy, silky wines.

🍷 **Ch. Malescasse** [ma-les-kas] (*Haut-Médoc Cru Bourgeois, Bordeaux, France*) Since 1993, wines have benefitted from being made by the former cellarmaster of *Pichon-Lalande*. 82 83 85 86 88 89 90 93 94 95 96

🍷 **Ch. Malescot-St-Exupéry** [ma-les-koh san tek-soo-peh-ree] (*Margaux 3ème Cru Classé, Bordeaux, France*) Understated but sometimes quite classy wines. 70 **82** 83 86 87 88 89 90 91 92 94 95 96 97 98 ☆☆☆ 1996 £££

🍷 **Ch. de Malle** [duh mal] (*Sauternes 2ème Cru Classé, Bordeaux, France*) Good *Sauternes* property near Preignac, famous for its beautiful *château*. 76 78 **81** 82 **83** 85 **86** 88 89 90 91 94 95 96 97 98 ☆☆☆☆ **1990 ££££**

Malolactic fermentation [ma-loh-lak-tik] Secondary "fermentation" in which appley *malic acid* is converted into the "softer," creamier *lactic* acid by naturally present or added strains of bacteria. Almost all red wines undergo a malolactic fermentation. For whites, it is common practice in *Burgundy*. It is varyingly used in the New World, where natural acid levels are often low. An excess is recognisable in wine as a buttermilky flavour.

🍷 **Ch. de la Maltroye** [mal-trwah] (*Burgundy, France*) Classy modern *Chassagne*-based estate with fingers in fourteen *AC* pies around *Burgundy*, all of whose wines are made by *Dom. Parent*. ☆☆☆☆ **1997 Chassagne-Montrachet Clos du Château de la Maltroye ££££**

🍇 **Malvasia** [mal-vah-see-ah] *Muscat*ty white grape vinified dry in Italy (as a component in *Frascati* for example), but far more successfully as good, sweet, traditional *Madeira*, where it is known as *Malmsey*. It is not the same grape as Malvoisie.

La Mancha [lah man-cha] (Spain) Huge region known for mostly dull and old-fashioned wines, but in recent times producing increasingly clean, modern examples. Also the place where the *Marquès de Griñon* is succeeding in his experiments with new vine-growing techniques and grapes, especially *Syrah*.

🍷 **Albert Mann** (*Alsace, France*) Top grower who always manages to express true varietal character without overblown flavours and excessive alcohol. ☆☆☆☆ **1997 Riesling Grand Cru Furstentum £££**

🍇 **Manseng (Gros M. & Petit M.)** [man-seng] (*South-West, France*) Two varieties of white grape grown in southwestern France. The Gros Manseng is a flavoursome workhorse for much of the dry white of the Armagnac region, whereas Petit Manseng is capable of extraordinary apricot-and-cream concentration in the great *vendange tardive* wines of *Jurançon*. The Manseng is one of the few noble varieties not to have found wide favour across the globe, possibly because it is low-yielding and hard to grow. *Dom. Cauhapé; Grassa; Producteurs de Plaimont*.

🍷 **Josef Mantler** [yoh-sef mant-lehr] (*Krems*, Austria) Reliable producer of both Grüner and Roter Veltliner as well as good *Riesling* and *Chardonnay*.

Manzanilla [man-zah-nee-yah] (*Jerez*, Spain) Dry tangy *sherry* – a fino style widely (though possibly mistakenly) thought to take on a salty tang from the coastal *bodegas* of Sanlucar de Barrameda. **Don Zoilo; Barbadillo; Hidalgo.**

🍷 **Maranges** [mah-ronzh] (*Burgundy*, France) A new hillside *appellation* promising potentially affordable, if a little rustic, *Côte d'Or* wines. White: 92 95 96 97 98 Red: **90** 92 95 96 97 98 **Bachelet;** Pierre Bresson; Chevrot; *Drouhin; Vincent Girardin; Claude Nouveau.*

Marc [mahr] (France) The residue of seeds, stalks, and skins left after the grapes are pressed – and often distilled into a fiery brandy of the same name, e.g. Marc de Bourgogne.

🍷 **Marcassin** (*Sonoma*, California) Helen Turley produces expressive – and, for some, sometimes a touch overblown – *Côte d'Or Grand Cru*-quality *Chardonnays* in tiny quantities from a trio of vineyards. Almost unobtainable.

Marches [mahr-kay] (Italy) Central wine region on the Adriatic coast, below Venice. Best known for *Rosso Conero* and good, dry, fruity *Verdicchio* whites. **Fazi Battaglia; Garofoli; Boccadigabbia; Fattoria Coroncino; Gioacchino Garafolli; Vallerosa Bonci; Umani Ronchi.**

🍷 **Marcillac** [mah-see-yak] (*South-West*, France) Full-flavoured country reds, made principally from the *Fer*, possibly blended with some *Cabernet* and *Gamay*. **Du Cros; Lacombe; Cave du Vallon-Valady.**

🍇 **Maréchal Foch** [mah-ray-shahl fohsh] A *hybrid* vine producing red grapes in Canada and Eastern North America. Inniskillin makes a good example.

Margaret River (*Western* Australia) Cool(ish) vineyard area on the coast of *Western Australia*, originally picked out by vinous academic, Dr. John Gladstones and *Robert Mondavi* when he contemplated expanding into Australia. The first vineyards were mostly planted by doctors, curiously enough. Now gaining notice for *Cabernet Sauvignon* and *Chardonnay*. Also one of Australia's only *Zinfandels*. White: 85 86 87 88 90 91 93 94 95 96 97 98 Red: **80 82 83 85 86 87** 88 **90** 91 92 93 94 95 96 97 98 99 **Brookland Valley;** *Cape Mentelle; Cullen;* Devil's Lair; *Evans & Tate; Moss Wood; Leeuwin; Pierro; Vasse Felix;* Voyager Estate; *Ch. Xanadu.*

🍷 **Margaux** [mahr-goh] (*Bordeaux*, France) Large, very varied *commune* with a concentration of *crus classés* including *Ch. Margaux*, *Palmer and Lascombes*. Sadly, other wines which should be deliciously blackberryish are variable, partly thanks to the diverse nature of the soil, and partly through the producers' readiness to sacrifice quality for the sake of yields. Curiously, though, if you want a good 1983, this vintage succeeded better here than elsewhere in the *Médoc*; 1995s are good too, and so, comparitively, are the 1999s. Also worth hunting out are generic *Margaux* from reputable *négociants*.

Ⅰ Ch. Margaux [mahr-goh] (*Margaux Premier Cru Classé, Bordeaux, France*) Peerless first growth, back on form since the dull 1970s, and producing intense wines with cedary perfume and velvet softness when mature. The second wine, *Pavillon Rouge* (red and matching white), is worth buying too. **61 78 79 81** 82 83 **84** 85 86 **87** 88 89 **90** 91 **92** 93 **94** 95 96 97 98 ☆☆☆☆☆ **1996 ££££**

Ⅰ Markham (*Napa Valley*, California) A producer to watch for fairly priced reds and whites. ☆☆☆☆ **1997 Markham Vineyards Reserve Chardonnay £££;** ☆☆☆☆ **1996 Markham Vineyards Reserve Merlot £££**

Marlborough [morl-buh-ruh] (New Zealand) An important wine area with cool climate in the South Island producing excellent *Sauvignon*, *Chardonnay*, and improving *Merlot* and *Pinot Noir*, as well as a number of impressive sparkling wines. White: **89 91 92** 96 97 **98** *Babich; Cellier le Brun; Cloudy Bay; Corbans Giesen; Grove Mill; Hunter's; Jackson Estate; Montana; Stoneleigh; Vavasour.*

Ⅰ Marne et Champagne [mahr-nay-shom-pan-y] (*Champagne*, France) Huge cooperative which owns the Besserat de Bellefon, *Lanson* and Alfred Rothschild labels, and can provide really good own-label wines for merchant and superstore buyers who are prepared to pay the price.

Ⅰ Ch. Marquis-de-Terme [mahr-kee duh tehrm] (*Margaux 4ème Cru Classé, Bordeaux*, France) Traditional property with quite tough wines. **81 82 83 85 86** 87 88 89 90 **93 95 96 98** ☆☆☆ **1996 £££**

Ⅰ Marsala [mahr-sah-lah] (*Sicily*, Italy) Rich, fortified wine from *Sicily* for use in recipes such as Zabaglione. *De Bartoli;* Cantine Florio; Pellegrino; Rallo.

Ⅰ Marsannay [mahr-sah-nay] (*Burgundy*, France) Northernmost village of the *Côte de Nuits* with a range of largely undistinguished but, for *Burgundy*, affordable *Chardonnay* and *Pinot Noir* (red and rosé). White: **79 84 85 86** 87 **88** 89 **90 92** 95 96 97 **98** Red: 76 **78** 79 **80** 83 **85** 86 87 **88 89 90** 92 95 96 97 **98** *Bruno Clair;* Fougeray de Beauclair; *Louis Jadot.*

❦ Marsanne [mahr-san] (*Rhône*, France) The grape usually responsible (in blends with *Roussanne*) for most of the northern *Rhône* white wines. Also successful in the *Goulburn Valley* in *Victoria* for *Ch. Tahbilk* and *Mitchelton* and in California for *Bonny Doon*. It has a delicate perfumed intensity when young and fattens out with age. Look out for un-oaked versions from Australia. **Tahbilk;** *Mitchelton;* Bonny Doon; *Guigal.*

Martinborough (New Zealand) Up-and-coming North Island region for *Pinot Noir* and *Chardonnay*. White: 87 88 **89 91** 92 **94** 96 97 **98** Red: **83 85** 87 89 90 **91 92** 93 94 95 96 97 98 *Ata Rangi;* Alana Estate; *Dry River;* Martinborough Vineyard; Palliser Estate.

☥ **Martinborough Vineyard** (*Martinborough*, New Zealand) Producer of the best Kiwi *Pinot Noir* and one of the best *Chardonnays*. Wines can be so *Burgundian* in style that the 1991 *Pinot Noir* was refused an export licence for being untypically "farmyardy" until a delegation of wine-loving politicians intervened. ☆☆☆☆ **1996 Martinborough Vineyard Reserve Pinot Noir £££**

☥ **Martinelli** (*Sonoma*, California) Century-old *Zinfandel* specialists, making rich intense reds from this variety and juicy *Pinot Noirs*.

☥ **Bodegas Martinez Bujanda** [mahr-tee-neth boo-han-dah] (*Rioja*, Spain) New-Wave producer of fruit-driven wines sold as *Conde de Valdemar*. Probably the most consistently recommendable producer in *Rioja*. ☆☆☆☆**1994 Finca Valpiedra Reserva £££**

☥ **Martini** (*Piedmont*, Italy) Good *Asti Spumante* from the producer of the vermouth house which invented "lifestyle" advertising – still, we're all guilty of something. ☆☆☆ **Asti Fratelli Martini ££**

☥ **Louis Martini** (*Napa Valley*, California) Grand old name right on form at the moment. Superlative long-lived *Cabernet* from the Monte Rosso vineyard. ☆☆☆☆ **1997 Sangiovese Heritage Collection 1997 £££**; ☆☆☆☆☆ **1995 Russian River Valley Reserve Merlot £££**

❀ **Marzemino** [mahrt-zeh-mee-noh] (Italy) Grape making spicy-plummy wines.

☥ **Mas Amiel** [mahs ah-mee-yel] (*Provence*, France) Producer of wonderful rich almost *port*-like wine in the small *appellation* of Maury in the west of *Provence*. ☆☆☆☆ **Maury 15 Ans d'Age £££**

☥ **Mas de Daumas Gassac** [mas duh doh-mas gas-sac] (*Midi*, France) Ground-breaking *Herault Vin de Pays* red, compared by some to top *claret*. Its flavours come from an eclectic blend of up to half a dozen varieties, including *Pinot Noir, Syrah, Mourvèdre* and *Cabernet* – and a unique "*terroir*". Approachable when young, but lasts for ages. A white blend including *Viognier* is similarly impressive. ☆☆☆☆ **1998 White £££**

☥ **Mas Jullien** [mas joo-lye'n] (*Languedoc-Roussillon*, France) The most stylish wines in the *Coteaux du Languedoc* (or elsewhere in southern France). Classic individual reds and whites from classic traditional grapes.

☥ **Clos Martinet** [mas mahr-tee-neht] (*Priorato*, Spain) One of a pair of dazzling Priorato wines that is catching the attention of US critics. The *second wine* is Martinet Bru.

☥ **Bartolo Mascarello** [mas-kah-reh-loh] (*Piedmont,* Italy) Great ultra-traditional *Barolo* specialist whose rose-petaly wine proves that the old ways can compete with the new. But they do call for patience.

☥ **Giuseppe Mascarello** [mas-kah-reh-loh] (*Piedmont*, Italy) Top-class *Barolo* estate (unconnected with that of *Bartolo Mascarello*), producing characterful wine from individual vineyards. Succeeds in tricky vintages. Great *Dolcetto*. ☆☆☆☆ **1995 Monprivato ££££**

☥ **Gianni Masciarelli** [mash-chee-yah-reh-lee] (*Abruzzo*, Italy) One of the starriest makers of Montepulciano d'Abruzzo.

☥ **Masi** [mah-see] (*Veneto*, Italy) Producer with reliable, affordable reds and whites and single-vineyard wines which serve as a justification for *Valpolicella's* denomination. ☆☆☆☆☆ **1995 Osar £££**

☥ **La Massa** [mah-sah] (*Tuscany*, Italy) Top class Chianti producer with a spectacularly good 1996 Chianti Classico Giorgio Primo.

☥ **Massandra** [mahsan-drah] (*Crimea*, Ukraine) Famous as the source of great, historic, dessert wines which were sold at a memorable Sotheby's auction in 1991, this is now the place to find good but not great *Cabernet Sauvignon*.

Master of Wine (MW) One of a small number of people (around 250) internationally who have passed a gruelling set of wine exams.

☥ **Mastroberadino** [maas tro be rah dino] (*Campania*, Italy) Top producer of rich Taurasi in Italy's south. ☆☆☆☆ **1993 Taurasi Radici £££**

Y **Matanzas Creek** [muh-tan-zuhs] (*Sonoma Valley,* California)
Top-class complex *Chardonnay* (one of California's best), good
Sauvignon, and high-quality accessible *Merlot.* ✰✰✰✰ 1996 Sonoma
Valley Merlot ££££

🍇 **Mataro** [muh-tah-roh] See *Mourvèdre.*

Y **Mateus** [ma-tay-oos] (Portugal) Highly commercial pink and white
off-dry *frizzante* wine made by *Sogrape,* Portugal's biggest producer,
sold in bottles traditional in Franken, Germany, and with a label
depicting a palace with which the wine has no connection. A 50-year-
old marketing masterpiece. The name is now being used for *Sogrape's*
more serious reds.

Y **Thierry Matrot** [tee-yer-ree ma-troh] (*Burgundy,* France) Top-class white
producer with great white and recommendable red *Blagny.* ✰✰✰✰ 1992
Meursault Les Charmes ££££

Y **Chateau Matsa** [maht-sah] (*Attica,* Greece) One of the Greece's best new
wave producers.

Y **Matteo Correggia** [mah-tey-yoh coh-rey-djee-yah] (*Piedmont,* Italy) One
of the best wine producers in Italy, excelling with Barbera d'Alba and
Nebbiolo d'Alba.

Y **Matthew Cellars** (*Washington State,* US) Up-and-coming producer of
Cabernet and *Sémillon.*

Y **Matua Valley** [ma-tyoo-wah] (*Auckland,* New Zealand) Reliable maker
of great (*Marlborough*) *Sauvignon,* (Judd Estate) *Chardonnay* and
Merlot. Also producer of the even better *Ararimu* red and white. Shingle
Peak is the *second label.* ✰✰✰✰ 1997 Dartmoor Smith Cabernet
Sauvignon £££

Y **Yvon Mau** [ee-von moh] (*Bordeaux & South-West,* France) Highly
commercial producer of *Bordeaux* and other, mostly white, wines from
South-West France. Occasionally good. ✰✰✰ 1996 Premius ££

Y **Ch. Maucaillou** [mow-kih-yoo] (*Moulis Cru Bourgeois, Bordeaux,*
France) *Cru Bourgeois* in the *commune* of *Moulis* regularly producing
approachable wines to beat some *crus classés.* 75 82 83 85 86 88 89 90
92 93 94 95 96 97 98

Maule [mow-lay] (Chile) Up-and-coming *Central Valley* region especially
for white wines but warm enough for red. *Santa Carolina;* Carta Vieja.

Y **Bernard Maume** [Mohm] (*Burgundy,* France) Small *Gevrey-Chambertin*
estate run by a biology professor and his son and making long-lived wines.
✰✰✰✰ 1997 Gevrey-Chambertin £££

Y **Bodegas Mauro** [mow-roh] (Spain) Just outside the *Ribera del Duero*
DO, but making very similar rich red wines.

Y **Maury** [moh-ree] (*Languedoc-Roussillon,* France) Potentially rich sweet
wine to compete with *Banyuls* and *port.* Sadly, too many examples are light
and feeble. ✰✰✰✰ 1995 Mas Amiel Vintage Reserve £££

🍇 **Mauzac** [moh-zak] (France) White grape used in southern France for *Vin
de Pays* and *Gaillac.* Can be characterful and floral or dull and earthy.

🍇 **Mavrodaphne** [mav-roh-daf-nee] (Greece) Characterful indigenous
Greek red grape, and the wine made from it. Dark and strong, it needs
ageing to be truly worth drinking. ✰✰✰✰ Kourtakis Mavrodaphne of
Patras ££

🍇 **Mavrud** [mah-vrood] (Bulgaria) Traditional red grape and the characterful,
if rustic, wine made from it.

Y **Maximin Grünhaus** [mak-siee min groon-hows] (*Mosel-Saar-Ruwer,*
Germany) Dr. Carl von Schubert's 1,000-year-old estate producing intense
Rieslings. ✰✰✰✰✰ 1996 Abtsberg Riesling Spätlese ££££

♈ **Maxwell** (*McLaren Vale*, Australia) Reliable producer of *Shiraz*, *Merlot* and *Semillon*, and good mead.

♈ **Mayacamas** [mih-yah-kah-mas] (*Napa Valley*, California) Long-established winery on *Mount Veeder* with *tannic* but good old-fashioned *Cabernet* and long-lived rich *Chardonnay*. ☆☆☆☆ 1994 Cabernet Sauvignon ££££

♈ **McGuigan Brothers** (*Hunter Valley*, Australia) Commercial and occasionally quite impressive stuff from the former owners of *Wyndham Estate*. ☆☆☆☆ 1997 McGuigan Shareholders Shiraz ££

McLaren Vale (*South Australia*) Region close to Adelaide renowned for European-style wines, but possibly too varied in topography, soil and climate to create its own identity. White: **86 87 88 90 91 94 95 97 98** Red: **80 82 84 85 86 87 88 90 91** 94 95 96 97 98 *D'Arenberg; Hardy's; Kays Amery, Maglieri; Geoff Merrill; Ch. Reynella; Wirra Wirra.*

♈ **McWilliams** (*Hunter Valley*, Australia) *Hunter Valley*-based, evidently non-republican firm with great traditional ("Elizabeth") *Semillon* and ("Philip") *Shiraz* which are now sold younger than previously and so may need time. Fortified wines can be good, too, as are the pioneering *Barwang* and improved *Brand's* wines. Surprisingly good at "Bag-in-box" wines! ☆☆☆☆ 1994 Elizabeth Semillon £££

♈ **Médoc** [may-dok] (*Bordeaux*, France) Area encompassing the region of *Bordeaux* south of the *Gironde* and north of the town of *Bordeaux* in which the *Cru Classés* as well as far more ordinary fare are made. Should be better than basic *Bordeaux* and less good than *Haut-Médoc*, which tend to have more flavour: experience, however, suggests that this is not always the case.

♈ **Meerlust Estate** [meer-loost] (*Stellenbosch*, South Africa) One of the *Cape's* best estates. Classy *Merlots* and a highly rated *Bordeaux*-blend called "Rubicon", both of which will hopefully, one day, benefit from being bottled on the estate rather than by the *Bergkelder*. ☆☆☆☆ 1995 Rubicon £££

♈ **Gabriel Meffre** [mef-fr] (*Rhône*, France) Sound commercial *Rhône* and, now, southern France producer under the Galet Vineyards and Wild Pig labels. However, a tradition of producing reliable, more classy wines is maintained. ☆☆☆ 1997 Seguret Les Villages des Papes ££

♈ **Ch. Megyer** [meg-yer] (*Tokaji*, Hungary) French-owned pioneer of *Tokaji* and *Furmint*.

🍇 **Melnik** [mehl-neek] (Bulgaria) Both a grape variety and a commune where rich reds are produced.

🍇 **Melon de Bourgogne** [muh-lon duh boor-goyn] (France) Grape originally imported from *Burgundy* (where it is no longer grown) to the *Loire* by Dutch brandy distillers who liked its resistance to frost. Amazingly, good producers now contrive to make decent *Muscadet* from it.

♈ **Charles Melton** (*Barossa Valley*, Australia) Small-scale producer of lovely still and sparkling *Shiraz* and world-class rosé called "Rose of Virginia", as well as Nine Popes, a wine based on, and mistakenly named after, *Châteauneuf-du-Pape*. ☆☆☆☆ NV Sparkling Red £££

Mendocino [men-doh-see-noh] (California) Northern, coastal wine county known for unofficial marijuana farming and for its laid back winemakers who successfully exploit cool microclimates to make "European-style" wines. Red: 84 **85** 86 87 **90 91** 92 93 95 96 97 98 White: **85 90 91** 92 95 96 97 98 *Fetzer; Handley Cellars; Hidden Cellars; Lazy Creek; Parducci; Roederer; Scharffenberger.*

Mendoza [men-doh-zah] (Argentina) Capital of a now up-and-coming principal wine region. Source of good rich reds from firms producing traditional-style reds but with more uplifting fruit. **La Agricola; Bianchi; *Catena; Etchart;* Finca Flichman; *Norton; Lurton; Morande; la Rural;* San Telmo; *Trapiche; Weinert.***

☫ **Menetou-Salon** [men-too sah-lon] (*Loire,* France) Bordering on *Sancerre,* making similar if earthier, less pricy *Sauvignon,* as well as some decent *Pinot Noir. Henri Pellé* makes the best. **De Beaurepaire; R Champault; Charet; Fournier; de Loye; *Pellé;* la Tour St Martin.**

☫ **Dom. Méo-Camuzet** [may-oh-ka-moo-zay] (*Burgundy,* France) Brilliant *Côte de Nuits* estate with top-class vineyards and intense, oaky wines, made, until his retirement, by the great *Henri Jayer.*

Mercaptans [mehr-kap-ton] See *hydrogen sulphide.*

☫ **Mercier** [mehr-see-yay] (*Champagne,* France) Subsidiary, or is it sister company, of *Moët & Chandon* and producer of improving but pretty commercial sparkling wine which, according to the advertisements, is the biggest seller in France. ☆☆☆☆ **Champagne Mercier Demi-Sec £££**

☫ **Mercouri** [mehr-koo-ree] (*Peleponnese,* Greece) Starry new wave producer with good reds and very successful Roditis.

☫ **Mercurey** [mehr-koo-ray] (*Burgundy,* France) Village in the *Côte Chalonnaise,* where *Faiveley* makes high-quality wine. Red: 78 80 **85** 86 87 **88 89** 90 92 95 96 97 98 99 White: 84 **85 86** 87 **88** 89 **90 92** 95 96 97 98 **Dom Brintet; Marguerite Carillon; Ch. de Chamirey; *Dom. Faiveley;* Genot-Boulanger; Michel Juillot; *Olivier Leflaive;* Meix-Foulot; *Pillot.***

☫ **Meridian** (*San Luis Obispo,* California) Unusually good-value *Pinot Noir* from *Santa Barbara.* The *Merlot* and *Chardonnay* are pretty impressive too.

🌢 **Merlot** [mehr-loh] "Flavour of the Month", if the ludicrous orgy of planting in California's *Central Valley* is anything to go by. Already becoming an unloved child, as grapegrowers and winemakers discover that this red variety only produces appealing soft, honeyed, even toffeeish wine with plummy fruit when it is planted in the right (ideally clay) soil, and kept to very moderate yields. In other words, quite the opposite of what it will get in the *Central Valley.* It is traditionally used to balance the more *tannic Cabernet Sauvignon* throughout the *Médoc,* where it is actually the most widely planted grape; as it is in *Pomerol* and *St. Emilion,* where clay also prevails. Also increasingly – though not spectacularly – successful in the *Languedoc* in southern France. California's best efforts include *Newton, Matanzas Creek,* and (recently) *Duckhorn.* Australia, South Africa, and New Zealand have had few real successes, but there are impressive efforts from *Washington State* and Chile.

☫ **Merricks Estate** (*Mornington Peninsula,* Australia) Small estate specialising in *Shiraz.* ☆☆☆☆ **1994 Shiraz**

☫ **Geoff Merrill** (*McLaren Vale,* Australia) The ebullient moustachioed winemaker who has nicknamed himself "The Wizard of Oz". Impressive if restrained *Semillon, Chardonnay,* and *Cabernet* in *McLaren Vale* under his own label, plus easier-going Mount Hurtle wines (especially the rosé).

☫ **Merryvale** (*Napa Valley,* California) Very starry winery with especially good Reserve and Silhouette *Chardonnay* and Profile *Cabernet.* ☆☆☆☆ **1996 Hillside Cabernet £££**

Ɏ Louis Métaireau [meht-teh-roh] (*Loire*, France) The Cadillac of *Muscadet*, which comes here in the form of individual *cuvées*. Cuvée One is the star.

Méthode Champenoise [may-tohd shom-puh-nwahz] Term now outlawed by the EU from wine labels but still used to describe the way *Champagne* and all other quality sparkling wines are produced. Labour intensive, because bubbles are made by secondary fermentation in bottle, rather than in a vat or by the introduction of gas. Bottles are individually given the "*dégorgement* process", topped up and recorked!

Methuselah Same size bottle as an *Imperiale* (six litres). Used in *Champagne*.

Ɏ Meursault [muhr-soh] (*Burgundy*, France) Superb white *Burgundy*; the *Chardonnay* ideally showing off its nutty, buttery richness in full-bodied dry wine. Like *Nuits-St.-Georges* and *Beaune*, it has no *Grands Crus* but great *Premiers Crus* such as Charmes, Perrières, and Genevrières. There is a little red here too, some of which is sold as *Volnay-Santenots*. White: 89 **90 92** 95 96 97 98 Ampeau; d'Auvenay; Coche-Dury; Drouhin; Henri Germain; Ropiteau; Jobard; Comtes Lafon; Michelot; Pierre Morey; Jacques Prieur; Ch. de Puligny-Montrachet; Roulot; Roux Père et Fils; Verget.

Ɏ Ch. de Meursault [muhr-soh] (*Burgundy*, France) One of *Burgundy's* few *châteaux* and well worth a visit. The wines – far better than most produced by its owner, *Patriarche* – are good too. ☆☆☆☆☆ 1996 Meursault Premier Cru £££

Mexico See *Baja California*.

Ɏ Ch. Meyney [may-nay] (*St. Estèphe Cru Bourgeois, Bordeaux*, France) Improving *St. Estèphe* property, with wines that are richer in flavour than some of its neighbours. 81 **82** 83 85 **86** 88 89 90 91 92 93 94 95 96 **97 98**

Ɏ Miani [mee-yah-nee] (*Friuli-Venezia Giulia*, Italy) Enzo Pontoni's scrupulous efforts to keep yields low make for brilliant examples of Bordeaux red varieties, *Riesling* and *Chardonnay*.

Ɏ Peter Michael (*Sonoma*, California) UK-born Sir Peter Michael produces stunning *Sonoma*, *Burgundy*-like *Chardonnays*, *Sauvignons*, and *Cabernets*. ☆☆☆☆☆ 1996 Belle Côte £££

Ɏ Louis Michel et Fils [mee-shel] (*Burgundy*, France) Top-class *Chablis* producer. ☆☆☆☆ 1997 Chablis Vaillons ££££

Ɏ Robert Michel (*Rhône*, France) Produces softer *Cornas* than most from this sometimes tough *appellation*: beautiful, strong yet silky wines.

Ɏ Alain Michelot [mee-shloh] (*Burgundy*, France) Producer of perfumed, elegant *Nuits-St.-Georges* that can be enjoyed young – but is well worth keeping too. ☆☆☆☆ 1994 Nuits-St.-Georges Vaucrains ££££

Ɏ Dom. Michelot-Buisson [mee-shloh bwee-son] (*Burgundy*, France) One of the great old *Meursault* properties. A pioneer of estate bottling – and of the use of new oak. Wines are rarely subtle, but then they never lack typical *Meursault* flavour either. ☆☆☆☆ 1995 Meursault Les Genevrières ££££

Micro-Wine / Micro-Vin Term used to describe limited-production wines such as *le Pin* and *Screaming Eagle*.

♀ **Mildara Blass** [mil-dah-rah] (*South Australia*) Dynamic, unashamedly "market-driven" Fosters-owned company whose varied portfolio of styles and (sometimes derivative labels) includes *Rothbury, Yarra Ridge, Yellowglen, Wolf Blass, Balgownia,* Mount Helen, *Stonyfell, Saltram,* and *Maglieri. Coonawarra* wines, including the very commercial *Jamieson's Run,* are best. ☆☆☆☆ **1995 Mildara Coonawarra Cabernet Sauvignon £££**

♀ **Millton Estate** (*Gisborne,* New Zealand) James Millton is an obsessive, not to say a masochist. He loves the hard-to-make *Chenin Blanc* and uses it to make first-class organic wine in *Gisborne.* Sadly, it seems, most people would rather buy his *Chardonnay.* ☆☆☆☆ **1999 Opou Riesling £££**

♀ **Milmanda** [mil-man-dah] (*Conca de Barbera,* Spain) *Torres'* top-label *Chardonnay.* Classy by any standards. ☆☆☆☆☆ **1997 £££**

♀ **Kym Milne** Antipodean *flying winemaker* who has been quietly expanding his empire with great success, particularly with Vinfruco in *South Africa,* at Le Trulle in southern *Italy,* and at *Nagyrede* in *Hungary.*

♀ **Minervois** [mee-nehr-vwah] (*South-West,* France) Fast leaving *Corbières* behind with its improving reds, Minervois' styles and qualities vary, depending on the part of the region, the grape and the maker. Wines made from old-vine *Carignan* can be richly intense; *maceration-carbonique* wines from younger *Carignan* can compete with *Beaujolais*; *Mourvèdre* can be perfumed, and *Syrah,* spicy. Some of the best wines come from a newly-recognised sub-region called la Livinière, where the leading producer Jean-Christophe Piccinini is based. Elsewhere, an enterprising Australian called Nerida Abbott is labelling a pure *Syrah* as "*Shiraz*" (a term that is apparently not recognised in France as a synonym for this variety). Whites and rosés are considerably less interesting. **Abbott's Cumulus; Clos Centeilles; Gourgazaud; Ch d'Oupia; Piccinini; Ste. Eulalie; la Tour Boisée; Villerambert-Julien.**

Mis en Bouteille au Ch./Dom. [mee zon boo-tay] (France) Estate-bottled.

🌱 **Misket** (Bulgaria) Dullish, sometimes faintly herby white grape.

♀ **Mission** (*Hawke's Bay,* New Zealand) Still run by monks, nearly 150 years after its foundation, this estate is now one of the best in New Zealand. ☆☆☆☆ **1997 Jewelstone Mission Cabernet Merlot £££**

♀ **Mission Hill** (*British Columbia,* Canada) Dynamic producer of various styles, ranging from *Riesling icewine* to *Merlot.*

♀ **Ch. la Mission-Haut-Brion** [lah mee-see-yon oh-bree-yon] (*Pessac-Léognan Cru Classé, Bordeaux,* France) Tough but rich reds which rival and – possibly in 1998 – even overtake its supposedly classier neighbour *Haut-Brion.* 78 79 **81 82 83** 84 **85 86 87** 88 89 90 91 92 **93 94** 95 96 97 98 99

♀ **Mitchell** (*Clare Valley,* Australia) Good producer of *Riesling* and of the Peppertree *Shiraz,* one of the *Clare Valley's* best reds. Also good for powerful *Grenache, Riesling, Semillon,* and sparkling *Shiraz.*

♀ **Mitchelton** (*Goulburn Valley,* Australia) A modern producer of *Marsanne* and *Semillon* which now belongs to *Petaluma. Late harvest Rieslings* are also good, as is a *Beaujolais*-style red, known as Cab Mac. The French-style Preece range – named after the former winemaker – is also worth seeking out.

Mittelhaardt [mit-tel-hahrt] (*Pfalz,* Germany) Central and best *Bereich* of the *Rheinpfalz.* QbA/Kab/Spät: **85** 86 **88 89 90** 91 92 93 94 95 96 97 98 Aus/Beeren/Tba: **83 85** 88 89 90 91 92 93 94 95 96 97 98

Mittelmosel [mit-tel-moh-zul] (*Mosel-Saar-Ruwer,* Germany) Middle and best section of the *Mosel,* including the *Bernkastel Bereich.* QbA/Kab/Spät: **85 86 88 89 90** 91 92 93 94 95 96 97 98 Aus/Beeren/Tba: **83 85** 88 89 90 91 92 93 94 95 96 97 98 99

Mittelrhein [mit-tel-rihne] (Germany) Small, northern section of the *Rhine.* Good *Rieslings* that sadly are rarely seen outside Germany. QbA/Kab/Spät: **85 86 88 89 90** 91 92 93 94 95 96 97 98 Aus/Beeren/Tba: **83 85** 88 89 90 91 92 93 94 95 96 97 98 *Toni Jost.*

☤ **Mittnacht-Klack** [mit-nakt-clack] (*Alsace,* France) Seriously high-quality wines with particular accent on *"vendange tardive"* and *late harvest* wines. ☆☆☆☆ 1996 Gewurztraminer Rosacker ££££
Moelleux [mwah-luh] (France) Sweet.

☤ **Moët & Chandon** [moh-wet ay shon-den] (*Champagne,* France) The biggest producer in *Champagne. Dom Pérignon,* the top wine, and *vintage* Moët are reliably good and new *cuvées* of "Brut Imperial Non-Vintage" though not always brilliant, show a welcome reaction to recent criticism. Watch out too for a good *Brut* rosé. ☆☆☆☆ 1993 Vintage Rosé £££

☤ **Clos Mogador** [kloh MOH-gah-dor] (*Priorato,* Spain) Juicy, modern, and more importantly, stylish red wine from the once ultra-traditional and rustic region of *Priorato.* The shape of things to come. ☆☆☆☆ 1995 £££

☤ **Moillard** [mwah-yar] (*Burgundy,* France) Middle-of-the-road *négociant* whose best wines are sold under the "Dom. Thomas Moillard" label.

Moldova Young republic next to Romania whose as yet uncertain potential was briefly exploited by *Hugh Ryman* at the Hincesti winery.

☤ **Mauro Molino** [mah-oo-roh moh-le-noh] (*Piedmont,* Italy) Small producer of exemplary *Barbera* (Vigna Gattere) and *Barolo.*

☤ **Monbazillac** [mon-ba-zee-yak] (*South-West,* France) *Bergerac AC* using the grapes of sweet *Bordeaux* to make improving alternatives to *Sauternes.*

☤ **Ch. Monbousquet** [mon-boo-skay] (*St. Emilion Grand Cru Classé, Bordeaux,* France) Newly taken over and now producing rich, concentrated wines. The 1994 was specially successful. **78** 79 82 **85** 86 88 89 90 92 93 94 95 96 97 98 ☆☆☆ 1995 Ch. Monbousquet, St. Emilion £££

☤ **Ch. Monbrison** [mon-bree-son] (*Margaux, Bordeaux,* France) Reliable, constant overperformer in this often disappointing *appellation.* A great 1999. **78** 79 82 **85** 86 88 89 90 92 94 95 96 97 98 ☆☆☆☆ 1990 ££££

☤ **Mönchof** [moon-chof] (*Mosel,* Germany) Top *Mosel* producer in *Urzig.*

☤ **Ch. de Moncontour** [mon-con-toor] (*Loire,* France) One of the more recommendable – and affordable – sources of still and sparkling *Vouvray.* ☆☆☆ 1995 Vouvray Demi-Sec ££

☤ **Robert Mondavi** [mawn-dah-vee] (*Napa Valley,* California) Pioneering producer of great Reserve *Cabernet* and *Pinot Noir,* and *Chardonnay,* and inventor of *oaky Fumé Blanc Sauvignon.* The new "IO" Italian-style and Coastal wines are good but the Woodbridge wines, though pleasant, are less interesting. Co-owner of *Opus One* and now in a joint venture with *Caliterra* in Chile and *Frescobaldi* in *Tuscany.* ☆☆☆☆ 1997 IO £££

☤ **la Mondotte** [mon-dot] (*St. Emilion, Bordeaux,* France) Ultra-intense rich micro-wine produced by the owner of Canon La Gaffelière.

☤ **Mongeard-Mugneret** [mon-zhahr moon-yeh-ray] (*Burgundy,* France) A source of invariably excellent and sometimes stunningly exotic red *Burgundy.* ☆☆☆☆ 1997 Vosne-Romanée £££

🍇 **Monica (di Cagliari/Sardegna)** [moh-nee-kah] (*Sardinia,* Italy) Red grape and wine of *Sardinia* producing drily tasty and fortified spicy wine.

🍷 **Marqués de Monistrol** [moh-nee-strol] (*Catalonia,* Spain) Single-estate *Cava.* Also successfully producing noble varietals.
  ☆☆☆☆ 1997 Merlot ££

Monopole [mo-noh-pohl] (France) Literally, exclusive – in *Burgundy* denotes single ownership of an entire vineyard. Romanée-Conti and Château Grillet are good examples.

🍷 **Mont Gras** [mon gra] (*Colchagua,* Chile) Fast-improving winery. ☆☆☆☆☆ 1999 Réserva Single Vineyard Carmenére £££

🍷 **Clos du Mont Olivet** [Mo(n)-toh-lee-vay] (*Rhône,* France) Good *Châteauneuf-du-Pape* producer. *Cuvée du Pape* is the top wine. ☆☆☆☆ 1998 Châteauneuf-du-Pape £££

🍷 **Les Producteurs du Mont Tauch** [mon-tohsh] (*Midi,* France) Southern cooperative with surprisingly good, top-of-the-range wines.
  ☆☆☆☆ 1998 Reserve Baron de la Tour ££

🍷 **Montagne St. Emilion** [mon-tan-yuh san tay-mee-yon] (*Bordeaux,* France) A "satellite" of *St. Emilion.* Often very good-value *Merlot*-dominant reds which can outclass supposedly finer fare from *St. Emilion* itself. Drink young. 82 83 85 86 88 89 90 94 95 96 97 98 99
Ch. d'Arvouet; *Beauséjour;* Bonfort; *Calon;* Corbin; Faizeau; Fauconnière; Vieux Château Calon.

🍷 **Montagny** [mon-tan-yee] (*Burgundy,* France) Small hillside *Côte Chalonnaise commune* producing good lean *Chardonnay* that can be a match for many *Pouilly-Fuissés.* Confusingly, unlike other parts of Burgundy *Premier Crus* here are not from better vineyards; they're just made from riper grapes. White: 90 92 93 95 96 97 98 Bertrand & Juillot; *J-M Boillot;* Cave de Buxy; *Ch. de Davenay; Joseph Faiveley; Louis Latour; Olivier Leflaive; Bernard Michel; Moillard; Antonin Rodet;* Ch. de la Saule; Jean Vachet.

🍷 **Montalcino** [mon-tal-chee-noh] (*Tuscany,* Italy) Village near Sienna known for *Brunello di Montalcino, Chianti's* big brother, whose reputation was largely created by *Biondi Santi,* whose wines no longer deserve the prices they command. *Rosso di Montalcino* is lighter. 78 79 82 85 88 90 94 95 96 97 98 *Altesino; Banfi; Costanti; Frescobaldi; Poggio Antico.*

🍷 **Montana** (*Marlborough,* New Zealand) Impressively consistent, huge firm with tremendous *Sauvignons,* improving *Chardonnays,* and good-value *Lindauer* and *Deutz Marlborough Cuvée* sparkling wine. Reds are improving but still tend to be on the green side. Look out for the Church Road wines and the smartly packaged single-estate wines such as the Brancott *Sauvignon.* ☆☆☆☆ 1998 Renwick Estate Chardonnay £££

🍷 **Monte Real** [mon-tay ray-al] (*Rioja,* Spain) Made by Bodegas Riojanos; generally decent, richly flavoured and *tannic Rioja.*

🍷 **Montecarlo** [mon-tay car-loh] (*Tuscany,* Italy) A wide variety of grapes are allowed here, including Rhône varieties such as the *Syrah* and *Roussanne* as well as the *Sangiovese* and the red and white *Bordeaux* varieties. Unsurprisingly, there are good *IGTs* too. Carmignani; Wandanna.

Y Fattoria di Montechiari [mon-tay-kee-yah-roh] (*Tuscany*, Italy) A fast-rising star in Montecarlo, producing rich berryish varietal reds under the Montechiari name using the *Cabernet Sauvignon*, *Sangiovese* and *Pinot Noir*. The *Chardonnay* is worth looking out for too.

Y Bodegas Montecillo [mon-tay-thee-yoh] (*Rioja*, Spain) Classy wines including the oddly named Viña Monty. The Cumbrero Blanco white is good, too. ☆☆☆ **1989 Viña Monty Gran Reserva ££**

Y Montée de Tonnerre [mon-tay duh ton-nehr] (*Burgundy*, France) Excellent *Chablis Premier Cru*.

Y Montefalco Sagrantino [mon-teh-fal-koh sag-ran-tee-noh] (*Umbria*, Italy) Intense and very characterful, cherryish red made from the local Sagrantino grape.

Y Ch. Montelena [mon-teh-lay-nah] (*Napa Valley*, California) Its two long-lived *Chardonnays* (from Napa and the rather better Alexander Valley) make this one of the more impressive producers in the state. The vanilla-and-blackcurranty *Cabernet* can be impenetrable. I prefer the *Zinfandel*.

❦Montepulciano [mon-tay-pool-chee-yah-noh] (Italy) Very confusingly, this is both a grape used to make rich red wines in central and south-eastern Italy (Montepulciano *d'Abruzzi*, etc) and the name of a wine-producing town in *Tuscany* (see *Vino Nobile di Montepulciano*) which (yes, you guessed) uses a different grape altogether.

Monterey [mon-teh-ray] (California) Underrated region south of San Francisco, producing potentially good if sometimes rather grassy wines. **Jekel; Sterling Redwood Trail; Estancia.**

Y The Monterey Vineyard (*Monterey*, California) Generally reliable inexpensive varietal wines now sold under the Redwood Trail label overseas. Go for the "Classic" range. Read the labels carefully though, especially if you might be expecting wines with these labels to reflect the vinous character of the *Monterey* region. In fact, as the small print reveals the contents may actually come from anywhere in California and have on occasion – when local stocks were low – been produced in the *Languedoc* region in France.

Y Monte Rossa [mon-teh ros-sah] (*Lombardy*, Italy) A really top class Franciacorta producer with two key wines in the Satèn and Cabochon cuvées.

Ï Viña Montes [mon-tehs] (*Curico*, Chile) Leading Chilean oenologist, Aurelio Montes' go-ahead winery with good reds, including the flagship Alpha M) and improved *Sauvignon*. ☆☆☆☆☆ 1997 Alpha M £££

Ï Fattoria di Montevertine [mon-ter-TEE-neh] (*Tuscany*, Italy) Less famous outside Italy than *Antinori* and *Frescobaldi* perhaps, but just as instrumental in the evolution of modern *Tuscan* wine, and of the rediscovery of the *Sangiovese* grape. Le Pergole Torte is the long-lived top wine. Il Sodaccio is fine too, however.

Ï Montevetrano [mon-teh-veh-trah-noh] (*Campania*, Italy) A highly innovative producer proving that applying skilled winemaking to a novel blend of the local Aglianico and the *Cabernet Sauvignon* and *Merlot* can make for a world class red wine.

Ï Monteviña [mon-tay-veen-yah] (*Amador County*, California) *Sutter Home* subsidiary, making exceptional *Zinfandel* from *Amador County* and reliable *Cabernet*, *Chardonnay* and *Fumé Blanc*. ☆☆☆ 1996 Monteviña Barbera ££

Ï Monthélie [mon-tay-lee] (*Burgundy*, France) Often overlooked *Côte de Beaune* village producing potentially stylish reds and whites. The appropriately named Dom. Monthélie-Douhairet is the most reliable estate. White: 85 86 88 89 90 92 95 96 97 98 Red: 78 80 83 85 86 87 88 89 90 92 95 96 97 98 99 **Coche-Dury; Jaffelin; Comtes Lafon; Olivier Leflaive; Leroy; Monthélie-Douhairet; Ch. de Puligny-Montrachet; Roulot.**

Montilla-Moriles [mon-tee-yah maw-ree-lehs] (Spain) *DO* region producing *sherry*-type wines in *solera* systems, often so high in alcohol that fortification is unnecessary. Good examples offer far better value than many sherries. Occasional successes achieve far more. **Pérez Barquero; Toro Albalá.**

Ï Dom. de Montille [duh mon-tee] (*Burgundy*, France) A lawyer-cum-winemaker whose *Volnays* and *Pommards*, if rather tough and astringent when young, are unusually fine and long-lived. Classy stuff.

Ï Montlouis [mon-lwee] (*Loire*, France) Neighbour of *Vouvray* making similar, lighter-bodied, dry, sweet, and sparkling wines. **Berger; Delétang; Levasseur; Moyer; la Taille aux Loups.**

Ï Le Montrachet [luh mon-ra-shay] (*Burgundy*, France) Shared between the villages of *Chassagne-* and *Puligny-Montrachet*, with its equally good neighbours *Bâtard-M.*, Chevalier-M., *Bienvenue-Bâtard-M*,.and Criots-Bâtard-M. Potentially the greatest, biscuitiest white *Burgundy* – and thus dry white wine – in the world. **Marc Colin; Drouhin (Marquis de Laguiche); Comtes Lafon; Leflaive; Ramonet; Domaine de la Romanée-Conti; Sauzet.**

Ï Montravel [mon'-ravel] (South West France) Region with three separate *appellations*: Montravel, for dry *Sémillon/Sauvignon*; *Côtes de Montravel* and Haut-Montravel for semi-sweet, medium-sweet and *late harvest* whites. **Ch du Bloy, Pique-Serre, la Roche-Marot, Viticulteurs de Port Ste Foy.**

Ï Ch. Montrose [mon-rohz] (*St. Estèphe 2ème Cru Classé, Bordeaux*, France) Back-on-form *St. Estèphe* renowned for its longevity. More typical of the *appellation* than *Cos d'Estournel* but often less approachable in its youth. However, still maintains a rich, tarry, inky style. Especially good in 1994, though less so in 1995 and 1996. **61 64** 66 **70 75** 76 78 79 81 **82** 83 85 86 88 89 90 91 92 93 94 95 96 97 98 99

Ch. Montus [mon-toos] (*South-West*, France) Ambitious producer in *Madiran* with carefully oaked examples of *Tannat* and *Pacherenc de Vic Bilh*. *Bouscassé* is a cheaper, more approachable label.

Moondah Brook (*Swan Valley*, Australia) An atypically (for the baking *Swan Valley*) cool vineyard belonging to *Houghtons* (and thus *Hardys*). The stars are the wonderful tangy *Verdelho* and richly oaky *Chenin Blanc*. The *Chardonnay* and reds are less impressive.

Moorilla Estate [moo-rillah] (*Tasmania*, Australia) Long-established, recently reconstituted estate with particularly good *Riesling*.

Mór [moh-uhr] (Hungary) Region gaining a name for its dry whites.

Moraga (*Bel Air*, California) Multi-million dollar homes were demolished to create this steeply sloping 7 acre vineyard in the heart of Bel Air. So, the $50 price tag on its Bordeaux-like wine seems almost modest.

Morande [moh-ran-day] (Argentina/Chile) Impressive winemaker, producing wine often from pioneering varieties on both sides of the Andes.

Morellino di Scansano [moh-ray-lee-noh dee skan-sah-noh] (*Tuscany*, Italy) Amazing cherry and raspberry, young-drinking red made from a clone of *Sangiovese*. Cantina Cooperativa; Motta; le Pupile.

Dom. Marc Morey [maw-ray] (*Burgundy*, France) Estate producing stylish white *Burgundy*. ☆☆☆☆ 1996 Chassagne-Montrachet Morgeot £££

Dom. Pierre Morey [maw-ray] (*Burgundy*, France) Top-class *Meursault* producer known for concentrated wines in good vintages. ☆☆☆☆ 1996 Meursault Perriéres £££

Bernard Morey et Fils [maw-ray] (*Burgundy*, France) Top-class producer in *Chassagne-Montrachet* with good vineyards here and in *St. Aubin*. ☆☆☆☆ 1996 Puligny-Montrachet La Truffière ££££

Morey-St.-Denis [maw-ray san duh-nee] (*Burgundy*, France) *Côtes de Nuits* village which produces deeply fruity, richly smooth reds, especially the *Grand Cru* "Clos de la Roche". Best producer is *Domaine Dujac*, which virtually makes this *appellation* its own. 76 **78** 79 **80** 82 83 **85** 86 87 **88 89 90** 92 95 96 *Bruno Clair; Dujac; Faiveley;* Georges Lignier; *Hubert Lignier; Ponsot.*

Morgon [mohr-gon] (*Burgundy*, France) One of the ten *Beaujolais Crus*. Worth maturing, as it can take on a delightful chocolate/cherry character. **89** 90 **91** 93 94 95 **96** 97 98 Dom. Calon; *Georges Duboeuf (aka Marc Dudet);* Jean Descombes; *Sylvain Fessy;* Jean Foillard; Lapierre; Piron; Savoye.

Morio Muskat [maw-ree-yoh moos-kat] White grape grown in Germany and Eastern Europe and making simple grapey wine.

Mornington Peninsula (*Victoria*, Australia) Some of Australia's newest and most southerly vineyards on a perpetual upward crescent. Close to Melbourne and under threat from housing developers. Good *Pinot Noir*, minty *Cabernet* and juicy *Chardonnay*, though the innovative T'Gallant is leading the way with other varieties. *Dromana; Paringa; Stonier;* T'Gallant.

Morris of Rutherglen (*Rutherglen*, Australia) Despite the takeover by *Orlando* and the retirement of local hero and champion winemaker Mick Morris, this is still an extraordinarily successful producer of delicious *Liqueur Muscat* and *Tokay* (seek out the Show Reserve). Also worth buying is a weird and wonderful *Shiraz-Durif* sparkling red. ☆☆☆☆ *Liqueur Muscat* £££

⚤ **Denis Mortet** [mor-tay] (*Burgundy*, France) Fast up-and-coming producer with straight *Gevrey-Chambertin* that is every bit as good as some of his neighbours' *Grands Crus*. ☆☆☆☆ 1995 Gevrey-Chambertin £££

⚤ **Morton Estate** (*Waikato*, New Zealand) Producer of fine *Sauvignon*, *Chardonnay* and *Bordeaux* styles. ☆☆☆☆ 1997 Colefield Sauvignon ££

⚤ **Mosbacher** [moss-bahk-kur] (*Pfalz*, Germany) High quality estate producing spicy *Rieslings* in Forst.

⚤ **Moscatel de Setúbal** [mos-kah-tel day say-too-bahl] (Portugal) See *Setúbal*.

🍇 **Moscato** [mos-kah-toh] (Italy) The Italian name for *Muscat*, widely used across Italy in all styles of white wine from *Moscato d'Asti*, through the more serious *Asti Spumante*, to dessert wines like *Moscato di Pantelleria*.

⚤ **Moscato d'Asti** [mos-kah-toh das-tee] (Italy) Delightfully grapey, sweet, and fizzy low alcohol wine from the *Muscat*, or *Moscato* grape. Far more flavoursome (and cheaper) than designer alcoholic lemonade. Drink young.

⚤ **Moscato Passito di Pantelleria** [pah-see-toh dee pan-teh-leh-ree-yah] (*Sicily*, Italy) Gloriously traditional sweet wine made on an island off *Sicily* from grapes that are dried out of doors until they have shrivelled into raisins.

⚤ **Mosel/Moselle** [moh-zuhl] (Germany) River and term loosely used for wines made around the Mosel and nearby Saar and Ruwer rivers. Equivalent to the "*Hock*" of the Rhine. (Moselblümchen is the equivalent of Liebfraumilch.) Not to be confused with France's uninspiring *Vins de Moselle*. The wines tend to have flavours of green fruits when young but develop a wonderful ripeness as they fill out with age. . QbA/Kab/Spät: **89 90** 91 92 93 94 95 96 97 98 Aus/Beeren/Tba: **83 85** 88 89 90 91 92 93 94 95 96 97 98 *Dr Loosen;* JJ Chriastobel; Jakoby-Mathy; Freiher von Heddesdorff; Willi Haag; Heribert Kerpen; Weingut Karlmuhle; Karp-Schreiber; *Immich Batterieberg*.

⚤ **Lenz Moser** [lents moh-zur] (Austria) Big producer whose range includes crisp dry whites and luscious dessert wines. Best efforts come from the Klosterkeller Siegendorf.

⚤ **Moss Wood** (*Margaret River*, Australia) Pioneer producer of *Pinot Noir*, *Cabernet*, and *Semillon*. The wines have long cellaring potential and have a very French feel to them. The *Semillon* is reliably good in both its oaked and unoaked form; the *Chardonnay* is big and forward and the *Pinot Noir* never quite living up to the promise of the early 1980s.

⚤ **La Motte Estate** [la mot] (*Franschhoek*, South Africa) Best known for top *Shiraz*. ☆☆☆☆ 1994 La Motte Millennium £££

⚤ **Herdade de Mouchão** [Hehr-dah-day dey moo sha-'oh] (*Alentejo*, Portugal) Estate producing high quality reds in this up-and-coming region.

⚤ **J.P. Moueix** [mwex] (*Bordeaux*, France) Top-class *négociant*/producer, Christian *Moueix* specialises in stylishly traditional *Pomerol* and *St. Emilion* and is responsible for *Pétrus*, *La Fleur-Pétrus*, *Bel Air*, Richotey and *Dominus* in California. (Do not confuse with any other Moueix's).

⚤ **Moulin Touchais** [moo-lan too-shay] (*Loire*, France) Producer of intensely honeyed, long-lasting, sweet white from *Coteaux du Layon*.

⚤ **Moulin-à-Vent** [moo-lan-na-von] (*Burgundy*, France) One of the ten *Beaujolais Crus* – big and rich at its best, like *Morgon*, it can benefit from ageing. **88 89** 90 **91** 93 95 96 97 98. Charvet; Degrange; *Duboeuf;* Paul Janin; Janodet; Lapierre; *Ch. du Moulin-à-Vent;* la Tour du Bief.

Ⓣ Ch. Moulin-à-Vent [moo-lan-na-von] (*Moulis Cru Bourgeois, Bordeaux,* France) Leading *Moulis* property. 82 83 85 86 89 90 94 96

Ⓣ Ch. du Moulin-à-Vent [moo-lan-na-von] (*Burgundy,* France) Reliable producer of *Moulin-à-Vent*. 85 88 89 90 91 93 94 95 96 97 98

Ⓣ Moulis [moo-lees] (*Bordeaux,* France) Red wine village of the *Haut-Médoc*; often paired with *Listrac*, but making far more approachable good-value *Crus Bourgeois*. 76 **78** 79 81 **82** 83 **85 86** 88 89 90 94 95 96 97 98 Ch. Anthonic; *Chasse-Spleen; Maucaillou;* Moulis; *Poujeaux.*

Mount Barker (Western Australia) Cooler-climate, southern region with great *Riesling, Verdelho,* impressive *Chardonnay,* and restrained *Shiraz.* White: 90 91 93 **94 95** 96 97 98 Red: **80 82 83** 85 86 87 88 **90** 91 92 93 94 95 96 97 98 Frankland Estate; *Goundrey; Howard Park; Plantagenet;* Wignalls.

Ⓣ Mount Horrocks (*Clare Valley,* Australia) Inventive *Shiraz* and *Riesling* producer that has made a speciality out of reviving an old method of winemaking called "Cordon Cut", which concentrates the flavour of the *Riesling* juice by cutting the canes some time before picking the grapes. ☆☆☆☆ 1999 Watervale Cordon Cut Riesling £££

Ⓣ Mount Hurtle (*McLaren Vale,* South Australia) See *Geoff Merrill.*

Ⓣ Mount Langi Ghiran [lan-gee gee-ran] (*Victoria,* Australia) A maker of excellent cool-climate *Riesling*, peppery *Shiraz* and very good *Cabernet*. ☆☆☆☆ 1998 Joanna Limestone Coast Cabernet Sauvignon £££

Ⓣ Mount Mary (*Yarra Valley,* Australia) Dr Middleton makes *Pinot Noir* and *Chardonnay* that are astonishingly and unpredictably *Burgundy*-like in the best and worst sense of the term. The *claret*y-like Quintet blend is more reliable. ☆☆☆☆☆ 1998 Pinot Noir £££

Mount Veeder (*Napa Valley,* California) Convincing hillside *appellation* producing impressive reds, especially from *Cabernet Sauvignon* and *Zinfandel.* Red: 84 **85** 86 87 **90 91** 92 **93** 95 96 97 98 White: **85 90** 91 92 95 96 97 98 Hess Collection; *Mayacamas; Mount Veeder Winery;* Ch. Potelle.

Ⓣ Mountadam (*High Eden Ridge,* Australia) Son of *David Wynn,* Adam makes classy Burgundian *Chardonnay* and *Pinot Noir* (both still and sparkling) and an impressive blend called "The Red". Also worth seeking out are the *Eden Ridge* organic wines, the fruity *David Wynn* range and the "Samuel's Bay" *second label.* ☆☆☆☆ 1998 Chardonnay £££

Ⓦ Mourvèdre [mor-veh-dr] (*Rhône,* France) Floral-spicy *Rhône* grape usually found in blends. Increasingly popular in France and California where, as in Australia, it is called *Mataro. Jade Mountain; Penfolds; Ridge.*

Mousse [mooss] The bubbles in *Champagne* and sparkling wines.

Mousseux [moo-sur] (France) Sparkling wine – generally cheap and unremarkable.

Ⓣ Mouton-Cadet [moo-ton ka-day] (*Bordeaux,* France) A brilliant commercial invention by Philippe de Rothschild who used it to profit handsomely from the name of *Mouton-Rothschild,* with which it has no discernible connection. The quality of – and more specifically the value for money offered by – these wines has traditionally been lamentable, but there have been heartening improvements recently. The "Réserve" is now better than the basic, and the recently launched white *Graves Réserve* creditable in its own right.

♀ Ch. Mouton-Baronne-Philippe [moo-ton ba-ron-fee-leep] (*Pauillac, 5ème Cru Classé, Bordeaux*, France) Known as Mouton d'Armailhac until 1933, then as Mouton-Baron-Philippe, then Mouton-Baronne-Philippe (in 1975) before becoming *Ch. d'Armailhac* in 1989.

♀ Ch. Mouton-Rothschild [moo-ton roth-child] (*Pauillac Premier Cru Classé, Bordeaux*, France) The only *château* to be elevated to a first growth from a second, Mouton can have gloriously rich, complex flavours of roast coffee and blackcurrant. Recent vintages were eclipsed by *Margaux*, *Lafite* and *Latour* but the 1998 and 1999 show a return to form. **61 62 66 70 75** 76 78 81 82 83 **85** 86 88 89 90 91 93 **94** 95 96 97 98 ☆☆☆☆ **1998 ££££**

Mudgee [mud-zhee] (*New South Wales*, Australia) Australia's first *appellation* region, a coolish-climate area now being championed by *Rosemount* as well as by *Rothbury*. **Botobolar; Huntington Estate.**

♀ Bodegas Muga [moo-gah] (*Rioja,* Spain) Producer of good old-fashioned *Riojas*, of which Prado Enea is the best.

♀ Jacques-Frederic Mugnier [moo-nee-yay] (*Burgundy,* France) *Chambolle-Musigny* estate that makes long-lived wines from great vineyards, including Bonnes-Mares and *Musigny*. ☆☆☆☆ **1997 Chambolle-Musigny £££**

♀ Mulderbosch [mool-duh-bosh] (*Stellenbosch,* South Africa) South Africa's answer to *Cloudy Bay*: exciting *Sauvignon* and *Meursault*-like *Chardonnay*, not to mention a red blend called Faithful Hound. ☆☆☆☆ **1998 Chardonnay ££**

♀ Weingut Müller-Catoir [moo-luh kah-twah] (*Pfalz,* Germany) Great new-wave producer using new-wave grapes as well as *Riesling*. Wines of all styles are impeccable and packed with flavour. Search out powerful Grauburgunder, Rieslaner, and *Scheurebe* wines. ☆☆☆☆☆ **1997 Haardter Herrenletten Riesling Spätlese ££**

♀ Egon Müller-Scharzhof [moo-luh shahtz-hof] (*Mosel-Saar-Ruwer,* Germany) Truly brilliant *Saar* producer. ☆☆☆☆☆ **1996 Scharzhofberger Riesling Spätlese £££**

⚑ Müller-Thurgau [moo-lur-toor-gow] (Germany) Workhorse white grape, a *Riesling* x *Sylvaner* cross – also known as *Rivaner* – making much unremarkable wine in Germany, but yielding some gems for producers like *Müller-Catoir*. Very successful in England.

♀ Mumm/Mumm Napa [murm] (*Champagne,* France/California) Maker of slightly improved Cordon Rouge *Champagne* and far better *Cuvée Napa* from California. Newly (1999) sold by its owners, Seagram. Hopefully new owners will have greater ambitions. ☆☆☆☆ **1995 Cuvée Limitée £££**

♀ René Muré [moo-ray] (*Alsace,* France) Producer of full-bodied wines, especially from the Clos St. Landelin vineyard. ☆☆☆☆ **1997 Tokay Pinot Gris Vorbourg, Clos St. Landelin £££**

Murfatlar [moor-fat-lah] (Romania) Major vineyard and research area that is having increasing success with *Chardonnay* (including some late-harvest sweet examples), and *Cabernet Sauvignon*.

♈ **Murphy-Goode** (*Alexander Valley*, California) Classy producer of quite Burgundian style whites which sell at – for California – affordable prices, as well as high quality Cabernet Sauvignon. ☆☆☆☆ **1996 Alexander Valley Brenda Block Reserve Cabernet £££**

♈ **Bodegas Marqués de Murrieta** [mar-kays day moo-ree-eh-tah] (*Rioja*, Spain) Probably Spain's best old-style *oaky* white (sold as Castillo Ygay). The red, at its best, is one of the most long-lived, elegant *Riojas* – look out for the old Castillo Ygays from the 1960s with their distinctive old-style labels. ☆☆☆☆ **1995 Blanco Reserva Especial £££**

♈ **Murrietta's Well** (*Livermore*, California) Blends of *Zinfandel* and *Cabernet*, *Merlot* are rare, but the berryish red sold by *Wente* under this name proves that it is an experiment more producers should try.

♈ **Ch. Musar** [moo-sahr] (*Ghazir*, Lebanon) *Serge Hochar* makes a different red every year, varying the blend of *Cabernet*, *Cinsault*, and *Syrah*. The style veers wildly between *Bordeaux*, the *Rhône*, and Italy, but there's never a risk of becoming bored. Good vintages easily keep for a decade. The *Chardonnay*-based whites are less than dazzling, though. 86 88 89 91 93 95

🍇 **Muscadelle** [mus-kah-del] Spicy ingredient in white *Bordeaux*. See *Tokay*.

♈ **Muscadet des Coteaux de la Loire / Côtes de Grand Lieu / de Sèvre et Maine** [moos-kah-day day koh-toh dur lah lwar / koht dur gron lyur / dur say-vr' eh mayn] (*Loire*, France) Emphatically non-aromatic wines made from the *Melon de Bourgogne*. Worthwhile examples are briefly matured and bottled on their dead yeasts or *lees* (*"sur lie"*). The Côtes de Grand Lieu is worth looking for, as can be the rare Coteaux de la *Loire*. Sèvre et Maine is less reliable. 98 99 *Dom. de Chasseloir;* Bossard; Chéreau-Carré; Couillaud; Guindon; *de Goulaine;* Pierre Luneau; Metaireau; Marcel Sautejeau; Sauvion.

🍇 **Muscat** [mus-kat] Generic name for a species of white grape (aka *Moscato* in Italy) of which there are a number of different sub-species.

🍇 **Muscat à Petits Grains** [moos-kah ah puh-tee gran] Aka *Frontignan*, the best variety of Muscat and the grape responsible for *Muscat de Beaumes de Venise*, *Muscat de Rivesaltes*, *Asti Spumante*, *Muscat of Samos*, *Rutherglen* Muscats, and dry *Alsace* Muscats.

♈ **Muscat de Cap Corse / Frontignan / Mireval / Rivesaltes / St. Jean de Minervois** (*Languedoc-Roussillon*, France) Potentially luscious fortified Muscats of which Rivesaltes and Minervois are possibly the best.

🍇 **Muscat of Alexandria** [moos-kah] Grape responsible for *Moscatel de Setúbal*, *Moscatel de Valencia*, and sweet South Australians. Also known as *Lexia*, and in South Africa it satisfies the sweet tooth of much of the Afrikaner population as *Hanepoot*.

🍇 **Muscat Ottonel** [moos-kah ot-oh-nel] *Muscat* variety grown in Middle and Eastern Europe.

🍷 **Musigny** [moo-zee-nyee] (*Burgundy*, France) Potentially wonderful *Grand Cru* from which *Chambolle-Musigny* takes its name. 76 79 82 83 88 89 90 91 92 93 94 95 96 97 98 *De Vogüé; Groffier; Leroy; Mugnier; Prieur.*

Must Unfermented grape juice.
MW See *Master of Wine*.

N

Nackenheim [nahk-ehn-hime] (*Rheinhessen*, Germany) Village in the *Nierstein Bereich*, sadly best known for its debased *Grosslage*, Gutes Domtal. QbA/Kab/Spät: **90** 91 92 93 95 96 97 98 99 Aus/Beeren/Tba: 90 91 92 93 94 95 96 **97** 98 *Gunderloch;* Kürfurstenhof; Heinrich Seip.

Nahe [nah-huh] (Germany) *Anbaugebiet* producing wines which can combine delicate flavour with full body. QbA/Kab/Spät: **88 89 90** 91 **92 93** 94 95 96 97 98 Aus/Beeren/Tba: **83 85** 88 89 90 91 92 **93 94** 95 96 97 98 *Crusius; Schlossgut Diel;* Hermann Donnhoff; Hehner Kiltz; *Kruger-Rumpf.*

🍷 **Ch. Nairac** [nay-rak] (*Barsac 2ème Cru Classé, Bordeaux,* France) Delicious, lush, long-lasting wine sometimes lacking a little complexity.

🍷 **Nalle** (*Sonoma*, California) Great *Dry Creek* producer of some of California's (and thus the world's) greatest *Zinfandel*.

Naoussa [nah-oosa] (Greece) Region producing dry red wines, often from the Xynomavro grape. *Boutari.*

Napa [na-pa] (California) Named after the Native American word for "plenty", this is a region with plentiful wines ranging from ordinary to sublime. Too many are hyped; none is cheap and the region as a whole is far too varied in altitude and conditions to make sense as a single *appellation*. The 20 or so smaller *appellations* within Napa, such as *Carneros, Stag's Leap, Howell Mountain* and *Mt. Veeder* deserve greater prominence – as do nearby regions like *Sonoma*. Red: 86 87 **90 91 92 93** 94 95 96 97 98 White: 85 **90 91** 92 **95** 96 97 98 *Atlas Peak; Beaulieu; Beringer; Cain; Cakebread; Caymus; Chimney Rock; Clos du Val; Crichton Hall; Cuvaison; Diamond Creek; Dom. Chandon; Duckhorn; Dunn; Flora Springs; Franciscan; Frog's Leap; Heitz; Hess Collection; Ch. Montelena; Monteviña; Mumm; Newton; Niebaum-Coppola; Opus One; Ch. Potelle; Phelps; Schramsberg; Screaming Eagle; Shafer; Stag's Leap; Sterling; Turley.*

🍷 **Napa Ridge** (California) Highly successful brand, most of whose pleasant, commercial wines are made with juice from grapes grown outside *Napa*. (Exports are less confusingly labelled as "Coastal Ridge".)

🍷 **Nautilus Estate** [naw-tih-luhs] (*Marlborough*, New Zealand) *Yalumba's* New Zealand offshoot. Sparkling wine and *Sauvignon*. ☆☆☆ **Nautilus Cuvée ££**

225

� **Navajas** [na-VA-khas] (*Rioja*, Spain) Small producer making impressive reds and *oaky* whites worth keeping. ✩✩✩✩ **1994 Tinto Reserva ££**

☒ **Navarra** [na-VAH-rah] (Spain) Northern *DO*, traditionally renowned for rosés and heavy reds but now producing wines to rival those from neighbouring *Rioja*, where prices are often higher. Look for innovative *Cabernet Sauvignon* and *Tempranillo* blends. **81 82 83 85 87 89 90** 91 **92** 94 95 96 **97 98 Chivite; Guelbenzu; Castillo de Monjardin; Vinicola Murchantina; Nekeas; Ochoa; Palacio de la Vega; Senorio de Sarria.**

🌿 **Nebbiolo** [neh-bee-oh-loh] (*Piedmont*, Italy) Grape of *Piedmont*, producing wines with tarry, cherryish, spicy flavours that are slow to mature but become richly complex – epitomised by *Barolo* and *Barbaresco*. Quality and style vary enormously depending on soil. Aka *Spanna*.

☒ **Nederburg** [neh-dur-burg] (*Paarl*, South Africa) Huge commercial producer. The Edelkeur *late harvest* wines are the gems of the cellar. Sadly, the best wines are only sold at the annual Nederburg Auction.

Négociant [nay-goh-see-yon] (France) Merchant who buys, matures, and bottles wine. See also *Eléveur*.

Négociant-manipulant (NM) [ma-nih-pyoo-lon] (*Champagne*, France) Buyer and blender of wines for *Champagne*, identifiable by the NM number which is mandatory on the label.

🌿 **Negroamaro** [nay-groh-ah-mah-roh] (*Puglia*, Italy) A Puglian grape whose name means "bitter-black" and produces fascinating, spicy-gamey reds. Found in *Salice Salentino* and *Copertino*.

Nelson (New Zealand) Small region, a glorious bus ride to the north-west of *Marlborough*. *Neudorf* and *Seifried/ Redwood Valley* are the stars. White: **96** 97 **98** Red: **91 92 94** 95 96 97 **98 99**

☒ **Nemea** [nur-may-yah] (Peloponnese, Greece) Improving cool(ish) climate region for reds made from Agiorgitiko. **Boutari; Semeli; Tsantalis.**

☒ **Nepenthe** [neh-pen-thi] (*Adelaide Hills*, South Australia) Instant star with dazzling *Chardonnay, Semillon, Sauvignon, Pinot Noir, Cabernet-Merlot* and *Zinfandel.* ✩✩✩✩ **1999 Unwooded Chardonnay £££**

☒ **Ch. La Nerthe** [nehrt] (*Rhône*, France) One of the most exciting estates in *Châteauneuf-du-Pape*, producing rich wines with seductive dark fruit.

☒ **Ch. Nenin** [nay-nan] (*Pomerol, Bordeaux*, France) A château to watch since its recent purchase by the extraordinary Michel Delon of *Ch. Léoville-Las-Cases*.

Neuchâtel [nur-sha-tel] (Switzerland) Lakeside region. Together with Les Trois Lacs, a source of good red and rosé, *Pinot Noir*, and *Chasselas* and *Chardonnay* whites. **Ch. d'Auvernier; Porret.**

☒ **Neudorf** [noy-dorf] (*Nelson*, New Zealand) Pioneering small-scale producer of beautifully made *Chardonnay, Semillon, Sauvignon, Riesling* and *Pinot Noir.* ✩✩✩✩✩ **1998 Moutere Chardonnay £££**

Neusiedlersee [noy-zeed-lur-zay] (Austria) *Burgenland* region on the Hungarian border. Great *late harvest* and improving whites and reds. **Fieler-Artinger; Kracher; Lang; Willi Opitz; Tschida.**

Nevers [nur-vehr] (France) Subtlest oak – from a forest in *Burgundy*.

New South Wales (Australia) Major wine-producing state, which is home to the famous *Hunter Valley*, along with the *Cowra, Mudgee, Orange,* and *Murrumbidgee* regions. White: 85 86 87 88 90 91 94 95 96 97 98 Red: 82 83 85 86 87 88 90 91 93 94 95 96 97 98

New Zealand Instant superstar with proven *Sauvignon Blanc* and *Chardonnay* and – despite most expectations – increasingly successful *Merlots* and more particularly *Pinot Noirs*. Syrah can work well too occasionally, as can *Pinot Gris* and *Gewürztraminer*. *Cabernet Sauvignon*, however, rarely ripens properly. Vintages vary, however (1998 was not a great year for *Marlborough*). See *Marlborough, Martinborough, Hawke's Bay, Nelson; Gisborne, Auckland.*

☘ **Newton Vineyards** (*Napa Valley*, California) High-altitude vineyards with top-class *Chardonnay, Merlot,* and *Cabernet*, now being made with help from *Michel Rolland*.

☘ **Neszmély** (Hungary) Go-ahead winery in Aszar-Neszmély producing good commercial white wines.

☘ **Ngatarawa** [na-TA-ra-wah] (*Hawke's Bay*, New Zealand) Small winery that can make impressive reds and even better *Chardonnay*s and *late harvest* whites. ☆☆☆☆ 1998 Glazebrook Merlot-Cabernet £££

Niagara (*Ontario*, Canada) Area close to the Falls and to Lakes Ontario and Erie where the *Vidal* is used to make good *Icewine*. The *Chardonnay, Riesling* and – though less successfully – red varieties such as *Pinot Noir* and *Merlot* are now being used too. *Ch. des Charmes; Henry of Pelham; Inniskillin; Magnotta; Reif; Southbrook.*

☘ **Nicholson River** (*Gippsland*, Australia) The temperamental *Gippsland* climate makes for a small production of stunning *Chardonnay*s. ☆☆☆☆ 1993 Chardonnay £££

☘ **Niebaum-Coppola** [nee-bowm coh-po-la] (*Napa Valley*, California) You've seen the movie. Now taste the wine. The "Dracula" and "Godfather" director's estate now includes the appropriately Gothic *Inglenook* winery, has some of the oldest vines about and makes intensely concentrated *Cabernet*s to suit the patient. ☆☆☆☆ 1995 Rubicon Napa Valley ££££

☘ **Niederhausen Schlossböckelheim** [nee-dur-how sen shlos-berk-ehl-hime] (*Nahe*, Germany) State-owned estate producing highly concentrated *Riesling* from great vineyards.

☘ **Dom. Michel Niellon** [nee-el-lon] (*Burgundy*, France) Estate ranking consistently in the top five white *Burgundy* producers and making highly concentrated wines. ☆☆☆☆ 1996 Chassagne-Montrachet £££

☘ **Niepoort** [nee-poort] (*Douro*, Portugal) Small, independent *port* house making subtle vintage and particularly impressive *colheita tawnies*. A name to watch. ☆☆☆☆ 1985 Colheita Port £££

Nierstein [neer-stine] (*Rheinhessen*, Germany) Village and (with *Piesport*) *Bereich* best known in the UK. Some fine wines, obscured by the notoriety of the reliably dull Niersteiner Gutes Domtal. QbA/Kab/Spät: 85 86 88 89 90 91 92 93 94 95 96 97 98 Aus/Beeren/Tba: 83 85 88 89 90 91 92 93 94 95 96 97 98 *Balbach; Gunderloch; Heyl zu Herrnsheim.*

℀ **Nieto & Senetiner** [nee-yeh-toh eh seh-neh-tee-nehr] (*Mendoza,* Argentina) Reliable wines sold under the Valle de Vistalba and Cadus labels.

℀ **Nigl** [nee-gel] (*Kremstal,* Austria) One of Austria's best producers of dry *Riesling* and *Grüner Veltliner.*

℀ **Weingut Nikolaihof** [nih-koh-li-hof] (*Niederösterreich,* Austria) One of the producers of some of the best *Grüner Veltliners* and *Rieslings* in Austria. ✩✩✩✩ 1997 Riesling Smaragd Wachau Vom Stein £££

℀ **Nipozzano** [nip-ots-zano] (*Tuscany,* Italy) See *Frescobaldi.*

℀ **Nino Negri** [nee-noh neh-gree] (*Lombardy,* Italy) Casimiro Maule makes one of the best examples of Valtellina Sfursat.

℀ **Nobilo** [nob-ih-loh] (*Huapai,* New Zealand) Kiwi colony of the BRL Hardy empire making good *Chardonnay* from *Gisborne,* "*Icon*" wines from *Marlborough* including a pleasant, commercial off-dry *White Cloud* blend.

Noble rot Popular term for *botrytis cinerea.*

℀ **Vino Nocetto** (Shenandoah Valley, California, US) Winery that has been unusually successful with Italian-style Sangiovese.

℀ **Normans** (*McLaren Vale,* Australia) Fast-improving *Cabernet* and *Shiraz* specialist. ✩✩✩✩ 1998 Old Vines Shiraz ££

℀ **Bodega Norton** [naw-ton] (Argentina) One of Argentina's most recommendable producers, producing a wide range of *varietal* wines. The "Privada" wines are the cream of the crop. ✩✩✩✩ 1998 Privada ££

Nouveau [noo-voh] New wine, most popularly used of *Beaujolais.*

℀ **Quinta da Noval** (*Douro,* Portugal) Fine and potentially finer estate. The ultra-rare Nacional **vintage ports** are the jewel in the crown, made from ungrafted vines. Also of note are great *colheita tawny ports.*

℀ **Albet i Noya** [al-bet-ee-noy-ya] (Spain) Innovative producer with red and white traditional and imported varieties. A superstar in the making.

℀ **Nuits-St.-Georges** [noo-wee san zhawzh] (*Burgundy,* France) *Commune* producing the most *claret*-like of red *Burgundies,* properly tough and lean when young but glorious with age. Whites are good but ultra-rare. Red 78 79 **80** 82 83 **85** 86 87 **88 89 90** 91 92 93 **94** 95 96 97 98 99 *Dom. de l'Arlot; Robert Chevillon; Jean-Jacques Confuron; Faiveley; Henri Gouges; Jean Grivot; Leroy; Alain Michelot;* Patrice Rion; Henri & Gilles Remoriquet.

℀ **Nuragus di Cagliari** [noo-rah-goos dee ka-lee-yah-ree] (*Sardinia,* Italy) Good-value, tangy, floral wine from the Nuragus grape.

NV Non-vintage, meaning a blend of wines from different years.

O

℀ **Oakville Ranch** (*Napa Valley,* California) Potentially one of the *Napa's* most exciting red wine producers, but wines have so far been a little too tough.

Oaky Flavour imparted by oak casks which will vary depending on the source of the oak (American is more obviously sweet than French). Woody is usually less complimentary.

℀ **Vin de Pays d'Oc** [pay-doc] (*Languedoc-Roussillon,* France) The world's biggest wine region, encompassing *appellations* such as *Corbières* and *Minervois* and several smaller *Vins de Pays* regions.

℀ **Bodegas Ochoa** [och-oh-wah] (*Navarra,* Spain) New-wave producer of creamy, fruitily fresh *Cabernet, Tempranillo* and *Viura.* ✩✩✩✩ 1990 Navarra Tinto Reserva ££

Ockfen [ok-fehn] (*Mosel-Saar-Ruwer,* Germany) Village producing some of the best, steeliest wines of the *Saar-Ruwer Bereich,* especially *Rieslings* from the *Bockstein* vineyard. QbA/Kab/Spät: 85 86 **88 89 90** 91 **92 93 94 95** 96 97 98 Aus/Beeren/Tba: **83 85 88 89 90** 91 **92 93 94 95** 96 97 98 ☆☆☆ **1996 Ockfener Bockstein Riesling Reichsgraf von Kesselstadt ££**

Oechsle [urk-slur] (Germany) Indication of the sugar level in grapes or wine.

Oeste [wes-teh] (Portugal) Western region in which a growing number of fresh, light, commercial wines are being made, of which the most successful has undoubtedly been Arruda. Red: 93 94 95 96 97 98

Oestrich [ur-strihckh] (*Rheingau,* Germany) Source of good *Riesling.* QbA/Kab/Spät: **85** 86 **88 89 90** 91 **92 93** 94 95 96 97 98 Aus/Beeren/ Tba: **89 90** 92 93 94 95 96 97 98 *Wegeler Deinhard; Balthazar Ress.*

♀ **Michel Ogier** [ogee-yay] (*Rhône,* France) *Côte Rôtie* producer, making less muscular wines than most of his neighbours. ☆☆☆☆ **1997 La Rosine Syrah, Côtes du Rhone £££**
Oïdium [oh-id-ee-yum] Fungal grape infection, shrivelling them, and turning them grey.

♀ **Ojai Vineyard** [oh-high] (*Santa Barbara,* California) The specialities here are a *Sauvignon-Semillon* blend and – more interestingly – a *Rhône*-like *Syrah.* ☆☆☆☆ **1995 Syrah Bien Nacido Vineyard £££**

Okanagan (*British Columbia,* Canada) Principal wine region in the west of Canada. Despite frosts, *Pinot Noir* can produce good wine here. *Mission Hill.*

🍇 **Olasz Rizling** [oh-lash-riz-ling] (Hungary) Term for the *Welschriesling.*
♀ **Ch. Olivier** [oh-liv-ee-yay] (*Pessac-Léognan Cru Classé, Bordeaux,* France) An underperformer which has yet to join the *Graves* revolution. Red: 82 83 85 86 88 89 90 91 92 93 94 95 96 98 White: 90 92 93 94 96 98
Oloroso [ol-oh-roh-soh] (*Jerez,* Spain) Style of full-bodied *sherry,* that is either dry or semi-sweet.

♀ **Oltrepò Pavese** [ohl-tray-poh pa-vay-say] (*Lombardy,* Italy) Still and sparkling *DOC* made from local grapes including the characterfully spicy red Gutturnio and white Ortrugo. Ca' Di Frara; *Tenuta Il Bosco;* Cabanon; Fugazza; Mazzolina; Bruno Verdi.

♀ **Omar Khayyam (Champagne India)** [oh-mah-ki-yam] (*Maharashtra,* India) *Champagne*-method wine which, when drunk young, has more than novelty value. The producer's cheeky name, "*Champagne* India", is a source of considerable annoyance to the Champenois, but they, in the shape of *Piper Heidsieck,* were happy enough to sell the Indians their expertise.
♀ **Willi Opitz** [oh-pitz] (*Neusiedlersee,* Austria) Oddball pet food-manufacturer-turned-producer of a magical mystery tour of *late harvest* and straw-dried (Schilfwein) wines, including an extraordinary *botrytis* red labelled – to the discomfort of some Californians – "Opitz One". ☆☆☆☆☆ **1997 Opitz One Schilfwein £££**

Oppenheim [op-en-hime] (*Rheinhessen,* Germany) Village in *Nierstein Bereich* best known – unfairly – for unexciting wines from the Krottenbrunnen. Elsewhere produces soft wines with concentrated flavour.

🍷 **Opus One** (*Napa Valley,* California) 20-year old co-production between *Mouton-Rothschild* and *Robert Mondavi.* Classy *claret*-like blackcurranty wine that sells at an appropriately classy *claret*-like price. ☆☆☆☆☆ **1995 ££££**

Orange (*New South Wales,* Australia) Coolish region which, with *Cowra,* is likely to eclipse the nearby *Hunter Valley.* Try the Orange *Chardonnay* made by Philip Shaw of *Rosemount* from vineyards of which he is proud co-owner.

🍇 **Orange Muscat** Another highly eccentric member of the *Muscat* family, best known for dessert wines in California by *Quady* and in Australia for the delicious *Brown Brothers Late Harvest Orange Muscat* and *Flora.*

Oregon (US) Fashionable cool-climate state, some of whose winemakers grow marijuana as keenly as their speciality, *Pinot Noir.* The *Chardonnay, Riesling, Pinot Gris,* and sparkling wines show promise too. *Adelsheim; Amity; Argyle; Beaux Freres; Cameron; Chehalem; Dom Drouhin;* Duck Pond; *Erath; Eyrie;* Henry Estate; King Estate; *Ponzi; Rex Hill; Sokol Blosser.*

🍷 **Oriachovitza** [oh-ree-ak-hoh-vit-sah] (Bulgaria) Major source of reliable *Cabernet Sauvignon* and *Merlot.*

🍷 **Orlando** (South Australia) Huge, French-owned (Pernod-Ricard) producer of the world-beating and surprisingly reliable *Jacob's Creek* wines. Look for "Reserve" and "Limited Release" efforts. The RF range is good but the harder-to-find Gramps and Flaxmans wines are more exciting, as are Jacaranda Ridge, Centenary, and the "Saints" series. ☆☆☆ **1995 Jacob's Creek Limited Release Shiraz Cabernet £££**

Orléanais [aw-lay-yo-nay] (*Loire,* France) A vineyard area around Orléans in the Central Vineyards region of the *Loire,* specialising in unusual white blends of *Chardonnay* and *Pinot Gris,* and reds of *Pinot Noir* and *Cabernet Franc.* White: **95 96 97** 98 Red: **90 95** 96 97 98

🍷 **Ch. Olivier** [oh-liv-ee-yay] (*Pessac-Léognan, Bordeaux,* France) Pretty chateau that was disappointing but seems better in 1999.

🍷 **Ch. Les Ormes-de-Pez** [awm dur-pay] (*St. Estèphe Cru Bourgeois, Bordeaux,* France) Often underrated stable-mate of *Lynch-Bages* and made with similar skill. **82 83** 85 **86** 88 89 90 92 93 94 95 96 97 98 99

🍷 **Tenuta dell'Ornellaia** [teh-noo-tah del-aw-nel-li-ya] (*Tuscany,* Italy) *Bordeaux*-blend *Bolgheri Super-Tuscan* from the brother of Piero Antinori. This is serious wine that is worth maturing. ☆☆☆☆ **1996 Ornellaia ££££**

🍇 **Ortega** [aw-tay-gah] Recently developed variety, and grown in Germany and England, though rarely to tasty advantage. *Biddenden* makes a good one, however, as does *Denbies,* which uses it to produce *late harvest* wine.

Orvieto [ohr-vee-yet-toh] (*Umbria*, Italy) White Umbrian *DOC* responsible for a quantity of dull wine. Orvieto *Classico* is better. Look out for Secco if you like your white wine dry; *Amabile* if you have a sweet tooth. **Antinori; Bigi; La Carraia; Covio Cardetto; Palazzone.**

Osbourne [os-sbaw-nay] (*Jerez*, Spain) Producer of a good range of *sherries* including a brilliant *Pedro Ximenez*.

Dom. Ostertag [os-tur-tahg] (*Alsace*, France) Poet and philosopher André Ostertag's superb *Alsace domaine.* ☆☆☆☆ 1997 Riesling Heissenberg £££

Oxidation The effect (usually detrimental, occasionally – as in *sherry* – intentional) of oxygen on wine.

Oxidative The opposite to reductive. Certain wines – most reds, and whites like *Chardonnay* – benefit from limited exposure to oxygen during their fermentation and maturation, such as barrel ageing.

Oyster Bay (*Marlborough*, New Zealand) See entry for *Delegats.* ☆☆☆ 1999 Sauvignon Blanc ££

P

Paarl [pahl] (South Africa) Warm region in which *Backsberg* and *Boschendal* make a wide range of appealing wines. Hotter and drier than neighbouring *Stellenbosch*. Red: **82 84** 86 **87** 89 **91 92** 93 94 95 96 97 98 White: 95 97 98 *Charles Back/Fairview; KWV; Backsberg; Glen Carlou; Villiera; Plaisir de Merle.*

Pacherenc du Vic-Bilh [pa-shur-renk doo vik beel] (*South-West*, France) Rare, dry or fairly sweet white wine made from the *Petit* and *Gros Manseng*. A speciality of *Madiran.* ☆☆☆☆☆ 1997 Alain Brumont les Jardins du Bouscasse Pacherenc du Vic-Bihl ££

Padthaway [pad-thah-way] (South Australia) Vineyard area just north of *Coonawarra* specialising in *Chardonnay* and *Sauvignon*, though reds work well here too. White: **94** 95 96 97 98 Red: **86 87** 88 **90 91** 94 95 96 97 98 *Angove's Hardys; Lindemans; Orlando; Penfolds.*

Pagadebit di Romagna [pah-gah-deh-bit dee roh-man-ya] (*Emilia-Romagna*, Italy) Dry, sweet, and sparkling whites from the Pagadebit grape.

Pago de Carrovejas [pah-goh deh kah-roh-vay-jash] (*Ribera del Duero*, Portugal) One of the best producers in Ribera del Duero.

Pahlmeyer (*Napa Valley*, California) One of California's most interesting winemakers, producing *Burgundian Chardonnay* and a complex *Bordeaux*-blend red. ☆☆☆☆ 1996 Napa Valley Chardonnay £££

Paitin [pih-teen] (*Piedmont*, Italy) The Sori Paitin vineyard in Barbaresco can offer Gaja quality at affordable prices.

Ch. Pajzos [pah-zhohs] (*Tokaji*, Hungary) Serious French-owned producer of new-wave *Tokay.* ☆☆☆☆ 1993 Tokay Aszú 5 Puttonyos £££

Bodegas Palacio [pa-las-see-yoh] (*Rioja*, Spain) Underrated *bodega* with stylish, fruit-driven reds and distinctively oaky whites. Also helped by wine guru *Michel Rolland.* ☆☆☆☆ 1995 Reserva Especial Rioja ££

♗ **Palacio de Fefiñanes** [pah-las-see-yoh day fay-feen-yah-nays] (*Galicia,* Spain) Fine producer of *Rias Baixas Albariño.*

♗ **Alvaro Palacios** [pah-las-see-yohs] (*Catalonia,* Spain) Superstar Priorato estate producing individual wines with rich, concentrated flavours. L'Ermita is the (very pricy) top wine. Finca Dofi and Les Terrasses are more affordable.

Palate Nebulous, not to say ambiguous, term describing the apparatus used for tasting (i.e., the tongue) as well as the skill of the taster ("he has a good palate").

♗ **Palette** [pa-let] (*Provence,* France) *AC* rosé and creamy white, well liked by holiday makers in St. Tropez who are so used to extortionate prices for cups of coffee that they don't notice paying more for a pink wine than for a serious red. The white, which can be very perfumed, is better value.

♗ **Palliser Estate** [pa-lih-sur] (*Martinborough,* New Zealand) Source of classy *Sauvignon Blanc, Chardonnay* and – increasingly – *Pinot Noir* from *Martinborough.* ☆☆☆☆ **1999 Pinot Noir ££**

♗ **Ch. Palmer** [pahl-mur] (*Margaux 3ème Cru Classé, Bordeaux,* France) The success story of the late Peter Sichel who died in 1998, this third growth *Margaux* stands alongside the best of the *Médoc* and often outclasses its more highly ranked neighbours. Wonderfully perfumed. **61 66 70 71 75 76 78 79** 80 82 **83** 84 85 **86** 87 **88 89** 90 91 92 93 **94** 95 96 97 98

♗ **Palo Cortado** [pah-loh kaw-tah doh] (*Jerez,* Spain) Rare *sherry* pitched between *amontillado* and *oloroso.* **Gonzalez Byass; Hidalgo; Lustau; Osborne; Pedro Romero; Valdespino.**

🍇 **Palomino** [pa-loh-mee-noh] (*Jerez,* Spain) White grape responsible for virtually all fine *sherries* – and almost invariably dull white wine, when unfortified. Also widely grown in South Africa.

♗ **Ch. Pape-Clément** [pap klay-mon] (*Pessac-Léognan Cru Classé, Bordeaux,* France) Great source of rich reds since the mid 1980s and, more recently, small quantities of delicious peach-oaky white. Red: 70 **75** 82 83 85 **86** 88 89 90 92 **93** 94 95 96 97 98

♗ **Parducci** [pah-doo-chee] (*Mendocino,* California) Steady producer whose *Petite Sirah* is a terrific bargain. ☆☆☆☆ **1997 Petite Sirah £££**

♗ **Dom. Alain Paret** [pa-ray] (*Rhône,* France) Producer of a great *St. Joseph* and *Condrieu,* in partnership with one of the world's best-known winemakers. (Though, to be fair, Gérard Dépardieu does owe his fame to the cinema rather than his efforts among the vines.) ☆☆☆☆ **1997 Condrieu Lys de Volan ££££**

♗ **Paringa Estate** (*Mornington, Victoria,* Australia) With *T'Galant* and *Stoniers,* this is one of the stars of *Mornington Peninsula.* Fine *Shiraz.*

♗ **Parker Estate** (*Coonawarra,* Australia) Small producer sharing its name with the US guru, and calling its (very pricy) red "First Growth". Marks for chutzpah. ☆☆☆☆ **1996 Terra Rossa First Growth ££££**

♗ **Parusso** [pah-roo-soh] (*Piedmont,* Italy) Very fine single-vineyard Barolos (Munie and Rocche) and wines sold under the Langhe designation.

Pasado/Pasada [pa-sah-doh/dah] (Spain) Term applied to old or fine *fino* and *amontillado sherries.* Worth seeking out.

♗ **C.J. Pask** [pask] (*Hawke's Bay,* New Zealand) *Cabernet* pioneer with excellent *Chardonnay* and *Sauvignon.* One of New Zealand's very best. ☆☆☆☆ **1998 Reserve Cabernet Merlot £££**

Paso Robles [pa-soh roh-blays] (*San Luis Obispo,* California) Warmish, long-established region, good for *Zinfandel* (especially *Ridge*), *Rhône,* and Italian varieties. Plus increasingly successful *Chardonnays* and *Pinots.* Red: **85** 86 87 **90 91** 92 93 95 White: **85 90 91** 92 **94** 95 96 97 98 99

♀ Pasqua [pas-kwah] (*Veneto*, Italy) Producer of fairly priced, reliable wines.
☆☆☆ 1998 Soave Superiore Sagramoso £

Passetoutgrains [pas-stoo-gran] (*Burgundy*, France) Wine supposedly
made from two-thirds *Gamay*, one third *Pinot Noir* - though few
producers respect these proportions. Once the Burgundians' daily red –
until they decided to sell it and drink cheaper wine from other regions.

♀ Passing Clouds (*Bendigo*, Australia) "We get clouds, but it never rains ..."
Despite a fairly hideous label, this is one of Australia's most serious red
blends.

Passito [pa-see-toh] (Italy) Raisiny wine made from sun-dried *Erbaluce*
grapes in Italy. This technique is now used in Australia by *Primo Estate*.

♀ Ch. Patache d'Aux [pa-tash-doh] (*Médoc Cru Bourgeois*, *Bordeaux*, France)
Traditional, toughish stuff. 83 85 88 **89 90** 93 95 96 97 98 ☆☆☆ 1996 £££

♀ Frederico Paternina [pa-tur-nee-na] (*Rioja*, Spain) Ernest Hemingway's
favourite *bodega*.

♀ Luis Pato [lweesh-pah-toh] (*Bairrada*, Portugal) One of Portugal's rare
superstar winemakers, proving, amongst other things, that the *Baga* grape
can make first-class spicy, berryish red wines. ☆☆☆☆ 1997 Quinta do
Ribeirinho Primeira Escolha ££

♀ Patriarche [pa-tree-arsh] (*Burgundy*, France) Huge merchant whose name
is not a watchword for great *Burgundy*. The *Ch. de Meursault domaine*,
however, is worthwhile.

♀ Patrimonio [pah-tree-moh-nee-yoh] (*Corsica*, France) One of the best
appellations in Corsica. Grenache reds and rosés and Vermintino whites.
Dom. Aliso-Rossi; , Arena, de Catarelli; Gentile; Leccia; Clos Marfisi;
Orenga de Gaffory.

♀ Patz & Hall (*Napa Valley*, California) The maker of delicious,
unashamedly full-flavoured *Chardonnays*.

♀ Pauillac [poh-yak] (*Bordeaux*, France) One of the four famous
"*communes*" of the *Médoc*, Pauillac is the home of *Châteaux Latour, Lafite*,
and *Mouton-Rothschild*, as well as the two *Pichons* and *Lynch-Bages*. The
epitome of full-flavoured blackcurranty *Bordeaux*; very classy (and pricy)
wine. 70 75 76 **78** 79 **82** 83 **85 86** 88 89 90 94 95 96 97 98

♀ Clos de Pauililles [poh-leey] (*Languedoc-Roussillon*, France) Top-class
producer of *Banyuls* and of the little-known *appellation* of *Collioure*.

♀ Neil Paulett [paw-let] (South Australia) Small, top-flight *Clare Valley*
Riesling producer. ☆☆☆☆ 1995 Polish Hill River Riesling ££

♀ Dr Pauly-Bergweiler [bur-gwi-lur] (*Mosel-Saar-Ruwer*, Germany)
Ultra-modern winery with really stylish modern dry and late-
harvest *Riesling*. ☆☆☆☆ 1997 Bernkasteler Badstube Riesling
Spätlese ££

Ch. Pavie [pa-vee] (*St. Emilion Premier Grand Cru Classé, Bordeaux,* France) Recently purchased, impeccably made, plummily rich *St. Emilion* wines. 79 81 82 83 85 86 87 88 89 90 91 93 94 95 96 98

Ch. Pavie-Decesse [pa-vee dur-ses] (*St. Emilion Grand Cru Classé, Bordeaux,* France) Neighbour to *Ch. Pavie,* but a shade less impressive. 82 83 85 86 88 89 90 92 94 95 96

Ch. Pavie-Macquin [pa-vee ma-kah'] (*St. Emilion Grand Cru Classé, Bordeaux*) Returned to form since the late 1980s – and the producer of a startlingly good 1993.

Le Pavillon Blanc de Ch. Margaux [pa-vee-yon blon] (*Bordeaux,* France) The (rare) *Sauvignon*-dominated white wine of *Ch. Margaux* which still acts as the yardstick for the growing number of *Médoc* white wines. 85 86 89 **90 91** 92 95 96 97

Pazo de Barrantes [pa-thoh de bah-ran-tays] (*Galicia,* Spain) One of the newest names in *Rias Baixas,* producing lovely spicy *Albariño.* Under the same ownership as *Marques de Murrieta,*

Ca' del Pazzo [kah-del-pat-soh] (*Tuscany,* Italy) Ultra-classy, *oaky Super-Tuscan* with loads of ripe fruit and oak.

Pécharmant [pay-shar-mon] (*South-West,* France) In the *Bergerac* area, producing light, *Bordeaux*-like reds. Worth trying.

Pedro Ximénez (PX) [peh-droh khee-MEH-nes] (*Jerez,* Spain) White grape, dried in the sun to create a sweet, curranty wine, which is used in the blending of the sweeter *sherry* styles, and in its own right by *Osbourne,* and by *Gonzalez Byass* for its brilliant Noe. Also produces a very unusual wine at *De Bortoli* in Australia. ☆☆☆☆ **Cream Of Creams, Manuel de Argueso £££**

Viña Pedrosa [veen-ya pay-droh-sah] (*Ribera del Duero,* Spain) Modern blend of *Tempranillo* and classic *Bordelais* varieties. The Spanish equivalent of a *Super-Tuscan.*

Clos Pegase [kloh-pay-gas] (*Napa Valley,* California) Showcase winery with improving but historically generally overpraised wines. ☆☆☆ **1996 Merlot Napa Valley £££**

Pelissero [peh-lee-seh-roh] (*Piedmont,* Italy) Oaky Barberas, rich, dark Dolcetto and lovely single-vineyard Barbaresco.

Dom. Henry Pellé [on-ree pel-lay] (*Loire,* France) Reliable producer of fruitier-than-usual *Menetou-Salon.* ☆☆☆☆ **1998 Menetou-Salon £££**

Pelorus [pe-law-rus] (*Marlborough,* New Zealand) Showy, big, buttery, yeasty, almost Champagne-style New Zealand sparkling wine from *Cloudy Bay.*

Pemberton (Western Australia) Up-and-coming cooler climate region for more restrained styles of *Chardonnay* and *Pinot Noir; Picardy, Plantagenet* and *Smithbrook* are the names to look out for.

Peñaflor [pen-yah-flaw] (Argentina) Huge, dynamic firm producing increasingly good-value wines. ☆☆☆☆☆ **1998 Malbec Barricas £££**

Penedés [peh-neh-dehs] (*Catalonia,* Spain) Largest *DOC* of *Catalonia* with varying altitudes, climates and styles ranging from *cava* to still wines pioneered by *Torres* and others, though some not as successfully. The use of *varietals* such as *Cabernet Sauvignon, Merlot,* and *Chardonnay* allows more French style winemaking without losing intrinsic Spanish character. Belatedly living up to some of its early promise. White: **95** 96 **97 98** Red: **85 87** 88 89 90 **91** 93 **94 95 96 97** 98 *Albet i Noya;* Can Feixes; Can Ráfols dels Caus; *Freixenet; Cavas Hill; Juvé y Camps;* Jean Leon; *Monistrol;* Puigi Roca; *Torres.*

♀ **Penfolds** (*South Australia*) The world's biggest premium wine company with a high-quality range, from Bin 2 to *Grange*. Previously a red wine specialist but now rapidly becoming a skilful producer of still white wines such as the improving Yattarna (good but not yet living up to its supposed role as the "White *Grange*"). Under the same ownership as *Wynns, Seaview, Rouge Homme, Lindemans, Tullochs, Leo Buring, Seppelt,* and now James Halliday's *Coldstream Hills* and *Devil's Lair* in the *Margaret River.* ☆☆☆☆☆ 1997 Bin 707 Cabernet Sauvignon £££; ☆☆☆☆☆ 1997 RWT Shiraz £££

♀ **Penley Estate** (*Coonawarra,* Australia) High-quality *Coonawarra* estate with rich *Chardonnay* and very blackcurranty *Cabernet.* ☆☆☆☆ 1996 Coonawarra Cabernet Sauvignon £££

♀ **Peppoli** [peh-poh-lee] (*Tuscany,* France) One of *Antinori's* most reliable *Chianti Classicos.*

♀ **Comte Peraldi** [peh-ral-dee] (*Corsica,* France) High-class *Corsican* wine producer, now also making good wine in Romania. ☆☆☆ 1997 Ajaccio Clos du Cardinal ££

♀ **Perez Pascuas** [peh-reth Pas-scoo-was] (*Ribera del Duero,* Spain) Producer of Viña Pedrosa, one of the top examples of *Ribera del Duero.*

♀ **Le Pergole Torte** [pur-goh-leh taw-teh] (*Tuscany,* Italy) Long-established pure *Sangiovese,* oaky *Super-Tuscan.* ☆☆☆☆☆ 1995 Montevertine ££

🌱 **Periquita** [peh-ree-kee-tah] (Portugal) Spicy, tobaccoey grape – and the wine *J.M. da Fonseca* makes from it.

Perlé/Perlant [pehr-lay/lon] (France) Lightly sparkling.

Perlwein [pehrl-vine] (Germany) Sparkling wine.

> **Pernand-Vergelesses** [pehr-non vehr-zhur-less] (*Burgundy,* France) *Commune* producing rather jammy reds but fine whites, including some *Côte d'Or* best buys. White: 85 86 87 **88** 89 **90 92** 95 96 97 98 Red: 78 83 **85** 87 **88** 89 **90** 92 95 96 97 98 Arnoux; Champy; *Chandon de Briailles; Dubreuil-Fontaine; Germain (Château de Chorey); Jadot; Laleure-Piot; Pavelot; Rapet; Dom. Rollin.*

♀ **André Perret** (*Rhône,* France) Producer of notable *Condrieu* and some unusually good examples of *St. Joseph.* ☆☆☆☆ 1997 St. Joseph £££

♀ **Joseph Perrier** [payh-ree-yay] (*Champagne,* France) Family-run producer whose long-lasting elegant *Champagnes* have a heavy *Pinot Noir* influence. ☆☆☆☆ 1995 Cuvée Royale Vintage ££££

♀ **Perrier-Jouët** [payh-ree-yay zhoo-way] (*Champagne,* France) Sadly underperforming *Champagne* house which, like *Mumm,* has now been sold by Canadian distillers, Seagram. Sidestep the non-vintage for the genuinely worthwhile – and brilliantly packaged – Belle Epoque prestige cuvée white and rosé sparkling wine. ☆☆☆☆ 1993 Belle Epoque ££££

♀ **Elio Perrone** [eh-lee-yoh peh-roh-nay] (*Piedmont,* Italy) There are good Barberas, Chardonnays and Dolcettos here, but the really distictive wine is the Moscato.

♀ **Pesquera** [peh-SKEH-ra] (*Ribera del Duero,* Spain) Robert Parker dubbed this the *Ch. Pétrus* of Spain. Well, maybe. I'd say it's a top-class *Tempranillo* often equal to *Vega Sicilia* and the best of *Rioja.* ☆☆☆☆ 1996 Tinto ££

> **Pessac-Léognan** [peh-sak lay-on-yon] (*Bordeaux,* France) *Graves commune* containing most of the finest *châteaux. Ch. Bouscat; Carbonnieux; Fieuzal; Domaine de Chevalier; Haut-Bailly; Haut Brion; Larrivet-Haut-Brion; Laville-Haut-Brion; La Louvière; Malartic-Lagravière. la Mission-Haut-Brion; Smith-Haut-Laffite; la Tour-Haut-Brion.*

☿ **Petaluma** [peh-ta-loo-ma] (*Adelaide Hills*, Australia) High-tech creation of *Brian Croser* and role model for other producers in the New World who are interested in combining innovative winemaking with the fruit of individually characterful vineyards. Classy *Chardonnay*s from Piccadilly in the *Adelaide Hills, Clare Rieslings* (particularly good *late harvest*) and *Coonawarra* reds. Now owns *Smithbrook* and *Mitchelton*. ☆☆☆☆ 1997 Chardonnay £££

PETALUMA

1986 COONAWARRA

750ml

PRODUCE OF AUSTRALIA BOTTLED AT PICCADILLY SA

Pétillant [pur-tee-yon] Lightly sparkling.

☿ **Petit Chablis** [pur-tee shab-lee] (*Burgundy*, France) (Theoretically) less fine than plain *Chablis* – though plenty of vineyards that were previously designated as Petit Chablis can now produce wines sold as *Chablis*. Hardly surprisingly, the ones that are left are often poor value. 95 96 97 98 *La Chablisienne; Jean-Paul Droin; William Fevre;* Dom des Malandes.

☙ **Petit Verdot** [pur-tee vehr-doh] (*Bordeaux*, France) Highly trendy and excitingly spicy, if *tannic* grape variety traditionally used in small proportions in red *Bordeaux*, but now also in California (rarely), and (increasingly often) as a pure varietal in Australia (*Leconfield, Pirramimma*), Italy and Spain (*Marqués de Griñon*). ☆☆☆☆ 1998 Dominio de Valdepusa ££

☿ **Ch. Petit Village** [pur-tee vee-lahzh] (*Pomerol, Bordeaux,* France) Classy, intense, blackcurranty-plummy *Pomerol* now under the same ownership as *Ch. Pichon-Longueville*. Worth keeping. 75 78 79 81 **82** 83 **85** 86 88 89 90 92 **93** 94 95 96 97 98 ☆☆☆☆ 1990 ££££

☙ **Petite Sirah** [peh-teet sih-rah] Spicy red cousin of the *Syrah* grown in California and Mexico and as *Durif* in the *Midi* and Australia. *LA Cetto; Carmen; Fetzer; Morris; Parducci; Ridge; Turley.*

Petrolly A not unpleasant overtone often found in mature *Riesling*. Arrives faster in Australia than in Germany.

☿ **Ch. Pétrus** [pay-trooss] (*Pomerol, Bordeaux,* France) Until recently the priciest of all *clarets* (until *le Pin* came along). Voluptuous *Pomerol* hits the target especially well in the US, and is finding a growing market in the Far East. Beware of fakes (especially big bottles) which crop up increasingly often. 61 62 **64** 66 **70 71** 75 76 78 **79** 81 82 83 85 86 88 89 90 92 93 94 95 96 97 98 99 ☆☆☆☆☆ 1989 ££££

☿ **Pewsey Vale** [pyoo-zee vayl] (*Adelaide Hills*, Australia) Classy, cool-climate wines from winery under the same ownership as *Yalumba, Hill-Smith* and *Heggies*. ☆☆☆☆ 1999 Riesling ££; ☆☆☆☆ 1998 Cabernet Sauvignon £££

☿ **Ch. de Pez** [dur pay] (*St. Estèphe Cru Bourgeois, Bordeaux,* France) Fast-improving *St. Estèphe*, especially since its recent purchase by *Louis Roederer*. In good vintages, well worth ageing. 78 79 **82** 83 85 **86** 88 89 **90 93** 94 95 96 97 98

Pfalz [Pfaltz] (Germany) Formerly known as the *Rheinpfalz*, and before that as the *Palatinate*. Warm, southerly *Anbaugebiet* noted for riper, spicier *Riesling*. Currently competing with the *Mosel* for the prize of best of Germany's wine regions. QbA/Kab/Spät: 85 86 **88 89 90** 91 92 93 94 95 96 97 98 Aus/Beeren/Tba: **83 85** 88 89 90 91 92 93 94 95 97 98 *Kurt Darting; Lingenfelder; Müller-Cattoir.*

⊗ **Ch. Phélan-Ségur** [fay-lon say-goor] (*St. Estèphe Cru Bourgeois, Bordeaux,* France) A good-value property since the mid-1980s, with ripe, well-made wines. Could do better. 75 **82** 85 88 89 90 92 93 **94** 95 96 97 98

⊗ **Joseph Phelps** (*Napa Valley,* California) Pioneer *Napa* user of *Rhône* varieties (*Syrah* and *Viognier*), and a rare source of *late harvest Riesling*. *Cabernet* is a strength. ☆☆☆☆ 1996 Insignia Napa Valley ££££

⊗ **Philipponnat** [fee-lee-poh-nah] (*Champagne,* France) Small producer famous for Clos des Goisses, but also notable for vintage and rosé.

⊗ **RH Phillips** (California, US) Producer whose great value California wines deserve to be better known. ☆☆☆☆ 1998 Toasted Head Chardonnay ££

Phylloxera vastatrix [fih-lok-seh-rah] Root-eating louse that wiped out Europe's vines in the 19th century. Foiled by grafting *vinifera* onto resistant American *labrusca* rootstock. Pockets of pre-phylloxera and/or ungrafted vines still exist in France (in a *Bollinger* vineyard and on the south coast – the louse hates sand), Portugal (in *Quinta do Noval's* "Nacional" vineyard), Australia and Chile. Elsewhere, phylloxera recently devastated *Napa Valley* vines.

Piave [pee-yah-vay] (*Veneto,* Italy) *DOC* in *Veneto* region, including reds made from a *Bordeaux*-like mix of grapes.

⊗ **Ch. Pibarnon** [pee-bah-non] (*Bandol,* France) Top-class producer of modern *Bandol*. 88 **89** 90 92 93 95 **96** 97 98 ☆☆☆☆☆ 1996 £££

⊗ **Ch. Pibran** [pee-bron] (*Pauillac Cru Bourgeois, Bordeaux,* France) Small but high-quality and classically *Pauillac* property. 88 **89** 90 95 96 98

⊗ **Picardy** (*Pemberton,* Western Australia) Impressive new *Pinot Noir* and *Shiraz* specialist by the former winemaker of *Moss Wood*.

⊗ **Pic St. Loup** [peek-sa'-loo] (*Languedoc-Roussillon,* France) Up-and-coming region within the *Coteaux du Languedoc* for *Syrah*-based, *Rhône*-style reds and whites. *Dom. l'Hortus;* Mas Bruguière.

⊗ **FX Pichler** [peek-lehr] (*Wachau Cru,* Austria) Arguably the best dry ("*Trocken*") winemaker in Austria – and certainly a great exponent of the *Grüner Veltliner* and *Riesling* at their richly dry best. ☆☆☆☆☆ 1998 Grüner Veltliner Smaragd Trocken Wachau Wösendorfer Kollmütz ££££

⊗ **Ch. Pichon-Lalande** [pee-shon la-lond] (*Pauillac 2ème Cru Classé, Bordeaux,* France) The new name for Pichon-Longueville-Lalande. Famed *super second* and tremendous success story, thanks to top-class winemaking and the immediate appeal of its unusually high *Merlot* content. A great 1996, but surprisingly a slightly less exciting 1998. **61** 66 **70 75 78 79 82 83** 85 86 88 89 **90 91** 92 93 94 95 96 97 98 ☆☆☆☆ 1989 ££££

⊗ **Ch. Pichon-Longueville** [pee-shon long-veel] (*Pauillac 2ème Cru Classé, Bordeaux,* France) New name for Pichon-Longueville-Baron. An under-performing second growth *Pauillac* until its purchase by *AXA* in 1988. Now level with, and sometimes ahead of, *Ch. Pichon-Lalande*, once the other half of the estate. Wines are intense and complex. Les Tourelles, the *second label*, is a good-value alternative. **86** 88 89 90 91 **92 93 94** 95 96 97 98

🌿 **Picolit** [pee-koh-leet] (*Friuli,* Italy) Grape used to make both sweet and dry white wine. *Jermann* makes a good one.

Piedmont/Piemonte [pee-yed-mont/pee-yeh-mon-tay] (Italy) Ancient and modern northwestern region producing old-fashioned, tough *Barolo* and *Barbaresco* and brilliant modern fruit-packed wines. Also makes *Oltrepò Pavese, Asti Spumante* and *Dolcetto d'Alba*. See *Nebbiolo*.

⚊ **Bodegas Piedmonte** [pee-yehd-mohn-teh] (*Navarra*, Spain) Confusingly named (see above), dynamic cooperative producing good reds from *Tempranillo, Cabernet* and *Merlot*.

⚊ **Pieropan** [pee-yehr-oh-pan] (*Veneto,* Italy) *Soave's* top producer, which more or less invented single-vineyard wines here and is still a great exception to the dull *Soave* rule. Lovely almondy wine. ✰✰✰✰ 1998 Vigneto ££

⚊ **Pieroth** [pee-roth] Huge company whose salesmen visit clients' homes offering wines that are rarely recommended by this or any other critic.

⚊ **Pierro** [pee-yehr-roh] (*Margaret River,* Australia) Small estate producing rich, buttery, *Meursault*-like *Chardonnay*. ✰✰✰✰ 1998 Chardonnay £££

Piesport [pees-sport] (*Mosel-Saar-Ruwer,* Germany) Produced in the *Grosslage Michelsberg*, a region infamous for dull German wine, and bought by people who think themselves above *Liebfraumilch*. Try a single-vineyard – Gunterslay or Goldtröpchen – for something more memorable.
QbA/Kab/Spät: **85 86 88 89 90** 91 **92 93 94 95** 96 97 98 99 Aus/Beeren/Tba: **83 85** 88 89 90 91 **92** 93 **94** 95 96 97 98 99

⚊ **Pighin** [pee-jeen] (*Friuli,* Italy) Good, rather than great Collio producer, with creditable examples of most of the styles produced here.

⚊ **Pikes** (*Clare Valley,* South Australia) Top-class estate with great *Riesling, Shiraz, Sangiovese* and *Sauvignon*. ✰✰✰✰ 1999 Sauvignon Blanc ££

⚊ **Jean Pillot** [pee-yoh] (*Burgundy,* France) There are three estates called Pillot in *Chassagne-Montrachet*. This one is the best – and produces by far the finest red.

⚊ **Ch. le Pin** [lur pan] (*Pomerol, Bordeaux,* France) Ultra-hyped, small, recently formed estate whose – admittedly delicious – wines sell at increasingly silly prices in the US and the Far East. The forerunner of a string of other similar honey-traps (see *Ch. Valandraud and la Mondotte*), and one of the wines that is helping to create a burgeoning trade in forged bottles.
81 82 83 85 86 87 88 89 90 92 93 94 95 96 97 98 99 ✰✰✰✰✰ 1995 ££££

⚊ **Pine Ridge** (*Napa Valley,* California) Greatly improved *Stag's Leap* producer that is now also making good quality reds on *Howell Mountain*. The Oregon *Archery Summit* wines are also worth seeking out.
✰✰✰✰✰ 1998 Stags Leap District Cabernet Sauvignon ££££

Pineau de Charentes [pee-noh dur sha-ront] (*South-West,* France) Fortified wine produced in the Cognac region.

⚊ **Pingus** [pin-goos] (*Ribeiro del Duero,* Spain) Probably the finest wine now being made in this region. Expect cleaner, richer, more modern wines than those from many of the neighbours. ✰✰✰✰✰ 1996 ££££

🍇 **Pinot Blanc/Bianco** [pee-noh blon] Rather like *Chardonnay* without all that fruit, and rarely as classy or complex. Fresh, creamy and adaptable. At its best in *Alsace* (Pinot d'Alsace), the Alto-Adige in Italy (as *Pinot Bianco*), and in Germany and Austria (as *Weissburgunder*). In California, confusingly, a synonym for *Melon de Bourgogne*.

🍇 **Pinot Chardonnay** (Australia) Misleading name for *Chardonnay*, still used by *Tyrrells*. Don't confuse with *Pinot Noir/Chardonnay* sparkling wine blends such as the excellent *Seaview* and *Yalumba*.

🍇 **Pinot Gris/Grigio** [pee-noh gree] (*Alsace*, France) White grape of uncertain origins, making full, rather heady, spicy wine. Best in *Alsace* (also known as *Tokay d'Alsace*), Italy (as *Pinot Grigio*) and Germany (as *Ruländer* or *Grauburgunder*). **Ernst Brun; Bott-Geyl; Dopff & Irion; Kreydenweiss; Ostertag; Piper's Brook; Schleret; Sorg; Cave de Turckheim; Weinbach (Faller); Zind–Humbrecht.**

🍇 **Pinot Meunier** [pee-noh-mur-nee-yay] (*Champagne*, France) Dark pink-skinned grape. Plays an unsung but major role in *Champagne*. Can also be used to produce a still varietal wine. **Best's; Bonny Doon; William Wheeler.**

🍇 **Pinot Noir** [pee-noh nwahr] Black grape responsible for all red *Burgundy* and in part for white *Champagne*. Also successfully grown in the New World in sites whose climate is neither too warm nor too cold. Winemakers need the dedication which might otherwise have destined them for a career in nursing. Buying is like Russian Roulette – once you've got a taste for that complex raspberryish flavour, you'll go on pulling the expensive trigger. See *Oregon, Carneros, Yarra, Santa Barbara, Tasmania, Burgundy, Martinborough*.

🍇 **Pinotage** [pee-noh-tazh] (South Africa) *Pinot Noir* x *Cinsault* cross with a spicy, plummy character, used in South Africa and (now very rarely) New Zealand. Good old examples are brilliant but rare; most taste muddy and rubbery. New winemaking and international demand are making for more exciting wines. **Beyerskloof; Clos Malverne; Fairview; Grangehurst; Kanonkop; Saxenberg; Simonsig; Warwick.**

🍸 **Piper Heidsieck** [pi-pur hide-seek] (*Champagne*, France) Greatly improved *Champagne* made by Daniel Thibaut of *Charles Heidsieck*. The "Rare" is worth looking out for.

🍸 **Pipers Brook Vineyards** (*Tasmania*, Australia) Dr. Andrew Pirie, who has just bought *Heemskerk*, is a pioneering producer of fine *Burgundian Chardonnay*, *Pinot Noir*, and *Pinot Gris*. Ninth Island, the *second label*, includes an excellent unoaked *Chablis*-like *Chardonnay*. The new Pirie sparkling wine is good too. ☆☆☆☆ **1998 Pinot Gris £££**

🍸 **Pira** [pee-rah] (*Piedmont*, Italy) Chiara Boschis's impressive small *Barolo* estate makes long-lived wines from top-class vineyards.

🍸 **Producteurs Plaimont** [play-mon] (*South-West*, France) Reliable cooperative in *Côtes de St. Mont* producing *Bordeaux*-lookalike reds and whites with some use of local grapes. See also *Pacherenc du Vic-Bilh* and *Madiran*.

🍸 **Plaisir de Merle** [play-zeer dur mehrl] (*Paarl*, South Africa) Paul Pontallier of *Ch. Margaux* is helping to make ripe, soft reds and New World-style whites for *Stellenbosch Farmers' Winery* in this new showcase operation. ☆☆☆☆ **1997 Chardonnay ££**

🍸 **Plantagenet** (*Mount Barker*, Western Australia) Good producer of *Chardonnay, Riesling, Cabernet*, and lean *Shiraz* in this increasingly successful region in the south-west corner of Australia. ☆☆☆☆ **1997 Mount Barker Cabernet Sauvignon £££**

🍸 **Il Podere dell'Olivos** [eel poh-deh-reh del-oh-lee-vohs] (California) Pioneering producer of Italian varietals.

🍸 **Poggio Antico** [pod-zhee-yoh an-tee-koh] (*Tuscany*, Italy) Ultra-reliable *Brunello* producer. ☆☆☆☆ **1995 Brunello di Montalcino ££££**

🍸 **Pojer & Sandri** [poh-zhehr eh san-dree] (*Trentino*, Italy) Good red and white and, especially, sparkling wines.

�र **Pol Roger** [pol rod-zhay] (*Champagne*, France) Fine producer, with an unusually subtle non-vintage that improves with keeping. The Cuvée Winston Churchill (named in honour of a faithful fan) is spectacular, and the *Demi-Sec* is a rare treat. ☆☆☆☆☆ 1990 Winston Churchill ££££

�र **Erich & Walter Polz** [poltz] (*Styria*, Austria) Producers of notable dry wines, including Pinot Blanc and Gris and one of Austria's best examples of Sauvignon Blanc.

�र **Poliziano** [poh-leet-zee-yah-noh] (*Tuscany*, Italy) Apart from a pack-leading *Vino Nobile di Montepulciano*, this is the place to find the delicious Elegia and Le Stanze *Vini da Tavola*. ☆☆☆☆☆ 1997 Vino Nobile di Montepulciano £££

�र **Pomerol** [pom-meh-rohl] (*Bordeaux*, France) With *St. Emilion*, the *Bordeaux* for lovers of the *Merlot*, which predominates in its rich, soft, plummy wines. *Ch. Pétrus* and *le Pin* are the big names but wines like *Petit Village* and *Clos René* abound. None are cheap because production is often limited to a few thousand cases (in the *Médoc*, 20–40,000 is more common). Quality is far more consistent than in *St. Emilion*. See *Pétrus*, *Moueix* and individual châteaux. 79 81 **82 83 85** 86 **88 89** 90 **93** 94 95 96 97 98 99

� **Pomino** [poh-mee-noh] (*Tuscany*, Italy) Small *DOC* within *Chianti Rufina*; virtually a monopoly for *Frescobaldi* who make a delicious buttery unwooded white *Pinot Bianco/Chardonnay*, the oaky-rich Il Benefizio and a tasty *Sangiovese/Cabernet*. ☆☆☆ 1996 Pomino Bianco ££

�I **Pommard** [pom-mahr] (*Burgundy*, France) Very variable quality *commune*, theoretically with a higher proportion of old vines, making slow-to-mature, then solid and complex reds. 78 **85** 86 87 **88 89 90** 92 93 94 95 96 97 98 *Comte Armand; Jean-Marc Boillot; Girardin; Dominique Laurent; Leroy; Château de Meursault; de Montille; Mussy; Dom. de Pousse d'Or.*

�I **Pommery** [pom-meh-ree] (*Champagne*, France) Returned-to-form big-name with rich full-flavoured style. The top-label Louise Pommery white and rosé are tremendous. ☆☆☆☆☆ 1989 Cuvée Louise ££££

�I **Pongràcz** [pon-gratz] (South Africa) Brand name for the *Bergkelder's* (excellent) *Cap Classique* sparkling wine. ☆☆☆☆ Cap Classique ££

�I **Dom. Ponsot** [pon-soh] (*Burgundy*, France) Top-class estate noted for *Clos de la Roche*, *Chambertin* and (rare) white *Morey-St.-Denis*. More affordable is the excellent *Gevrey*. ☆☆☆☆ 1995 Clos de la Roche £££

�I **Ch. Pontet-Canet** [pon-tay ka-nay] (*Pauillac 5ème Cru Classé*, *Bordeaux*, France) Rich, concentrated, up-and-coming *Pauillac* benefitting since the early 1980s from the dedicated ambition of its owners who also have *Lafon-Rochet*. **82** 83 85 **86** 88 89 90 91 **93 94** 95 96 97 98 99

�I **Ponzi** [pon-zee] (*Oregon*, US) The ideal combination: a maker of good *Pinot Noir*, *Chardonnay* and even better beer. ☆☆☆☆ 1994 Pinot Noir Reserve £££

Port (*Douro*, Portugal) Fortified wine made in the upper *Douro* valley. Comes in several styles; see *Tawny*, *Ruby*, *LBV*, *Vintage*, *Crusted* and *White port*.

�I **Viña Porta** [veen-yah por-ta] (*Rapel*, Chile) Dynamic winery that specialises in juicy *Cabernet* and *Merlot*. The *Chardonnay* is good too.

�I **Ch. Potelle** (*Napa Valley*, California) French-owned *Mount Veeder* winery that won fame when its stylish wines were served at the White House. Great Zinfandel. ☆☆☆☆ 1997 Chardonnay £££

�I **Ch. Potensac** [po-ton-sak] (*Médoc Cru Bourgeois*, *Bordeaux*, France) Under the same ownership as the great *Léoville-Las-Cases*, and offering a more affordable taste of the winemaking that goes into that wine.

Pouilly-Fuissé [poo-yee fwee-say] (*Burgundy,* France) Variable white often sold at vastly inflated prices. Pouilly-Vinzelles, Pouilly-Loché, and other *Mâconnais* wines are often better value, though top-class Pouilly-Fuissé from producers like *Ch. Fuissé,* Dom. Noblet, or Dom. Ferret can compete with the best of the *Côte d'Or.* 88 89 **90 92 95** 96 97 98 *Barraud; Corsin;* Ferret; *Ch. Fuissé;* Lapierre; Noblet; Philibert; *Verget.*

☖ **Pouilly-Fumé** [poo-yee foo-may] (*Loire,* France) Potentially ultra-elegant *Sauvignon Blanc* with classic gooseberry fruit and "smoky" overtones derived from flint ("silex") subsoil. Like *Sancerre,* rarely repays cellaring. See *Ladoucette* and *Didier Dagueneau.* 94 95 96 97

☖ **Ch. Poujeaux** [poo-joh] (*Moulis Cru Bourgeois, Bordeaux,* France) Up-and-coming. reliable, plummy-blackcurranty wine. 79 **82 83 85 86** 88 89 90 91 92 93 94 **95 96** 97 98 99 ☆☆☆ 1993 £££
Pourriture noble [poo-ree-toor nohbl] (France) See *Botrytis cinerea* or *noble rot.*

☖ **Dom. de la Pousse d'Or** [poos-daw] (*Burgundy,* France) One of the top estates in *Volnay.* (The *Pommard* and *Santenay* wines are good too.) ☆☆☆☆ 1997 Volnay Clos de la Bousse d'Or ££££
Prädikat [pray-dee-ket] (Germany) As in Qualitätswein mit Prädikat (*QmP*), the (supposedly) higher quality level for German and Austrian wines, indicating a greater degree of natural ripeness.

☖ **Franz Prager** [prah-gur] (*Wachau,* Austria) Top class producer of a wide range of impressive *Grüner-Veltliners,* and, now, *Rieslings.*
Precipitation The creation of a harmless deposit, usually of *tartrate* crystals, in white wine, which the Germans romantically call "diamonds".
Premier Cru [prur-mee-yay kroo] In *Burgundy,* indicates wines that fall between *village* and *Grand Cru* quality. Some major *communes* such as *Beaune* and *Nuits-St.-Georges* have no *Grand Cru.* Wine simply labelled Meursault Premier Cru, for example is probably a blend from two or more vineyards.

☖ **Premières Côtes de Blaye** See *Côtes de Blaye*

☖ **Premières Côtes de Bordeaux** [prur-mee-yay koht dur bohr-doh] (*Bordeaux,* France) Up-and-coming riverside *appellation* for reds and (often less interestingly) sweet whites. Whites: 76 **83 85 86 88 89 90 95** 96 **97** 98 99 *Carsin;* Grand-Mouëys; *Reynon.*

Prestige Cuvée [koo-vay] (*Champagne,* France) The top wine of a *Champagne* house. Expensive and elaborately packaged. Some, like *Dom Pérignon,* are brilliant; others less so. Other best-known examples include *Veuve Clicquot's* Grand Dame and *Roederer's* Cristal.

☖ **Preston Vineyards** (*Sonoma,* California) Winery making the most of *Dry Creek Zinfandel* and *Syrah.* A white Meritage blend is pretty good too and there is an improving *Viognier.*

☖ **Dom. Jacques Prieur** [pree-yur] (*Burgundy,* France) Estate with fine vineyards. Increasingly impressive since takeover by *Antonin Rodet.*

☖ **Ch. Prieuré-Lichine** [pree-yur-ray lih-sheen] (*Margaux 4ème Cru Classé, Bordeaux,* France) Recently (1999) sold and – in 2000 – much improved *château* making good if rarely subtle blackcurranty wine which benefits from input by *Michel Rolland.* (Thanks to its flamboyant previous owner) this is one of the only *châteaux* with a gift shop and a helicopter landing pad on its roof. 70 **82 83 85 86** 88 89 90 **93 94** 95 96 97 98 99

Primeur [pree-mur] (France) New wine, e.g. *Beaujolais* Primeur (the same as *Beaujolais Nouveau*) or, as in *en primeur*, wine which is sold while still in barrel (known in the US as "Futures").

℣ **Primitivo** [pree-mih-tee-voh] (*Puglia*, Italy) Another name for the *Zinfandel*.

℣ **Primo Estate** [pree-moh] (South Australia) Extraordinarily imaginative venture among the fruit farms of the Adelaide Plains. Passion-fruity *Colombard*, sparkling *Shiraz*, and *Bordeaux* blends made *Amarone*-style, using grapes partially dried in the sun. The olive oil is good too.
☆☆☆☆ 1998 Joseph Cabernet Merlot £££

℣ **Principe de Viana** [preen-chee-pay de vee-yah-nah] (*Navarra*, Spain) Highly commercial winery producing large amounts of good value red and white wine. The Agramont label is particularly worthwhile.

℣ **Prinz zu Salm-Dalberg** [zoo sahlm dal-burg] (*Nahe*, Germany) Innovative producer with good red *Spätburgunder* and (especially) *Scheurebe*.

℣ **Priorato / Priorat** [pree-yaw-rah-toh / raht] (*Catalonia*, Spain) Highly prized / priced, sexy New-Wave wines from a region once known for hefty alcoholic reds from *Cariñena* and *Garnacha* grapes. **Rene Barbier (Clos Mogador); Costers del Siurana; Mas Martinet;** Clos i Terrasses; J.M. Fuentes; Daphne Glorian; *Alvaro Palacios;* Pasanau Germans; Scala Dei; Vilella de la Cartoixa. ☆☆☆☆ 1997 Clos de l'Obac £££

Propriétaire (Récoltant) [pro-pree-yeh-tehr ray-kohl-ton] (France) Vineyard owner-manager.

℣ **Prosecco di Conegliano-Valdobbiàdene** [proh-sek-koh dee coh-nay-lee-anoh val-doh-bee-yah-day-nay] (*Veneto*, Italy) Soft, slightly earthy, dry and sweet sparkling wine made from the *Prosecco* grape. Less boisterous and fruity than *Asti Spumante*. Drink young. Bisol; Bortolin; Canevel; Produttori de Valdobbiadene; Ruggeri; Zardetto.

Provence [proh-vons] (France) Southern region producing fast-improving wine with a number of minor *ACs*. Rosé de Provence should be dry and fruity with a hint of peppery spice. See *Bandol, Coteaux d'Aix en-Provence, Palette*.

℣ **Provins** [proh-vah'] (*Valais*, Switzerland) Dynamic cooperative, making the most of *Chasselas* and more interesting varieties such as the *Arvine*.

℣ **J.J. Prüm** [proom] (*Mosel-Saar-Ruwer*, Germany) Top *Riesling* producer with fine *Wehlener* vineyards. ☆☆☆☆ 1997 Wehlener Sonnenuhr Riesling Kabinett £££

℣ **Dom. Michel Prunier** [proo-nee-yay] (*Burgundy*, France) Best estate in *Auxey-Duresses*. ☆☆☆☆ 1997 Auxey-Duresses Vieilles Vignes ££

℣ **Alfredo Prunotto** [proo-not-toh] (*Piedmont*, Italy) Good *Barolo* producer recently bought by *Antinori*. ☆☆☆☆ 1994 Barolo Bussia £££

Puglia [poo-lee-yah] (Italy) Hot region, now making cool wines, thanks to *flying winemakers* like *Kym Milne*. Also see *Salice Salentino* and *Copertino*.

℣ **Puiatti** [pwee-yah-tee] (*Friuli-Venezia Giulia*, Italy) Producer of some of Italy's most stylish *Chardonnay, Pinot Bianco, Pinot Grigio,* and *Tocai Friulano*. The Archetipi wines are the cream of the crop.

℣ **Puisseguin St. Emilion** [pwees-gan san tay-mee-lee-yon] (*Bordeaux*, France) Satellite of *St. Emilion* making similar, *Merlot*-dominant wines which are often far better value. **82 83 85** 86 **88 89** 90 94 95 97 98

Vins de — Bourgogne

PULIGNY-MONTRACHET
1ᵉʳ CRU LES PERRIÈRES
APPELLATION PULIGNY-MONTRACHET 1ᵉʳ CRU CONTRÔLÉE

13,5% vol. **1994** 750 ml

Mis en bouteille au Domaine par Louis CARILLON et Fils
VITICULTEURS
Puligny-Montrachet Côte-d'Or - France

PRODUCE OF FRANCE

ℐ **Puligny-Montrachet** [poo-lee-nee mon-ra-shay] (*Burgundy*, France) Aristocratic white *Côte d'Or commune* that shares the *Montrachet* vineyard with *Chassagne*. Should be complex buttery *Chardonnay* with a touch more elegance than *Meursault*. *Carillon, Sauzet, Ramonet, Drouhin,* and *Dom. Leflaive* are all worth their money. **85 86 88** 89 **90 92** 95 96 97 98 99 *D'Auvenay; Carillon; Chavy; Drouhin; Leflaive (Olivier & Domaine); Marquis de Laguiche; Ch de Puligny-Montrachet; Ramonet; Sauzet.*

Putto [poot-toh] (Italy) See *Chianti*.

Puttonyos [poot-toh-nyos] (*Tokaji*, Hungary) The measure of sweetness (from 1 to 6) of *Tokaji*. The number indicates the number of puttonyos (baskets) of sweet *aszú* paste that are added to the base wine.

ℐ **Ch. Puygeraud** [Pwee-gay-roh] (*Bordeaux*, France) Perhaps the best property on the *Côtes de Francs*. 85 86 88 **89** 90 **94 95** 96 97 98 99

Pyrenees (*Victoria*, Australia) One of the classiest regions in *Victoria*, thanks to the efforts of *Taltarni* and *Dalwhinnie*. White: **92 94 95 96** 97 98 Red: **85 86 87 88 90 91 92 94 95** 96 97 98

ℐ **Pyrus** [pi-rus] (Australia) *Lindemans Coonawarra* wine that's right back on form in 1997. ☆☆☆☆☆ **1997 Pyrus £££**

Q

QbA *Qualitätswein bestimmter Anbaugebiet:* [kvah-lih-tayts-vine behr-shtihmt-tuhr ahn-bow-geh-beet] (Germany) Basic-quality German wine from one of the 11 *Anbaugebiete*, e.g. *Rheinhessen*.

QmP *Qualitätswein mit Prädikat:* [pray-dee-kaht] (Germany) *QbA* wine (supposedly) with "special qualities". The QmP blanket designation is broken into five sweetness rungs, from *Kabinett* to *Trockenbeerenauslese* plus *Eiswein*.

ℐ **Quady** [kway-dee] (*Central Valley*, California) Quirky producer of the wittily named "Starboard" (served in a decanter), *Orange Muscat* Essencia (great with chocolate), *Black Muscat* Elysium, low-alcohol Electra, and now, the brilliant Vya Sweet Vermouth. ☆☆☆☆ **Quady's Starboard Batch 88 £££**

ℐ **Quarles Harris** [kwahrls] (*Douro*, Portugal) Underrated *port* producer with a fine 1980 and 1983. ☆☆☆☆ **1983 Vintage Port £££**

ℐ **Quarts de Chaume** [kahr dur shohm] (*Loire*, France) Luscious but light sweet wines, uncloying, ageing beautifully, from the *Coteaux du Layon*. The *Dom. des Baumard* is exceptional. Sweet white: **76** 83 **85 86 88 89** 90 **94** 95 96 97 98 *Dom des Baumard; Pierre Soulez.*

Y **Querciabella** [kehr-chee-yah-BEH-lah] (*Tuscany,* Italy) Top class *Chianti Classico* estate with a great *Sangiovese-Cabernet* blend called Camartina.

Y **Quilceda Creek** [kwil-see-dah] (*Washington State,* US) Producer of one of the best, most blackcurranty *Cabernets* in the Northwest.

Y **Quincy** [kan-see] (*Loire,* France) Dry *Sauvignon,* lesser-known and sometimes good alternative to *Sancerre* or *Pouilly-Fumé.* **Joseph Mellot.**

Quinta [keen-ta] (Portugal) Vineyard or estate, particularly in the *Douro,* where "single Quinta" *vintage ports* are increasingly being taken as seriously as the big-name blends. See *Crasto, Vesuvio* and *de la Rosa.*

Y **Quintessa** (*Napa,* Caifornia) Exciting new venture from Agustin Huneeus, the man behind *Franciscan* and *Veramonte*

Y **Guiseppe Quintarelli** [keen-ta-reh-lee] (*Veneto,* Italy) Old-fashioned *Recioto*-maker producing some of the quirkiest, most sublime *Valpolicella,* recognisable by the apparently hand-written labels.Try the more affordable Molinara. ☆☆☆☆☆ **1995 Molinara ££**

Y **Quivira** (*Sonoma,* California) Great *Dry Creek* producer of intense *Zinfandel* and *Syrah* and a deliciously clever *Rhône*-meets-California blend that includes both varieties.

Y **Qupé** [kyoo-pay] (*Central Coast,* California) Run by one of the founders of *Au Bon Climat,* this *Santa Barbara* winery produces brilliant *Syrah* and *Rhône*-style whites. ☆☆☆☆ **1997 Bien Nacido Syrah £££**

R

Y **Ch. Rabaud-Promis** [rrah-boh prraw-mee] (*Sauternes Premier Cru Classé, Bordeaux,* France) Under-performing until 1986; now making top-class wines. 83 85 **86** 87 **88 89 90 95** 96 97 98 ☆☆☆☆☆ **1990 £££**

Racking The drawing off of wine from its *lees* into a clean cask or vat.

Y **Rafael Estate** [raf-fay-yel] (*Mendoza,* Argentina) Dynamic producer of great value *Malbec*-based reds with the assistance of *flying winemaker, Hugh Ryman.*

Y **A Rafanelli** [ra-fur-nel-lee] (*Sonoma,* California) Great *Dry Creek* winery with great *Cabernet* Sauvignon. The *Zinfandel* is the jewel in the crown though. ☆☆☆☆ **1995 Zinfandel £££**

Y **Olga Raffault** [ra-foh] (*Loire,* France) There are several Raffaults in *Chinon;* this is the best – and the best source of some of the longest-lived examples of this *appellation.*

Y **Le Ragose** [lay-rah-goh-say] (*Veneto,* Italy) A name to look out for in *Valpolicella* – for great *Amarone, Recioto* and Valpolicella Classico (le Sassine).

Y **Raïmat** [ri-mat] (*Catalonia,* Spain) Innovative *Codorníu*-owned winery in the *Costers del Segre* region. Merlot, a *Cabernet/Merlot* blend called Abadia and *Tempranillo* are interesting and *Chardonnay* – both still and sparkling – are good. ☆☆☆☆ **1994 Cabernet Sauvignon Reserva ££**

Rainwater (*Madeira,* Portugal) Light dry style of *Madeira* popular in the US. ☆☆☆ **Berry Bros & Rudd's Selected Rainwater ££**

Y **Ch. Ramage-la-Batisse** [ra-mazh la ba-teess] (*Haut-Médoc Cru Bourgeois, Bordeaux,* France) Good-value wine from St. Laurent, close to *Pauillac.*

Y **Ramitello** [ra-mee-tel-loh] (*Molise,* Italy) Spicy-fruity reds and creamy citric whites produced by di Majo Norante in Biferno on the Adriatic coast.

Y **Adriano Ramos Pinto** [rah-mosh pin-toh] (*Douro,* Portugal) Family-run winery that belongs to *Roederer. Colheita tawnies* are a delicious speciality, but the *vintage* wines and *single quintas* are good too.

Dom. Ramonet [ra-moh-nay] (*Burgundy,* France) Supreme *Chassagne-Montrachet* estate with top-flight *Montrachet, Bâtard* and *Bienvenues-Bâtard-Montrachet* and fine complex *Premiers Crus.* Pure class; worth waiting for too.
☆☆☆☆☆ 1995 Bâtard-Montrachet ££££.

Castello dei Rampolla [kas-teh-lohday-ee ram-poh-la] (*Tuscany,* Italy) Good *Chianti*-producer whose wines need time to soften. The berryish Sammarco *Vino da Tavola* is also impressive.

Rancio [ran-see-yoh] Term for the peculiarly tangy yet prized *oxidised* flavour of certain fortified wines, particularly in France (e.g. *Banyuls*) and Spain.

Randersacker [ran-dehr-sak-kur] (*Franken,* Germany) One of the most successful homes of the *Sylvaner*, especially when made by Weingut *Juliusspital.*

Rapel [ra-pel] (Central Valley, Chile) Important subregion of the *Central Valley*, especially for reds. Includes *Colchagua* and *Cachapoal.*

Rapitalà [ra-pih-tah-la] (*Sicily,* Italy) Estate producing a fresh, peary white wine from a blend of local grapes.

Kent Rasmussen (*Carneros,* California) One of California's too-small band of truly inventive winemakers, producing great *Burgundy*-like *Pinot Noir* and *Chardonnay* and Italianate *Sangiovese* and *Dolcetto.*
☆☆☆☆ 1998 Chardonnay £££

Rasteau [ras-stoh] (*Rhône,* France) Southern village producing peppery reds with rich, berry fruit. The fortified *Muscat* can be good too. Red: **88 89 90 95 96** 97 98 99 Bressy-Masson; des Coteaux des Travers; Dom des Girasols; de la Grangeneuve; Marie-France Masson; Rabasse-Charavin; La Soumade; François Vache.

Renato Ratti [rah-tee] (*Piedmont,* Italy) One of the finest, oldest producers of *Barolo.*

Rauenthal [row-en-tahl-tee] (*Rheingau,* Germany) *Georg Breur* is the most interesting producer in this beautiful village. Other names to look for include *Schloss Schönborn* and *Schloss Rheinhartshausen.*

Ch. Rauzan-Ségla [roh-zon say-glah] (*Margaux 2ème Cru Classé, Bordeaux,* France) For a long time an under-performing *Margaux.* Now, since its purchase by Chanel in 1994, one of the best buys in *Bordeaux.*
70 82 83 85 **86** 88 89 90 **91 92 93 94** 95 96 97 98 99

Ch. Rauzan-Gassies [roh-zon ga-sees] (*Margaux 2ème Cru Classé, Bordeaux*, France) Compared to *Rauzan-Ségla* its neighbour, this property is still underperforming magnificently.

Jean-Marie Raveneau [rav-noh] (*Burgundy*, France) The long-established king of *Chablis*, with impeccably made *Grand* and *Premier Cru* wines that last brilliantly. ☆☆☆☆☆ **1996 Chablis Valmur £££**

Ravenswood (*Sonoma Valley*, California) Brilliant *Zinfandel*-maker whose individual-vineyard wines are wonderful examples of this variety. The *Merlots* and *Cabernet* are fine too.

Ravenswood (South Australia) Label confusingly adopted by *Hollick* for its top *Coonawarra* reds (no relation to the above entry).

Raventos i Blanc [ra-vayn-tos ee blank] (*Catalonia*, Spain) Josep Raventos' ambition is to produce the best sparkling wine in Spain, adding *Chardonnay* to local varieties. ☆☆☆☆☆ **Cava Brut Reserva £££**

Ch. Rayas [rih-yas] (*Rhône*, France) The only chance to taste *Châteauneuf-du-Pape* made solely from the *Grenache*. Pricy but good.

Raymond (*Napa Valley*, California) Tasty, intense *Cabernets* and *Chardonnays*. ☆☆☆☆ 1996 **Cabernet Sauvignon Napa Valley Generations £££**

Ch. Raymond-Lafon [ray-mon la-fon] (*Sauternes, Bordeaux*, France) Very good small producer whose wines deserve keeping. **75 80 82 83 85 86 89** 90 92 94 95 96 97 98

Ch. de Rayne-Vigneau [rayn veen-yoh] (*Sauternes Premier Cru Classé, Bordeaux*, France) *Sauternes* estate, located at *Bommes*, producing a deliciously rich complex wine. 85 86 88 89 90 92 94 95 96 97 98 99 ☆☆☆☆ **1998 ££££**

RD (*Récemment Dégorgée*) (*Champagne*, France) A term invented by *Bollinger* for their delicious vintage *Champagne*, which has been allowed a longer-than-usual period (as much as fifteen years) on its *lees*.

Real Companhia Vinicola do Norte de Portugal [ray-yahl com-pah-nee-yah vee-nee-koh-lah doh nor-tay day por-too-gahl] (*Douro*, Portugal) The full name of the firm better known as the *Royal Oporto Wine Co*. The best wines are the *tawny* ports sold under the Quinta dos Carvalhas label. Other efforts – especially the *vintage ports* are rarely worth buying

Ignacio Recabarren [ig-na-see-yoh reh-ka-ba-ren] (Chile) Superstar winemaker and Casablanca pioneer.

Recioto [ray-chee-yo-toh] (*Veneto*, Italy) Sweet or dry alcoholic wine made from semi-dried, ripe grapes. Usually associated with *Valpolicella* and *Soave*.

Récoltant-manipulant (RM) [ray-kohl-ton ma-nih-poo-lon] (*Champagne*, France) Individual winegrower and blender, identified by mandatory RM number on label.

Récolte [ray-kohlt] (France) Vintage, literally 'harvest'.

Dom. de la Rectorie [rehc-toh-ree] (*Languedoc-Roussillon*, France) One of the two top names (with *Mas Blanc*) in *Banyuls*, and also a brilliant producer of *Collioure*.

Redman (South Australia) Improved *Coonawarra* estate with intense reds. ☆☆☆☆ **1997 Cabernet Sauvignon ££**

Redoma [ray-doh-mah] (*Douro*, Portugal) New wave red and white table wines from the dynamic, yet reliable port producer Dirk *Nieport*.

Redwood Valley Estate See *Seifried*.

Refosco [re-fos-koh] (*Friuli-Venezia Giulia*, Italy) Red grape and its dry and full-bodied *DOC* wine. Benefits from ageing.

Regaleali [ray-ga-lay-ah-lee] (*Sicily*, Italy) Ambitious aristocratic estate, using local varieties to produce some of *Sicily's* most serious wines. ☆☆☆☆ **1995 Cabernet Sauvignon £££**.

Régisseur [rey-jee-sur] (*Bordeaux*, France) In *Bordeaux* (*only*), the cellar-master.

Ɏ Régnié [ray-nyay] (*Burgundy*, France) Once sold as *Beaujolais Villages*, Régnié now has to compete with *Chiroubles*, *Chénas* and the other *crus*. It is mostly like an amateur competing against pros. Fortunately for Régnié, those pros often aren't on great form. *Duboeuf* makes a typical example. 90 **91** 93 94 95 96 97 98 99 *Duboeuf;* Dubost; Piron; Sapin; Trichard.

Ɏ Reguengos (*Alentejo*, Portugal) Richly flavoursome reds pioneered by Esporão and the Reguengos de Monsaraz cooperative.

🍇 Reichensteiner [rike-en-sti-ner] Recently developed white grape, popular in England (and Wales).

Ɏ Reif Estate Winery [reef] (*Ontario*, Canada) Impressive *icewine* specialist. ☆☆☆☆ 1998 Vidal Icewine ££££

Ɏ Remelluri [ray-may-yoo-ree] (*Rioja*, Spain) For most modernists, this is the nearest *Rioja* has got to a top-class, small-scale organic estate. Wines are more serious (and *tannic*) than most, but they're fuller in flavour too and they're built to last. ☆☆☆☆ 1996 Rioja ££

Remuage [reh-moo-wazh] (*Champagne*, France) Part of the *méthode champenoise*, the gradual turning and tilting of bottles so that the yeast deposit collects in the neck ready for *dégorgement*.

Reserva [ray-sehr-vah] (Spain) Wine aged for a period specified by the relevant *DO*: usually one year for reds and six months for whites and pinks.

Réserve [reh-surv] (France) Legally meaningless, as in "Réserve Personelle," but implying a wine selected and given more age.

Residual sugar Term for wines which have retained grape sugar not converted to *alcohol* by yeasts during fermentation. In France 4 grams per litre is the threshold. In the US, the figure is 5 and many so-called "dry" white wines contain as much as 10 and some supposedly dry red *Zinfandels* definitely have more than a trace of sweetness. New Zealand Sauvignons are rarely bone dry, but their *acidity* balances and conceals any residual sugar.

Ɏ Weingut Balthasar Ress [bul-ta-zah rress] (*Rheingau*, Germany) Good producer in *Hattenheim*, blending delicacy with concentration. ☆☆☆☆ 1996 Hattenheimer Riesling Qualitätswein Halbtrocken £££

Retsina [ret-see-nah] (Greece) Wine made the way the ancient Greeks used to make it – resinating it with pine to keep it from spoiling. Today, it's an acquired taste for non-holidaying, non-Greeks. Pick the freshest examples you can find (though this isn't easy when labels mention no vintage).

Reuilly [rur-yee] (*Loire*, France) (Mostly) white *AC* for dry *Sauvignons*, good-value, if sometimes rather earthy alternatives to nearby *Sancerre* and *Pouilly-Fumé* and spicy *Pinot* rosé. *Henri Beurdin;* Bigonneau; *Lafond.*

�152 **Rex Hill Vineyards** (*Oregon*, US) Greatly improved *Pinot* specialist.

�152 **Chateau Reynella** [ray-nel-la] (*McLaren Vale*, Australia) *BRL Hardy* subsidiary, mastering both reds and whites. ☆☆☆☆ **Chateau Reynella Shiraz 1997 ££**

�152 **Ch. Reynon** [ray-non] (*Premier Côtes de Bordeaux*, France) Fine red and especially recommendable white wines from *Denis Dubourdieu*.

Rheingau [rine-gow] (Germany) Traditional home of the finest *Rieslings* of the 11 *Anbaugebiete*, but now often overshadowed by the *Pfalz* and *Mosel*. There are still great things to be found, however. QbA/Kab/Spät: **85 86 88 89 90** 92 93 94 95 96 97 98 Aus/Beeren/Tba: **83 85** 88 89 90 92 93 94 95 96 97 98 *Künstler; Balthasar Ress; Domdechant Werner'sches; HH Eser.*

Rheinhessen [rine-hehs-sen] (Germany) Largest of the 11 *Anbaugebiete*, now well known for *Liebfraumilch* and *Niersteiner*. Fewer than one vine in 20 is now *Riesling*; sadly, easier-to-grow varieties, and lazy cooperative wineries, generally prevail. There are a few stars, however. QbA/Kab/Spät: **85** 86 **88 89 90** 91 **92 93** 94 95 96 97 98 Aus/Beeren/Tba: **83 85 88 89 90** 91 92 93 94 95 96 97 98 *Balbach; Keller; Gunderloch.*

�152 **Rhône** [rohn] (France) Fast-improving, exciting, packed with increasingly sexy *Grenache, Syrah* and *Viognier* wines. See *St. Joseph, Crozes-Hermitage, Hermitage, Condrieu, Côtes du Rhône, Châteauneuf-du-Pape, Tavel, Lirac, Gigondas, Ch. Grillet, Beaumes de Venise*. White: **88 89 90** 91 **94** 95 96 97 98 Northern Rhône Red: **76 78 82 83 85 88** 89 90 91 95 96 Southern Rhône Red: **78 82 83 85 88** 89 **90 95** 96 97 98

�152 **Rias Baixas** [ree-yahs bi-shahs] (*Galicia*, Spain) The place to find spicy *Albariño*. **Lagar de Cervera;** *Pazo de Barrantes; Santiago Ruiz;* **Valdamor.**

�152 **Ribatejo** [ree-bah-tay-joh] (Portugal) *DO* area north of Lisbon where *Peter Bright* and the cooperatives are beginning to make highly commercial white and red wine, but traditional *Garrafeiras* are worth watching out for too.

�152 **Ribera del Duero** [ree-bay-rah del doo-way-roh] (Spain) One of the regions to watch in Spain for good reds. Unfortunately, despite the established success of *Vega Sicilia* and of producers like *Pesquera, Pingus, Arroyo,* and *Alion*, there is still far too much poor winemaking. 82 **83 85** 87 89 90 91 92 94 95 96 97 98 *Arroyo;* Pago de Carraovejas; Balbas; *Pesquera; Pedrosa; Pingus;* Hermanos Sastre; Valtravieso; *Vega Sicilia.*

�152 **Dom. Richeaume** [ree-shohm] (*Provence*, France) Dynamic producer of good, earthy, long-lived, organic *Cabernet* and *Syrah*. Sadly, as with many other smaller organic wineries, quality can vary from bottle to bottle. Recommendable, nonetheless. ☆☆☆☆ **1998 Cuvée Columelle Rouge £££**

Richebourg [reesh-boor] (*Burgundy*, France) Top-class *Grand Cru* vineyard just outside *Vosne-Romanée* with a recognisable floral-plummy style. 76 **78** 79 **80** 82 83 **85** 86 87 **88 89 90** 92 93 94 95 96 97 98 *Grivot;* Anne Gros; Leroy; Méo-Camuzet; D&D Mugneret; Noëllat; Romanée-Conti.

�152 **Richou** [ree-shoo] (*Loire,* France) Fine *Anjou* producer with reliable reds and whites and fine, affordable, sweet whites from Coteaux de l'Aubance.

Y Weingut Max Ferd Richter [rikh-tur] (*Mosel-Saar-Ruwer,* Germany) Excellent producer of long-lived concentrated-yet-elegant *Mosel Rieslings* from high-quality vineyards. The *cuvée* Constantin is the unusually successful dry wine, while at the other end of the scale, the *Eisweins* are sublime. ☆☆☆☆☆ **1997 Graacher Himmelreich Riesling Kabinett £££**

Y John Riddoch (South Australia) Classic *Wynn's Coonawarra* red. One of Australia's best and longest-lasting wines. (Not to be confused with the wines that *Katnook Estate* sells under its own "Riddoch" label.)

RIDGE
CALIFORNIA
ZINFANDEL
GEYSERVILLE
1985

83% ZINFANDEL, 10% PETITE SIRAH, 5% CARIGNANE
SONOMA COUNTY   ALCOHOL 13.3% BY VOLUME
PRODUCED AND BOTTLED BY RIDGE VINEYARDS, BW 4488
17100 MONTE BELLO RD, BOX A1, CUPERTINO, CALIFORNIA

Y Ridge Vineyards (*Santa Cruz,* California) Paul Draper, and Ridge's hilltop *Santa Cruz* and *Sonoma* vineyards, consistently produce some of California's very finest *Zinfandel, Cabernet, Mataro,* and *Chardonnay.* ☆☆☆☆☆ **1997 Ridge Geyserville Zinfandel ££££**

Y Riecine [ree-eh-chee-nay] (*Tuscany,* Italy) Modern estate with fine *Chiantis* and an even more impressive la Gioia *Vino da Tavola.*

℣ Riesling [reez-ling] The noble grape responsible for Germany's finest offerings, ranging from light, floral, everyday wines, to the delights of *botrytis*-affected sweet wines which retain their freshness for decades. Reaching its zenith in the superbly balanced racy wines of the *Mosel,* and the richer offerings from the *Rheingau,* it also performs well in *Alsace,* California, South Africa, and Australia. Watch out for the emergence of the *Wachau* region as a leader of the Austrian *Riesling* pack.

℣ Riesling Italico See *Italian Riesling,* etc.

Y Ch. Rieussec [ree-yur-sek] (*Sauternes Premier Cru Classé, Bordeaux,* France) Fantastically rich and concentrated *Sauternes,* often deep in colour and generally at the head of the pack chasing *d'Yquem.* Now owned by the Rothschilds of *Lafite.* R de Rieussec is the unexceptional dry white wine. **75** 79 82 **83 85 86** 88 89 90 92 93 94 95 **96** 97 98 99

Rioja [ree-ok-hah] (Spain) Spain's best-known wine region is split into three parts. The Alta produces the best wines, followed by the Alavesa, while the Baja is by far the largest. Most Riojas are blends made by large *bodegas* using grapes grown in two or three of the regions. Small *Bordeaux*- and *Burgundy*-style estates are rare, thanks to restrictive Spanish rules which require wineries to store unnecessarily large quantities of wine. Things are happening in the vineyards, however, including plantings of "experimental" *Cabernet* alongside the traditional *Tempranillo* and lesser-quality *Garnacha.* Such behaviour breaks all sorts of local rules – as does the irrigation which is also now in evidence – but is already paying off for producers like *Martinez Bujanda.* With luck, this kind of innovative thinking will help the region as a whole to live up to its reputation. Reds: **79 80 81** 82 **83 85 87** 89 90 91 92 94 95 *Amézola de la Mora; Ardanza; Artadi; Baron de Ley; Berberana; Breton; Campillo; Campo Viejo; Contino; El Coto; Lopez de Heredia; Marqués de Griñon; Marqués de Murrieta; Marqués de Riscal; Marqués de Vargas; Martinez Bujanda; Montecillo; Ondarre; Palacio; Remelluri; La Rioja Alta; Riojanos.*

☿ **La Rioja Alta** [ree-ok-hah ahl-ta] (*Rioja,* Spain) Of all the big companies in *Rioja,* this is the name to remember. Its Viña Ardanza, Reserva 904, and (rarely produced) Reserva 890 are all among the most reliable and recommendable wines in the region. ☆☆☆ **1990 Viña Ardanza Reserva £££**

☿ **Dom. Daniel Rion** [ree-yon] (*Burgundy,* France) Patrice Rion produces impeccably made modern Nuits-St.-Georges and Vosne-Romanées. ☆☆☆☆ **1996 Vosne-Romanee Les Beaux Monts £££**

Ripasso [ree-pas-soh] (*Veneto,* Italy) Method whereby newly made *Valpolicella* is partially refermented in vessels recently vacated by *Recioto* and *Amarone.* Ripasso wines made in this way are richer, alcoholic, and raisiny. Increases the *alcohol* and *body* of the wine. *Tedeschi; Quintarelli; Masi.*

☿ **Marqués de Riscal** [ris-kahl] (*Rioja,* Spain) Historic *Rioja* name now back on form thanks to more modern winemaking for both reds and whites. The Baron de Chirel is the recently launched top wine. ☆☆☆☆☆ **1996 Reserva £££**

Riserva [ree-zEHr-vah] (Italy) *DOC* wines aged for a specified number of years – often an unwelcome term on labels of wines like *Bardolino,* which are usually far better drunk young.

❦ **Rivaner** [rih-vah-nur] (Germany) The name used for *Müller-Thurgau* (a cross between *Riesling* and *Sylvaner*) in parts of Germany and *Luxembourg.*

☿ **Rivera** [ree-vay-ra] (*Puglia,* Italy) One of the new wave of producers who are turning the southern region of *Puglia* into a source of interesting wines. The red Riserva il Falcone is the star wine here.

Riverina [rih-vur-ee-na] (*New South Wales,* Australia) Irrigated *New South Wales* region which produces basic-to-good wine, much of which ends up in *"South-East Australian"* blends. Late harvest *Semillons* can, however, be surprisingly spectacular. *Cranswick Estate, McWilliams.*

☿ **Rivesaltes** [reev-zalt] (*Languedoc-Roussillon,* France) Fortified dessert wine of both colours. The white made from the *Muscat* is lighter and more lemony than *Beaumes de Venise,* while the *Grenache* red is like liquid Christmas pudding and ages wonderfully. *Cazes;* Ch. de Corneilla; *Força Réal;* Ch. de Jau; *Sarda-Malet.*

☿ **Giorgio Rivetti** [ree-VAY-tee] (*Piedmont,* Italy) Star producer of wonderfully aromatic Moscato d'Asti, *Barberesco* and *Barbera.*

Riviera Ligure di Ponente [reev-ee-yeh-ra lee-goo-ray dee poh-nen-tay] (*Liguria,* Italy) Little-known northwestern region, close to Genoa, where local grapes like the *Vermentino* produce light aromatic reds and whites.

Robertson (South Africa) Warm area where *Chardonnays* and *Sauvignons* are taking over from the *Muscats* that used to be the region's pride. *Graham Beck; Springfield;* Robertson Winery; *Van Loveren;* Weltevrede.

☿ **Rocche dei Manzoni** [rok-keh day-yee mant-zoh-nee] (*Piedmont,* Italy) The Nebbiolo-Barbera Bricco Manzoni is the top wine here, but the single-vineyard *Barolo* is good too and there's some lovely *Chardonnay.*

☿ **Rocca delle Macie** [ro-ka del leh mah-chee-yay] (*Tuscany,* Italy) Reliable if unspectacular *Chianti* producer.

☿ **La Roche aux Moines** [rosh oh mwahn] See *Nicolas Joly.*

☿ **Joe Rochioli** [roh-kee-yoh-lee] (*Sonoma,* California) Brilliant *Russian River Pinot Noir* and *Chardonnay* producer whose name also appears on single-vineyard wines from *Williams Selyem.*

ℹ Rockford (*Barossa Valley*, Australia) Robert "Rocky" O'Callaghan makes a great intense *Barossa Shiraz* using 100-year-old vines and 50-year-old equipment. There's a mouthfilling *Semillon*, a wonderful Black *Shiraz* sparkling wine, and a magical *Alicante Bouschet* rosé, which is sadly only to be found at the winery. ☆☆☆☆ **1997 Basket Press Shiraz, Barossa Valley £££**

ℹ Antonin Rodet [on-toh-nan roh-day] (*Burgundy*, France) Very impressive *Mercurey*-based *négociant*, which has also improved the wines of the *Jacques Prieur domaine* in *Meursault*. **Ch. de Chamery; de Rully.**

ℹ Louis Roederer [roh-dur-rehr] (*Champagne*, France) Family-owned, and still one of the most reliable *Champagne* houses, whose delicious non-vintage wine benefits from being cellared for a few years. Roederer's prestige Cristal remains a most deliciously "wine-like" *Champagne*.
☆☆☆☆☆ **1990 Cristal ££££**

Roederer Estate [roh-dur-rehr] (*Mendocino,* California) No longer involved with the *Jansz* sparkling wine in *Tasmania* but making top-class wine in California which is sold in the US as Roederer Estate and in the UK as Quartet. ☆☆☆☆ **Quartet Anderson Valley £££**

ℹ Roero [roh-weh-roh] (*Piedmont,* Italy) *Nebbiolo* red and *Arneis* white (sold as Roero Arneis) which are now among Italy's most interesting wines. *Ceretto; Bruno Giacosa; Prunotto;* **Serafino; Vietti.**

Michel Rolland [roh-lon] Based in *Pomerol, St. Emilion,* and now increasingly international guru-oenologist, whose taste for ripe fruit flavours is influencing wines from *Ch. Ausone* to Argentina and beyond.

ℹ Rolly-Gassmann [rroh-lee gas-sman] (*Alsace,* France) Fine producer of subtle, long-lasting wines which are sometimes slightly marred by an excess of *sulphur dioxide.*

ℹ Dom. de la Romanée-Conti [rroh-ma-nay kon-tee] (*Burgundy,* France) Aka "DRC". Small *Grand Cru* estate. The jewel in the crown is the Romanée-Conti vineyard itself, though *La Tâche* runs it a close second. Both can be extraordinary, ultra-concentrated spicy wine, as can the *Romanée-St.-Vivant.* The *Richebourg, Echézeaux,* and *Grands Echézeaux* and *Montrachet* are comparable to those produced by other estates – and sold by them for less kingly ransoms. ☆☆☆☆☆ **1996 Romanée St Vivant ££££**

Romania Traditional source of sweet reds and whites, now developing drier styles from classic European varieties. *Flying winemakers* are helping, as is the owner of the *Comte Peraldi* estate in *Corsica. Note* that Romania's well-praised *Pinot Noirs* may be made from a different variety, mistaken for the *Pinot.*

🍇 Romarantin [roh-ma-ron-tan] (*Loire,* France) Interesting, limey grape found in obscure white blends in the *Loire.* See *Cheverny.*

Römerlay [rrur-mehr-lay] (*Mosel,* Germany) One of the *Grosslagen* in the *Ruwer* river valley. QbA/Kab/Spät: **85** 86 **88 89 90** 91 **92 93 94** 95 96 97 98 99 Aus/Beeren/Tba: **83 85** 88 89 90 91 **92 93 94** 95 96 97 98 99

ℹ Ronchi di Manzano [ron-kee dee mant-zoh-noh] (*Friuli-Venezia Giulia,* Italy) Famed in Italy for its *Merlot* (Ronc di Subule), this producer's most interesting wine may well be its rich white *Picolit.*

ℹ Ronco del Gnemiz [ron-koh del gneh-meez] (*Friuli-Venezia Giulia,* Italy) One of the world's few producers of great *Müller-Thurgau,* and some pretty good *Chardonnay* in the *Colli Orientali.*

ℹ Ronco delle Betulle [ron-koh deh-leh beh-too-leh] (*Friuli-Venezia Giulia,* Italy) Try the *Bordeaux*-blend Narciso here – or the *Tocai Friulano, Sauvignon, Pinot Bianco* or *Grigio.* You won't be disappointed.

� **Rongopai** [ron-goh-pi] (*Te Kauwhata,* New Zealand) Estate in a region of the North Island pioneered by *Cooks,* but which has fallen out of favour with that company and with other producers. The speciality here is *botrytis* wines, but the *Chardonnay* is good too.

☰ **La Rosa** (Chile) One of the fastest-growing wineries in Chile, with new vineyards and great winemaking from *Ignacio Recabarren.* Las Palmeras is a *second label.* ☆☆☆☆ 1999 Viña la Rosa La Palmeria Chardonnay £££

☰ **Quinta de la Rosa** (*Douro,* Portugal) Recently established estate producing excellent port and exemplary dry red wine, under guidance from David Baverstock, Australian-born former winemaker at *Dow's* and responsible for the wines of *Esperao.* ☆☆☆☆ 1998 Douro Tinto £££
Rosato (Italy) Rosé.

☰ **Rosé d'Anjou** [roh-zay don-joo] (*Loire,* France) Usually dull, semi-sweet pink from the *Malbec, Groslot* and (less usually) *Cabernet Franc.*

☰ **Rosé de Loire** [roh-zay duh-lwahr] (*Loire,* France) The wine *Rosé d'Anjou* ought to be. Dry, fruity stuff. *Richou;* Cave des Vignerons de Saumur.

☰ **Rosé de Riceys** [roh-zay dur ree-say] (*Champagne,* France) Rare and occasionally delicious still rosé from the *Pinot Noir.* Pricy. Alexandre Bonnet.

☰ **Rosemount Estate** (*Hunter Valley,* Australia) Ultradynamic company which introduced the world to *oaky Hunter Chardonnay* with its Show Reserve and Roxburgh. Reliably good-value blends from other areas have followed, including impressive *Syrahs* and *Chardonnays* from the newly developed region of *Orange* and *Mountain Blue from Mudgee.* ☆☆☆☆ 1998 GSM £££; ☆☆☆☆☆ 1999 Orange Vineyard Shiraz £££

☰ **Rosenblum** (*Alameda,* California) Terrific characterful *Zinfandels* from a wide variety of individual vineyards in *Napa, Sonoma, Contra Costa,* and *Paso Robles.* There are also some great multi-regional Californian blends.

☰ **Rossese di Dolceaqua** [ros-seh-seh di dohl-chay-ah-kwah] (*Liguria,* Italy) Attractive, generally early-drinking wines made from the Rossese. Single-vineyard examples like Terre Bianche's Bricco Arcagna are more serious.

☰ **Dom. Rossignol-Trapet** [ros-seen-yol tra-pay] (*Burgundy,* France) Once old-fashioned, now more recommendable estate in *Gevrey-Chambertin.*

☰ **Rosso Conero** [ros-doh kon-neh-roh] (*Marches,* Italy) Big, *Montepulciano* and *Sangiovese* red, with a rich, herby flavour. Good-value characterful stuff. ☆☆☆☆ 1995 Umani Ronchi Cumaro £££

☰ **Rosso di Montalcino** [ros-soh dee mon-tal-chee-noh] (*Tuscany,* Italy) *DO* for lighter, earlier-drinking versions of the more famous *Brunello di Montalcino.* Often better – and better value – than that wine. 82 85 88 90 91 93 **94** 95 96 97 98 *Altesino; Caparzo;* Fattoria dei Barbi; Talenti.

☰ **Rosso Piceno** [ros-soh pee-chay-noh] (*Marche,* Italy) Traditionally rustic red made from a blend of the *Montepulciano* and *Sangiovese.*

☰ **René Rostaing** [ros-tang] (*Rhône,* France) Producer of serious northern *Rhône* reds, including a (somewhat) more affordable alternative to *Guigal's* la Landonne. ☆☆☆☆ 1996 Côte Rôtie la Côte Blonde £££

☥ **Rothbury Estate** (*Hunter Valley,* Australia) Founded by Len Evans, Svengali of the Australian wine industry and now – via *Mildara* – a subsidiary of Fosters, this is a great source of *Shiraz, Semillon,* and *Chardonnay* from the *Hunter Valley.* There are also wines from nearby *Cowra* and first-class *Sauvignon* from the bit of the estate that surfaces in *Marlborough,* New Zealand.
    ☆☆☆☆ 1998 Brokenback Shiraz £££

☥ **Joseph Roty** [roh-tee] (*Burgundy,* France) Superstar producer of a range of intensely concentrated but unsubtle wines in *Gevrey-Chambertin.*
    ☆☆☆☆ 1995 Charmes-Chambertin ££££

☥ **Rouge Homme** (*Coonawarra,* Australia) Founded by the linguistically talented *Mr. Redman,* but now under the same ownership as *Penfolds* and *Lindemans.* This is increasingly one of the most reliable producers in *Coonawarra.* ☆☆☆☆ 1998 Shiraz-Cabernet £££

☥ **Dom. Guy Roulot** [roo-loh] (*Burgundy,* France) One of the greatest *domaines* in *Meursault.* ☆☆☆☆ 1997 Meursault Perrières £££

☥ **Georges Roumier** [roo-me-yay] (*Burgundy,* France) Blue-chip winery with great quality at every level, from village *Chambolle-Musigny* to the *Grand Cru,* Bonnes Mares, and (more rarely seen) white *Corton-Charlemagne.* ☆☆☆☆ 1996 Bonnes Mares ££££

☥ **Round Hill** (*Napa,* California) A rare source of Californian bargains. Large-production, inexpensive *Merlots* and *Chardonnays* that outclass many a pricier offering from smart boutique wineries.

☘ **Roussanne** [roos-sahn] (*Rhône,* France) With the *Marsanne,* one of the key white grapes of the northern *Rhône.*

☥ **Armand Rousseau** [roos-soh] (*Burgundy,* France) *Gevrey-Chambertin* estate on top form with a range of *Premiers* and *Grands Crus.* Well-made, long-lasting wines. ☆☆☆☆ 1997 Chambertin ££££

☘ **Roussette de Savoie** [roo-sette] (*Savoie,* France) The local name for the equally local Altesse grape. Fresh, easy-drinking fare.

Roussillon [roos-see-yon] (*Languedoc-Roussillon,* France) Vibrant up-and-coming region, redefining traditional varieties, especially *Muscat.*

☥ **Ch. Routas** [roo-tahs] (*Provence,* France) Impressive producer of intense reds and whites in the *Coteaux Varois.* 1995 Rouvier £££

☥ **Royal Oporto Wine Co.** (*Douro,* Portugal) Occasionally (very occasionally) successful, large producer.

☥ **The Royal Tokaji Wine Co.** (*Tokaji,* Hungary) Recently-founded company that has – with other foreign investors – helped to drag *Tokaji* into the late 20th century with great single-vineyard wines.
    ☆☆☆☆ 1993 Aszú 4 Puttonyos £££

☥ **Rozendal Farm** [roh-zen-dahl] (*Stellenbosch,* South Africa) Impeccably made, organic, Bordeaux-style reds from a producer whose quality consciousness made him decide not to release the 1997 vintage.

☥ **Rubesco di Torgiano** [roo-bes-koh dee taw-jee-yah-noh] (*Umbria,* Italy) Modern red *DOCG*; more or less the exclusive creation of *Lungarotti.*
    ☆☆☆ 1990 Vigna Monticchio Riserva £££

☥ **Rubino** [roo-bee-noh] (*Umbria,* Italy) Rich "Super-Umbrian" red from the la Pazzola estate. Matches many a *Super Tuscan.*

Ruby (*Douro,* Portugal) Cheapest, basic *port*; young, blended, sweetly fruity.

☘ **Ruby Cabernet** [roo-bee ka-behr-nay] (California) A *Cabernet Sauvignon* and *Carignan* cross producing unsubtly fruity wines in California, Australia, and South Africa.

☘ **Ruche** [roo-kay] (*Piedmont,* Italy) Raspberryish red grape from northern Italy producing early-drinking wines. Best from *Bava.*

Rüdesheim [rroo-des-hime] (*Rheingau*, Germany) Tourist town producing powerful *Rieslings*. QbA/Kab/Spät: **85** 86 **88 89 90** 91 **92 93** 94 95 96 97 98 Aus/Beeren/Tba: **83 85 88 89** 90 91 92 93 94 95 96 97 98 99 *Georg Breuer; August Kesseler; Josef Leitz; Schloss Schönborn; Staatsweingüter Kloster Eberbach*

☖ **Rueda** [roo-way-dah] (Spain) *DO* in northwest Spain for clean, dry whites from the local *Verdejo*. Progress is being led most particularly by the *Lurtons, Marqués de Riscal* and *Marqués de Griñon*.

☖ **Ruffino** [roof-fee-noh] (*Tuscany*, Italy) Big *Chianti* producer with impressive top-of-the-range wines, including the reliable *Cabreo Vino da Tavola*. **93 94** 95 96 97 98 ☆☆☆☆ **1993 Riserva Ducale Gold £££**

Rufina [roo-fee-na] (*Tuscany*, Italy) A subregion within *Chianti*, producing supposedly classier wine. **78 79** 81 **82 85 88 90** 94 95 96 97 98

☖ **Ruinart** [roo-wee-nahr] (*Champagne*, France) High-quality sister to *Moët & Chandon*, with superlative *Blanc de Blancs*. ☆☆☆☆☆ **1995 R. de Ruinart £££**

🍇 **Rülander** [roo-len-dur] (Germany) German name for *Pinot Gris*.

☖ **Rully** [roo-yee] (*Burgundy*, France) *Côte Chalonnaise commune* producing rich white and a red that's been called the "poor man's" *Volnay*. See *Antonin Rodet, Jadot* and *Olivier Leflaive*. Red: 86 87 **88 89 90** 92 95 96 97 98 White: **85 88** 89 **90 92** 95 96 97 98 *Faiveley;* Jacqueson; *Jadot; Olivier Leflaive; Antonin Rodet.*

Ruppertsberg [roo-purt-sbehrg] (*Pfalz*, Germany) Top-ranking village with a number of excellent vineyards making vigorous fruity *Riesling*. QbA/Kab/Spät: **88 89 90** 91 **92 93** 94 95 96 97 98 Aus/Beeren/ Tba: 83 85 88 89 90 91 92 93 94 95 96 97 98 99 *Bürklin-Wolf; Kimich;* Werlé.

☖ **la Rural** [lah roo-rahl] (*Mendoza*, Argentina) Old-established producer, now making good, commercial wines. The Malbec is the strongest card.

☖ **Rusden** (*Barossa*, South Australia) Small, new estate gaining instant recognition in the US for its rich Barossa Cabernets and Grenaches.

Russe [rooss] (Bulgaria) Danube town best known in Britain for its reliable red blends but vaunted in *Bulgaria* as a source of modern whites.

Russian River Valley (California) Cult, cool-climate area to the north of *Sonoma* and west of *Napa*. Ideal for apples and good sparkling wine, as is proven by the excellent *Iron Horse*, which also makes impressive table wines. Great *Pinot Noir* country. Red: **90 91 92** 93 95 96 97 98 99 White: 92 **95** 96 97 98 *Dehlinger; de Loach; Iron Horse; Kistler; Martinelli; Rochioli; Sonoma-Cutrer;* Joseph Swann; *Marimar Torres; Williams Selyem.*

Rust [roost] (*Burgenland*, Austria) Wine centre of *Burgenland*, famous for Ruster *Ausbruch* sweet white wine.

☖ **Rust-en-Vrede** (*Stellenbosch*, South Africa) Well-regarded producer but could improve. ☆☆☆ **1996 Estate Red ££**

Rustenberg (*Stellenbosch,* South Africa) On a roll since 1996 with investment in the cellars (which put an end to musty flavours encountered in previous vintages) this is now a leading light in the Cape. The lower-priced Brampton efforts are quite good too, but are decidedly less reliable. ☆☆☆☆ **1999 Stellenbosch Chardonnay £££**

Rutherford (California) *Napa* region in which some producers believe sufficiently to propose it – and its geological "bench" – as an *appellation*.
Red: **85** 86 87 **90 91** 92 **93 95** 96 97 98 White: **90 91** 92 **94 95** 96 97 98 99

Rutherglen (*Victoria,* Australia) Hot area on the *Murray River* pioneered by gold miners. Today noted for rich *Muscat* and *Tokay* dessert and *port*-style wines.The reds are often tough and the *Chardonnays* are used by cool-region winemakers to demonstrate why *port* and light dry whites are hard to make in the same climate. *All Saints; Campbells; Chambers; Morris; Pfeiffer; Seppelt; Stanton & Killeen.*

Ruwer [roo-vur] (*Mosel-Saar-Ruwer,* Germany) *Mosel* tributary alongside which is to be found the *Römerlay Grosslage,* and includes Kasel, *Eitelsbach* and the great *Maximin Grünhaus* estate. QbA/Kab/Spät: **85** 86 **88 89 90 92 93 94** 95 96 97 98 Aus/Beeren/Tba: 83 **85 88 89 90 92** 93 94 95 **96 97 98**

Hugh Ryman [ri-man] *Flying winemaker* whose team turns grapes into wine under contract in *Bordeaux, Burgundy,* southern France, Spain, Germany, Moldova, Chile, California, South Africa, and Hungary. Wines tend to bear the initials HDR at the foot of the label – or one of Ryman's own brands: Santara, Kirkwood, Richemont, Rafael Estate.

Rymill [ri-mil] (South Australia) One of several *Coonawarra* wineries to mention *Riddoch* on its label (in its Riddoch Run) and a rising star. Rymill at least has the legitimacy of a family link to *John Riddoch,* the region's founder. The *Shiraz* and *Cabernet* are first class, as are the whites and the sparkling wine. ☆☆☆☆ **1997 Shiraz £££**

S

Saale-Unstrut [zah-luhr oon-struht] (Germany) Remember East Germany? Well, this is where poor wines used to be made there in the bad old days. Today good ones are being produced, by producers like Lützkendorf.

Saar [zahr] (*Mosel-Saar-Ruwer,* Germany) The other *Mosel* tributary associated with lean, slatey *Riesling.* Villages include *Ayl, Ockfen,* Saarburg, Serrig, *Wiltingen.* QbA/Kab/Spät: **85 88 89 90** 91 **92 93** 94 95 96 97 98 Aus/Beeren/Tba: **83 85 88 89 90** 91 92 93 94 95 96 97 98 99

Sablet [sa-blay] (*Rhône,* France) Good *Côtes du Rhône* village. Red: **78** 81 **82 83 85 88** 89 **90 95** 96 97 98 99

♈ **Sachsen** [zak-sen] (Germany) Revived former East German region where Klaus Seifert is producing good *Riesling.*

♈ **St. Amour** [san ta-moor] (*Burgundy,* France) One of the ten *Beaujolais Crus* – usually light and fruity. 94 95 **96 97** 98 **Billards; la Cave Lamartine; Duboeuf; Patissier; Revillon.**

♈ **St. Aubin** [san toh-ban] (*Burgundy,* France) Underrated *Côte d'Or* village for (jammily rustic) reds and rich, nutty, rather classier white; affordable alternatives to *Meursault.* White: **86 88** 89 **90 92 95 96** 97 98 Red: **85** 86 87 **88 89 90** 92 95 96 97 98 *Jean-Claude Bachelet; Champy; Marc Colin;* Hubert Lamy-Monnot; *Olivier Leflaive;* Henri Prudhon; *Ch de Puligny-Montrachet;* Roux Père et Fils; Gérard Thomas.

♈ **St. Bris** [san bree] (*Burgundy,* France) Best-known for its VDQS *Sauvignon de St Bris,* this village close to *Chablis* can also make unusually good examples of the *Aligoté grape. Jean-Marc Brocard; la Chablisienne;* Joel et David Griffe; St Prix; Sorin Defrance.

♈ **St. Chinian** [san shee-nee-yon] (*South-West,* France) Neighbour of *Faugères* in the *Coteaux du Languedoc,* producing mid-weight wines from *Carignan* and other *Rhône* grapes. **Ch. des Albières; de Astide Rousse; Babeau; Mas Champart; Clos Bagatelle; Canet-Valette; Cazel-Viel; Coujan; Cooperative de Roquebrun; Mas de la Tour; Maurel Fonsalade; Ch. Quartironi de Sars.**

♈ **St. Clement** (*Napa Valley,* California) Japanese-owned winery whose best wine is the Oroppas red blend. In case you were wondering, the name isn't a Native American word, but that of the owner spelled backward.

♈ **St. Emilion** [san tay-mee-lee-yon] (*Bordeaux,* France) Large *commune* with varied soils and wines. At best, sublime *Merlot*-dominated *claret*; at worst dull, earthy and fruitless. 170 or so *"Grand Cru"* St. Emilions are made in better-sited vineyards and have to undergo a tasting every vintage to be able to use these words on their labels and too few fail. *Grand Cru Classé* refers to 68 *châteaux,* of which two – *Ausone* and *Cheval-Blanc* – are rated as *"Premier Grands Crus Classés"* and 11 are *"Premiers Grands Crus Classés B".* These ratings are reviewed every decade. Supposedly "lesser" satellite neighbours – *Lussac, Puisseguin, St. Georges* etc. – often make better value wine than basic St. Emilion. **70 75** 78 79 81 **82 83 85** 86 **88 89** 90 94 95 96 97 98 99 *Angelus; Ausone;* Beau-Séjour-Bécot; *Beauséjour; Belair; Canon; Canon la Gaffelière; Cheval Blanc; Clos des Jacobins; Clos Fourtet; Figeac; Franc Mayne; Grand Mayne; Larcis Ducasse; Magdelaine; la Mondotte; Pavie; Tertre Roteboeuf; Troplong-Mondot; Trottevieille; Valandraud.*

St. Estèphe [san teh-stef] (*Bordeaux*, France) Northernmost *Médoc commune* with clay soil and wines which can be a shade more rustic than those of neighbouring *Pauillac* and *St. Julien*, but which are often longer-lived and more structured than some of the juicy, easy-to-drink *St. Emilions* and *Pomerols* that tend to win approval from critics. **78 82 83 85 86** 88 89 90 92 93 94 95 96 97 98 **Calon-Ségur; Cos d'Estournel; Haut-Marbuzet; Lafon-Rochet; Marbuzet; Montrose; de Pez; Ormes de Pez; Phélan-Ségur.**

St. Francis (*Sonoma*, California) Innovative winery with great *Zinfandels*, and Reserve *Chardonnays* and *Cabernets*. The first Californian to introduce artificial corks to protect wine drinkers from faulty bottles. ☆☆☆☆ **1996 Cabernet Sauvignon £££;** ☆☆☆☆ **1997 Zinfandel £££**

St. Georges-St.Emilion [san jorrzh san tay-mee-lee-yon] (*Bordeaux*, France) Satellite of *St. Emilion* with good *Merlot*-dominant reds, often better value than *St. Emilion* itself. **Ch. Maquin St. Georges; St. Georges.**

St. Hallett (*Barossa Valley*, Australia) Superstar *Barossa* winery specialising in wines from old ("old block") *Shiraz* vines. Whites (especially *Semillon* and *Riesling*) are good too. ☆☆☆☆ **1998 Blackwell Shiraz £££**

St. Hubert's (*Victoria*, Australia) Pioneering *Yarra* winery with ultra-fruity *Cabernet* and mouth-filling *Roussanne* whites. ☆☆☆☆ **1996 Roussanne ££**

Chateau St. Jean [jeen] (*Sonoma*, California) Named after the founder's wife; now Japanese-owned and a source of good single-vineyard *Chardonnays*, late harvest *Rieslings* and *Bordeaux*-style reds. ☆☆☆☆ **1996 Robert Young Vineyard Chardonnay £££**

St. Joseph [san joh-sef] (*Rhône*, France) Potentially vigorous, fruity *Syrah* from the northern *Rhône*. Whites range from flabby to fragrant *Marsannes*. Red: **82 83 85 88** 89 **90** 91 **95** 96 97 98 **Chapoutier; Chave; Courbis; Coursodon; Cuilleron; Delas; de Fauturie; Gacho-Pascal; Gaillard; Graillot; Gripa; Grippat; Perret; Pichon; St.-Désirat; Trollo; Vernay.**

St. Julien [san-joo-lee-yen] (*Bordeaux*, France) Aristocratic *Médoc commune* producing classic rich wines, full of cedar and deep, ripe fruit. 70 75 76 **78** 79 81 **82** 83 **85 86** 88 89 90 94 95 96 97 98 99 **Beychevelle; Branaire; Ducru-Beaucaillou; Gruaud-Larose; Lagrange; Langoa-Barton; Léoville-Barton; Léoville-Las-Cases; Léoville-Poyferré; Talbot.**

St. Laurent [sant loh-rent] (Austria) *Pinot Noir*-like berryish red grape, mastered, in particular, by *Umathum*.

St. Nicolas de Bourgueil [san nee-koh-lah duh boor-goy] (*Loire*, France) Lightly fruity *Cabernet Franc*; needs a warm year to ripen its raspberry fruit, but then can last for up to a decade. Lighter than *Bourgueil*. **Yannick Amirault; Caslot; Max Cognard; Delauney; Druet; Jamet; Mabileau; Vallée.**

St. Péray [san pay-reh] (*Rhône*, France) AC near *Lyon* for full-bodied, still white and *méthode champenoise* sparkling wine, at risk from encroaching housing. **J-F Chapoud; Auguste Clape; Bernard Gripa; Marcel Juge; Jean Lionnet; Alain Voge.**

Ch. St. Pierre [san pee-yehr] (*St. Julien 4ème Cru Classé, Bordeaux*, France) Reliable *St. Julien* under the same ownership as *Ch. Gloria*.

♆ St. Romain [san roh-man] (*Burgundy*, France) *Hautes Côtes de Beaune* village producing undervalued fine whites and rustic reds. **Christophe Buisson; Chassorney; Germain et Fils; Iain Gras;** *Jaffelin;* **Thévenin-Monthélie.**

♆ St. Véran [san vay-ron] (*Burgundy*, France) Once sold as *Beaujolais Blanc*; affordable alternative to *Pouilly-Fuissé*; better than most *Mâconnais* whites. Ch. Fuissé is first class. White: **92 93 94 95 96** 97 **98 99** *Barraud; Corsin;* **Dom des Deux Roches;** *Duboeuf; Ch. Fuissé;* **Luquet; Pacquet.**

♆ Ste. Croix-du-Mont [sant crwah doo mon] (*Bordeaux*, France) Never as luscious, rich and complex as the better efforts of its neighbour *Sauternes* – but often a far more worthwhile buy than wines unashamedly sold under that name. Sweet white: **88 90 92 93 94 95 96** 97 98

♆ Saintsbury (*Carneros*, California) Superstar *Carneros* producer of unfiltered *Chardonnay* and – more specially – *Pinot Noir*. The slogan: "Beaune in the USA" refers to the winery's Burgundian aspirations! The Reserve *Pinot* is a world-beater, while the easy-going Garnet is the good *second label.* ☆☆☆☆ **1997 Carneros Pinot Noir £££**

Sakar [sa-kah] (Bulgaria) Long-time source of much of the best *Cabernet Sauvignon* to come from *Bulgaria.*

♆ Castello della Sala [kas-tel-loh del-la sah-lah] (*Umbria*, Italy) *Antinori's* over-priced but sound *Chardonnay, Sauvignon.* Also good *Sauvignon*/Procanico blend. ☆☆☆☆ **1996 Sauvignon della Sala ££**

♆ Ch de Sales [duh sahl] (*Pomerol, Bordeaux*) Good but generally unexciting wine for relatively early drinking. Also worth looking out for is Stonyfell, which matches rich Shiraz flavours with an appealingly "retro" label. ☆☆☆☆ **1998 Mamre Brook Chardonnay £££; 1997 No.1 Shiraz £££**

♆ Salice Salentino [sa-lee-chay sah-len-tee-noh] (*Puglia*, Italy) Spicy, intense red made from the characterful *Negroamaro.* Great value, especially when mature. *Candido; Leone de Castris;* **Taurino; Vallone.**

♆ Salomon-Undhof [sah-loh-mon oond-hohf] (*Kremstal*, Austria) Top class producer, with especially notable *Riesling.*

♆ Salon le Mesnil [sah-lon lur may-neel] (*Champagne*, France) Small, traditional subsidiary of *Laurent Perrier* with cult following for pure long-lived *Chardonnay Champagne.* Only sold as a single-vintage cuvée.

♆ Saltram [sawl-tram] (South Australia) Fast-improving part of the *Mildara-Blass* empire. Rich, fairly priced *Barossa* reds and whites (also under the Mamre Brook label) and top-flight *"ports".* ☆☆☆☆ **1996 No 1 Shiraz £££**

♆ Samos [sah-mos] (Greece) Aegean island producing sweet, fragrant, golden *Muscat* once called "the wine of the Gods".

♆ Cellier des Samsons [sel-yay day som-son] (*Burgundy*, France) Source of better-than-average *Beaujolais.*

San Luis Obispo [san loo-wis oh-bis-poh] (California) Californian region gaining a reputation for *Chardonnay* and *Pinot Noir.* Try *Edna Valley.* Red: 84 **85** 86 87 **90 91** 92 **93 95** 96 97 98 White: 92 **95 96** 97 98

⟁ **Viña San Pedro** [veen-ya san-pay-droh] (*Curico*, Chile) Huge *Curico* firm whose wines are quietly and steadily improving thanks to the efforts of consultant *Jacques Lurton*. ☆☆☆☆ 1997 Cabo de Hornos Cabernet Sauvignon £££

⟁ **Sancerre** [son-sehr] (*Loire*, France) At its best, the epitome of elegant, steely dry *Sauvignon*; at its worst, oversulphured and fruitless. Reds and rosés, though well regarded and highly priced by French restaurants, are often little better than quaffable *Pinot Noir*. 90 94 **95 96 97** 98 99 Bailly-Reverdy; Jean-Paul Balland; *Henri Bourgeois;* Cotat; Lucien Crochet; Vincent Delaporte; Pierre Dézat; Fouassier; de la Garenne; Gitton; les Grands Groux; *Pascal Jolivet; de Ladoucette;* Serge Laporte; Mellot; Thierry Merlin-Cherrier; Paul Millerioux; Natter; Vincent Pinard; Jean-Max Roger; *Vacheron;* André Vatan.

⟁ **Sanchez Romate** (*Jerez*, Spain) Top quality, old-established sherry producer with delicious NPU (Non Plus Ultra) Amontillado.

⟁ **Sandeman** (Spain/Portugal) North American-owned, generally under-performing but occasionally dazzling *port* and *sherry* producer. Port: 55 57 58 **60 62 63** 65 66 67 68 **70** 72 75 80 94 97 ☆☆☆☆☆ Royal Corregidor Sherry £££

⟁ **Sanford Winery** (*Santa Barbara*, California) *Santa Barbara* superstar producer of *Chardonnay* and especially distinctive, slightly horseradishy *Pinot Noir*. ☆☆☆☆ 1997 Pinot Noir Sanford & Benedict Vineyard £££

🍇 **Sangiovese** [san-jee-yoh vay-seh] (Italy) The tobaccoey, herby-flavoured red grape of *Chianti* and *Montepulciano*, now being used increasingly in *Vino da Tavola* and – though rarely impressively – in California. *Antinori; Atlas Peak; Bonny Doon; Isole e Olena.*

⟁ **Castello di San Polo in Rosso** [san-poh-loh in -ros-soh] (*Tuscany*, Italy) Reliable, quite traditional *Chianti Classico* estate.

⟁ **Luciano Sandrone** [loo-chee-yah-noh sahn-droh-nay] (*Piedmont*. Italy) With fellow revolutionaries *Clerico*, *Roberto Voerzio* and *Altare*, Luciano Sandrone has spearheaded the move to modern *Barolo*. Great *Dolcetto* too.

Santa Barbara (California) Successful southern, cool-climate region for *Pinot Noir* and *Chardonnay*. *Au Bon Climat; Byron; Ojai; Qupé; Sanford.*

⟁ **Viña Santa Carolina** [ka-roh-lee-na] (Chile) Greatly improved producer, thanks to *Ignacio Recabarren* and vineyards in *Casablanca*. Good reds. ☆☆☆☆☆ 1999 Santa Carolina Barrica Selection Chardonnay £££

Santa Cruz Mountains [krooz] (California) Exciting region to the south of San Francisco. See *Ridge* and *Bonny Doon*. Red: 84 **85** 86 87 **90 91** 92 **93** 95 **96** 97 98 White: **91** 92 95 96 97 98 99

🍷 **Santa Emiliana** (*Aconcagua*, Chile) Large producer with good Andes Peak offerings from *Casablanca*, and wines from the new southern region of Mulchen. ☆☆☆☆ **1999 Andes Peak Cabernet Sauvignon ££**

🍷 **Santa Maddalena** [san-tah mah-dah-LAY-nah] (*Alto Adige*, Italy) Light spicy-fruity red made from the Schiava. Rarely found outside the region, but well worth seeeking out. **Cantina Produttori Sta. Maddalena; Gojer.**

🍷 **Santa Rita** [ree-ta] (*Maipo*, Chile) Back on track after a slightly bumpy patch. The Casa Real is not only one of Chile's best and most fairly priced reds; it is also truly world class and the Carmenere, Cabernet "Triple C" a great value new arrival on the scene. ☆☆☆☆☆ **1997 Triple C 1997 £££**

🍷 **Santenay** [sont-nay] (*Burgundy*, France) Southern *Côte d'Or* village, producing pretty whites and good, though occasionally rather rustic, reds. Look for *Girardin* and *Pousse d'Or*. White: 88 89 **90 92 95** 96 97 98 Red: 78 79 **80** 83 **85** 86 87 **88 89 90** 92 95 96 97 98 **Roger Belland;** *Fernand* **Chevrot;** *Marc Colin;* **Colin-Deléger;** *Girardin; Olivier Leflaive; Bernard Morey;* **Lucien Muzet; Claude Nouveau;** *Pousse d'Or;* **Prieur Brunet.**

🍷 **Caves São João** [sow-jwow] (*Bairrada*, Portugal) Small company which produces high-quality *Bairrada*.

Sardinia (Italy) Traditionally the source of powerful reds (try *Santadi*) and whites, increasingly interesting *DOC* fortified wines, and new-wave modern reds to match the best *Super Tuscans*. **Sella e Mosca.**

🍷 **Paolo Saracco** [pow-loh sah-rak-koh] (*Piedmont*, Italy) Competing with *Vietti* for the role of top *Moscato*-maker. His *Chardonnay* Bianch del Luv is pretty impressive too.

🍷 **Sarget de Gruaud-Larose** [sahr-jay dur groowoh lah-rohs] (*St. Julien*, *Bordeaux*, France) *Second label* of *Ch. Gruaud-Larose.*

🍷 **Sassicaia** [sas-see-ki-ya] (*Tuscany*, Italy) World-class *Cabernet*-based *Super Tuscan* with more of an Italian than a *claret* taste. No longer a mere *Vino da Tavola* since the *DOC* Bolgheri was introduced in 1994.

🍷 **Saumur** [soh-moor] (*Loire*, France) Heartland of variable *Chenin*-based sparkling and still wine, and potentially more interesting *Saumur-Champigny*. Red: **85 88 89 90 95** 96 97 98 White: **90** 94 95 96 **97** 98 Sweet White: **76** 83 **85** 86 **88 89 90** 94 **95** 96 97 98 *Ch. du Hureau;* **Langlois-Château; Roches Neuves; Vatan; Cave des Vignerons de Saumur; Villeneuve.**

🍷 **Saumur-Champigny** [soh-moor shom-pee-nyee] (*Loire*, France) Crisp *Cabernet Franc* red; best served slightly chilled. Good examples are worth cellaring. **88 89 90 95** 96 97 98 *Bouvet-Ladubay; Couly-Dutheil; Filliatreau;* **Foucault;** *Ch. du Hureau;* **Langlois-Château; Targé; Vatan; de Villeneuve.**

🍷 **Saussignac** [soh-sin-yak] (*South West*, France) Historically in the shadow both of *Sauternes* and nearby Monbazillac, this sweet wine region is enjoying a minor boom at the moment, thanks to a set of quality-conscious producers who are making wines to put many a Sauternes to shame. **Ch la Chabrier; des Eyssards; Ch Grinou; Dom. Léonce Cuisset; Dom de Richard, Ch. les Miaudoux, Tourmentine; le Payral; Clos d'Yvigne.**

Sauternes [soh-turn] (*Bordeaux*, France) Rich, potentially sublime, honeyed dessert wines from *Sauvignon* and *Sémillon* (and possibly *Muscadelle*) blends. Should be affected by *botrytis* but the climate does not always allow this. That's one explanation for disappointing generic and minor-producer Sauternes; the other is careless winemaking, and,in particular, a tendency to be heavy-handed with *sulphur dioxide*. 78 79 80 81 82 **83 85 86 88 89 90 91** 92 95 97 98   *Bastor-Lamontagne; Doisy-Daëne; Fargues; Filhot; Guiraud; Rieussec; Suduiraut; Yquem.*

Sauvignon Blanc [soh-vin-yon-blon] "Grassy", "catty", "asparagussy", "gooseberryish" grape widely grown but rarely really loved, so often blended, oaked or made sweet. In France at home in the *Loire* and *Bordeaux*. New Zealand gets it right – especially in *Marlborough*. In Australia, *Knappstein*, *Cullens*, *Stafford Ridge*, and *Shaw & Smith* are right on target. *Mondavi's* oaked *Fumé Blanc* and *Kendall Jackson's* sweet versions are successful but *Monteviña*, *Quivira*, *Dry Creek*, *Simi*, and – in blends with the *Sémillon* – *Carmenet* are the stars. Chile makes better versions every year, despite starting out with a lesser variety. See *Caliterra*, *Casablanca*, *Canepa*, *Sta. Carolina*, and *Villard*. In South Africa, see *Thelema*, *Klein Constantia* and *Neil Ellis*.

Sauvignon de St. Bris [soh-vin-yon-dur san bree] (*Burgundy*, France) *Burgundy's* only *VDQS*. An affordable and often worthwhile alternative to *Sancerre*, produced in vineyards near *Chablis*. *Jean-Marc Brocard; Moreau.*

Etienne Sauzet [soh-zay] (*Burgundy*, France) First-rank estate whose white wines are almost unfindable outside collectors' cellars and Michelin-starred restaurants. ☆☆☆☆ **1998 Puligny-Montrachet ££££**

Savagnin [sa-van-yan] (*Jura*, France) No relation of the *Sauvignon*; a white *Jura* variety used for *Vin Jaune* and blended with *Chardonnay* for *Arbois*. Also, confusingly, the Swiss name for the *Gewürztraminer*.

Savennières [sa-ven-yehr] (*Loire*, France) Fine, if sometimes aggressively dry *Chenin Blanc* whites. Very long-lived. **86 88 89 90 94 95** 96 97 98   *des Baumard; Bise; du Closel; Coulée de Serrant; d'Epiré; La Roche aux Moines; de Plaisance; Soulez.*

Savigny-lès-Beaune [sa-veen-yee lay bohn] (*Burgundy*, France) Distinctive whites (sometimes made from *Pinot Blanc*) and raspberry reds. At their best can compare with *Beaune*. *Simon Bize; Chandon de Briailles; Ecard; Girard-Voillot; Girardin; Pavelot; Tollot-Beaut.*

Savoie [sav-wah] (Eastern France) Mountainous region near Geneva producing crisp floral whites such as *Abymes*, *Apremont*, *Seyssel* and *Crépy*.

☒ **Saxenburg** (*Stellenbosch*, South Africa) Reliable producer of ripely flavoursome wines. Particularly good *Pinotage* and *Sauvignon Blanc*.

☒ **Scavino** [ska-vee-noh] (*Piedmont*, Italy) Terrific new-wave, juicy reds, including single-vineyard *Barolos*, *Barberas* and *Dolcettos*. ☆☆☆☆ 1995 Barolo Rocche £££

☒ **Scharffenberger** [shah-fen-bur-gur] (*Mendocino*, California) Pommery-owned, independently-run producer of top-class, top-value sparkling wine. ☆☆☆☆ Scharffenberger Brut £££

Scharzhofberg [shahts-hof-behrg] (*Mosel-Saar-Ruwer*, Germany) Top-class *Saar* vineyard, producing great *Riesling*. QbA/Kab/Spät: **85 86 88 89 90** 91 **92 93 94 95** 96 97 98 Aus/Beeren/Tba: **83 85 88 89 90** 91 **92 93** 94 95 96 97 98 Reichsgraf von Kesselstadt.

Schaumwein [showm-vine] (Germany) Low-priced sparkling wine.

🍇 **Scheurebe** [shoy-ray-bur] (Germany) *Riesling* x *Sylvaner* cross, grown in Germany and in England. Tastes deliciously like pink grapefruit. In Austria, where it makes brilliant sweet wines, they sometimes call it Samling 88. *Kurt Darting; Hafner; Kadlec; Alois Kracher; Lingenfelder.*

🍇 **Schiava** [skee yah-vah] (*Alto-Adige*, Italy) Grape used in *Lago di Caldaro* and *Santa Maddalena* to make light reds.

Schilfwein [shilf-vine] (Austria) Luscious "reed wine" – Austrian *vin de paille* pioneered by *Willi Opitz*.

☒ **Schiopetto** [skee yoh-peh-toh] (*Friuli-Venezia Giulia*, Italy) Gloriously intense, perfumed *Collio* white varietals to rival those of *Jermann*.

Schloss [shloss] (Germany) Literally "castle", vineyard or estate.

☒ **Schloss Böckelheim** [shloss ber-kell-hime] (*Nahe*, Germany) Varied southern part of the *Nahe*. Wines from the Kupfergrube vineyard and the State Wine Domaine are worth buying. QbA/Kab/Spät: **85 86 88 89 90** 91 92 93 94 95 96 97 98 Aus/Beeren/Tba: **83 85 88 89** 90 91 92 93 94 95 96 97 98 99.

☒ **Schloss Lieser** [shloss lee-zuh] (*Mosel*, Germany) Excellent small estate related to *Fritz Haag*.

☒ **Schloss Reinhartshausen** [shloss rine-harts-how-zehn] (*Rheingau*, Germany) Innovative estate, successful with *Pinot Blanc* and *Chardonnay* (the latter introduced following a suggestion by *Robert Mondavi*). The *Rieslings* are good too. QbA/Kab/Spät: **85 88 89 90** 91 **92 93 94** 95 96 97 98 Aus/Beeren/Tba: **83 85 88 89 90** 91 **92 93 94** 95 96 97 98

☒ **Schloss Saarstein** [shloss sahr-shtine] (*Mosel-Saar-Ruwer*, Germany) High-quality *Riesling* specialist in *Serrig*. QbA/Kab/Spät: **85 86 88 89 90** 91 92 93 94 95 96 97 98 Aus/Beeren/Tba: **83 85 88 89 90** 91 **92 93 94** 95 96 97 98

☒ **Schloss Schönborn** [shloss shern-born] (*Mosel-Saar-Ruwer*, Germany) Unreliable but sometimes brilliant estate.

☒ **Schloss Vollrads** [shloss fol-rahts] (*Rheingau*, Germany) Long-time underperforming *Charta* pioneer. Following the death of the man behind it – Graf Matuschka-Greiffenclau – things may change.

☒ **Schloss Wallhausen** [shloss val-how-zen] (*Nahe*, Germany) Prinz zu Salm-Dalberg's estate is one of the top best in the Nahe, producing fine dry Riesling. ☆☆☆☆ 1998 Riesling Eiswein Gold Cap £££

Schlossböckelheim [shloss berk-el-hime] (*Nahe*, Germany) Village which gives its name to a large *Nahe Bereich*, producing elegant *Riesling*. QbA/Kab/Spät: **88 89 90** 91 92 93 94 95 96 97 98 Aus/Beeren/Tba: **83 85 88** 89 90 91 92 93 94 95 96 97 98 99 Staatsweingut Niederhausen.

Schlossgut Diel [deel] (*Nahe,* Germany) Armin Diel is both wine writer and winemaker. Co-author of the excellent German Wine Guide, his Dorsheimer Goldloch wines are worth seeking out.

Dom. Schlumberger [shloom-behr-jay] (*Alsace,* France) Great, sizeable estate whose subtle top-level wines can often rival those of the somewhat more showy *Zind-Humbrecht.* ☆☆☆☆ 1997 Riesling Les Princes Abbés £££

Schramsberg [shram-sberg] (*Napa Valley,* California) The winery that single-handedly put Californian sparkling wine on the quality trail. Wines used to be too big for their boots, possibly because too many of the grapes were from warm vineyards in *Napa.* The J. Schram is aimed at *Dom Pérignon* and gets pretty close to the target.
☆☆☆☆ 1992 J Schram ££££

Scotchman's Hill (Victoria, Australia) *Pinot Noir* specialist in *Geelong. Sauvignons* and *Chardonnays* have been less exciting.

Screaming Eagle (*Napa Valley,* California) Minuscule winery the size of many people's living room, and producing around 200 of intense *Cabernet* per year since 1992 – and selling them at £100 a bottle. The owners are avowedly trying to make California's greatest wine. Sadly most people will only ever read about it.

Seaview (South Australia) *Penfold's* brand for brilliantly reliable sparkling wine and (less frequently) *McLaren Vale* red table wines. Look out for the Edwards & Chaffey label too. ☆☆☆☆ 1996 Chardonnay Blanc de Blancs £££

Sebastiani/ Cecchetti Sebastiani [seh-bas-tee-yan-nee] (*Sonoma Valley,* California) Sebastiani makes unexceptional wine from *Central Valley* grapes. The associated but separate Cecchetti Sebastiani however, like the top end of *Gallo,* makes really good stuff in *Sonoma.* The Pepperwood Grove wines are good too. ☆☆☆☆ 1996 Cecchetti Sebastiani Napa Valley Merlot £££

Sec/secco/seco [se-koh] (France/Italy/Spain) Dry.

Second label (*Bordeaux,* France) Wine from a producer's (generally a *Bordeaux Château*) lesser vineyards, younger vines, and/or lesser *cuvées* of wine. Especially worth buying in good vintages. See *Les Forts de Latour.*

Segura Viudas [say-goo-rah vee-yoo-dass] (*Catalonia,* Spain) The quality end of the Freixenet Cava giant. ☆☆☆ Brut Reserva £££

Seifried Estate [see-freed] (*Nelson,* New Zealand) Also known as *Redwood Valley Estate.* Superb *Riesling,* especially *late harvest* style, and very creditable *Sauvignon* and *Chardonnay.*

Sekt [zekt] (Germany) Very basic sparkling wine – best won in carnival games. Watch out for anything that does not state that it is made from *Riesling* – other grape varieties almost invariably make highly unpleasant wines. Only the prefix "Deutscher" guarantees German origin.

Selaks [see-lax] (*Auckland,* New Zealand) Large company in Kumeu best known for the piercingly fruity *Sauvignon* originally made by a young man called Kevin Judd, who went on to produce *Cloudy Bay.*
☆☆☆☆ 1999 Drylands Estate Sauvignon Blanc £££

☰ **Weingut Selbach-Oster** [zel-bahkh os-tehr] (*Mosel-Saar-Ruwer,* Germany) Archetypical *Mosel Riesling.*

Sélection de Grains Nobles (SGN) [say-lek-see-yon day gran nohbl] (Alsace, France) Equivalent to German *Beerenauslese;* rich, sweet *botrytised* wine from specially selected grapes.

☰ **Sella e Mosca** [seh-la eh mos-kah] (*Sardinia,* Italy) Dynamic firm with a good *Cabernet* called Villamarina, the rich *Anghelu Ruju* and traditional *Cannonau.* ☆☆☆☆ 1997 Cannonau di Sardegna Riserva £££

☰ **Fattoria Selvapiana** [fah-taw-ree-ya sel-va-pee-yah-nah] (*Tuscany,* Italy) Great *Chianti Rufina, vin santo,* and olive oil. ☆☆☆☆ 1996 Riserva Fornace £££

☰ **Château Semeli** [seh-meh-lee] (*Attica,* Greece) Producer of classy Cabernet and Nemea reds.

🌿 **Sémillon** [in France: say-mee-yon; in Australia: seh-mil-lon and even seh-mih-lee-yon] Peachy grape generally blended with *Sauvignon* to make sweet and dry *Bordeaux,* and vinified separately in Australia, where it is also sometimes blended with *Chardonnay.* Rarely as successful in other New World countries where many versions taste more like *Sauvignon.* **Carmenet; Geyser Peak; McWilliams; Rothbury; Tyrrell; Xanadu.**

☰ **Seña** [sen-ya] (Chile) A *Mondavi* and *Caliterra* co-production. A Mercedes of a wine: impeccably put together but, so far, still somehow unexciting.

☰ **Sepp Moser** [sep-moh-zur] (*Kremstal,* Austria) Serious producer of – especially – good *Grüner Veltiner* and late harvest *Chardonnay* and *Riesling.*

☰ **Seppelt** (South Australia) *Penfolds* subsidiary and pioneer of the *Great Western* region where it makes rich still and sparkling *Shiraz* and Dorrien *Cabernet.* Other Seppelt sparkling wines are recommendable too, though the once-fine Salinger seems to have lost its way. ☆☆☆☆ 1997 Great Western Shiraz £££; ☆☆☆☆ DP63 Rutherglen Show Muscat £££

☰ **Serafini & Vidotto** [seh-rah-fee-noh eh vee-dot-toh] (*Veneto,* Italy) Francesco Serafini and Antonello Vidotto make great Pinot Nero.

☰ **Seresin** [seh-ra-sin] (*Marlborough,* New Zealand) New venture launched by a British movie cameraman. Impeccable vineyards and really impressive *Chardonnay, Sauvignon,* and a promising *Pinot Noir.*

Servir frais (France) Serve chilled.

☰ **Setúbal** [shtoo-bal] (Portugal) *DOC* on the *Setúbal Peninsula.*

Setúbal Peninsula (Portugal) Home of the *Setúbal DOC,* but now notable for the rise of two new wine regions, Arrabida and Palmela, where *JM Fonseca Succs* and *JP Vinhos* are making excellent wines from local and international grape varieties. The lusciously rich *Moscatel de Setúbal,* however, is still the star of the show.

☰ **Seyssel** [say-sehl] (*Savoie,* France) *AC* region near Geneva producing light white wines that are usually enjoyed in après-ski mood when no-one is overly concerned about value for money. **Maison Mollex; Varichon et Clerc.**

🌿 **Seyval Blanc** [say-vahl blon] *Hybrid* grape – a cross between French and US vines – unpopular with EU authorities but successful in eastern US, Canada, and England, especially at *Breaky Bottom.*

☰ **Shafer** [shay-fur] (*Napa Valley,* California) Top *Cabernet* producer in the *Stag's Leap* district, and maker of classy *Carneros Chardonnay* and *Merlot.* ☆☆☆☆ 1997 Hillside Select Cabernet Sauvignon Stag's Leap District £££

☰ **Shaw & Smith** (*Adelaide Hills,* Australia) Recently founded winery producing one of Australia's best *Sauvignons* and a pair of increasingly *Burgundian Chardonnays* that demonstrate how good wines from this variety can taste with and without oak. ☆☆☆☆☆ 1999 Sauvignon Blanc £££

Sherry (*Jerez*, Spain) The fortified wine made in the area surrounding *Jerez*. Wines made elsewhere – Australia, England, South Africa, etc. – may no longer use the name. See also *Almacenista; Fino; Amontillado; Manzanilla; Cream Sherry. Barbadillo; Gonzalez Byass; Hidalgo; Lustau.*

Shiraz [shee-raz] (Australia, South Africa) The *Syrah* grape in Australia and South Africa, named after its supposed birthplace in Iran. South African versions are lighter (and generally greener) than the Australians, while the Australians are usually riper and oakier than efforts from the *Rhône*. The move to cooler sites is broadening the range of Australian *Shiraz*, however. *Hardy's; Henschke; Maglieri; Lindemans; Rockford; Rothbury; Penfolds; Picardy; Plantagenet; St. Hallett; Saxenburg; Wolf Blass.*

Sicily (Italy) Historically best known for *Marsala* and sturdy "southern" table wine. Now, however, there is an array of other unusual fortified wines and a fast-growing range of new-wave reds and whites, many of which are made from grapes grown nowhere else on earth. *De Bartoli; Corvo; Planeta; Regaleali; Terre di Ginestra.*

Sieur d'Arques [see-uhr dark] (*Languedoc-Roussillon,* France) High-tech cooperative in *Limoux* that ought to serve as a role model to its neighbours. Good *Blanquette de Limoux* sparkling wine and truly impressive *Chardonnays* sold under the Toques et Clochers label.

Ch. Sigalas-Rabaud [see-gah-lah rah-boh] (*Bordeaux,* France) Fine Sauternes estate, producing rich, but delicate wines.

Siglo [seeg-loh] (*Rioja,* Spain) Good brand of modern red (traditionally sold in a burlap "sack") and old-fashioned whites.

Signorello (*Napa Valley,* California) Small winery making *Burgundian Chardonnay* with lots of yeasty richness, *Bordeaux*-style *Semillon* and *Sauvignon* as well as *Cabernets* that are both blackcurranty and stylish.

Silex [see-lex] (France) Term describing flinty soil, used by *Didier Dagueneau* for his oak-fermented *Pouilly-Fumé*.

Silver Oak Cellars (*Napa Valley,* California) Superb specialist *Cabernet* producers favouring fruitily accessible, but still classy, wines which benefit from long ageing in (American oak) barrels and bottle before release. Look out for older vintages of the single-vineyard Bonny's Vineyard wines, the last of which was made in 1991.

Silverado [sil-veh-rah-doh] (*Napa Valley,* California) Reliable *Cabernet, Chardonnay* and now *Sangiovese* winery that belongs to Walt Disney's widow. ☆☆☆☆ **1997 Napa Valley Chardonnay £££**

Simi Winery [see-mee] (*Sonoma Valley,* California) Recently sold (to the giant Canandaigua) and made famous by the thoughtful Zelma Long and her complex, long-lived Burgundian *Chardonnay*, archetypical *Sauvignon*, and lovely, blackcurranty *Alexander Valley Cabernet*. The current (excellent) Kiwi-born winemaker has so far remained in place, thank goodness. ☆☆☆☆ **1997 Carneros Chardonnay £££**

Ⓣ Bert Simon (*Mosel-Saar-Ruwer*, Germany) Newish estate in the *Saar* river valley with super-soft *Rieslings* and unusually elegant *Weissburgunder*.

Ⓣ Simonsig Estate [see-mon-sikh] (*Stellenbosch*, South Africa) Big estate with a very impressive commercial range, and the occasional gem – try the *Shiraz*, *Cabernet*, *Pinotage*, *Chardonnay* the Kaapse Vonkel sparkler. ✰✰✰ **1998 Chardonnay ££**

Sin Crianza [sin cree-an-tha] (Spain) Not aged in wood.

Ⓣ Sion [see-yo'n] (*Valais*, Switzerland) One of the proud homes of the grape the Swiss call the Fendant and outsiders know as *Chasselas*. Dull elsewhere, it can produce creditable (and even occasionally ageworthy) wines.

Ⓣ Ch. Siran [see-ron] (*Margaux Cru Bourgeois, Bordeaux*, France) Beautiful *château* outperforming its classification and producing increasingly impressive and generally fairly priced wines. 70 **75 78** 81 **82** 83 85 86 88 89 90 93 94 95 96 97 98 99

Ⓣ Skillogalee [skil-log-gah-lee] (*Clare Valley*, Australia) Well-respected *Clare* producer, specialising in *Riesling*, but also showing his skill with reds. ✰✰✰✰ **1999 Riesling ££**

Skin contact The longer the skins of black grapes are left in with the juice after the grapes have been crushed, the greater the *tannin* and the deeper the colour. Some non-aromatic white varieties (*Chardonnay* and *Semillon* in particular) can also benefit from extended skin contact (usually between six and twenty-four hours) to increase flavour.

Ⓣ Skouras (*Peleponnese*, Greece) Go-ahead producer, making good Nemea reds and Viognier whites.

Sliven [slee-ven] Bulgarian region offering good-value, simple reds and better-than-average whites.

Slovakia Up-and-coming source of wines from grapes little seen elsewhere, such as the *Muscat*ty Irsay Oliver.

Slovenia Former Yugoslavian region in which *Laski Rizling* is king. Other grapes show greater promise.

Ⓣ Smith & Hook (*Mendocino*, California) Winery with a cult following for its zippy blackcurranty *Cabernet Sauvignon*. These lack the ripe richness sought by most US critics, however.

Ⓣ Smith-Madrone (*Napa*, California) Long-established winery which bucks the trend by using the *Riesling* (which is being uprooted elsewhere) to make good wine. *Chardonnay* is good too.

Ⓣ Smith Woodhouse (*Douro*, Portugal) Part of the same empire as *Dow's*, *Graham's*, and *Warre's* but often overlooked. *Vintage ports* can be good, as is the house speciality *Traditional Late Bottled Vintage Port*. 60 **63 66** 70 75 **77 85** 94 97 ✰✰✰✰ **1990 Traditional Late Bottled Vintage Port £££**

Ⓣ Ch. Smith-Haut-Lafitte [oh-lah-feet] (*Pessac-Léognan Cru Classé, Bordeaux*, France) Estate flying high since its purchase by a former French sportsman and his wife. Increasingly classy reds and (specially) pure *Sauvignon* whites. Grape seeds from the estate are also used to make an anti-ageing skin cream called Caudalie. Red: **82** 85 86 **89 90** 93 94 95 96 97 98 White: 92 **93** 94 **95** 96 97 98 ✰✰✰✰ **1998 White ££££**

Ⓣ Smithbrook (Western Australia) *Pinot Noir* specialist in the southerly region of *Pemberton*. Now owned by *Petaluma*. ✰✰✰✰ **1999 Sauvignon Blanc £££**

℞ **Soave** [swah-veh] (*Veneto*, Italy) Mostly dull stuff, but *Soave Classico* is better; single-vineyard versions are best. Sweet *Recioto* di Soave is delicious. *Pieropan* is almost uniformly excellent. **Anselmi; La Cappuccina; Inama; Masi; Pieropan; Pra; Tedeschi; Zenato.**

℞ **Ch. Sociando-Mallet** [soh-see-yon-doh ma-lay] (*Haut-Médoc Cru Bourgeois, Bordeaux*, France) A *Cru Bourgeois* whose oaked, fruity red wines are way above its status. 82 83 85 86 88 89 90 91 93 95 96 97 98

℞ **Sogrape** [soh-grap] (Portugal) Having invented *Mateus* Rosé half a century ago, this large firm is now modernising the wines of *Dão* (with the new Quinta dos Carvalhais), *Douro* and *Bairrada*, and *Alentejo* (Vinha do Monte) bringing out flavours these once-dull wines never seemed to possess. *Sogrape* also owns the *port* house of *Ferreira* and is thus also responsible for *Barca Velha*, Portugal's top red table wine. The *Penfolds* of Portugal. ☆☆☆☆☆ **1996 Quinta dos Carvalhais Touriga Nacional ££**

℞ **Sokol Blosser** (*Oregon*, US) Highly successful makers of rich *Chardonnay*. The *Pinot* is good too. ☆☆☆☆☆ **1994 Redland Chardonnay £££**

℞ **Solaia** [soh-li-yah] (*Tuscany*, Italy) Yet another *Antinori Super Tuscan*. A phenomenal blend of *Cabernet Sauvignon* and *Franc*, with a little *Sangiovese*. Italy's top red? ☆☆☆☆☆ **1996 Solaia Antinori ££££**

Solera [soh-leh-rah] (*Jerez*, Spain) Ageing system involving older wine being continually "refreshed" by slightly younger wine of the same style.

℞ **Bodegas Felix Solís** [fay-leex soh-lees] (*Valdepeñas*, Spain) By far the biggest, most go-ahead winery in *Valdepeñas*.

Somontano [soh-mon-tah-noh] (Spain) *DO* region in the foothills of the Pyrénées in Aragon, now experimenting with international grape varieties. **COVISA; Enate; Pirineos; Viñas Del Vero.**

Sonnenuhr [soh-neh-noor] (*Mosel*, Germany) Vineyard site in the famous village of *Wehlen*. See *Dr Loosen*. QbA/Kab/Spät: **85 86 88 89 90 91 92 93 94 95** 96 97 98 Aus/Beeren/Tba: **85 88 89 90 91 92** 93 94 95 96 97 98

Sonoma Valley [so-noh-ma] (California) Despite the *Napa* hype, this lesser-known region not only contains some of the state's top wineries, it is also home to *E&J Gallo*'s super-premium vineyard and *Dry Creek*, home of some of California's best *Zinfandels*. The region is sub-divided into the *Sonoma, Alexander* and *Russian River Valleys* and *Dry Creek*. Red: **85 90 91 92** 93 95 **96** 97 **98** White: **90 91 92 95** 96 97 **98 Adler Fels; Arrowood; Carmenet; Ch. St Jean Clos du Bois; Dry Creek; Duxoup; E&J Gallo; Geyser Peak; Gundlach Bundschu; Cecchetti Sebastiani; Iron Horse; Jordan; Kenwood; Kistler; Laurel Glen; Matanzas Creek; Peter Michael; Quivira; Ravenswood; Ridge; St. Francis; Sonoma-Cutrer; Simi; Marimar Torres; Joseph Swan.**

⊤ **Sonoma-Cutrer** [soh-noh-ma koo-trehr] (*Sonoma Valley*, California) Recently sold producer of world-class single-vineyard *Chardonnay* that can rival *Puligny-Montrachet*. The "Les Pierres" is the pick of the litter.

⊤ **Marc Sorrel** [sor-rel] (*Rhône*, France) *Hermitage* producer who is – unusually – as successful in white as red. The "le Gréal" single-vineyard red is the wine to buy, though the "les Roccoules" white ages well.

⊤ **Pierre Soulez** [soo-layz] (*Loire*, France) Producer of *Savennières* from several vineyards. The Clos du Papillon and Roche-aux-Moines *late harvest* wines are the ones to buy.

⊤ **Ch. Soutard** [soo-tahr] (*St. Emilion, Bordeaux*, France) Highly traditional *St. Emilion* estate with long-lived wines that rely on far less oak than many of its neighbours.

South Africa The wine revolution is as dramatic as the ones affecting the rest of South African society. Quality is patchy but improving and better producers are leading the way toward producing riper, more characterful wine that apes neither France nor Australia. Elsewhere, look for inexpensive, simple dry and off-dry *Chenins*, lovely *late harvest* and fortified wines, and surprisingly good *Pinotages*; otherwise very patchy. Red: 86 **87** 89 **91 92** 93 94 **95** 96 97 98 White: 92 93 94 **95** 96 97 98
Fairview; Grangehurst; Klein Constantia; Jordan; Kanonkop; Mulderbosch; Plaisir de Merle; Saxenburg; Simonsig; Thelema; Vergelegen.

South Australia Home of almost all the biggest wine companies, and still producing over 50 per cent of Australia's wine. The *Barossa Valley* is one of the country's oldest wine producing regions, but like its neighbours *Clare* and *McLaren Vale*, faces competition from cooler areas like the *Adelaide Hills*, *Padthaway* and *Coonawarra*. Red: **82 84 85 86 87** 88 **90 91 94** 95 96 97 98 White: **87** 88 **90 91 94** 95 96 97 98

South-East Australia A cleverly meaningless regional description which sidesteps Europe's pettier *appellation*-focused rules. Technically, it covers around 85 per cent of Australia's vineyards.

South-West France An unofficial umbrella term covering the areas between *Bordeaux* and the *Pyrénées, Bergerac, Madiran, Cahors, Jurançon* and the *Vins de Pays de Côtes de Gascogne*.

🍇 **Spanna** [spah-nah] (*Piedmont*, Italy) The *Piedmontese* name for the *Nebbiolo* grape and the more humble wines made from it.

⊤ **Pierre Sparr** (*Alsace*, France) Big producer offering a rare chance to taste traditional *Chasselas*. ☆☆☆☆ **1996 Tokay Pinot Gris Reserve ££**

⊤ **Spätburgunder** [shpayt-bur-goon-dur](Germany) German name for *Pinot Noir*.
Spätlese [shpayt-lay-zeh] (Germany) Second step in the *QmP* scale, *late harvest*ed grapes making wine a notch drier than *Auslese*.

⊤ **Fratelli Speri** [speh-ree] (*Veneto*, Italy) A fast-rising star with delicious . Monte Sant'Urbano Amarone della Valpolicella Classico.

⊤ **Domaine Spiropoulos** [spee-ro-poo-los] (*Peloponnese*, Greece) Fine producer of organic wine, including Porfyros, one of Greece's best modern reds. ☆☆☆☆ **1999 Porfyros ££**

⊤ **Spottswoode** (*Napa Valley*, California) Excellent small producer of complex *Cabernet* and unusually good *Sauvignon Blanc*. Deserves greater recognition. ☆☆☆☆☆ **1996 Cabernet Sauvignon £££**

Ⴑ **Spring Mountain** (*Napa Valley*, California) Revived old winery with great vineyards and classy berryish *Cabernet*.

Ⴑ **Springfield Estate** (*Robertson*, South Africa) Decent, rather than great producer, with crisp dry *Sauvignons*. ☆☆☆ **1999 Special Cuvée Sauvignon Blanc £££**

Spritz/ig [shprit-zig] Slight sparkle or sparkling wine. Also *pétillance*.

Spumante [spoo-man-tay] (Italy) Sparkling.

Ⴑ **Squinzano** [skeen-tzah-noh] (*Puglia*, Italy) Traditional, often rustic reds from the warm south. The *Santa Barbara* cooperative makes the best wines.

Staatsweingut [staht-svine-goot] (Germany) A state-owned wine estate such as Staatsweingüter *Eltville* (*Rheingau*), a major cellar in *Eltville*.

Ⴑ **Standing Stones** (*New York State*, US) Recommendable Finger Lakes producer with an especially good Riesling.

Ⴑ **Stafford Ridge** (*Adelaide Hills*, Australia) Fine *Chardonnay* and especially *Sauvignon* from *Lenswood* by Geoff Weaver, former winemaker of *Hardys*.

Stag's Leap District (*Napa Valley*, California) A long-established hillside region, specialising in blackcurranty *Cabernet Sauvignon*. Red: 84 **85** 86 87 **90 91** 92 93 95 96 S. Anderson; *Clos du Val*; Cronin; Hartwell; *Pine Ridge; Shafer; Silverado Vineyards; Stag's Leap;* Steltzner.

Ⴑ **Stag's Leap Wine Cellars** (*Napa Valley*, California) Pioneering supporter of the *Stag's Leap appellation*, and one of the finest wineries in California. The best wines are the Faye Vineyard, SLV and Cask 23 *Cabernets*. ☆☆☆☆☆ **1997 SLV-FAYE Cabernet Sauvignon £££**

Ⴑ **Staglin** (*Napa Valley*, California) Classy producer of stylish, Bordeaux-like *Cabernet* and pioneering *Sangiovese*. ☆☆☆☆☆ **1995 Cabernet Sauvignon £££**

Stalky or stemmy Flavour of the stem rather than of the juice.

Ⴑ **Stanton & Killeen** (*Rutherglen*, Australia) Reliable producer of *Liqueur Muscat*. ☆☆☆☆ **Rutherglen Liqueur Muscat ££**

Ⴑ **Steele** (*Lake County*, California) The former winemaker of *Kendall Jackson* and a master when it comes to producing fruitily crowd-pleasing *Chardonnays* from various regions and more complex *Zinfandel*.

Steely Refers to young wine with evident *acidity*. A compliment when paid to *Chablis* and dry *Sauvignons*.

🍇 **Steen** [steen] (South Africa) Local name for (and possibly odd *clone* of) *Chenin Blanc*. Widely planted (over 30 per cent of the vineyard area). The best come from *Boschendal* and *Fairview*.

Ⴑ **Steiermark / Styria** (Austria) Sunny southern region where the *Chardonnay* is now being used (under the name of "Morillon") to produce rich, buttery but often quite Burgundian wines.

Stellenbosch [stel-len-bosh] (South Africa) Centre of the *Cape* wine industry, and climatically and topographically diverse region that, like the *Napa Valley*, is taken far too seriously as a regional *appellation*. Hillside sub-regions like Helderberg make more sense. Red: 82 84 86 **87** 89 **91 92** 93 94 **95** 96 97 98 White: **95 96** 97 98 99 00 *Bergkelder; Delheim; Neil Ellis; Grangehurst;* Hartenburg; *Jordan;* Kanonkop; *Meerlust; Mulderbosch; Rustenberg;* Saxenburg; Stellenzicht; *Thelema;* Warwick.

Ⴑ **Stellenbosch Farmers' Winery** (*Stellenbosch*, South Africa) South Africa's biggest producer; wines include Sable View, Libertas, *Nederburg*, and, now, *Plaisir de Merle*.

☥ **Stellenzicht Vineyards** [stel-len-zikht] (*Stellenbosch*, South Africa) Sister estate of Neethlingshof, with a good *Sauvignon* and a *Shiraz* good enough to beat *Penfolds Grange* in a blind tasting. ☆☆☆☆ **1997 Shiraz £££**

☥ **Sterling Vineyards** (*Napa Valley*, California) Founded by Peter Newton (now at *Newton* vineyards) and once the plaything of Coca-Cola, this showcase estate now belongs to Canadian liquor giant Seagram. Among the current successes are the Reserve *Cabernet*, *Pinot Noir*, and fairly priced Redwood Trail wines. ☆☆☆☆ **1995 Reserve Cabernet Sauvignon ££**

☥ **Weingut Georg Stiegelmar** [stee-gel-mahr] (*Burgenland*, Austria) Producer of pricy, highly acclaimed, dry whites from *Chardonnay* and *Pinot Blanc*, late harvest wines, and some particularly good reds from *Pinot Noir* and *St. Laurent*. ☆☆☆☆☆ **1995 Juris Trockenbeerenauslese £££**

☥ **Stoneleigh** (*Marlborough*, New Zealand) Reliable *Marlborough* label used by *Corbans*. ☆☆☆☆ **1999 Sauvignon Blanc ££**

☥ **Stonestreet** (*Sonoma*, California) Highly commercial wines from the *Kendall-Jackson* stable. ☆☆☆☆ **1995 Alexander Valley Legacy £££**

☥ **Stonier's** [stoh-nee-yurs] (*Mornington Peninsula*, Australia) Small *Mornington* winery, successful with impressive *Pinot Noir*, *Chardonnay* and *Merlot*. (Previously known as Stoniers-Merrick; and now a subsidiary of *Petaluma*). ☆☆☆☆ **1998 Reserve Pinot Noir ££**

☥ **Stony Hill** (*Napa Valley*, California) Unfashionable old winery with the guts to produce long-lived, complex *Chardonnay* that tastes like unoaked *Grand Cru Chablis*, rather than follow the herd in apeing buttery-rich *Meursault*. Individual wine for individualist winedrinkers.

☥ **Stonyridge** (*Auckland*, New Zealand) Rapidly rising star on the fashionable Waiheke Island, making impressive, if pricy, *Bordeaux*-style reds.

☥ **Storybook Mountain** (*Napa Valley*, California) Great individual-vineyard *Zinfandels* that taste good young but are built for the long haul. The *Howell Mountain* vines are – after the 1997 vintage – being replanted with *Cabernet Sauvignon*.

Structure The "structural" components of a wine include *tannin*, *acidity*, and *alcohol*. They provide the skeleton or backbone that supports the "flesh" of the fruit. A young wine with good structure should age well.

☥ **Ch. de Suduiraut** [soo-dee-rroh] (*Sauternes Premier Cru Classé*, *Bordeaux*, France) Producing greater things since its purchase by French insurance giant, AXA. Top wines: "*Cuvée* Madame," "Crème de Tête." The 1999 was probably the Sauternes of the vintage 75 **76** 78 **79** 81 **82 83** 85 86 **88 89** 90 94 96 97 98 99 ☆☆☆☆ **1998 ££££**

Suhindol [soo-win-dol] (Bulgaria) One of *Bulgaria's* best-known regions, the source of widely available, fairly-priced *Cabernet Sauvignon*.

Sulphites US labelling requirement alerting those suffering from an (extremely rare) allergy to the presence of *sulphur dioxide*. Curiously, no such requirement is made of cans of baked beans and dried apricots, which contain twice as much of the chemical.

Sulphur dioxide/SO2 Antiseptic routinely used by food packagers and winemakers to protect their produce from bacteria and *oxidation*.

☥ **Super Second** (*Bordeaux*, France) *Médoc* second growths: *Pichon-Lalande*, *Pichon-Longueville*, *Léoville-Las-Cases*, *Ducru-Beaucaillou*, *Cos d'Estournel*; whose wines are thought to rival – and cost nearly as much as – the first growths. Other over-performers include: *Rauzan-Ségla* and *Léoville-Barton*, *Lynch-Bages*, *Palmer*, *La Lagune*, *Montrose*.

Super Tuscan (Italy) New-Wave *Vino da Tavola / IGT* (usually red) wines, pioneered by producers like *Antinori*, which stand outside traditional *DOC* rules. Generally *Bordeaux*-style blends or *Sangiovese* or a mixture of both.

Supérieur/Superiore [soo-pay-ree-ur/soo-pay-ree-ohr-ray] (France/Italy) Often relatively meaningless in terms of discernible quality. Denotes wine (well or badly) made from riper grapes.

Sur lie [soor-lee] (France) The ageing "on its *lees*" – or dead yeasts – most commonly associated with *Muscadet*, but now being used to make other fresher, richer and sometimes slightly sparkling wines in southern France.

Süssreserve [soos-sreh-zurv] (Germany) Unfermented grape juice used to bolster sweetness and fruit in German and English wines.

♟ **Sutter Home Winery** (*Napa Valley*, California) Home of robust red *Zinfandel* in the 1970s, and responsible for the invention of successful sweet "white" (or, as the non-colour-blind might say, pink) *Zinfandel*. *Amador County Zinfandels* are still good, but rarely exceptional. The M Trinchero Founders Estate *Cabernet* and *Chardonnay* are worth looking out for.

♟ **Joseph Swan** (*Sonoma*, California) Small Burgundian-scale winery whose enthusiastic winemaker, Rod Berglund, produces great single-vineyard, often attractively quirky, *Pinot Noir* and *Zinfandel*.

Swan Valley (*Western Australia*) Hot old vineyard area; good for fortified wines and a source of fruit for *Houghton's* successful *HWB*. *Houghton* also produces cooler-climate wines in the microclimate of *Moondah Brook*.

♟ **Swanson** [swon-son] (*Napa Valley*, California) Top-flight, innovative producer of *Cabernet, Chardonnay, Sangiovese, Syrah* and *late harvest Semillon*. ☆☆☆☆☆ **1996 Alexis £££**

Switzerland Produces increasingly enjoyable wines from grapes ranging from the *Chasselas, Marsanne, Syrah* and *Pinot Noir* to the local *Cornallin* and *Petite Arvine*. See *Dôle, Fendant, Chablais*. Also the only country to use screw caps for much of its wine, thus facilitating recycling and avoiding the problems of faulty corks. Clever people, the Swiss.

♣ **Sylvaner/Silvaner** [sihl-vah-nur] Relatively non-aromatic white grape, originally from *Austria* but adopted by other European areas, particularly *Alsace* and *Franken*. Elsewhere, wines are often dry and earthy, though there are some promising efforts with it in South Africa.

♣ **Syrah** [see-rah] (*Rhône,* France) The red *Rhône* grape, an exotic mix of ripe fruit and spicy, smoky, gamey, leathery flavours. Skilfully adopted by Australia, where it is called *Shiraz* and in southern France for *Vin de Pays d'Oc*. Increasingly popular in California, thanks to "*Rhône* Rangers" like *Bonny Doon* and *Phelps*. See *Qupé, Marqués de Griñon* in Spain and *Isole e Olena* in Italy, plus *Côte Rôtie, Hermitage, Shiraz*.

T

♟ **La Tâche** [la tash] (*Burgundy*, France) Wine from the La Tâche vineyard, exclusively owned by the *Dom. de la Romanée Conti*. Frequently as good as the rarer and more expensive "La Romanée Conti". ☆☆☆☆☆ **1994 ££££**

Tafelwein [tah-fel-vine] (Germany) Table wine. Only the prefix "Deutscher" guarantees German origin.

♟ **Ch. Tahbilk** [tah-bilk] (*Victoria*, Australia) Old-fashioned winemaking in the Goulbourn Valley. Great long-lived *Shiraz* from 130-year-old vines, surprisingly good *Chardonnay*, and lemony *Marsanne* which needs a decade. The second wine is Dalfarras. ☆☆☆☆ **1998 Marsanne ££**

♟ **Cave de Tain L'Hermitage** (*Rhône*, France) Reliable cooperative for *Crozes-Hermitage*, and *Hermitage*. ☆☆☆☆ **1998 Crozes-Hermitage Nobles Rives £££**

� **Taittinger** [tat-tan-jehr] (*Champagne,* France) Producer of reliable non-vintage, and fine Comtes de *Champagne Blanc de Blancs* and Rosé.

☃ **Ch. Talbot** [tal-boh] (*St. Julien 4ème Cru Classé, Bordeaux,* France) Reliable, if sometimes slightly jammy, wine. In the same stable as Ch. Gruaud Larose. Connêtable Talbot is the *second label.* 75 **78** 79 81 **82 83** 84 **85** 86 88 89 90 92 93 94 95 96 97 98.

☃ **Talley** (*San Luis Obispo,* California) Serious small producer of elegant *Chardonnay* and *Pinot Noir* that lasts.

☃ **Taltarni** [tal-tahr-nee] (*Victoria,* Australia) Until his recent departure, Dominique Portet made great European-style *Shiraz Cabernets* in this beautiful *Pyrénées* vineyard. ✰✰✰✰ **1997 Merlot Cabernet £££**

🍇 **Tannat** [ta-na] (France) Rustic French grape variety, traditionally widely used in the blend of *Cahors* and in South America, principally in *Uruguay.*
Tannic See *Tannin.*
Tannin Astringent component of red wine which comes from the skins, seeds, and stalks and helps the wine to age.

☃ **Tardy & Ange** [tahr-dee ay onzh] (*Rhône,* France) Partnership producing classy *Crozes-Hermitage* at the Dom. de Entrefaux.

☃ **Tarragona** [ta-ra-go-nah] (*Catalonia,* Spain) *DO* region south of *Penedés* and home to many cooperatives. Contains the better-quality *Terra Alta.*

☃ **Tarrawarra** [ta-ra-wa-ra] (*Yarra Valley,* Australia) Increasingly successful *Pinot* pioneer in the cool-climate region of the *Yarra Valley. Second label* is Tunnel Hill. ✰✰✰✰ **1998 *Chardonnay £££***
Tarry Red wines from hot countries often have an aroma and flavour reminiscent of tar. The *Syrah* and *Nebbiolo* exhibit this characteristic.
Tartaric Type of acid found in grapes. Also the form in which acid is added to wine in hot countries whose legislation allows this.
Tartrates [tar-trayts] Harmless white crystals often deposited by white wines in the bottle. In Germany, these are called "diamonds".

Tasmania (Australia) Cool-climate island, showing potential for sparkling wine, *Chardonnay, Riesling* and *Pinot Noir.* White: 92 94 95 96 97 98 Red: **91 92 94 95** 96 97 98 *Freycinet; Heemskerk; Moorilla; Piper's Brook; Pirie.*

Tastevin [tat-van] The silver *Burgundy* tasting-cup used as an insignia by vinous brotherhoods (*confréries*), as a badge of office by sommeliers and as ashtrays by the author. The *Chevaliers de Tastevin* organise annual tastings, awarding a mock-medieval Tastevinage label to the best wines. *Chevaliers de Tastevin* attend banquets, often wearing similarly mock-medieval clothes.

☃ **Taurasi** [tow-rah-see] (*Campania,* Italy) Big old-fashioned *Aglianico.* Needs years to soften and develop a burned, cherry taste. **Mastroberardino.**

☃ **Cosimo Taurino** [tow-ree-noh] (*Puglia,* Italy) The name to look for when buying Salice Salentino. The red Patrigliono and Notapanaro and the Chardonnay are worth looking for too.

☃ **Tavel** [ta-vehl] (*Rhône,* France) Dry rosé. Often very disappointing. Seek out young versions and avoid the bronze colour revered by traditionalists. **Ch. d'Aquéria; Dom. de la Forcadière; de la Mordorée; du Prieuré; Ch. de Trinquevedel; de Valéry.**

Tawny (*Douro,* Portugal) In theory, pale browny-red *port* that acquires its mature appearance and nutty flavour from long ageing in oak casks. *Port* houses, however, legally produce '"tawny" by mixing basic *ruby* with *white port* and skipping the tiresome business of barrel-ageing altogether. The real stuff comes with an indication of age, such as 10 or 20-year-old, but these figures are approximate. A 10-year-old *port* only has to "taste as though it is that old". *Colheita ports* are tawnies of a specific vintage. **Noval; Taylor's; Graham's; Cockburn's; Dow's; Niepoort; Ramos Pinto; Calem.**

☂ **Taylor (Fladgate & Yeatman)** (*Douro,* Portugal) With *Dow's,* one of the "first growths" of the *Douro*. Outstanding *vintage port,* "modern" *Late Bottled Vintage.* Also owns *Fonseca* and *Guimaraens,* and produces the excellent *Quinta de Vargellas* Single-*Quinta port.* 55 60 63 66 70 75 77 83 85 92 94 97 **1987 Quinta de Vargellas £££**

☂ **Te Mata** [tay mah-tah] (*Hawke's Bay,* New Zealand) Pioneer John Buck proves what *New Zealand* can do with *Chardonnay* (in the Elston Vineyard) and pioneered reds with his Coleraine and (lighter) Awatea.

☂ **Fratelli Tedeschi** [tay-dehs-kee] (*Veneto,* Italy) Reliable producer of rich and concentrated *Valpolicellas* and good *Soaves.* The *Amarones* are particularly impressive. ☆☆☆☆☆ **1996 Capitel Recioto Classico Monte Fontana £££**

☂ **Tement** [teh-ment] (*Steiermark,* Austria) Producer of a truly world-class barrel-fermented *Sauvignon Blanc* which competes directly with top *Pessac-Léognan* whites. *Chardonnays* are impressive too.

☂ **Dom. Tempier** [tom-pee-yay] (*Provence,* France) *Provence* superstar estate, producing single-vineyard red and rosé *Bandols* that support the claim that the *Mourvèdre* (from which they are largely made) ages well. The rosé is also one of the best in the region.

🍇 **Tempranillo** [tem-prah-nee-yoh] (Spain) The red grape of *Rioja* – and just about everywhere else in Spain, thanks to the way in which its strawberry fruit suits the vanilla/oak flavours of barrel-ageing. In *Navarra,* it is called *Cencibel;* in *Ribera del Duero,* Tinto Fino; in the *Penedés, Ull de Llebre;* in *Toro,* Tinto de Toro; and in Portugal – where it is used for *port* – it's known as *Tinto Roriz.* So far, though, it is rarely grown outside Spain.

Tenuta [teh-noo-tah] (Italy) Estate or vineyard.

☂ **Terlano/Terlaner** [tehr-LAH-noh/tehr-LAH-nehr] (*Trentino-Alto-Adige,* Italy) Northern Italian village and its wine: usually fresh, crisp and carrying the name of the grape from which it was made.

🍇 **Teroldego Rotaliano** [teh-rol-deh-goh roh-tah-lee-AH-noh] (*Trentino-Alto-Adige,* Italy) Dry reds, quite full-bodied, with lean, slightly bitter berry flavours which make them better accompaniments to food. **Foradori.**

Terra Alta [tay ruh al-ta] (*Catalonia,* Spain) Small DO within the much larger *Tarragona DO,* producing wines of higher quality due to the difficult climate and resulting low yields. **Pedro Rovira.**

☂ **Terrazas** [teh-rah-zas] (Mendoza, Argentina) The brand name of Moët & Chandon's recently launched impressive red and white Argentinian wines.

☂ **Terre Rosse** [teh-reh roh-seh] (*Liguria,* Italy) One of the best estates in Liguria, with good examples of *Vermentino* and Pigato.

☂ **Ch. du Tertre** [doo tehr-tr] (*Margaux 5ème Cru Classé, Bordeaux,* France) Recently restored to former glory by the owners of *Calon-Ségur.*

☂ **Ch. Tertre-Daugay** [doo tehr-tr] (*St. Emilion, Grand Cru, Bordeaux,* France) Steadily improving property whose wines are cast in a classic mould and do not always have the immediate appeal of bigger, oakier neighbours.

� **Ch. Tertre-Rôteboeuf** [Tehr-tr roht-burf] (*St. Emilion Grand Cru Classé, Bordeaux,* France) Good, rich, concentrated if sometimes atypical, crowd-pleasing wines. 85 86 88 89 90 91 **93 94** 95 96 97 98

Tête de Cuvée [teht dur coo-vay] (France) An old expression still used by traditionalists to describe their finest wine.

☐ **Thackrey** (*Marin County,* California) Rich, impressively concentrated wines that seek to emulate the *Rhône,* but actually come closer to Australia in style.

☐ **Thames Valley Vineyard** (*Reading,* England) England's most reliable and dynamic winery – and consultancy – thanks to Australian expertise.

☐ **Dr H Thanisch** [tah-nish] (*Mosel-Saar-Ruwer,* Germany) Two estates with confusingly similar labels. The best of the pair which has a *VDP* logo offers usually decent though potentially disappointing examples of *Bernkasteler* Doctor, one of the finest vineyards in Germany.

☐ **Thelema Mountain Vineyards** [thur-lee-ma] (*Stellenbosch,* South Africa) One of the very best wineries in South Africa, thanks to Gyles Webb's skill and to stunning hillside vineyards. *Chardonnay* and *Sauvignon* are the stars, though Webb is coming to terms with his reds too.

☐ **Thermenregion** [thehr -men-ray-gee-yon] (Austria) Big region close to Vienna, producing good reds and sweet and dry whites.

☐ **Ch. Thieuley** [tee-yur-lay] (*Entre-Deux-Mers, Bordeaux,* France) Classy property forging the way for concentrated *Sauvignon*-based, well-oaked whites, and silky reds. With *Château Bonnet,* this is one of the leading lights of this region. ☆☆☆☆ **1999 Cuvée Francis Courselle Blanc ££**

☐ **Michel Thomas** [toh-mah] (*Loire,* France) Producer of reliable modern Sancerre with rich flavours. ☆☆☆☆ **1999 £££**

☐ **Paul Thomas** (*Washington State,* US) Dynamic brand now under the same ownership as Columbia Winery, and producing a broad range of wines, including good *Chardonnay* and *Semillon* whites and *Cabernet-Merlot* reds.

☐ **Three Choirs Vineyard** (*Gloucestershire,* England) Named for the three cathedrals of Gloucester, Hereford, and Worcester, this is one of England's most reliable estates. Try the oaky "Barrique-matured" whites and the annual "New Release" *Nouveau.*

☐ **Thurston Wolfe** (*Washington State,* US) Enthusiastic supporter of the local speciality, the mulberryish red Lemberger – and producer too of good fortified "port" and Black Muscat.

☐ **Ticino** [tee-chee-noh] (Switzerland) One of the best parts of Switzerland to go looking for easy-drinking and (relatively) affordable reds, the best of which are made from *Merlot.* Interestingly, this region has also quietly pioneered White Merlot, a style of wine we will be encountering quite frequently in the next few years, as Californian grapegrowers and winemakers struggle to find ways of disposing of the surplus of this grape. ☆☆☆☆ **1998 Guido Brivia Bianco Rovere Bianco di Uve Merlot £££**

☐ **Tiefenbrunner** [tee-fen-broon-nehr] (*Trentino-Alto-Adige,* Italy) Consistent producer of fair-to-good varietal whites, most particularly *Chardonnay* and *Gewürztraminer.*

☐ **Tignanello** [teen-yah-neh-loh] (*Tuscany,* Italy) *Antinori's Sangiovese – Cabernet Super Tuscan* is one of Italy's original superstars. Should last for a decade. 82 83 **85** 88 **90** 93 **94** 95 96 97 ☆☆☆☆ **1994 ££££**

☞ **Tinta Roriz** [teen-tah roh-reesh] (Portugal) See *Tempranillo*

☐ **Tio Pepe** [tee-yoh peh-peh] (*Jerez,* Spain) Ultra-reliable fino *sherry* from *Gonzalez Byass.* ☆☆☆☆ **££**

☞ **Tocai** [toh-kay] (Italy) Lightly herby Venetian white grape, confusingly unrelated to others of similar name. Drink young.

Tokaji [toh-ka-yee] (Hungary) Not to be confused with Australian *liqueur Tokay*, Tocai Friulano or *Tokay d'Alsace*, *Tokaji Aszú* is a dessert wine made in a specific region of Eastern *Hungary* (and a small corner of *Slovakia*) by adding measured amounts (*puttonyos*) of *eszencia* (a paste made from individually-picked, overripe, and/or *botrytis*-affected grapes) to dry wine made from the local *Furmint* and *Hárslevelu* grapes. Sweetness levels, which depend on the amount of *eszencia* added, range from one to six *puttonyos*, anything beyond which is labelled *Aszú Eszencia*. This last is often confused with the pure syrup which is sold – at vast prices – as *Eszencia*. Wines have become fresher and finer (less *oxidised*) since the arrival of outside investment, which has also revived interest in making individual-vineyard wines from the best sites. **Disznókö; *Royal Tokaji Wine Co; Ch. Megyer; Oremus; Pajzos;* Tokajkovago.**

Tokay [in France: to-kay; in Australia: toh-kih] Various different regions have used Tokay as a local name for other grape varieties. In Australia it is the name of a fortified wine from *Rutherglen* made from the *Muscadelle*; in *Alsace*, it is *Pinot Gris*; while the Italian *Tocai* is quite unrelated. Hungary's Tokay – now helpfully renamed *Tokaji* – is largely made from the *Furmint*.

Tokay d'Alsace [toh-ki dal-sas] (Alsace, France) See *Pinot Gris*.

Tollana [to-lah-nah] (South Australia) Another part of the Southcorp (*Penfolds, Lindeman* etc) empire – and a source of great value. ☆☆☆☆ 1996 TR222 Cabernet Sauvignon ££; ☆☆☆☆ 1998 Eden Valley Riesling ££

Dom. Tollot-Beaut [to-loh-boh] (Burgundy, France) Wonderful *Burgundy* domaine in *Chorey-lès-Beaune*, with top-class *Corton* vineyards and a mastery over modern techniques and new oak. Wines have lots of rich fruit flavour. Some traditionalists find them overly showy. ☆☆☆☆☆ 1997 Corton Bressandes £££

Torcolato [taw-ko-lah-toh] (Veneto, Italy) See *Maculan*.

Torgiano [taw-jee-yah-noh] (Umbria, Italy) Zone in *Umbria* and modern red wine made famous by *Lungarotti*. See *Rubesco*.

Michel Torino [Toh-ree-noh] (Cafayate, Argentina) Reliable producer of various wine styles from Salta – and a leading light in the move towards organic wine in Argentina. ☆☆☆☆ 1999 Coleccion Malbec ££££

Toro [to-roh] (Spain) Fast up-and-coming region on the *Douro*, close to Portugal, producing intense reds such as Fariña's *Collegiata* from the *Tempranillo*, confusingly known here as the Tinta de Toro. **Bajoz; *Fariña,* Vega Saúco.**

🍷 **Torre de Gall** [to-ray day-gahl] (*Catalonia,* Spain) *Moët & Chandon's* Spanish sparkling wine – now better-known as Cava Chandon. As good it gets using traditional *cava* varieties. ☆☆☆☆ **££**

🍷 **Torres** [TO-rehs] (*Catalonia,* Spain) *Miguel Torres* revolutionised Spain's wine industry with reliable wines like Viña Sol, Gran Sangre de Toro, Esmeralda, and Gran Coronas, before doing the same for Chile. Today, while these wines face heavier competition, efforts at the top end of the scale, like the *Milmanda Chardonnay,* Fransola *Sauvignon Blanc* and Mas Borras ("Black Label") *Cabernet Sauvignon,* still look good. ☆☆☆☆ **1998 Milmanda £££**

🍷 **Marimar Torres** [TO-rehs] (*Sonoma,* California) *Miguel Torres'* sister is producing some of the most impressive *Pinot Noir* and *Chardonnay* from a spectacular little vineyard in *Russian River.* ☆☆☆☆ **1998 Pinot Noir £££**

🍷 **Miguel Torres** [TO-rehs] (*Curico,* Chile) Improving offshoot of the Spanish giant. The Santa Digna *Cabernet* and the new Manso de Velasco are the star wines. ☆☆☆☆☆ **1997 Manso de Velasco £££**

🍇 **Torrontes** [to-ron-tehs] (Argentina) Aromatic grape variety related to the *Muscat,* and highly successful in Argentina. *Etchart* and la Agricola are star producers. Smells sweet even when the wine is bone dry.

Toscana [tos-KAH-nah] (Italy) See *Tuscany.*

🍷 **Ch. la Tour Blanche** [lah toor blonsh] (*Sauternes Premier Cru Classé, Bordeaux,* France) Since the late 1980s, one of the finest, longest-lasting *Sauternes.* Also a well-run wine school. 86 **88** 89 90 92 94 95 96 97 98

🍷 **Ch. la Tour-Carnet** [lah toor kahr-nay] (*Haut-Médoc 4ème Cru Classé, Bordeaux,* France) Picturesque but *Cru Bourgeois*-level fourth growth.

🍷 **Ch. la Tour-de-By** [lah toor dur bee] (*Médoc Cru Bourgeois, Bordeaux,* France) Reliable, especially in ripe years. **85** 86 88 89 90 91 94 95 96 98.

🍷 **Ch. Tour-du-Haut-Caussin** [toor doo oh koh-sa'n] (*Haut-Médoc Cru Bourgeois, Bordeaux,* France) Highly reliable modern estate.

🍷 **Ch. Tour-du-Haut-Moulin** [toor doo oh moo-lan] (*Haut-Médoc Cru Bourgeois, Bordeaux,* France) An under-appreciated producer of what often can be *cru classé* quality wine. **82** 83 **85** 86 88 **89 90** 92 94 95 96 97 98

🍷 **Ch. la Tour-Martillac** [lah toor mah-tee-yak] (*Graves Cru Classé, Bordeaux,* France) Recently revolutionised organic *Pessac-Léognan* estate with juicy reds and good whites. **82** 83 85 86 88 89 90 91 **92** 93 94 95 96 97 98.

🍷 **Touraine** [too-rayn] (*Loire,* France) Area encompassing the *ACs Chinon, Vouvray* and *Bourgueil.* Also an increasing source of quaffable *varietal* wines – *Sauvignon, Gamay* de Touraine, etc. White: 96 97 98 Red: **88 89** 90 95 96 97 98 **Bellevue; de la Besnerie; Briare; Paul Buisse; Charmoise; de la Gabillière; Henry Marionet; Octavie; Oisly & Thésée; Oudin Frères.**

🍷 **Les Tourelles de Longueville** [lay too-rel dur long-ur-veel] (*Pauillac, Bordeaux,* France) The *second label* of *Pichon-Longueville.*

🍇 **Touriga (Nacional/Francesa)** [too-ree-ga nah-see-yoh-nahl/fran-say-sa] (Portugal) Red *port* grapes, also (though rarely) seen in the New World. Now being used for *varietal* wines by *Sogrape*.

Traditional Generally meaningless term, except in sparkling wines where the "méthode traditionelle" is the new way to say "*méthode champenoise*" and in Portugal where "Traditional *Late Bottled Vintage*" refers to *port* that unlike non-traditional LBV, hasn't been filtered. ("Tradition" in some parts of France can also refer to – unappealingly – old-fashioned winemaking.)

🍇 **Traminer** [tra-mee-nur; in Australia: trah-MEE-nah] A less aromatic variant of the *Gewürztraminer* grape widely grown in Eastern Europe and Italy, although the term is confusingly also used as a pronounceable, alternative name for the latter grape – particularly in Australia.

Transfer Method A way of making sparkling wine, involving a second fermentation in the bottle, but unlike the *méthode champenoise* in that the wine is separated from the lees by pumping it out of the bottle into a pressurised tank for clarification before returning it to another bottle.

🍷 **Bodegas Trapiche** [tra-pee-chay] (Argentina) Huge go-ahead producer with noteworthy barrel-fermented *Chardonnay* and *Cabernet/Malbec*.
☆☆☆☆ 1997 Oak Cask Cabernet £££

Tras-os-Montes [tras-ohsh-montsh] (*Douro,* Portugal) Up-and-coming wine region of the *Upper Douro*, right up at Spanish border and source of *Barca Velha.*

🍇 **Trebbiano** [treh-bee-yah-noh] (Italy) Ubiquitous white grape in Italy. Less vaunted in France, where it is called *Ugni Blanc.*

🍷 **Trebbiano d'Abruzzo** [treh-bee-yah-noh dab-root-zoh] (*Abruzzo,* Italy) A *DOC* region where they grow a clone of *Trebbiano,* confusingly called Trebbiano di Toscana, and use it to make unexceptional dry whites.

🍷 **Trefethen** [treh-feh-then] (*Napa Valley,* California) Pioneering estate whose *Chardonnay* and *Cabernet* now taste oddly old-fashioned. The Eshcol wines, though cheaper, are curiously often a better buy.

Trentino [trehn-tee-noh] (Italy) Northern *DOC* in Italy. *Trentino* specialities include crunchy red *Marzemino*, nutty white Nosiola, and excellent *Vin Santo*. Winemaking here often suffers from over-production, but less greedy winemakers can offer lovely, soft, easy-drinking wines. Càvit; Ferrari; Foradori; Pojer & Sandri; San Leonardo; Vallarom; Roberto Zeni.

Trentino-Alto-Adige [trehn-tee-noh al-toh ah-dee-jay] (Italy) Northern region confusingly combining the two *DOC* areas *Trentino* and *Alto-Adige.*

🍷 **Dom. de Trévallon** [treh-vah-lon] (*Provence,* France) Superstar long-lived blend of *Cabernet Sauvignon* and *Syrah* that was sold under the Les Baux de Provence appellation but has now (because of crazily restrictive rules regarding grape varieties) been demoted to *Vin de Pays des Bouches du Rhône.* ☆☆☆☆ 1995 £££

🍷 **Triebaumer** [tree-bow-mehr] (*Burgenland,* Austria) Fine producer of late harvest wines (including good Sauvignon) and well-made reds.
☆☆☆☆☆ 1998 Ausbruch Sauvignon Blanc £££

🍷 **Dom. Frédéric-Emile Trimbach** [tram-bahkh] (*Alsace,* France) Distinguished grower and merchant with subtle complex wines. Top *cuvées* are the Frédéric Emile, Clos St. Hune, and Seigneurs de Ribeaupierre.
☆☆☆☆☆ 1995 Riesling Alsace Cuvée Frédéric Emile £££

Trittenheim [trit-ten-hime] (*Mosel-Saar-Ruwer,* Germany) Village whose vineyards are said to have been the first in Germany planted with *Riesling,* making honeyed wine. QbA/Kab/Spät: **85 88 89 90** 91 **92 93 94 95** 96 97 98 Aus/Beeren/Tba: **83 85 88 89 90** 91 92 93 **94** 95 96 97 98 99

Trocken [trok-ken] (Germany) Dry, often aggressively so. Avoid Trocken *Kabinett* from such northern areas as the *Mosel, Rheingau* and *Rheinhessen.* QbA (*chaptalised*) and *Spätlese* Trocken wines (made, by definition, from riper grapes) are better. See also *Halbtrocken.*

Trockenbeerenauslese [trok-ken-beh-ren-ows-lay-zeh] (Austria/ Germany) Fifth rung of the *QmP* ladder, wine from selected dried grapes which are usually *botrytis*-affected and full of natural sugar. Only made in the best years, rare and expensive, though less so in Austria than Germany.

❦ **Trollinger** [troh-ling-gur] (Germany) The German name for the Black Hamburg grape, used in *Württemberg* to make light red wines.

Tronçais [tron-say] (France) Forest producing some of the best oak for barrels.

❦ **Ch. Tronquoy-Lalande** [trron-kwah-lah-lond] (*St. Estèphe Cru Bourgeois, Bordeaux,* France) Traditional wines to buy in ripe years. 79 **82** 83 **85** 86 88 89 90 93 94 95 96 97 98 ☆☆☆☆ **1995 £££**

❦ **Ch. Troplong-Mondot** [trroh-lon mondoh] (*St. Emilion Grand Cru Classé, Bordeaux,* France) Brilliantly-sited, top-class property whose wines now sell for top-class prices. **82** 83 **85** 86 88 89 90 91 92 93 94 95 96 98

❦ **Ch. Trotanoy** [trrot-teh-nwah] (*Pomerol, Bordeaux,* France) Never less than fine and back on especially roaring form since the beginning of the 1990s to compete with *Pétrus.* Some may, however, prefer the lighter style of some of the 1980s. **61 64 67 70 71 75** 76 78 79 81 **82** 83 **85** 86 **88 89** 90 **93 94** 95 96 97 98 ☆☆☆☆ **1994 ££££**

❦ **Ch. Trottevieille** [trrott-vee-yay] (*St. Emilion Premier Grand Cru, Bordeaux,* France) Steadily improving property. **79** 81 **82** 83 **85** 86 88 89 90 91 92 93 94 95 96 97 98 ☆☆☆☆ **1986 ££££**

❦ **Trousseau** [troo-soh] (Eastern France) Grape variety found in *Arbois.*

❦ **Tsantalis** [tsan-tah-lis] (*Nemea,* Greece) Increasingly impressive producer, redefining traditional varieties.

❦ **Tua Rita** [too-wah ree-tah] (*Tuscany,* Italy) Young estate making tiny quantities of wines using grapes from vines that previously went into *Sassicaia.* Giusto dei Notri is the *Bordeaux* blend; Redigaffi is the pure *Merlot.*

❦ **Tulloch** [tul-lurk] (*Hunter Valley,* Australia) Under-performing backwater of the *Penfolds* empire.

Tunisia [too-nee-shuh] Best known for dessert *Muscat* wines.

☿ **Cave Vinicole de Turckheim** [turk-hime] (*Alsace*, France) Cooperative whose top wines can often rival those of some the region's best estates. ☆☆☆☆ 1998 Tokay Pinot Gris Heimbourg £££

☿ **Turkey Flat** (South Australia) Small maker of intensely rich *Barossa*, *Shiraz* and *Grenache*. ☆☆☆☆☆ 1997 Shiraz £££

☿ **Turley Cellars** (*Napa Valley*, California) US guru *Robert Parker's* favourite, Helen Turley, who is winemaker here and consultant elsewhere, makes intense but not overblown *Petite Sirahs* and *Zinfandels*, including small quantities from very old vines.

Tuscany (Italy) Major region, the famous home of *Chianti* and reds such as *Brunello di Montalcino* and the new wave of *Super Tuscan Vini da Tavola*. Red: 78 79 81 82 85 88 90 94 95 96 97 98 99

☿ **Tyrrell's** (*Hunter Valley*, Australia) *Chardonnay* (confusingly sold as *Pinot Chardonnay*) pioneer, and producer of old-fashioned *Shiraz* and (probably most impressively) *Semillon* and even older-fashioned *Pinot Noir* which tastes curiously like old-fashioned *Burgundy*. ☆☆☆☆ 1999 Vat 47 Pinot Chardonnay £££; ☆☆☆☆☆ 1997 Vat 8 Shiraz Cabernet £££

U

🍇 **Ugni Blanc** [oo-nee blon] (France) Undistinguished white grape whose neutrality makes it ideal for distillation. It needs modern winemaking to produce a wine with flavour. In Italy, where it is known as the *Trebbiano*, it takes on a mantle of (spurious) nobility. Try *Vin de Pays des Côtes de Gascogne*.

🍇 **Ull de Llebre** [ool dur yay-bray] (Spain) Literally "hare's eye". See *Tempranillo*.

Ullage Space between surface of wine and top of cask or, in a bottle, the cork. The wider the gap, the greater the danger of oxidation. Older wines almost always have some degree of ullage; the less the better.

☿ **Umani Ronchi** [oo-mah-nee ron-kee] (*Marches*, Italy) Innovative producer whose wines, like the extraordinary new Pelago, prove that *Tuscany* is not the only exciting region in Italy. ☆☆☆☆☆ 1998 le Busche £££

☿ **Umathum** [oo-ma-toom] (*Neusiedlersee*, Austria) Producer of unusually good red wines including a brilliant *St. Laurent*.

Umbria [uhm-bree-ah] (Italy) Central wine region, best known for white *Orvieto* and *Torgiano*, but also producing the excellent red *Rubesco*.

☿ **Viña Undurraga** [oon-dur-rah-ga] (*Central Valley*, Chile) Family-owned estate with a range of single varietal wines, including good *Carmenère*.

Unfiltered Filtering a wine can remove flavour – as can *fining* it with egg white or bentonite (clay). Most winemakers traditionally argue that both practices are necessary if the finished wine is going to be crystal-clear and free from bacteria that could turn it to vinegar. Many quality-conscious New-Wave producers, however, are now cutting back on *fining* and/or filtering.

Uruguay Outside consultants and investment from firms like *Freixenet* are turning this into a new source of *Cabernet Sauvignon* and *Tannat*. Castel Pujol; Castillo Viejo; Juanico.

Urzig [oort-zig] (*Mosel-Saar-Ruwer,* Germany) Village on the *Mosel* with steeply sloping vineyards and some of the very best producers, including Christoffel, *Mönchhof,* and *Dr. Loosen.* QbA/Kab/Spät: **88 89 90** 92 93 95 96 97 98 Aus/Beeren/Tba: **83 85 88 89 90** 91 92 93 **94** 95 96 97 98 99

♈ **Utiel-Requena** [oo-tee-yel reh-kay-nah] (*Valencia,* Spain) *DO* of *Valencia,* producing heavy red and good fresh rosé from the Bobal grape.

V

♈ **Dom. Vacheron** [va-shur-ron] (*Loire,* France) Reliable, if unspectacular, producer of *Sancerre* – including a better-than-average red.

♈ **Vacqueyras** [va-kay-ras] (*Rhône,* France) *Côtes du Rhône* village with full-bodied, peppery reds which compete with (pricier) *Gigondas.* Red: 90 95 **96** 97 98 99. Cazaux; Combe; Couroulu; Fourmone; *Jaboulet Aîné;* Dom. de Mont Vac; Montmirail; de la Soleïade; Tardieu-Laurent; Ch. des Tours; *Cave de Vacqueyras; Vidal-Fleury.*

♈ **Aldo Vajra** [vi-rah] (*Piedmont,* Italy) Producer of rich, complex *Barolo* and the deliciously different gamey Freisa delle Langhe.

Valais [va-lay] (Switzerland) Vineyard area on the upper *Rhône,* making good *Fendant* (*Chasselas*) which surmounts the usual innate dullness of that grape. There are also some reasonable – in all but price – light reds made from the *Pinot Noir.* Bonvin; Imesch; Provins.

Val/Valle d'Aosta [val-day-yos-tah] (Italy) Small, spectacularly beautiful area between *Piedmont* and the French/Swiss border. Better for tourism than wine.

♈ **Vignerons du Val d'Orbieu** [val-dor-byur] (*Languedoc-Roussillon,* France) Would-be innovative association of over 200 cooperatives and growers that now also owns the Cordier brand. Apart from the generally excellent Cuvée Mythique, however, too many wines leave room for improvement. Reds are far better than whites. ✩✩✩✩ **1998 Cuvée Mythique ££**

♈ **Valbuena** [val-boo-way-nah] (*Ribera del Duero,* France) The – relatively – younger version of *Vega Sicilia* hits the streets when it is around five years old.

♈ **Ch. Valandraud** [va-lon-droh] (*St. Emilion, Bordeaux,* France) An instant superstar launched in 1991 as competition for *le Pin.* Production is tiny (of *Pomerol* proportions), quality meticulous, and the price astronomical. Values quintupled following demand from the US and Far East, where buyers seem uninterested in the fact that these wines are – however delicious – actually no finer than *Médoc* classics costing far less.

♈ **Valdeorras** [bahl-day-ohr-ras] (*Galicia,* Spain) A barren and mountainous *DO* in *Galicia* beginning to exploit the *Cabernet Franc*-like local grape Mencia and the indigenous white Godello.

☲ **Valdepeñas** [bahl-deh-pay-nyass] (*La Mancha,* Spain) *La Mancha DO* striving to refine its rather hefty strong reds and whites. Progress is being made, particularly with reds. **Miguel Calatayud; *Los Llanos;* Felix Solis.**

☲ **Valdespino** [bahl-deh-spee-noh] (*Jerez,* Spain) Old-fashioned *sherry* company that uses wooden casks to ferment most of its wines. Makes a classic *fino* Innocente and an excellent *Pedro Ximénez.*

☲ **Valdivieso** [val-deh-vee-yay-soh] (*Curico,* Chile) Dynamic winery with good commercial wines, high-quality *Chardonnay* and *Pinot Noir* and an award-winning blend of grapes, regions, and years called Caballo Loco whose heretical philosophical approach gives Gallic traditionalists apoplexy. ☆☆☆☆☆ **1998 Reserve Cabernet Sauvignon £££**

☲ **Abazzia di Vallechiara** [ah-bat-zee-yah dee val-leh-kee-yah-rah] (*Piedmont,* Italy) Following the lead of fellow actor Gérard Départdieu, Ornella Muti now has her own wine estate, with some first class Dolcetto wines.

☲ **Valençay** [va-lon-say] (*Loire,* France) *AC* within Touraine, near *Cheverny,* making comparable whites: light and clean, if rather sharp. 90 94 95 96 97 98 99

☲ **Valencia** [bah-len-thee-yah] (Spain) Produces quite alcoholic red wines from the Monastrell and also deliciously sweet grapey *Moscatel de Valencia.*

☲ **Edoardo Valentini** [vah-len-tee-nee] (*Abruzzo,* Italy) Good, old-fashioned Montepulciano d'Abruzzo and unusually good Trebbiano d'Abruzzo.

☲ **Vallet Frères** [va-lay frehr] (*Burgundy,* France) Good, small, traditional – not to say old-fashioned – merchant based in *Gevrey-Chambertin.* Also known as Pierre Bourrée. ☆☆☆☆ **1987 Charmes-Chambertin £££**

☲ **Valpolicella** [val-poh-lee-cheh-lah] (*Veneto,* Italy) Over-commercialised, light, red wine which should – with rare exceptions – be drunk young to catch its interestingly bitter-cherryish flavour. Bottles labelled *Classico* are better; best are *Ripasso* versions, made by refermenting the wine on the *lees* of an earlier vat. For a different experience, buy *Amarone* or *Recioto.* 86 88 90 91 93 94 95 96 97 98 99. *Allegrini; Bertani; Bolla; Boscaini;* Brunelli; *dal Forno; Guerrieri-Rizzardi; Masi;* Mazzi; *Quintarelli; Le Ragose;* Serego Alighieri; *Tedeschi;* Villa Spinosa; *Zenato;* Fratelli Zeni.

☲ **Valréas** [val-ray-yas] (*Rhône,* France) Peppery, inexpensive red wine from a *Côtes du Rhône* village. 78 83 85 88 89 90 95 96 97. *Earl Gaia*

⟨Y⟩ **Valtellina** [val-teh-lee-na] (*Lombardy*, Italy) Red *DOC* mostly from the *Nebbiolo* grape, of variable quality. Improves with age. The raisiny Sfursat, made from dried grapes, is more interesting.

⟨Y⟩ **Varichon et Clerc** [va-ree-shon ay klayr] (*Savoie*, France) Good producer of sparkling wine.
Varietal A wine made from and named after one or more grape variety, e.g., California *Chardonnay*. The French authorities are trying to outlaw such references from the labels of most of their *appellation contrôlée* wines. "*Shiraz*" has so far escaped this edict because it is considered a foreign word.

⟨Y⟩ **Viña Los Vascos** [los vas-kos] (*Colchagua Valley*, Chile) Estate belonging to Eric de *Rothschild* of *Ch. Lafite*, and shamelessly sold with a *Lafite*-like label. The *Cabernet* Grande Reserve has improved but the standard *Cabernet* is uninspiring and the white disappointing, not to say downright poor.

⟨Y⟩ **Vasse Felix** [vas-fee-liks] (*Margaret River*, Australia) Very classy *Margaret River* winery belonging to the widow of millionaire Rupert Holmes à Court, specialising in juicy, high-quality (multi-regional) *Cabernet*, *Shiraz*, *Semillon*, and *Riesling*. ☆☆☆☆☆ 1998 Heytesbury £££

⟨Y⟩ **Vaucluse** [voh-klooz] (*Rhône*, France) *Côtes du Rhône* region with good *Vin de Pays* and peppery reds and rosés.

Vaud [voh] (Switzerland) Swiss wine area on the shores of Lake Geneva, famous for unusually tangy *Chasselas* (Dorin) and light reds.

⟨Y⟩ **Vaudésir** [voh-day-zeer] (*Burgundy*, France) Possibly the best of the seven *Chablis Grands Crus*.

⟨Y⟩ **Vavasour** [va-va-soor] (*Marlborough*, New Zealand) Pioneers of the Awatere Valley sub-region of *Marlborough*, hitting high standards with *Bordeaux*-style reds, powerful *Sauvignons*, and impressive *Chardonnays*. Dashwood is the *second label*. ☆☆☆☆ 1999 Sauvignon Blanc £££
VDP (Germany) Association of high-quality producers. Look for the eagle.
VDQS (*Vin Délimité de Qualité Supérieur*) (France) Official, neither-fish-nor-fowl, designation for wines better than *Vin de Pays* but not fine enough for an *AC*. Enjoying a strange half-life (amid constant rumours of its imminent abolition), this includes such oddities as *Sauvignon de St. Bris*.

⟨Y⟩ **Veenwouden** [fehn-foh-den] (*Paarl*, South Africa) A chance to taste what happens when Michel Rolland of Bordeaux gets his hands on vineyards in South Africa. Hardly surprisingly, riper and rich-tasting Merlots than most of the others traditionally associated with South Africa. ☆☆☆☆☆ 1997 Veenwouden Merlot £££
Vecchio [veh-kee-yoh] (Italy) Old.

⟨Y⟩ **Vecchio Samperi** [veh-kee-yoh sam-peh-ree] (*Sicily*, Italy) Best *Marsala* estate, belonging to De Bartoli. Although not DOC, a dry aperitif similar to an *amontillado sherry*.

⟨Y⟩ **Vega Sicilia** [bay-gah sih-sih-lyah] (*Ribera del Duero*, Spain) Spain's top wine is a long (10 years) barrel-matured, eccentric *Tempranillo-Bordeaux* blend called Unico sold for extravagant prices. For a cheaper, slightly fresher taste of the Vega Sicilia-style, try the supposedly lesser Valbuena. 62 64 66 67 69 **70** 72 74 75 76 79 80 82 83 ☆☆☆☆☆ 1994 Valbuena £££
Vegetal Often used of *Sauvignon Blanc*, like "grassy". Can be complimentary – though not in California or Australia, where it is held to mean "unripe".

� **Velich** [veh-likh] (*Burgenland*, Austria) High quality producers of a wide range of wines including recommendable Chardonnay.

☐ **Caves Velhas** [kah-vash-vay-yash] (Portugal) Large merchants who blend wine from all over the country, almost single-handedly saved the *Bucelas DO* from extinction. Wines are good, but rarely outstanding.
Velho/velhas [vay-yoh/vay-yash] (Portugal) Old, as of red wine.

Velletri [veh-leh-tree] (Italy) Town in the Alban hills (*Colli Albani*), producing mainly *Trebbiano* and *Malvasia*-based whites, similar to *Frascati*.

☙ **Veltliner** See *Grüner Veltliner*.
Vendange [Von-donzh] (France) Harvest or vintage.
Vendange tardive [von-donzh tahr-deev] (France) Particularly in *Alsace*, wine from *late harvested* grapes, usually lusciously sweet.
Vendemmia/Vendimia [ven-deh-mee-yah/ven-dee-mee-yah] (Italy, Spain) Harvest or vintage.

☐ **Venegazzú** [veh-neh-gaht-zoo] (*Veneto*, Italy) Fine, understated *claret*-like *Cabernet Sauvignon Vino da Tavola* "Super-Veneto" to compete with those *Super Tuscans*. Needs five years. The black label is better.

Veneto [veh-neh-toh] (Italy) Northeastern wine region, the home of *Soave*, *Valpolicella* and *Bardolino*.

Venica e Venica [veh-ni-ca] (*Friuli Venezia Giulia*, Italy) Two brothers who make some of the most flavoursome whites in Collio, including Sauvignon, Pinot Bianco and Chardonnay.

☐ **Veramonte** [vay-rah-mon-tay] (*Casablanca*, Chile) New venture by Augustin Huneeus of *Franciscan Vineyards* in *California*, already producing impressive reds, especially the *Merlot* (which, like many others, is actually *Carmenère*).

☙ **Verdejo** [vehr-de-khoh] (Spain) Interestingly herby white grape; confusingly not the *Verdelho* of *Madeira* and Australia, but the variety used for new-wave *Rueda*.

☙ **Verdelho** [in *Madeira*: vehr-deh-yoh; in *Australia*: vur-del-loh] (Madeira/Australia) White grape used for fortified *Madeira* and *white port* and for limey, dry, table wine in Australia, especially in the Hunter Valley. **Capel Vale; Chapel Hill; Moondah Brook; Sandalford.**

☙ **Verdicchio** [vehr-dee-kee-yoh] (*Marches,* Italy) Spicy white grape seen in a number of *DOCs* in its own right, the best of which is *Verdicchio dei Castelli di Jesi*. In *Umbria* this grape is a major component of *Orvieto*.

☐ **Verdicchio dei Castelli di Jesi** [vehr-dee-kee-yoh day-ee kas-tay-lee dee yay-zee] (*Marches,* Italy) Light, clean, and crisp wines to drink with seafood. **Bucci;** *Garofoli;* **Monacesca; Umani Ronchi.**

☙ **Verduzzo** [vehr-doot-soh] (*Friuli-Venezia Giulia,* Italy) Flavoursome white grape making a dry and a fine *amabile-style* wine in the *Colli Orientale*.

☐ **Vergelegen** [vehr-kur-lek-hen] (*Somerset West,* South Africa) Hi-tech winery producing some of the Cape's more reliable wines.

☐ **Verget** [vehr-jay] (*Burgundy,* France) Young *negociant* based in the Mâconnais and producing impeccable white wines ranging from *Mâcon Villages* to *Meursault* and *Chablis*.

☙ **Vermentino** [vayr-men-tee-noh] (*Liguria,* Italy) The spicy, dry white grape of the Adriatic and, increasingly, in modern southern French *Vin de Table*.

🍇 **Vernaccia** [vayr-naht-chah] (*Tuscany*, Italy) White grape making the Tuscan *DOCG* Vernaccia di San Gimignano (where it's helped by a dash of *Chardonnay*) and *Sardinian* Vernaccia di Oristano. At best with a distinct nut 'n' spice flavour. **Casale-Falchini; Teruzzi & Puthod**

🍷 **Georges Vernay** [vayr-nay] (*Rhône*, France) The great master of *Condrieu* who can do things with *Viognier* that few seem able to match. ☆☆☆☆☆ 1997 Condrieu Les Chaillées de l'Enfer £££

🍷 **Noël Verset** [vehr-say] (*Cornas, Rhône*) Top-class *Cornas* producer.

🍷 **Quinta do Vesuvio** [veh-soo-vee-yoh] (*Douro*, Portugal) Single *quinta port* from the family that owns *Dow's, Graham's, Warre's*, etc.

🍷 **Veuve Clicquot-Ponsardin** [vurv klee-koh pon-sahr-dan] (*Champagne*, France) The distinctive orange label is the mark of reliable non-vintage *Brut*. The *prestige cuvée* is called Grand Dame after the famous Widow Clicquot, the *Demi-Sec* is a lovely honeyed wine and the vintage rosé is now one of the best pink wines in the region. ☆☆☆☆ 1993 Grande Dame ££££

Victoria (Australia) Huge variety of wines from the *Liqueur Muscats* of *Rutherglen* to the peppery *Shirazes* of *Bendigo* and the elegant *Chardonnays* and *Pinot Noirs* of the *Yarra Valley*.

🍷 **Vidal** [vee-dahl] (*Hawke's Bay*, New Zealand) One of New Zealand's top four red wine producers. Associated with *Villa Maria* and *Esk Valley*. *Chardonnays* are the strongest suit. ☆☆☆☆ 1999 Hawke's Bay Riesling. £££

🍇 **Vidal** [vi-dahl] (Canada) A *hybrid* and highly frost-resistant variety looked down on by European authorities but widely and successfully grown in *Canada* for spicily exotic *icewine*. *Iniskillin; Rief Estate.*

🍷 **J. Vidal-Fleury** [vee-dahl flur-ree] (*Rhône*, France) High-quality grower and shipper that belongs to *Guigal*.

VIDE [vee-day] (Italy) Syndicate supposedly denoting finer estate wines.

🍷 **Vi di Romans** [vee-dee roh-mans] (*Friuli-Venezia Giulia*, Italy) If you thought the only winemaking Gallos were in California, meet Gianfranco Gallo's delicious *Tocai Friulano, Pinot Grigio* and *Sauvignon Blanc*.

🍷 **la Vieille Ferme** [vee-yay fairm] (*Rhône*, France) Delicious organic red and white *Côtes du Rhône* from the Perrin family who are best known for their *Châteauneuf du Pape* estate *Château de Beaucastel*.

Vieilles Vignes [vee-yay veen] (France) Wine (supposedly) made from a producer's oldest vines. (In reality, while real vine maturity begins at 25, Vieilles Vignes can mean anything between 15 and 90 years of age.)

🍷 **Vietti** [vee-yet-tee] (*Piedmont*, Italy) Impeccable single-vineyard *Barolo* (Rocche di Castiglione; Brunate and Villero), *Barbaresco* and *Barbera*. The white *Arneis* is pretty impressive too.

🍷 **Vieux Château Certan** [vee-yur-cha-toh-sehr-tan] (*Pomerol, Bordeaux*, France) Ultra-classy, small *Pomerol* property, known as "VCC" to its fans, producing reliable, concentrated, complex wine. ☆☆☆☆☆ 1996 ££££

� **Dom. du Vieux-Télégraphe** [vee-yor tay-lay-grahf] (*Rhône,* France) Modern *Châteauneuf-du-Pape* domaine now back on form after a dull patch. Great whites too. ☆☆☆☆ **1996 Châteauneuf-du-Pape £££**

� **Vignalta** [veen-yal-tah] (*Veneto,* Italy) Colli Eugeanei producer brewing up a storm with its Gemola (*Merlot-Cabernet Franc*) and Sirio (*Muscat*).

� **Ch. Vignelaure** [veen-yah-lawrr] (*Provence,* France) Pioneering estate, now owned by David O'Brien, son of Vincent the Irish racehorse trainer.

Vignoble [veen-yohbl] (France) Vineyard; vineyard area.

� **Villa Maria** (*Auckland,* New Zealand) One of New Zealand's biggest producers, and one which is unusual in coming close to hitting the target with its reds as well as its whites. *Riesling* is a particular success.

� **Villa Sachsen** [zak-zen] (*Rheinhessen,* Germany) Estate with good-rather-than-great, low-yielding vineyards in *Bingen.*

Villages (France) The suffix "villages" e.g., *Côtes du Rhône* or *Mâcon* generally – like *Classico* in Italy – indicates a slightly superior wine from a smaller delimited area encompassing certain village vineyards.

Villany [vee-lah-nyee] (Hungary) Warm area of Hungary with a promising future for soft young drinking reds.

� **Villard** [vee-yarr] (Chile) Improving wines from French-born Thierry Villard, especially *Chardonnays* from *Casablanca.* ☆☆☆☆ **1999 Premium Reserve Chardonnay £££**

� **Ch. Villemaurine** [veel-maw-reen] (*St. Emilion Grand Cru Classé, Bordeaux,* France) Often hard wines which are not helped by heavy-handedness with oak. **82 83 85 86 88 89** 90 **92 94 96 98**

� **Villiera Estate** [vil-lee-yeh-rah] (*Paarl,* South Africa) Reliable range of affordable sparkling and still wines from the go-ahead Grier family. The *Sauvignons* and Cru Monro red and now a very impressive *Merlot* are the wines to buy. ☆☆☆☆ **1999 Gewurztraminer £££**

� **Viñas del Vero** [veen-yas del veh-roh] (*Somontano,* Spain) Modern producer of New Wave varietal wines, including recommendable Cabernet Sauvignon.

Vin de Corse [van dur kaws] (*Corsica,* France) *Appellation* within *Corsica.* Good sweet *Muscats* too. **Gentile;** *Peraldi;* **Skalli; Toraccia.**

Vin de garde [van dur gahrd] (France) Wine to keep.

� **Vin de l'Orléanais** [van dur low-lay-yon-nay] (*Loire,* France) Small *VDQS* in the Central Vineyards of the *Loire.* See *Orléanais.*

Vin de Paille [van dur piy] (*Jura,* France) Traditional, now quite rare regional speciality; sweet golden wine from grapes dried on straw mats.

Vin de Pays [van dur pay-yee] (France) Lowest/broadest geographical designation. In theory, these are simple country wines with certain regional characteristics. In fact, the producers of some of France's most exciting wines – such as *Dom. de Trévallon* and *Mas de Daumas Gassac* – prefer this designation and the freedom it offers from the restrictions imposed on *appellation contrôlée* wines. See *Côtes de Gascogne* and *Vin de Pays d'Oc.*

Vin de Savoie [van dur sav-wah] (Eastern France) Umbrella appellation encompassing mountainous sub-appellations such as *Aprément* and Chignon.

Vin de table [van dur tahbl] (France) Table wine from no particular area.

� **Vin de Thouarsais** [twar-say] (*Loire,* France) *VDQS* for a soft light red from the *Cabernet Franc*; whites from the *Chenin Blanc.*

Vin doux naturel [doo nah-too-rrel] (France) Fortified – so not really "naturel" at all – dessert wines, particularly the sweet, liquorous *Muscats* of the south, such as *Muscat de Beaumes de Venise, Mireval* and *Rivesaltes*.

Vin Gris [van gree] (France) Chiefly from *Alsace* and the *Jura*, pale rosé from red grapes pressed after crushing or following a few hours of skin contact.

Vin Jaune [van john] (*Jura*, France) Golden-coloured *Arbois* speciality; slightly *oxidised* – like *fino sherry*. See *Ch. Chalon*.

Vin ordinaire (France) A simple local wine, usually served in carafes.

Vin Santo [vin sahn-toh] (Italy) Powerful, highly traditional white dessert wine made from bunches of grapes hung to dry in airy barns for up to six years, especially in *Tuscany* and *Trentino*. Often very ordinary, but at its best competes head-on with top-quality medium *sherry*. Best drunk with sweet almond ("Cantuccine") biscuits. *Altesino; Avignonesi; Badia a Coltibuono; Berardenga; Felsina Isole e Olena; Poliziano; Selvapiana.*

Vin vert [van vehrr] (*Languedoc-Roussillon*, France) Light, refreshing, *acidic* white wine.

♟ Vinsobres [van sohb-rruh] (*Rhône*, France) One of the weirdest wine names – it sounds like a brand of non-alcoholic Chardonnay – this is in fact one of the Côtes du Rhône Villages. *Dom des Aussellons; Haume-Arnaud; Dom du Coriançon; du Moulin.*

♟ Vine Cliff [(*Napa*, California) A well-regarded young estate with flavour- and oak-packed, quite unsubtle *Cabernet Sauvignon* and *Chardonnay*.

Viña de Mesa [vee-nah day may-sah] (Spain) Spanish for table wine.

♟ Vinho Verde [vee-noh vehrr-day] (Portugal) Literally "green" wine, confusingly red or pale white often tinged with green. At worst, dull and sweet. At best delicious, refreshing and slightly sparkling. Drink young.

♟ Vinícola Navarra [vee-nee-koh-lah na-vah-rah] (*Navarra*, Spain) Ultra-modern winemaking and newly-planted vineyards beginning to come on stream. Owned by *Bodegas y Bebida*.

Vinifera [vih-nih-feh-ra] Properly *Vitis vinifera*: Species of all European vines – and thus most of the vines used globally for quality wine.

Vino da Tavola [vee-noh dah tah-voh-lah] (Italy) Table wine, but the *DOC* quality designation net is so riddled with holes that producers of many superb – and pricey – wines have contented themselves with this "modest" *appellation*. Now being replaced by *IGT*.

Vino de la Tierra [bee-noh day la tyay rah] (Spain) Spanish wine designation which can offer interesting, affordable, regional wines.

♟ Vino Nobile di Montepulciano [vee-noh noh-bee-lay dee mon-tay-pool-chee-ah-noh] (*Tuscany*, Italy) *Chianti* in long pants; potentially truly noble (though not often), and made from the same grapes. Can age well. Rosso di Montepulciano is the lighter, more accessible version. The *Montepulciano* of the title is the *Tuscan* town, not the grape variety. *Avignonesi; Boscarelli; Carpineto; Casale; del Cerro; Poliziano; Tenuta Trerose.*

Vino novello [vee-noh noh-vay-loh] (Italy) New wine; equivalent to French *nouveau*.

Vinopolis Recently (1999) launched London wine museum / theme park.

Vintage Year of production.

Vintage Champagne (*Champagne*, France) Wine from a single "declared" year.

Vintage Character (port) (*Douro*, Portugal) Smartly packaged up-market *ruby* made by blending various years' wines.

Vintage (port) (*Douro,* Portugal) Produced only in "declared" years, aged in wood then in the bottle for many years. In "off" years, *port* houses release wines from their top estates as single *quinta ports*. This style of *port* must be decanted, as it throws a sediment.

�$ **Viognier** [vee-YoN-nee-yay] (*Rhône,* France) Infuriating white variety which, at its best, produces floral peachy wines that startle with their intensity and originality. Once limited to the *Rhône* – *Condrieu* and *Ch. Grillet* – but now increasingly planted in southern France, California and Australia. Benefits from a little – but not too much – contact with new oak. Controversially, rumours now abound that some of the the Viognier grown in California may in fact be *Roussanne* – another variety altogether. *Calera; Duboeuf; Guigal; Heggies; Andre Perret; Georges Vernay.*

Viré [vee-ray] (*Burgundy,* France) *Mâconnais* village, famous for whites.

☧ **Virgin Hills** [*Victoria,* Australia] A single red blend that is unusually lean in style for Australia and repays keeping. Making valiant efforts to make sulphur-free wine. ☆☆☆☆ **1996** £££
Viticulteur (-Propriétaire) (France) Vine grower/vineyard owner.

�$ **Viura** [vee-yoo-ra] (Spain) Dull white grape of the *Rioja* region and elsewhere, now being used to greater effect.

☧ **Dom. Michel Voarick** [vwah-rik] (*Burgundy,* France) Old-fashioned wines that avoid the use of new oak. Fine *Corton-Charlemagne.*

☧ **Dom. Vocoret** [vok-ko-ray] (*Burgundy,* France) Classy *Chablis* producer whose wines age well. ☆☆☆☆☆ **1997 Chablis Motmains** £££

☧ **Gianni Voerzio** [vwayrt-zee-yoh] (*Piedmont,* Italy) Not quite as impressive a *Barolo* producer as *Roberto* (see below), but a fine source of *Barbera, Freisa, Arneis* and *Dolcetto.*

☧ **Roberto Voerzio** [vwayrt-zee-yoh] (*Piedmont,* Italy) One of the new-wave producers of juicy, spicy reds, including a first-rate *Barolo.* ☆☆☆☆ **1996 Barolo Cerequio** £££

☧ **Alain Voge** [vohzh] (*Rhône,* France) Traditional *Cornas* producer who also makes good *St. Péray.*

☧ **De Vogüé** [dur voh-gway] (*Burgundy,* France) *Chambolle-Musigny* estate whose ultra-concentrated red wines deserve to be kept – for ages. Not cheap, but nor are many of life's true luxuries.
Volatile acidity (VA) Vinegary character evident in wines which have been spoiled by bacteria.

☧ **Volnay** [vohl-nay] (*Burgundy,* France) Red wine village in the *Côte de Beaune* (the Caillerets vineyard, now a *Premier Cru,* was once ranked equal to *le Chambertin*). This is the home of fascinating, plummy, violety reds. 78 80 83 **85 88 89 90 92** 93 94 95 96 97 98 99 *Ampeau; d'Angerville; J-M Boillot; Bouchard Père et Fils; Joseph Drouhin; Vincent Girardin; Camille Giroud; François Buffet; Michel Lafarge; Comtes Lafon; Leroy; Dom de Montille; Pousse d'Or;* Régis Rossignol-Changarnier, Vaudoisey; Voillot.

☧ **Castello di Volpaia** [vol-pi-yah] (*Tuscany,* Italy) Top *Chianti* estate with *Super Tuscans* Coltassala and Balifico. ☆☆☆☆ **1995 Chianti Classico Riserva** £££

☧ **Vosne-Romanée** [vohn roh-ma-nay] (*Burgundy,* France) *Côte de Nuits* red wine village with *Romanée-Conti* among its many grand names, and other potentially gorgeous, plummy, rich wines, from many different producers. 78 79 80 82 83 **85 88 89 90** 92 95 96 97 98 99 *Arnoux; Cacheux; Confuron-Cotetidot; Engel; Anne Gros; Faiveley; Grivot; Hudelot-Noëllat; Jayer-Gilles; Laurent; Leroy; Méo-Camuzet; Mongeard-Mugneret; Mugneret-Gibourg; Rion; Romanée-Conti; Rouget; Jean Tardy; Thomas-Moillard.*

Voss (*Sonoma*, California) Californian venture by *Yalumba*, producing lovely intense *Zinfandel*.

Vougeot [voo-joh] (*Burgundy*, France) *Côte de Nuits commune* comprising the famous *Grand Cru Clos de Vougeot* and numerous growers of varying skill. Red: 78 79 83 **85 88 89 90** 92 93 95 96 97 98. **Amiot-Servelle;** *Bertagna; Bouchard Père et Fils;* Chopin-Groffier; *J-J Confuron; Joseph Drouhin; Engel; Faiveley; Anne & François Gros; Louis Jadot; Leroy; Méo-Camuzet; Denis Mortet;* Mugneret-Gibourg; *Jacques Prieur;* Prieuré Roch; Henri Rebourseau; *Rion;* Ch. de la Tour.

la Voulte Gasparets [voot-gas-pah-ray] (*Languedoc-Roussillon*, France) Unusually ambitious estate with single-vineyard bottlings (Romain Pauc is the best) that show just how good *Corbières* can be from the best sites.

Vouvray [voov-ray] (*Loire*, France) White wines from the *Chenin Blanc*, ranging from clean dry whites and refreshing sparkling wines to *Demi-Secs* and honeyed, long-lived, sweet *Moelleux* wines. Often spoiled by massive doses of *sulphur dioxide*. Sweet white: **76** 83 **85** 86 **88 89 90** 94 95 96 97 98 White: 83 **85 86 88 89 90 94** 95 96 97 98. *Des Aubuisières; Champalou; Huët;* Foreau; Fouquet; Gaudrelle; Jarry; Mabille; Clos de Nouys; Pichot; Vaugondy.

VQA (Canada) Acronym for Vintners Quality Alliance, a group of Canadian producers with a self-styled quality designation.

Vriesenhof [free-zen-hof] (*Stellenbosch*, South Africa) Tough, occasionally classic reds and so-so *Chardonnay*. ☆☆☆ 1997 Pinotage ££

W

Wachau [vak-kow] (Austria) Major wine region producing some superlative *Riesling* from steep, terraced vineyards. Alzinger; *Pichler; Hirtzberger;* Jamek; *Nikolaihof; Prager; Freie Weingärtner Wachau.*

Wachenheim [vahkh-en-hime] (*Pfalz*, Germany) Superior *Mittelhaardt* village which should produce full, rich, unctuous *Riesling*. QbA/Kab/Spät: **85 88 89 90** 91 **92 93** 94 95 96 97 98 Aus/Beeren/Tba: **83 85 88 89 90** 91 92 93 94 95 96 97 98 *Biffar; Bürklin-Wolf.*

Waiheke Island (*Auckland*, New Zealand) Tiny island off Auckland where holiday cottages compete for space with vineyards. Land – and the resulting wines – is pricy, but this microclimate does produce some of New Zealand's best reds. *Goldwater Estate; Stonyridge;* Te Motu.

Waipara Springs [wi-pah-rah] (*Canterbury*, New Zealand) Tiny producer offering the opportunity to taste wines from this southern region at their best.

Wairau River [wi-row] (*Marlborough*, New Zealand) Classic Kiwi *Chardonnays* and *Sauvignons* with piercing fruit character. ☆☆☆☆ 1999 Sauvignon Blanc ££

Walker Bay (South Africa) Promising region for *Pinot Noir* and *Chardonnay*. Established vineyards include *Hamilton Russell* and *Bouchard-Finlayson*.

Warre's [waw] (*Douro*, Portugal) Oldest of the big seven *port* houses and a stablemate to *Dow's*, *Graham's*, and *Smith Woodhouse*. Traditional *port* which is both rather sweeter and more *tannic* than most. The old-fashioned *Late-Bottled Vintage* is particularly worth seeking out too. Quinta da Cavadinha is the recommendable *single-quinta*.. 55 58 60 **63 66 70 75** 77 83 85 91 94 97 ☆☆☆☆☆ **1988 Quinta da Cavadinha £££**

Warwick Estate [wo-rik] (*Stellenbosch*, South Africa) Source of some of South Africa's best reds, including a good *Bordeaux*-blend called Trilogy. The *Cabernet Franc* grows extremely well here.

Washington State (US) Underrated (especially in the US) state whose dusty irrigated vineyards produce classy *Riesling*, *Sauvignon*, and *Merlot*. Red: 85 88 **89** 91 92 94 **95** 96 97 98 White: **95 96** 97 98. *Col Solare; Columbia; Columbia Crest; 'Ecole 41; Hedges; Hogue; Kiona; Leonetti Cellars; Quilceda Creek;* Staton Hills; Ch. Ste. Michelle; *Paul Thomas; Walla Walla Vintners; Waterbrook; Andrew Will; Woodward Canyon.*

Waterbrook (*Washington State*, US) High quality winery with stylish *Sauvignon Blanc*, *Viognier* and *Chardonnay* as well as berryish reds.

Jimmy Watson Trophy (*Victoria*, Australia) Coveted trophy given annually to the best young (still-in-barrel) red at the Melbourne Wine Show. Apparently "worth" $(Aus) 1,000,000 in increased sales to the winner, it is often criticised for hyping stuff that is not necessarily representative of what you'll actually be drinking when the wine gets in the bottle.

Geheimrat J. Wegeler Deinhard [vayg-lur-dine-hard] (*Rheingau*, Germany) Once family-owned producer recently bought by the huge sparkling wine producer Henkell Söhnlein. Wines that made Deinhard famous include recommendable top *Mosel*s such as *Bernkasteler Doctor* and *Wehlener Sonnenuhr*. It remains to be seen whether the new owners continue to produce wines of the same standard.

Wehlen [vay-lehn] (*Mosel-Saar-Ruwer*, Germany) *Mittelmosel village* making fresh, sweet, honeyed wines; look for the *Sonnenuhr* vineyard. QbA/Kab/Spät: **85 86 88 89 90** 91 92 93 94 95 Aus/Beeren/Tba: **83 85** 88 89 90 **91** 92 93 94 95 96. *Dr Loosen;* JJ Prum; SA Prum; *Richter; Wegeler Deinhard; Selbach-Oster.*

Weingut Dr Robert Weil [vile] (*Rheingau*, Germany) Suntory-owned, family-run winery with stunning dry and *late harvest* wines. ☆☆☆☆☆ **1998 Kiedrich Gräfenberg, Riesling Spätlese £££**

Dom. Weinbach [vine-bahkh] (*Alsace*, France) Laurence Faller regularly turns out wonderful, concentrated, but gloriously subtle wines. The Cuvée Laurence is a personal favourite. ☆☆☆☆☆ **1997 Riesling Grand Cru Schlossberg Cuvee Ste Catherine Cuvee de Centenaire ££££**

� **Bodegas y Cavas de Weinert** [vine-nurt] (Argentina) Excellent *Cabernet Sauvignon* specialist, whose soft, ripe wines last extraordinarily well. ☆☆☆☆ **1995 Malbec ££**

Weingut [vine-goot] (Germany) Wine estate.

Weinkellerei [vine-keh-lur-ri] (Germany) Cellar or winery.

☆ **Weissburgunder** [vi-sbur-goon-dur] (Germany/Austria) The *Pinot Blanc* in Germany and Austria. Relatively rare, so often made with care.

☆ **Weissherbst** [vi-sairb-st] (*Baden,* Germany) Spicy, berryish dry rosé made from various different grape varieties.

☆ **Welschriesling** [velsh-rreez-ling] Aka *Riesling Italico, Lutomer, Olasz, Laski Rizling.* Dull grape, unrelated to the *Rhine Riesling,* but with many synonyms. Comes into its own when affected by *botrytis.*

☆ **Wendouree** (*Clare,* Australia) Small winery with a cult following for its often *Malbec*-influenced reds. Wines are very hard to find outside Australia but are well worth seeking out. ☆☆☆☆ **1992 Cabernet Malbec £££**

☆ **Wente Brothers** (*Livermore,* California) Improving family company which, despite – or perhaps because of – such distracting enterprises as producing cigars and joint ventures in Mexico, Israel, and Eastern Europe, is still trailing in quality and value behind firms like *Fetzer. Murrieta's Well* is the strongest card in the Wente pack. ☆☆☆☆ **1997 Herman Wente Reserve Chardonnay ££**

☆ **Weingut Domdechant Werner'sches** [dom-dekh-ahnt vayr-nehr-ches vine-goot] (*Rheingau,* Germany) Excellent vineyard sites at *Hochheim* and *Riesling* grapes combine to produce a number of traditional wines that age beautifully.

☆ **De Wetshof Estate** [vets-hof] (*Robertson,* South Africa) *Chardonnay* pioneer, Danie de Wet makes up to seven different styles of wine for different markets.

☆ **William Wheeler Winery** (*Sonoma,* California) Inventive producer whose Quintet brings together such diverse grapes as the *Pinot Meunier,* the *Pinot Noir, Grenache,* and *Cabernet Sauvignon.* ☆☆☆☆☆ **1995 Napa Valley Reserve Cabernet Sauvignon ££**

☆ **White Cloud** (New Zealand) Commercial white made by *Nobilo.*

White port (*Douro,* Portugal) Semi-dry aperitif, drunk by its makers with tonic water and ice, which shows what they think of it. *Churchill's* make a worthwhile version. ☆☆☆☆ **Churchill's White Port ££**

☆ **Whitehall Lane** (*Napa Valley,* California) Impressive *Merlots* and *Cabernets.* ☆☆☆☆☆ **1996 Cabernet Sauvignon Napa Valley Leonardini Vineyard.**

☆ **Wien** [veen] (Austria) Region close to the city of Vienna, producing ripe-tasting whites and reds. **Mayer; Wieninger.**

☆ **Wild Horse** (*San Luis Obispo,* California) *Chardonnays, Pinot Blancs* and *Pinot Noirs* are all good, but the perfumed *Malvasia Bianca* is the star.

Willamette Valley [wil-AM-et] (*Oregon,* US) The heart of Oregon's *Pinot Noir* vineyards.

☆ **Williams Selyem** [sel-yem] (*Sonoma,* California) Recently dissolved partnership producing world-class *Burgundian*-style *Chardonnay* and *Pinot Noir.*

Wiltingen [vihl-ting-gehn] (*Mosel-Saar-Ruwer,* Germany) Distinguished *Saar* village, making elegant, slatey wines. Well known for the *Scharzhofberg* vineyard. QbA/Kab/Spät: **85** 86 **88 89 90** 91 **92 93 94** 95 96 97 98 Aus/Beeren/Tba: **83 85 88 89** 90 91 92 93 94 95 96 97 98 99

☲ **Wing Canyon** (*Mount Veeder,* California) Small *Cabernet Sauvignon* specialist with vineyards high in the hills of *Mount Veeder.* Great, intense, blackcurranty wines. ☆☆☆☆ 1995 Mount Veeder Cabernet Sauvignon ££££

Winkel [vin-kel] (*Rheingau,* Germany) Village with a reputation for complex delicious wine, housing *Schloss Vollrads* estate. QbA/Kab/Spät: **85** 86 **88 89 90** 91 **92 93** 94 95 96 97 98 Aus/Beeren/Tba: **83 85 88 89** 90 91 **92 93** 94 95 96 97 98 99

Wintrich [vin-trikh] (*Mosel,* Germany) Less famous – but often more recommendable commune close to *Piesport.* Ohligsberg is the vineyard to look out for. *Rheinhold Haart.*

Winzerverein/Winzergenossenschaft [vint-zur-veh-rine/vint-zur-geh-nosh-en-shaft] (Germany) Cooperative.

☲ **Wirra Wirra Vineyards** (*McLaren Vale,* Australia) Reliable producer making first-class *Riesling* and *Cabernet* which, in best vintages, is sold as The Angelus.

☲ **Wither Hills** (*Marlborough,* New Zealand) Instantly successful new venture from Brent Marris former winemaker at *Delegat's.*

☲ **WO (Wine of Origin)** (South Africa) Official European-style certification system that is taken seriously in South Africa.

☲ **J.L. Wolf** [volf] (*Pfalz,* Germany) Classy estate, recently reconstituted by *Dr Loosen.* ☆☆☆☆☆ 1998 Forster Pechstein Riesling Spätlese Trocken £££

☲ **Wolfberger** [volf-behr-gur] (*Alsace,* France) Brand used by the dynamic Eguisheim cooperative for highly comercial wines. ☆☆☆☆ 1998 Gewurztraminer ££

☲ **Wolffer Estate** (*New York,* US) Long Island winery gaining a local following for its *Merlot* and *Chardonnay.*

☲ **Wolff-Metternich** [volf met-tur-nikh] (*Baden,* Germany) Good, rich *Riesling* from the granite slopes of *Baden.*

☲ **Woodward Canyon** (*Washington State,* US) Small producer of characterful but subtle *Chardonnay* and *Bordeaux*-style reds that compete with the best of California. *Semillons* are pretty impressive too. ☆☆☆☆ 1996 Cabernet Sauvignon Washington Canoe Ridge Vineyard Artist Series £££

Württemberg [foor-thm-behrg] (Germany) *Anbaugebiet* surrounding the Neckar area, producing more red than any other German region.

☲ **Würzburg** [foor-ts-burg] (*Franken,* Germany) Great *Sylvaner* country, though there are some fine *Rieslings* too. **Bürgerspital; *Juliusspital.***

☲ **Wyken** (*Suffolk,* UK) Producer of one of England's most successful red wines (everything's relative) and rather better *Bacchus* white.

☲ **Wyndham Estate** (*Hunter Valley,* Australia) Ultra-commercial *Hunter/Mudgee* producer which, like *Orlando,* now belongs to Pernod-Ricard. Quite what that firm's French customers would think of these often rather jammy blockbusters is anybody's guess. ☆☆☆☆ 1998 Bin 555 Shiraz ££

☲ **Wynns** (*Coonawarra,* Australia) Subsidiary of *Penfolds,* based in *Coonawarra* and producer of the *John Riddoch Cabernet* and Michael *Shiraz,* both of which are only produced in good vintages and sell fast at high prices. There is also a big buttery *Chardonnay* and a commercial *Riesling.* ☆☆☆☆☆ 1997 Coonawarra Estate Michael Shiraz £££

Ch. Xanadu [za-na-doo] (*Margaret River,* Australia) The reputation here was built on *Semillon,* but the *Cabernet* is good too. ☆☆☆☆ **1998 Cabernet Reserve £££**

Xarel-lo [sha-rehl-loh] (*Catalonia,* Spain) Fairly basic grape exclusive to *Catalonia.* Used for *Cava;* best in the hands of *Jaume Serra.*

Xynasteri [ksee-nahs-teh-ree] (Cyprus) Indigenous white grape.

"Y" d'Yquem [ee-grek dee-kem] (*Bordeaux,* France) Hideously expensive dry wine of *Ch. d'Yquem* which, like other such efforts by *Sauternes châteaux,* is of greater academic than hedonistic interest. (Under ludicrous Appellation Contrôlée rules, dry Sauternes has to be labelled as "Bordeaux" – like the region's very cheapest, nastiest dry white wine.

Yakima Valley [yak-ih-mah] (*Washington State,* US) Principal region of *Washington State.* Particularly good for *Merlot, Riesling* and *Sauvignon.* Red: 85 88 **89** 91 92 94 95 96 97 98 White: **90 91 92 94 95** 96 97 98 Blackwood Canyon; Chinook; *Columbia Crest; Columbia Winery; Hogue; Kiona;* Ch. Ste. Michelle; Staton Hills; Stewart; Tucker; Yakima River.

Yalumba [ya-lum-ba] (*Barossa Valley,* Australia) Associated with *Hill-Smith, Heggies, Pewsey-Vale,* and *Jansz* in Australia, *Nautilus* in New Zealand and *Voss* in California. Producers of good-value reds and whites under the Oxford Landing label; more serious vineyard-designated reds and dry and sweet whites, fortified wines (including *Rutherglen Muscat*) and some of Australia's most appealing sparkling wine, including *Angas Brut* and the brilliant Cuvée One *Pinot Noir-Chardonnay.*
☆☆☆☆ **1995 Cabernet Sauvignon Shiraz £££;** ☆☆☆☆ **1998 The Virgilius Viognier £££**

Yarra Ridge [ya-ra] (Australia) *Mildara-Blass* label that might lead buyers to imagine that its wines all come from vineyards in the *Yarra Valley.* In fact, like *Napa Ridge,* this is a brand that is used for wine from vineyards in other regions. European laws, which are quite strict on this kind of thing, apply to non-European wines, so bottles sold in the EU will be from Yarra.

Yarra Valley [ya-ra] (*Victoria*, Australia) Historic wine district whose "boutiques" make top-class *Burgundy*-like *Pinot Noir* and *Chardonnay* (*Coldstream Hills* and *Tarrawarra*), some stylish *Bordeaux*-style reds and, at *Yarra Yering*, a brilliant *Shiraz*. **De Bortoli; Coldstream Hills; Dom. Chandon (Green Point);** Diamond Valley; Long Gully; **Mount Mary;** Oakridge; St Huberts; Seville Estate; *Tarrawarra; Yarra Yering;* Yering Station.

♟ **Yarra Yering** [ya-ra yeh-ring] (*Yarra Valley*, Australia) Bailey Carrodus proves that the *Yarra Valley* is not just *Pinot Noir* country by producing a complex *Cabernet* blend, including a little *Petit Verdot* (Dry Red No.1) and a *Shiraz* (Dry Red No.2), in which he puts a bit of *Viognier*. Underhill is the *second label*. ☆☆☆☆ **1994 Underhill Shiraz £££**

♟ **Yecla** [yeh-klah] (Spain) Generally uninspiring red wine region.

♟ **Yellowglen** (South Australia) Producer of uninspiring basic sparkling wine, and some really fine top-end fare, including the "Y" which looks oddly reminiscent of a sparkling wine called "J" from *Jordan* in California.

♟ **Yering Station** (*Victoria*, Australia) High quality young *Yarra* estate, with rich, but stylish Chardonnay and Pinot Noir.

♟ **Yeringberg** (*Victoria*, Australia) Imposing old Yarra estate that used to produce disappointing wines. Now making Rhône style reds and whites that are worth looking out for.

♟ **Yonder Hill** (*Stellenbosch*, South Africa) New winery making waves with well-oaked reds. ☆☆☆☆ **1997 Merlot ££**

Yonne [yon] (*Burgundy*, France) Northern *Burgundy* département in which *Chablis* is to be found.

♟ **Ch. d'Yquem** [dee-kem] (*Sauternes Premier Cru Supérieur, Bordeaux*, France) Sublime *Sauternes*. The grape pickers are sent out several times to select the best grapes. Not produced every year. Recently bought by the giant Louis-Vuitton Moët Hennessy group which wants to sell the wine through its duty-free shops in the Far East. Such is the wine world. **67 71** 73 **75 76** 77 78 79 **80 81 82** 83 84 85 86 87 88 89 90 91 93 94 95 96 97 98 ☆☆☆☆☆ **1998 ££££**

Z

♟ **Zaca Mesa** [za-ka may-sa] (*Santa Barbara*, California) Fast-improving winery with a focus on spicy *Rhône* varietals.

♟ **Zandvliet** [zand-fleet] (*Robertson*, South Africa) Estate well thought-of in South Africa for its Merlot.

♟ **ZD** [zee-dee] (*Napa*, California) Long-established producer of very traditional California oaky, tropically fruity Chardonnay and plummy Pinot Noir.

Zell [tzell] (*Mosel-Saar-Ruwer*, Germany) Bereich of lower *Mosel* and village, making pleasant, flowery *Riesling*. Famous for the *Schwarze Katz* (black cat) *Grosslage*. QbA/Kab/Spät: **85 88 89 90** 91 **92** 93 94 95 96 97 98 Aus/Beeren/Tba: **83 85 88 89** 90 91 **92** 93 94 95 96 97 98

Zema Etate [zee-mah] (*South Australia*) High quality Coonawarra estate with characteristically rich, berryish reds.

ℐ **Zenato** [zay-NAH-toh] (*Veneto*, Italy) Successful producer of modern *Valpolicella* (particularly *Amarone*), *Soave*, and *Lugana*. ☆☆☆☆☆ **1999 Cortechiaia Soave Classico £££**

Zentralkellerei [tzen-trahl-keh-lur-ri] (Germany) Massive central cellars for groups of cooperatives in six of the *Anbaugebiete* – the *Mosel-Saar-Ruwer* Zentralkellerei is Europe's largest cooperative.

ℐ **Fattoria Zerbina** [zehr-bee-nah] (*Emilia-Romagna*, Italy) The eye-catching wine here is the Marzeno di Marzeno *Sangiovese-Cabernet*, but this producer deserves credit for making one of the only examples of Albana di Romagna to warrant the region's DOCG status.

ℐ **Zevenwacht** [zeh-fen-fakht] (*Stellenbosch*, South Africa) One of South Africa's better producers of both Shiraz and Pinotage. ☆☆☆☆ **1998 Shiraz £££**

ℐ **Zibibbo** [zee-BEE-boh] (*Sicily*, Italy) Good, light *Muscat* for easy summer drinking.

🍇 **Zierfandler** [zeer-fen-dlur] (Austria) Indigenous grape used in Thermenregion to make lightly spicy white wines.

ℐ **Zilliken** [tsi-li-ken] (*Saar*, Germany) Great *late harvest Riesling* producer. ☆☆☆☆☆ **1997 Riesling Beerenauslese Gold Cap Saarburger Rausch £££**

Zimbabwe An industry started by growing grapes in ex-tobacco fields is slowly attaining a level of international adequacy.

ℐ **Dom. Zind-Humbrecht** [zind-hoom-brekht] (*Alsace*, France) Extraordinarily consistent producer of ultra-concentrated, single-vineyard wines and good *varietals* that have won numerous awards from the *International Wine Challenge* and drawn *Alsace* to the attention of a new generation of wine drinkers. ☆☆☆☆ **1998 Pinot Gris Heimbourg £££**

🍇 **Zinfandel** [zin-fan-del] (California, Australia, South Africa) Versatile red grape, producing everything from dark, jammy, leathery reds in California, to (with a little help from sweet *Muscat*) pale pink "blush" wines, and even a little fortified wine that bears comparison with *port*. Also grown by *Cape Mentelle* and *Nepenthe* in Australia, and *Blauwklippen* in South Africa. *Chateau Potelle; Cline; Clos la Chance; De Loach; Edmeades; Elyse; Gary Farrell; Green & Red; Lamborn Family Vineyards; Quivira, Rafanelli; Ravenswood; Ridge; Rocking Horse; Rosenblum; St. Francis; Steele; Storybook Mountain, Joseph Swan; Turley; Wellington.*

ℐ **Don Zoilo** [don zoy-loh] (*Jerez*, Spain) Classy *sherry* producer. ☆☆☆☆ **Don Zoilo Oloroso ££**

ℐ **Zonin** [zoh-neen] (*Veneto*, Italy) Dynamic company producing good wines in the *Veneto*, *Piedmont* and *Tuscany*.

🍇 **Zweigelt** [zvi-gelt] (Austria) Distinctive berryish red wine grape, more or less restricted to Austria and Hungary. **Angerer; Hafner; Kracher; Müller; Umathum.**

UK
AND EIRE
MERCHANTS

WHAT THIS CHAPTER CONTAINS

The following chapter has been conceived in order to help you to find almost everything – short of a congenial companion – you are likely to need to enjoy wine. If you are looking for a good local retailer, a wine from a specific region/country, or perhaps a wine course/school, vacation, tour, cellar, rack, or chiller, this is the place to look.

WINE MERCHANTS

3D Wines ☆☆☆☆
Holly Lodge, High Street, Swineshead, Lincolnshire, PE20 3LH. 01205 820 745. FAX 01205 821 042. E-mail: info@3dwines.com Website: www.3dwines.com
By the case only, credit cards, delivery, tastings, mail order only.
French wine club with an outlet near Calais.

W.M. Addison ☆☆☆☆
The Warehouse, Village Farm, Lilleshall, Newport, Shropshire, TF10 9HB. 01952 670 200. FAX 01952 677 309.
Credit cards, delivery, en primeur, cellarage, glass hire/loan, tastings.
Australian and classic French wines.

Adnams ☆☆☆☆☆
The Crown, High Street, Southwold, Suffolk, IP18 6DP. 01502 727 222. FAX 01502 727 223.
E-mail: wines@adnams.co.uk
Credit cards, delivery, tastings, en primeur, cellarage, glass hire, mail order case only.
Brilliantly eclectic, innovative and imaginative merchant.

Allez Vins! ☆☆☆
PO Box 1019, Long Itchington, Rugby, Warwickshire, CV23 8ZU. +FAX 01926 811 969. E-mail: av@bigfoot.com
Website:www.allezvins.co.uk
Credit cards, tastings, delivery, glass hire, mail order only.
Family company specialising in French regional wines from small producers.

The Antique Wine Co. ☆☆☆☆
The Old Stables, Thorpe Constantine, Staffs, B79 0LH. 01827 830 707. FAX 01827 830 539.
E-mail: celebrate@antiquewine.co.uk
Website: www.antiquewine.co.uk
Mail order only, credit cards, delivery, cellarage, en primeur.
Specialists in anniversary wines.

John Armit Wines ☆☆☆☆☆
5 Royalty Studios, 105 Lancaster Road, London, W11 1QF. 020 7727 6846. FAX 020 7727 7133. E-mail: info@armit.co.uk Website: www. armit.co.uk
By the case only, credit cards, delivery, tastings, en primeur, cellarage, mail order only.
Superb clarets, Burgundies and Italians. Specialised wine events for women.

Arriba Kettle ☆☆☆☆
Buckle Street, Honeybourne, Evesham, Worcs, WR11 5QB. 01386 833 024. FAX 01386 833 541. Mail order only, by the case only, glass hire, delivery.
Focus is on France. Good small growers from Loire, Burgundy and the South.

Asda Stores ☆☆☆
Asda House, Southbank, Great Wilson Street, Leeds, LS11 5AD. 01132 435 435. FAX 01132 417 766.
Website: www.asda.co.uk
Credit cards, tastings, glass hire/loan.
US-owned supermarket offering value-for-money wines. Six big-saver lines are available by the case only.

Australian Wine Club ☆☆☆☆☆
Freepost WC5500, Slough, Berks, SL3 9BH. 020 8538 0718. Order line: 0800 856 2004. FAX 0800 856 2114.
E-mail: sales@austwine.demon. co. uk
Website: www.australian-wine.co.uk
Mail order only, by the case only, credit cards, delivery.
Rare wines and an annual wine fair.

Averys of Bristol ☆☆☆☆
Orchard House, Southfield Road, Nailsea, Bristol, BS48 1JN. 01275 811 100. FAX 01275 811 101.
Credit cards, delivery, tastings, en primeur, cellarage, glass hire/loan.
Personal service, expert advice and great wines from traditional as well as up-and-coming areas.

Ballantynes of Cowbridge ☆☆☆☆

3 Westgate, Cowbridge, Vale of
Glamorgan CF71 7AQ. ☎ 01446 774
840. FAX 01446 775 253. E-mail: richard@
ballantynes.co.uk Website:
www.ballantynes.co.uk Credit cards,delivery,
tastings, en primeur, cellarage, glass loan.
Dynamic list, featuring Italy, Spain,
Australia, Burgundy and the Languedoc.

Balls Brothers ☆☆☆☆

313 Cambridge Heath Road, London, E2
9LQ. ☎ 020 7739 6466. FAX 020 7729
0258. E-mail: sales@ballsbrothers.co.uk
Website: www.ballsbrothers.co.uk
By the case only, mail order, credit cards,
delivery, en primeur, tastings, glass hire/loan.
Good French and Italian wines.

Georges Barbier ☆☆☆☆

267 Lee High Road, London, SE12 8RU.
☎ 020 8852 5801. FAX 020 8463 0398.
E-mail: georgesbarbier@telinco.co.uk
By the case only, delivery, cellarage.
Eclectic wine selection from Spain,
Uruguay and a great range from France.

Barrels & Bottles ☆☆☆☆

3 Oak Street, Heeley Bridge, Sheffield S8
9UB. ☎ 0114 2556611. FAX 0114 255
1010.
E-mail: sales@barrelsandbottles.co.uk
Website:www.barrelsandbottles.co.uk
Credit cards, delivery, tastings, en primeur,
cellarage, glass hire/loan.
German specialist with retail wine store.

Bat & Bottle ☆☆☆☆

Knightley Grange Office, Grange Road,
Woodseaves, Staffs, ST20 0JU. ☎ 01785
284 495.FAX 01785 284 877.
E-mail: sales@batandbottle-wine.co.uk
Website: www.batandbottlewine.co.uk
Credit cards, delivery, tastings, en primeur, glass
loan, mail order, cellarage.
Focusing on small growers from Italy,
France and Iberia.

Bennetts Wines ☆☆☆☆☆

High Street, Chipping Campden, Glos,
GL55 6AG. ☎ 01386 840 392.
FAX 01386 840 974. E-mail:
enquiries@bennettsfinewines.com
Website: www.bennettsfinewines.com
Credit cards, delivery, tastings, en primeur.
A terrific selection of classic French and
great New World wines, including good
older bottles.

Berkmann Wine Cellars ☆☆☆☆

12 Brewery Road, London, N7 9NH.
☎ 020 7609 4711. FAX 020 7607 0018.
E-mail: karenm@berkmann.co.uk
Website: www.berkmann.co.uk
Credit cards, delivery.
Focus on France, plus good Italian,
Spanish and American wines.

Berry Bros. & Rudd ☆☆☆☆☆

3 St. James's Street, London, SW1A 1EG.
☎ 020 7396 9600. / 020 7396 9669.
FAX 020 7396 9611. E-mail: orders@
bbr.co.uk Website: www.bbr.co.uk
Credit cards, delivery, en primeur, cellarage,
glass hire/loan, mail order worldwide.
Fantastic French and New World wines.
Great, comprehensive Internet service.

Bibendum ☆☆☆☆☆

113 Regents Park Road, London, NW1
8UR. ☎ 020 7916 7706. FAX 020 7722
7354. E-mail: sales@bibendum-
wine.co.uk Website: www.bibendum-
wine.co.uk By the case only, mail order only,
credit cards, delivery, tastings, glass loan, en
primeur, cellarage.
This enthusiastic firm still offers an
excellent range of individual Old and
New World wines backed up by excellent
customer service.

Booths of Stockport ☆☆☆☆

62 Heaton Moor Road, Heaton Moor,
Stockport, SK4 4ND. ☎+FAX 0161 432
3309.
Credit cards, delivery, tastings, glass hire/loan.
Good Iberian, Australian and Chileans.

Booths Supermarkets ☆☆☆☆☆

4-6 Fishergate, Preston, PR1 3LJ.
☎ 01772 251 701. FAX 01772 255 642.
Credit cards, glass hire/loan, tastings.
One of Britain's most enterprising
supermarket groups. The firm behind
everywineco.uk

Bordeaux Direct ☆☆☆☆

New Aquitaine House, Exeter Way,
Theale, Reading, Berkshire, RG7 4Pl.
☎ 0118 903 0903. FAX 0118 903 1073.
E-mail: orders@bordeaux-direct.co.uk
Website: www.bordeauxdirect.co.uk
Mail order, credit cards, delivery, tastings, en
primeur, cellarage, glass hire/loan.
Part of the world's biggest home delivery
wine group. French country wines,
newsletters and a great tasting festival.

Bordeaux Index Ltd ☆☆☆☆

1st Floor, 3-5 Spafield Street, London EC1 4QB. [📞] 020 7278 9495. / 278 9795. [FAX] 020 7278 9707.
E-mail: sales@bordeaux.com
Website: www.bordeauxindex.com
By the case only, delivery, en primeur, cellarage.
Young, dynamic, high-tech wine traders.

The Bottleneck ☆☆☆

7 & 9 Charlotte Street, Broadstairs, Kent, CT10 1LR. [📞]+[FAX] 01843 861 095.
Credit cards, delivery, tastings, glass loan.
A good range of New World wines.

Bottoms Up ☆☆☆☆

Sefton House, 42 Church Road, Welwyn Garden City, Herts, AL8 6PJ. [📞] 01707 385 110. [FAX] 01707 385 004.
Website: www.enjoyment.co.uk
Credit cards, delivery, tastings, glass hire/loan.
Quirky chain from the same group as Victoria Wine, Wine Rack and Thresher.

La Bouteille d'Or ☆☆☆☆

Queens Lodge, Queens Club Gardens, London W14 9TA [📞] 020 7385 3122. [FAX] 0207 385 3122.
E-mail: labouteilledor@newbury.net
By the case only, mail order, delivery, tastings.
Focus on Champagne from small growers.

The Burgundy Shuttle ☆☆☆☆

13 Mandeville Courtyard, 142 Battersea Park Road, London, SW11 4NB.
[📞] 020 7498 0755. [FAX] 020 7498 0724.
E-mail: peter@burgundyshuttle.ltd.uk
By the case only, credit cards, en primeur, cellarage, glass loan, delivery.
Excellent Burgundy specialist.

The Butlers Wine Cellar ☆☆☆☆

247 Queens Park Road, Brighton, East Sussex, BN2 2XJ. [📞] 01273 698 724. [FAX] 01273 622 761.
E-mail: ButlersWine.cellar@cwcom.net
Website: www.altura.co.uk/Butlers.htm
Credit cards, delivery, tastings, glass hire/loan.
Great range from the classic to the eclectic.

Andrew Bruce ☆☆☆☆

Fourth Floor, 22 Hans Place, London, SW1X 0EP. [📞] 020 7591 1982 [FAX] 020 7225 0366.
E-mail: abrucewine@compuserve.com
Website: www.abruce.co.uk
By the case only, en primeur, cellarage, delivery.
Small list specialising in fine and rare.

Anthony Byrne ☆☆☆☆

Ramsey Business Park, Stocking Fen Road, Ramsey, Huntingdon, Cambs, PE17 1UR. [📞] 01487 814 555. [FAX] 01487 814 962.
E-mail: anthony.byrne@dial.pipex.com
Website: dspace.dial.pipex.com/anthony.byrne
Delivery, en primeur, cellarage, tastings, by the case only.
Fine wines from Alsace and Burgundy.

D Byrne & Co. ☆☆☆☆☆

Victoria Buildings, 12 King Street, Clitheroe, Lancs, BB7 2EP. [📞] 01200 423 152. [FAX] 01200 429 386. En primeur, credit cards, glass loan, delivery, tastings.
Family business with a great combination of traditional and new wave wines.

Cape Province Wines ☆☆☆

77 Laleham Road, Staines, Middlesex, TW18 2EA. [📞] 01784 451 860. [FAX] 01784 469 267. E-mail: capewines@msn.com Website: www.cape-wines.com
Credit cards, mail order, delivery.
The best place for hard-to-find modern South African wines.

Cave Cru Classé ☆☆☆☆

Unit 13, The Leathermarket, Weston Street, London, SE1 3ER. [📞] 020 7378 8579. [FAX] 020 7378 8544.
E-mail: enquiries@ccc.co.uk
Website: www.cave-cru-classe.com
By the case only, cellarage, credit cards, delivery, en primeur, tastings.
Top vintages of top wines from Rhône, Bordeaux and Burgundy.

The Celtic Vintner ☆☆☆☆

Star Trading Estate, Ponthir Road, Caerleon, Newport, Gwent, NP18 1PQ.
[📞] 01633 430 055. [FAX] 01633 430 154.
E-mail: info@celticvintner.co.uk Website: www.thewinemarket.co.uk
By the case only, credit cards, delivery, glass hire.
Award-winning merchant strong on Australia, Spain and South Africa.

Andrew Chapman ☆☆☆☆

14 Haywards Road, Drayton, Abingdon, Oxon OX14 4LB. [📞] 01235 550707. [FAX] 01235 55080. E-mail: info@acfw.co.uk
Website: www.acfw.co.uk
By the case only, mail order, credit cards, glass loan, delivery, tastings.
Interesting wines and a lively list.

Charterhouse Emporium ☆☆☆☆

82 Goding Street, London, SE11 5AW.
📞 020 7587 1302. FAX 020 7587 0982.
E-mail: charterhousewineemporium@
ukgateway.net
Website: www.charterhousewine.co.uk
Credit cards, delivery, en primeur, cellarage,
tastings, glass loan.
*Well-chosen wines, particularly from
Australia, Chile and Spain.*

Châteaux Wines ☆☆☆

Paddock House, Upper Tockington
Road, Tockington, Bristol, BS32 4LQ.
📞+FAX 01454 613 959.
E-mail: cheryl.miller@bris.ac.uk
Website: www.btinternet.com
By the case only, credit cards, mail order,
delivery, en primeur, cellarage, tastings.
Decent French selection.

Brian Coad Fine Wines ☆☆☆☆

Grape Expectations Wine Warehouse,
Stray Park, off Park St., Ivybridge, Devon,
PL21 9DW. 📞 01752 698 632. FAX 01752
691 160. Mail order,by the case only, delivery,
tastings, en primeur (port only), glass loan.
Gems here include great Loires.

Cockburns of Leith ☆☆☆☆

The Wine Emporium, 7 Devon Place,
Edinburgh, Scotland EH12 5HJ.
📞 0131 346 1113. FAX 0131 313 2607.
Website: www.winelist.co.uk
Credit cards, delivery, tastings, en primeur, glass
loan, cellarage.
*Reliable, traditional merchant. Good for
Claret and Burgundy.*

Compendium Wine Merchants
☆☆☆

Alanbrooke Road, Castlereagh, Belfast
BT6 9PR. 📞 01232 791197.
FAX 01232 798001.
E-mail: info@compendiumwines.com
Credit cards, delivery, glass loan/hire, tastings.
*New kids on the block with an exciting
portfolio and an approachable, informal
manner. Australian range is particularly
impressive.*

Co-op (CWS Retail) ☆☆☆

New Century House, PO Box 53,
Manchester, M60 4ES. 📞 0800 317
827. FAX 0161 827 5117.
Website: www.co-op.co.uk Credit cards.
*A good list of wines at good bargain
prices.*

Corkscrew Wines ☆☆☆☆

Arch 5, Viaduct Estate, Carlisle, CA2 5BN.
📞+FAX 01228 543033. E-mail:wines@
corkscrewwines.demon.co.uk
Website:www.corkscrew-wines.com
Credit cards, delivery, tastings, en primeur, glass
loan.
*Small merchant with a big list. Good
Australian wines across-the-board.*

Corney and Barrow ☆☆☆☆

12 Helmet Row, London, EC1V 3TD.
📞 020 7251 4051. FAX 020 7608 1373.
E-mail: andrew.gordon@corbar.co.uk
Website: www.corbar1.demon.co.uk
Credit cards, mail order, delivery, en primeur,
cellarage, glass hire/loan, tastings.
*Fine wine specialists with an eye for the
world's most desirable wines.*

Croque-en-Bouche ☆☆☆☆☆

221 Wells Road, Malvern Wells,
Worcester, WR14 4HF. 📞 01684 565
612. FAX 0870 7066282.
E-mail: mail@croque-en-bouche.co.uk
Website: www.croque-en-bouche.co.uk
By the case only, credit cards, delivery, cellarage.
*Great restaurant-cum-wine merchant. A
list packed with delights.*

Rodney Densem Wines ☆☆☆☆

4 Pillory Street, Nantwich, Cheshire,
CW5 7JW. 📞 01270 212 200. Retail:
01270 626 999. FAX 01270 212 300.
E-mail: sales@onestopwine.com
Website: www.onestopwine.com
Credit cards, delivery, tastings, en primeur,
cellarage, glass loan.
All-France focus. Many half-bottles.

Direct Wine Shipments ☆☆☆☆☆

5/7 Corporation Square, Belfast, N.
Ireland, BT1 3AJ. 📞 01232 508000.
FAX 01232 240 202. E-mail: enquiry@
directwine.co.uk Website: www.
directwine.co.uk Credit cards, delivery,
tastings, en primeur, cellarage, glass hire/loan.
*A good merchant offering tastings and
courses. Strong on Spain and Australia.*

Domaine Direct ☆☆☆☆☆

10 Hardwick Street, London, EC1R 4RB.
📞 020 7837 1142. FAX 020 7837 8605.
Website: www.domainedirect.co.uk
By the case only, credit cards, delivery, cellarage,
tastings, en primeur.
*A serious list with fine Burgundy and
New World estates at competitive prices.*

Eckington Wines ☆☆☆☆

2 Ravencar Road, Eckington, Sheffield,
S21 4JZ. [C]+FAX 01246 433 213.
E-mail: qandrewloughran@supanet.com
By the case only, delivery, tastings, glass loan.
*A compact list covering most areas, styles
and prices. Friendly service.*

Edencroft Fine Wines ☆☆☆

8-10 Hospital Street, Nantwich,
Cheshire, CW5 5RJ. [C] 01270 629975.
FAX 01270 625302. E-mail:
Edencroftfinewines@btinternet.com
Website:www.edencroft.com
Credit cards, en primeur, delivery,tastings, glass
hire.
*A compact range focusing on the New
World.*

El Vino Co. ☆☆☆

Vintage House, 1-2 Hare Place, Fleet
Street, London, EC4Y 1BJ. [C] 020 7353
5384. FAX 020 7936 2367.
E-mail: graham.mitchell@btinternet.com
Website: www.elvino.co.uk
Credit cards, delivery, tastings, en primeur,
cellarage, glass hire.
*Specialists in France but now introducing
more New World wines.*

Farr Vintners ☆☆☆☆☆

19-21 Sussex Street, Pimlico, London,
SW1V 4RR. [C] 020 7821 2000.
FAX 020 7821 2020.
E-mail: sales@farr-vintners.com
Website: www.farr-vintners.com
By the case only (min. order £500), cellarage, en
primeur.
*The reference point for the world's finest
and rarest wines.*

Ferrers Le Mesurier & Son ☆☆☆

"Turnsloe", North Street, Titchmarsh,
Kettering, Northants, NN14 3DH.
[C]+FAX 01832 732 660.
By the case only, delivery, cellarage, en primeur.
*A French-biased list with its share of
treats. A second outlet is now open near
Norwich.*

Fine & Rare Wines ☆☆☆☆☆

Unit 17-18 Pall Mall Deposit, 124-128
Barlby Road, London, W10 6BL.
[C] 020 8960 1995. FAX 020 8960 1911.
E-mail: wine@frw.co.uk
Website: www.frw.co.uk
Mail order, delivery, en primeur.
Wide-ranging list of serious wines.

Fine Wines Limerick ☆☆☆

Vintage House, 48 Roches Street,
Limerick, Ireland [C] (00 353) 61 417
784. FAX (00 353) 61 417 276.
E-mail: finewine@indigo.ie
Website: www.websters.
Credit cards, glass loan, delivery, cellarage,
tastings, en primeur.
Specialists in Bordeaux and Chile.

Fine Wines of New Zealand
☆☆☆☆

PO Box 476, London, NW5 2NZ.
[C] 020 7482 0093. FAX 020 7267 8400.
E-mail: margaret.harvey@btinternet.com
Website: www.fwnz.co.uk
By the case only, mail order, tastings, credit
cards, delivery.
*A great place to find some of New
Zealand's up-and-coming new
winemakers.*

Le Fleming Wines ☆☆☆☆

19 Spenser Rd., Harpenden, Herts, AL5
5NW. [C]+FAX 01582 760 125.
E-mail: CJEN101984@aol.com
By the case only, delivery, en primeur, tastings,
wine club.
*One-woman band with great wines from
across the world.*

Forth Wines ☆☆☆☆

Crawford Place, Milnathort, Kinross-
shire, Scotland KY13 9XF. [C] 01577 866
001. FAX 01577 866 020.
By the case only, credit cards, delivery, en
primeur, delivery, glass loan/hire.
*Wines from first rate producers in the old
as well as the New World.*

Fortnum & Mason ☆☆☆☆☆

181 Piccadilly, London, WIA IER.
[C] 020 7734 8040. FAX 020 7437 3278.
E-mail: info@fortnumandmason.co.uk
Website: www.fortnumandmason.co.uk
Credit cards, delivery, tastings, en primeur.
*Ultra-smart store with classic wines and
a 24 hour UK-wide delivery service.*

Four Walls Wine Co. ☆☆☆☆☆

1 High Street, Chilgrove, Nr Chichester,
W. Sussex, PO18 9HX. [C] 01243 535
360. FAX 01243 535 418.
E-mail: fourwallswine@compuserve.com
Credit cards, delivery, en primeur, tastings,
cellarage, glass hire/loan.
*A super list of 3,500 blue-chip Bordeaux,
Burgundies, Germans and Loires.*

John Frazier ☆☆☆☆

Stirling Road, Cranmore Industrial Estate, Shirley. Solihull B40 4XD. 0121 704 3415. FAX 0121 711 2710. E-mail: info@fraziers.co.uk Website: www.fraziers.co.uk Credit cards, cellarage, en primeur. *Comprehensive range with small growers as well as the big names.*

Friarwood ☆☆☆☆

26 New Kings Road, London, SW6 4ST. 020 7736 2628. FAX 020 7731 0411. E-mail: sales@friarwood.com Website: www.friarwood.com Credit cards, delivery, tastings, en primeur, cellarage, glass loan. *Specialists in Bordeaux, Loire and Burgundy.*

Gauntleys ☆☆☆☆☆

4 High Street, Exchange Arcade, Nottingham, NG1 2ET. 0115 9110 55. FAX 0115 911 0557. E-mail: rhone@innotts.co.uk Website: www.gauntleywine.com Credit cards, mail order, delivery, tastings, glass loan, en primeur. *Superb on Alsace, Rhône and Loire, expanding into Germany, Spain and Italy.*

Goedhuis & Co. ☆☆☆☆☆

6 Rudolf Place, Miles Street, London, SW8 IRP. 020 7793 7900. FAX 020 7793 7170. E-mail: goedhuis@btinternet.com Website: www.goedhuis.com By the case only, delivery, en primeur, cellarage, glass hire/loan. *Source of serious Old and New World wine. En primeur, Bordeaux and Burgundy.*

Gordon & MacPhail ☆☆☆☆

58-60 South Street, Elgin, Moray, Scotland, IV30 1JY. 01343 545 110. FAX 01343 540 155. E-mail: mail@gordonandmacphail.com Website: www.gordonandmacphail.com Credit cards, delivery, tastings, glass hire/loan. *Brilliant malt whisky from your birthyear, French country wines and good examples from the New World.*

Grapevine (inc. BH Wines) ☆☆☆

Embleton, Cockermouth, Cumbria, CA13 9YA. 017687 76100 FAX 017687 76767 E-mail: Grapevyn@aol.com Credit cards, delivery. *Interesting Vins de Pays are among the finds from this restructured company.*

The Great Northern Wine Co. ☆☆☆☆

The Old Bank, 342 Kirkstall Road, Leeds, LS4 2DS. 0113 230 4455. FAX 0113 230 4488. E-mail: gnw.leeds@ onyxnet.co.uk Credit cards, delivery, mail order, en primeur, glass loan, tastings. *One of the best merchants between Edinburgh and Watford. Friendly service.*

The Great Western Wine Co. ☆☆☆☆

Wells Road, Bath, BA2 3AP. 01225 322 800. FAX 01225 442 139. E-mail: post@greatwesternwine.co.uk By the case only, credit cards, delivery, tastings, cellarage, glass loan, en primeur. *Great range, especially good French country wines. Plenty of half-bottles too and an enticing diary of tastings.*

The Greek Wine Centre ☆☆☆☆

48 Underdale Road, Shrewsbury, Shrops, SY2 5DT. 01743 364 636. FAX 01743 367 960. E-mail: greekwines.uk@ clara.net Website: greekwines.uk.clara.net Delivery, tastings. *Exciting new-wave wines from Greece.*

Peter Green ☆☆☆☆☆

37 A/B Warrender Park Road, Edinburgh, Scotland, EH9 1HJ. +FAX 0131 229 5925. Credit cards, mail order, delivery, tastings, glass loan, en primeur. *Top-class wines from Germany, Italy and Australia.*

Growers & Chateaux ☆☆☆

Hartland House, Church Street, Reigate, Surrey, RH2 0DA. 01372 374 239. FAX 01372 377 610. E-mail: info@ winesite.net Website: www.winesite.net By the case only, en primeur, credit cards, delivery, tastings. *A broad ranging list focusing on France. Fun new Monty Python range.*

H. & H. Bancroft ☆☆☆☆

East Bridge Office North, New Covent Garden Market, London SW8 5JB 0207 6278700. FAX 0207 6278766. Orders: 01480 469449. E-mail: mail@hhfinewines.co.uk Website: www.hhfinewines.co.uk Credit cards, delivery, cellarage, en primeur. *The amalgamation of Adam Bancroft and H&H has created a portfolio of individual wines from France, Italy and Australia.*

Hall Batson & Co. ☆☆☆☆

168 Wroxham Road, Norwich, Norfolk, NR7 8DE. ☎ 01603 415 115. FAX 01603 484 096. E-mail:hbwine@paston.co.uk
Mail order, by case only, credit cards, delivery, glass loan, tastings, en primeur.
A broad international range that's strong on France, South America and Australia.

Handford-Holland Park ☆☆☆☆

12 Portland Road, London, W11 4LE. ☎ 020 7221 9614. FAX 020 7221 9613. E-mail: james@handford-wine.demon. co.uk Website: www.handford-wine. demon.co.uk
Credit cards, delivery, tastings, en primeur, cellarage, glass loan.
Great place to buy and learn about wine, especially from France and Spain.

Roger Harris Wines Ltd. ☆☆☆☆☆

Loke Farm, Weston Longville, Norfolk, NR9 5LG. ☎ 01603 880 171. FAX 01603 880 291. E-mail: sales@rhwine.co.uk Website: www.rhwine.co.uk Mail order only, by the case only, credit cards, delivery.
The best of Beaujolais and the Mâconnais with the promise of next day delivery.

Harrods Ltd ☆☆☆☆☆

87-135 Brompton Road, Knightsbridge, London, SW1X 7XL. ☎ 020 7730 1234. FAX 020 7225 5823.
Website: www.harrods.com Credit cards, delivery, cellarage, en primeur, tastings.
State of the art wine shop. 1,600 wines in stock and still hot on the classics.

Harvey Nichols & Co. ☆☆☆☆☆

109-125 Knightsbridge, London, SW1X 7RJ. ☎ 020 7201 8537. FAX 020 7235 5020.
E-mail: wineshop@harveynichols.co.uk
Credit cards, mail order, delivery.
A great collection of both Old World and New World classics which can also be enjoyed in the 5th Floor restaurant.

Richard Harvey Wines ☆☆☆☆

Bucknowle House, Bucknowle, Wareham, Dorset. BH20 5PQ.
☎ 01929 481 437 FAX 01929 481 275.
E-mail: harvey@lds.co.uk
By the case only, en primeur, glass loan, delivery, tastings.
A combination of wine and food. A good selection of clarets and other non-vinous delights such as oils, olives etc.

The Haslemere Cellar ☆☆☆☆

Rear of 2 Lower Street, Haslemere, Surrey, GU27 2NX. ☎ 01428 645 081. FAX 01428 645 108.
E-mail:hcellar@haslemere.com
Credit cards, delivery, tastings, en primeur, cellarage, glass loan.
Skilfully chosen French wines are the principal attraction.

Haynes Hanson & Clark ☆☆☆☆

25 Eccleston Street, London, SW1W 9NP. ☎ 020 7259 0102. FAX 020 7259 0103. E-mail: london@hhandc.co.uk
Credit cards, delivery, tastings, en primeur, glass loan.
France is the area of focus here, and Burgundy the particular strength.

Hedley Wright Wine Merchant Ltd (inc. Castle Growers) ☆☆☆☆

Twyford Business Centre, London Road, Bishops Stortford, Herts, CM23 3YT. ☎ 01279 465818. FAX 01279 465819. By the case only, credit cards, delivery, tastings, en primeur, cellarage, glass loan.
A good country merchant offering classy Chileans and Old World stars.

Charles Hennings ☆☆☆

London House, Lower Street, Pulborough, Sussex, RH20 2BW. ☎ 01798 872 485. FAX 01798 873 163. Credit cards, delivery, tastings, glass loan.
A traditional range of wines from Europe and interesting offerings from the New World.

Heyman Barwell Jones ☆☆☆☆

130 Ebury Street, London, SW1W 9QQ. ☎ 020 7881 0050. FAX 020 7730 0575. E-mail: sales@heyman.co.uk Website: www.heyman.co.uk
By the case only, mail order, credit cards, delivery, tastings, en primeur, cellarage, wine club.
A very good range from all corners of the globe. Especially interesting Burgundy.

High Breck Vintners ☆☆☆

11 Nelson Road, London N8 9RX ☎ 020 8340 1848. FAX 020 8340 5162. E-mail: hbv@richanl.freeserve.co.uk
Mail order only, by the case only, delivery, en primeur, glass loan.
Traditional wine merchant with a focus on boutique French producers.

George Hill of Loughborough
☆☆☆☆
59 Wards End, Loughborough, Leics, LE11 3HB. 📞 01509 212717. FAX 01509 236963 E-mail: geo-hill-wines@gmtnet.co.uk En primeur, cellarage, credit cards, glass hire/loan, delivery, tastings.
Informative, easy to follow list with a broad range of interesting wines.

House of Townend ☆☆☆☆
Red Duster House, 101 York Street, Hull. HU2 0QX. 📞 01482 586582. FAX 01482 218796.
E-mail: info@houseoftownend.co.uk
Website: www.houseoftownend.co.uk
Delivery, en primeur, mail order, cellarage, glass loan, tastings.
Burgundy, South Africa and Australia are particular strengths.

Jeroboams ☆☆☆☆
8-12 Brook Street, London, W1Y 2BH. 📞 020 7629 7916. FAX 020 7495 3314.
E-mail: sales@jeroboams.co.uk
Website: www.jeroboams.co.uk
Credit cards, delivery, en primeur, cellarage, delivery, glass hire, tastings.
Specialists in wine and cheese from claret to Caerphilly. Now incorporates Laytons.

Michael Jobling Wines ☆☆☆☆
Baltic Chambers, 3-7 Broad Chare, Newcastle-upon-Tyne NE1 3DQ.
📞 0191 261 5298. FAX 0191 261 4543.
Website: www.michaeljoblingwines.co.uk
Mail order, by the case only, en primeur, credit cards, glass loan, delivery, tastings.
Well-chosen wines backed up with personal advice, tastings and dinners.

S.H. Jones & Co. ☆☆☆☆
27 High Street, Banbury, Oxon, OX16 8EW. 📞 01295 251 179. FAX 01295 272 352. E-mail: SHJwork@aol.com
Credit cards, delivery, tastings, en primeur, cellarage, glass loan.
Frequent tastings and malt whisky club. Dependable for French and Spanish wines.

Justerini & Brooks ☆☆☆☆☆
61 St. James's Street, London, SW1A 1LZ. 📞 020 7493 8721. FAX 020 7499 4653. Also 45 George St. Edinburgh EH2 2HT. Mail order, credit cards, delivery, en primeur, cellarage, glass loan.
Second-to-none in the quality of the range across the board and in the service offered.

King & Barnes ☆☆☆☆
16 Bishopric, Horsham, W. Sussex, RH12 1QP. 📞 01403 270 870.
FAX 01403 270 570.
E-mail: king.barnes@btinternet.com
Website: www.king&barnes.co.uk
Credit cards, delivery, tastings, glass loan.
Sussex brewer/wine merchant. Good and fairly priced range.

Lay & Wheeler ☆☆☆☆☆
Gosbecks Park, Gosbecks Road, Colchester, Essex, CO2 9JT. 📞 01206 764 446. FAX 01206 560 002.
E-mail: laywheeler@ndirect.co.uk
Website: www.layandwheeler.co.uk
Credit cards, delivery, tastings, en primeur, cellarage, glass loan.
One of the best regional and mail-order sources of Old and New World classics.

Laymont & Shaw ☆☆☆☆
The Old Chapel, Millpool, Truro, Cornwall, TR1 1EX. 📞 01872 270 545.
FAX 01872 223 005.
E-mail: info@laymont-shaw.co.uk
Website: www.laymont-shaw.co.uk
Mail order, by the case only, delivery, tastings, glass loan.
A treasure-trove of both new wave and traditional wines from Spain and Portugal.

Laytons Wine Merchants ☆☆☆☆
20 Midland Road, London, NW1 2AD. 📞 020 7388 4567. FAX 020 7383 7419.
E-mail: sales@laytons.co.uk
Website: www.laytons.co.uk Credit cards, delivery, en primeur, cellarage, glass loan, tastings.
Now trading as Jeroboams.

Lea & Sandeman ☆☆☆☆☆
170 Fulham Road, London, SW10 9QH. 📞 0207 2440522. FAX 0207 2440533.
E-mail: sales@leaandsandeman.co.uk
Credit cards, delivery, en primeur, cellarage, tastings, glass loan.
First class London merchant with shops in Fulham, Notting Hill and Barnes.

Lloyd Taylor Wines ☆☆☆
Bute House, Arran Road, Perth, Scotland, PH1 3DZ. 📞 01738 447 878.
FAX 01738 447 979.
E-mail: sales@lloyd.taylor.wines.com
Website: www.lloyd-taylor-wines.com
Credit cards, delivery, tastings, glass loan, en primeur, cellarage.
One of Scotland's best wine merchants.

O.W. Loeb & Co. ☆☆☆☆

82 Southwark Bridge Road, London, SE1
0AS. **C** 020 7928 7750. FAX 020 7928
1855. E-mail: finewine@owloeb.com
Website: www.owloeb.com

Mail order, delivery, by the case only, en
primeur, credit cards, tastings, cellarage.

*A well-chosen list with some superstars
from Burgundy, Germany and Alsace.
Bordeaux is also worth a look.*

Longford Wines ☆☆☆☆

Great North Barn, Hamsey, Lewes, E.
Sussex, BN8 5TB. **C** 01273 480 761.
FAX 01273 480 861.
Email: longwine@aol.com

By the case only, mail order, delivery, en primeur,
glass hire/loan, credit cards, cellarage.

French and German specialists.

Magnum Fine Wines ☆☆☆☆

43 Pall Mall, London, SW1Y 5JG.
C 020 7839 5732. FAX 020 7321 0848.
E-mail: wine@magnum.u-net.com
Website: www.magnum.co.uk

By the case only, credit cards, delivery, en
primeur, tastings, wine club.

*Impressive selection of French fine wines,
especially Bordeaux – at a price.*

Majestic Wine ☆☆☆☆☆

Odhams Trading Estate, St. Albans Road,
Watford, Herts, WD2 5RE. **C** 01923
298 200. FAX 01923 819 105.
E-mail: info@majestic.co.uk
Website: www.majestic.co.uk

By the case only, credit cards, delivery, tastings,
en primeur, glass loan.

*A very good range of interesting wines,
with bargain one-off purchases.*

Marks & Spencer ☆☆☆☆

Michael House, Baker Street, London,
W1A 1DN. **C** 020 7935 4422. FAX 020
7268 2674. Website: www.marks-and-
spencer.co.uk M&S chargecard and switch.

*New World and Champagne are the areas
of interest in this limited but reliable range.*

Martinez Fine Wines ☆☆☆☆

35 The Grove, Ilkley, W. Yorks, LS29
9NJ. **C** 01943 603241. FAX 01943
816489. E-mail: martinez@ilkley.co.uk
Website: www.martinez.co.uk

Credit cards, delivery, tastings, en primeur,
cellarage, glass hire/loan, mail order.

*Shops in Halifax, Ilkley, Horsforth and
Harrogate stock well chosen wines.*

F. & E. May ☆☆☆☆

27 Brownlow Mews, Bloomsbury,
London, WC1N 2LA. **C** 020 7405
6249. FAX 020 7404 4472.
E-mail: fandemay@netcomuk.co.uk

Credit cards, cellarage, glass loan, delivery,
tastings, en primeur.

*A great range of classic wines from
Germany, Alsace, Bordeaux and
Champagne.*

Mayor Sworder ☆☆☆☆

7 Aberdeen Road, Croydon, CR0 1EQ.
C 020 8686 1155. FAX 020 8686 2017.
E-mail: mayor.sworder@btinternet.com
Website: www.mayorsworder.uk.com

By the case only, credit cards, delivery, en
primeur, cellarage, tastings, glass loan.

*Classy Old World list and some unusual
New World offerings. Very good service.*

Mills Whitcombe Fine Wines ☆☆☆

The Sett, Lower Maescoed, Hereford.
HR2 0HS **C** 01873 860224.

Mail order, by the case only, en primeur,
cellarage, delivery, credit cards, tastings.

*Country merchant specialising in growers'
wines with tastings in a rural setting.*

Milton Sandford Wines ☆☆☆☆

The Old Chalk Mine, Warren Row Road,
Knowl Hill, Reading. Berks RG10 8QS.
C 01628 829449. FAX 01628 829424.

By the case only, delivery.

*Compact list with some interesting small
growers from Australia.*

Mitchells Wine Merchants ☆☆☆☆

354 Meadowhead, Sheffield, S. Yorks, S8
7UJ. **C** 0114 274 5587. FAX 0114 274
8481. E-mail:
wine@mitchellswine.freeserve.co.uk
Website:
www.mitchellswinemerchantsltd.co.uk

Credit cards, delivery, tastings, en primeur,
cellarage, glass loan.

*Characterful wines, both Old World and
New. Great whisky too.*

Montrachet ☆☆☆☆

59 Kennington Road, Waterloo, London,
SE1 7PZ. **C** 020 7928 1990. FAX 020
7928 3415.
E-mail: montrachetwine@aol.com

Credit cards, mail order only, by the case only,
delivery, tastings, en primeur.

*Superb domaine Burgundies, the best
German estates and classic Bordeaux.*

Moreno Wine ☆☆☆☆
2 Norfolk Place, London, W2 1QN.
📞 020 7706 3055. 📠 020 7724 3813.
E-mail: sales@moreno-wines.co.uk
Credit cards, mail order, glass loan, tastings, delivery.
Dynamic Spanish and South American specialist. Tutored tastings monthly.

Morris & Verdin ☆☆☆☆☆
10 The Leathermarket, Weston Street, London, SE1 3ER. 📞 020 7357 8866. 📠 020 7357 8877. E-mail: sales@m-v.co.uk
Website: www.morris-verdin.co.uk
By the case only, delivery, tastings, en primeur, cellarage.
Brilliant Burgundies, sublime sherries and "new classic" Californians.

Wm. Morrison ☆☆☆☆
Wakefield 41 Industrial Estate, Carrgate, Wakefield, W. Yorks. WF2 0XF.
📞 01924 870 000. 📠 01924 875 300.
Credit cards, tastings, glass loan.
Great-value mid-price wines.

Nadder Wines ☆☆☆☆
2 Netherhampton Road, Harnham, Salisbury, Wilts, SP2 8HE. 📞 01722 325 418. 📠 01722 421 617.
E-mail: nadderwines@btinternet.com
By the case only, mail order, wine warehouse, credit cards, delivery, tastings, glass loan.
Laudable range from France plus some great new wines from South America.

James Nicholson ☆☆☆☆☆
27a Killyleagh Street, Crossgar, Co. Down, Northern Ireland, BT30 9DQ.
📞 01396 830 091. 📠 01396 830 028.
E-mail: info@jnwine.co.uk
Website: www.jnwine.co.uk
Credit cards (no Amex, Diners), mail order, delivery, cellarage, tastings, en primeur, wine club, glass loan.
Superb growers' wines from Burgundy, California and the Midi.

Nickolls and Perks ☆☆☆☆
37 High Street, Stourbridge, West Midlands, DY8 1TA. 📞 01384 394 518.
📠 01384 440 786.
E-mail: sales@nickollsandperks.co.uk
Website: www.nickollsandperks.co.uk
Credit cards, mail order, wine club, delivery, tastings, en primeur, cellarage, glass loan.
Superb Champagnes and classics from Bordeaux. Investigate the en primeurs.

Nicolas UK ☆☆☆☆
157 Great Portland Street, London, W1N 5FB. 📞 020 7436 9338. 📠 020 7637 1691. Website: www.nicolas.tm.fr
Credit cards, delivery, tastings, glass hire, en primeur, cellarage.
Reliable range from little-known French regional wines to top flight clarets.

Noble Rot ☆☆☆☆
18 Market Street, Bromsgrove, Worcs, B61 8DA. 📞 01527 575 606. 📠 01527 833 133. Credit cards, delivery, tastings, glass loan, wine club.
Majestic-style warehouse emporium.

The Nobody Inn ☆☆☆☆☆
Doddiscombsleigh, Nr Exeter, Devon, EX6 7PS. 📞 01647 252 394. 📠 01647 252 978. E-mail: inn.nobody@virgin.net
Mail order, credit cards, delivery, tastings, glass hire/loan.
Country pub with brilliant malts too.

Oddbins ☆☆☆☆☆
31-33 Weir Road, Wimbledon, London, SW19 8UG. 📞 020 8944 4400. 📠 020 8944 4411. Website: www.oddbins.com
Credit cards, en primeur, delivery, tastings, glass loan.
A great range with wine-mad staff. Those wanting more should try Oddbins Fine Wine shops. Also now near Calais.

Pallant Wines ☆☆☆☆
17 High Street, Arundel, W. Sussex, BN18 9AD. 📞 01903 882 288.
📠 01903 882 801.
E-mail: contact@Pallant-Wines.co.uk
Credit cards, delivery, tastings, glass hire/loan.
With a great delicatessen this is a Mecca for foodies as well as wine buffs.

Parfrements ☆☆☆☆
68 Cecily Road, Cheylesmore, Coventry, CV3 5LA. 📞 01203 503646. 📠 01203 506406. E-mail: sales@parfrements.co.uk
Website: www.parfrements.co.uk
En primeur, cellarage, glass hire, delivery, tastings.
Includes a good Portuguese range.

The Pavilion Wine Co. ☆☆☆☆
Finsbury Circus Gardens, Finsbury Circus, London, EC2M 7AB. 📞 020 7628 8224. 📠 020 7628 6205.
By the case only, credit cards, delivery, en primeur, cellarage.
Hand-picked wines from small producers.

Thos. Peatling ☆☆☆☆

Westgate House, Westgate Street, Bury St
Edmunds, Suffolk, IP33 1QS. [C] 01284
714 285. [FAX] 01284 714 483.
Credit cards, cellarage (small scale), delivery, glass
loan, tastings.
*Bordeaux specialist stocking over fifty
malt whiskies.*

Penistone Court ☆☆☆☆

No 5 The Railway Station, Penistone,
Sheffield S36 6HP [C] 01226 766037.
[FAX] 01226 767310.
E-mail: pcwc@dircon.co.uk
By the case only, delivery, glass loan.
*Austrian specialists with a short list of
well-chosen wines.*

Philglas & Swiggot ☆☆☆☆

21 Northcote Road, Battersea, London,
SW11 1NG. [C] 020 7924 4494. [FAX] 020
7642 1308.
E-mail: karen@philglasandswiggot.co.uk
Credit cards, tastings, delivery, glass loan.
*Antipodean specialists par excellence but
good for Spain and Italy too.*

Christopher Piper Wines ☆☆☆☆

1 Silver Street, Ottery St. Mary, Devon,
EX11 1DB. [C] 01404 814 139.
[FAX] 01404 812 100.
E-mail: chrispiperwines@freeserve.co.uk
Credit cards, mail order, delivery, tastings, en
primeur, cellarage, glass loan.
*A dependable list with good Burgundies,
southern French and Australian wines.*

Terry Platt ☆☆☆☆☆

Council St. West, Llandudno, Conwy,
Wales, LL30 1ED. [C] 01492 874099.
[FAX] 01492 874788.
E-mail: plattwines@clara.co.uk
Credit cards, delivery, tastings, cellarage, glass
hire/loan.
*A range to satisfy bargain-seekers and
enthusiasts alike.*

Le Pont de la Tour ☆☆☆☆☆

The Butlers Wharf Building, 36d Shad
Thames, Butlers Wharf, London, SE1 2YE.
[C] 020 7403 2403. [FAX] 020 7403 0267.
E-mail:
emmanuels@conran-restaurants.co.uk
Website: www.conran-restaurants.co.uk
Credit cards, delivery, glass loan.
*Essentially, the Pont de la Tour's
restaurant's excellent and in some cases
exclusive wine list at retail prices.*

Portland Wine Co. ☆☆☆

152a Ashley Road, Hale, Cheshire,
WA15 9SA. [C] 0161 962 8752. [FAX]
0161 905 1291.
E-mail: portwineco@aol.com
Website: www.portlandwine.co.uk
Credit cards, en primeur, tastings, delivery, glass
loan.
*A broad range with particularly choice
wines from the New World.*

R.S. Wines ☆☆☆☆

Avonleigh Parklands Road, Bower
Ashton, Bristol, BS3 2JW. [C] 0117 963
1780. [FAX] 0117 953 3797.
By the case only, delivery, cellarage, tastings, en
primeur.
Good New and Old World wines.

Raeburn Fine Wines ☆☆☆☆☆

21/23 Comely Bank Road, Edinburgh,
EH4 1DS. [C] 0131 343 1159. [FAX] 0131
332 5166.
E-mail:raeburn@netcomuk.co.uk
Website: www.raeburnfinewines.com
Credit cards, delivery, tastings, en primeur, glass
hire/loan, cellarage.
*Still enjoying a cult following both sides of
the border. The list includes enticing names
from the Mosel and Burgundy.*

Reid Wines (1992) ☆☆☆☆☆

The Mill, Marsh Lane, Hallatrow, Bristol,
BS39 6EB. [C] 01761 452 645. [FAX] 01761
453 642. Mail order only, credit cards, delivery,
tastings, glass loan.
*Eccentric merchant with a witty list
brimming with classic and rare wines.*

La Réserve ☆☆☆☆☆

56 Walton Street, Knightsbridge, London,
SW3 1RB. [C] 020 7589 2020. [FAX] 020
7581 0250. E-mail: realwine@la-reserve.
co.uk Website: www.la-reserve.co.uk
Credit cards, delivery, tastings, en primeur,
cellarage, glass loan
*Impeccable Burgundies and top wines
from most other regions. Unique themed
tastings of top-notch wines.*

Howard Ripley ☆☆☆☆☆

35 Eversley Crescent, London, N21 1EL.
[C] 020 8360 8904. [FAX] 020 8351 6564.
By the case only, mail order, delivery, tastings, en
primeur, glass loan.
*Burgundy-loving dentist-turned-specialist
wine merchant. Lists 42 of the best
domaines.*

Roberson ☆☆☆☆
348 Kensington High Street, London,
W14 8NS. ☏ 020 7371 2121. FAX 020
7371 4010. E-mail: wines@roberson
co.uk Website: www.roberson.co.uk
Credit cards, delivery, tastings, cellarage, glass
loan, mail order.
*An eclectic range of young and mature
wines from all over the world.*

The Rogers Wine Co. ☆☆☆
Rectory Cottage, 20 Lower Street,
Sproughton, Ipswich, Suffolk, IP8 3AA.
☏ 01473 748 464. FAX 01473 744 245.
E-mail: rogers.co@fsbdial.co.uk
By the case only, delivery, en primeur, tastings,
glass hire/loan.
Broad range with good Loire and Alsace.

C.A. Rookes ☆☆☆
7 Western Road Ind. Estate, Stratford
upon Avon, Warks. CV37 0AH. ☏ 01789
297 777. FAX 01789 297 752. Website:
www.carookes.co.uk En Primeur, cellarage,
glass hire, delivery, tastings.
*Hand-written list, hand sold wines
including some fine Loires.*

Safeway Stores ☆☆☆☆
Safeway House, 6 Millington Road,
Hayes, Middlesex, UB3 4AY. ☏ 020
8848 8744. FAX 020 8970 3605/573
1865. Credit cards, glass loan.
Good-value wines in all sectors.

J. Sainsbury ☆☆☆☆
Stamford House, Stamford Street, London,
SE1 9LL. ☏ 020 7695 6000. FAX 020
7695 7610. Website: www.sainsburys.
co.uk Credit cards, glass loan.
*Increasingly customer focused chain. New
ideas include recipes on wine labels.*

Sandiway Wine Co. ☆☆☆☆☆
Chester Road, Sandiway, Cheshire, CW8
2NH. ☏ 01606 882 101. FAX 01606 888
407. E-mail: graham@sandiway.com
Website: www.sandiwaywine.com
Credit cards, delivery, tastings, glass loan.
Merchants bursting with enthusiasm.

Scatchard Ltd. ☆☆☆☆
Scatchard Building, 38 Vernon Street,
Liverpool, L2 2AY. ☏ 0151 236 6468.
FAX 0151 236 7003.
E-mail: info@scatchard.com
Credit cards, delivery, tastings, glass loan.
Spain is the specialist subject.

Sebastopol Wines ☆☆☆☆
Sebastopol Barn, London Road, Blewbury,
Oxon, OX11 9HB. ☏ 01235 850 471.
FAX 01235 850 776. By the case only, credit
cards, en primeur, delivery, glass hire, tastings.
Fine French wines, port and Madeira.

Seckford Wines ☆☆☆☆
Dock Lane, Melton, Ipswich, IP12 1PE.
☏ 01394 446622. FAX 01394 446633.
E-mail: marcus@seckfordwines.co.uk
Website: www.seckfordwines.co.uk
By the case only, mail order, credit cards,
delivery, en primeur, cellarage.
*Exciting new wines from South Africa and
Australia – plus the classics.*

Selfridges ☆☆☆☆☆
400 Oxford Street, London, W1A 1AB.
☏ 020 7318 3730. FAX 020 7491 1880.
(Manchester: ☏ 0161 629 1220.)
Credit cards, mail order, delivery, tastings,
cellarage, glass hire/loan.
*Fairly priced and highly comprehensive
range to choose from.*

Edward Sheldon ☆☆☆☆
New Street, Shipston on Stour, Warks.
CV36 4EN. ☏ 01608 661 409.
FAX 01608 663 166.
E-mail: finewine@edward-sheldon.co.uk
Credit cards, delivery, tastings, en primeur,
cellarage, glass loan.
*Wide selection. Strong on Bordeaux and
Burgundy.*

Somerfield Stores ☆☆☆
Somerfield House, Whitchurch Lane,
Bristol, BS14 OTJ. ☏ 01179 359 359.
FAX 01179 780 629. Credit cards, delivery.
Price-conscious supermarket chain.

Sommelier Wine Co. ☆☆☆☆
23 St. George's Esplanade, St. Peter Port,
Guernsey, Channel Islands, GY1 2BG.
☏ 01481 721 677. FAX 01481 716 818.
Credit cards, delivery, cellarage, tastings, glass loan.
*Great New World and sweet wines
available. Individually described and
VAT-free.*

South African Wine Centre ☆☆☆☆
5-6 Roxby Place, London, SW6 1RU.
☏ 020 7903 8311. FAX 020 7903 8313.
E-mail: sawc@swig.co.uk
Credit cards,delivery, tastings, glass loan/hire.
*Comprehensive South African range.
Some gems are unavailable elsewhere.*

Frank E. Stainton Wines ☆☆☆☆
3 Berry's Yard, Finkle Street, Kendal, Cumbria, LA9 4AB. ℂ 01539 731 886. FAX 01539 730 396.
Credit cards, delivery, tastings, en primeur.
Broad range. Good Rieslings, Bordeaux, New World and half-bottles.

John Stephenson & Sons ☆☆☆
Darwil House, Bradley Hall Road, Nelson, Lancs, BB9 8HE.
ℂ 01282 614 618. FAX 01282 601 161.
E-mail: wbannp@aol.com
Credit cards, delivery.
You must choose carefully, but the best wines will repay your efforts.

Stevens Garnier ☆☆☆☆
47 West Way, Botley, Oxford, OX2 0JF.
ℂ 01865 263 303. FAX 01865 791 594.
E-mail: info@stevensgarnier.co.uk
Credit cards, delivery, glass loan, tastings, en primeur, cellarage (on request).
A good range from the Loire, Burgundy, Portugal, South Africa and South America benefits from this firm's separate role as an importer-wholesaler.

Stratford's ☆☆☆☆
High St, Cookham-on-Thames, Berks, SL6 9SQ. ℂ 01628 810 606. FAX 01628 810 605. E-mail: hayley@stratfordwine.co.uk Website: www.stratfordwine.co.uk
Credit cards, delivery, tastings, glass loan.
A good international range. Chile and Australia are particularly inspiring.

The Sunday Times Wine Club ☆☆☆☆
New Aquitaine House, Exeter Way, Theale, Reading, Berks, RG7 4PL.
ℂ 0118 903 0903. FAX 0118 903 1073.
E-mail: orders@wine-club.co.uk
Website: www.sundaytimeswineclub.co.uk
Credit cards, delivery, tastings, en primeur, cellarage, glass hire/loan.
Part of the same empire as Bordeaux Direct (qv) and offering an excellent new Internet service.

SWIG Wine Merchants ☆☆☆☆
206 Haverstock Hill, London, NW3 2AG.
ℂ 020 7431 4412. FAX 020 7431 1326.
E-mail: imbibe@swig.co.uk Website: www.swig.co.uk Credit cards, delivery, tastings, glass loan, mail order nationwide.
Innovative list with some fine and rare wines. Good wedding list service.

T. & W. Wines ☆☆☆☆☆
51 King Street, Thetford, Norfolk, IP24 2AU. ℂ 01842 765 646. FAX 01842 766 407. E-mail:contact@tw-wines.co.uk
Website: www.tw-wines.co.uk
Mail order, credit cards, delivery, tastings, en primeur, cellarage, glass loan.
Superb range from France and California.

Tanners Wines ☆☆☆☆☆
26 Wyle Cop, Shrewsbury, Shrops, SY1 1XD. ℂ 01743 234 500/234 455. FAX 01743 234 501.
E-mail: sales@tanners-wines.co.uk
Website: www.tanners-wines.co.uk
Credit cards, delivery, tastings, en primeur, glass hire/loan, regional chain, mail order.
Merchant with strengths in France and Germany, featuring small growers.

Tesco Stores ☆☆☆☆
Delamare Road, Cheshunt, Herts, EN8 9SL. ℂ 01992 632 222. FAX 01992 658 225. Website: www.tesco.co.uk
Credit cards, tastings, glass loan.
Ultra-dynamic supermarket chain.

Thresher Wine Shop ☆☆☆☆
Sefton House, 42 Church Rd, Welwyn Garden City, Herts, AL8 6PJ. ℂ 01707 385 110. FAX 01707 385 004.
Website: www.enjoyment.co.uk
Credit cards, delivery, tastings.
The country's largest high street chain offering a broad selection.

Transatlantic Wines ☆☆☆
The Magpies, Eye Kettleby Drive, Eye Kettleby, Melton Mowbray, LE14 2TD.
ℂ 01664 565013. FAX 01664 564938.
E-mail: pjwb@clara.net Mail order, by the case only, glass loan, cellarage, delivery, tastings.
Trans-world wines with a focus on small, top quality domaines.

Trout Wines ☆☆☆☆
The Trout, Nether Wallop, Stockbridge, Hants, SO20 8EW. ℂ+FAX 01264 781 472. Credit cards, delivery, tastings, glass loan.
A short, affordable, exciting list.

Turville Valley Wines ☆☆☆☆☆
The Firs, Potter Row, Great Missenden, Bucks, HP16 9LT. ℂ+FAX 01494 868 818. E-mail: tvwine@aol.com
Mail order only, by the case only, delivery, en primeur, cellarage.
Classic Bordeaux and port of all ages.

The Ubiquitous Chip ☆☆☆☆☆

12 Ashton Lane, Glasgow, G12 8SJ.
☎ 0141 334 5007. FAX 0141 337 1302.
E-mail: mail@ubiquitouschip.co.uk
Website: www.ubiquitouschip.co.uk
Credit cards, delivery, tastings, glass loan.
Glasgow's top merchant; part of the award winning restaurant.

Unwins Wine Merchants ☆☆☆

Birchwood House, Victoria Road,
Dartford, Kent, DA1 5AJ. ☎ 01322 272
711. FAX 01322 294 469.
Credit cards, delivery, tastings, glass hire/loan.
Home Counties chain now making an impact on London with the acquisition of Fullers' shops. Good Portuguese wines.

Valvona & Crolla ☆☆☆☆☆

19 Elm Row, Edinburgh, EH7 4AA.
☎ 0131 556 6066. FAX 0131 556 1668.
E-mail: sales@valvonacrolla.co.uk
Website: www.valvonacrolla.co.uk
Credit cards, delivery, tastings, glass loan.
Stunning Italian wines and an expanding range from elsewhere. Tutored tastings.

The Victoria Wine Co. ☆☆☆☆

Sefton House, 42 Church Road, Welwyn
Garden City, Herts. AL8 6PJ. ☎ 01707
385 110. FAX 01707 385 004.
Website: www.enjoyment.co.uk
Credit cards, local delivery, glass loan, tastings.
Martha's Vineyard shops have the most exciting wines, but V.W. still have good stuff. Part of the same group as Thresher.

La Vigneronne ☆☆☆☆☆

105 Old Brompton Road, London, SW7
3LE. ☎ 020 7589 6113. FAX 020 7581
2983. E-mail: michael@lavigneronne.
co.uk Website: www.lavigneronne.co.uk
Mail order, credit cards, delivery, tastings, en premier.
Good range including fantastic old Bordeaux and Burgundy wines. Frequent, well-run tastings and dinners.

Villeneuve Wines ☆☆☆☆

One Venlaw Court, Peebles, Scotland
EH45 8AE. ☎ 01721 722 500.
FAX 01721 729 922.
E-mail: wines@villeneuvewines.com
Website: www.villeneuvewines.com
En premier, cellarage, mail order, tastings, delivery, credit cards, glass.
Three shops, with a range including rare vintages of Château Musar.

Vin du Van ☆☆☆☆

Colthups, The Street, Appledore, Kent,
TN26 2BX. ☎ 01233 758 727.
FAX 01233 758 389.
Mail order, by the case only, delivery, credit cards, glass loan.
Wacky, unpretentious yet informative list. Superb portfolio of Aussie wines.

Vinceremos ☆☆☆☆

19 New St., Leeds. LS18 4BH
☎ 0113 205 4545. FAX 0113 205 4546.
E-mail: info@vinceremos.co.uk
Website: www.vinceremos.co.uk
By the case only, mail order, glass hire/loan, en premier, cellarage, credit cards, delivery, tastings.
One of the best sources for organic and new Moroccan wines.

Vino Vino ☆☆☆☆

Freepost, SEA5662, New Malden, KT3
3BR. ☎ 0403 436 949. FAX 020 8942
4003. E-mail: vinovino@dircon.co.uk
Mail order, credit cards, delivery.
Specializing in wonderful classic and new Italian wines. Regular, informative mailings.

Vintage Roots ☆☆☆☆☆

Farley Farms, Bridge Farm, Reading
Road, Arborfield, RG2 9HT. ☎ 0800
980 4992. FAX 0118 976 1998.
Website: www.vintageroots.co.uk
By the case only, mail order only, credit cards, delivery, tastings, glass hire/loan.
All wines 100% certified organic, some biodynamic, all full of character.

Vintage Wines ☆☆☆☆

116-118 Derby Road, Nottingham, NG1
5FB. ☎ 0115 947 6565. FAX 0115 950
5276.
Credit cards, cellarage, en premier, delivery, tastings, glass hire/loan.
A good list to pick from. France, Germany and Australia are explored in some depth.

The Vintry ☆☆☆☆

Park Farm, Milland, Liphook, Hants,
GU30 7JT. ☎ 01428 741 389. FAX 01428
741 368. E-mail: sales@vintry.co.uk
Website: www.vintry.co.uk
By the case only, glass loan/hire, credit cards (internet only), delivery, tastings.
Six outlets, offering a good general selection, including British-made French wines such as Ch. Méaume.

Waitrose Wine Direct ☆☆☆☆

Freepost (SW1647), Bracknell, Berks.
RG12 8HX. 📞 0800 188 881. FAX 0800
1888.
E-mail: waitrose-direct@johnlewis.co.uk
Website: www.waitrose-direct.co.uk
Mail order only, credit cards, delivery, en
primeur, cellarage.
*Mail order arm of Waitrose with a wide
and balanced range of global styles.*

Waitrose ☆☆☆☆☆

Southern Industrial Area, Bracknell,
Berks, RG12 8YA. 📞 01344 424 680.
FAX 01344 825 255. Credit cards. en
primeur, glass loan, cellarage, delivery, tastings.
*Traditional wines are always to the fore,
but there are plenty of innovative bottles
to look out for.*

Waterloo Wine Co. ☆☆☆☆

61 Lant Street, London, SE1 1QN.
📞 020 7403 7967. FAX 020 7357 6976.
E-mail: sales@waterloowine.co.uk
Credit cards, delivery, tastings, glass hire/loan.
*The Waipara West vineyard owners focus
on New Zealand. Great Loire, German
and Midi offerings too with older vintages
often available.*

Waters of Coventry ☆☆☆☆

Collins Road, Heathcote, Warwick, CV34
6TF. 📞 01926 888 889. FAX 01926 887
416. E-mail: rc@wildbunch.co.uk
Website: waters-wine-merchants.co.uk
Credit cards, delivery, mail order.
*Top Rhônes, Burgundies and Spanish. New
world offerings include fine olive oils.*

Waverley Direct ☆☆☆☆

Nest Road, Gateshead, NE10 0ES.
📞 0870 6040210. FAX 0191 438 2658.
E-mail:
customer.inquiries@waverley-direct.co.uk
Website: www.waverley-direct.co.uk
Mail order only, delivery, tastings,
en primeur.
*Bordeaux, Burgundy and the New World
in abundance.*

Weavers of Nottingham ☆☆☆☆

1 Castle Gate, Nottingham, NG1 7AQ.
📞 0115 958 0922. FAX 0115 950 8076.
E-mail: weavers@weavers-wine.co.uk
Website: www.weavers-wine.co.uk
Credit cards, delivery, tastings, glass hire/loan
*Traditional merchant with wide range of
wines, accessories, malts and liqueurs.*

Whitebridge Wines ☆☆☆☆

Unit 21, Whitebridge Estate, Stone,
Staffs, ST15 8LQ. 📞 01785 817 229.
FAX 01785 811 181. E-mail: francispeel@
whitebridgewines.freeserve.co.uk
Cellarage, glass loan, delivery, credit cards en
primeur (port), tastings.
*Particularly good on wines from France,
Spain and the New World.*

Whiteside's of Clitheroe ☆☆☆☆☆

Shawbridge Street, Clitheroe, Lancs, BB7
1NA. 📞 01200 422 281. FAX 01200 427
129. Credit cards, glass loan, delivery, tastings,
cellarage.
*A good New World selection with a fine
range of whiskies and Spanish wines.*

The Wine Bureau ☆☆☆☆

58 Tower Street, Harrogate, N. Yorks,
HG1 1HS. 📞 01423 527 772.
FAX 01423 566 330.
E-mail: sales@winebureau.co.uk
Website: www.winebureau.co.uk
Mail order, credit cards, delivery, tastings, en
primeur, cellarage, glass loan.
*A broad international selection which has
grown out of their Tannin Level Wine Bar.*

Wine Cellar ☆☆☆☆

PO Box 476, Loushers Lane,
Warrington, Cheshire, WA4 6RR.
📞 01925 444 555. FAX 01925 415 474.
Website: www.winecellar.co.uk Credit
cards, delivery, en primeur, glass hire/loan.
*Steaming ahead following a management
buy-out. This is an innovative chain.
Some shops include cafés.*

The Wine Cellar ☆☆☆☆

10 Station Parade, Sanderstead Road,
South Croydon, Surrey, CR2 0PH.
📞 020 8657 6936. FAX 020 8657 9391.
E-mail: woodgeraldine@aol.com
Credit cards, delivery, tastings, en primeur,
cellarage, glass loan.
*This independent merchant offers a
commendable selection, including a great
range of malts.*

Wine Rack ☆☆☆☆

Sefton House, 42 Church Rd, Welwyn
Garden City, Herts, AL8 6PJ. 📞 01707
385 110. FAX 01707 385 004. Website:
www.enjoyment.co.uk
Credit cards, delivery, tastings, glass hire/loan.
*The up-market, high street face of
Thresher.*

Wine Raks (Scotland) ☆☆☆☆

21 Springfield Rd, Aberdeen, AB15 7RJ.
📞 01224 311 460. FAX 01224 312 186.
E-mail:
wineraks@wine-raks.freeserve.co.uk
Website: www.wineraks.co.uk
Credit cards, delivery, tastings, en primeur, glass hire/loan, cellarage.
An interesting list of Old World growers' wines and exciting New World wines.

The Wine Society ☆☆☆☆☆

Gunnels Wood Road, Stevenage,
Hertfordshire, SG1 2BG. 📞 01438 741
177. FAX 01438 761 167.
E-mail: winesociety@dial.pipex.com
Mail order, credit cards, delivery, tastings, glass loan, en primeur, cellarage.
Mail order merchant offering French classics and South American wines.

The Wine Treasury ☆☆☆☆

69-71 Bondway, London, SW8 1SQ.
📞 020 7793 9999. FAX 020 7793 8080.
E-mail: quality@winetreasury.com
Website: www.winetreasury.com
Mail order, by the case only, credit cards, en primeur, delivery, tastings (syndicate members).
Premium Californian wines, plus top names from Italy, Australia and elsewhere.

Winefinds ☆☆☆☆

Dinton Business Park, Dinton, nr.
Salisbury, Wilts. SP3 5SR. 📞 01722 716
916. FAX 01722 716 179.
E-mail: sales@winefinds.co.uk
By the case only, credit cards, delivery, tastings.
A team of Masters of Wine seeking out treats from Burgundy, Languedoc, Italy and Spain.

The Winery ☆☆☆☆

4 Clifton Road, Maida Vale, London, W9
1SS. 📞 020 7286 6475. FAX 020 7286
2733. E-mail: dmotion@globalnet.co.uk
Credit cards, delivery, tastings, glass loan.
Great exclusivities in California, Italy and Burgundy direct from the growers.

The Wright Wine Co. ☆☆☆☆

The Old Smithy, Raikes Road, Skipton,
N. Yorks, BD23 1NP. 📞 01756 700 886.
FAX 01756 798 580.
E-mail: Bob@wineandwhisky.co.uk
Website: www.wineandwhisky.co.uk
Credit cards, delivery, cellarage, glass loan.
Great wines from Alsace, South Africa and Australia, including many halves.

Wrightson & Company ☆☆☆☆

Manfield Grange, Manfield, Darlington,
N. Yorks, DL2 2RE. 📞 01325 374 134.
FAX 01325 374 135. E-mail:
ed.wrightson.wines@onyxnet.co.uk
Website: www.wrightsonwines.co.uk
By the case only, mail order, credit cards, delivery, tastings, en primeur, cellarage, glass loan.
An informative, elegant and easy to follow wine list. Some interesting tasting cases.

Peter Wylie Fine Wines ☆☆☆☆☆

Plymtree Manor, Plymtree, Cullompton,
Devon, EX15 2LE. 📞 01884 277 555.
FAX 01884 277 557. E-mail:
peter@wylie-fine-wines.demon.co.uk
Website: www.wyliefinewines.co.uk
Mail order only, delivery (worldwide), en primeur, cellarage.
A veritable treasure-trove of rare and fine wines. Check out their website to take advantage of worldwide delivery.

Yapp Brothers ☆☆☆☆☆

The Old Brewery, Mere, Wiltshire, BA12
6DY. 📞 01747 860 423. FAX 01747 860
929. E-mail: sales@yapp.co.uk
Website: www.yapp.co.uk
Credit cards, delivery, tastings, cellarage.
Britain's most faithful and probably best Loire and Rhône specialists. A fine general selection.

York Wines ☆☆☆☆

Wellington House, Sheriff Hutton, Yorks,
YO60 6QY. 📞 01347 878 716.
FAX 01347 878 546.
E-mail: york_wines@lineone.net
Website: yorkwines.co.uk
Credit cards, delivery, tastings, en primeur, glass hire/loan.
Traditional merchant with a good all-round range, and an original selection from both the Old and New Worlds.

Noel Young Wines ☆☆☆☆☆

56 High Street, Trumpington,
Cambridge, CB2 2LS. 📞 01223 844
744/566 744. FAX 01223 844 736.
E-mail: noel.young@dial.pipex.com
Website: www.nywines.co.uk
Credit cards, mail order, en primeur, delivery, tastings, glass hire/loan.
Good broad range with some brilliant Austrian wines. Educative and entertaining tastings.

COUNTRY AND REGIONAL SPECIALISTS

THE AMERICAS

NORTH AMERICA
Adnams (see page 296)
The Antique Wine Co.
(see page 296)
Asda Stores (see page 296)
Averys of Bristol (see page 296)
Bennetts Wines (see page 297)
Bibendum (see page 297)
Booths (see page 297)
The Bottleneck (see page 298)
Corkscrew Wines (see page 299)
Gordon and MacPhail
(see page 301)
Great Northern Wine Co.
(see page 301)
Charles Hennings
(see page 302)
King & Barnes (see page 303)
Lea & Sandeman (see page 303)
Lay & Wheeler (see page 303)
Morris & Verdin (see page 305)
Nadder Wines (see page 305)
New Fine Wines (see page 277)
James Nicholson (see page 305)
Oddbins (see page 305)
Terry Platt (see page 306)
R.S. Wines (see page 306)
Raeburn Fine Wines
(see page 306)
Sommelier Wine Co.
(see page 307)
Frank E. Stainton Wines
(Page 308)
Stevens Garnier (see page 308)
Stratford's (see page 308)
T.&W. Wines (see page 308)
Waverley Direct (see page 310)
The Wine Treasury
(see page 311)

SOUTH AMERICA
Georges Barbier of London
(see page 297)
Booths of Stockport
(see page 297)
The Bottleneck (see page 298)
Charterhouse Emporium
(see page 299)
Ben Ellis Wines (see page 272)
Fine Wines of Limerick
(see page 300)
Forth Wines (see page 300)
Hall Batson & Co. (see page 302)

Hedley Wright (see page 302)
Moreno Wine (see page 305)
Stevens Garnier (see page 308)
The Wine Society
(see page 311)
The Wright Wine Co.
(see page 311)

AUSTRALIA
Adnams (see page 296)
Australian Wine Club
(see page 296)
Bennetts (see page 297)
Booths of Stockport
(see page 297)
Charterhouse Emporium
(see page 299)
Direct Wine Shipments
(see page 299)
Eckington Wines (see page 300)
Edencroft Fine Wines
(see page 300)
Great Northern Wine Co
(see page 301)
Peter Green (see page 301)
H.& H. Fine Wines
(see page 273)
Hall Batson & Co. (see page 302)
Jeroboams (see page 303)
Mitchells (see page 260)
Philglas & Swiggott
(see page 306)
Christopher Piper (see page 306)
Portland Wine Co. (see page 306)
R.S. Wines (see page 306)
Sandiway Wine Co.
(see page 307)
Vin du Van (see page 309)
Vintage Wines (see page 309)

AUSTRIA
Ben Ellis Wines (see page 272)
Forth Wines (see page 300)
T.&W. Wines (see page 308)
Morris & Verdin (305)
Penistone Court (see page 306)
Noel Young Wines
(see page 311)

EASTERN EUROPE
Wines of Westhorpe
(see page 283)

ENGLAND

Stratford's Wine Shippers
(see page 308)

FRANCE

ALSACE

Ballantynes of Cowbridge
(see page 297)
Anthony Byrne (see page 298)
Gauntleys of Nottingham
(see page 301)
The Haslemere Cellar
(see page 302)
O.W. Loeb (see page 304)
Scatchard Wines (see page 307)
Tanners Wines (see page 308)
Wine Rack (see page 310)
The Wine Society (see page 311)

BEAUJOLAIS

Roger Harris (see page 302)

BORDEAUX

The Antique Wine Co.
(see page 296)
John Armit Wines (see page 296)
Averys of Bristol (see page 296)
Balls Brothers (see page 297)
Berry Bros. & Rudd (see page 297)
Bibendum (see page 297)
Bordeaux Index (see page 298)
The Butlers Wine Cellar
(see page 298)
Anthony Byrne (see page 298)
Cave Cru Classé (see page 298)
Brian Coad (see page 299)
Corney and Barrow (see page 299)
Direct Wine Shipments
(see page 299)
Farr Vintners (see page 300)
Fortnum & Mason (see page 300)
Four Walls Wine Co.
(see page 300)
Friarwood (see page 301)
Goedhuis & Co. (see page 301)
Harrods (see page 302)
Harvey Nichols (see page 302)
Justerini & Brooks (see page 303)
Lay & Wheeler (see page303)
O.W. Loeb (see page 304)
Magnum Fine Wines (see page 304)
F. & E. May (see page 304)
Montrachet (see page 304)
Nickolls & Perks (see page 305)
Nicolas (see page 305)
Oddbins Fine Wines (see page 305)

Thos. Peatling (see page 306)
Le Pont de la Tour (see page 306)
Reid Wines (see page 306)
Roberson (see page 307)
Edward Sheldon (see page 307)
Tanners Wines (see page 308)
Turville Valley Wines
(see page 308)
The Ubiquitous Chip
(see page 309)
Waverley Direct (see page 310)
Wilkinson Vintners (see page 282)
The Wine Society (see page 311)
Peter Wylie Fine Wines
(see page 311)

BURGUNDY

3D Wines (see page 296)
The Antique Wine Co.
(see page 296)
John Armit Wines (see page 296)
Averys of Bristol (see page 296)
Georges Barbier (see page 297)
Bibendum (see page 297)
The Burgundy Shuttle
(see page 298)
The Butlers Wine Cellar
(see page 298)
Anthony Byrne (see page 298)
Cave Cru Classé (see page 298)
Brian Coad (see page 299)
Corney and Barrow (see page 299)
Domaine Direct (see page 299)
Farr Vintners (see page 300)
Fortnum & Mason (see page 300)
Four Walls Wine Co. (see page 300)
Goedhuis & Co. (see page 301)
Harrods (see page 302)
Harvey Nichols (see page 302)
Haynes Hanson & Clark
(see page 302)
House of Townsend (see page 303)
Jeroboams (see page 303)
Lay & Wheeler (see page 303)
Lea & Sandeman (see page 303)
O.W. Loeb (see page 304)
Montrachet (see page 305)
Morris & Verdin (see page 305)
James Nicholson (see page 305)
Oddbins Fine Wines (see page 305)
Christopher Piper (see page 306)
Le Pont de la Tour (see page 306)
Raeburn Fine Wines (see page 306)
Howard Ripley (see page 306)
Stevens Garnier (see page 308)
T.&W. Wines (see page 308)
Turville Valley Wines (see page 308)
The Ubiquitous Chip (see page 309)

La Vigneronne (see page 309)
Waverley Direct (see page 310)
The Wine Press (see page 282)

CHAMPAGNE
3D Wines (see page 296)
Farr Vintners (see page 300)
Fortnum & Mason (see page 300)
Marks & Spencer
(see page 304)
Harrods (see page 302)
Majestic Wine (see page 304)
Oddbins (see page 305)

COUNTRY WINES
Allez Vins! (see page 296)
Bordeaux Direct (see page 297)
The Great Western Wine Co.
(see page 301)
Nadder Wines (see page 305)

LOIRE
Brian Coad (see page 299)
Four Walls Wine Co.
(see page 300)
Growers & Chateaux (see page 301)
Yapp Brothers (see page 311)

RHONE
Bibendum (see page 297)
Croque-en-Bouche (see page 299)
Farr Vintners (see page 300)
Gauntleys of Nottingham
(see page 301)
Waters of Coventry (see page 310)
Yapp Brothers (see page 311)

GERMANY

Adnams (see page 296)
Four Walls Wine Co. (see page 300)
Justerini & Brooks (see page 303)
Laytons Wine Merchants
(see page 303)
O.W. Loeb (see page 304)
Longford Wines (see page 304)
Majestic Wine (see page 304)
F.&E. May (see page 304)
Tanners Wines (see page 308)

ITALY

John Armit (see page 296)
Averys of Bristol (see page 296)
Bat & Bottle
(see page 297)
Peter Green (see page 301)
Hall Batson (see page 302)
Laytons Wine Merchants
(see page 303)
Valvona & Crolla (see page 309)
Vino Vino (see page 309)
Winefinds (see page 311)

NEW ZEALAND

Fine Wines of New Zealand
(see page 300)
Vin du Van (see page 309)
Waterloo Wine Co. (see page 310)

PORTUGAL

Moreno Wine Importers
(see page 305)
Raeburn Fine Wines (see page 306)

SOUTH AFRICA

Cape Province (see page 298)
King & Barnes (see page 303)
South African Wine Centre
(see page 307)

SPAIN

Arriba Kettle (see page 296)
Georges Barbier (see page 297)
Direct Wine Shipments
(see page 299)
S. H. Jones (see page 303)
Laymont & Shaw (see page 303)
Mitchells Wine Merchants
(see page 304)
Moreno Wine Importers
(see page 305)
Oddbins (see page 305)
Scatchard (see page 307)
Waters of Coventry (see page 310)

FORTIFIED WINE SPECIALISTS

PORT & MADEIRA
Ballantynes of Cowbridge
(see page 297)
Farr Vintners (see page 300)
Fortnum & Mason (see page 300)

Moreno Wine Importers
(see page 305)
Pallant Wines (see page 305)
Thos. Peatling (see page 306)
Quellyn-Roberts (see page 278)

Reid Wines (see page 306)
T.&W. Wines (see page 308)
Turville Valley Wines (see page 308)
Peter Wylie (see page 311)

SHERRY
Ballantynes of Cowbridge
(see page 297)
El Vino (see page 300)

Fortnum & Mason (see page 300)
Laymont & Shaw (see page 303)
Lea & Sandeman (see page 303)
Martinez (see page 304)
Moreno Wine Importers
(see page 305)
Morris & Verdin (see page 305)
Scatchard (see page 307)
Reid Wines (see page 306)

BEER SPECIALISTS

Adnams (see page 296)
Fullers (see page 272)
King & Barnes
(see page 303)
Majestic Wine (see page 304)

Mitchells Wine Merchants
(see page 304)
Oddbins (see page 305)
Unwins (see page 309)
Wine Cellar (see page 310)

SPIRIT SPECIALISTS

ARMAGNAC & COGNAC
Georges Barbier (see page 297)
Justerini & Brooks (see page 303)
Nicolas (see page 305)
The Ubiquitous Chip
(see page 309)

WHISKY
Berry Bros. & Rudd (see page 297)

Harrods (see page 302)
Charles Hennings (see page 302)
S.H. Jones (see page 303)
The Nobody Inn (see page 305)
Oddbins (see page 305)
Pallant Wines (see page 305)
La Réserve (see page 278)
The Ubiquitous Chip
(see page 309)

FINE AND RARE WINE SPECIALISTS

John Armit Wines (see page 296)
Bennetts Wines (see page 297)
Berry Bros. & Rudd (see page 297)
Bibendum (see page 297)
Bordeaux Index (see page 298)
Anthony Byrne (see page 298)
Cave Cru Classé (see page 298)
Corney and Barrow (see page 299)
Farr Vintners (see page 300)
Fine and Rare Wines
(see page 300)
Fortnum & Mason (see page 300)
Four Walls Wine Co. (see page 300)
Goedhuis & Co. (see page 301)
Harrods (see page 302)
Harvey Nichols (see page 302)
Lay & Wheeler (see page 303)
Nickolls & Perks (see page 305)
Nicolas (see page 305)
The Pavilion Wine Co.
(see page 305)
Oddbins Fine Wines
(see page 305)

Thos. Peatling (see page 306)
Raeburn Fine Wines
(see page 306)
Reid Wines (see page 306)
La Réserve (see page 278)
Roberson (see page 307)
T.&W. Wines (see page 308)
Tanners Wines (see page 308)
Turville Valley Wines
(see page 308)
Whiteside's of Clitheroe
(see page 310)
Peter Wylie Fine Wines
(see page 311)
Yapp Brothers (see page 311)
Noel Young Wines (see page 311)

AUCTIONEERS

Bigwood Auctioneers
☎ 01789 269 415. FAX 01789 294 168.
Website: www.bigwoodauctioneers.co.uk
Christie's
☎ 020 7839 9060. FAX 020 7839 1611.
Website: www.christies.com
Lithgow
☎ 01642 710 158. FAX 01642 712 641.
E-mail: lithgows.auctions@onyxnet.co.uk

Morphets
☎ 01423 530030. FAX 01423 500717.
Phillip's
☎ 01225 310 609. FAX 01225 446 675.
Sotheby's
☎ 020 7293 6423. FAX 020 7293 5961.
Website: www.sothebys.com
J. Straker Chadwick & Sons
☎ 01873 852 624. FAX 01873 857 311.

WINE COURSES

Association of Wine Educators
☎ +FAX 020 8995 2277.
Challenge Educational Services
☎ 01273 220 261. FAX 01273 220 376.
E-mail: enquiries@challengeuk.com
Christie's
☎ 020 7839 9060. FAX 020 7839 1611.
German Wine Institute
☎ (0049) 6131 282918.
Grape Sense
☎ +FAX 01359 270318.
E-mail: grapesense@aol.com
Kensington & Chelsea College
☎ 020 7573 5333. FAX 020 8960 2693.
Leicestershire Wine School
☎ 0116 254 2702. FAX 0116 254 2702.
Leith's
☎ 020 7229 0177. FAX 020 7937 5257.
E-mail: info@leiths.com
Maurice Mason
☎ +FAX 020 8841 8732.
North West Wine and Spirit Assoc.
☎ +FAX 01244 678 624.

Plumpton College
☎ 01273 890 454. FAX 01273 890 071.
E-mail: enquiries@plumpton.ac.uk
Scala School
☎ 020 7281 3040. FAX 020 7281 3001
E-mail: scalawine@compuserve.com
Sotheby's
☎ 020 7293 6423. FAX 020 7293 5961.
Vinform ☎ 0181 876 0110.
Wensum Lodge
☎ 01603 666 021. FAX 01603 765 633.
Wine Associates Ltd. (courses in UK &
France) ☎ 01803 299292.
France: 0033 553 588 148.
Website: www.wineassociates.co.uk
Wine & Spirit Education Trust
☎ 020 7236 3551. FAX 020 7329 8712.
E-mail: wset@wset.co.uk
Wine Education Service
☎ 020 8423 6338. FAX 020 8723 3751.
E-mail:info@wine-education-service.co.uk
Wine Wise
☎ 020 7254 9734. FAX 020 7249 3663.

WINE HOLIDAYS

Allez France & Great Escapes
☎ 01903 748 100. / 748 138.
FAX 01903 745 044.
Arblaster & Clarke Wine Tours
☎ 01730 893 344. FAX 01730 892 888.
E-mail: sales@winetours.co.uk
Backroads
☎ 01425 655 022. FAX 01425 655 177.
The Cape Vine
☎ 01604 648 768. FAX 01604 644 013.
DER Travel
☎ 020 7290 1111. FAX 020 7629 7442.
Edwin Doran Travel
☎ 020 8288 1000.
FAX 020 8288 2955.

Fine Wine Travel Company
☎ 020 7229 1243.
Francophiles Discover France
☎ +FAX 01362 851 076.
In the French Alps with Wink Lorch
☎ 01494 677 728. FAX 01494 677729.
Grenadier Travel
☎ 01206 549 585. FAX 01206 561 337.
HGP Wine Tours
☎ 01803 299 292. FAX 01803 292 008.
KD River Cruises Europe
☎ 01372 742 033. FAX 01372 724 871.
Millers House Hotel
☎ 01969 622 630.
FAX 01969 623 570.

Moswin Tours
☎ 0116 271 4982. FAX 0116 271 6016.
Ski Gourmet and Winetrails
☎ 01306 712 111. FAX 01306 713 504.
The Sunday Times Wine Club Tours
☎ 01730 895 353. FAX 01730 892 888.
Tanglewood Wine Tours
☎ 01932 348 720. FAX 01932 350 861.
Website:www.tanglewoodwine.co.uk

Travel Club of Upminster
☎ 01708 227 260. FAX 01708 229 678.
UK Vineyards Association.
☎ 01728 638 080. FAX 01728 638 442.
Wessex Continental Travel
☎+FAX 01752 846 880.
Wine Journeys Alternative Travel Group
☎ 01865 315 678. FAX 01865 315 697/8/9.

ACCESSORIES

GLASSES
Conran Shop (Riedel range)
☎ 020 7589 7401. FAX 020 7823 7015.
Dartington Crystal
☎ 01805 626 262. FAX 01805 626 267.
Equinox (Belfast) (Riedel range)
☎ 01232 230 089.
Oneida/Schott UK
☎ 01753 212500.

CORKSCREWS
Screwpull
☎ 01264 343 900.

STORAGE
Access Storage Space
☎ 020 8991 9717. FAX 020 8991 9611.
Consort Wine Care Systems
☎ 01635 550055. FAX 01635 41733.
Euro-cave
☎ 020 8200 1266. FAX 020 8200 1792.
Website: www.artofwine.co.uk
Smith & Taylor
☎ 020 7627 5070. FAX 020 7622 8235.
Vin-Garde
☎+FAX 01926 811 376.

WINE RACKS
A.&W. Moore
☎ 0115 944 1434.
FAX 0115 932 0735.
R.T.A Wine Racks
☎ 01328 829 666.

Spiral Cellars
☎ 01372 279 166.
The Wine Rack Company
☎+FAX 01243 543 253.

ANTIQUES
Bacchus Gallery
☎ 01798 342 844. FAX 01798 342 634.

GENERAL WINE ACCESSORIES
In addition to the 2 specialists listed most independent wine merchants now stock a good range of wine accessories.
Birchgrove Products Ltd.
☎ 01483 533 400. FAX 01483 533 700.
The Hugh Johnson Collection
☎ 020 7491 4912. FAX 020 7493 0602.

CHILLING DEVICES
Chilla ☎ 0181 891 6464.
Coolbags & Boxes UK
☎ 0118 9333 331. FAX 0118 9333 579.
Vacu Products
☎ 01299 250 480. FAX 01299 251 559.

BOOKS
Books for Cooks
☎ 020 7221 1992. FAX 020 7221 1517
Website: www.booksforcooks.com
Cooking The Books
☎+FAX 01633 400 150.
Richard Stanford
☎ 020 7836 1321.

WINE CLUBS

Académie du Vin
☎ 01803 299 292. FAX 01803 292 008.
E-mail: hgpwine@aol.com
Alston Wine Club
☎ 01434 381 338.
Amersham
☎ 01494 771 983.

Association of Wine Cellarmen
☎ 020 8871 3092.
Barrels and Bottles
☎ 0114 255 6611.
FAX 0114 255 1010.
Charlemagne
☎ 020 8567 1733.

Cirencester
☎ 01285 641 126.
Confrérie Internationale de St. Vincent
☎ 0113 267 9258. FAX 0113 228 9307.
E-mail: asmalley@cwcom.net
Cornwall
☎ 01872 223 570.
Decant & Taste
☎ 01507 605 758.
Eastbourne
☎ 01323 727675.
Goring & Streatley
☎ 01491 873 620.
Guild of Sommeliers
☎ 0161 928 0852.
Harrogate Medical
☎ 01423 503 129. FAX 01423 561 820.
Herefordshire
☎ 01432 275 656.
Hextable Wine Club
☎ 01732 823 345.
Hollingworth
☎ 01706 374 765. E-mail: peter-l@msn.com
Ightham Wine Club
☎ 01732 885 557.
Institute of Wines & Spirits (Scotland)
☎ +FAX 01324 554 162.
The Interesting Wine Club
☎ 020 7272 2457 / 5767. FAX 020 7272 4312.
International Wine and Food Society
☎ 020 7495 4191. FAX 020 7495 4172.
E-mail: iwandfs@aol.com
Leicester Evington
☎ 0116 231 4760. FAX 0116 287 5371.
Leicester Grand Union
☎ 0116 287 1662.

Lincoln Wine Society
☎ +FAX 01522 680 388.
London Branch of IWFS
☎ 0208 349 2260. FAX 0208 346 4360.
Manchester
☎ 01706 824 283.
Moreno
☎ 020 7286 0678.
Myster Wine Club
☎ 01633 893 485.
Notting Hill
☎ 0181 969 9668.
Preston
☎ 01772 254 251. FAX 01772 203 858.
Rochester
☎ 01634 848 345.
Scottish
☎ 0131 664 8855.
Tanglewood Wine Society
☎ 01932 348 720. FAX 01932 350 861.
West Hampstead
☎ 020 7794 3926.
Windsor and Eton
☎ 01753 790 188. FAX 01753 790 189.
E-mail: enquiries@etonvintners.co.uk
Wine and Dine
☎ 020 8673 4439.
FAX 020 8675 5543. E-mail:
bensonwines@connectingbusiness.com
Wine Collectors (WineShare)
☎ 01306 742 164.
Wine Schoppen
☎ 0114 255 6611. FAX 0114 255 1010.
The Winetasters
☎ 01753 889 720.
York ☎ +FAX 01904 691 628.

Cross-channel Shopping

EastEnders Bulk Beer Warehouse
14 Rue Gustave Courbet, 62100 Calais,
France. ☎ (33) 3 21 34 53 33.
FAX (33) 3 21 97 61 22.
Normandy Wine Warehouse
(4 branches – 2 in Cherbourg, 2 in
Ouistreham) 71 Avenue Carnot, 50100
Cherbourg, France. ☎ (33) 2 33 43 39 79.
FAX: (33) 2 33 43 22 69.
Oddbins
Cité Europe, 139 Rue de Douvres, 62901
Coquelles, Cedex, France. ☎ (33) 3 21
82 07 32. FAX (33) 3 21 82 05 83.
Perardel Wine Market
Z.A. Marcel Doret, Calais, France.
☎ (33) 3 21 97 21 22.
Sainsbury's Wine Store
Centre Commercial Auchon, Route de

Boulogne, Calais, France. ☎ (33) 3 21
82 38 48. FAX (33) 3 21 36 01 91
Le Tastevin
9 Rue Val, 35400 St.-Malo, France. ☎ (33)
2 99 82 46 56. FAX (33) 2 99 81 09 69.
Tesco Vin Plus
Espace 122, Boulevard du Kent, Cité
Europe, 62231 Coquelles, France.
☎ (33) 3 21 46 02 70. FAX (33) 3 21 46
02 79.
The Wine & Beer Company
Rue de Judée, Zone Industrielle Marcel
Doret, 62100 Calais, France. ☎ (33) 3
21 97 63 00. FAX (33) 3 21 97 70 15.
The Wine Society
1 Rue de la Paroisse, 62140 Hesdin,
France. ☎ (33) 3 21 86 52 07.
FAX (33) 3 21 86 52 13.

The world of wine online is changing so rapidly that the following list can only offer a snapshot of what you may find if you go looking for wine on the web. But it should give you a pretty good start.

ONLINE RETAILERS

Apart from the specialist online merchants listed here, you will also find websites for many of the companies profiled on pages 296-311

www.a-bestfixture.com
Wine accessories, supplies and gifts.
www.auswine.com.au
Australian wines shipped worldwide.
www.avalonwine.com
Wines from the Pacific Northwest.
www.bbr.co.uk
Traditional merchant. Worldwide delivery.
www.cawineclub.com
California wine club.
www.chateau-online.com
French wines shipped throughout Europe.
www.clarets.com
Not just claret. Ship worldwide.
www.connseries.com
US site with limited-production wines.
www.esquin.com
Superstore and wine club.
www.everywine.co.uk
UK site offering 35,000 wines.
www.evineyard.com
Ship to most US States.

www.finestwine.com
Global supply of collectable wines.
www.libation.com
Wine and beer delivered worldwide.
www.madaboutwine.com
Wine delivered worldwide.
www.planetwine.com
Australian-turned-international site.
www.tinamou.com
Premium French wines and vintage port.
www.virginwine.com
Dynamic UK-based site.
www.wine.com
Wines, gifts, accessories and wine links.
www.winebroker.com
Fine wine specialists.
www.thewinebrokers.com
Worldwide delivery and online wineclub.
www.winepros.com
Contributors include this Guide's author.
www.winex.com
Good general catalogue of wine. US only.

ONLINE AUCTIONEERS

www.auctionvine.com
A central online auction site.
www.amazon.com
Online giant associated with Sotheby's.
www.brentwoodwine.com
Auction site with fixed price sales too.
www.tcwc.com
The Chicago Wine Company.
www.internetauctionlist.com
Network of auction company web sites.
www.magnumwines.com
Speciality wines.

www.wine-auction-gazette.com
Calendar of wine auctions.
www.winebid.com
Fine wines and spirit auctions in the USA, the UK and Australia.
www.winetoday.com
An updated archive of articles on auctions.
www.vines.netauctions.net.au
Five annual auctions in Australia.
www.winesonauction.com
Wine sold by producers.

NEWS, REVIEWS & GENERIC SITES

www.4wine.com
US dominant link to worldwide wines.
www.ambrosiawine.com
A search engine to find almost any wine, clubs and a live online chat feature.
www.decanter.com
The UK wine magazine online.
www.connectingdrinks.com
The route to WINE Magazine online.

www.drinkwine.com
All about wine.
www.food-and-drink.com
Links to food and drink sites.
www.foodandwine.com
Food and Wine Magazine online.
www.gangofpour.com
Loads of general information about wine. Reviews and tasting notes.

www.goodwineguide.com
The online partner to this Guide.
www.grapevineweekly.com
An online magazine with lots of links.
www.hotwine.com
A link to winesites, plus poetic quotes.
www.interaxus.com/pages/wine.html
Wine reviews.
www.intlwinechallenge.com
The world's biggest wine competition.
www.intowine.com
Winemaking and wine-and-the-bible.
www.purplepages.com
Directory of wine-related websites.
www.orgasmicwines.com
News and wines to buy.
www.smartwine.com
Market news for the investor.
www.thewinenews.com
News and reviews.
www.vine2wine.com
Links to over 2,000 wine sites.
www.wineadvocate.com
The guru Robert Parker @ home.
www.wine-and-health.com
Comment and news about the
healthiness – and otherwise – of wine.
www.wine-asia.com
News of this growing wine market.
www.winebrats.org
New wave, emphatically unstuffy wine
news and chat.
www.winecellar.com
A complete source of wine links.
www.wine-collector.com
Swap and chat about collectable bottles.

www.wineculture.com
A hip guide to wine on the web.
www.wineenthusiastmag.com
Articles and the latest news.
www.wineinfonet.com
A multi-language portal.
www.wine-investor.com
How to spend your cash.
www.wineplace.com
Winemaking galore.
www.wineontheweb.com
The talking online wine magazine.
www.winepros.com
Experts including James Halliday and
the author of this Guide.
www.wineratings.com
Wine reviews and advice.
www.wine-searcher.com
Search the web for all aspects of wine.
www.winesense.com
Wine appreciation and women in wine.
www.winexwired.com
The online presence of the irreverent
Wine X Magazine.
www.winetoday.com
News from the New York Times.
www.thewinenews.com
Features, reviews and recommendations.
www.winespectator.com
The Wine Spectator's online magazine.
www.wino.net
Wine laws, investment and health.
www.worldsgreatestwines.com
Competition winners galore.
www.worldwine.com
A website dedicated to wine links.

WINERIES

www.cawinemall.com
Comprehensive directory of Californian
web wineries by region or grape variety.
www.champagnes.com
An introduction to Champagne.
www.edgamesandart.com/wine.html
A database of wine and wineries.
www.hiddenwineries.com
Lesser known US wineries.
www.vinosearch.com
Wines and wineries across the globe.

www.winecollection.com
An online collection of France's wineries.
www.wines.com
An award-winning guide to wine and
wineries.
www.winetoday.com
A comprehensive list of wineries.
www.wineweb.com
Wines and wineries across the world.
www.worldwine.com
Lots of links.

ONLINE WINE EDUCATION

www.WineEducation.com
Certified Wine Educator, Stephen Reiss.
www.wine.gurus.com
Society of Wine Educators'
home page.

www.wine-school.com
An online diploma wine course.
www.wineprofessor.com
Food and wine pairing; wine
labels etc.

REGIONAL SITES

www.argentinewines.com
Argentina's new-wave wines.

www.barossa.com
Wines of the Barossa Valley.

www.bordeaux.com
A virtual tour of Bordeaux.

www.coonawarra.com
Australia's most famous region.

www.germanwines.de
Multilingual official site.

www.indagegroup.com
Promoting India's wine.

www.ivp.pt
The Port Wine Institute's web site.

www.liwines.com
Long Island wine country.

www.napawine.com
Visit Napa wineries and wine sites.

www.madeirawine.com
All about Madeira's wines and history.

www.nothingbutchampagne.com
For lovers of bubbles.

www.nywine.com
New York uncorked.

www.nzwine.com
The official site of New Zealand wine.

www.sonomawine.com
Sonoma County Wineries Association.

www.twgga.com
Wines from Texas.

www.washingtonwine.org
All about wine in Washington.

www.wine.co.za
A guide to South African wines.

www.winecountry.com
The gateway to wines of California.

www.winesofchile.com
Ever-expanding guide to Chilean wines.

www.wineinstitute.com
Californian wineries with lots of links.

www.wine.it
Wines of Italy.

www.wines-france.com
User-friendly guide to French wines.

www.winetitles.com.au
A complete guide to wine Downunder.

www.winetour.com
A guide to Ontario's wineries.

ONLINE WINE CHATROOMS AND CLUBS

www.4wine.com
Lists a multitude of chatrooms.

www.auswine.com.au/cgi-bin/ auswine/browse
The Australian Wine Centre's virtual shop provides a search feature, a forum and a chatroom.

www.drinkwine.com
Bulletin board and extensive listing of associations.

www.evineyard.com
Offers live talk and a lively wine club.

www.iglou.com/wine/chat
Join a crowd of other wine lovers and compare notes.

www.nobilevineyards.com
International wine club and chatroom.

www.secretcellars.com
A virtual wine club that brings California's small vineyards to your door.

www.vineswinger.com
Plentiful chat rooms and busy wine forums.

www.winebrats.org
Access to various wine chatrooms.

www.wineculture.com
A resource of various chatrooms.

www.wineinstitute.org
Lists discussion groups and chatrooms focusing on California wine.

www.wine-lovers-page.com/wine.shtml
Wine chatroom.

www.winerave.com
Website with its own wine chatroom – arguably the liveliest on the net..

www.wines.com
Bulletin board where questions can be posed to wine experts.

www.winesite.com
Extensive list of links to international wine clubs.

www.winespectator.com.
Regular opportunities to interview wine personalities.

www.zinfans.com
For lovers of the Zinfandel – in its every form.

*To assist me in keeping these lists up to date for future editions, please email recommendations of other sites to robertjoseph@goodwineguide.com.
In return, I will send copies of my book French Wines to senders of the most useful tips.*

INDEX

This index can be used as a supplement to the *A–Z of Wine*.(pages 97–294)

C

D

E

F

G

M

Q

R

V

W

X

Y

Z

WINE ON THE WEB

Apart from our lists of recommended websites
on pages 16–19 and 319–321
if you enjoy
The Sunday Telegraph Good Wine Guide
visit Robert Joseph's
Good Wine Guide
site on the World Wide Web at
www.goodwineguide.com
for news, competitions,
an electronic Wine Atlas, comment and
links to over 200 wineries and merchants
throughout the world

Visit
www.wine-school.com
www.robertjoseph.com
for interactive food and wine updates
and, of course
www.dk.com
for details of other Dorling Kindersley titles